Mysticism:
A Study in Nature and Development of Spiritual Consciousness

by Evelyn Underhill

Edited by Anthony Uyl

Woodstock, Ontario, 2017

Mysticism: A Study in Nature and Development of Spiritual Consciousness

by Evelyn Underhill (1875 -1941)
Edited by Anthony Uyl

Originally Published in 1910
Twelfth Edition Published in 1930

The text of Mysticism: A Study in Nature and Development of Spiritual Consciousness is all in the Public Domain. This edition is published by Devoted Publishing a division of 2165467 Ontario Inc.

What kind of philosophies do you have?
Let us know!

Contact us at: devotedpub@hotmail.com
Visit our shop on Facebook: @DevotedPublishing
Published in Woodstock, Ontario, Canada 2017.

For bulk educational rates, please contact us at the above email address.

ISBN: 9781520610382

Table of Contents

PREFACE TO THE TWELFTH EDITION

Since this book first appeared, nineteen years ago, the study of mysticism--not only in England, but also in France, Germany and Italy--has been almost completely transformed. From being regarded, whether critically or favourably, as a byway of religion, it is now more and more generally accepted by theologians, philosophers and psychologists, as representing in its intensive form the essential religious experience of man. The labours of a generation of religious psychologists--following, and to some extent superseding the pioneer work of William James--have already done much to disentangle its substance from the psycho-physical accidents which often accompany mystical apprehension. Whilst we are less eager than our predecessors to dismiss all accounts of abnormal experience as the fruit of superstition or disease, no responsible student now identifies the mystic and the ecstatic; or looks upon visionary and other "extraordinary phenomena" as either guaranteeing or discrediting the witness of the mystical saints. Even the remorseless explorations and destructive criticisms of the psycho-analytic school are now seen to have effected a useful work; throwing into relief the genuine spiritual activities of the psyche, while explaining in a naturalistic sense some of their less fortunate psycho-physical accompaniments. The philosophic and theological landscape also, with its increasing emphasis on Transcendence, its new friendliness to the concept of the Supernatural, is becoming ever more favourable to the metaphysical claims of the mystics. On one hand the prompt welcome given to the work of Rudolf Otto and Karl Barth, on the other the renewed interest in Thomist philosophy, seem to indicate a growing recognition of the distinctness and independence of the Spiritual Order. and a revival of the creaturely sense, strongly contrasting with the temper of late nineteenth-century thought.

Were I, then, now planning this book for the first time, its arguments would be differently stated. More emphasis would be given (a) to the concrete, richly living yet unchanging character of the Reality over against the mystic, as the first term, cause and incentive of his experience; (b) to that paradox of utter contrast yet profound relation between the Creator and the creature, God and the soul, which makes possible his development; (c) to the predominant part played in that development by the free and prevenient action of the Supernatural--in theological language, by "grace"--as against all merely evolutionary or emergent theories of spiritual transcendence. I feel more and more that no psychological or evolutionary treatment of man's spiritual history can be adequate which ignores the element of "given-ness" in all genuine mystical knowledge. Though the mystic Life means organic growth, its first term must be sought in ontology; in the Vision of the Principle, as St. Gregory the Great taught long ago. For the real sanction of that life does not inhere in the fugitive experiences or even the transformed personality of the subject; but in the metaphysical Object which that subject apprehends.

Again, it now seems to me that a critical realism, which found room for the duality of our full human experience--the Eternal and the Successive, supernatural and natural reality--would provide a better philosophic background to the experience of the mystics than the vitalism which appeared, twenty years ago, to offer so promising a way of escape from scientific determinism. Determinism--more and more abandoned by its old friends the physicists--is no longer the chief enemy to such a spiritual interpretation of life as is required by the experience of the mystics. It is rather a naturalistic monism, a shallow doctrine of immanence unbalanced by any adequate sense of transcendence, which now threatens to re-model theology in a sense which leaves no room for the noblest and purest reaches of the spiritual life.

Yet in spite of the adjustments required by such a shifting at the philosophic outlook, and by nearly twenty years of further study and meditation, the final positions which seem to me to be required by the existence of mysticism remain substantially unchanged. Twenty years ago, I was already convinced that the facts of man's spiritual experience pointed to a limited dualism; a diagram which found place for his contrasting apprehension of Absolute and Contingent, Being and Becoming, Simultaneous and Successive. Further, that these facts involved the existence in him too of a certain doubleness, a higher and lower, natural and transcendental self--something equivalent to that "Funklein" spark, or apex of the soul on which the mystics have always insisted as the instrument of their special experience. Both these opinions were then unpopular. The second, in particular, has been severely criticized by Professor Pratt and other authorities on the psychology of religion. Yet the constructive work which has since been done on the metaphysical implications of mystical experience has tended more and more to establish their necessity, at least as a basis of analysis; and they can now claim the most distinguished support.

The recovery of the concept of the Supernatural--a word which no respectable theologian of the last generation cared to use--is closely linked with the great name of Friedrich von Hügel. His persistent opposition to all merely monistic, pantheist and immanental philosophies of religion, and his insistence on the need of a "two-step diagram" of the Reality accessible to man, though little heeded in his life-time, are now bearing fruit. This re-instatement of the Transcendent, the "Wholly Other," as the religious fact, is perhaps the most fundamental of the philosophic changes which have directly affected the study of mysticism. It thus obtains a metaphysical background which harmonizes with its greatest declarations, and supports its claim to empirical knowledge of the Truth on which all religion rests. Closely connected with the transcendence of its Object, are the twin doctrines emphasized in all Von Hügel's work. First, that while mysticism is an essential element in full human religion, it can never be the whole content of such religion. It requires to be embodied in some degree in history, dogma and institutions if it is to reach the sense-conditioned human mind. Secondly, that the antithesis between the religions of "authority" and of "spirit," the "Church" and the "mystic," is false. Each requires the other. The "exclusive" mystic, who condemns all outward forms and rejects the support of the religious complex, is an abnormality. He inevitably tends towards pantheism, and seldom exhibits in its richness the Unitive Life. It is the "inclusive" mystic, whose freedom and originality are fed but not hampered by the spiritual tradition within which he appears, who accepts the incarnational status of the human spirit, and can "find the inward in the outward as well as the inward in the inward," who shows us in their fullness and beauty the life-giving possibilities of the soul transfigured in God.

Second in importance among the changes which have come over the study of mysticism, I should reckon the work done during the last decade upon the psychology of prayer and contemplation. I cannot comment here upon the highly technical discussions between experts as to the place where the line is to be drawn between "natural" and "supernatural," "active" and "infused" operations of the soul in communion with God; or the exact distinction between "ordinary" and "extraordinary" contemplation. But the fact that these discussions have taken place is itself significant; and requires from religious psychology the acknowledgement of a genuine two-foldness in human nature--the difference in kind between Animus the surface-self and Anima the transcendental self, in touch with supernatural realities. Here, the most important work has been done in France; and especially by the Abbé Bremond, whose "Prière et Poésie" and "Introduction a la Philosophie de la Prière"--based on a vast acquaintance with mystical literature--mark, I believe, the beginning of a new understanding of the character of contemplation. The Thomist philosophy of Maritain, and the psychological researches of Maréchal, tend to support this developing view of the mystical experience, even in its elementary forms, as an activity of the transcendental self; genuinely supernatural, yet not necessarily involving any abnormal manifestations, and linked by the ascending "degrees of prayer" with the subject's "ordinary" religious life. This disentangling of the substance of mysticism from the psycho-physical accidents of trance, ecstasy, vision and other abnormal phenomena which often accompany it, and its vindication as something which gives the self a genuine knowledge of transcendental Reality--with its accompanying demonstration of the soberness and sanity of the greatest contemplative saints--is the last of the beneficent changes which have transformed our study of the mystics. In this country it is identified with the work of two Benedictine scholars; Abbot Chapman of Downside and Dom Cuthbert Butler, whose "Western Mysticism" is a masterly exhibition of the religious and psychological normality of the Christian contemplative life, as developed by its noblest representatives.

Since this book was written, our knowledge of the mystics has been much extended by the appearance of critical texts of many writings which had only been known to us in garbled versions; or in translations made with an eye to edification rather than accuracy. Thus the publication of the authentic revelations of Angela of Foligno--one of the most interesting discoveries of recent years--has disclosed the unsuspected splendour of her mystical experience. The critical texts of St. Teresa and St. John of the Cross which are now available amend previous versions in many important respects. We have reliable editions of Tauler and Ruysbroeck; of "The Cloud of Unknowing," and of Walter Hilton's works. The renewed interest in seventeenth-century mysticism, due in part to the Abbé Bremond's great work, has resulted in the publication of many of its documents. So too the literary, social and historical links between the mystics, the influence of environment, the great part played by forgotten spiritual movements and inarticulate saints, are beginning to be better understood. Advantage has been taken of these facts in preparing the present edition. All quotations from the mystics have been revised by comparison with the best available texts. The increased size of the historical appendix and bibliography is some indication of the mass of fresh material which is now at the disposal of students; material which must be examined with truth-loving patience, with sympathy, and above all with humility, by those who desire to make valid additions to our knowledge of the conditions under which the human spirit has communion with God.

Easter 1930 E. U.

PREFACE TO THE FIRST EDITION

This book falls naturally into two parts; each of which is really complete in itself, though they are in a sense complementary to one another. Whilst the second and longest part contains a somewhat detailed study of the nature and development of man's spiritual or mystical consciousness, the first is intended rather to provide an introduction to the general subject of mysticism. Exhibiting it by turns from the point of view of metaphysics, psychology, and symbolism, it is an attempt to gather between the covers of one volume information at present scattered amongst many monographs and text-books written in divers tongues, and to give the student in a compact form at least the elementary facts in regard to each of those subjects which are most closely connected with the study of the mystics.

Those mystics, properly speaking, can only be studied in their works: works which are for the most part left unread by those who now talk much about mysticism. Certainly the general reader has this excuse, that the masterpieces of mystical literature, full of strange beauties though they be, offer considerable difficulties to those who come to them unprepared. In the first seven chapters of this book I have tried to remove a few of these difficulties; to provide the necessary preparation; and to exhibit the relation in which mysticism stands to other forms of life. If, then, the readers of this section are enabled by it to come to the encounter of mystical literature with a greater power of sympathetic comprehension than they previously possessed, it will have served the purpose for which it has been composed.

It is probable that almost every such reader, according to the angle from which he approaches the subject, will here find a good deal which seems to him superfluous. But different types of mind will find this unnecessary elaboration in different places. The psychologist, approaching from the scientific standpoint, eager for morbid phenomena, has little use for disquisitions on symbolism, religious or other. The symbolist, approaching from the artistic standpoint, seldom admires the proceedings of psychology. I believe, however, that none who wish to obtain an idea of mysticism in its wholeness, as a form of life, can afford to neglect any of the aspects on which these pages venture to touch. The metaphysician and the psychologist are unwise if they do not consider the light thrown upon the ideas of the mystics by their attitude towards orthodox theology. The theologian is still more unwise if he refuse to hear the evidence of psychology. For the benefit of those whose interest in mysticism is chiefly literary, and who may care to be provided with a clue to the symbolic and allegorical element in the writings of the contemplatives, a short section on those symbols of which they most often make use has been added. Finally, the persistence amongst us of the false opinion which confuses mysticism with occult philosophy and psychic phenomena, has made it necessary to deal with the vital distinction which exists between it and every form of magic.

Specialists in any of these great departments of knowledge will probably be disgusted by the elementary and superficial manner in which their specific sciences are here treated. But this book does not venture to address itself to specialists. From those who are already fully conversant with the matters touched upon, it asks the indulgence which really kindhearted adults are always ready to extend towards the efforts of youth. Philosophers are earnestly advised to pass over the first two chapters, and theologians to practise the same charity in respect of the section dealing with their science.

The giving of merely historical information is no part of the present plan: except in so far as chronology has a bearing upon the most fascinating of all histories, the history of the spirit of man. Many books upon mysticism have been based on the historical method: amongst them two such very different works as Vaughan's supercilious and unworthy "Hours with the Mystics" and Dr. Inge's scholarly Bampton lectures. It is a method which seems to be open to some objection: since mysticism avowedly deals with the individual not as he stands in relation to the civilization of his time, but as he stands in relation to truths that are timeless. All mystics, said Saint-Martin, speak the same language and come from the same country. As against that fact, the place which they happen to occupy in the kingdom of this world matters little. Nevertheless, those who are unfamiliar with the history of mysticism properly so called, and to whom the names of the great contemplatives convey no accurate suggestion of period or nationality, may be glad to have a short statement of their order in time and distribution in space. Also, some knowledge of the genealogy of mysticism is desirable if we are to distinguish the original contributions of each individual from the mass of speculation and statement which he inherits from the past. Those entirely unacquainted with these matters may find it helpful to glance at the Appendix before proceeding to the body of the work; since few things are more disagreeable than the constant encounter of persons to whom we have not been introduced.

The second part of the book, for which the first seven chapters are intended to provide a preparation, is avowedly psychological. It is an attempt to set out and justify a definite theory of the nature of man's mystical consciousness: the necessary stages of organic growth through which the typical mystic passes, the state of equilibrium towards which he tends. Each of these stages--and also the characteristically mystical and still largely mysterious experiences of visions and voices, contemplation and ecstasy--though viewed from the standpoint of psychology, is illustrated from the lives of the mystics; and where possible in their own words. In planning these chapters I have been considerably helped by M. Delacroix's brilliant "Etudes sur le Mysticisme," though unable to accept his conclusions: and here gladly take the opportunity of acknowledging my debt to him and also to Baron von Hügel's classic "Mystical Element of Religion." This book, which only came into my hands when my own was planned and partly written, has since been a constant source of stimulus and encouragement.

Finally, it is perhaps well to say something as to the exact sense in which the term "mysticism" is here understood. One of the most abused words in the English language, it has been used in different and often mutually exclusive senses by religion, poetry, and philosophy: has been claimed as an excuse for every kind of occultism, for dilute transcendentalism, vapid symbolism, religious or aesthetic sentimentality, and bad metaphysics. On the other hand, it has been freely employed as a term of contempt by those who have criticized these things. It is much to be hoped that it may be restored sooner or later to its old meaning, as the science or art of the spiritual life.

Meanwhile, those who use the term "Mysticism" are bound in self-defence to explain what they mean by it. Broadly speaking, I understand it to be the expression of the innate tendency of the human spirit towards complete harmony with the transcendental order; whatever be the theological formula under which that order is understood. This tendency, in great mystics, gradually captures the whole field of consciousness; it dominates their life and, in the experience called "mystic union," attains its end. Whether that end be called the God of Christianity, the World-soul of Pantheism, the Absolute of Philosophy, the desire to attain it and the movement towards it--so long as this is a genuine life process and not an intellectual speculation--is the proper subject of mysticism. I believe this movement to represent the true line of development of the highest form of human consciousness.

It is a pleasant duty to offer my heartiest thanks to the many kind friends and fellow students, of all shades of opinion, who have given me their help and encouragement. Amongst those to whom my heaviest debt of gratitude is due are Mr. W. Scott Palmer, for much valuable, generous, and painstaking assistance, particularly in respect of the chapter upon Vitalism: and Miss Margaret Robinson, who in addition to many other kind offices, has made all the translations from Meister Eckhart and Mechthild of Magdeburg here given.

Sections of the MS. have been kindly read by the Rev. Dr. Inge, by Miss May Sinclair, and by Miss Eleanor Gregory; from all of whom I have received much helpful and expert advice. To Mr. Arthur Symons my thanks and those of my readers are specially due; since it is owing to his generous permission that I am able to make full use of his beautiful translations of the poems of St. John of the Cross. Others who have given me much help in various directions, and to whom most grateful acknowledgments are here offered, are Miss Constance Jones, Miss Ethel Barker, Mr. J. A. Herbert of the British Museum--who first brought to my notice the newly discovered "Mirror of Simple Souls"--the Rev. Dr. Arbuthnot Nairn, Mr. A. E. Waite, and Mr. H. Stuart Moore, F.S.A. The substance of two chapters--those upon "The Characteristics of Mysticism" and "Mysticism and Magic"--has already appeared in the pages of The Quest and The Fortnightly Review. These sections are here reprinted by kind permission of their respective editors.

Feast of St. John of the Cross E. U. 1910

PART I: THE MYSTIC FACT

"What the world, which truly knows nothing, calls mysticism' is the science of ultimates, . . . the science of self-evident Reality, which cannot be reasoned about,' because it is the object of pure reason or perception. The Babe sucking its mother's breast, and the Lover returning, after twenty years' separation, to his home and food in the same bosom, are the types and princes of Mystics."

COVENTRY PATMORE,

"The Rod, the Root, and the Flower"

CHAPTER I

The most highly developed branches of the human family have in common one peculiar characteristic. They tend to produce--sporadically it is true, and often in the teeth of adverse external circumstances--a curious and definite type of personality; a type which refuses to be satisfied with that which other men call experience, and is inclined, in the words of its enemies, to "deny the world in order that it may find reality." We meet these persons in the east and the west; in the ancient, mediaeval, and modern worlds. Their one passion appears to be the prosecution of a certain spiritual and intangible quest: the finding of a "way out" or a "way back" to some desirable state in which alone they can satisfy their craving for absolute truth. This quest, for them, has constituted the whole meaning of life. They have made for it without effort sacrifices which have appeared enormous to other men: and it is an indirect testimony to its objective actuality, that whatever the place or period in which they have arisen, their aims, doctrines and methods have been substantially the same. Their experience, therefore, forms a body of evidence, curiously self-consistent and often mutually explanatory, which must be taken into account before we can add up the sum of the energies and potentialities of the human spirit, or reasonably speculate on its relations to the unknown world which lies outside the boundaries of sense.

All men, at one time or another, have fallen in love with the veiled Isis whom they call Truth. With most, this has been a passing passion: they have early seen its hopelessness and turned to more practical things. But others remain all their lives the devout lovers of reality: though the manner of their love, the vision which they make to themselves of the beloved object varies enormously. Some see Truth as Dante saw Beatrice: an adorable yet intangible figure, found in this world yet revealing the next. To others she seems rather an evil but an irresistible enchantress: enticing, demanding payment and betraying her lover at the last. Some have seen her in a test tube, and some in a poet's dream: some before the altar, others in the slime. The extreme pragmatists have even sought her in the kitchen; declaring that she may best be recognized by her utility. Last stage of all, the philosophic sceptic has comforted an unsuccessful courtship by assuring himself that his mistress is not really there.

Under whatsoever symbols they have objectified their quest, none of these seekers have ever been able to assure the world that they have found, seen face to face, the Reality behind the veil. But if we may trust the reports of the mystics--and they are reports given with a strange accent of certainty and good faith--they have succeeded where all these others have failed, in establishing immediate communication between the spirit of man, entangled as they declare amongst material things, and that "only Reality," that immaterial and final Being, which some philosophers call the Absolute, and most theologians call God. This, they say--and here many who are not mystics agree with them--is the hidden Truth which is the object of man's craving; the only satisfying goal of his quest. Hence, they should claim from us the same attention that we give to other explorers of countries in which we are not competent to adventure ourselves; for the mystics are the pioneers of the spiritual world, and we have no right to deny validity to their discoveries, merely because we lack the opportunity or the courage necessary to those who would prosecute such explorations for themselves.

It is the object of this book to attempt a description, and also--though this is needless for those who read that description in good faith--a justification of these experiences and the conclusions which have been drawn from them. So remote, however, are these matters from our ordinary habits of thought, that their investigation entails, in those who would attempt to understand them, a definite preparation: a purging of the intellect. As with those who came of old to the Mysteries, purification is here the gate of knowledge. We must come to this encounter with minds cleared of prejudice and convention, must deliberately break with our inveterate habit of taking the "visible world" for granted; our lazy assumption that somehow science is "real" and metaphysics is not. We must pull down our own card houses--descend, as the mystics say, "into our nothingness"--and examine for ourselves the foundations of all possible human experience, before we are in a position to criticize the buildings of the visionaries, the poets, and the saints. We must not begin to talk of the unreal world of these dreamers until we have discovered--if we can--a real world with which it may be compared.

Such a criticism of reality is of course the business of philosophy. I need hardly say that this book is not written by a philosopher, nor is it addressed to students of that imperial science. Nevertheless, amateurs though we be, we cannot reach our starting-point without trespassing to some extent on philosophic ground. That ground covers the whole area of first principles: and it is to first principles that we must go, if we would understand the true significance of the mystic type.

Let us then begin at the beginning: and remind ourselves of a few of the trite and primary facts which all practical persons agree to ignore. That beginning, for human thought, is of course the I, the Ego, the self-conscious subject which is writing this book, or the other self-conscious subject which is reading it; and which declares, in the teeth of all arguments, I AM. [1] Here is a point as to which we all feel quite sure. No metaphysician has yet shaken the ordinary individual's belief in his own existence. The uncertainties only begin for most of us when we ask what else is .

To this I, this conscious self "imprisoned in the body like an oyster in his shell," [2] come, as we know, a constant stream of messages and experiences. Chief amongst these are the stimulation of the tactile nerves whose result we call touch, the vibrations taken up by the optic nerve which we call light, and those taken up by the ear and perceived as sound.

What do these experiences mean? The first answer of the unsophisticated Self is, that they indicate the nature of the external world: it is to the "evidence of her senses" that she turns, when she is asked what the world is like. From the messages received through those senses, which pour in on her whether she will or no, battering upon her gateways at every instant and from every side, she constructs that "sense-world" which is the "real and solid world" of normal men. As the impressions come in--or rather those interpretations of the original impressions which her nervous system supplies--she pounces on them, much as players in the spelling game pounce on the separate letters dealt out to them. She sorts, accepts, rejects, combines: and then triumphantly produces from them a "concept" which is, she says, the external world. With an enviable and amazing simplicity she attributes her own sensations to the unknown universe. The stars, she says, are bright; the grass is green. For her, as for the philosopher Hume, "reality consists in impressions and ideas."

It is immediately apparent, however, that this sense-world, this seemingly real external universe--though it may be useful and valid in other respects--cannot be the external world, but only the Self's projected picture of it. [3] It is a work of art, not a scientific fact; and, whilst it may well possess the profound significance proper to great works of art, is dangerous if treated as a subject of analysis. Very slight investigation shows that it is a picture whose relation to reality is at best symbolic and approximate, and which would have no meaning for selves whose senses, or channels of communication, happened to be arranged upon a different plan. The evidence of the senses, then, cannot be accepted as evidence of the nature of ultimate reality: useful servants, they are dangerous guides. Nor can their testimony disconcert those seekers whose reports they appear to contradict.

The conscious self sits, so to speak, at the receiving end of a telegraph wire. On any other theory than that of mysticism, it is her one channel of communication with the hypothetical "external world." The receiving instrument registers certain messages. She does not know, and--so long as she remains dependent on that instrument--never can know, the object, the reality at the other end of the wire, by which those messages are sent; neither can the messages truly disclose the nature of that object. But she is justified on the whole in accepting them as evidence that something exists beyond herself and her receiving instrument. It is obvious that the structural peculiarities of the telegraphic instrument will have exerted a modifying effect upon the message. That which is conveyed as dash and dot, colour and shape, may have been received in a very different form. Therefore this message, though it may in a partial sense be relevant to the supposed reality at the other end, can never be adequate to it. There will be fine vibrations which it fails to take up, others which it confuses together. Hence a portion of the message is always lost; or, in other language, there are aspects of the world which we can never know.

The sphere of our possible intellectual knowledge is thus strictly conditioned by the limits of our own personality. On this basis, not the ends of the earth, but the external termini of our own sensory nerves, are the termini of our explorations: and to "know oneself" is really to know one's universe. We are locked up with our receiving instruments: we cannot get up and walk away in the hope of seeing whither the lines lead. Eckhart's words are still final for us: "the soul can only approach created things by the voluntary reception of images." Did some mischievous Demiurge choose to tickle our sensory apparatus in a new way, we should receive by this act a new universe.

William James once suggested as a useful exercise for young idealists, a consideration of the changes which would be worked in our ordinary world if the various branches of our receiving instruments exchanged duties; if, for instance, we heard all colours and saw all sounds. Such a remark throws a sudden light on the strange and apparently insane statement of the visionary Saint-Martin, "I heard flowers that sounded, and saw notes that shone"; and on the reports of other mystics concerning a rare moment of consciousness in which the senses are fused into a single and ineffable act of perception, and colour and sound are known as aspects of one thing. [4]

Since music is but an interpretation of certain vibrations undertaken by the ear, and colour an interpretation of other vibrations performed by the eye, this is less mad than it sounds and may yet be brought within the radius of physical science. Did such an alteration of our senses take place the world would still send us the same messages--that strange unknown world from which, on this hypothesis, we are hermetically sealed--but we should interpret them differently. Beauty would still be ours, though speaking another tongue. The bird's song would then strike our retina as a pageant of colour: we should see the magical tones of the wind, hear as a great fugue the repeated and harmonized greens of the forest, the cadences of stormy skies. Did we realize how slight an adjustment of our organs is needed to initiate us into such a world, we should perhaps be less contemptuous of those mystics who tell us that they apprehended the Absolute as "heavenly music" or "Uncreated Light": less fanatical in our determination to make the solid "world of common sense" the only standard of reality. This "world of common sense" is a conceptual world. It may represent an external universe: it certainly does represent the activity of the human mind. Within that mind it is built up: and there most of us are content "at ease for aye to dwell," like the soul in the Palace of Art.

A direct encounter with absolute truth, then, appears to be impossible for normal non-mystical consciousness. We cannot know the reality, or even prove the existence, of the simplest object: though this is a limitation which few people realize acutely and most would deny. But there persists in the race a type of personality which does realize this limitation: and cannot be content with the sham realities that furnish the universe of normal men. It is necessary, as it seems, to the comfort of persons of this type to form for themselves some image of the Something or Nothing which is at the end of their telegraph lines: some "conception of being," some "theory of knowledge." They are tormented by the Unknowable, ache for first principles, demand some background to the shadow show of things. In so far as man possesses this temperament, he hungers for reality, and must satisfy that hunger as best he can: staving off starvation, though he many not be filled.

It is doubtful whether any two selves have offered themselves exactly the same image of the truth outside their gates: for a living metaphysic, like a living religion, is at bottom a strictly personal affair--a matter, as William James reminded us, of vision rather than of argument. [5] Nevertheless such a living metaphysic may--and if sound generally does--escape the stigma of subjectivism by outwardly attaching itself to a traditional School; as personal religion may and should outwardly attach itself to a traditional church. Let us then consider shortly the results arrived at by these traditional schools--the great classic theories concerning the nature of reality. In them we see crystallized the best that the human intellect, left to itself, has been able to achieve.

I. The most obvious and generally accepted explanation of the world is of course that of Naturalism, or naive Realism: the point of view of the plain man. Naturalism states simply that we see the real world, though we may not see it very well. What seems to normal healthy people to be there, is approximately there. It congratulates itself on resting in the concrete; it accepts material things as real. In other words, our corrected and correlated sense impressions, raised to their highest point of efficiency, form for it the only valid material of knowledge: knowledge itself being the classified results of exact observation.

Such an attitude as this may be a counsel of prudence, in view of our ignorance of all that lies beyond: but it can never satisfy our hunger for reality. It says in effect, "The room in which we find ourselves is fairly comfortable. Draw the curtains, for the night is dark: and let us devote ourselves to describing the furniture." Unfortunately, however, even the furniture refuses to accommodate itself to the naturalistic view of things. Once we begin to examine it attentively, we find that it abounds in hints of wonder and mystery: declares aloud that even chairs and tables are not what they seem.

We have seen that the most elementary criticism, applied to any ordinary object of perception, tends to invalidate the simple and comfortable creed of "common sense"; that not merely faith but gross credulity, is needed by the mind which would accept the apparent as the real. I say, for instance, that I "see" a house. I can only mean by this that the part of my receiving instrument which undertakes the duty called vision is affected in a certain way, and arouses in my mind the idea "house." The idea "house" is now treated by me as a real house, and my further observations will be an unfolding, enriching, and defining of this image. But what the external reality is which evoked the image that I call "house," I do not know and never can know. It is as mysterious, as far beyond my apprehension, as the constitution of the angelic choirs. Consciousness shrinks in terror from contact with the mighty verb "to be." I may of course call in one sense to "corroborate," as we trustfully say, the evidence of the other; may approach the house, and touch it. Then the nerves of my hand will be affected by a sensation which I translate as hardness and solidity; the eye by a peculiar and wholly incomprehensible sensation called redness; and from these purely personal changes my mind constructs and externalizes an idea which it calls red bricks. Science herself, however, if she be asked to verify the reality of these perceptions, at once declares that though the material world be real, the ideas of solidity and colour are but hallucination. They belong to the human animal, not to the physical universe: pertain to accident not substance, as scholastic philosophy would say.

"The red brick," says Science, "is a mere convention. In reality that bit, like all other bits of the universe, consists, so far as I know at present, of innumerable atoms whirling and dancing one about the other. It is no more solid than a snowstorm. Were you to eat of Alice-in-Wonderland's mushroom and shrink to the dimensions of the infra-world, each atom with its electrons might seem to you a solar system and the red brick itself a universe. Moreover, these atoms themselves elude me as I try to grasp them. They are only manifestations of something else. Could I track matter to its lair, I might conceivably discover that it has no extension, and become an idealist in spite of myself. As for redness, as you call it, that is a question of the relation between your optic nerve and the light waves which it is unable to absorb. This evening, when the sun slopes, your brick will probably be purple, a very little deviation from normal vision on your part would make it green. Even the sense that the object of perception is outside yourself may be fancy; since you as easily attribute this external quality to images seen in dreams, and to waking hallucinations, as you do to those objects which, as you absurdly say, are really there.'"

Further, there is no trustworthy standard by which we can separate the "real" from the "unreal" aspects of phenomena. Such standards as exist are conventional: and correspond to convenience, not to truth. It is no argument to say that most men see the world in much the same way, and that this "way" is the true standard of reality: though for practical purposes we have agreed that sanity consists in sharing the hallucinations of our neighbours. Those who are honest with themselves know that this "sharing" is at best incomplete. By the voluntary adoption of a new conception of the universe, the fitting of a new alphabet to the old Morse code--a proceeding which we call the acquirement of knowledge--we can and do change to a marked extent our way of seeing things: building up new worlds from old sense impressions, and transmuting objects more easily and thoroughly than any magician. "Eyes and ears," said Heracleitus, "are bad witnesses to those who have barbarian souls": and even those whose souls are civilized tend to see and hear all things through a temperament. In one and the same sky the poet may discover the habitation of angels, whilst the sailor sees only a promise of dirty weather ahead. Hence, artist and surgeon, Christian and rationalist, pessimist and optimist, do actually and truly live in different and mutually exclusive worlds, not only of thought but also of perception. Only the happy circumstance that our ordinary speech is conventional, not realistic, permits us to conceal from one another the unique and lonely world in which each lives. Now and then an artist is born, terribly articulate, foolishly truthful, who insists on "Speaking as he saw." Then other men, lapped warmly in their artificial universe, agree that he is mad: or, at the very best, an "extraordinarily imaginative fellow."

Moreover, even this unique world of the individual is not permanent. Each of us, as we grow and change, works incessantly and involuntarily at the re-making of our sensual universe. We behold at any specific moment not "that which is," but "that which we are", and personality undergoes many readjustments in the course of its passage from birth through maturity to death. The mind which seeks the Real, then, in this shifting and subjective "natural" world is of necessity thrown back on itself: on images and concepts which owe more to the "seer" than to the "seen." But Reality must be real for all, once they have found it: must exist "in itself" upon a plane of being unconditioned by the perceiving mind. Only thus can it satisfy that mind's most vital instinct, most sacred passion--its "instinct for the Absolute," its passion for truth.

You are not asked, as a result of these antique and elementary propositions, to wipe clean the slate of normal human experience, and cast in your lot with intellectual nihilism. You are only asked to acknowledge that it is but a slate, and that the white scratches upon it which the ordinary man calls facts, and the Scientific Realist calls knowledge, are at best relative and conventionalized symbols of that aspect of the unknowable reality at which they hint. This being so, whilst we must all draw a picture of some kind on our slate and act in relation therewith, we cannot deny the validity--though we may deny the usefulness--of the pictures which others produce, however abnormal and impossible they may seem; since these are sketching an aspect of reality which has not come within our sensual field, and so does not and cannot form part of our world. Yet as the theologian claims that the doctrine of the Trinity veils and reveals not Three but One, so the varied aspects under which the universe appears to the perceiving consciousness hint at a final reality, or in Kantian language, a Transcendental Object, which shall be, not any one, yet all of its manifestations; transcending yet including the innumerable fragmentary worlds of individual conception. We begin, then, to ask what can be the nature of this One; and whence comes the persistent instinct which--receiving no encouragement from sense experience--apprehends and desires this unknown unity, this all-inclusive Absolute, as the only possible satisfaction of its thirst for truth.

2. The second great conception of Being-- Idealism-- has arrived by a process of elimination at a tentative answer to this question. It whisks us far from the material universe, with its interesting array of "things," its machinery, its law, into the pure, if thin, air of a metaphysical world. Whilst the naturalist's world is constructed from an observation of the evidence offered by the senses, the Idealist's world is constructed from an observation of the processes of thought. There are but two things, he says in effect, about which we are sure: the existence of a thinking subject, a conscious Self, and of an object, an Idea, with which that subject deals. We know, that is to say, both Mind and Thought. What we call the universe is really a collection of such thoughts; and these, we agree, have been more or less distorted by the subject, the individual thinker, in the process of assimilation. Obviously, we do not think all that there is to be thought, conceive all that there is to be conceived; neither do we necessarily combine in right order and proportion those ideas which we are capable of grasping. Reality, says Objective Idealism, is the complete, undistorted Object, the big thought, of which we pick up these fragmentary hints: the world of phenomena which we treat as real being merely its shadow show or "manifestation in space and time."

According to the form of Objective Idealism here chosen from amongst many as typical--for almost every Idealist has his own scheme of metaphysical salvation [6] --we live in a universe which is, in popular language, the Idea, or Dream of its Creator. We, as Tweedledum explained to Alice in the most philosophic of all fairy tales, are "just part of the dream." All life, all phenomena, are the endless modifications and expressions of the one transcendent Object, the mighty and dynamic Thought of one Absolute Thinker, in which we are bathed. This Object, or certain aspects of it--and the place of each individual consciousness within the Cosmic Thought, or, as we say, our position in life, largely determines which these aspects shall be--is interpreted by the senses and conceived by the mind, under limitations which we are accustomed to call matter, space and time. But we have no reason to suppose that matter, space, and time are necessarily parts of reality; of the ultimate Idea. Probability points rather to their being the pencil and paper with which we sketch it. As our vision, our idea of things, tends to approximate more and more to that of the Eternal Idea, so we get nearer and nearer to reality: for the idealist's reality is simply the Idea, or Thought of God. This, he says, is the supreme unity at which all the illusory appearances that make up the widely differing worlds of "common sense," of science, of metaphysics, and of art dimly hint. This is the sense in which it can truly be said that only the supernatural possesses reality; for that world of appearance which we call natural is certainly largely made up of preconception and illusion, of the hints offered by the eternal real world of Idea outside our gates, and the quaint concepts which we at our receiving instrument manufacture from them.

There is this to be said for the argument of Idealism: that in the last resort, the destinies of mankind are invariably guided, not by the concrete "facts" of the sense world, but by concepts which are acknowledged by every one to exist only on the mental plane. In the great moments of existence, when he rises to spiritual freedom, these are the things which every man feels to be real. It is by these and for these that he is found willing to live, work suffer, and die. Love, patriotism, religion, altruism, fame, all belong to the transcendental world. Hence, they partake more of the nature of reality than any "fact" could do; and man, dimly recognizing this, has ever bowed to them as to immortal centres of energy. Religions as a rule are steeped in idealism: Christianity in particular is a trumpet call to an idealistic conception of life, Buddhism is little less. Over and over again, their Scriptures tell us that only materialists will be damned.

In Idealism we have perhaps the most sublime theory of Being which has ever been constructed by the human intellect: a theory so sublime, in fact, that it can hardly have been produced by the exercise of "pure reason" alone, but must be looked upon as a manifestation of that natural mysticism, that instinct for the Absolute, which is latent in man. But, when we ask the idealist how we are to attain communion with the reality which he describes to us as "certainly there," his system suddenly breaks down; and discloses itself as a diagram of the heavens, not a ladder to the stars. This failure of Idealism to find in practice the reality of which it thinks so much is due, in the opinion of the mystics, to a cause which finds epigrammatic expression in the celebrated phrase by which St. Jerome marked the distinction between religion and philosophy. "Plato located the soul of man in the head; Christ located it in the heart." That is to say, Idealism, though just in its premises, and often daring and honest in their application, is stultified by the exclusive intellectualism of its own methods: by its fatal trust in the squirrel-work of the industrious brain instead of the piercing vision of the desirous heart. It interests man, but does not involve him in its processes: does not catch him up to the new and more real life which it describes. Hence the thing that matters, the living thing, has somehow escaped it; and its observations bear the same relation to reality as the art of the anatomist does to the mystery of birth.

3. But there is yet another Theory of Being to be considered: that which may be loosely defined as Philosophic Scepticism. This is the attitude of those who refuse to accept either the realistic or the idealistic answer to the eternal question: and, confronted in their turn with the riddle of reality, reply that there is no riddle to solve. We of course assume for the ordinary purposes of life that for every sequence a: b: present in our consciousness there exists a mental or material A: B: in the external universe, and

that the first is a strictly relevant, though probably wholly inadequate, expression of the second. The bundle of visual and auditory sensations, for instance, whose sum total I am accustomed to call Mrs. Smith, corresponds with something that exists in the actual as well as in my phenomenal world. Behind my Mrs. Smith, behind the very different Mrs. Smith which the X rays would exhibit, there is, contends the Objective Idealist, a transcendental, or in the Platonic sense an ideal Mrs. Smith, at whose qualities I cannot even guess; but whose existence is quite independent of my apprehension of it. But though we do and must act on this hypothesis, it remains only a hypothesis; and it is one which philosophic scepticism will not let pass.

The external world, say the sceptical schools, is--so far as I know it--a concept present in my mind. If my mind ceased to exist, so far as I know the concept which I call the world would cease to exist too. The one thing which for me indubitably is, the self's experience, its whole consciousness. Outside this circle of consciousness I have no authority to indulge in guesses as to what may or may not Be. Hence, for me, the Absolute is a meaningless diagram, a superfluous complication of thought: since the mind, wholly cut off from contact with external reality, has no reason to suppose that such a reality exists except in its own ideas. Every effort made by philosophy to go forth in search of it is merely the metaphysical squirrel running round the conceptual cage. In the completion and perfect unfolding of the set of ideas with which our consciousness is furnished, lies the only reality which we can ever hope to know. Far better to stay here and make ourselves at home: only this, for us, truly is.

This purely subjective conception of Being has found representatives in every school of thought: even including by a curious paradox, that of mystical philosophy--its one effective antagonist. Thus Delacroix, after an exhaustive and even sympathetic analysis of St. Teresa's progress towards union with the Absolute, ends upon the assumption that the God with whom she was united was the content of her own subconscious mind. [7] Such a mysticism is that of a kitten running after its own tail: a different path indeed from that which the great seekers for reality have pursued. The reductio ad absurdum of this doctrine is found in the so-called "philosophy" of New Thought, which begs its disciples to "try quietly to realize that the Infinite is really You." [8] By its utter denial not merely of a knowable, but of a logically conceivable Transcendent, it drives us in the end to the conclusion of extreme pragmatism; that Truth, for us, is not an immutable reality, but merely that idea which happens to work out as true and useful in any given experience. There is no reality behind appearance; therefore all faiths, all figments with which we people that nothingness are equally true, provided they be comfortable and good to live by.

Logically carried out, this conception of Being would permit each man to regard other men as non-existent except within his own consciousness: the only place where a strict scepticism will allow that anything exists. Even the mind which conceives consciousness exists for us only in our own conception of it; we no more know what we are than we know what we shall be. Man is left a conscious Something in the midst, so far as he knows, of Nothing: with no resources save the exploring of his own consciousness.

Philosophic scepticism is particularly interesting to our present inquiry, because it shows us the position in which "pure reason," if left to itself, is bound to end. It is utterly logical; and though we may feel it to be absurd, we can never prove it to be so. Those who are temperamentally inclined to credulity may become naturalists, and persuade themselves to believe in the reality of the sense world. Those with a certain instinct for the Absolute may adopt the more reasonable faith of idealism. But the true intellectualist, who concedes nothing to instinct or emotion, is obliged in the end to adopt some form of sceptical philosophy. The horrors of nihilism, in fact, can only be escaped by the exercise of faith, by a trust in man's innate but strictly irrational instinct for that Real "above all reason, beyond all thought" towards which at its best moments his spirit tends. If the metaphysician be true to his own postulates, he must acknowledge in the end that we are all forced to live, to think, and at last to die, in an unknown and unknowable world: fed arbitrarily and diligently, yet how we know not, by ideas and suggestions whose truth we cannot test but whose pressure we cannot resist. It is not by sight but by faith--faith in a supposed external order which we can never prove to exist, and in the approximate truthfulness and constancy of the vague messages which we receive from it--that ordinary men must live and move. We must put our trust in "laws of nature" which have been devised by the human mind as a convenient epitome of its own observations of phenomena, must, for the purposes of daily life, accept these phenomena at their face value: an act of faith beside which the grossest superstitions of the Neapolitan peasant are hardly noticeable.

The intellectual quest of Reality, then, leads us down one of three blind alleys: (1) To an acceptance of the symbolic world of appearance as the real; (2) to the elaboration of a theory also of necessity symbolic--which, beautiful in itself, cannot help us to attain the Absolute which it describes; (3) to a hopeless but strictly logical skepticism.

In answer to the "Why? Why?" of the bewildered and eternal child in us, philosophy, though always ready to postulate the unknown if she can, is bound to reply only, "Nescio! Nescio!" In spite of all her busy map-making, she cannot reach the goal which she points out to us, cannot explain the curious conditions under which we imagine that we know; cannot even divide with a sure hand the subject and object of thought. Science, whose business is with phenomena and our knowledge of them, though she too is an idealist at heart, has been accustomed to explain that all our ideas and instincts, the pictured world that we take so seriously, the oddly limited and illusory nature of our experience, appear to minister to one great end: the preservation of life, and consequent fulfilment of that highly mystical hypothesis, the Cosmic Idea. Each perception, she assures us, serves a useful purpose in this evolutionary scheme: a scheme, by the way, which has been invented--we know not why--by the human mind, and imposed upon an obedient universe.

By vision, hearing, smell, and touch, says Science, we find our way about, are warned of danger, obtain our food. The male perceives beauty in the female in order that the species may be propagated. It is true that this primitive instinct has given birth to higher and purer emotions; but these too fulfil a social purpose and are not so useless as they seem. Man must eat to live, therefore many foods give us agreeable sensations. If he overeats, he dies; therefore indigestion is an unpleasant pain. Certain facts of which too keen a perception would act detrimentally to the life-force are, for most men, impossible of realization: i.e. , the uncertainty of life, the decay of the body, the vanity of all things under the sun. When we are in good health, we all feel very real, solid, and permanent; and this is of all our illusions the most ridiculous, and also the most obviously useful from the point of view of the efficiency and preservation of the race.

But when we look closer, we see that this brisk generalization does not cover all the ground--not even that little tract of ground of which our senses make us free; indeed, that it is more remarkable for its omissions than for its inclusions. Récéjac has well said that "from the moment in which man is no longer content to devise things useful for his existence under the exclusive action of the will-to-live, the principle of (physical) evolution has been violated." [9] Nothing can be more certain than that man is not so content. He has been called by utilitarian philosophers a tool-making animal--the highest praise they knew how to bestow. More surely he is a vision-making animal; [10] a creature of perverse and unpractical ideals, dominated by dreams no less than by appetites--dreams which can only be justified upon the theory that he moves towards some other goal than that of physical perfection or intellectual supremacy, is controlled by some higher and more vital reality than that of the determinists. We are driven to the conclusion that if the theory of evolution is to include or explain the facts of artistic and spiritual experience--and it cannot be accepted by any serious thinker if these great tracts of consciousness remain outside its range--it must be rebuilt on a mental rather than a physical basis.

Even the most ordinary human life includes in its range fundamental experiences--violent and unforgettable sensations--forced on us as it were against our will, for which science finds it hard to account. These experiences and sensations, and the hours of exalted emotion which they bring with them--often recognized by us as the greatest, most significant hours of our lives--fulfil no office in relation to her pet "functions of nutrition and reproduction." It is true that they are far-reaching in their effects on character; but they do little or nothing to assist that character in its struggle for physical life. To the unprejudiced eye many of them seem hopelessly out of place in a universe constructed on strictly physico-chemical lines--look almost as though nature, left to herself, tended to contradict her own beautifully logical laws. Their presence, more, the large place which they fill in the human world of appearance, is a puzzling circumstance for deterministic philosophers; who can only escape from the dilemma here presented to them by calling these things illusions, and dignifying their own more manageable illusions with the title of facts.

Amongst the more intractable of these groups of perceptions and experiences are those which we connect with religion, with pain and with beauty. All three, for those selves which are capable of receiving their messages, possess a mysterious authority far in excess of those feelings, arguments, or appearances which they may happen to contradict. All three, were the universe of the naturalists true, would be absurd; all three have ever been treated with the reverence due to vital matters by the best minds of the race.

A. I need not point out the hopelessly irrational character of all great religions: which rest, one and all, on a primary assumption that can never be intellectually demonstrated, much less proved--the assumption that the supra-sensible is somehow important and real, and is intimately connected with the life of man. This fact has been incessantly dwelt upon by their critics, and has provoked many a misplaced exercise of ingenuity on the part of their intelligent friends. Yet religion--emphasizing and pushing to extremes that general dependence on faith which we saw to be an inevitable condition of our lives--is one of the most universal and ineradicable functions of man, and this although it constantly acts detrimentally to the interests of his merely physical existence, opposes "the exclusive action of the will-to-live," except in so far as that will aspires to eternal life. Strictly utilitarian, almost logical in the savage, religion becomes more and more transcendental with the upward progress of the race. It begins as black magic; it ends as Pure Love. Why did the Cosmic Idea elaborate this religious instinct, if the construction put upon its intentions by the determinists be true?

B. Consider again the whole group of phenomena which are known as "the problem of suffering":

the mental anguish and physical pain which appear to be the inevitable result of the steady operation of "natural law" and its voluntary assistants, the cruelty, greed, and injustice of man. Here, it is true, the naturalist seems at first sight to make a little headway, and can point to some amongst the cruder forms of suffering which are clearly useful to the race: punishing us for past follies, spurring to new efforts, warning against future infringements of "law." But he forgets the many others which refuse to be resumed under this simple formula: forgets to explain how it is that the Cosmic Idea involves the long torments of the incurable, the tortures of the innocent, the deep anguish of the bereaved, the existence of so many gratuitously agonizing forms of death. He forgets, too, the strange fact that man's capacity for suffering tends to increase in depth and subtlety with the increase of culture and civilization; ignores the still more mysterious, perhaps most significant circumstance that the highest types have accepted it eagerly and willingly, have found in Pain the grave but kindly teacher of immortal secrets, the conferrer of liberty, even the initiator into amazing joys.

Those who "explain" suffering as the result of nature's immense fecundity--a by-product of that overcrowding and stress through which the fittest tend to survive--forget that even were this demonstration valid and complete it would leave the real problem untouched. The question is not, whence come those conditions which provoke in the self the experiences called sorrow, anxiety, pain: but, why do these conditions hurt the self? The pain is mental; a little chloroform, and though the conditions continue unabated the suffering is gone. Why does full consciousness always include the mysterious capacity for misery as well as for happiness--a capacity which seems at first sight to invalidate any conception of the Absolute as Beautiful and Good? Why does evolution, as we ascend the ladder of life, foster instead of diminishing the capacity for useless mental anguish, for long, dull torment, bitter grief? Why, when so much lies outside our limited powers of perception, when so many of our own most vital functions are unperceived by consciousness, does suffering of some sort form an integral part of the experience of man? For utilitarian purposes acute discomfort would be quite enough; the Cosmic Idea, as the determinists explain it, did not really need an apparatus which felt all the throes of cancer, the horrors of neurasthenia, the pangs of birth. Still less did it need the torments of impotent sympathy for other people's irremediable pain the dreadful power of feeling the world's woe. We are hopelessly over-sensitized for the part science calls us to play.

Pain, however we may look at it, indicates a profound disharmony between the sense-world and the human self. If it is to be vanquished, either the disharmony must be resolved by a deliberate and careful adjustment of the self to the world of sense, or, that self must turn from the sense-world to some other with which it is in tune. [11] Pessimist and optimist here join hands. But whilst the pessimist, resting in appearance, only sees "nature red in tooth and claw" offering him little hope of escape, the optimist thinks that pain and anguish--which may in their lower forms be life's harsh guides on the path of physical evolution--in their higher and apparently "useless" developments are her leaders and teachers in the upper school of Supra-sensible Reality. He believes that they press the self towards another world, still "natural" for him, though "supernatural" for his antagonist, in which it will be more at home. Watching life, he sees in Pain the complement of Love: and is inclined to call these the wings on which man's spirit can best take flight towards the Absolute. Hence he can say with A Kempis, "Gloriari in tribulatione non est grave amanti," [12] and needs not to speak of morbid folly when he sees the Christian saints run eagerly and merrily to the Cross. [13]

He calls suffering the "gymnastic of eternity," the "terrible initiative caress of God"; recognizing in it a quality for which the disagreeable rearrangement of nerve molecules cannot account. Sometimes, in the excess of his optimism, he puts to the test of practice this theory with all its implications. Refusing to be deluded by the pleasures of the sense world, he accepts instead of avoiding pain, and becomes an ascetic; a puzzling type for the convinced naturalist, who, falling back upon contempt--that favourite resource of the frustrated reason--can only regard him as diseased.

Pain, then, which plunges like a sword through creation, leaving on the one side cringing and degraded animals and on the other side heroes and saints, is one of those facts of universal experience which are peculiarly intractable from the point of view of a merely materialistic philosophy.

C. From this same point of view the existence of music and poetry, the qualities of beauty and of rhythm, the evoked sensations of awe, reverence, and rapture, are almost as difficult to account for. The question why an apparent corrugation of the Earth's surface, called for convenience' sake an Alp, coated with congealed water, and perceived by us as a snowy peak, should produce in certain natures acute sensations of ecstasy and adoration, why the skylark's song should catch us up to heaven, and wonder and mystery speak to us alike in "the little speedwell's darling blue" and in the cadence of the wind, is a problem that seems to be merely absurd, until it is seen to be insoluble. Here Madam How and Lady Why alike are silent. With all our busy seeking, we have not found the sorting house where loveliness is extracted from the flux of things. We know not why "great" poetry should move us to unspeakable emotion, or a stream of notes, arranged in a peculiar sequence, catch us up to heightened levels of vitality: nor can we guess how a passionate admiration for that which we call "best" in art or letters can possibly contribute to the physical evolution of the race. In spite of many lengthy disquisitions on

Esthetics, Beauty's secret is still her own. A shadowy companion, half seen, half guessed at, she keeps step with the upward march of life: and we receive her message and respond to it, not because we understand it but because we must .

Here it is that we approach that attitude of the self, that point of view, which is loosely and generally called mystical. Here, instead of those broad blind alleys which philosophy showed us, a certain type of mind has always discerned three strait and narrow ways going out towards the Absolute. In religion, in pain, and in beauty--and not only in these, but in many other apparently useless peculiarities of the empirical world and of the perceiving consciousness--these persons insist that they recognize at least the fringe of the real. Down these three paths, as well as by many another secret way, they claim that news comes to the self concerning levels of reality which in their wholeness are inaccessible to the senses: worlds wondrous and immortal, whose existence is not conditioned by the "given" world which those senses report. "Beauty," said Hegel, who, though he was no mystic, had a touch of that mystical intuition which no philosopher can afford to be without, "is merely the Spiritual making itself known sensuously." [14] In the good, the beautiful, the true," says Rudolph Eucken, "we see Reality revealing its personal character. They are parts of a coherent and substantial spiritual world." [15] Here, some of the veils of that substantial world are stripped off: Reality peeps through and is recognized, dimly or acutely, by the imprisoned self.

Récéjac only develops this idea when he says, [16] "If the mind penetrates deeply into the facts of aesthetics, it will find more and more, that these facts are based upon an ideal identity between the mind itself and things. At a certain point the harmony becomes so complete, and the finality so close that it gives us actual emotion. The Beautiful then becomes the sublime; brief apparition, by which the soul is caught up into the true mystic state, and touches the Absolute. It is scarcely possible to persist in this Esthetic perception without feeling lifted up by it above things and above ourselves, in an ontological vision which closely resembles the Absolute of the Mystics." It was of this underlying reality--this truth of things--that St. Augustine cried in a moment of lucid vision, "Oh, Beauty so old and so new, too late have I loved thee!" [17] It is in this sense also that "beauty is truth, truth beauty": and as regards the knowledge of ultimate things which is possible to ordinary men, it may well be that

"That is all
Ye know on earth, and all ye need to know."

"Of Beauty," says Plato in an immortal passage, "I repeat again that we saw her there shining in company with the celestial forms; and coming to earth we find her here too, shining in clearness through the clearest aperture of sense. For sight is the most piercing of our bodily senses: though not by that is wisdom seen; her loveliness would have been transporting if there had been a visible image of her, and the other ideas, if they had visible counterparts, would be equally lovely. But this is the privilege of Beauty, that being the loveliest she is also the most palpable to sight. Now he who is not newly initiated, or who has been corrupted, does not easily rise out of this world to the sight of true beauty in the other. . . . But he whose initiation is recent, and who has been the spectator of many glories in the other world, is amazed when he sees anyone having a godlike face or form, which is the expression of Divine Beauty; and at first a shudder runs through him, and again the old awe steals over him. . . ." [18]

Most men in the course of their lives have known such Platonic hours of initiation, when the sense of beauty has risen from a pleasant feeling to a passion, and an element of strangeness and terror has been mingled with their joy. In those hours the world has seemed charged with a new vitality; with a splendour which does not belong to it but is poured through it, as light through a coloured window, grace through a sacrament, from that Perfect Beauty which "shines in company with the celestial forms" beyond the pale of appearance. In such moods of heightened consciousness each blade of grass seems fierce with meaning, and becomes a well of wondrous light: a "little emerald set in the City of God." The seeing self is indeed an initiate thrust suddenly into the sanctuary of the mysteries: and feels the "old awe and amazement" with which man encounters the Real. In such experiences, a new factor of the eternal calculus appears to be thrust in on us, a factor which no honest seeker for truth can afford to neglect; since, if it be dangerous to say that any two systems of knowledge are mutually exclusive, it is still more dangerous to give uncritical priority to any one system. We are bound, then, to examine this path to reality as closely and seriously as we should investigate the most neatly finished safety-ladder of solid ash which offered a salita alle stelle.

Why, after all, take as our standard a material world whose existence is affirmed by nothing more trustworthy than the sense-impressions of "normal men"; those imperfect and easily cheated channels of communication? The mystics, those adventurers of whom we spoke upon the first page of this book, have always declared, implicitly or explicitly, their distrust in these channels of communication. They have never been deceived by phenomena, nor by the careful logic of the industrious intellect. One after another, with extraordinary unanimity, they have rejected that appeal to the unreal world of appearance which is the standard of sensible men: affirming that there is another way, another secret, by which the conscious self may reach the actuality which it seeks. More complete in their grasp of experience than the votaries of intellect or of sense, they accept as central for life those spiritual messages which are mediated by religion, by beauty, and by pain. More reasonable than the rationalists, they find in that very hunger for reality which is the mother of all metaphysics, an implicit proof that such reality exists; that there is something else, some final satisfaction, beyond the ceaseless stream of sensation which besieges consciousness. "In that thou hast sought me, thou hast already found me," says the voice of Absolute Truth in their ears. This is the first doctrine of mysticism. Its next is that only in so far as the self is real can it hope to know Reality: like to like: Cot ad cot loquitur. Upon the propositions implicit in these two laws the whole claim and practice of the mystic life depends.

"Finite as we are," they say--and here they speak not for themselves, but for the race--"lost though we seem to be in the woods or in the wide air's wilderness, in this world of time and of chance, we have still, like the strayed animals or like the migrating birds, our homing instinct. . . . We seek. That is a fact. We seek a city still out of sight. In the contrast with this goal, we live. But if this be so, then already we possess something of Being even in our finite seeking. For the readiness to seek is already something of an attainment, even if a poor one." [19]

Further, in this seeking we are not wholly dependent on that homing instinct. For some, who have climbed to the hill-tops, that city is not really out of sight. The mystics see it and report to us concerning it. Science and metaphysics may do their best and their worst: but these pathfinders of the spirit never falter in their statements concerning that independent spiritual world which is the only goal of "pilgrim man." They say that messages come to him from that spiritual world, that complete reality which we call Absolute: that we are not, after all, hermetically sealed from it. To all who will receive it, news comes of a world of Absolute Life, Absolute Beauty, Absolute Truth, beyond the bourne of time and place: news that most of us translate--and inevitably distort in the process--into the language of religion, of beauty, of love, or of pain.

Of all those forms of life and thought with which humanity has fed its craving for truth, mysticism alone postulates, and in the persons of its great initiates proves, not only the existence of the Absolute, but also this link: this possibility first of knowing, finally of attaining it. It denies that possible knowledge is to be limited (a) to sense impressions, (b) to any process of intellection, (c) to the unfolding of the content of normal consciousness. Such diagrams of experience, it says, are hopelessly incomplete. The mystics find the basis of their method not in logic but in life: in the existence of a discoverable "real," a spark of true being, within the seeking subject, which can, in that ineffable experience which they call the "act of union," fuse itself with and thus apprehend the reality of the sought Object. In theological language, their theory of knowledge is that the spirit of man, itself essentially divine, is capable of immediate communion with God, the One Reality. [20]

In mysticism that love of truth which we saw as the beginning of all philosophy leaves the merely intellectual sphere, and takes on the assured aspect of a personal passion. Where the philosopher guesses and argues, the mystic lives and looks; and speaks, consequently, the disconcerting language of first-hand experience, not the neat dialectic of the schools. Hence whilst the Absolute of the metaphysicians remains a diagram--impersonal and unattainable--the Absolute of the mystics is lovable, attainable, alive.

"Oh, taste and see!" they cry, in accents of astounding certainty and joy. "Ours is an experimental science. We can but communicate our system, never its result. We come to you not as thinkers, but as doers. Leave your deep and absurd trust in the senses, with their language of dot and dash, which may possibly report fact but can never communicate personality. If philosophy has taught you anything, she has surely taught you the length of her tether, and the impossibility of attaining to the doubtless admirable grazing land which lies beyond it. One after another, idealists have arisen who, straining frantically at the rope, have announced to the world their approaching liberty; only to be flung back at last into the little circle of sensation. But here we are, a small family, it is true, yet one that refuses to die out, assuring you that we have slipped the knot and are free of those grazing grounds. This is evidence which you are bound to bring into account before you can add up the sum total of possible knowledge; for you will find it impossible to prove that the world as seen by the mystics, unimaginable, formless, dark with excess of bright,' is less real than that which is expounded by the youngest and most promising demonstrator of a physicochemical universe. We will be quite candid with you. Examine us as much as you like: our machinery, our veracity, our results. We cannot promise that you shall see what we have seen, for here each man must adventure for himself; but we defy you to stigmatize our experiences as impossible or invalid. Is your world of experience so well and logically founded that you dare make of it a standard? Philosophy tells you that it is founded on nothing better than the reports of your sensory apparatus and the traditional concepts of the race. Certainly it is imperfect, probably it is illusion in any event, it never touches the foundation of things. Whereas what the world, which truly knows nothing, calls "mysticism" is the science of ultimates, . . . the science of self-evident Reality, which cannot be "reasoned about," because it is the object of pure reason or perception.'" [21]

Footnotes:

1. Even this I AM, which has seemed safe ground to most metaphysicians, is of course combated by certain schools of philosophy. "The word Sum ," said Eckhart long ago, "can be spoken by no creature but by God only: for it becomes the creature to testify of itself Non Sum ." In a less mystical strain Lotze, and after him Bradley and other modern writers, have devoted much destructive criticism to the concept of the Ego as the starting-point of philosophy: looking upon it as a large, and logically unwarrantable, assumption.

2. Plato, "Phaedrus," § 250.

3. Thus Eckhart, "Every time that the powers of the soul come into contact with created things, they receive the create images and likenesses from the created thing and absorb them. In this way arises the soul's knowledge of created things. Created things cannot come nearer to the soul than this, and the soul can only approach created things by the voluntary reception of images. And it is through the presence of the image that the soul approaches the created world: for the image is a Thing, which the soul creates with her own powers. Does the soul want to know the nature of a stone--horse--a man? She forms an image."---Meister Eckhart, Pred. i. ("Mystische Schriften," p. 15).

4. Thus Edward Carpenter says of his own experience of the mystical consciousness, "The perception seems to be one in which all the senses unite into one sense" (quoted in Bucke's "Cosmic Consciousness," p. 198).

5. "A Pluralistic Universe," p. 10.

6. There are four main groups of such schemes: (1) Subjective; (2) Objective; (3) Transcendental (Kantian); (4) Absolute (Hegelian). To this last belongs by descent the Immanental Idealism of Croce and Gentile.

7. Delacroix, "Études sur le Mysticisme," p. 62.

8. E. Towne, "Just how to Wake the Solar Plexus," p. 25.

9. "Fondements de la Connaissance Mystique," p. 15.

10. Or, as Aristotle, and after him St. Thomas Aquinas, suggest, a contemplative animal, since "this act alone in man is proper to him, and is in no way shared by any other being in this world" ("Summa Contra Gentiles," l. iii, cap. xxxvii., Rickaby's translation).

11. All the healing arts, from Aesculapius and Galen to Metchnikoff and Mrs. Eddy, have virtually accepted and worked upon these two principles.

12. "De Imitatione Christi." I. ii. cap. vi.

13. "Such as these, I say, as if enamoured by My honour and famished for the food of souls, run to the table of the Most holy Cross, willing to suffer pain. . . . To these, My most dear sons, trouble is a pleasure, and pleasure and every consolation that the world would offer them are a toil" (St. Catherine of Siena, Dialogo, cap. xxviii.). Here and throughout I have used Thorold's translation.

14. "Philosophy of Religion," vol. ii. p. 8.

15. "Der Sinn und Wert des Lebens," p. 148.

16. "Fondements de la Connaissance Mystique," p. 74.

17. Aug. Conf., bk. x. cap. xxvii.

18. "Phaedrus," § 250 (Jowett's translation). The reference in the phrase "he whose initiation is recent" is to the rite of admission into the Orphic Mysteries. It is believed by some authorities that the neophyte may have been cast into an hypnotic sleep by his "initiator," and whilst in this condition a vision of the "glories of the other world" suggested to him. The main phenomena of "conversion" would thus be artificially produced: but the point of attack being the mind rather than the heart, the results, as would appear from the context, were usually transient.

19. Royce, "The World and the Individual," vol. i. p. 181.

20. The idea of Divine Union as man's true end is of course of great antiquity. Its first definite appearance in the religious consciousness of Europe seems to coincide with the establishment of the Orphic Mysteries in Greece and Southern Italy in the sixth century B.C. See Rohde: "Psyche," cap. 10, and Adam, "The Religious Teachers of Greece," p. 92.

21. Coventry Patmore, "The Rod, the Root, and the Flower," "Aurea Dicta," cxxviii.

CHAPTER II

W e glanced, at the beginning of this inquiry, at the universes which result from the various forms of credulity practised by the materialist, the idealist, and the sceptic. We saw the mystic denying by word and act the validity of the foundations on which those universes are built: substituting his living experience for their conceptual schemes. But there is another way of seeing reality or, more correctly, one aspect of reality. This scheme of things possesses the merit of accepting and harmonizing many different forms of experience; even those supreme experiences and intuitions peculiar to the mystics. The first distinct contribution of the twentieth century to man's quest of the Real, it entered the philosophic arena from several different directions; penetrating and modifying current conceptions not only of philosophy but of religion, science, art and practical life. It was applied by Driesch [22] and other biologists in the sphere of organic life. Bergson, [23] starting from psychology, developed its intellectual and metaphysical implications; whilst Rudolph Eucken [24] constructed from, or beside it, a philosophy of the Spirit, of man's relations to the Real.

In all these we find the same principle; the principle of a free spontaneous and creative life as the essence of Reality. Not law but aliveness, incalculable and indomitable, is their subject-matter: not human logic, but actual living experience is their criterion of truth. Vitalists, whether the sphere of their explorations be biology, psychology or ethics, see the whole Cosmos, the physical and spiritual worlds, as instinct with initiative and spontaneity: as above all things free. For them, nature, though conditioned by the matter with which she works, is stronger than her chains. Pushing out from within, ever seeking expression, she buds and breaks forth into original creation. [25] The iron "laws" of the determinists are merely her observed habits, not her fetters: and man, seeing nature in the terms of "cause and effect," has been the dupe of his own limitations and prejudices.

Bergson, Nietzsche, Eucken, differing in their opinion as to life's meaning, are alike in this vision: in the stress which they lay on the supreme importance and value of life--a great Cosmic life transcending and including our own. This is materialism inside out: for here what we call the universe is presented as an expression of life, not life as an expression or by-product of the universe. The strange passionate philosophy of Nietzsche is really built upon an intense belief in this supernal nature and value of Life, Action and Strength: and spoilt by the one-sided individualism which prevented him from holding a just balance between the great and significant life of the Ego and the greater and more significant life of the All.

Obviously, the merit of vitalistic philosophy lies in its ability to satisfy so many different thinkers, starting from such diverse points in our common experience. On the phenomenal side it can accept and transfigure the statements of physical science. In its metaphysical aspect it leaves place for those ontological speculations which seem to take their rise in psychology. It is friendly to those who demand an important place for moral and spiritual activity in the universe. Finally--though here we must be content with deduction rather than declaration--it leaves in the hands of the mystics that power of attaining to Absolute Reality which they have always claimed: shows them as the true possessors of freedom, the torch-bearers of the race.

Did it acknowledge its ancestors with that reverence which is their due, Vitalism would identify itself with the mystic philosopher, Heracleitus; who, in the fifth century B.C., introduced its central idea to the European world [26] : for his "Logos" or Energizing Fire is but another symbol for that free and living Spirit of Becoming, that indwelling creative power, which Vitalism acknowledges as the very soul or immanent reality of things. It is in essence both a Hellenic and a Christian system of thought. In its view of the proper function of the intellect it has some unexpected affinities with Aristotle, and after him with St. Thomas Aquinas; regarding it as a departmental affair, not the organ of ultimate knowledge. Its theory of knowledge is close to that of the mystics: or would be, if those gazers on reality had interested themselves in any psychological theory of their own experiences.

A philosophy which can harmonize such diverse elements as these, and make its influence felt in so many fields of thought, may be useful in our present attempt towards an understanding of mysticism: for it illustrates certain aspects of perceived reality which other systems ignore. It has the further recommendation of involving not a mere diagram of metaphysical possibilities, but a genuine theory of knowledge. Its scope includes psychology as well as philosophy: the consideration, not only of the nature of Reality but also of the self's power of knowing it--the machinery of contact between the mind and the flux of things. Thus it has an inclusive quality lacking in the tidy ring-fenced systems of other schools of thought. It has no edges, and if it be true to itself should have no negations. It is a vision, not a map.

The primary difference between Vitalism and the classic philosophic schools is this. Its focal point is not Being but Becoming. [27] Translated into Platonic language, not the changeless One, the Absolute, transcending all succession, but rather His energizing Thought--the Son, the Creative Logos--is the supreme reality which it proposes as accessible to human consciousness.

"All things," said Heracleitus, "are in a state of flux." "Everything happens through strife." "Reality is a condition of unrest." [28] Such is also the opinion of Bergson and Alexander; who, agreeing in this with the conclusions of physical science, look upon the Real as dynamic rather than static, as becoming rather than being perfect, and invite us to see in Time--the precession or flux of things--the very stuff of reality--

"From the fixed lull of Heaven she saw
Time like a pulse shake fierce
Through all the worlds"-- [29]

said Rossetti of the Blessed Damozel. So Bergson, while ignoring if he does not deny the existence of the "fixed lull," the still Eternity, the point of rest, finds everywhere the pulse of Time, the vast unending storm of life and love. Reality, says Bergson, is pure creative Life; a definition which excludes those ideas of perfection and finality involved in the idealist's concept of Pure Being as the Absolute and Unchanging One. [30] This life, as he sees it, is fed from within rather than upheld from without. It evolves by means of its own inherent and spontaneous creative power. The biologist's Nature "so careful of the type"; the theologian's Creator transcending His universe, and "holding all things in the hollow of His hand": these are gone, and in their place we have a universe teeming with free individuals, each self-creative, each evolving eternally, yet towards no term.

Here, then, the deep instinct of the human mind that there must be a unity, an orderly plan in the universe, that the strung-along beads of experience do really form a rosary, though it be one which we cannot repeat, is deliberately thwarted. Creation, Activity, Movement; this, says Vitalism, rather than any merely apparent law and order, any wholeness, is the essential quality of the Realms the Real: and life is an eternal Becoming, a ceaseless changefulness. At its highest it may be conceived as "the universe flowering into deity," [31] As the Hermetic philosophers found in the principle of analogy, "Quod inferius sicut quod superius," [32] the Key of Creation, so we are invited to see in that uninterrupted change which is the condition of our normal consciousness, a true image, a microcosm of the living universe as a part of which that consciousness has been evolved.

If we accept this theory, we must then impute to life in its fullness--the huge, many levelled, many coloured life, the innumerable worlds which escape the rhythm of our senses; not merely that patch of physical life which those senses perceive--a divinity, a greatness of destiny far beyond that with which it is credited by those who hold to a physico-chemical theory of the universe. We must perceive in it, as some mystics have done, "the beating of the Heart of God"; and agree with Heracleitus that "there is but one wisdom, to understand the knowledge by which all things are steered through the All." [33] Union with reality--apprehension of it--will upon this hypothesis be union with life at its most intense point: in its most dynamic aspect. It will be a deliberate harmony set up with the Logos which that same philosopher described as "man's most constant companion." Ergo, says the mystic, union with a Personal and Conscious spiritual existence, immanent in the world--one form, one half of the union which I have always sought, since this is clearly life in its highest manifestation. Beauty, Goodness, Splendour, Love, all those shining words which exhilarate the soul, are but the names of aspects or qualities picked out by human intuition as characteristic of this intense and eternal Life in which is the life of men.

How, then, may we knew this Life, this creative and original soul of things, in which we are bathed; in which, as in a river, swept along? Not, says Bergson bluntly, by any intellectual means. The mind which thinks it knows Reality because it has made a diagram of Reality, is merely the dupe of its own categories. The intellect is a specialized aspect of the self, a form of consciousness: but specialized for very different purposes than those of metaphysical speculation. Life has evolved it in the interests of life; has made it capable of dealing with "solids," with concrete things. With these it is at home. Outside of them it becomes dazed, uncertain of itself; for it is no longer doing its natural work, which is to help life, not to know it. In the interests of experience, and in order to grasp perceptions, the intellect breaks up experience, which is in reality a continuous stream, an incessant process of change and response with no separate parts, into purely conventional "moments," "periods," or psychic "states." It picks out from the flow of reality those bits which are significant for human life; which "interest" it, catch its attention. From these it makes up a mechanical world in which it dwells, and which seems quite real until it is subjected to criticism. It does, says Bergson, the work of a cinematograph: takes snapshots of something which is always moving, and by means of these successive static representations--none of which are real, because Life, the object photographed, never was at rest--it recreates a picture of life, of motion. This rather jerky representation of divine harmony, from which innumerable moments are left out, is useful for practical purposes: but it is not reality, because it is not alive. [34]

This "real world," then, is the result of your selective activity, and the nature of your selection is largely outside your control. Your cinematograph machine goes at a certain pace, takes its snapshots at certain intervals. Anything which goes too quickly for these intervals, it either fails to catch, or merges with preceding and succeeding movements to form a picture with which it can deal. Thus we treat, for instance, the storm of vibrations which we convert into "sound" and "light." Slacken or accelerate its clock-time, change its rhythmic activity, and at once you take a different series of snapshots, and have as a result a different picture of the world. Thanks to the time at which the normal human machine is set, it registers for us what we call, in our simple way, "the natural world." A slight accession of humility or common sense might teach us that a better title would be " our natural world."

Let human consciousness change or transcend its rhythm, and any other aspect of any other world may be ours as a result. Hence the mystics' claim that in their ecstasies they change the conditions of consciousness, and apprehend a deeper reality which is unrelated to human speech, cannot be dismissed as unreasonable. Do not then confuse that surface-consciousness which man has trained to be an organ of utility and nothing more--and which therefore can only deal adequately with the "given" world of sense--with that mysterious something in you, that ground of personality, inarticulate but inextinguishable, by which you are aware that a greater truth exists. This truth, whose neighbourhood you feel, and for which you long, is Life. You are in it all the while, "like a fish in the sea, like a bird in the air," as St. Mechthild of Hackborn said many centuries ago. [35]

Give yourself, then, to this divine and infinite life, this mysterious Cosmic activity in which you are immersed, of which you are born. Trust it. Let it surge in on you. Cast off, as the mystics are always begging you to do, the fetters of the senses, the "remora of desire"; and making your interests identical with those of the All, rise to freedom, to that spontaneous, creative life which, inherent in every individual self, is our share of the life of the Universe. You are yourself vital --a free centre of energy--did you but know it. You can move to higher levels, to greater reality, truer self-fulfilment, if you will. Though you be, as Plato said, like an oyster in your shell, you can open that shell to the living waters without, draw from the "Immortal Vitality." Thus only--by contact with the real--shall you know reality. Cot ad cot loquitur.

The Indian mystics declare substantially the same truth when they say that the illusion of finitude is only to be escaped by relapsing into the substantial and universal life, abolishing individuality. So too, by a deliberate self-abandonment to that which Plato calls the "saving madness" of ecstasy, did the initiates of Dionysus "draw near to God." So their Christian cousins assert that "self-surrender" is the only way: that they must die to live, must lose to find: that knowing implies being: that the method and secret which they have always practiced consists merely in a meek and loving union--the synthesis of passion and self-sacrifice--with that divine and unseparated life, that larger consciousness in which the soul is grounded, and which they hold to be an aspect of the life of God. In their hours of contemplation, they deliberately empty themselves of the false images of the intellect, neglect the cinematograph of sense. Then only are they capable of transcending the merely intellectual levels of consciousness, and perceiving that Reality which "hath no image."

"Pilgrimage to the place of the wise," said Jalalu ddin, "is to find escape from the flame of separation." It is the mystics' secret in a nutshell. "When I stand empty in God's will and empty of God's will and of all His works and of God Himself," cries Eckhart with his usual violence of language, "then am I above all creatures and am neither God nor creature, but I am what I was and evermore shall be."[36] He attains, that is to say, by this escape from a narrow selfhood, not to identity with God--that were only conceivable upon a basis of pantheism--but to an identity with his own substantial life, and through it with the life of a real and living universe; in symbolic language, with "the thought of the Divine Mind" whereby union with that Mind in the essence or ground of the soul becomes possible. The first great message of Vitalistic philosophy is then seen to be--Cease to identify your intellect and your self: a primary lesson which none who purpose the study of mysticism may neglect. Become at least aware of, if you cannot "know," the larger, truer self: that root and depth of spirit, as St. François de Sales calls it, from which intellect and feeling grow as fingers from the palm of the hand--that free creative self which constitutes your true life, as distinguished from the scrap of consciousness which is its servant.

How then, asks the small consciously-seeking personality of the normal man, am I to become aware of this, my larger self, and of the free, eternal, spiritual life which it lives?

Here philosophy, emerging from the water-tight compartment in which metaphysics have lived too long retired, calls in psychology; and tells us that in intuition, in a bold reliance on contact between the totality of the self and the external world--perhaps too in those strange states of lucidity which accompany great emotion and defy analysis--lies the normal man's best chance of attaining, as it were, a swift and sidelong knowledge of this real. Smothered in daily life by the fretful activities of our surface-mind, reality emerges in our great moments; and, seeing ourselves in its radiance, we know, for good or evil, what we are. "We are not pure intellects . . . around our conceptional and logical thought there remains a vague, nebulous Somewhat, the substance at whose expense the luminous nucleus we call the intellect is formed." [37] In this aura, this diffused sensitiveness, we are asked to find man's medium of communication with the Universal Life.

Such fragmentary, dim and unverifiable perceptions of the Real, however, such "excursions into the Absolute," cannot be looked upon as a satisfaction of man's hunger for Truth. He does not want to peep, but to live. Hence he cannot be satisfied with anything less than a total and permanent adjustment of his being to the greater life of reality. This alone can resolve the disharmonies between the self and the world, and give meaning and value to human life. [38] The possibility of this adjustment--of union between man's life and that "independent spiritual life" which is the stuff of reality--is the theme alike of mysticism and of Eucken's spiritual vitalism or Activistic Philosophy. [39] Reality, says Eucken, is an independent spiritual world, unconditioned by the apparent world of sense. To know it and to live in it is man's true destiny. His point of contact with it is personality: the inward fount of his being: his heart, not his head. Man is real, and in the deepest sense alive, in virtue of this free personal life-principle within him; but he is bound and blinded by the ties set up between his surface-intelligence and the sense-world. The struggle for reality must be a struggle on man's part to transcend the sense-world, escape its bondage. He must renounce it, and be "re-born" to a higher level of consciousness; shifting his centre of interest from the natural to the spiritual plane. According to the thoroughness with which he does this, will be the amount of real life he enjoys. The initial break with the "world," the refusal to spend one's life communing with one's own cinematograph picture, is essential if the freedom of the infinite is to be attained. We are amphibious creatures: our life moves upon two levels at once--the natural and the spiritual. The key to the puzzle of man lies in the fact that he is "the meeting point of various stages of Reality." [40] All his difficulties and triumphs are grounded in this. The whole question for him is, which world shall be central for him--the real, vital, all-embracing life we call spirit, or the lower life of sense? Shall "Existence," the superficial obvious thing, or "Substance," the underlying verity, be his home? Shall he remain the slave of the senses with their habits and customs, or rise to a plane of consciousness, of heroic endeavour, in which--participating in the life of spirit--he knows reality because he is real?

The mystics, one and all, have answered this question in the same sense, and proved in their own experience that the premises of "Activism" are true. This application of the vitalistic idea to the transcendental world, does in fact fit the observed facts of mysticism far more closely even than it fits the observed facts of man's ordinary mental life.

(1) The primary break with the sense-world. (2) The "new" birth and development of the spiritual consciousness on high levels--in Eucken's eyes an essential factor in the attainment of reality. (3) That ever closer and deeper dependence on and appropriation of the fullness of the Divine Life; a conscious participation, and active union with the infinite and eternal. These three imperatives, as we shall see later, form an exact description of the psychological process through which the mystics pass. If then this transcendence is the highest destiny of the race, mysticism becomes the crown of man's ascent towards Reality; the orderly completion of the universal plan.

The mystics show us this independent spiritual life, this fruition of the Absolute, enjoyed with a fullness to which others cannot attain. They are the heroic examples of the life of spirit; as the great artists, the great discoverers, are the heroic examples of the life of beauty and the life of truth. Directly participating, like all artists, in the Divine Life, they are usually persons of great vitality: but this vitality expresses itself in unusual forms, hard of understanding for ordinary men. When we see a picture or a poem, hear a musical composition, we accept it as an expression of life, an earnest of the power which brought it forth. But the deep contemplations of the great mystic, his visionary reconstructions of reality, and the fragments of them which he is able to report, do not seem to us--as they are--the equivalents, or more often the superiors of the artistic and scientific achievements of other great men.

Mysticism, then, offers us the history, as old as civilization, of a race of adventurers who have carried to its term the process of a deliberate and active return to the divine fount of things. They have surrendered themselves to the life-movement of the universe, hence have lived with an intenser life than other men can ever know; have transcended the "sense-world" in order to live on high levels the spiritual life. Therefore they witness to all that our latent spiritual consciousness, which shows itself in the "hunger for the Absolute," can be made to mean to us if we develop it; and have in this respect a unique importance for the race. It is the mystics, too, who have perfected that method of intuition, that knowledge by union, the existence of which philosophy has been driven to acknowledge. But where the metaphysician obtains at best a sidelong glance at that Being "unchanging yet elusive," whom he has so often defined but never discovered, the artist a brief and dazzling vision of the Beauty which is Truth, they gaze with confidence into the very eyes of the Beloved.

The mystics, again, are, by their very constitution, acutely conscious of the free and active "World of Becoming," the Divine Immanence and its travail. It is in them and they are in it: or, as they put it in their blunt theological way, "the Spirit of God is within you." But they are not satisfied with this statement and this knowledge; and here it is that they part company with vitalism. It is, they think, but half a truth. To know Reality in this way, to know it in its dynamic aspect, enter into "the great life of the All": this is indeed, in the last resort, to know it supremely from the point of view of man--to liberate from selfhood the human consciousness--but it is not to know it from the point of view of God. There are planes of being beyond this; countries dark to the intellect, deeps into which only the very greatest contemplatives have looked. These, coming forth, have declared with Ruysbroeck that "God according to the Persons is Eternal Work, but according to the Essence and Its perpetual stillness He is Eternal Rest." [41]

The full spiritual consciousness of the true mystic is developed not in one, but in two apparently opposite but really complementary directions:--

". . . io vidi
Ambo le corte del ciel manifeste." [42]

On the one hand he is intensely aware of, and knows himself to be at one with that active World of Becoming, that immanent Life, from which his own life takes its rise. Hence, though he has broken for ever with the bondage of the senses, he perceives in every manifestation of life a sacramental meaning; a loveliness, a wonder, a heightened significance, which is hidden from other men. He may, with St. Francis, call the Sun and the Moon, Water and Fire, his brothers and his sisters: or receive, with Blake, the message of the trees. Because of his cultivation of disinterested love, because his outlook is not conditioned by "the exclusive action of the will-to-live," he has attained the power of communion with the living reality of the universe; and in this respect can truly say that he finds "God in all and all in God." Thus, the skilled spiritual vision of Lady Julian, transcending the limitations of human perception, entering into harmony with a larger world whose rhythms cannot be received by common men, saw the all-enfolding Divine Life, the mesh of reality. "For as the body is clad in the cloth," she said, "and the flesh in the skin and the bones in the flesh and the heart in the whole, so are we, soul and body, clad in the Goodness of God and enclosed. Yea, and more homely: for all these may waste and wear away, but the Goodness of God is ever whole." [43] Many mystical poets and pantheistic mystics never pass beyond this degree of lucidity.

On the other hand, the full mystic consciousness also attains to what is, I think, its really characteristic quality. It develops the power of apprehending the Absolute, Pure Being, the utterly Transcendent: or, as its possessor would say, can experience "passive union with God." This all-round expansion of consciousness, with its dual power of knowing by communion the temporal and eternal, immanent and transcendent aspects of reality--the life of the All, vivid, flowing and changing, and the changeless, conditionless life of the One--is the peculiar mark, the ultimo sigillo of the great mystic, and must never be forgotten in studying his life and work.

As the ordinary man is the meeting-place between two stages of reality--the sense-world and the world of spiritual life--so the mystic, standing head and shoulders above ordinary men, is again the meeting-place between two orders. Or, if you like it better, he is able to perceive and react to reality under two modes. On the one hand he knows, and rests in, the eternal world of Pure Being, the "Sea Pacific" of the Godhead, indubitably present to him in his ecstasies, attained by him in the union of love. On the other, he knows--and works in--that "stormy sea," the vital World of Becoming which is the expression of Its will. "Illuminated men," says Ruysbroeck, "are caught up, above the reason, into naked vision. There the Divine Unity dwells and calls them. Hence their bare vision, cleansed and free, penetrates the activity of all created things, and pursues it to search it out even to its height." [44]

Though philosophy has striven since thought began--and striven in vain--to resolve the paradox of Being and Becoming, of Eternity and Time, she has failed strangely enough to perceive that a certain type of personality has substituted experience for her guesses at truth; and achieved its solution, not by the dubious processes of thought, but by direct perception. To the great mystic the "problem of the Absolute" presents itself in terms of life, not in terms of dialectic. He solves it in terms of life: by a change or growth of consciousness which--thanks to his peculiar genius--enables him to apprehend that two-fold Vision of Reality which eludes the perceptive powers of other men. It is extraordinary that this fact of experience a central fact for the understanding of the contemplative type--has received so little attention from writers upon mysticism. As we proceed with our inquiry, its importance, its far-reaching implications in the domains of psychology, of theology, of action, will become more and more evident. It provides the reason why the mystics could never accept the diagram of the Vitalists or Evolutionists as a complete statement of the nature of Reality. "Whatever be the limits of your knowledge, we know"--they would say--"that the world has another aspect than this: the aspect which is present to the Mind of God." "Tranquillity according to His essence, activity according to His nature: perfect stillness, perfect fecundity," [45] says Ruysbroeck again, this is the two-fold character of the Absolute. That which to us is action, to Him, they declare, is rest, "His very peace and stillness coming from the brimming fullness of

His infinite life." [46] That which to us is Many, to that Transcendent Knower is One. Our World of Becoming rests on the bosom of that Pure Being which has ever been the final Object of man's quest: the "river in which we cannot bathe twice" is the stormy flood of life flowing toward that divine sea. "How glorious," says the Voice of the Eternal to St. Catherine of Siena, "is that soul which has indeed been able to pass from the stormy ocean to Me, the Sea Pacific, and in that Sea, which is Myself, to fill the pitcher of her heart." [47]

The evolution of the mystic consciousness, then, brings its possessors to this transcendent point of view: their secret is this unity in diversity, this stillness in strife. Here they are in harmony with Heracleitus rather than with his modern interpreters. That most mystical of philosophers discerned a hidden unity beneath the battle, transcending all created opposites, and taught his disciples that "Having hearkened not unto me but unto the Logos, it is wise to confess that all things are one." [48] This is the secret at which the idealists' and concept of Pure Being has tried, so timidly, to hint: and which the Vitalists' more intimate, more actual concept of Becoming has tried, so unnecessarily, to destroy. We shall see the glorious raiment in which the Christian mystics deck it when we come to consider their theological map of the quest.

If it be objected--and this objection has been made by advocates of each school of thought--that the existence of the idealists' and mystics' "Absolute" is utterly inconsistent with the deeply alive, striving life which the Vitalists identify with reality, I reply that both concepts at bottom are but symbols of realities which the human mind can never reach: and that the idea of stillness, unity and peace is and has ever been humanity's best translation of its intuition of the achieved Perfection of God. "In the midst of silence a hidden word was spoken to me.' Where is this Silence, and where is the place in which this word is spoken? It is in the purest that the soul can produce, in her noblest part, in the Ground, even the Being of the Soul." [49] So Eckhart: and here he does but subscribe to a universal tradition. The mystics have always insisted that "Be still, be still, and know " is the condition of man's purest and most direct apprehensions of reality: that he experiences in quiet the truest and deepest activity: and Christianity when she formulated her philosophy made haste to adopt and express this paradox.

"Quid es ergo, Deus meus?" said St. Augustine, and gave an answer in which the vision of the mystic, the genius of the philosopher, combined to hint something at least of the paradox of intimacy and majesty in that all-embracing, all-transcending One. "Summe, optime, potentissime, omnipotentissime, misericordissime et justissime, secretissime et presentissime, pulcherrime et fortissime; stabilis et incomprehensibilis; immutabilis, mutans omnia. Numquam novus, nunquam vetus. . . . Semper agens, semper quietus: colligens et non egens: portans et implens et protegens; creans et nutriens et perficiens: quaerens cum nihil desit tibi. . . . Quid dicimus, Deus meus, vita mea, dulcedo mea sancta? Aut quid dicit aliquis, cum de te dicit?" [50]

It has been said that "Whatever we may do, our hunger for the Absolute will never cease." This hunger--that innate craving for, and intuition of, a final Unity, an unchanging good--will go on, however heartily we may feed on those fashionable systems which offer us a dynamic or empirical universe. If, now, we admit in all living creatures--as Vitalists must do--an instinct of self-preservation, a free directive force which may be trusted and which makes for life: is it just to deny such an instinct to the human soul? The "entelechy" of the Vitalists, the "hidden steersman," drives the phenomenal world on and up. What about that other sure instinct embedded in the race, breaking out again and again, which drives the spirit on and up; spurs it eternally towards an end which it feels to be definite yet cannot define? Shall we distrust this instinct for the Absolute, as living and ineradicable as any other of our powers, merely because philosophy finds it difficult to accommodate and to describe?

"We must," says Plato in the "Timaeus," "make a distinction of the two great forms of being, and ask, What is that which Is and has no Becoming, and what is that which is always becoming and never Is?" [51] Without necessarily subscribing to the Platonic answer to this question, we may surely acknowledge that the question itself is sound and worth asking; that it expresses a perennial demand of human nature; and that the analogy of man's other instincts and cravings assures us that these his fundamental demands always indicate the existence of a supply. [52] The great defect of Vitalism, considered as a system, is that it only answers half the question; the half which Absolute Idealism disdained to answer at all.

We have seen that the mystical experience, the fullest all-round experience in regard to the transcendental world which humanity has attained, declares that there are two aspects, two planes of discoverable Reality. We have seen also that hints of these two planes--often clear statements concerning them--abound in mystical literature of the personal first-hand type. [53] Pure Being, says Boutroux in the course of his exposition of Boehme, [54] has two characteristic manifestations. It shows itself to us as Power, by means of strife, of the struggle and opposition of its own qualities. But it shows itself to us as Reality, in harmonizing and reconciling within itself these discordant opposites.

Its manifestation as Power, then, is for us in the dynamic World of Becoming, amidst the thud and surge of that life which is compounded of paradox, of good and evil, joy and sorrow, life and death.

Here, Boehme declares that the Absolute God is voluntarily self-revealing. But each revelation has as its condition the appearance of its opposite: light can only be recognized at the price of knowing darkness, life needs death, love needs wrath. Hence if Pure Being--the Good, Beautiful and True--is to reveal itself, it must do so by evoking and opposing its contrary: as in the Hegelian dialectic no idea is complete without its negative. Such a revelation by strife, however, is rightly felt by man to be incomplete. Absolute Reality, the Player whose sublime music is expressed at the cost of this everlasting friction between bow and lyre, is present, it is true, in His music. But He is best known in that "light behind," that unity where all these opposites are lifted up into harmony, into a higher synthesis; and the melody is perceived, not as a difficult progress of sound, but as a whole.

We have, then, (a) The achieved Reality which the Greeks, and every one after them, meant by that seemingly chill abstraction which they called Pure Being: that Absolute One, unconditioned and undiscoverable, in Whom all is resumed. In the undifferentiated Godhead of Eckhart, the Transcendent Father of orthodox Christian theology, we see the mind's attempt to conceive that "wholly other" Reality, unchanging yet changer of all. It is the great contribution of the mystics to humanity's knowledge of the real that they find in this Absolute, in defiance of the metaphysicians, a personal object of love, the goal of their quest, a "Living One who lives first and lives perfectly, and Who, touching me, the inferior, derivative life, can cause me to live by Him and for His sake" [55] .

(b) But, contradicting the nihilism of Eastern contemplatives, they see also a reality in the dynamic side of things: in the seething pot of appearance. They are aware of an eternal Becoming, a striving, free, evolving life; not merely as a shadow-show, but as an implicit of their Cosmos felt also in the travail of their own souls--God's manifestation or showing, in which He is immanent, in which His Spirit truly works and strives. It is in this plane of reality that all individual life is immersed: this is the stream which set out from the Heart of God and "turns again home."

The mystic knows his task to be the attainment of Being, Eternal Life, union with the One, the "return to the Father's heart": for the parable of the Prodigal Son is to him the history of the universe. This union is to be attained, first by cooperation in that Life which bears him up, in which he is immersed. He must become conscious of this "great life of the All," merge himself in it, if he would find his way back whence he came. Vae soli . Hence there are really two distinct acts of "divine union," two distinct kinds of illumination involved in the Mystic Way: the dual character of the spiritual consciousness brings a dual responsibility in its train. First, there is the union with Life, with the World of Becoming: and parallel with it, the illumination by which the mystic "gazes upon a more veritable world." Secondly, there is the union with Being, with the One: and that final, ineffable illumination of pure love which is called the "knowledge of God." It is through the development of the third factor, the free, creative "spirit," the scrap of Absolute Life which is the ground of his soul, that the mystic can (a) conceive and (b) accomplish these transcendent acts. Only Being can know Being: we "behold that which we are, and are that which we behold." But there is a spark in man's soul, say the mystics, which is real--which in fact is--and by its cultivation we may know reality. "Thus," says Von Hügel "a real succession, real efforts, and the continuous sense of limitation and inadequacy are the very means in and through which man apprehends increasingly (if only he thus loves and wills) the contrasting yet sustaining Simultaneity, Spontaneity, Infinity, and pure action of the Eternal Life of God." [56]

Over and over again--as Being and Becoming, as Eternity and Time, as Transcendence and Immanence, Reality and Appearance, the One and the Many--these two dominant ideas, demands, imperious instincts of man's self will reappear; the warp and woof of his completed universe. On the one hand is his intuition of a remote, unchanging Somewhat calling him: on the other there is his longing for and as clear intuition of an intimate, adorable Somewhat, companioning him. Man's true Real, his only adequate God, must be great enough to embrace this sublime paradox, to take up these apparent negations into a higher synthesis. Neither the utter transcendence of extreme Absolutism, nor the utter immanence of the Vitalists will do. Both these, taken alone, are declared by the mystics to be incomplete. They conceive that Absolute Being who is the goal of their quest as manifesting Himself in a World of Becoming: working in it, at one with it yet though semper agens, also semper quietus .The Divine spirit which they know to be immanent in the heart and in the universe comes forth from and returns to the Transcendent One; and this division of persons in unity of substance completes the "Eternal Circle, from Goodness, through Goodness, to Goodness."

Absolute Being and Becoming, the All and the One, are found to be alike inadequate to their definition of this discovered Real; the "triple star of Goodness, Truth, and Beauty." Speaking always from experience--the most complete experience achieved by man--they assure us of an Absolute which overpasses and includes the Absolute of philosophy, far transcends that Cosmic life which it fills and sustains, and is best defined in terms of Transcendent Personality; which because of its unspeakable richness and of the poverty of human speech, they have sometimes been driven to define only by negations. At once static and dynamic, above life and in it, "all love yet all law," eternal in essence though working in time, this vision resolves the contraries which tease those who study it from without, and swallows up whilst it kindles to life all the partial interpretations of metaphysics and of science.

Here then stands the mystic. By the help of two types of philosophy, eked out by the resources of symbolic expression and suggestion, he has contrived to tell us something of his vision and his claim. Confronted by that vision--that sublime intuition of eternity--we may surely ask, indeed are bound to ask, "What is the machinery by which this self, akin to the imprisoned and sense-fed self of our daily experience, has contrived to slip its fetters and rise to those levels of spiritual perception on which alone such vision can be possible to man? How has it brought within the field of consciousness those deep intuitions which fringe upon Absolute Life; how developed powers by which it is enabled to arrive at this amazing, this superhuman concept of the nature of Reality?" Psychology will do something, perhaps, to help us to an answer to this question; and it is her evidence which we must examine next. But for the fullest and most satisfying answer we must go to the mystics; and they reply to our questions, when we ask them, in the direct and uncompromising terms of action, not in the refined and elusive periods of speculative thought.

"Come with us," they say to the bewildered and entangled self, craving for finality and peace, "and we will show you a way out that shall not only be an issue from your prison, but also a pathway to your Home. True, you are immersed, fold upon fold, in the World of Becoming; worse, you are besieged on all sides by the persistent illusions of sense. But you too are a child of the Absolute. You bear within you the earnest of your inheritance. At the apex of your spirit there is a little door, so high up that only by hard climbing can you reach it. There the Object of your craving stands and knocks; thence came those persistent messages--faint echoes from the Truth eternally hammering at your gates--which disturbed the comfortable life of sense. Come up then by this pathway, to those higher levels of reality to which, in virtue of the eternal spark in you, you belong. Leave your ignoble ease, your clever prattle, your absurd attempts to solve the apparent contradictions of a Whole too great for your useful little mind to grasp. Trust your deep instincts: use your latent powers. Appropriate that divine, creative life which is the very substance of your being. Remake yourself in its interest, if you would know its beauty and its truth. You can only behold that which you are. Only the Real can know Reality."

NOTE TO THE TWELFTH EDITION

THE changed philosophic outlook since this chapter was first written, eighteen years ago, has now given to it a somewhat old-fashioned air. The ideas of Bergson and Eucken no longer occupy the intellectual foreground. Were I now writing it for the first time, my examples would be chosen from other philosophers, and especially from those who are bringing back into modern thought the critical realism of the scholastics. But the position which is here defended--that a limited dualism, a "Two-step philosophy," is the only type of metaphysic adequate to the facts of mystical experience remains in my own mind as true as before. Now that mysticism enjoys the patronage of many pious monists and philosophic naturalists, this view seems more than ever in need of strong and definite statement.

Footnotes:

22. "The Science and Philosophy of Organism," Gifford Lectures. 1907-8.

23. "Les Données Immédiates de la Conscience" (1889), "Matière et Mémoire" (1896), "L'Evolution Créatrice" (1907).

24."Der Kampf um einen geistigen Lebensinhalt" (1896), "Der Sinn und Wert den Lebens" (1908), &c. See Bibliography.

25. The researches of Driesch (op. cit .) and of de Pries ("The Mutation Theory," 1910) have done much to establish the truth of this contention upon the scientific plane. Now particularly Driesch's account of the spontaneous responsive changes in the embryo sea-urchin, and de Vries' extraordinary description of the escaped stock of evening primrose, varying now this way, now that, "as if swayed by a restless internal tide."

26. The debt to Heracleitus is acknowledged by Schiller. See "Studies in Humanism," pp. 39, 40.

27. See, for the substance of this and the following pages, the works of Henri Bergson already mentioned. I am here also much indebted to the personal help of my friend "William Scott Palmer," whose interpretations have done much towards familiarizing English readers with Bergson's philosophy; and to Prof. Willdon Carr's paper on "Bergson's Theory of Knowledge, read before the Aristotelian Society, December 1908.

28. Heracleitus, Fragments, 46, 84.

29. First edition, canto x.

30. E.g. St. Augustine's "That alone is truly real whichabides unchanged" (Conf., bk. vii. cap. 10), and among modern thinkers F. von Hügel: "An absolute Abidingness, pure Simultaneity, Eternity, in God . . . stand out, in man's deepest consciousness, with even painful contrast, against all mere Succession, all sheer flux and change." ("Eternal Life," p. 365.)

31. S. Alexander, "Space, Time and Deity," vol. ii, p. 410.

32. See below, Pt. I. Cap. VII.

33. Heracleitus, op. cit .

34. On the complete and undivided nature of our experience in its wholeness," and the sad work our analytic brains make of it when they come to pull it to pieces, Bradley has some valuable contributory remarks in his "Oxford Lectures on Poetry," p. 15.

35. "Liber Specialis Gratiae," I. ii. cap. xxvi.

36. Meister Eckhart, Pred. lxxxvii.

37. Willdon Carr, op. cit .

38. "It seems as if man could never escape from himself, and yet, when shut in to the monotony of his own sphere, he is overwhelmed with a sense of emptiness. The only remedy here is radically to alter the conception of man himself, to distinguish within him the narrower and the larger life, the life that is straitened and finite and can never transcend itself, and an infinite life through which he enjoys communion with the immensity and the truth of the universe. Can man rise to this spiritual level? On the possibility of his doing so rests all our hope of supplying any meaning or value to life" ("Der Sinn und Wert des Lebens," p. 81).

39. The essentials of Eucken's teaching will be found conveniently summarized in "Der Sinn und Wert des Lebens."

40. "Der Sinn und Wert den Lebens," p. 121.

41. "De Septem Gradibus Amoral" cap. xiv.

42. Par. xxx. 95.

43. "Revelations of Divine Love." cap. vi.

44. Ruysbroeck, "Samuel," cap. viii.

45. Ibid., "De Vera Contemplatione," cap. xii.

46. Von Hügel, "The Mystical Element of Religion," vol. ii. p. 132.

47. St. Catherine of Siena, Dialogo, cap. lxxxix.

48. Heracleitus, op. cit .

49. Meister Eckhart, Pred. i.

50. Aug. Conf., bk. i. cap. iv. "What art Thou, then, my God? . . . Highest, best, most potent [i.e. , dynamic], most omnipotent [i.e, transcendent], most merciful and most just, most deeply hid and yet most near. Fairest, yet strongest: steadfast, yet unseizable; unchangeable yet changing all things: never new, yet never old. . . . Ever busy, yet ever at rest; gathering yet needing not: bearing, filling, guarding: creating, nourishing and perfecting; seeking though Thou hast no wants. . . . What can I say, my God, my life, my holy joy? or what can any say who speaks of Thee?" Compare the strikingly similar Sufi definition of the Nature of God, as given in Palmer's "Oriental Mysticism," pp. 22,23. "First and last, End and Limit of all things, incomparable and unchangeable, always near yet always far," &c. This probably owes something to Platonic influence.

51. "Timaeus," § 27.

52. "A natural craving," said Aquinas, "cannot be in vain." Philosophy is creeping back to this "mediaeval' point of view. Compare "Summa Contra Gentiles," I. ii. cap. lxxix.

53. Compare Dante's vision in Par. xxx., where he sees Reality first as the streaming River of Light, the flux of things; and then, when his sight has been purged, as achieved Perfection, the Sempiternal Rose.

54. E. Boutroux, "Le Philosophe Allemand, Jacob Boehme." p. 18.

55. F. von Hügel: "Eternal Life, p. 385.

56. Op. Cit ., p. 387.

CHAPTER III

We come now to consider the mental apparatus which is at the disposal of the self: to ask what it can tell us of the method by which she may escape from the prison of the sense-world, transcend its rhythm, and attain knowledge of--or conscious contact with--a supra-sensible Reality. We have seen the normal self shut within that prison, and making, by the help of science and of philosophy, a survey of the premises and furniture: testing the thickness of the walls and speculating on the possibility of trustworthy news from without penetrating to her cell. Shut with her in that cell, two forces, the desire to know more and the desire to love more, are ceaselessly at work. Where the first of these cravings predominates, we call the result a philosophical or a scientific temperament; where it is overpowered by the ardour of unsatisfied love, the self's reaction upon things becomes poetic, artistic, and characteristically--though not always explicitly--religious.

We have seen further that a certain number of persons declare that they have escaped from the prison. Have they done so, it can only be in order to satisfy these two hungry desires, for these, and these only, make that a prison which might otherwise be a comfortable hotel; and since, in varying degrees, these desires are in all of us, active or latent, it is clearly worth while to discover, if we can, the weak point in the walls, and method of achieving this one possible way of escape.

Before we try to define in psychological language the way in which the mystic slips the fetters of sense, sets out upon his journey towards home, it seems well to examine the machinery which is at the disposal of the normal, conscious self: the creature, or part of a creature, which we recognize as "ourselves." The older psychologists were accustomed to say that the messages from the outer world awaken in that self three main forms of activity. (1) They arouse movements of attraction or repulsion, of desire or distaste; which vary in intensity from the semi-conscious cravings of the hungry infant to the passions of the lover, artist, or fanatic. (2) They stimulate a sort of digestive process, in which she combines and cogitates upon the material presented to her; finally absorbing a certain number of the resulting concepts and making them part of herself or of her world, (3) The movements of desire, or the action of reason, or both in varying combinations, awaken in her a determination by which percept and concept issue in action; bodily, mental, or spiritual. Hence, the main aspects of the self were classified as Emotion, Intellect, and Will: and the individual temperament was regarded as emotional, intellectual, or volitional, according to whether feeling, thought, or will assumed the reins.

Modern psychologists have moved away from this diagrammatic conception, and incline more and more to dwell upon the unity of the psyche--that hypothetical self which none have ever seen--and on some aspect of its energetic desire, its libido, or "hormic drive" as the ruling factor of its life. These conceptions are useful to the student of mysticism, though they cannot be accepted uncritically or regarded as complete.

Now the unsatisfied psyche in her emotional aspect wants, as we have said, to love more; her curious intellect wants to know more. The awakened human creature suspects that both appetites are being kept on a low diet; that there really is more to love, and more to know, somewhere in the mysterious world without, and further that its powers of affection and understanding are worthy of some greater and more durable objective than that provided by the illusions of sense. Urged therefore by the cravings of feeling or of thought, consciousness is always trying to run out to the encounter of the Absolute, and always being forced to return. The neat philosophical system, the diagrams of science, the "sunset-touch," are tried in turn. Art and life, the accidents of our humanity, may foster an emotional outlook; till the moment in which the neglected intellect arises and pronounces such an outlook to have no validity. Metaphysics and science seem to offer to the intellect an open window towards truth; till the heart looks out and declares this landscape to be a chill desert in which she can find no nourishment. These diverse aspects of things must be either fused or transcended if the whole self is to be satisfied; for the reality which she seeks has got to meet both claims and pay in full.

When Dionysius the Areopagite divided those angels who stand nearest God into the Seraphs who are aflame with perfect love, and the Cherubs who are filled with perfect knowledge, he only gave expression to the two most intense aspirations of the human soul, and described under an image the two-fold condition of that Beatific Vision which is her goal.[57]

There is a sense in which it may be said, that the desire of knowledge is a part of the desire of perfect love: since one aspect of that all inclusive passion is clearly a longing to know, in the deepest, fullest, closest sense, the thing adored. Love's characteristic activity--for Love, all wings, is inherently active, and "cannot be lazy," as the mystics say--is a quest, an outgoing towards an object desired, which only when possessed will be fully known, and only when fully known can be perfectly adored.[58] Intimate communion, no less than worship, is of its essence. Joyous fruition is its proper end. This is true of all Love's quests, whether the Beloved be human or divine--the bride, the Grail, the Mystic Rose, the Plenitude of God. But there is no sense in which it can be said that the desire of love is merely a part of the desire of perfect knowledge: for that strictly intellectual ambition includes no adoration, no self-spending, no reciprocity of feeling between Knower and Known. Mere knowledge, taken alone, is a matter of receiving, not of acting: of eyes, not wings: a dead alive business at the best. There is thus a sharp distinction to be drawn between these two great expressions of life: the energetic love, the passive knowledge. One is related to the eager, outgoing activity, the dynamic impulse to do somewhat, physical, mental, or spiritual, which is inherent in all living things and which psychologists call conation: the other to the indwelling consciousness, the passive knowing somewhat, which they call cognition.

Now "conation" is almost wholly the business of will, but of will stimulated by emotion: for wilful action of every kind, however intellectual it may seem, is always the result of interest, and interest involves feeling. We act because we feel we want to; feel we must. Whether the inspiring force be a mere preference or an overwhelming urge, our impulse to "do" is a synthesis of determination and desire. All man's achievements are the result of conation, never of mere thought. "The intellect by itself moves nothing," said Aristotle, and modern psychology has but affirmed this law. Hence his quest of Reality is never caused, though it may be greatly assisted, by the intellectual aspect of his consciousness; for the reasoning powers as such have little initiative. Their province is analytic, not exploratory. They stay at home, dissecting and arranging matter that comes to hand; and do not adventure beyond their own region in search of food. Thought does not penetrate far into an object in which the self feels no interest-- i.e. , towards which she does not experience a "conative" movement of attraction, of desire--for interest is the only method known to us of arousing the will, and securing the fixity of attention necessary to any intellectual process. None think for long about anything for which they do not care; that is to say, which does not touch some aspect of their emotional life. They may hate it, love it, fear it, want it; but they must have some feeling about it. Feeling is the tentacle we stretch out to the world of things.

Here the lesson of psychology is the same as that which Dante brought back from his pilgrimage; the supreme importance and harmonious movement of il desiro and il velle. Si come rota ch'egualmente è mossa ,[59] these move together to fulfil the Cosmic Plan. In all human life, in so far as it is not merely a condition of passive "awareness," the law which he found implicit in the universe is the law of the individual mind. Not logic, not "common sense,"but l'amor che move il sole e le altre stelle the motive force of the spirit of man: in the inventors, the philosophers, and the artists, no less than in the heroes and in the saints.

The vindication of the importance of feeling in our life, and in particular its primacy over reason in all that has to do with man's contact with the transcendental world, has been one of the great achievements of modern psychology. In the sphere of religion it is now acknowledged that "God known of the heart" gives a better account of the character of our spiritual experience than "God guessed at by the brain"; that the loving intuition is more fruitful and more trustworthy than the dialectic proof. One by one the commonplaces of mysticism are thus rediscovered by official science, and given their proper place in the psychology of the spiritual life. Thus Leuba, hardly a friendly witness, is found to agree with the Fourth Evangelist that "Life, more life, a larger, richer, more satisfying life, is in the last analysis the end of religion,"[60] and we have seen that life, as we know it, has the character of a purposive striving, more directly dependent on will and feeling then on thought. Of this drive, this urge, thought indeed is but the servant; a skilled and often arrogant servant, with a constant tendency to usurpation. Some form of feeling--interest, desire, fear, appetite--must supply the motive power. Without this, the will would be dormant, and the intellect lapse into a calculating machine.

Further, "the heart has its reasons which the mind knows not of." It is a matter of experience that in our moments of deep emotion, transitory though they be, we plunge deeper into the reality of things than we can hope to do in hours of the most brilliant argument. At the touch of passion doors fly open which logic has battered on in vain: for passion rouses to activity not merely the mind, but the whole vitality of man. It is the lover, the poet, the mourner, the convert, who shares for a moment the mystic's privilege of lifting that Veil of Isis which science handles so helplessly, leaving only her dirty fingermarks behind. The heart, eager and restless, goes out into the unknown, and brings home, literally and actually, "fresh food for thought." Hence those who "feel to think" are likely to possess a richer, more real, if less orderly, experience than those who "think to feel."

This psychological law, easily proved in regard to earthly matters, holds good also upon the supersensual plane. It was expressed once for all by the author of "The Cloud of Unknowing" when he said of God, "By love He may be gotten and holden, but by thought of understanding, never."[61] That exalted feeling, that "secret blind love pressing," not the neat deductions of logic, the apologist's "proofs" of the existence of the Absolute, unseals the eyes to things unseen before. "Therefore," says the same mystic "what time that thou purposest thee to this work, and feelest by grace that thou art called of God, lift then up thine heart unto God with a meek stirring of love; and mean God that made thee and bought thee, and that graciously hath called thee to thy degree and receive none other thought of God. And yet not all these but if thou list; for it sufficeth thee enough, a naked intent direct unto God without any other cause than Himself." [62] Here we see emotion at its proper work; the movement of desire passing over at once into the act of concentration, the gathering up of all the powers of the self into a state of determined attention, which is the business of the Will. "This driving and drawing," says Ruysbroeck, "we feel in the heart and in the unity of all our bodily powers, and especially in the desirous powers." [63] This act of perfect concentration, the passionate focussing of the self upon one point, when it is applied "with a naked intent" to real and transcendental things, constitutes in the technical language of mysticism the state of recollection: [64] a condition which is peculiarly characteristic of the mystical consciousness, and is the necessary prelude of pure contemplation, that state in which the mystic enters into communion with Reality.

We have then arrived so far in our description of the mechanism of the mystic. Possessed like other men of powers of feeling, thought, and will, it is essential that his love and his determination, even more than his thought, should be set upon Transcendent Reality. He must feel a strong emotional attraction toward the supersensual Object of his quest: that love which scholastic philosophy defined as the force or power which causes every creature to follow out the trend of its own nature. Of this must be born the will to attain communion with that Absolute Object. This will, this burning and active desire, must crystallize into and express itself by that definite and conscious concentration of the whole self upon the Object, which precedes the contemplative state. We see already how far astray are those who look upon the mystical temperament as passive in type.

Our next concern, then, would seem to be with this condition of contemplation: what it does and whither it leads. What is (a) its psychological explanation and (b) its empirical value? Now, in dealing with this, and other rare mental conditions, we are of course trying to describe from without that which can only adequately be described from within; which is as much as to say that only mystics can really write about mysticism. Fortunately, many mystics have so written; and we, from their experiences and from the explorations of psychology upon another plane, are able to make certain elementary deductions. It appears generally from these that the act of contemplation is for the mystic a psychic gateway; a method of going from one level of consciousness to another. In technical language it is the condition under which he shifts his "field of perception" and obtains his characteristic outlook on the universe. That there is such a characteristic outlook, peculiar to no creed or race, is proved by the history of mysticism; which demonstrates plainly enough that in some men another sort of consciousness, another "sense," may be liberated beyond the normal powers we have discussed. This "sense" has attachments at each point to emotion, to intellect, and to will. It can express itself under each of the aspects which these terms connote. Yet it differs from and transcends the emotional, intellectual, and volitional life of ordinary men. It was recognized by Plato as that consciousness which could apprehend the real world of the Ideas. Its development is the final object of that education which his "Republic" describes. It is called by Plotinus "Another intellect, different from that which reasons and is denominated rational." [65] Its business, he says, is the perception of the supersensual--or, in Neoplatonic language, the intelligible world. It is the sense which, in the words of the "Theologia Germanica," has "the power of seeing into eternity," [66] the "mysterious eye of the soul" by which St. Augustine saw "the light that never changes." [67] It is, says Al Ghazzali, a Persian mystic of the eleventh century, "like an immediate perception, as if one touched its object with one's hand." [68] In the words of his great Christian successor, St. Bernard, "it may be defined as the soul's true unerring intuition, the unhesitating apprehension of truth": [69] which "simple vision of truth," says St. Thomas Aquinas, "ends in a movement of desire." [70]

It is infused with burning love, for it seems to its possessors to be primarily a movement of the heart: with intellectual subtlety, for its ardour is wholly spent upon the most sublime object of thought: with unflinching will, for its adventures are undertaken in the teeth of the natural doubts, prejudices, languors, and self-indulgence of man. These adventures, looked upon by those who stay at home as a form of the Higher Laziness, are in reality the last and most arduous labours which the human spirit is called to perform. They are the only known methods by which we can come into conscious possession of all our powers; and, rising from the lower to the higher levels of consciousness, become aware of that larger life in which we are immersed, attain communion with the transcendent Personality in Whom that life is resumed.

Mary has chosen the better, not the idler part; for her gaze is directed towards those First Principles without which the activity of Martha would have no meaning at all. In vain does sardonic common sense, confronted with the contemplative type, reiterate the sneer of Mucius, "Encore sont-ils heureux que la pauvre Marthe leur fasse la cuisine." It remains a paradox of the mystics that the passivity at which they appear to aim is really a state of the most intense activity: more, that where it is wholly absent no great creative action can take place. In it, the superficial self compels itself to be still, in order that it may liberate another more deep-seated power which is, in the ecstasy of the contemplative genius, raised to the highest pitch of efficiency.

"This restful travail," said Walter Hilton, "is full far from fleshly idleness and from blind security. It is full of ghostly work but it is called rest, for grace looseth the heavy yoke of fleshly love from the soul and maketh it mighty and free through the gift of the holy ghostly love for to work gladly, softly, and delectably. . . . Therefore is it called an holy idleness and a rest most busy; and so is it in stillness from the great crying and the beastly noise of fleshly desires." [71]

If those who have cultivated this latent power be correct in their statements, the self was mistaken in supposing herself to be entirely shut off from the true external universe. She has, it seems certain tentacles which, once she learns to uncurl them, will stretch sensitive fingers far beyond that limiting envelope in which her normal consciousness is contained, and give her news of a higher reality than that which can be deduced from the reports of the senses. The fully developed and completely conscious human soul can open as an anemone does, and know the ocean in which she is bathed. This act, this condition of consciousness, in which barriers are obliterated, the Absolute flows in on us, and we, rushing out to its embrace, "find and feel the Infinite above all reason and above all knowledge," [72] is the true "mystical state." The value of contemplation is that it tends to produce this state, release this transcendental sense; and so turns the "lower servitude" in which the natural man lives under the sway of his earthly environment to the "higher servitude" of fully conscious dependence on that Reality "in Whom we live and move and have our being."

What then, we ask, is the nature of this special sense--this transcendental consciousness--and how does contemplation liberate it?

Any attempt to answer this question brings upon the scene another aspect of man's psychic life: an aspect of paramount importance to the student of the mystic type. We have reviewed the chief ways in which our surface consciousness reacts upon experience: a surface consciousness which has been trained through long ages to deal with the universe of sense. We know, however, that the personality of man is a far deeper and more mysterious thing than the sum of his conscious feeling, thought and will: that this superficial self--this Ego of which each of us is aware--hardly counts in comparison with the deeps of being which it hides. "There is a root or depth in thee," says Law, "from whence all these faculties come forth as lines from a centre, or as branches from the body of a tree. This depth is called the centre, the fund, or bottom, of the soul. This depth is the unity, the Eternity, I had almost said the infinity of thy soul, for it is so infinite that nothing can satisfy it, or give it any rest, but the infinity of God." [73]

Since normal man is utterly unable to set up relations with spiritual reality by means of his feeling, thought, and will, it is clearly in this depth of being--in these unplumbed levels of personality--that we must search, if we would find the organ, the power, by which he is to achieve the mystic quest. That alteration of consciousness which takes place in contemplation can only mean the emergence from this "fund or bottom of the soul" of some faculty which diurnal life keeps hidden "in the deeps."

Modern psychology, in its doctrine of the unconscious or subliminal personality, has acknowledged this fact of a range of psychic life lying below and beyond the conscious field. Indeed, it has so dwelt upon and defined this shadowy region--which is really less a "region" than a useful name--that it sometimes seems to know more about the unconscious than about the conscious life of man. There it finds, side by side, the sources of his most animal instincts, his least explicable powers, his most spiritual intuitions: the "ape and tiger," and the "soul." Genius and prophecy, insomnia and infatuation, clairvoyance, hypnotism, hysteria, and "Christian" science--all are explained by the "unconscious mind." In his destructive moods the psychologist has little apparent difficulty in reducing the chief phenomena of religious and mystical experience to activities of the "unconscious," seeking an oblique satisfaction of repressed desires. Where he undertakes the more dangerous duties of apologetic, he explains the same phenomena by saying that "God speaks to man in the subconsciousness," [74] by which he can only mean that our apprehensions of the eternal have the character of intuition rather than of thought. Yet the "unconscious" after all is merely a convenient name for the aggregate of those powers, parts, or qualities of the whole self which at any given moment are not conscious, or that the Ego is not conscious of. Included in the unconscious region of an average healthy man are all those automatic activities by which the life of the body is carried on: all those "uncivilized" instincts and vices, those remains of the ancestral savage, which education has forced out of the stream of consciousness and which now only send their messages to the surface in a carefully disguised form. There too work in the hiddenness those longings for which the busy life of the world leaves no place: and there lies that deep pool, that heart of personality, from which in moments of lucidity a message may reach the conscious field. Hence in normal men the best and worst, most savage and most spiritual parts of character, are bottled up "below the threshold." Often the partisans of the "unconscious" forget to mention this.

It follows, then, that whilst we may find it convenient and indeed necessary to avail ourselves of the symbols and diagrams of psychology in tracking out the mystic way, we must not forget the large and vague significance which attaches to these symbols, and the hypothetical character of many of the entities they represent. Nor must we allow ourselves to use the "unconscious" as the equivalent of man's transcendental sense. Here the mystics have surely displayed a more scientific spirit, a more delicate power of analysis, than the psychologists. They, too, were aware that in normal men the spiritual sense lies below the threshold of consciousness. Though they had not at their command the spatial metaphors of the modern school, and could not describe man's ascent toward God in those picturesque terms of levels and uprushes, margins and fields, projection, repression, and sublimation, which now come so naturally to investigators of the spiritual life, they leave us in no doubt as to their view of the facts. Further, man's spiritual history primarily meant for them, as it means for us, the emergence of this transcendental sense; its capture of the field of consciousness, and the opening up of those paths which permit the inflow of a larger spiritual life, the perception of a higher reality. This, in so far as it was an isolated act, was "contemplation." When it was part of the general life process, and had permanent results, they called it the New Birth, which "maketh alive." The faculty or personality concerned in the "New Birth"--the "spiritual man," capable of the spiritual vision and life, which was dissociated from the "earthly man" adapted only to the natural life--was always sharply distinguished by them from the total personality, conscious or unconscious. It was something definite; a bit or spot of man which, belonging not to Time but to Eternity, was different in kind from the rest of his human nature, framed in all respects to meet the demands of the merely natural world. [75] The business of the mystic in the eyes of these old specialists was to remake, transmute, his total personality in the interest of his spiritual self; to bring it out of the hiddenness, and unify himself about it as a centre, thus "putting on divine humanity."

The divine nucleus, the point of contact between man's life and the divine life in which it is immersed and sustained, has been given many names in course of the development of mystical doctrine. All clearly mean the same thing, though emphasizing different aspects of its life. Sometimes it is called the Synteresis, [76] the keeper or preserver of his being: sometimes the Spark of the Soul, the Fünklein of the German mystics: sometimes its Apex the point at which it touches the heavens. Then, with a sudden flight to the other end of the symbolic scale, and in order to emphasize its participation in pure Being, rather than its difference from mere nature, it is called the Ground of the Soul, the foundation or basal stuff indwelt by God, whence springs all spiritual life. Clearly all these guesses and suggestions aim at one goal and are all to be understood in a symbolic sense; for, as Malaval observed in answer to his disciples' anxious inquiries on this subject, "since the soul of man is a spiritual thing and thus cannot have divisions or parts, consequently it cannot have height or depth, summit or surface. But because we judge spiritual things by the help of material things, since we know these better and they are more familiar to us, we call the highest of all forms of conception the summit, and the easier way of comprehending things the surface, of the understanding." [77]

Here at any rate, whatever name we may choose to give it, is the organ of man's spiritual consciousness; the place where he meets the Absolute, the germ of his real life. Here is the seat of that deep "Transcendental Feeling," the "beginning and end of metaphysics" which is, says Professor Stewart, "at once the solemn sense of Timeless Being--of That which was and is and ever shall be' overshadowing us--and the conviction that Life is good." "I hold," says the same writer, "that it is in Transcendental Feeling, manifested normally as Faith in the Value of Life, and ecstatically as sense of Timeless Being, and not in Thought proceeding by way of speculative construction, that Consciousness comes nearest to the object of metaphysics, Ultimate Reality." [78]

The existence of such a "sense," such an integral part or function of the complete human being, has been affirmed and dwelt upon not only by the mystics, but by seers and teachers of all times and creeds: by Egypt, Greece, and India, the poets, the fakirs, the philosophers, and the saints. A belief in its actuality is the pivot of the Christian position; indeed of every religion worthy of the name. It is the justification of mysticism, asceticism, the whole machinery of the self-renouncing life. That there is an extreme point at which man's nature touches the Absolute: that his ground, or substance, his true being, is penetrated by the Divine Life which constitutes the underlying reality of things; this is the basis on which the whole mystic claim of possible union with God must rest. Here, they say, is our link with reality; and in this place alone can be celebrated the "marriage from which the Lord comes." [79]

To use another of their diagrams, it is thanks to the existence within him of this immortal spark from the central fire, that man is implicitly a "child of the infinite." The mystic way must therefore be a life, a discipline, which will so alter the constituents of his mental life as to include this spark within the conscious field; bring it out of the hiddenness, from those deep levels where it sustains and guides his normal existence, and make it the dominant element round which his personality is arranged.

It is clear that under ordinary conditions, and save for sudden gusts of "Transcendental Feeling" induced by some saving madness such as Religion, Art, or Love, the superficial self knows nothing of the attitude of this silent watcher--this "Dweller in the Innermost"--towards the incoming messages of the external world: nor of the activities which they awake in it. Concentrated on the sense-world, and the messages she receives from it, she knows nothing of the relations which exist between this subject and the unattainable Object of all thought. But by a deliberate inattention to the messages of the senses, such as that which is induced by contemplation, the mystic can bring the ground of the soul, the seat of "Transcendental Feeling," within the area of consciousness: making it amenable to the activity of the will. Thus becoming unaware of his usual and largely fictitious "external world," another and more substantial set of perceptions, which never have their chance under normal conditions, rise to the surface. Sometimes these unite with the normal reasoning faculties. More often, they supersede them. Some such exchange, such "losing to find," appears to be necessary, if man's transcendental powers are to have their full chance.

"The two eyes of the soul of man," says the "Theologia Germanica," here developing a profound Platonic image, "cannot both perform their work at once: but if the soul shall see with the right eye into eternity, then the left eye must close itself and refrain from working, and be as though it were dead. For if the left eye be fulfilling its office toward outward things, that is holding converse with time and the creatures; then must the right eye be hindered in its working; that is, in its contemplation. Therefore, whosoever will have the one must let the other go; for no man can serve two masters."' [80]

There is within us an immense capacity for perception, for the receiving of messages from outside; and a very little consciousness which deals with them. It is as if one telegraph operator were placed in charge of a multitude of lines: all may be in action, but he can only attend to one at a time. In popular language, there is not enough consciousness to go round. Even upon the sensual plane, no one can be aware of more than a few things at once. These fill the centre of our field of consciousness: as the object on which we happen to have focussed our vision dominates our field of sight. The other matters within that field retreat to the margin. We know, dimly, that they are there; but we pay them no attention and should hardly miss them if they ceased to exist.

Transcendental matters are, for most of us, always beyond the margin; because most of us have given up our whole consciousness to the occupation of the senses, and permitted them to construct there a universe in which we are contented to remain. Only in certain states--recollection, contemplation, ecstasy and their allied conditions--does the self contrive to turn out the usual tenants, shut the "gateways of the flesh," and let those submerged powers which are capable of picking up messages from another plane of being have their turn. Then it is the sense-world which retreats beyond the margin, and another landscape that rushes in. At last, then, we begin to see something of what contemplation does for its initiates. It is one of the many names applied to that chain of processes which have for their object this alteration of the mental equilibrium: the putting to sleep of that "Normal Self" which usually wakes, and the awakening of that "Transcendental Self" which usually sleeps. To man, "meeting-point of various stages of reality," is given--though he seldom considers it--this unique power of choosing his universe.

The phenomenon known as double or disintegrated personality may perhaps give us a hint as to the mechanical nature of the change which contemplation effects. In this psychic malady the total character of the patient is split up; a certain group of qualities are, as it were, abstracted from the surface-consciousness and so closely associated as to form in themselves a complete "character" or "personality"--necessarily poles asunder from the "character" which the self usually shows to the world, since it consists exclusively of those elements which are omitted from it. Thus in the classical case of Miss Beauchamp, the investigator, Dr. Morton Prince, called the three chief "personalities," from their ruling characteristics, "the Saint," "the Woman," and "the Devil." [81] The totality of character which composed the "real Miss Beauchamp" had split up into these contrasting types; each of which was excessive, because withdrawn from the control of the rest. When, voluntarily or involuntarily, the personality which had possession of the field of consciousness was lulled to sleep, one of the others emerged. Hypnotism was one of the means which most easily effected this change.

Now in persons of mystical genius, the qualities which the stress of normal life tends to keep below the threshold of consciousness are of enormous strength. In these natural explorers of Eternity the "transcendental faculty," the "eye of the soul," is not merely present in embryo, but is highly developed; and is combined with great emotional and volitional power. The result of the segregation of such qualities below the threshold of consciousness is to remove from them the friction of those counterbalancing traits in the surface mind with which they might collide. They are "in the hiddenness," as Jacob Boehme would say. There they develop unchecked, until a point is reached at which their strength is such that they break their bounds and emerge into the conscious field: either temporarily dominating the subject as in ecstasy, or permanently transmuting the old self, as in the "unitive life." The attainment of this point may be accelerated by processes which have always been known and valued by the mystics; and which tend to produce a state of consciousness classed by psychologists with dreams, reverie, and the results of hypnosis. In all these the normal surface-consciousness is deliberately or involuntarily lulled, the images and ideas connected with normal life are excluded, and images or faculties from "beyond the threshold" are able to take their place.

Of course these images or faculties may or may not be more valuable than those already present in the surface-consciousness. In the ordinary subject, often enough, they are but the odds and ends for which the superficial mind has found no use. In the mystic, they are of a very different order: and this fact justifies the means which he instinctively employs to secure their emergence. Indian mysticism founds its external system almost wholly on (a) Asceticism, the domination of the senses, and (b) the deliberate practice of self-hypnotization; either by fixing the eyes on a near object, or by the rhythmic repetition of the mantra or sacred word. By these complementary forms of discipline, the pull of the phenomenal world is diminished and the mind is placed at the disposal of the subconscious powers. Dancing, music, and other exaggerations of natural rhythm have been pressed into the same service by the Greek initiates of Dionysus, by the Gnostics, by innumerable other mystic cults. That these proceedings do effect a remarkable change in the human consciousness is proved by experience: though how and why they do it is as yet little understood. Such artificial and deliberate production of ecstasy is against the whole instinct of the Christian contemplatives; but here and there amongst them also we find instances in which ecstatic trance or lucidity, the liberation of the "transcendental sense," was inadvertently produced by purely physical means. Thus Jacob Boehme, the "Teutonic theosopher," having one day as he sat in his room "gazed fixedly upon a burnished pewter dish which reflected the sunshine with great brilliance," fell into an inward ecstasy, and it seemed to him as if he could look into the principles and deepest foundations of things. [82] The contemplation of running water had the same effect on St. Ignatius Loyola. Sitting on the bank of a river one day, and facing the stream, which was running deep, "the eyes of his mind were opened, not so as to see any kind of vision, but so as to understand and comprehend spiritual things . . . and this with such clearness that for him all these things were made new." [83] This method of attaining to mental lucidity by a narrowing and simplification of the conscious field, finds an apt parallel in the practice of Immanuel Kant, who "found that he could better engage in philosophical thought while gazing steadily at a neighbouring church steeple." [84]

It need hardly be said that rationalistic writers, ignoring the parallels offered by the artistic and philosophic temperaments, have seized eagerly upon the evidence afforded by such instances of apparent mono-ideism and self-hypnotization in the lives of the mystics, and by the physical disturbances which accompany the ecstatic trance, and sought by its application to attribute all the abnormal perceptions of contemplative genius to hysteria or other disease. They have not hesitated to call St. Paul an epileptic, St. Teresa the "patron saint of hysterics"; and have found room for most of their spiritual kindred in various departments of the pathological museum. They have been helped in this grateful task by the acknowledged fact that the great contemplatives, though almost always persons of robust intelligence and marked practical or intellectual ability--Plotinus, St. Bernard, the two Ss. Catherine, St. Teresa, St. John of the Cross, and the Sufi poets Jàmi and Jalalu ddin are cases in point--have often suffered from bad physical health. More, their mystical activities have generally reacted upon their bodies in a definite and special way; producing in several cases a particular kind of illness and of physical disability, accompanied by pains and functional disturbances for which no organic cause could be discovered, unless that cause were the immense strain which exalted spirit puts upon a body which is adapted to a very different form of life.

It is certain that the abnormal and highly sensitized type of mind which we call mystical does frequently, but not always, produce or accompany strange and inexplicable modifications of the physical organism with which it is linked. The supernatural is not here in question, except in so far as we are inclined to give that name to natural phenomena which we do not understand. Such instances of psycho-physical parallelism as the stigmatizations of the saints--and indeed of other suggestible subjects hardly to be ranked as saints--will occur to anyone. [85] I here offer to the reader another less discussed and more extraordinary example of the modifying influence of the spirit on the supposed "laws" of bodily life.

We know, as a historical fact, unusually well attested by contemporary evidence and quite outside the sphere of hagiographic romance, that both St. Catherine of Siena and her namesake St. Catherine of Genoa--active women as well as ecstatics, the first a philanthropist, reformer, and politician, the second an original theologian and for many years the highly efficient matron of a large hospital--lived, in the first case for years, in the second for constantly repeated periods of many weeks, without other food than the consecrated Host which they received at Holy Communion. They did this, not by way of difficult obedience to a pious vow, but because they could not live in any other way. Whilst fasting, they were well and active, capable of dealing with the innumerable responsibilities which filled their lives. But the attempt to eat even a few mouthfuls--and this attempt was constantly repeated, for, like all true saints, they detested eccentricity [86] --at once made them ill and had to be abandoned as useless. [87]

In spite of the researches of Murisier, [88] Janet, [89] Ribot, [90] and other psychologists, and their persevering attempts to find a pathological explanation which will fit all mystic facts, this and other marked physical peculiarities which accompany the mystical temperament belong as yet to the unsolved problems of humanity. They need to be removed both from the sphere of marvel and from that of disease--into which enthusiastic friends and foes force them by turn--to the sphere of pure psychology; and there studied dispassionately with the attention which we so willingly bestow on the less interesting eccentricities of degeneracy and vice. Their existence no more discredits the sanity of mysticism or the validity of its results than the unstable nervous condition usually noticed in artists--who share to some extent the mystic's apprehension of the Real--discredits art. "In such cases as Kant and Beethoven," says Von Hügel justly, "a classifier of humanity according to its psycho-physical phenomena alone would put these great discoverers and creators, without hesitation, amongst hopeless and useless hypochondriacs." [91]

In the case of the mystics the disease of hysteria, with its astounding variety of mental symptoms, its strange power of disintegrating, rearranging and enhancing the elements of consciousness, its tendencies to automatism and ecstasy, has been most often invoked to provide an explanation of the observed phenomena. This is as if one sought the source of the genius of Taglioni in the symptoms of St. Vitus's dance. Both the art and the disease have to do with bodily movements. So too both mysticism and hysteria have to do with the domination of consciousness by one fixed and intense idea or intuition, which rules the life and is able to produce amazing physical and psychical results. In the hysteric patient this idea is often trivial or morbid [92] but has become--thanks to the self's unstable mental condition--an obsession. In the mystic the dominant idea is a great one: so great in fact, that when it is received in its completeness by the human consciousness, almost of necessity it ousts all else. It is nothing less than the idea or perception of the transcendent reality and presence of God. Hence the mono-ideism of the mystic is rational, whilst that of the hysteric patient is invariably irrational.

On the whole then, whilst psycho-physical relations remain so little understood, it would seem more prudent, and certainly more scientific, to withhold our judgment on the meaning of the psychophysical phenomena which accompany the mystic life; instead of basing destructive criticism on facts which are avowedly mysterious and at least capable of more than one interpretation. To deduce the nature of a compound from the character of its byproducts is notoriously unsafe.

Our bodies are animal things, made for animal activities. When a spirit of unusual ardour insists on using its nerve-cells for other activities, they kick against the pricks; and inflict, as the mystics themselves acknowledge, the penalty of "mystical ill-health." "Believe me, children," says Tauler, "one who would know much about these high matters would often have to keep his bed, for his bodily frame could not support it." [93] "I cause thee extreme pain of body," says the voice of Love to Mechthild of Magdeburg. "If I gave myself to thee as often as thou wouldst have me, I should deprive myself of the sweet shelter I have of thee in this world, for a thousand bodies could not protect a loving soul from her desire. Therefore the higher the love the greater the pain." [94]

On the other hand the exalted personality of the mystic--his self-discipline, his heroic acceptance of labour and suffering, and his inflexible will--raises to a higher term that normal power of mind over body which all possess. Also the contemplative state--like the hypnotic state in a healthy person--seems to enhance life by throwing open deeper levels of personality. The self then drinks at a fountain which is fed by the Universal Life. True ecstasy is notoriously life-enhancing. In it a bracing contact with Reality seems to take place, and as a result the subject is himself more real. Often, says St. Teresa, even the sick come forth from ecstasy healthy and with new strength; for something great is then given to the soul. [95] Contact has been set up with levels of being which the daily routine of existence leaves untouched. Hence the extraordinary powers of endurance, and independence of external conditions, which the great ecstatics so often display.

If we see in the mystics, as some have done, the sporadic beginning of a power, a higher consciousness, towards which the race slowly tends; then it seems likely enough that where it appears nerves and organs should suffer under a stress to which they have not yet become adapted, and that a spirit more highly organized than its bodily home should be able to impose strange conditions on the flesh. When man first stood upright, a body long accustomed to go on all fours, legs which had adjusted themselves to bearing but half his weight, must have rebelled against this unnatural proceeding; inflicting upon its author much pain and discomfort if not absolute illness. It is at least permissible to look upon the strange "psycho-physical" state common amongst the mystics as just such a rebellion on the part of a normal nervous and vascular system against the exigencies of a way of life to which it has not yet adjusted itself. [96]

In spite of such rebellion, and of the tortures to which it has subjected them, the mystics, oddly enough, are a long-lived race: an awkward fact for critics of the physiological school. To take only a few instances from amongst marked ecstatics, St. Hildegarde lived to be eighty-one, Mechthild of Magdeburg to eighty-seven, Ruysbroeck to eighty-eight, Suso to seventy, St. Teresa to sixty-seven, St. Catherine of Genoa and St. Peter of Alcantara to sixty-three. It seems as though that enhanced life which is the reward of mystical surrender enabled them to triumph over their bodily disabilities: and to live and do the work demanded of them under conditions which would have incapacitated ordinary men.

Such triumphs, which take heroic rank in the history of the human mind, have been accomplished as a rule in the same way. Like all intuitive persons, all possessors of genius, all potential artists--with whom in fact they are closely related--the mystics have, in psychological language, "thresholds of exceptional mobility." That is to say, a slight effort, a slight departure from normal conditions, will permit their latent or "subliminal" powers to emerge and occupy the mental field. A "mobile threshold" may make a man a genius, a lunatic, or a saint. All depends upon the character of the emerging powers. In the great mystic, these powers, these tracts of personality lying below the level of normal consciousness, are of unusual richness; and cannot be accounted for in terms of pathology. "If it be true," says Delacroix, "that the great mystics have not wholly escaped those nervous blemishes which mark nearly all exceptional organizations, there is in them a vital and creative power, a constructive logic, an extended scale of realization--in a word, a genius--which is, in truth, their essential quality. . . . The great mystics, creators and inventors who have found a new form of life and have justified it . . . join, upon the highest summits of the human spirit, the great simplifiers of the world." [97]

The truth, then, so far as we know it at present, seems to be that those powers which are in contact with the Transcendental Order, and which constitute at the lowest estimate half the self, are dormant in ordinary men; whose time and interest are wholly occupied in responding to the stimuli of the world of sense. With those latent powers sleeps the landscape which they alone can apprehend. In mystics none of the self is always dormant. They have roused the Dweller in the Innermost from its slumbers, and round it have unified their life. Heart, Reason, Will are there in full action, drawing their incentive not from the shadow-show of sense, but from the deeps of true Being; where a lamp is lit, and a consciousness awake, of which the sleepy crowd remains oblivious. He who says the mystic is but half a man, states the exact opposite of the truth. Only the mystic can be called a whole man, since in others half the powers of the self always sleep. This wholeness of experience is much insisted on by the mystics. Thus the Divine Voice says to St. Catherine of Siena, "I have also shown thee the Bridge and the three general steps, placed there for the three powers of the soul; and I have told thee how no one can attain to the life of grace unless he has mounted all three steps, that is, gathered together all the three powers of the soul in My Name." [98]

In those abnormal types of personality to which we give the name of genius, we seem to detect a hint of the relations which may exist between these deep levels of being and the crust of consciousness. In the poet, the musician, the great mathematician or inventor, powers lying below the threshold, and hardly controllable by their owner's conscious will, clearly take a major part in the business of perception and conception. In all creative acts, the larger share of the work is done subconsciously: its emergence is in a sense automatic. This is equally true of mystics, artists, philosophers, discoverers, and rulers of men. The great religion, invention, work of art, always owes its inception to some sudden uprush of intuitions or ideas for which the superficial self cannot account; its execution to powers so far beyond the control of that self, that they seem, as their owner sometimes says, to "come from beyond." This is "inspiration"; the opening of the sluices, so that those waters of truth in which all life is bathed may rise to the level of consciousness.

The great teacher, poet, artist, inventor, never aims deliberately at his effects. He obtains them he knows not how: perhaps from a contact of which he is unconscious with that creative plane of being which the Sufis call the Constructive Spirit, and the Kabalists Yesod, and which both postulate as lying next behind the world of sense. "Sometimes," said the great Alexandrian Jew Philo, "when I have come to my work empty, I have suddenly become full; ideas being in an invisible manner showered upon me, and implanted in me from on high; so that through the influence of divine inspiration, I have become greatly excited, and have known neither the place in which I was, nor those who were present, nor myself, nor what I was saying, nor what I was writing; for then I have been conscious of a richness of interpretation, an enjoyment of light, a most penetrating insight, a most manifest energy in all that was to be done; having such an effect on my mind as the clearest ocular demonstration would have on the eyes." [99] This is a true creative ecstasy, strictly parallel to the state in which the mystic performs his mighty works.

To let oneself go, be quiet, receptive, appears to be the condition under which such contact with the Cosmic Life may be obtained. "I have noticed that when one paints one should think of nothing: everything then comes better," says the young Raphael to Leonardo da Vinci. [100] The superficial self must here acknowledge its own insufficiency, must become the humble servant of a more profound and vital consciousness. The mystics are of the same opinion. "Let the will quietly and wisely understand," says St. Teresa, "that it is not by dint of labour on our part that we can converse to any good purpose with God." [101] "The best and noblest way in which thou mayst come into this Life," says Eckhart, "is by keeping silence and letting God work and speak. Where all the powers are withdrawn from their work and images, there is this word spoken . . . the more thou canst draw in all thy powers and forget the creature the nearer art thou to this, and the more receptive." [102]

Thus Boehme says to the neophyte, [103] "When both thy intellect and will are quiet and passive to the expressions of the eternal Word and Spirit, and when thy soul is winged up above that which is temporal, the outward senses and the imagination being locked up by holy abstraction, then the eternal Hearing, Seeing, and Speaking will be revealed in thee. Blessed art thou therefore if thou canst stand still from self thinking and self willing, and canst stop the wheel of thy imagination and senses." Then, the conscious mind being passive, the more divine mind below the threshold--organ of our free creative life--can emerge and present its reports. In the words of an older mystic, "The soul, leaving all things and forgetting herself, is immersed in the ocean of Divine Splendour, and illuminated by the Sublime Abyss of the Unfathomable Wisdom." [104]

The "passivity" of contemplation, then, is a necessary preliminary of spiritual energy: an essential clearing of the ground. It withdraws the tide of consciousness from the shores of sense, stops the "wheel of the imagination." "The Soul," says Eckhart again, "is created in a place between Time and Eternity: with its highest powers it touches Eternity, with its lower Time." [105] These, the worlds of Being and Becoming, are the two "stages of reality" which meet in the spirit of man. By cutting us off from the temporal plane, the lower kind of reality, Contemplation gives the eternal plane, and the powers which can communicate with that plane, their chance. In the born mystic these powers are great, and lie very near the normal threshold of consciousness. He has a genius for transcendental--or as he would say, divine--discovery in much the same way as his cousins, the born musician and poet, have a genius for musical or poetic discovery. In all three cases, the emergence of these higher powers is mysterious, and not least so to those who experience it. Psychology on the one hand, theology on the other, may offer us diagrams and theories of this proceeding: of the strange oscillations of the developing consciousness, the fitful visitations of a lucidity and creative power over which the self has little or no control, the raptures and griefs of a vision by turns granted and withdrawn. But the secret of genius still eludes us, as the secret of life eludes the biologist.

The utmost we can say of such persons is, that reality presents itself to them under abnormal conditions and in abnormal terms, and that subject to these conditions and in these terms they are bound to deal with it. Thanks to their peculiar mental make up, one aspect of the universe is for them focussed so sharply that in comparison with it all other images are blurred, vague, and unreal. Hence the sacrifice which men of genius--mystics, artists, inventors--make of their whole lives to this one Object, this one vision of truth, is not self-denial, but rather self-fulfilment. They gather themselves up from the unreal, in order to concentrate on the real. The whole personality then absorbs or enters into communion with certain rhythms or harmonies existent in the universe, which the receiving apparatus of other selves cannot take up. "Here is the finger of God, a flash of the Will that can!" exclaims Abt Vogler, as the sounds grow under his hand. "The numbers came!" says the poet. He knows not how, certainly not by deliberate intellection.

So it is with the mystic. Madame Guyon states in her autobiography, that when she was composing her works she would experience a sudden and irresistible inclination to take up her pen; though feeling wholly incapable of literary composition, and not even knowing the subject on which she would be impelled to write. If she resisted this impulse it was at the cost of the most intense discomfort. She would then begin to write with extraordinary swiftness; words, elaborate arguments, and appropriate quotations coming to her without reflection, and so quickly that one of her longest books was written in one and a half days. "In writing I saw that I was writing of things which I had never seen: and during the time of this manifestation, I was given light to perceive that I had in me treasures of knowledge and understanding which I did not know that I possessed." [106]

Similar statements are made of St. Teresa, who declared that in writing her books she was powerless to set down anything but that which her Master put into her mind. [107] So Blake said of "Milton" and "Jerusalem," "I have written the poems from immediate dictation, twelve or sometimes twenty or thirty lines at a time, without premeditation and even against my will. The time it has taken in writing was thus rendered non-existent, and an immense poem exists which seems to be the labour of a long life, all produced without labour or study." [108]

These are, of course, extreme forms of that strange power of automatic composition, in which words and characters arrive and arrange themselves in defiance of their authors' will, of which most poets and novelists possess a trace. Such composition is probably related to the automatic writing of "mediums" and other sensitives; in which the often disorderly and incoherent subliminal mind seizes upon this channel of expression. The subliminal mind of the great mystic, however, is not disorderly. It is abnormally sensitive, richly endowed and keenly observant--a treasure house, not a lumber room--and becomes in the course of its education, a highly disciplined and skilled instrument of knowledge. When, therefore, its contents emerge, and are presented to the normal consciousness in the form of lucidity, "auditions," visions, automatic writing, or any other translations of the supersensible into the terms of sensible perception, they cannot be discredited because the worthless unconscious region of feebler natures sometimes manifests itself in the same way. Idiots are often voluble: but many orators are sane.

Now, to sum up: what are the chief characteristics which we have found to concern us in this sketch-map of the mental life of man?

(1) We have divided that life, arbitrarily enough, along the fluctuating line which psychologists call the "threshold of his consciousness" into the surface life and the unconscious deeps.

(2) In the surface life, though we recognized its essential wholeness, we distinguished three outstanding and ever-present aspects: the Trinity in Unity of feeling, thought, and will. Amongst these we were obliged to give the primacy to feeling, as the power which set the machinery of thought and

will to work.

(3) We have seen that the expression of this life takes the two complementary forms of conation, or outgoing action and cognition, or indwelling knowledge; and that the first, which is dynamic in type, is largely the work of the will stimulated by the emotions; whilst the second, which is passive in type, is the business of the intellect. They answer to the two main aspects which man discerns in the universal life: Being and Becoming.

(4) Neither conation nor cognition--action nor thought--as performed by this surface mind, concerned as it is with natural existence and dominated by spatial conceptions, is able to set up any relations with the Absolute or transcendental world. Such action and thought deal wholly with material supplied directly or indirectly by the world of sense. The testimony of the mystics, however, and of all persons possessing an "instinct for the Absolute," points to the existence of a further faculty--indeed, a deeper self--in man; a self which the circumstances of diurnal life usually keep "below the threshold" of his consciousness, and which thus becomes one of the factors of his "subliminal life." This hidden self is the primary agent of mysticism, and lives a "substantial" life in touch with the real or transcendental world. [109]

(5) Certain processes, of which contemplation has been taken as a type, can so alter the state of consciousness as to permit the emergence of this deeper self; which, according as it enters more or less into the conscious life, makes man more or less a mystic.

The mystic life, therefore, involves the emergence from deep levels of man's transcendental self; its capture of the field of consciousness; and the "conversion" or rearrangement of his feeling, thought, and will--his character--about this new centre of life.

We state, then, as the conclusion of this chapter, that the object of the mystic's adventure, seen from within, is the apprehension of, or direct communion with, that transcendental Reality which we tried in the last section to define from without. Here, as in the fulfilment of the highest earthly love, knowledge and communion are the same thing; we must be "oned with bliss" if we are to be aware of it. That aspect of our being by which we may attain this communion--that "marrow of the Soul," as Ruysbroeck calls it--usually lies below the threshold of our consciousness; but in certain natures of abnormal richness and vitality, and under certain favourable conditions, it may be liberated by various devices, such as contemplation. Once it has emerged, however, it takes up, to help it in the work, aspects of the conscious self. The surface must co-operate with the deeps, and at last merge with those deeps to produce that unification of consciousness upon high levels which alone can put a term to man's unrest. The heart that longs for the All, the mind that conceives it, the will that concentrates the whole self upon it, must all be called into play. The self must be surrendered: but it must not be annihilated, as some Quietists have supposed. It only dies that it may live again. Supreme success,--the permanent assurance of the mystic that "we are more verily in heaven than in earth,"--says the Lady Julian, in a passage which anticipates the classification of modern psychology, "cometh of the natural Love of our soul, and of the clear light of our Reason, and of the steadfast Mind." [110]

But what is the order of precedence which these three activities are to assume in the work which is one ?All, as we have seen, must do their part; for we are concerned with the response of man in his wholeness to the overwhelming attraction of God. But which shall predominate? The ultimate nature of the self's experience of reality will depend on the answer she gives to this question. What, here, are the relative values of Mind and Heart? Which will bring her closest to the Thought of God; the real life in which she is bathed? Which, fostered and made dominant, is most likely to put her in harmony with the Absolute? The Love of God, which is ever in the heart and often on the lips of the Saints, is the passionate desire for this harmony; the "malady of thought" is its intellectual equivalent. Though we may seem to escape God, we cannot escape some form of this craving; except at the price of utter stagnation. We go back, therefore, to the statement with which this chapter opened: that of the two governing desires which share the prison of the self. We see them now as representing the cravings of the intellect and the emotions for the only end of all quests. The disciplined will--the "conative power"--with all the dormant faculties which it can wake and utilize, can come to the assistance of one of them. Which? The question is a crucial one, for the destiny of the self depends on the partner which the will selects.

Footnotes:

57. The wise Cherubs, according to the beautiful imagery of Dionysius, are "all eyes," but the loving Seraphs are "all wings." Whilst the Seraphs, the figure of intensest Love, " move perpetually

towards things divine," ardour and energy being their characteristics, the characteristic of the Cherubs is receptiveness their power of absorbing the rays of the Supernal Light. (Dionysius the Areopagite, "De Caelesti Ierarchia," vi. 2, and vii. 1.)

58. So Récéjac says of the mystics, they desire to know, only that they may love; and their desire for union with the principle of things in God, Who is the sum of them all, is founded on a feeling which is neither curiosity nor self-interest" ("Fondements de la Connaissance Mystique," p. 50).

59. Par. xxxiii. 143.

60. The Monist , July, 1901, p. 572.

61. "The Cloud of Unknowing," cap. vi.

62. Op. cit., cap. vii.

63. "De Ornatu Spiritalium Nuptiarum," I. ii. cap. v.

64. See below, Pt. II. Cap. VI.

65. Plotinus, Ennead vi. 9.

66. "Theologia Germanica," cap. vii. (trans. Winkworth).

67. Aug. Conf., bk. vii. cap. x.

68. A. Schmölders, "Essai sur les Écoles Philosophique chez les Arabes," p. 68.

69. "De Consideration," bk. ii. cap. ii.

70. "Summa Theologica," ii. ii. q. clxxx, art. 3. eds. 1 and 3.

71. Walter Hilton, "The Scale of Perfection," bk. ii. cap. xl.

72. Ruysbroeck, "De Septem Gradibus Amoris," cap. xiv.

73. "The Spirit of Prayer" ("Liberal and Mystical Writings of William Law," p, 14). So too St. François de Sales says: "This root is the depth of the spirit, Mens , which others call the Kingdom of God." The same doctrine appears, under various symbols, in all the Christian Mystics.

74. Cutten, "Psychological Phenomena of Christianity," p. 18. James, "Varieties of Religious Experience," p. 155. For a temperate and balanced discussion, see Pratt: "The Religious Consciousness."

75. Note to the 12th Edition. During the eighteen years which have elapsed since this chapter was written, much work has been done on the psychology of mysticism. After suffering severely at the hands of the "new psychologists" the contemplative faculty is once more taken seriously; and there is even some disposition to accept or restate the account of it given by the mystics. Thus Bremond ("Prière et Poésie" and "Introduction à la Philosophie de la Prière") insists on the capital distinction between the surface-mind, capable of rational knowledge, and the deeper mind, organ of mystical knowledge, and operative in varying degrees in religion poetic, and Esthetic apprehensions.

76. An interesting discussion of the term "Synteresis" will be found in Dr. Inge's "Christian Mysticism," Appendix C, pp. 359, 360.

77. "La Pratique de la Vraye Theologie Mystique," vol. 1. p. 204.

78. J. A. Stewart, *The Myths of Plato," pp. 41, 43. Perhaps I may point out that this Transcendental Feeling--the ultimate material alike of prayer and of poetry--has, like the mystic consciousness, a dual perception of Reality: static being and dynamic life. See above, p. 42.

79. Tauler, Sermon on St. Augustine ("The Inner Way," p. 162).

80. "Theologia Germanica," cap. vii. Compare "De Imitatione Christi," 1. iii. cap. 38.

81. Morton Prince, "The Dissociation of a Personality," p. 16.

82. Martensen, "Jacob Boehme," p. 7.

83. Testament, cap. iii.

84. Starbuck, "The Psychology of Religion," p. 388.

85. See, for instances, Cutten, The Psychological Phenomena of Christianity," cap. viii.

86. "Singularity," says Gertrude More, "is a vice which Thou extremely hatest." (The Spiritual Exercises of the most vertuous and religious Dame Gertrude More," p. 40). All the best and sanest of the mystics are of the same opinion.

87. See E. Gardner, "St. Catherine of Siena," pp. 12and 48; and E. von Hügel, "The Mystical Element of Religion," vol. i. p. 135.

88. "Les Maladies des Sentiments Religieux."

89. "L'État Mentale des Hysteriques," and "Une Extatique" (Bulletin de l'Institut Psychologique , 1901).

90. "La Psychologie des Sentiment," 1896.

91. Op. cit ., vol. ii. p. 42.

92. For examples consult Pierre Janet, op. cit.

93. Sermon for First Sunday after Easter (Winkworth, p. 302).

94. "Das Fliessende Licht der Gottheit," pt. ii. cap. xxv.

95. Vida, cap. xx. sect. 29.

96. Boyce Gibson ("God with Us," cap. iii.) has drawn a striking parallel between the ferment and "interior uproar" of adolescence and the profound disturbances which mark man's entry into a conscious

spiritual life. His remarks are even more applicable to the drastic rearrangement of personality which takes place in the case of the mystic, whose spiritual life is more intense than that of other men.

97. Delacroix, "Études sur le Mysticisme," p. iii.

98. Dialogo, cap. lxxxvi.

99. Quoted by James ("Varieties of Religious Experience," p. 481) from Clissold's "The Prophetic Spirit in Genius and Madness," p. 67.

100. "Mérejkowsky, "Le Roman do Leonard de Vinci," p. 638.

101. Vida, cap. xv. 9.

102. Meister Eckhart, Pred. i. ("Mystische Schriften," p. 18).

103. "Three Dialogues of the Supersensual Life," p. 14.

104. Dionysius the Areopagite, "De Divinis Nominibus," vii. 3.

105. Pred. xxiii. Eckhart obtained this image from St. Thomas Aquinas, "Summa Contra Gentiles," I. iii. cap. lxi. "The intellectual soul is created on the confines of eternity and time."

106. Vie, t. ii. pp. 120, 223, 229. It might reasonably be objected that Madame Guyon does not rank high among the mystics and her later history includes some unfortunate incidents. This is true. Nevertheless she exhibit such a profusion of mystical phenomena and is so candid in her self-disclosures, that she provides much valuable material for the student.

107. G. Cunninghame Graham, "Santa Teresa," vol. i. p. 202.

108. "Letters of William Blake," April 25, 1803.

109. This insistence on the twofold character of human personality is implicit in the mystics. "It is" says Bremond, "the fundamental dogma of mystical psychology--the distinction between the two selves: Animus, the surface self; Anima , the deep self; Animus , rational knowledge; and Anima , mystical or poetic knowledge . . . the I, who feeds on notions and words, and enchants himself by doing so; the Me, who is united to realities" (Bremond "Prière et Poésie," cap. xii.).

110. Julian of Norwich, "Revelations of Divine Love," cap, lv.

CHAPTER IV

The spiritual history of man reveals two distinct and fundamental attitudes towards the unseen; and two methods whereby he has sought to get in touch with it. For our present purpose I will call these methods the "way of magic" and the "way of mysticism." Having said this, we must at once add that although in their extreme forms these methods are sharply contrasted, their frontiers are far from being clearly defined: that, starting from the same point, they often confuse the inquirer by using the same language, instruments, and methods. Hence, much which is really magic is loosely and popularly described as mysticism. They represent as a matter of fact the opposite poles of the same thing: the transcendental consciousness of humanity. Between them lie the great religions, which might be described under this metaphor as representing the ordinarily habitable regions of that consciousness. Thus, at one end of the scale, pure mysticism "shades off" into religion--from some points of view seems to grow out of it. No deeply religious man is without a touch of mysticism; and no mystic can be other than religious, in the psychological if not in the theological sense of the word. At the other end of the scale, as we shall see later, religion, no less surely, shades off into magic.

The fundamental difference between the two is this: magic wants to get, mysticism wants to give--immortal and antagonistic attitudes, which turn up under one disguise or another in every age of thought. Both magic and mysticism in their full development bring the whole mental machinery, conscious and unconscious, to bear on their undertaking: both claim that they give their initiates powers unknown to ordinary men. But the centre round which that machinery is grouped, the reasons of that undertaking, and the ends to which those powers are applied differ enormously. In mysticism the will is united with the emotions in an impassioned desire to transcend the sense-world, in order that the self may be joined by love to the one eternal and ultimate Object of love; whose existence is intuitively perceived by that which we used to call the soul, but now find it easier to refer to as the "cosmic" or "transcendental" sense. This is the poetic and religious temperament acting upon the plane of reality. In magic, the will unites with the intellect in an impassioned desire for supersensible knowledge. This is the intellectual, aggressive, and scientific temperament trying to extend its field of consciousness, until it includes the supersensual world: obviously the antithesis of mysticism, though often adopting its title and style.

It will be our business later to consider in more detail the characteristics and significance of magic. Now it is enough to say that we may class broadly as magical all forms of self-seeking transcendentalism. It matters little whether the apparatus which they use be the incantations of the old magicians, the congregational prayer for rain of orthodox Churchmen, or the consciously self-hypnotizing devices of "New Thought": whether the end proposed be the evocation of an angel, the power of transcending circumstance, or the healing of disease. The object is always the same: the deliberate exaltation of the will, till it transcends its usual limitations and obtains for the self or group of selves something which it or they did not previously possess. It is an individualistic and acquisitive science: in all its forms an activity of the intellect, seeking Reality for its own purposes, or for those of humanity at large.

Mysticism, whose great name is too often given to these supersensual activities, has nothing in common with this. It is non-individualistic. It implies, indeed, the abolition of individuality; of that hard separateness, that "I, Me, Mine" which makes of man a finite isolated thing. It is essentially a movement of the heart, seeking to transcend the limitations of the individual standpoint and to surrender itself to ultimate Reality; for no personal gain, to satisfy no transcendental curiosity, to obtain no other-worldly joys, but purely from an instinct of love. By the word heart, of course we here mean not merely "the seat of the affections," "the organ of tender emotion," and the like: but rather the inmost sanctuary of personal being, the deep root of its love and will, the very source of its energy and life. The mystic is "in love with the Absolute" not in any idle or sentimental manner, but in that vital sense which presses at all costs and through all dangers towards union with the object beloved. Hence, whilst the practice of magic--like the practice of science--does not necessarily entail passionate emotion, though of course it does and must entail interest of some kind, mysticism, like art, cannot exist without it. We must feel, and feel acutely, before we want to act on this hard and heroic scale.

We see, then, that these two activities correspond to the two eternal passions of the self, the desire of love and the desire of knowledge: severally representing the hunger of heart and intellect for ultimate truth. The third attitude towards the supersensual world, that of transcendental philosophy, hardly comes within the scope of the present inquiry; since it is purely academic, whilst both magic and mysticism are practical and empirical. Such philosophy is often wrongly called mysticism, because it tries to make maps of the countries which the mystic explores. Its performances are useful, as diagrams are useful, so long as they do not ape finality; remembering that the only final thing is personal experience--the personal and costly exploration of the exalted and truth-loving soul.

What then do we really mean by mysticism? A word which is impartially applied to the performances of mediums and the ecstasies of the saints, to "menticulture" and sorcery, dreamy poetry and mediaeval art, to prayer and palmistry, the doctrinal excesses of Gnosticism, and the tepid speculations of the Cambridge Platonists--even, according to William James, to the higher branches of intoxication [111] --soon ceases to have any useful meaning. Its employment merely confuses the inexperienced student, who ends with a vague idea that every kind of supersensual theory and practice is somehow "mystical." Hence the need of fixing, if possible, its true characteristics: and restating the fact that Mysticism, in its pure form, is the science of ultimates, the science of union with the Absolute, and nothing else, and that the mystic is the person who attains to this union, not the person who talks about it. Not to know about but to Be, is the mark of the real initiate.

The difficulty lies in determining the point at which supersensual experience ceases to be merely a practical and interesting extension of sensual experience--an enlarging, so to speak, of the boundaries of existence--and passes over into that boundless life where Subject and Object, desirous and desired, are one. No sharp line, but rather an infinite series of gradations separate the two states. Hence we must look carefully at all the pilgrims on the road; discover, if we can, the motive of their travels, the maps which they use, the luggage which they take, the end which they attain.

Now we have said that the end which the mystic sets before him is conscious union with a living Absolute. That Divine Dark, that Abyss of the Godhead, of which he sometimes speaks as the goal of his quest, is just this Absolute, the Uncreated Light in which the Universe is bathed, and which--transcending, as it does, all human powers of expression--he can only describe to us as dark. But there is--must be--contact "in an intelligible where" between every individual self and this Supreme Self, this Ultimate. In the mystic this union is conscious, personal, and complete. "He enjoys," says St. John of the Cross, "a certain contact of the soul with the Divinity; and it is God Himself who is then felt and tasted." [112] More or less according to his measure, he has touched--or better, been touched by--the substantial Being of Deity, not merely its manifestation in life. This it is which distinguishes him from the best and most brilliant of other men, and makes his science, in Patmore's words, "the science of self-evident Reality." Gazing with him into that unsearchable ground whence the World of Becoming comes forth "eternally generated in an eternal Now," we may see only the icy darkness of perpetual negations: but he, beyond the coincidence of opposites, looks upon the face of Perfect Love.

As genius in any of the arts is--humanly speaking--the final term of a power of which each individual possesses the rudiments, so mysticism may be looked upon as the final term, the active expression, of a power latent in the whole race: the power, that is to say, of so perceiving transcendent reality. Few people pass through life without knowing what it is to be at least touched by this mystical feeling. He who falls in love with a woman and perceives--as the lover really does perceive--that the categorical term "girl" veils a wondrous and unspeakable reality: he who, falling in love with nature, sees the landscape "touched with light divine,"--a charming phrase to those who have not seen it, but a scientific statement to the rest--he who falls in love with the Holy, or as we say "undergoes conversion": all these have truly known for an instant something of the secret of the world. [113]

". . . Ever and anon a trumpet sounds
From the hid battlement of Eternity,
Those shaken mists a space unsettle, then
Round the half-glimpsèd turrets slowly wash again."

At such moments "Transcendental Feeling, welling up from another Part of the Soul' whispers to Understanding and Sense that they are leaving out something. What? Nothing less than the secret plan of the Universe. And what is that secret plan? The other Part of the Soul' indeed comprehends it in silence as it is, but can explain it to the Understanding only in the symbolical language of the interpreter, Imagination--in Vision." [114]

Here, in this spark or "part of the soul" where the spirit, as religion says, "rests in God who made it," is the fountain alike of the creative imagination and the mystic life. Now and again something stings it into consciousness, and man is caught up to the spiritual level, catches a glimpse of the "secret plan." Then hints of a marvellous truth, a unity whose note is ineffable peace, shine in created things; awakening in the self a sentiment of love, adoration, and awe. Its life is enhanced, the barrier of personality is broken, man escapes the sense-world, ascends to the apex of his spirit, and enters for a brief period into the more extended life of the All.

This intuition of the Real lying at the root of the visible world and sustaining its life, is present in a modified form in the arts: perhaps it were better to say, must be present if these arts are so justify themselves as heightened forms of experience. It is this which gives to them that peculiar vitality, that strange power of communicating a poignant emotion, half torment and half joy, which baffle their more rational interpreters. We know that the picture which is "like a photograph," the building which is at once handsome and commodious, the novel which is a perfect transcript of life, fail to satisfy us. It is difficult to say why this should be so, unless it were because these things have neglected their true business; which was not to reproduce the illusions of ordinary men but to catch and translate for us something of that "secret plan," that reality which the artistic consciousness is able, in a measure, to perceive. "Painting as well as music and poetry exists and exults in immortal thoughts," says Blake.[115] That "life-enhancing power" which has been recognized as the supreme quality of good painting,[116] has its origin in this contact of the artistic mind with the archetypal--or, if you like, the transcendental--world: the underlying verity of things.

A critic, in whom poetic genius has brought about the unusual alliance of intuition with scholarship, testifies to this same truth when he says of the ideals which governed early Chinese painting, "In this theory every work of art is thought of as an incarnation of the genius of rhythm, manifesting the living spirit of things with a clearer beauty and intenser power than the gross impediments of complex matter allow to be transmitted to, our senses in the visible world around us. A picture is conceived as a sort of apparition from a more real world of essential life." [117]

That "more real world of essential life" is the world in which the "free soul" of the great mystic dwells; hovering like the six-winged seraph before the face of the Absolute. [118] The artist too may cross its boundaries in his brief moments of creation: but he cannot stay. He comes back to us, bearing its tidings, with Dante's cry upon his lips--

". . . Non eran da ciò le proprie penne
se non che la mia mente fu percossa
da un fulgore, in che sua voglia venne." [119]

The mystic may say--is indeed bound to say--with St. Bernard, "My secret to myself." Try how he will, his stammering and awestruck reports can hardly be understood but by those who are already in the way. But the artist cannot act thus. On him has been laid the duty of expressing something of that which he perceives. He is bound to tell his love. In his worship of Perfect Beauty faith must be balanced by works. By means of veils and symbols he must interpret his free vision, his glimpse of the burning bush, to other men. He is the mediator between his brethren and the divine, for art is the link between appearance and reality. [120]

But we do not call every one who has these partial and artistic intuitions of reality a mystic, any more than we call every one a musician who has learnt to play the piano. The true mystic is the person in whom such powers transcend the merely artistic and visionary stage, and are exalted to the point of genius: in whom the transcendental consciousness can dominate the normal consciousness, and who has definitely surrendered himself to the embrace of Reality. As artists stand in a peculiar relation to the phenomenal world, receiving rhythms and discovering truths and beauties which are hidden from other men, so this true mystic stands in a peculiar relation to the transcendental world, there experiencing actual, but to us unimaginable tension and delight. His consciousness is transfigured in a particular way, he lives at different levels of experience from other people: and this of course means that he sees a different world, since the world as we know it is the product of certain scraps or aspects of reality acting upon a normal and untransfigured consciousness. Hence his mysticism is no isolated vision, no fugitive glimpse of reality, but a complete system of life carrying its own guarantees and obligations. As other men are immersed in and react to natural or intellectual life, so the mystic is immersed in and reacts to spiritual life. He moves towards that utter identification with its interests which he calls "Union with God." He has been called a lonely soul. He might more properly be described as a lonely body: for his soul, peculiarly responsive, sends out and receives communications upon every side.

The earthly artist, because perception brings with it the imperative longing for expression, tries to give us in colour, sound or words a hint of his ecstasy, his glimpse of truth. Only those who have tried, know how small a fraction of his vision he can, under the most favourable circumstance, contrive to represent. The mystic, too, tries very hard to tell an unwilling world his secret. But in his case, the difficulties are enormously increased. First, there is the huge disparity between his unspeakable experience and the language which will most nearly suggest it. Next, there is the great gulf fixed between his mind and the mind of the world. His audience must be bewitched as well as addressed, caught up to something of his state, before they can be made to understand.

Were he a musician, it is probable that the mystic could give his message to other musicians in the terms of that art, far more accurately than language will allow him to do: for we must remember that there is no excuse but that of convenience for the pre-eminence amongst modes of expression which we accord to words. These correspond so well to the physical plane and its adventures, that we forget that they have but the faintest of relations with transcendental things. Even the artist, before he can make use of them, is bound to re-arrange them in accordance with the laws of rhythm: obeying unconsciously the rule by which all arts "tend to approach the condition of music."

So too the mystic. Mysticism, the most romantic of adventures, from one point of view the art of arts, their source and also their end, finds naturally enough its closest correspondences in the most purely artistic and most deeply significant of all forms of expression. The mystery of music is seldom realized by those who so easily accept its gifts. Yet of all the arts music alone shares with great mystical literature the power of waking in us a response to the life-movement of the universe: brings us--we know not how--news of its exultant passions and its incomparable peace. Beethoven heard the very voice of Reality, and little of it escaped when he translated it for our ears. [121]

The mediaeval mind, more naturally mystical than ours, and therefore more sharply aware of the part which rhythmic harmony plays in the worlds of nature and of grace, gave to music a cosmic importance, discerning its operation in many phenomena which we now attribute to that dismal figment, Law. "There are three kinds of music," says Hugh of St. Victor, "the music of the worlds, the music of humanity, the music of instruments. Of the music of the worlds, one is of the elements, another of the planets, another of Time. Of that which is of the elements, one is of number, another of weights, another of measure. Of that which is of the planets, one is of place, another of motion, another of nature. Of that which is of Time, one is of the days and the vicissitudes of light and darkness; another of the months and the waxing and waning of the moon; another of the years and the changes of spring, summer, autumn and winter. Of the music of humanity, one is of the body, another of the soul, another in the connexion that is between them." [122] Thus the life of the visible and invisible universe consists in a supernal fugue.

One contemplative at least, Richard Rolle of Hampole, "the father of English mysticism," was acutely aware of this music of the soul, discerning in it a correspondence with the measured harmonies of the spiritual universe. In those enraptured descriptions of his inward experience which are among the jewels of mystical literature, nothing is more remarkable than his constant and deliberate employment of musical imagery. This alone, it seems, could catch and translate for him the character of his experience of Reality. The condition of joyous and awakened love to which the mystic passes when his purification is at an end is to him, above all else, the state of Song. He does not "see" the spiritual world: he "hears" it. For him, as for St. Francis of Assisi, it is a "heavenly melody, intolerably sweet." [123]

"Song I call," he says, "when in a plenteous soul the sweetness of eternal love with burning is taken, and thought into song is turned, and the mind into full sweet sound is changed." [124] He who experiences this joyous exaltation "says not his prayers like other righteous men" but "is taken into marvellous mirth: and, goodly sound being descended into him, as it were with notes his prayers he sings." [125] So Gertrude More--"O lett me sitt alone, silent to all the world and it to me, that I may learn the song of Love." [126]

Rolle's own experience of mystic joy seems actually to have come to him in this form: the perceptions of his exalted consciousness presenting themselves to his understanding under musical conditions, as other mystics have received them in the form of pictures or words. I give in his own words the classic description of his passage from the first state of "burning love" to the second state of "songful love"--from Calor to Canor-- when "into song of joy meditation is turned." "In the night, before supper, as I my psalms sung, as it were the sound of readers or rather singers about me I beheld. Whilst, also praying, to heaven with all desire I took heed, suddenly, in what manner I wot not, in me the sound of song I felt; and likeliest heavenly melody I took, with me dwelling in mind. Forsooth my thought continually to mirth of song was changed, and my meditation to praise turned; and my prayers and psalm-saying, in sound I showed." [127]

The song, however, is a mystic melody having little in common with its clumsy image, earthly music. Bodily song "lets it"; and "noise of janglers makes it turn again to thought," "for sweet ghostly song accords not with outward song, the which in churches and elsewhere is used. It discords much: for all that is man's voice is formed with bodily ears to be heard; but among angels' tunes it has an acceptable melody, and with marvel it is commended of them that have known it." To others it is incommunicable. "Worldly lovers soothly words or ditties of our song may know, for the words they read: but the tone and sweetness of that song they may not learn." [128]

Such symbolism as this--a living symbolism of experience and action, as well as of statement--seems almost essential to mystical expression. The mind must employ some device of the kind if its transcendental perceptions--wholly unrelated as they are to the phenomena with which intellect is able to deal--are ever to be grasped by the surface consciousness. Sometimes the symbol and the perception which it represents become fused in that consciousness; and the mystic's experience then presents itself to him as "visions" or "voices" which we must look upon as the garment he has himself provided to veil that Reality upon which no man may look and live. The nature of this garment will be largely conditioned by his temperament--as in Rolle's evident bias towards music, St. Catherine of Genoa's leaning towards the abstract conceptions of fire and light--and also by his theological education and environment. Cases in point are the highly dogmatic visions and auditions of St. Gertrude, Suso, St. Catherine of Siena, the Blessed Angela of Foligno; above all of St. Teresa, whose marvellous self-analyses provide the classic account of these attempts of the mind to translate transcendental intuitions into concepts with which it can deal.

The greatest mystics, however--Ruysbroeck, St. John of the Cross, and St. Teresa herself in her later stages--distinguish clearly between the ineffable Reality which they perceive and the image under which they describe it. Again and again they tell us with Dionysius and Eckhart, that the Object of their contemplation "hath no image": or with St. John of the Cross that "the soul can never attain to the height of the divine union, so far as it is possible in this life, through the medium of any forms or figures." [129] Therefore the attempt which has sometimes been made to identify mysticism with such forms and figures--with visions, voices, "supernatural favours" and other abnormal phenomena--is clearly wrong.

"The highest and most divine things which it is given us to see and to know," says Dionysius the Areopagite plainly, "are but the symbolic language of things subordinate to Him who Himself transcendeth them all: through which things His incomprehensible Presence is shown, walking on those heights of His Holy Places which are perceived by the mind. [130]

The mystic, as a rule, cannot wholly do without symbol and image, inadequate to his vision though they must always be: for his experience must be expressed if it is to be communicated, and its actuality is inexpressible except in some side-long way, some hint or parallel which will stimulate the dormant intuition of the reader, and convey, as all poetic language does, something beyond its surface sense. Hence the large part which is played in all mystical writings by symbolism and imagery; and also by that rhythmic and exalted language which induces in sensitive persons something of the languid ecstasy of dream. The close connection between rhythm and heightened states of consciousness is as yet little understood. Its further investigation will probably throw much light on ontological as well as psychological problems. Mystical, no less than musical and poetic perception, tends naturally--we know not why--to present itself in rhythmical periods: a feature which is also strongly marked in writings obtained in the automatic state. So constant is this law in some subjects that Baron von Hügel adopted the presence or absence of rhythm as a test whereby to distinguish the genuine utterances of St. Catherine of Genoa from those wrongly attributed to her by successive editors of her legend. [131]

All kinds of symbolic language come naturally to the articulate mystic, who is often a literary artist as well: so naturally, that he sometimes forgets to explain that his utterance is but symbolic--a desperate attempt to translate the truth of that world into the beauty of this. It is here that mysticism joins hands with music and poetry: had this fact always been recognized by its critics, they would have been saved from many regrettable and some ludicrous misconceptions. Symbol--the clothing which the spiritual borrows from the material plane--is a form of artistic expression. That is to say, it is not literal but suggestive: though the artist who uses it may sometimes lose sight of this distinction. Hence the persons who imagine that the "Spiritual Marriage" of St. Catherine or St. Teresa veils a perverted sexuality, that the vision of the Sacred Heart involved an incredible anatomical experience, or that the divine inebriation of the Sufis is the apotheosis of drunkenness, do but advertise their ignorance of the mechanism of the arts: like the lady who thought that Blake must be mad because he said that he had touched the sky with his finger.

Further, the study of the mystics, the keeping company however humbly with their minds, brings with it as music or poetry does--but in a far greater degree--a strange exhilaration, as if we were brought near to some mighty source of Being, were at last on the verge of the secret which all seek. The symbols displayed, the actual words employed, when we analyse them, are not enough to account for such effect. It is rather that these messages from the waking transcendental self of another, stir our own deeper selves in their sleep. It were hardly an extravagance to say, that those writings which are the outcome of true and first-hand mystical experience may be known by this power of imparting to the reader the sense of exalted and extended life. "All mystics," says Saint-Martin, "speak the same language, for they come from the same country." The deep undying life within us came from that country too: and it recognizes the accents of home, though it cannot always understand what they would say.

Now, returning to our original undertaking, that of defining if we can the characteristics of true mysticism, I think that we have already reached a point at which William James's celebrated "four marks" of the mystic state, Ineffability, Noetic Quality, Transiency, and Passivity, [132] will fail to satisfy us. In their place I propose to set out, illustrate and, I hope, justify four other rules or notes which may be applied as tests to any given case which claims to take rank amongst the mystics.

1. True mysticism is active and practical, not passive and theoretical. It is an organic life-process, a something which the whole self does; not something as to which its intellect holds an opinion.

2. Its aims are wholly transcendental and spiritual. It is in no way concerned with adding to, exploring, re-arranging, or improving anything in the visible universe. The mystic brushes aside that universe, even in its supernormal manifestations. Though he does not, as his enemies declare, neglect his duty to the many, his heart is always set upon the changeless One.

3. This One is for the mystic, not merely the Reality of all that is, but also a living and personal Object of Love; never an object of exploration. It draws his whole being homeward, but always under the guidance of the heart.

4. Living union with this One--which is the term of his adventure--is a definite state or form of enhanced life. It is obtained neither from an intellectual realization of its delights, nor from the most acute emotional longings. Though these must be present they are not enough. It is arrived at by an arduous psychological and spiritual process--the so-called Mystic Way--entailing the complete remaking of character and the liberation of a new, or rather latent, form of consciousness; which imposes on the self the condition which is sometimes inaccurately called "ecstasy," but is better named the Unitive State.

Mysticism, then, is not an opinion: it is not a philosophy. It has nothing in common with the pursuit of occult knowledge. On the one hand it is not merely the power of contemplating Eternity: on the other, it is not to be identified with any kind of religious queerness. It is the name of that organic process which involves the perfect consummation of the Love of God: the achievement here and now of the immortal heritage of man. Or, if you like it better--for this means exactly the same thing--it is the art of establishing his conscious relation with the Absolute.

The movement of the mystic consciousness towards this consummation, is not merely the sudden admission to an overwhelming vision of Truth: though such dazzling glimpses may from time to time be vouchsafed to the soul. It is rather an ordered movement towards ever higher levels of reality, ever closer identification with the Infinite. "The mystic experience," says Récéjac, "ends with the words, I live, yet not I, but God in me.' This feeling of identification, which is the term of mystical activity, has a very important significance. In its early stages the mystic consciousness feels the Absolute in opposition to the Self . . . as mystic activity goes on, it tends to abolish this opposition. . . . When it has reached its term the consciousness finds itself possessed by the sense of a Being at one and the same time greater than the Self and identical with it: great enough to be God, intimate enough to be me." [133]

This is that mystic union which is the only possible fulfilment of mystic love: since

"All that is not One must ever
Suffer with the wound of Absence
And whoever in Love's city
Enters, finds but room for One
And but in One-ness, Union." [134]

The history of mysticism is the history of the demonstration of this law upon the plane of reality.

Now, how do these statements square with the practice of the great mystics; and with the various forms of activity which have been classified at one time or another as mystical?

(1) Mysticism is practical, not theoretical.

This statement, taken alone, is not, of course, enough to identify mysticism; since it is equally true of magic, which also proposes to itself something to be done rather than something to be believed. It at once comes into collision, however, with the opinions of those who believe mysticism to be "the reaction of the born Platonist upon religion."

The difference between such devout philosophers and the true mystic, is the difference which George Tyrrell held to distinguish revelation from theology. [135] Mysticism, like revelation, is final and personal. It is not merely a beautiful and suggestive diagram but experience in its most intense form. That experience, in the words of Plotinus, is the soul's solitary adventure: "the flight of the Alone to the Alone." [136] It provides the material, the substance, upon which mystical philosophy cogitates; as theologians cogitate upon the revelation which forms the basis of faith. Hence those whom we are to accept as mystics must have received, and acted upon, intuitions of a Truth which is for them absolute. If we are to acknowledge that they "knew the doctrine" they must have "lived the life"; submitted to the interior travail of the Mystic Way, not merely have reasoned about the mystical experiences of others. We could not well dispense with our Christian Platonists and mystical philosophers. They are our stepping-stones to higher things; interpret to our dull minds, entangled in the sense-world, the ardent vision of those who speak to us from the dimension of Reality. But they are no more mystics than the milestones on the Dover Road are travellers to Calais. Sometimes their words--the wistful words of those who know but cannot be--produce mystics; as the sudden sight of a signpost pointing to the sea will rouse the spirit of adventure in a boy. Also there are many instances of true mystics, such as Eckhart, who have philosophized upon their own experiences, greatly to the advantage of the world; and others--Plotinus is the most characteristic example--of Platonic philosophers who have passed far beyond the limits of their own philosophy, and abandoned the making of diagrams for an experience, however imperfect, of the reality at which these diagrams hint. It were more accurate to reverse the epigram above stated, and say, that Platonism is the reaction of the intellectualist upon mystical truth.

Over and over again the great mystics tell us, not how they speculated, but how they acted. To them, the transition from the life of sense to the life of spirit is a formidable undertaking, which demands effort and constancy. The paradoxical "quiet" of the contemplative is but the outward stillness essential to inward work. Their favourite symbols are those of action: battle, search, and pilgrimage.

"In an obscure night
Fevered with love's anxiety
(O hapless, happy plight!)
I went , none seeing me
Forth from my house, where all things quiet be," [137]

said St. John of the Cross, in his poem of the mystic quest.

"It became evident to me," says Al Ghazzali of his own search for mystic truth, "that the Sufis are men of intuition and not men of words. I recognized that I had learnt all that can be learnt of Sufiism by study, and that the rest could not be learnt by study or by speech." [138] "Let no one suppose," says the "Theologia Germanica," "that we may attain to this true light and perfect knowledge . . . by hearsay, or by reading and study, nor yet by high skill and great learning." [139] "It is not enough," says Gerlac Petersen, "to know by estimation merely: but we must know by experience." [140] So Mechthild of Magdeburg says of her revelations, "The writing of this book was seen, heard, and experienced in every limb. . . . I see it with the eyes of my soul, and hear it with the ears of my eternal spirit." [141]

Those who suppose mystical experience to be merely a pleasing consciousness of the Divine in the world, a sense of the "otherness" of things, a basking in the beams of the Uncreated Light, are only playing with Reality. True mystical achievement is the most complete and most difficult expression of life which is as yet possible to man. It is at once an act of love, an act of surrender, and an act of supreme perception; a trinity of experiences which meets and satisfies the three activities of the self. Religion might give us the first and metaphysics the third of these processes. Only Mysticism can offer the middle term of the series; the essential link which binds the three in one. "Secrets," says St. Catherine of Siena, "are revealed to a friend who has become one thing with his friend and not to a servant." [142]

(2) Mysticism is an entirely Spiritual Activity.

This rule provides us with a further limitation, which of course excludes all the practisers of magic and of magical religion: even in their most exalted and least materialistic forms. As we shall see when we come to consider these persons, their object--not necessarily an illegitimate one--is to improve and elucidate the visible by help of the invisible: to use the supernormal powers of the self for the increase of power, virtue, happiness or knowledge. The mystic never turns back on himself in this way, or tries to combine the advantages of two worlds. At the term of his development he knows God by communion, and this direct intuition of the Absolute kills all lesser cravings. He possesses God, and needs nothing more. Though he will spend himself unceasingly for other men, become "an agent of the Eternal Goodness," he is destitute of supersensual ambitions and craves no occult knowledge or power. Having his eyes set on eternity, his consciousness steeped in it, he can well afford to tolerate the entanglements of time. "His spirit," says Tauler, "is as it were sunk and lost in the Abyss of the Deity, and loses the consciousness of all creature-distinctions. All things are gathered together in one with the divine sweetness, and the man's being is so penetrated with the divine substance that he loses himself therein, as a drop of water is lost in a cask of strong wine. And thus the man's spirit is so sunk in God in divine union, that he loses all sense of distinction . . . and there remains a secret, still union, without cloud or colour." [143] "I wish not," said St. Catherine of Genoa, "for anything that comes forth from Thee, but only for Thee, oh sweetest Love!" [144] "Whatever share of this world," says Rabi'a, "Thou dost bestow on me, bestow it on Thine enemies, and whatever share of the next world thou dost give me, give it to Thy friends. Thou art enough for me!" [145] "The Soul," says Plotinus in one of his most profound passages, "having now arrived at the desired end, and participating of Deity, will know that the Supplier of true life is then present. She will likewise then require nothing farther; for, on the contrary it will be requisite to lay aside other things, to stop in this alone, amputating everything else with which she is surrounded." [146]

(3) The business and method of Mysticism is Love.

Here is one of the distinctive notes of true mysticism; marking it off from every other kind of transcendental theory and practice and providing the answer to the question with which our last chapter closed. It is the eager, outgoing activity whose driving power is generous love, not the absorbent, indrawing activity which strives only for new knowledge, that is fruitful in the spiritual as well as in the physical world.

Having said this, however, we must add--as we did when speaking of the "heart"--that the word Love as applied to the mystics is to be understood in its deepest, fullest sense; as the ultimate expression of the self's most vital tendencies, not as the superficial affection or emotion often dignified by this name. Mystic Love is a total dedication of the will; the deep-seated desire and tendency of the soul towards its Source. It is a condition of humble access, a life-movement of the self: more direct in its methods, more valid in its results--even in the hands of the least lettered of its adepts--than the most piercing intellectual vision of the greatest philosophic mind. Again and again the mystics insist upon this. "For silence is not God, nor speaking is not God; fasting is not God nor eating is not God; onliness is not God nor company is not God; nor yet any of all the other two such quantities, He is hid between them, and may not be found by any work of thy soul, but all only by love of thine heart. He may not be known by reason. He may not be gotten by thought, nor concluded by understanding; but he may be loved and chosen with the true lovely will of thine heart. . . . Such a blind shot with the sharp dart of longing love may never fail of the prick, the which is God." [147]

"Come down quickly,'" says the Incomprehensible Godhead to the soul that has struggled like Zaccheus to the topmost branches of the theological tree, "for I would dwell with you to-day.' And this hasty descent to which he is summoned by God is simply a descent by love and desire in to that abyss of the Godhead which the intellect cannot understand. But where intelligence must rest without, love and desire can enter in." [148]

Volumes of extracts might be compiled from the works of the mystics illustrative of this rule, which is indeed their central principle. "Some there are," says Plotinus, "that for all their effort have not attained the Vision; the soul in them has come to no sense of the splendour there. It has not taken warmth; it has not felt burning within itself the flame of love for what is there to know." [149] "Love," says Rolle, "truly suffers not a loving soul to bide in itself, but ravishes it out to the Lover, that the soul is more there where it loves, than where the body is that lives and feels it." "Oh singular joy of love everlasting," he says again, "that ravishes all his to heavens above all worlds, them binding with bands of virtue! Oh dear charity, in earth that has thee not is nought wrought, whatever it hath! He truly in thee that is busy, to joy above earthly is soon lifted! Thou makest men contemplative, heaven-gate thou openest, mouths of accusers thou dost shut, God thou makest to be seen and multitude of sins thou hidest. We praise thee, we preach thee, by thee the world we quickly overcome, by whom we joy and the heavenly ladder we ascend." [150]

Love to the mystic, then, is (a) the active, conative, expression of his will and desire for the Absolute; (b) his innate tendency to that Absolute, his spiritual weight. He is only thoroughly natural, thoroughly alive, when he is obeying its voice. For him it is the source of joy, the secret of the universe, the vivifying principle of things. In the words of Récéjac, "Mysticism claims to be able to know the Unknowable without any help from dialectics; and believes that, by the way of love and will it reaches a point to which thought alone is unable to attain." Again, "It is the heart and never the reason which leads us to the Absolute." [151] Hence in St. Catherine of Siena's exquisite allegory it is the feet of the soul's affection which brings it first to the Bridge, "for the feet carry the body as affection carries the soul."[152]

The jewels of mystical literature glow with this intimate and impassioned love of the Absolute; which transcends the dogmatic language in which it is clothed and becomes applicable to mystics of every race and creed. There is little difference in this between the extremes of Eastern and Western thought: between A Kempis the Christian and Jalalu d Din the Moslem saint.

"How great a thing is Love, great above all other goods: for alone it makes all that is heavy light, and bears evenly all that is uneven. . . .

"Love would be aloft, nor will it be kept back by any lower thing. Love would be free, and estranged from all worldly affection, that its inward sight be not hindered: that it may not be entangled by any temporal comfort, nor succumb to any tribulation.

"Nought is sweeter than love, nought stronger, nought higher, nought wider: there is no more joyous, fuller, better thing in heaven or earth. For love is born of God, and cannot rest save in God, above all created things.

"The lover flies, runs, and, rejoices: he is free, and cannot be restrained. He gives all for all, and has all in all; for he rests in One Supreme above all, from whom all good flows and proceeds.

"He looks not at the gift, but above all goods turns himself to the giver.

". . . He who loves knows the cry of this voice. For this burning affection of the soul is a loud cry in the ears of God when it saith My God, My Love, Thou art all mine, and I am all Thine."' [153]

So much for the Christian. Now for the Persian mystic.

"While the thought of the Beloved fills our hearts
All our work is to do Him service and spend life for Him.
Wherever He kindles His destructive torch
Myriads of lovers' souls are burnt therewith.
The lovers who dwell within the sanctuary
Are moths burnt with the torch of the Beloved's face.
O heart, hasten thither! for God will shine upon you,
And seem to you a sweet garden instead of a terror.
He will infuse into your soul a new soul,

So as to fill you, like a goblet, with wine.
Take up your abode in His Soul!
Take up your abode in heaven, oh bright full moon!
Like the heavenly Scribe, He will open your heart's book
That he may reveal mysteries unto you." [154]

Well might Hilton say that "Perfect love maketh God and the soul to be as if they both together were but one thing," [155] and Tauler that "the well of life is love, and he who dwelleth not in love is dead." [156]

These, nevertheless, are objective and didactic utterances; though their substance may be--probably is--personal, their form is not. But if we want to see what it really means to be "in love with the Absolute,"--how intensely actual to the mystic is the Object of his passion, how far removed from the spheres of pious duty or philosophic speculation, how concrete, positive and dominant such a passion may be--we must study the literature of autobiography, not that of poetry or exhortation. I choose for this purpose, rather than the well-known self-analyses of St. Augustine, St. Teresa or Suso, which are accessible to every one, the more private confessions of that remarkable mystic Dame Gertrude More, contained in her "Spiritual Exercises."

This nun, great-great-granddaughter of Sir Thomas More, and favourite pupil of the celebrated Benedictine contemplative, the Ven. Augustine Baker, exhibits the romantic and personal side of mysticism more perfectly than even St. Teresa, whose works were composed for her daughters' edification. She was an eager student of St. Augustine, "my deere deere Saint," as she calls him more than once. He had evidently influenced her language; but her passion is her own.

Remember that Gertrude More's confessions represent the most secret conversations of her soul with God. They were not meant for publication; but, written for the most part on blank leaves in her breviary, were discovered and published after her death. "She called them," says the title-page with touching simplicity, " Amor ordinem nescit: an Ideot's Devotions. Her only spiritual father and directour, Father Baker, styled them Confessiones Amantis, A Lover's Confessions. Amans Deum anima sub Deo despicit universa. A soul that loveth God despiseth all things that be inferiour unto God." [157]

The spirit of her little book is summed up in two epigrams: epigrams of which her contemporary, Crashaw, might have been proud. "To give all for love is a most sweet bargain." [158] "O let me love, or not live!" [159] Love indeed was her life: and she writes of it with a rapture which recalls at one moment the exuberant poetry of Jacopene da Todi, at another the love songs of the Elizabethan poets.

"Never was there or can there be imagined such a Love, as is between an humble soul and thee. Who can express what passeth between such a soul and thee? Verily neither man nor Angell is able to do it sufficiently. . . . In thy prayse I am only happy, in which, my Joy, I will exult with all that love thee. For what can be a comfort while I live separated from thee, but only to remember that my God, who is more myne than I am my owne, is absolutely and infinitely happy? . . . Out of this true love between a soul and thee, there ariseth such a knowledge in the soul that it loatheth all that is an impediment to her further proceeding in the Love of thee. O Love, Love, even by naming thee, my soul loseth itself in thee. . . . Nothing can Satiate a reasonable soul but only thou: and having of thee, who art indeed all, nothing could be said to be wanting to her. . . . Blessed are the cleans of hart for they shall see God. O sight to be wished, desired, and longed for; because once to have seen thee is to have learnt all things. Nothing can bring us to this sight but love. But what love must it be? not a sensible love only, a childish love, a love which seeketh itself more than the beloved. No, no, but it must be an ardent love, a pure love, a courageous love, a love of charity, an humble love, and a constant love, not worn out with labours, not daunted with any difficulties. . . . For that soul that hath set her whole love and desire on thee, can never find any true satisfaction, but only in thee." [160]

Who will not see that we have here no literary exercise, but the fruits of an experience of peculiar intensity? It answers exactly to one of the best modern definitions of mysticism as "in essence, the concentration of all the forces of the soul upon a supernatural Object, conceived and loved as a living Person." [161] "Love and desire," says the same critic, "are the fundamental necessities; and where they are absent man, even though he be a visionary, cannot be called a mystic." [162] Such a definition, of course, is not complete. It is valuable however, because it emphasizes the fact that all true mysticism is rooted in personality; and is therefore fundamentally a science of the heart.

Attraction, desire, and union as the fulfilment of desire; this is the way Life works, in the highest as in the lowest things. The mystic's outlook, indeed, is the lover's outlook. It has the same element of wildness, the same quality of selfless and quixotic devotion, the same combination of rapture and humility. This parallel is more than a pretty fancy: for mystic and lover, upon different planes, are alike responding to the call of the Spirit of Life. The language of human passion is tepid and insignificant beside the language in which the mystics try to tell the splendours of their love. They force upon the unprejudiced reader the conviction that they are dealing with an ardour far more burning for an Object far more real.

"This monk can give lessons to lovers!" exclaimed Arthur Symons in astonishment of St. John of the Cross. [163] It would be strange if he could not; since their finite passions are but the feeble images of his infinite one, their beloved the imperfect symbol of his First and only Fair. "I saw Him and sought Him: I had Him and I wanted Him," says Julian of Norwich, in a phrase which seems to sum up all the ecstasy and longing of man's soul. Only this mystic passion can lead us from our prison. Its brother, the desire of knowledge, may enlarge and improve the premises to an extent as yet undreamed of: but it can never unlock the doors.

(4) Mysticism entails a definite Psychological Experience.

That is to say, it shows itself not merely as an attitude of mind and heart, but as a form of organic life. It is not only a theory of the intellect or a hunger, however passionate, of the heart. It involves the organizing of the whole self, conscious and unconscious, under the spur of such a hunger: a remaking of the whole character on high levels in the interests of the transcendental life. The mystics are emphatic in their statement that spiritual desires are useless unless they initiate this costly movement of the whole self towards the Real.

Thus in the visions of Mechthild of Magdeburg, "The soul spake thus to her Desire, Fare forth and see where my Love is. Say to him that I desire to love.' So Desire sped forth, for she is quick of her nature, and came to the Empyrean and cried, Great Lord, open and let me in!' Then said the Householder of that place: What means this fiery eagerness?' Desire replied, Lord I would have thee know that my lady can no longer bear to live. If Thou wouldst flow forth to her, then might she swim: but the fish cannot long exist that is left stranded on the shore.' Go back,' said the Lord, I will not let thee in unless thou bring to me that hungry soul, for it is in this alone that I take delight.'" [164]

We have said [165] that the full mystic consciousness is extended in two distinct directions. So too there are two distinct sides to the full mystical experience. (A) The vision or consciousness of Absolute Perfection. (B) The inward transmutation to which that Vision compels the mystic, in order that he may be to some extent worthy of that which he has beheld: may take his place within the order of Reality. He has seen the Perfect; he wants to be perfect too. The "third term," the necessary bridge between the Absolute and the Self, can only, he feels, be moral and spiritual transcendence--in a word, Sanctity-- for "the only means of attaining the Absolute lies in adapting ourselves to It." [166] The moral virtues are for him, then, the obligatory "ornaments of the Spiritual Marriage" as Ruysbroeck called them: though far more than their presence is needed to bring that marriage about. Unless this impulse for moral perfection be born in him, this travail of the inner life begun, he is no mystic: though he may well be a visionary, a prophet, a "mystical" poet.

Moreover, this process of transmutation, this rebuilding of the self on higher levels, will involve the establishment within the field of consciousness, the making "central for life," of those subconscious spiritual perceptions which are the primary material of mystical experience. The end and object of this "inward alchemy" will be the raising of the whole self to the condition in which conscious and permanent union with the Absolute takes place and man, ascending to the summit of his manhood, enters into that greater life for which he was made. In its journey towards this union, the subject commonly passes through certain well-marked phases, which constitute what is known as the "Mystic Way." This statement rules out from the true mystic kingdom all merely sentimental and affective piety and visionary poetry, no less than mystical philosophy. It brings us back to our first proposition--the concrete and practical nature of the mystical act.

More than the apprehension of God, then, more than the passion for the Absolute, is needed to make a mystic. These must be combined with an appropriate psychological make-up, with a nature capable of extraordinary concentration, an exalted moral emotion, a nervous organization of the artistic type. All these are necessary to the successful development of the mystic life process. In the experience of those mystics who have left us the records of their own lives, the successive stages of this life process are always traceable. In the second part of this book, they will be found worked out at some length. Rolle, Suso, St. Teresa, and many others have left us valuable self-analyses for comparison: and from them we see how arduous, how definite, and how far removed from mere emotional or intellectual activity, is that educational discipline by which "the eye which looks upon Eternity" is able to come to its own. "One of the marks of the true mystic," says Leuba--by no means a favourable witness--"is the tenacious and heroic energy with which he pursues a definite moral ideal." [167] "He is," says Pacheu, "the pilgrim of an inward Odyssey." [168] Though we may be amazed and delighted by his adventures and discoveries on the way, to him the voyage and the end are all. "The road on which we enter is a royal road which leads to heaven," says St. Teresa. "Is it strange that the conquest of such a treasure should cost us rather dear?" [169]

It is one of the many indirect testimonies to the objective reality of mysticism that the stages of this road, the psychology of the spiritual ascent, as described to us by different schools of contemplatives, always present practically the same sequence of states. The "school for saints" has never found it necessary to bring its curriculum up to date. The psychologist finds little difficulty, for instance, in reconciling the "Degrees of Orison" described by St. Teresa [170] --Recollection, Quiet, Union, Ecstasy, Rapt, the "Pain of God," and the Spiritual Marriage of the soul--with the four forms of contemplation enumerated by Hugh of St. Victor, or the Sufi's "Seven Stages" of the soul's ascent to God, which begin in adoration and end in spiritual marriage. [171] Though each wayfarer may choose different landmarks, it is clear from their comparison that the road is one.

(5) As a corollary to these four rules, it is perhaps well to reiterate the statement already made, that True Mysticism is never self-seeking. It is not, as many think, the pursuit of supernatural joys; the satisfaction of a high ambition. The mystic does not enter on his quest because he desires the happiness of the Beatific Vision, the ecstasy of union with the Absolute, or any other personal reward. That noblest of all passions, the passion for perfection for Love's sake, far outweighs the desire for transcendental satisfaction. "O Love," said St. Catherine of Genoa, "I do not wish to follow thee for sake of these delights, but solely from the motive of true love." [172] Those who do otherwise are only, in the plain words of St. John of the Cross, "spiritual gluttons": [173] or, in the milder metaphor here adopted, magicians of the more high-minded sort. The true mystic claims no promises and makes no demands. He goes because he must, as Galahad went towards the Grail: knowing that for those who can live it, this alone is life. He never rests in that search for God which he holds to be the fulfilment of his highest duty; yet he seeks without any certainty of success. He holds with St. Bernard that "He alone is God who can never be sought in vain: not even when He cannot be found." [174] With Mechthild of Magdeburg, he hears the Absolute saying in his soul, "O soul, before the world was I longed for thee: and I still long for thee, and thou for Me. Therefore, when our two desires unite, Love shall be fulfilled."[175]

Like his type, the "devout lover" of romance, then, the mystic serves without hope of reward. By one of the many paradoxes of the spiritual life, he obtains satisfaction because he does not seek it; completes his personality because he gives it up. "Attainment," says Dionysius the Areopagite in words which are writ large on the annals of Christian ecstasy, "comes only by means of this sincere, spontaneous, and entire surrender of yourself and all things." [176] Only with the annihilation of selfhood comes the fulfilment of love. Were the mystic asked the cause of his often extraordinary behaviour, his austere and steadfast quest, it is unlikely that his reply would contain any reference to sublime illumination or unspeakable delights. It is more probable that he would answer in some such words as those of Jacob Boehme, "I am not come to this meaning, or to this work and knowledge through my own reason or through my own will and purpose; neither have I sought this knowledge, nor so much as to know anything concerning it. I sought only for the heart of God, therein to hide myself."[177]

"Whether we live or whether we die," said St. Paul, "we are the Lord's." The mystic is a realist, to whom these words convey not a dogma but an invitation: an invitation to the soul to attain that fullness of life for which she was made, to "lose herself in That which can be neither seen nor touched; giving herself entirely to this sovereign Object without belonging either to herself or to others; united to the Unknown by the most noble part of herself and because of her renouncement of knowledge; finally drawing from this absolute ignorance a knowledge which the understanding knows not how to attain.[178] Mysticism, then, is seen as the "one way out" for the awakened spirit of man; healing that human incompleteness which is the origin of our divine unrest. "I am sure," says Eckhart, "that if a soul knew the very least of all that Being means, it would never turn away from it." [179] The mystics have never turned away: to do so would have seemed to them a self-destructive act. Here, in this world of illusion, they say, we have no continuing city. This statement, to you a proposition, is to us the central fact of life. "Therefore, it is necessary to hasten our departure from hence, and detach ourselves in so far as we may from the body to which we are fettered, in order that with the whole of our selves, we may fold ourselves about Divinity, and have no part void of contact with Him." [180]

To sum up. Mysticism is seen to be a highly specialized form of that search for reality, for heightened and completed life, which we have found to be a constant characteristic of human consciousness. It is largely prosecuted by that "spiritual spark," that transcendental faculty which, though the life of our life, remains below the threshold in ordinary men. Emerging from its hiddenness in the mystic, it gradually becomes the dominant factor in his life; subduing to its service, and enhancing by its saving contact with reality, those vital powers of love and will which we attribute to the heart, rather than those of mere reason and perception, which we attribute to the head. Under the spur of this love and will, the whole personality rises in the acts of contemplation and ecstasy to a level of consciousness at which it becomes aware of a new field of perception. By this awareness, by this "loving sight," it is stimulated to a new life in accordance with the Reality which it has beheld. So strange and exalted is this life, that it never fails to provoke either the anger or the admiration of other men. "If the great Christian mystics," says Leuba, "could by some miracle be all brought together in the same place, each in his habitual environment, there to live according to his manner, the world would soon perceive that they constitute one of the most amazing and profound variations of which the human race has yet been witness." [181]

A discussion of mysticism, regarded as a form of human life, will therefore include two branches.

First the life process of the mystic: the remaking of his personality; the method by which his peculiar consciousness of the Absolute is attained, and faculties which have been evolved to meet the requirements of the phenomenal, are enabled to do work on the transcendental, plane. This is the "Mystic Way" in which the self passes through the states or stages of development which were codified by the Neoplatonists, and after them by the mediaeval mystics, as Purgation, Illumination, and Ecstasy. Secondly, the content of the mystical field of perception; the revelation under which the contemplative becomes aware of the Absolute. This will include a consideration of the so called doctrines of mysticism: the attempts of the articulate mystic to sketch for us the world into which he has looked, in language which is only adequate to the world in which the rest of us dwell. Here the difficult question of symbolism, and of symbolic theology, comes in: a point upon which many promising expositions of the mystics have been wrecked. It will be our business to strip off as far as may be the symbolic wrapping, and attempt a synthesis of these doctrines; to resolve the apparent contradictions of objective and subjective revelations, of the ways of negation and affirmation, emanation and immanence, surrender and deification, the Divine Dark and the Inward Light; and finally to exhibits if we can, the essential unity of that experience in which the human soul enters consciously into the Presence of God.

Footnotes:

111. See "Varieties of Religious Experience," p. 387, "The Drunken Consciousness is a bit of the Mystic Consciousness."

112. Llama de Amor Viva, II. 26.

113. Compare above, pp. 24, 26, 57.

114. J. A. Stewart, "The Myths of Plato," p. 40.

115. "Descriptive Catalogue."

116. See T. Rolleston, "Parallel Paths."

117. Laurence Binyon, "Painting in the Far East," p. 9.

118. "The Mirror of Simple Souls," Pt. III, cap. 1.

119. Par. xxxiii. 139. "Not for this were my wings fitted: save only that my mind was smitten by a lightning flash wherein came to it its desire."

120. In this connexion Godfernaux (Revue Philosophique, February, 1902) has a highly significant remark to the effect that romanticism represents the invasion of secular literature by mystic or religious emotion. It is, he says, the secularization of the inner life. Compare also Bremond, "Prière et Poesie."

121. I take from Hebert's monograph "Le Divin" two examples of the analogy between mystical and musical emotion. First that of Gay, who had "the soul, the heart, and the head full of music, of another beauty than that which is formulated by sounds." Next that of Ruysbroeck, who, in a passage that might have been written by Keats, speaks of contemplation and Love as "two heavenly pipes" which, blown upon by the Holy Spirit, play "ditties of no tone" (op. cit . p. 29).

122. Hugh of St. Victor, "Didascalicon de Studio Legendi."

123. "Fioretti." Delle Istimati. (Arnold's translation.)

124. Richard Rolle, The Fire of Love" (Early English Text Society), bk. i. cap. xv. In this and subsequent quotations from Rolle's Incendium Amoris I have usually adopted Misyn's fifteenth-century translation; slightly modernizing the spelling, and, where necessary, correcting from the Latin his errors and obscurities.

125. Op. cit., bk. i. cap. xxiii. Compare bk. ii. caps. v. and vi.

126. "Spiritual Exercises," p. 30.

127. Op. cit., bk. i. cap. xv.

128. Op. cit., bk. ii. caps, iii. and xii. Shelley is of the same opinion:-- "The world can hear not the sweet notes that move The Sphere whose light is melody to lovers." ("The Triumph of Life ")

129. "Subida del Monte Carmelo," I. ii. cap. xv.

130. "De Mystica Theologia," i. 3.

131. Von Hügel, "The Mystical Element of Religion," vol. i. p. 189.

132. "Varieties of Religious Experience," p. 380.

133. "Les Fondements de la Connaissance Mystique," p. 45.

134. Jámí. Quoted in "Jalalu d Din" (Wisdom of the East Series), p. 25.

135. "Through Scylla and Charybdis," p. 264.

136. Ennead vi. 9.

137. "En una Noche Escura," Stanza 1. I quote from Arthur Symons's beautiful translation, which will be found in vol. ii. of his Collected Poems.

138. Schmölders, "Les Écoles Philosophiques chez les Arabes," p. 55.

139. Cap. xix.

140. "Ignitum cum Deo Soliloquium," cap. xi.

141. "Das Fliessende Licht der Gottheit," pt. iv. cap, 13.

142. Dialogo, cap. lx.

143. Tauler, Sermon for Septuagesima Sunday (Winkworth's translation, p. 253).

144. Vita e Dottrina, cap. vi.

145. M. Smith, "Rabi'a the Mystic," p. 30.

146. Ennead vi. 9.

147. "An Epistle of Discretion." This beautiful old English tract, probably by the author of "The Cloud of Unknowing," is printed by E. Gardner, The Cell of Self Knowledge," p. 108.

148. Ruysbroeck, "De Ornatu Spiritalium Nuptiarum," I. i. cap. xxvi.

149. Ennead, vi. 9.

150. "The Mending of Life," cap. xi.

151. "Fondements de la Connaissance Mystique," p. 7.

152. Dialogo, cap. xxvi.

153. "De Imitatione Christi," I. ii. cap. v.

154. Jalalu d Din (Wisdom of the East Series), p. 79.

155. Treatise to a Devout Man, cap. viii.

156. Sermon for Thursday in Easter Week (Winkworth's translation, p. 294).

157. They were printed in 1658, "At Paris by Lewis de la Fosse in the Carme Street at the Signe of the Looking Glass," and have lately been republished. I quote from the original edition.

158. P. 138.

159. P. 181.

160. Op. cit. pp. 9, 16, 25, 35, 138, 175.

161. Berger, "William Blake," p. 72.

162. Ibid ., p. 74.

163. Contemporary Review, April, 1899.

164. "Das Fliessende Licht der Gottheit," pt. iii. cap. 1.

165. Supra. p. 35.

166. Récéjac, op. cit ., p. 35.

167. Revue Philosophique, July, 1902.

168. "Psychologie des Mystiques Chrétiens," p 14.

169. "Camino de Perfeccion," cap. xxiii.

170. In "El Castillo Interior."

171. See Palmer, "Oriental Mysticism," pt. v. ch. v.

172. Vita, p. 8.

173. "Subida del Monte Carmelo," l. ii. cap. vii.

174. "De Consideratione," I. v. cap. xi.

175. "Das Fliessende Light der Gottheit," pt. vii. cap. 16.

176. "De Mystica Theologia," i. 1.

177. "Aurora," English translation, 1764, p. 237.

178. Dionysius the Areopagite. "De Mystica Theologia," i. 3.

179. "Mystische Schriften," p. 137.

180. Plotinus, Ennead vi. 9.

181. Op. cit.

CHAPTER V

In the last chapter we tried to establish a distinction between the mystic who tastes supreme experience and the mystical philosopher who cogitates upon the data so obtained. We have now, however, to take account of the fact that often the true mystic is also a mystical philosopher; though there are plenty of mystical philosophers who are not and could never be mystics.

Because it is characteristic of the human self to reflect upon its experience, to use its percepts as material for the construction of a concept, most mystics have made or accepted a theory of their own adventures. Thus we have a mystical philosophy or theology--the comment of the intellect on the proceedings of spiritual intuition--running side by side with true or empirical mysticism: classifying its data, criticizing it, explaining it, and translating its vision of the supersensible into symbols which are amenable to dialectic.

Such a philosophy is most usually founded upon the formal creed which the individual mystic accepts. It is characteristic of him that in so far as his transcendental activities are healthy he is generally an acceptor and not a rejector of such creeds. The view which regards the mystic as a spiritual anarchist receives little support from history; which shows us, again and again, the great mystics as faithful sons of the great religions. Almost any religious system which fosters unearthly love is potentially a nursery for mystics: and Christianity, Islam, Brahmanism, and Buddhism each receives its most sublime interpretation at their hands. Thus St. Teresa interprets her ecstatic apprehension of the Godhead in strictly Catholic terms, and St. John of the Cross contrives to harmonize his intense transcendentalism with incarnational and sacramental Christianity. Thus Boehme believed to the last that his explorations of eternity were consistent with the teaching of the Lutheran Church. The Sufis were good Mohammedans, Philo and the Kabalists were orthodox Jews. Plotinus even adapted--though with what difficulty--the relics of paganism to his doctrine of the Real.

Attempts, however, to limit mystical truth--the direct apprehension of the Divine Substance--by the formula of any one religion, are as futile as the attempt to identify a precious metal with the die which converts it into current coin. The dies which the mystics have used are many. Their peculiarities and excrescences are always interesting and sometimes highly significant. Some give a far sharper, more coherent, impression than others. But the gold from which this diverse coinage is struck is always the same precious metal: always the same Beatific Vision of a Goodness, Truth, and Beauty which is one. Hence its substance must always be distinguished from the accidents under which we perceive it: for this substance has an absolute, and not a denominational, importance.

Nevertheless, if we are to understand the language of the mystics, it is evident that we must know a little of accident as well as of substance: that is to say, of the principal philosophies or religions which they have used in describing their adventures to the world. This being so, before we venture to apply ourselves to the exploration of theology proper, it will be well to consider the two extreme forms under which both mystics and theologians have been accustomed to conceive Divine Reality: that is to say, the so-called "emanation-theory" and "immanence-theory" of the transcendental world.

Emanation and Immanence are formidable words; which though perpetually tossed to and fro by amateurs of religious philosophy, have probably, as they stand, little actuality for practical modern men. They are, however, root-ideas for the maker of mystical diagrams: and his best systems are but attempts towards their reconciliation. Since the aim of every mystic is union with God, it is obvious that the vital question in his philosophy must be the place which this God, the Absolute of his quest, occupies in the scheme. Briefly, He has been conceived--or, it were better to say, presented--by the great mystics under two apparently contradictory modes.

(1) The opinion which is represented in its most extreme form by the theory of Emanations, declares His utter transcendence. This view appears early in the history of Greek philosophy. It is developed by Dionysius, by the Kabalists, by Dante: and is implied in the language of Rulman Merswin, St. John of the Cross and many other Christian ecstatics.

The solar system is an almost perfect symbol of this concept of Reality; which finds at once its most rigid and most beautiful expression in Dante's "Paradiso." [182] The Absolute Godhead is conceived as removed by a vast distance from the material world of sense; the last or lowest of that system of dependent worlds or states which, generated by or emanating from the Unity or Central Sun, become less in spirituality and splendour, greater in multiplicity, the further they recede from their source. That

Source--the Great Countenance of the Godhead--can never, say the Kabalists, be discerned by man. It is the Absolute of the Neoplatonists, the Unplumbed Abyss of later mysticism: the Cloud of Unknowing wraps it from our sight. Only by its "emanations" or manifested attributes can we attain knowledge of it. By the outflow of these same manifested attributes and powers the created universe exists, depending in the last resort on the latens Deitas: Who is therefore conceived as external to the world which He illuminates and vivifies.

St. Thomas Aquinas virtually accepts the doctrine of Emanations when he writes: [183] "As all the perfections of Creatures descend in order from God, who is the height of perfection, man should begin from the lower creatures and ascend by degrees, and so advance to the knowledge of God. . . . And because in that roof and crown of all things, God, we find the most perfect unity, and everything is stronger and more excellent the more thoroughly it is one; it follows that diversity and variety increase in things, the further they are removed from Him who is the first principle of all." Suso, whose mystical system, like that of most Dominicans, is entirely consistent with Thomist philosophy, is really glossing Aquinas when he writes: "The supreme and superessential Spirit has ennobled man by illuminating him with a ray from the Eternal Godhead. . . . Hence from out the great ring which represents the Eternal Godhead there flow forth . . . little rings, which may be taken to signify the high nobility of natural creatures." [184]

Obviously, if this theory of the Absolute be accepted the path of the soul's ascent to union with the divine must be literally a transcendence: a journey "upward and outward," through a long series of intermediate states or worlds till, having traversed the "Thirty-two paths of the Tree of Life," she at last arrives, in Kabalistic language, at the Crown: fruitive knowledge of God, the Abyss or Divine Dark of the Dionysian school, the Neoplatonic One. Such a series of worlds is symbolized by the Ten Heavens of Dante, the hierarchies of Dionysius, the Tree of Life or Sephiroth of the Kabalah: and receives its countersign in the inward experience, in the long journey of the self through Purgation and Illumination to Union. "We ascend," says St. Augustine, "thy ways that be in our heart, and sing a song of degrees; we glow inwardly with thy fire, with thy good fire, and we go, because we go upwards to the peace of Jerusalem." [185]

This theory postulates, under normal and non-mystical conditions, the complete separation of the human and the divine; the temporal and the eternal worlds. "Never forget," says St. John of the Cross, "that God is inaccessible. Ask not therefore how far your powers may comprehend Him, your feeling penetrate Him. Fear thus to content yourself with too little, and deprive your soul of the agility which it needs in order to mount up to Him." [186] The language of pilgrimage, of exile, comes naturally to the mystic who apprehends reality under these terms. To him the mystical adventure is essentially a "going forth" from his normal self and from his normal universe. Like the Psalmist "in his heart he hath disposed to ascend by steps in this vale of tears" from the less to the more divine. He, and with him the Cosmos--for to mystical philosophy the soul of the individual subject is the microcosm of the soul of the world--has got to retrace the long road to the Perfection from which it originally came forth; as the fish in Rulman Merswin's Vision of Nine Rocks must struggle upwards from pool to pool until they reach their Origin.

Such a way of conceiving Reality accords with the type of mind which William James called the "sick soul." [187] It is the mood of the penitent; of the utter humility which, appalled by the sharp contrast between itself and the Perfect which it contemplates, can only cry "out of the depths." It comes naturally to the temperament which leans to pessimism, which sees a "great gulf fixed" between itself and its desire, and is above all things sensitive to the elements of evil and imperfection in its own character and in the normal experience of man. Permitting these elements to dominate its field of consciousness, wholly ignoring the divine aspect of the World of Becoming, such a temperament constructs from its perceptions and prejudices the concept of a material world and a normal self which are very far from God.

(2) Immanence. At the opposite pole from this way of sketching Reality is the extreme theory of Immanence, which plays so large a part in modern theology. To the holders of this theory, who commonly belong to James's "healthy minded" or optimistic class, the quest of the Absolute is no long journey, but a realization of something which is implicit in the self and in the universe: an opening of the eyes of the soul upon the Reality in which it is bathed. For them earth is literally "crammed with heaven." "Thou wert I, but dark was my heart, I knew not the secret transcendent," says Téwekkul Bég, a Moslem mystic of the seventeenth century. [188] This is always the cry of the temperament which leans to a theology of immanence, once its eyes are opened on the light. "God," says Plotinus, "is not external to anyone, but is present with all things, though they are ignorant that He is so." [189] In other and older words, "The Spirit of God is within you." The Absolute Whom all seek does not hold Himself aloof from an imperfect material universe, but dwells within the flux of things: stands as it were at the very threshold of consciousness and knocks awaiting the self's slow discovery of her treasures. "He is not far from any one of us, for in Him we live and move and have our being," is the pure doctrine of Immanence: a doctrine whose teachers are drawn from amongst the souls which react more easily to the

touch of the Divine than to the sense of alienation and of sin, and are naturally inclined to love rather than to awe.

Unless safeguarded by limiting dogmas, the theory of Immanence, taken alone, is notoriously apt to degenerate into pantheism; and into those extravagant perversions of the doctrine of "deification" in which the mystic holds his transfigured self to be identical with the Indwelling God. It is the philosophical basis of that practice of introversion, the turning inward of the soul's faculties in contemplation, which has been the "method" of the great practical mystics of all creeds. That God, since He is in all--in a sense, is all--may most easily be found within ourselves, is the doctrine of these adventurers; [190] who, denying or ignoring the existence of those intervening "worlds" or "planes" between the material world and the Absolute, which are postulated by the theory of Emanations, claim with Ruysbroeck that "by a simple introspection in fruitive love" they "meet God without intermediary."[191] They hear the Father of Lights "saying eternally, without intermediary or interruption, in the most secret part of the spirit, the one, unique, and abysmal Word." [192]

This discovery of a "divine" essence or substance, dwelling, as Ruysbroeck says, at the apex of man's soul is that fundamental experience--found in some form or degree in all genuine mystical religion--which provides the basis of the New Testament doctrine of the indwelling spirit. It is, variously interpreted, the "spark of the soul" of Eckhart, the "ground" of Tauler, the Inward Light of the Quakers, the "Divine Principle" of some modern transcendentalists; the fount and source of all true life. At this point logical exposition fails mystic and theologian alike. A tangle of metaphors takes its place. We are face to face with the "wonder of wonders"--that most real, yet most mysterious, of all the experiences of religion, the union of human and divine, in a nameless something which is "great enough to be God, small enough to be me." In the struggle to describe this experience, the "spark of the soul," the point of juncture, is at one moment presented to us as the divine to which the self attains: at another, as that transcendental aspect of the self which is in contact with God. On either hypothesis, it is here that the mystic encounters Absolute Being. Here is his guarantee of God's immediate presence in the human heart; and, if in the human heart, then in that universe of which man's soul resumes in miniature the essential characteristics.

According to the doctrine of Immanence, creation, the universe, could we see it as it is, would be perceived as the self-development, the self-revelation of this indwelling Deity. The world is not projected from the Absolute, but immersed in God. "I understood," says St. Teresa, "how our Lord was in all things, and how He was in the soul: and the illustration of a sponge filled with water was suggested to me." [193] The world-process, then, is the slow coming to fruition of that Divine Spark which is latent alike in the Cosmos and in man. "If," says Boehme, "thou conceivest a small minute circle, as small as a grain of mustard seed, yet the Heart of God is wholly and perfectly therein: and if thou art born in God, then there is in thyself (in the circle of thy life) the whole Heart of God undivided." [194] The idea of Immanence has seldom been more beautifully expressed.

It is worth noticing that both the theological doctrines of reality which have been acceptable to the mystics implicitly declare, as science does, that the universe is not static but dynamic; a World of Becoming. According to the doctrine of Immanence this universe is free, self-creative. The divine action floods it: no part is more removed from the Godhead than any other part. "God," says Eckhart, "is nearer to me than I am to myself; He is just as near to wood and stone, but they do not know it." [195]

These two apparently contradictory explanations of the Invisible have both been held, and that in their extreme form, by the mystics: who have found in both adequate, and indeed necessary, diagrams by which to suggest something of their rich experience of Reality. [196] Some of the least lettered and most inspired amongst them--for instance, St. Catherine of Siena, Julian of Norwich--and some of the most learned, as Dionysius the Areopagite and Meister Eckhart, have actually used in their rhapsodies language appropriate to both the theories of Emanation and of Immanence. It would seem, then, that both these theories convey a certain truth; and that it is the business of a sound mystical philosophy to reconcile them. It is too often forgotten by quarrelsome partisans of a concrete turn of mind that at best all these transcendental theories are only symbols, methods, diagrams; feebly attempting the representation of an experience which in its fullness is always the same, and of which the dominant characteristic is ineffability. Hence they insist with tiresome monotony that Dionysius must be wrong if Tauler be right: that it is absurd to call yourself the Friend of God if unknowableness be that God's first attribute: that Plato's Perfect Beauty and St. Catherine of Siena's Accepter of Sacrifices cannot be the same: that the "courteous and dear-worthy Lord" who said to Lady Julian, "My darling, I am glad that thou art come to Me, in all thy woe I have ever been with thee," [197] rules out the formless and impersonal One of Plotinus, the "triple circle" of Suso and Dante. Finally, that if God be truly immanent in the material world it is either sin or folly to refuse that world in order that we may find Him; and if introversion be right, a plan of the universe which postulates intervening planes between Absolute Being and the phenomenal world must be wrong.

Now as regards the mystics, of whom we hold both these doctrines, these ways of seeing truth--for what else is a doctrine but that?--it is well to remind ourselves that their teaching about the relation of the Absolute to the finite, of God to the phenomenal world, must be founded in the first instance on what they know by experience of the relation between that Absolute and the individual self. This experience is the valid part of mysticism, the thing which gives to it its unique importance amongst systems of thought, the only source of its knowledge. Everything else is really guessing aided by analogy. When therefore the mystic, applying to the universe what he knows to be true in respect of his own soul, describes Divine Perfection as very far removed from the material world, yet linked with it by a graduated series of "emanations"--states or qualities which have each of them something of the godlike, though they be not God--he is trying to describe the necessary life-process which he has himself passed through in the course of his purgation and spiritual ascent from the state of the "natural man" to that other state of harmony with the spiritual universe, sometimes called "deification," in which he is able to contemplate, and unite with, the divine. We have in the "Divina Commedia" a classic example of such a twofold vision of the inner and the outer worlds: for Dante's journey up and out to the Empyrean Heaven is really an inward alchemy, an ordering and transmuting of his nature, a purging of his spiritual sight till--transcending all derived beatitude--it can look for an instant on the Being of God.

The mystic assumes--because he tends to assume an orderly basis for things--that there is a relation, an analogy, between this microcosm of man's self and the macrocosm of the world-self. Hence his experience, the geography of the individual quest, appears to him good evidence of the geography of the Invisible. Since he must transcend his natural life in order to attain consciousness of God, he conceives of God as essentially transcendent to the natural world. His description of that geography, however--of his path in a land where there is no time and space, no inner and no outer, up or down--will be conditioned by his temperament, by his powers of observation, by the metaphor which comes most readily to his hand, above all by his theological education. The so-called journey itself is a psychological and spiritual experience: the purging and preparation of the self, its movement to higher levels of consciousness, its unification with that more spiritual but normally unconscious self which is in touch with the transcendental order, and its gradual or abrupt entrance into union with the Real. Sometimes it seems to the self that this performance is a retreat inwards to that "ground of the soul" where, as St. Teresa says, "His Majesty awaits us": sometimes a going forth from the Conditioned to the Unconditioned, the "supernatural flight" of Plotinus and Dionysius the Areopagite. Both are but images under which the self conceives the process of attaining conscious union with that God who is "at once immanent and transcendent in relation to the Soul which shares His life." [198]

He has got to find God. Sometimes his temperament causes him to lay most stress on the length of the search; sometimes the abrupt rapture which brings it to a close makes him forget that preliminary pilgrimage in which the soul is "not outward bound but rather on a journey to its centre." The habitations of the Interior Castle through which St. Teresa leads us to that hidden chamber which is the sanctuary of the indwelling God: the hierarchies of Dionysius, ascending from the selfless service of the angels, past the seraphs' burning love, to the God enthroned above time and space: the mystical paths of the Kabalistic Tree of Life which lead from the material world of Malkuth through the universes of action and thought, by Mercy, Justice and Beauty, to the Supernal Crown; [199] all these are different ways of describing this same pilgrimage.

As every one is born a disciple of either Plato or Aristotle, so every human soul leans to one of these two ways of apprehending reality. The artist, the poet, every one who looks with awe and rapture on created things, acknowledges in this act the Immanent God. The ascetic, and that intellectual ascetic the metaphysician, turning from the created, denying the senses in order to find afar off the uncreated, unconditioned Source, is really--though often he knows it not--obeying that psychological law which produced the doctrine of Emanations.

A good map then, a good mystical philosophy, will leave room for both these ways of interpreting our experience. It will mark the routes by which many different temperaments claim to have found their way to the same end. It will acknowledge both the aspects under which the patria splendida Truth has appeared to its lovers: the aspects which have called forth the theories of emanation and immanence and are enshrined in the Greek and Latin names of God. Deus, whose root means day, shining, the Transcendent Light; and Theos, whose true meaning is supreme desire or prayer--the Inward Love--do not contradict, but complete each other. They form, when taken together, an almost perfect definition of that Godhead which is the object of the mystic's desire: the Divine Love which, immanent in the soul spurs on that soul to union with the transcendent and Absolute Light--at once the source, the goal, the life of created things.

The true mystic--the person with a genius for God--hardly needs a map himself. He steers a compass course across the "vast and stormy sea of the divine." It is characteristic of his intellectual humility, however, that he is commonly willing to use the map of the community in which he finds himself, when it comes to showing other people the route which he has pursued. Sometimes these maps have been adequate. More, they have elucidated the obscure wanderings of the explorer; helped him; given him landmarks; worked out right. Time after time he puts his finger on some spot--some great hill of vision, some city of the soul--and says with conviction, "Here have I been." At other times the maps have embarrassed him, have refused to fit in with his description. Then he has tried, as Boehme did and after him Blake, to make new ones. Such maps are often wild in drawing, because good draughtsmanship does not necessarily go with a talent for exploration. Departing from the usual convention, they are hard--sometimes impossible--to understand. As a result, the orthodox have been forced to regard their makers as madmen or heretics: when they were really only practical men struggling to disclose great matters by imperfect means.

Without prejudice to individual beliefs, and without offering an opinion as to the exclusive truth of any one religious system or revelation--for here we are concerned neither with controversy nor with apologetics--we are bound to allow as a historical fact that mysticism, so far, has found its best map in Christianity. Christian philosophy, especially that Neoplatonic theology which, taking up and harmonizing all that was best in the spiritual intuitions of Greece, India, and Egypt, was developed by the great doctors of the early and mediaeval Church, supports and elucidates the revelations of the individual mystic as no other system of thought has been able to do.

We owe to the great fathers of the first five centuries--to Clement of Alexandria and Irenaeus, Gregory of Nyssa and Augustine; above all to Dionysius the Areopagite, the great Christian contemporary of Proclus--the preservation of that mighty system of scaffolding which enabled the Catholic mystics to build up the towers and bulwarks of the City of God. The peculiar virtue of this Christian philosophy, that which marks its superiority to the more coldly self-consistent systems of Greece, is the fact that it re-states the truths of metaphysics in terms of personality: thus offering a third term, a "living mediator" between the Unknowable God, the unconditioned Absolute, and the conditioned self. This was the priceless gift which the Wise Men received in return for their gold, frankincense, and myrrh. This solves the puzzle which all explorers of the supersensible have sooner or later to face: come si convenne l'imago al cerchio, [200] the reconciliation of Infinite and intimate, both known and felt, but neither understood. Such a third term, such a stepping-stone, was essential if mysticism were ever to attain that active union that fullness of life which is its object, and develop from a blind and egoistic rapture into fruitful and self-forgetting love.

Where non-Christian mystics, as a rule, have made a forced choice between the two great dogmatic expressions of their experience, (a) the long pilgrimage towards a transcendent and unconditioned Absolute, (b) the discovery of that Absolute in the "ground" or spiritual principle of the self; it has been possible to Christianity, by means of her central doctrine of the Trinity, to find room for both of them and to exhibit them as that which they are in fact--the complementary parts of a whole. Even Dionysius, the godfather of the emanation doctrine, combines with his scheme of descending hierarchies the dogma of an indwelling God: and no writer is more constantly quoted by Meister Eckhart, who is generally considered to have preached immanence in its most extreme and pantheistic form.

Further, the Christian atmosphere is the one in which the individual mystic has most often been able to develop his genius in a sane and fruitful way; and an overwhelming majority of the great European contemplatives have been Christians of a strong impassioned and personal type. This alone would justify us in regarding it as embodying, at any rate in the West, the substance of the true tradition: providing the "path of least resistance" through which that tradition flows. The very heretics of Christianity have often owed their attraction almost wholly to the mystical element in their teachings. The Gnostics, the Fraticelli, the Brethren of the Free Spirit, the Quietists, the Quakers, are instances of this. In others, it was to an excessive reliance on reason when dealing with the suprarational, and a corresponding absence of trust in mystical intuition that heresy was due. Arius and Pelagius are heretics of this type.

The greatest mystics, however, have not been heretics but Catholic saints. In Christianity the "natural mysticism" which like "natural religion," is latent in humanity, and at a certain point of development breaks out in every race, came to itself; and attributing for the first time true and distinct personality to its Object, brought into focus the confused and unconditioned God which Neoplatonism had constructed from the abstract concepts of philosophy blended with the intuitions of Indian ecstatics, and made the basis of its meditations on the Real. It is a truism that the chief claim of Christian philosophy on our respect does not lie in its exclusiveness but in its Catholicity: in the fact that it finds truth in a hundred different systems, accepts and elucidates Greek, Jewish, and Indian thought, fuses them in a coherent theology, and says to speculative thinkers of every time and place, "Whom therefore ye ignorantly worship, Him declare I unto you."

The voice of that Truth which spoke once for all on Calvary, and there declared the ground plan of the universe, was heard more or less perfectly by all the great seers, the intuitive leaders of men, the possessors of genius for the Real. There are few of the Christian names of God which were not known to the teachers of antiquity. To the Egyptians He was the Saviour, to the Platonists the Good, Beautiful and True, to the Stoics the Father and Companion. The very words of the Fourth Gospel are anticipated by Cleanthes. Heracleitus knew the Energizing Fire of which St. Bonaventura and Mechthild of Magdeburg speak. Countless mystics, from St. Augustine to St. John of the Cross, echo again and again the language of Plotinus. It is true that the differentia which mark off Christianity from all other religions are strange and poignant: but these very differentia make of it the most perfect of settings for the mystic life. Its note of close intimacy, of direct and personal contact with a spiritual reality given here and now--its astonishing combination of splendour and simplicity, of the sacramental and transcendent--all these things minister to the needs of the mystical type.

Hence the Christian system, or some colourable imitation of it, has been found essential by almost all the great mystics of the West. They adopt its nomenclature, explain their adventures by the help of its creed, identify their Absolute with the Christian God. Amongst European mystics the most usually quoted exception to this rule is Blake; yet it is curious to notice that the more inspired his utterance, the more passionately and dogmatically Christian even this hater of the Churches becomes:--

"We behold
Where Death eternal is put off eternally. O Lamb
Assume the dark satanic body in the Virgin's womb!
O Lamb divine ! it cannot thee annoy! O pitying One
Thy pity is from the foundation of the world, and thy Redemption
Begins already in Eternity." [201]

This is the doctrine of the Incarnation in a nutshell: here St. Thomas himself would find little to correct. Of the two following extracts from "Jerusalem," the first is but a poet's gloss on the Catholic's cry, "O felix culpa!" the second is an almost perfect epitome of Christian theology and ethics:--

"If I were pure, never could I taste the sweets
Of the forgiveness of sins. If I were holy I never could behold the tears
Of Love . . . O Mercy! O divine Humanity!
O Forgiveness, O Pity and Compassion! If I were pure I should never
Have known Thee."
"Wouldst thou love one who never died
For thee, or ever die for one who had not died for thee?
And if God dieth not for man, and giveth not Himself
Eternally for Man, Man could not exist, for Man is Love
As God is Love. Every kindness to another is a little death
In the Divine Image, nor can Man exist but by brotherhood." [202]

Whether the dogmas of Christianity be or be not accepted on the scientific and historical plane, then, those dogmas are necessary to an adequate description of mystical experience--at least, of the fully developed dynamic mysticism of the West. We must therefore be prepared in reading the works of the contemplatives for much strictly denominational language; and shall be wise if we preface the encounter by some consideration of this language, and of its real meaning for those who use and believe it.

No one needs, I suppose, to be told that the two chief features of Christian schematic theology are the dogmas of the Trinity and the Incarnation. They correlate and explain each other: forming together, for the Christian, the "final key" to the riddle of the world. The history of practical and institutional Christianity is the history of the attempt to exhibit their meaning in space and time. The history of mystical philosophy is the history--still incomplete--of the demonstration of their meaning in eternity.

Some form of Trinitarian dogma is found to be essential, as a method of describing observed facts, the moment that mysticism begins either (a) to analyse its own psychological conditions, or (b) to philosophize upon its intuitive experience of God. It must, that is to say, divide the aspects under which it knows the Godhead, if it is to deal with them in a fruitful or comprehensible way. The Unconditioned One, which is, for Neoplatonic and Catholic mystic alike, the final object of their quest, cannot of itself satisfy the deepest instincts of humanity: for man is aware that diversity in unity is a necessary condition if perfection of character is to be expressed. Though the idea of unity alone may serve to define the End--and though the mystics return to it again and again as a relief from that "heresy of multiplicity" by which they are oppressed--it cannot by itself be adequate to the description of the All.

The first question, then, must be--How many of such aspects are necessary to a satisfactory presentment of the mystic's position? How many faces of Reality does he see? We observe that his experience involves at least a twofold apprehension. (a) That Holy Spirit within, that Divine Life by which his own life is transfused and upheld, and of which he becomes increasingly conscious as his education proceeds. (b) That Transcendent Spirit without, the "Absolute," towards union with which the indwelling and increasingly dominant spirit of love presses the developing soul. In his ecstasy, it seems to the mystic that these two experiences of God become one. But in the attempt to philosophize on his experiences he is bound to separate them. Over and over again the mystics and their critics acknowledge, explicitly or implicitly, the necessity of this discrimination for human thought.

Thus even the rigid monotheism of Israel and Islam cannot, in the hands of the Kabalists and the Sufis, get away from an essential dualism in the mystical experience. According to the Zohar "God is considered as immanent in all that has been created or emanated, and yet is transcendent to all." [203] So too the Sufis. God, they say, is to be contemplated (a) outwardly in the imperfect beauties of the earth; (b) inwardly, by meditation. Further, since He is One, and in all things, "to conceive one's self as separate from God is an error: yet only when one sees oneself as separate from God, can one reach out to God. " [204]

Thus Delacroix, speaking purely as a psychologist, and denying to the mystical revelation--which he attributes exclusively to the normal content of the subliminal mind--any transcendental value, writes with entire approval of St. Teresa, that she "set up externally to herself the definite God of the Bible, at the same time as she set up within her soul the confused God of the Pseudo-Areopagite: the One of Neoplatonism. The first is her guarantee of the orthodoxy of the second, and prevents her from losing herself in an indistinction which is non-Christian. The confused God within is highly dangerous. . . . St. Teresa knew how to avoid this peril, and, served by her rich subconscious life, by the exaltation of her mental images, by her faculty of self-division on the one hand, on the other by her rare powers of unification, she realized simultaneously a double state in which the two Gods [i.e. , the two ways of apprehending God, transcendence and immanence] were guarantees of each other, mutually consolidating and enriching one another: such is the intellectual vision of the Trinity in the Seventh Habitation." [205]

It is probable that St. Teresa, confronted by this astonishing analysis, would have objected that her Trinity, unlike that of her eulogist, consisted of three and not two Persons. His language concerning confused interior and orthodox exterior Gods would certainly have appeared to her delicate and honest mind both clumsy and untrue: nor could she have allowed that the Unconditioned One of the Neoplatonists was an adequate description of the strictly personal Divine Majesty, Whom she found enthroned in the inmost sanctuary of the Castle of the Soul. What St. Teresa really did was to actualize in her own experience, apprehend in the "ground of her soul" by means of her extraordinarily developed transcendental perceptions, the three distinct and personal Aspects of the Godhead which are acknowledged by the Christian religion.

First, the Father, pure transcendent Being, creative Source and Origin of all that Is: the Unconditioned and Unknowable One of the Neoplatonists: Who is "neither This nor That" and must be conceived, pace M. Delacroix, as utterly transcendent to the subject rather than "set up within the soul."

Secondly, in the Person of Christ, St. Teresa isolated and distinguished the Logos or Creative Word; the expression, or outbirth, of the Father's thought. Here is the point at which the Divine Substance first becomes apprehensible by the spirit of man; that mediating principle "raised up between heaven and earth" which is at once the Mirror of Pure Being and the Light of a finite world. The Second Person of the Christian Trinity is for the believer not only the brightness or express image of Deity, but also the personal, inexhaustible, and responsive Fount of all life and Object of all love: Who, because of His taking up (in the Incarnation) of humanity into the Godhead, has become the Bridge between finite and infinite, between the individual and the Absolute Life, and hence in mystic language the "true Bridegroom" of every human soul.

Thirdly, she recognized within herself the germ of that Absolute Life, the indwelling Spirit which is the source of man's transcendental consciousness and his link with the Being of God. That is to say, the Holy Spirit of Divine Love, the Real Desirous seeking for the Real Desired, without Whose presence any knowledge of or communion with God on man's part would be inconceivable.

In the supreme Vision of the Trinity which was vouchsafed to St. Teresa in the Seventh Habitation of the soul, these three aspects became fused in One. In the deepest recesses of her spirit, in that abyss where selfhood ceases to have meaning, and the individual soul touches the life of the All, distinction vanished and she "saw God in a point." Such an experience, such an intuition of simple and undifferentiated Godhead--the Unity--beyond those three centres of Divine Consciousness which we call the Trinity of Persons, is highly characteristic of mysticism. The German mystics--temperamentally miles asunder from St. Teresa--described it as the attainment of the "still wilderness" or "lonely desert of Deity": the limitless Divine Abyss, impersonal, indescribable, for ever hid in the Cloud of Unknowing, and yet the true Country of the Soul. [206]

These statements, which appear when thus laid down to be hopelessly academic, violently divorced from life, were not for St. Teresa or any other Christian mystic abstract propositions; but attempts towards the description of first-hand experience.

"By some mysterious manifestation of the truth," she says, "the three Persons of the most Blessed Trinity reveal themselves, preceded by an illumination which shines on the spirit like a most dazzling cloud of light. The three Persons are distinct from one another; a sublime knowledge is infused into the soul, imbuing it with a certainty of the truth that the Three are of one substance, power, and knowledge, and are one God. Thus that which we hold as a doctrine of faith, the soul now, so to speak, understands by sight, though it beholds the Blessed Trinity neither by the eyes of the body nor of the soul, this being no imaginary vision. All the Three Persons here communicate Themselves to the soul, speak to it, and make it understand the words of our Lord in the Gospel, that He and the Father and the Holy Ghost will come and make their abode with the soul which loves Him and keeps His commandments.

O my God, how different from merely hearing and believing these words is it to realize their truth in this way! Day by day a growing astonishment takes possession of this soul, for the three Persons of the Blessed Trinity seem never to depart; that They dwell far within its own centre and depths; though for want of learning it cannot describe how, it is conscious of the indwelling of these divine Companions." [207]

Mystical writers constantly remind us that life as perceived by the human minds shows an inveterate tendency to arrange itself in triads: that if they proclaim the number Three in the heavens, they can also point to it as dominating everywhere upon the earth. Here Christianity did but give form to a deep instinct of the human mind: an instinct which made Pythagoras call Three the number of God, because beginning, middle, and end were contained therein. Thus to Hindu thought the Absolute Godhead was unknowable, but He disclosed three faces to man--Brahma the Creator, Shiva the Destroyer, Krishna the Repairer--and these three were One. So too the Neoplatonists distinguished three worlds; the Sensible or Phenomenal, the Rational or Intellectual, the Intelligible or Spiritual; and three aspects of God--the Unconditioned Absolute, the Logos or Artificer, and the divine Essence or Soul of the World which is both absolute and created. Perhaps we have in such triads a first sketch of the Christian Trinity; though falling far short of the requirements of man's spiritual experience. The dry bones await the breath of more abundant life. Corresponding with this diagram of God's nature the Platonists see also three grades of beauty; the Corporeal, the Spiritual, and the Divine.

Man, that "thing of threes," of body, soul and spirit, of understanding, memory and will, follows in his path towards unity the Threefold Way: for "our soul," says Lady Julian, "is made-trinity like to the unmade blissful Trinity, known and loved from without beginning, and in the making oned to the Maker." [208] We still tend to analyse our psychic life into emotional, volitional, and intellectual elements. Even the Subject and Object implied in every experience required a third term, the relation between them, without which no thought can be complete. Thus the very principle of analogy imposes upon man a Trinitarian definition of Reality as the one with which his mind is best able to cope. [209] It is easy for the hurried rationalist to demonstrate the absurdity of this fact but he will find it a very different matter when it comes to disproving it.

"I could wish," says St. Augustine, "that men would consider these three things that are in themselves . . . To Be, to Know, and to Will. For I am, and I know, and I will, I am knowing and willing, and I know myself to be and to will; and I will to be and to know. In these three therefore let him who can, see how inseparable a life there is--even one life, one mind, one essence: finally how inseparable is the distinction, and yet a distinction. Surely a man hath it before him: let him look into himself and see and tell me. But when he discovers and can see anything of these, let him not think that he has discovered that which is above these Unchangeable: which Is unchangeably and Knows unchangeably and Wills unchangeably." [210]

In a well-known passage, Julian of Norwich tells us how she saw the Trinity of the Divine Nature shining in the phenomenal as well as in the spiritual world. "He showed me," she says, "a little thing, the quantity of an hazel nut, in the palm of my hand; and it was as round as a ball. I looked thereupon with the eye of my understanding, and thought, What may this be? And it was answered generally thus: It is all that is made. . . . In this Little Thing I saw three properties. The first is that God made it, the second is that God loveth it, the third is that God keepeth it. But what is to me verily the Maker, the Keeper, and the Lover, I cannot tell." [211]

Julian, a simple and deeply human Englishwoman of middle age dwelling alone in her churchyard cell, might well be called the poet of the Trinity. She treats this austere and subtle dogma--of which the mediaeval mystics write with a passion little understood by those who look upon it as "orthodoxy reduced to mathematics"--with an intimacy and vigour which carry with them a conviction of her own direct and personal apprehension of the theological truth she struggles to describe. "I beheld," she says of a vision which is close to that of St. Teresa in the "Seventh Habitation of the Soul," and more lucidly if less splendidly expressed, "the working of all the blessed Trinity: in which beholding, I saw and understood these three properties: the property of the Fatherhood, the property of the Motherhood, and the property of the Lordhood, in one God. In our Father Almighty we have our keeping and our bliss as anent our natural Substance, [212] which is to us by our making, without beginning. And in the Second Person in wit and wisdom we have our keeping as anent our Sense-soul: our restoring and our saving; for He is our Mother, Brother, and Saviour. And in our good Lord, the Holy Ghost, we have our rewarding and our meed-giving for our living and our travail, and endless overpassing of all that we desire, in His marvellous courtesy of His high plenteous grace. For all our life is in three: in the first we have our Being, in the second we have our Increasing, and in the third we have our Fulfilling; the first is Nature, the second is Mercy, and the third is Grace. [213] . . . The high Might of the Trinity is our Father, and the deep Wisdom of the Trinity is our Mother, and the great Love of the Trinity is our Lord: and all this we have in Nature and in our Substantial Making." [214]

Again, in a passage of exquisite tenderness, "As verily as God is our Father, so verily God is our Mother; and that shewed He in all [her revelations] and especially in these sweet words where He saith: I it am. That is to say, I it am, the Might and the Goodness of the Fatherhood; I it am, the Wisdom of the Motherhood, I it am the Light and the Grace that is all blessed Love. I it am, the Trinity, I it am, the Unity: I am the sovereign Goodness of all manner of things. I am that maketh thee to love. I am that maketh thee to long: I it am, the endless fulfilling of all true desires. " [215]

So Christopher Hervey--

"The whole world round is not enough to fill
The heart's three corners, but it craveth still.
Only the Trinity that made it can
Suffice the vast triangled heart of Man." [216]

Any attempt towards a definition of God which does not account for and acknowledge these three aspects is found in experience to be incomplete. They provide objectives for the heart, the intellect, and the will: for they offer to the Self material for its highest love, its deepest thought, its act of supreme volition. Under the familiar Platonic terms of Goodness, Truth, and Beauty, they represent the divine source and end of Ethics, Science, and Art, the three supreme activities of man. Thus the ideals of artist, student, and philanthropist, who all seek under different modes the same reality, are gathered up in the mystic's One; as the pilgrimage of the three kings ended in the finding of one Star

"What is God?" says St. Bernard. "Length, breadth, height, and depth. What,' you say, you do after all profess to believe in the fourfold Godhead which was an abomination to you?' Not in the least. . . . God is designated One to suit our comprehension, not to describe his character. His character is capable of division, He Himself is not. The words are different, the paths are many, but one thing is signified; the paths lead to one Person." [217]

All possible ways of conceiving this One Person in His living richness are found in the end to range themselves under three heads. He is "above all and through all and in you all," [218] said St. Paul, anticipating the Councils in a flash of mystic intuition and giving to the infant Church the shortest and most perfect definition of its Triune God. Being, which is above all, manifests itself as Becoming; as the dynamic omnipresent Word of Life. The Divine Love immanent in the heart and in the world comes forth from, and returns to, the Absolute One. "Thou, my God, who art Love," says Nicolas of Cusa, "art Love that loveth, and Love that is loveable, and Love that is the bond between these twain." [219] Thus is completed "the Eternal Circle from Goodness, through Goodness, to Goodness." It is true that to these fundamental respects of the perceived Godhead--that Being, Becoming, and Desire whereto the worlds keep time--the mystics have given many and various names; for they have something of the freedom of true intimates in treating of the Reality which they love. In particular, those symbols of the Absolute which are drawn from the great and formless forces of the universe, rather than from the orthodox but necessarily anthropomorphic imagery of human relationship, have always appealed to them. Their intense apprehension of Spirit seems to find freer and more adequate expression in such terms, than in those in which the notion of space is involved, or which suggest a concrete picture to the mind. Though they know as well as the philosophers that "there must always he something symbolic in our way of expressing the spiritual life," since "that unfathomable infinite whose spiritual character is first recognized in our human experience, can never reveal itself fully and freely under the limitations of our earthly existence"; [220] yet they ever seek, like the artists they are, some new and vital image which is not yet part of the debased currency of formal religion, and conserves its original power of stinging the imagination to more vivid life.

Thus "the Kingdom of Heaven," says Law, "stands in this threefold life, where three are one, because it is a manifestation of the Deity, which is Three and One; the Father has His distinct manifestation in the Fire, which is always generating the Light; the Son has His distinct manifestation in the Light, which is always generated from the Fire; the Holy Ghost has His manifestation in the Spirit, that always proceeds from both, and is always united with them. It is this eternal unbeginning Trinity in Unity of Fire, Light, and Spirit, that constitutes Eternal Nature, the Kingdom of Heaven, the heavenly Jerusalem, the Divine Life, the Beatific Visibility, the majestic Glory and Presence of God. Through this Kingdom of Heaven, or Eternal Nature, is the invisible God, the incomprehensible Trinity, eternally breaking forth and manifesting itself in a boundless height and depth of blissful wonders, opening and displaying itself to all its creatures as in an infinite variation and endless multiplicity of its powers, beauties, joys, and glories." [221]

Perhaps an easier, better, more beautiful example of these abstract symbols of the Trinity than Law's Fire, Light, and Spirit is that of Light, Life, and Love: a threefold picture of the Real which is constantly dwelt upon and elaborated by the Christian mystics. Transcendent Light, intangible but unescapable, ever emanating Its splendour through the Universe: indwelling, unresting, and energizing

Life: desirous and directive Love--these are cardinal aspects of Reality to which they return again and again in their efforts to find words which will express something of the inexpressible truth.

(a) LIGHT, ineffable and uncreated, the perfect symbol of pure undifferentiated Being: above the intellect, as St. Augustine reminds us, but known to him who loves. [222] This Uncreated Light is the "deep yet dazzling darkness" of the Dionysian school, "dark from its surpassing brightness . . . as the shining of the sun on his course is as darkness to weak eyes." [223] It is St. Hildegarde's lux vivens, Dante's somma luce, wherein he saw multiplicity in unity, the ingathered leaves of all the universe [224]: the Eternal Father, or Fount of Things. "For well we know," says Ruysbroeck "that the bosom of the Father is our ground and origin, wherein our life and being is begun." [225]

(b) LIFE, the Son, hidden Steersman of the Universe, the Logos, Fire, or cosmic Soul of Things. This out-birth or Concept of the Father's Mind, which He possesses within Himself, as Battista Vernazza was told in her ecstasy, [226] is that Word of Creation which since It is alive and infinite, no formula can contain. the Word eternally "spoken" or generated by the Transcendent Light. "This is why," says Ruysbroeck again, "all that lives in the Father unmanifested in the Unity, is also in the Son actively poured forth in manifestation." [227] This life, then, is the flawless expression or character of the Father, Sapientia Patris. It is at once the personal and adorable comrade of the mystic's adventure and the inmost principle, the sustaining power, of a dynamic universe; for that which intellect defines as the Logos or Creative Spirit, contemplative love knows as Wonderful, Counsellor, and Prince of Peace.

Since Christ, for the Christian philosopher, is Divine Life Itself--the drama of Christianity expressing this fact and its implications "in a point"--it follows that His active spirit is to be discerned, not symbolically, but in the most veritable sense, in the ecstatic and abounding life of the world. In the rapturous vitality of the birds, in their splendid glancing flight: in the swelling of buds and the sacrificial beauty of the flowers: in the great and solemn rhythms of the sea--there is somewhat of Bethlehem in all these things, somewhat too of Calvary in their self-giving pains. It was this re-discovery of Nature's Christliness which Blake desired so passionately when he sang--

"I will not cease from mental fight,
Nor shall my sword sleep in my hand
Till we have built Jerusalem
In England's green and pleasant land."

Here then it is, on this pinnacle of faith, at the utmost boundaries of human speech, that mystical theology suddenly shows herself--not as the puzzle-headed constructor of impossible creeds, but as accepting and transmuting to a more radiant life those two profound but apparently contradictory metaphysical definitions of Reality which we have already discussed. [228] Eternal Becoming, God immanent and dynamic, striving with and in His world: the unresting "flux of things" of Heracleitus, the crying aloud of that Word "which is through all things everlastingly"--the evolutionary world-process beloved of modern philosophers--is here placed once for all in true relation with pure transcendent and unmoved Being; the Absolute One of Xenophanes and the Platonists. This Absolute is discerned by mystic intuition as the "End of Unity" in whom all diversities must cease; [229] the Ocean to which that ceaseless and painful Becoming, that unresting river of life, in which we are immersed, tends to return: the Son going to the Father.

(c) LOVE, the principle of attraction, which seems to partake at once of the transcendental and the created worlds. If we consider the Father as Supreme Subject--"origin," as Aquinas says, "of the entire procession of Deity" [230] --and the Son or generated Logos as the Object of His thought, in whom, says Ruysbroeck, "He contemplates Himself and all things in an eternal Now"; [231] then this personal Spirit of Love, il desiro e il velle, represents the relation between the two, and constitutes the very character of God. "The heavenly Father," says Ruysbroeck, "as a living Ground, with all that lives in Him, is actively turned towards His Son as to His own Eternal Wisdom. And that same Wisdom, with all that lives in it, is actively turned back towards the Father, that is towards that very ground from which it comes forth. And of this meeting is born the third Person, between the Father and the Son, that is the Holy Spirit, their mutual Love." [232] Proceeding, according to Christian doctrine, from Light and Life, the Father and Son--implicit, that is, in both the Absolute Source and dynamic flux of things--this divine spirit of desire is found enshrined in our very selfhood; and is the agent by which that selfhood is merged in the Absolute Self. "My love is my weight," said St. Augustine. [233] It is the spiritual equivalent of that gravitation which draws all things to their place. Thus Bernard Holland says in his Introduction to Boehme's "Dialogues," "In a deep sense, the desire of the Spark of Life in the Soul to return to its Original Source is part of the longing desire of the universal Life for its own heart or centre. Of this longing, the universal attraction striving against resistance, towards a universal centre, proved to govern the phenomenal or physical world, is but the outer sheath and visible working." Again, "Desire is everything in Nature; does everything. Heaven is Nature filled with divine Life attracted by Desire." [234]

"The best masters say," says Eckhart, "that the love wherewith we love is the Holy Spirit. [235] Some deny it. But this is always true: all those motives by which we are moved to love, in these is nothing else than the Holy Spirit." [236]

"God wills," says Ruysbroeck, gathering these scattered symbols to unity again, "that we should come forth from ourselves in this Eternal Light; that we should reunite ourselves in a supernatural manner with that image which is our true Life, and that we should possess it with Him actively and fruitively in eternal blessedness . . . this going forth of the contemplative is also in Love: for by fruitive love he overpasses his created being and finds and tastes the riches and delights which are God Himself, and which He causes to pour forth without ceasing in the most secret chamber of the soul, at that place where it is most like unto the nobility of God." [237]

Here only, in the innermost sanctuary of being, the soul's "last habitation," as St. Teresa said, is the truth which these symbols express truly known: for "as to how the Trinity is one and the Trinity in the Unity of the nature is one, whilst nevertheless the Trinity comes forth from the Unity, this cannot be expressed in words," says Suso, "owing to the simplicity of that deep abyss. Hither it is, into this intelligible where that the spirit, spiritualizing itself, soars up; now flying in the measureless heights, now swimming in the soundless deeps, of the sublime marvels of the Godhead!" [238]

Mystical philosophy, then, has availed itself gladly of the doctrine of the Trinity in expressing its vision of the nature of that Absolute which is found, by those who attain the deep Abyss of the Godhead, to be essentially One. But it is by the complementary Christian dogma of the Incarnation that it has best been able to describe and explain the nature of the inward and personal mystic experience. The Incarnation, which is for traditional Christianity synonymous with the historical birth and earthly life of Christ, is for mystics of a certain type, not only this but also a perpetual Cosmic and personal process. It is an everlasting bringing forth, in the universe and also in the individual ascending soul, of the divine and perfect Life, the pure character of God, of which the one historical life dramatized the essential constituents. Hence the soul, like the physical embryo, resumes in its upward progress the spiritual life-history of the race. "The one secret, the greatest of all," says Patmore, is "the doctrine of the Incarnation, regarded not as an historical event which occurred two thousand years ago, but as an event which is renewed in the body of every one who is in the way to the fulfilment of his original destiny." [239]

We have seen that for mystical theology the Second Person of the Trinity is the Wisdom of the Father, the Word of Life. The fullness of this Word could therefore only be communicated to the human consciousness by a Life. In the Incarnation this Logos, this divine character of Reality, penetrated the illusions of the sensual world--in other words, the illusions of all the selves whose ideas compose that world--and "saved" it by this infusion of truth. A divine, suffering, self-sacrificing Personality was then shown as the sacred heart of a living, striving universe: and for once the Absolute was exhibited in the terms of finite human existence. Some such event as this breaking through of the divine and archetypal life into the temporal world is perceived by the mystical philosopher to be a necessity, if man was ever to see in terms of life that greatness of life to which he belongs: learn to transcend the world of sense, and rebuild his life upon the levels of reality. "For Thou art," says Nicolas of Cusa, "the Word of God humanified, and Thou art man deified." [240] Thus it is that the Catholic priest in the Christmas Mass gives thanks, not for the setting in hand of any commercial process of redemption, but for a revelation of reality, "Quia per incarnati Verbi mysterium nova mentis nostrae oculis lux tuae claritatis infulsit: ut dum visibiliter Deum cognoscimus, per hunc in invisibilium amorem rapiamur." The essence of mystical Christianity seems to be summed up in these lovely words. [241]

"The Son of God, the Eternal Word in the Father, who is the glance, or brightness, and the power of the light eternity" says Boehme, "must become man and be born in you, if you will know God: otherwise you are in the dark stable and go about groping." [242] "The Word," says Ruysbroeck finely, "is no other than See. And this is the coming forth and the birth of the Son of the Eternal Light, in Whom all blessedness is seen and known." [243] Once at any rate, they say in effect, the measure of that which it was possible for the Spirit of Life to do and for living creatures to be, was filled to the brim. By this event, all were assured that the ladder of Creation was made whole; in this hypostatic union, the breach between appearance and reality, between God and man, was healed. The Bridge so made--to use St. Catherine of Siena's allegory again--is eternal, since it was "laid before the foundation of the world" in the "Eternal Now." Thus the voice of the Father says to her in that vision, "I also wish thee to look at the Bridge of My only-begotten Son, and see the greatness thereof, for it reaches from Heaven to earth; that is, that the earth of your humanity is joined to the greatness of the Deity thereby. I say, then, that this Bridge reaches from Heaven to earth, and constitutes the union which I have made with man. . . . So the height of the Divinity, humbled to the earth, and joined with your humanity made the Bridge and reformed the road. Why was this done? In order that man might come to his true happiness with the angels. And observe that it is not enough, in order that you should have life, that My son should have made you this Bridge, unless you walk thereon." [244] "Our high Father God Almighty, which is Being," says Lady Julian, "He knew and loved us from afore any time. Of which knowing, in His marvellous deep charity, and the foreseeing counsel of all the blessed Trinity, He willed that the Second Person should become our Mother." [245]

It is of course this assertion of the quickening communication of grace to nature, of God to man--an influx of ultimate reality, possible of assimilation by all--which constitutes the strength of the Christian religion. Instead of the stony diet of the philosophers, it offers to the self hungry for the Absolute that Panis Angelorum, the vivifying principle of the world. That is to say, it gives concrete and experimental knowledge of a supreme Personality--absorption into His mystical body--instead of the artificial conviction produced by concentration on an idea. It knits up the universe; shows the phenomenal pierced in all directions by the real, the natural as the vehicle of the supernatural. It provides a solid basis for mysticism, a basis which is at once metaphysical and psychological: and shows that state towards which the world's deepest minds have always instinctively aspired, as a part of the cosmic return through Christ to God.

"Quivi è la sapienza e la possanza
ch' apri le strade intra il cielo e la terra
onde fu già si lunga disianza." [246]

This is what the Christian mystics mean to express when they declare over and over again that the return to the Divine Substance, the Absolute, which is the end of the soul's ascent, can only be made through the humanity of Christ. The Son, the Word, is the character of the Father: that in which the Ineffable Godhead knows Himself, as we only know ourselves in our own characters. He is thus a double link: the means of God's self-consciousness, the means of man's consciousness of God. How then, asks mystic theology, could such a link complete its attachments without some such process as that which the Incarnation dramatized in time and space? The Principle of Life is also the Principle of Restitution; by which the imperfect and broken life of sense is mended and transformed into the perfect life of spirit. Hence the title of Repairer applied by Boehme to the Second Person of the Trinity.

In the last resort, the doctrine of the Incarnation is the only safeguard of the mystics against the pantheism to which they always tend. The Unconditioned Absolute, so soon as it alone becomes the object of their contemplation, is apt to be conceived merely as Divine Essence; the idea of Personality evaporates. The union of the soul with God is then thought of in terms of absorption. The distinction between Creator and creature is obliterated and loving communion is at an end. This is probably the reason why many of the greatest contemplatives--Suso and St. Teresa are cases in point--have found that deliberate meditation upon the humanity of Christ, difficult and uncongenial as this concrete devotion sometimes is to the mystical temperament, was a necessity if they were to retain a healthy and well-balanced inner life.

Further, these mystics see in the historic life of Christ an epitome--or if you will, an exhibition--of the essentials of all spiritual life. There they see dramatized not only the cosmic process of the Divine Wisdom, but also the inward experience of every soul on her way to union with that Absolute "to which the whole Creation moves." This is why the expressions which they use to describe the evolution of the mystical consciousness from the birth of the divine in the spark of the soul to its final unification with the Absolute Life are so constantly chosen from the Drama of Faith. In this drama they see described under veils the necessary adventures of the spirit. Its obscure and humble birth, its education in poverty, its temptation, mortification and solitude, its "illuminated life" of service and contemplation, the desolation of that "dark night of the soul" in which it seems abandoned by the Divine: the painful death of the self, its resurrection to the glorified existence of the Unitive Way, its final reabsorption in its Source--all these, they say, were lived once in a supreme degree in the flesh. Moreover, the degree of closeness with which the individual experience adheres to this Pattern is always taken by them as a standard of the healthiness, ardour, and success of its transcendental activities.

"Apparve in questa forma
Per dare a noi la norma."

sang Jacopone da Todi. "And he who vainly thinketh otherwise," says the "Theologia Germanica" with uncompromising vigour, "is deceived. And he who saith otherwise, lieth." [247]

Those to whom such a parallel seems artificial should remember that according to the doctrine of mysticism that drama of the self-limitation and self-sacrifice of the Absolute Life, which was once played out in the phenomenal world--forced, as it were, upon the consciousness of dim-eyed men--is eternally going forward upon the plane of reality. To them the Cross of Calvary is implicit in the Rose of the World. The law of this Infinite Life which was in the Incarnation expressing Its own nature in human terms, must then also be the law of the finite life; in so far as that life aspires to transcend individual limitations, rise to freedom, and attain union with Infinity. It is this governing idea which justifies the apparently fanciful allegorizations of Christian history which swarm in the works of the mystics.

To exhibit these allegorizations in detail would be tedious. All that is necessary is that the principle underlying them should be understood. I give, then, but one example: that which is referred by mystical writers to the Nativity, and concerns the eternal Birth or Generation of the Son or Divine Word.

This Birth is in its first, or cosmic sense, the welling forth of the Spirit of Life from the Divine Abyss of the unconditioned Godhead. "From our proper Ground, that is to say from the Father and all that which lives in Him, there shines," says Ruysbroeck, "an eternal Ray, the which is the Birth of the Son." [248] It is of this perpetual generation of the Word that Meister Eckhart speaks, when he says in his Christmas sermon, "We are celebrating the feast of the Eternal Birth which God the Father has borne and never ceases to bear in all Eternity: whilst this birth also comes to pass in Time and in human nature. Saint Augustine says this Birth is ever taking place." At this point, with that strong practical instinct which is characteristic of the mystics, Eckhart turns abruptly from speculation to immediate experience, and continues "But if it takes not place in me, what avails it? Everything lies in this, that it should take place in me." [249] Here in a few words the two-fold character of this Mystic Birth is exhibited. The interest is suddenly deflected from its cosmic to its personal aspect; and the individual is reminded that in him, no less than in the Archetypal Universe, real life must be born if real life is to be lived. "When the soul brings forth the Son," says Eckhart in another place, "it is happier than Mary."[250]

Since the soul, according to mystic principles, can only perceive Reality in proportion as she is real, know God by becoming Godlike, it is clear that this birth is the initial necessity. The true and definitely directed mystical life does and must open with that most actual, though indescribable phenomenon, the coming forth into consciousness of man's deeper, spiritual self, which ascetical and mystical writers of all ages have agreed to call Regeneration or Re-birth. Nothing that is within him is able of its own power to achieve this. It must be evoked by an energy, a quickening Spirit, which comes from beyond the soul, and "secretly initiates what He openly crowns." [251]

We nave already considered [252] the New Birth in its purely psychological aspect, as the emergence of the transcendental sense. Here its more profound and mystical side is exhibited. By a process which may indifferently be described as the birth of something new or the coming forth of something which has slept--since both these phrases are but metaphors for another and more secret operation--the eye is opened on Eternity, the self, abruptly made aware of Reality, comes forth from the cave of illusion like a child from the womb and begins to live upon the supersensual plane. Then she feels in her inmost part a new presence, a new consciousness--it were hardly an exaggeration to say a new Person--weak, demanding nurture, clearly destined to pass through many phases of development before its maturity is reached; yet of so strange a nature, that in comparison with its environment she may well regard it as Divine.

"This change, this upsetting, is called re-birth. To be born simply means to enter into a world in which the senses dominate, in which wisdom and love languish in the bonds of individuality. To be re-born means to return to a world where the spirit of wisdom and love governs and animal-man obeys."[253] So Eckartshausen. It means, says Jane Lead, "the bringing forth of a new-created Godlike similitude in the soul." [254] He is brought forth, says Eckartshausen again, in the stable previously inhabited by the ox of passion and the ass of prejudice. [255] His mother, says Boehme, is the Virgin Sophia, the Divine Wisdom, or Mirror of the Being of God. With the emergence of this new factor into the conscious field--this spiritual birth--the mystic life begins: as the Christian epoch began with the emergence of Divine Spirit in the flesh. Paradise, says Boehme, is still in the world, but man is not in Paradise unless he be born again. In that case, he stands therein in the New Birth, [256] and tastes here and now that Eternal Life for which he has been made.

Here then are some characteristics of the map which the Christian mystics are most inclined to use. There are, of course, other great landmarks upon it: and these we shall meet as we follow in detail the voyages of the questing soul. One warning, however, must be given to amateur geographers before we go on. Like all other maps, this one at its best can but represent by harsh outline and conventional colour the living earth which those travellers trod and the mysterious seas on which they sailed. It is a deliberately schematic representation of Reality, a flat and sometimes arid symbol of great landscapes, rushing rivers, awful peaks: dangerous unless these its limitations be always kept in mind. The boy who defined Canada as "very pink" was not much further off the track than those who would limit the Adorable Trinity to the definitions of the "Athanasian" Creed; however useful that chart may be, and is, within the boundaries imposed by its form.

Further, all such maps, and we who treat of them, can but set down in cold blood and with a dreadful pretence of precision, matters which the true explorers of Eternity were only able to apprehend in the ardours of such a passion, in the transports of such a union as we, poor finite slaves of our frittered emotions, could hardly look upon and live. "If you would truly know how these things come to pass," says St. Bonaventura, in a passage which all students of theology should ever keep in mind, "ask it of grace, not of doctrine; of desire, not of intellect; of the ardours of prayer, not of the teachings of the schools; of the Bridegroom, not of the Master; of God, not of man; of the darkness, not of the day; not of illumination, but of that Fire which enflames all and wraps us in God with great sweetness and most ardent love. The which Fire most truly is God, and the hearth thereof is in Jerusalem."[257]

Footnotes:

182. "La gloria di colui che tutto move per l'universo penetra, e resplende in una parte più e meno altrove" (Par. i. 1-3). The theological ground-plan of the Cantica is epitomized in this introductory verse.

183. "Summa Contra Gentiles," 1. iv. cap. 1. (Rickaby's translation).

184. Leben, cap. lvi.

185. Aug. Conf., bk. xiii. cap. xi.

186. Avisos y Sentencias Espirituales, N. 51.

187. "Varieties of Religious Experience," Lecture vi.

188. Quoted by W. L. Lilly, "Many Mansions," p. 140.

189. Ennead vi. 9.

190. Thus Aquinas says, "Since God is the universal cause of all Being, in whatever region Being can be found, there must be the Divine Presence" ("Summa Contra Gentiles," 1. iii. cap. lxviii.). And we have seen that the whole claim of the mystics ultimately depends on man's possession of pure being in "the spark of the soul."

191. "De Ornatu Spiritualium Nuptiarum," I. ii. cap. lxvii.

192. Op. cit., I. iii. cap. i.

193. Relaccion ix. 10. But this image of a sponge, which also suggested itelf to St. Augustine, proved an occasion of stumbling to his more metaphysical mind: tending to confuse his idea of the nature of God with the category of space. Vide Aug. Conf., bk. vii. cap. v.

194. "The Threefold Life of Man," cap. vi. § 71.

195. Eckhart, Pred, lxix. So too we read in the Oxyrhyncus Papyri, "Raise the stone and there thou shalt find Me. Cleave the wood and there am I."

196. Compare above, cap. ii.

197. "Revelations of Divine Love," cap. xl.

198. Boyce Gibson, "God with Us," p. 24.

199. See A. E. Waite, " TheDoctrine and Literature of the Kabalah," pp. 36-53.

200. Par. xxxiii. 137.

201. "Vala," viii. 237.

202. "Jerusalem," lxi. 44 and xcv. 23.

203. A. E. Waite, "The Doctrine and Literature of the Kabalah," p. 35.

204. Palmer. "Oriental Mysticism," pt. i. cap. i

205. Delacroix, "Études sur le Mysticisme," p. 75. The reference in the last sentence is to St. Teresa's "Castillo Interior."

206. See Tauler, Sermon on St. John Baptist, and Third Instruction (" The Inner Way," pp. 97 and 321); Suso, "Buchlein von der Warheit," cap. v.; Ruysbroeck, "De Ornatu Spiritalium Nuptiarum," 1. iii. caps. ii. and vi.

207. St. Teresa, "El Castillo Interior," Moradas; Sétimas, cap. i.

208. Julian of Norwich, "Revelations of Divine Love." cap. lv. Julian here repeats a familiar Patristic doctrine. So St. Thomas says ("Summa Contra Gentiles," 1. iv. cap. xxvi), "A likeness of the Divine Trinity is observable in the human mind."

209. "The three Persons of the Trinity," said John Scotus Erigena, "are less modes of the Divine Substance than modes under which our mind conceives the Divine Substance"--a stimulating statement of dubious orthodoxy.

210. Aug. Conf., bk. xiii. cap. xi.

211. Op. cit., cap. v.

212. Substance is here, of course, to be understood in the scholastic sense, as the reality which underlies merely phenomenal existence.

213. I.e. , the Second Person of the Christian Trinity is the redemptive, "fount of mercy," the medium by which Grace, the free gift of transcendental life, reaches and vivifies human nature: "permeates it," in Eucken's words, "with the Infinite and Eternal" ("Der Sinn und Wert des Lebens," p. 181).

214. "Revelations of Divine Love," cap. lviii.

215. Op. cit. , cap. lix.

216. "The School of the Heart," Epigram x. This book, which is a free translation of the "Scola Cordis" of Benedict Haeften (1635), is often, but wrongly attributed to Francis Quarles.

217. "De Consideratione," bk. v. cap. viii.

218. Ephesians iv. 6.

219. "De Visione Dei," cap. xvii.

220. Eucken, "Der Sinn und Wert des Lebens," p. 131.

221. "An Appeal to All who Doubt" ("Liberal and Mystical Writings of William Law" p. 54). Law's symbols are here borrowed from the system of his master, Jacob Boehme. (See the "De Signatura Rerum" of Boehme, cap. xiv.)

222. Aug. Conf., bk. vii. cap. x.

223. Tauler, 3rd Instruction ("The Inner Way," p. 324).

224. Par. xxxiii 67, 85.

225. "De Ornatu Spiritalium Nuptiarum," I. iii. cap. iii.

226. Von Hügel, "The Mystical Element of Religion," vol. i. p. 357.

227. Ruysbroeck, op. cit. ., loc. cit.

228. Supra, Cap. II.

229. Tauler, op. cit., loc. cit.

230. "Summa Contra Gentiles," I. iv. cap. xxvi.

231. "De Ornatu Spiritalium Nuptiarum," I. ii. cap. iv.

232. Op. cit., I. ii. cap. xxxvii.

233. Aug. Conf., bk. xiii. cap. ix.

234. Introduction to "Three Dialogues of the Supersensual Life," p. xxx.

235. The doctrine is found in St. Augustine, and is frequently reproduced by the mediaeval mystics. Eckhart is perhaps here quoting St. Thomas Aquinas, a usual source of his more orthodox utterances. Compare "Summa Contra Gentiles," I. iv. cap. xxiii: "Since the Holy Ghost proceeds as the love wherewith God loves Himself, and since God loves with the same love Himself and other beings for the sake of His own goodness, it is clear that the love wherewith God loves us belongs to the Holy Ghost. In like manner also the love wherewith we love God."

236. Pred. xii.

237. "De Ornatu Spiritalium Nuptiarum " I. iii. cap. iii.

238. Suso, Leben, cap. lvi.

239. "The Rod, the Root, and the Flower," "Homo," xix.

240. "De Visione Dei," cap. xxiii.

241. "Because by the mystery of the Incarnate Word the new light of Thy brightness hath shone upon the eyes of our mind: that we, knowing God seen of the eyes, by Him may be snatched up into the love of that which eye hath not seen" (Missale Romanum. Praefatio Solemnis de Nativitate).

242. "The Threefold Life of Man, cap. iii. § 31.

243. Ruysbroeck, op. cit ., l. iii. cap. i.

244. Dialogo, cap. xxii.

245. "Revelations of Divine Love," cap. lix.

246. Par. xxiii. 37. "Here is the Wisdom and the Power which opened the ways betwixt heaven and earth, for which there erst had been so long a yearning."

247. "Theologia Germanica," cap. xviii.

248. "De Ornatu Spiritalium Nuptiarum," l. iii. cap. v. The extreme antiquity of this idea is illustrated by the Catholic practice, dating from Patristic times, of celebrating three Masses on Christmas Day. Of these the first, at midnight, commemorates the Eternal Generation of the Son; the second, at dawn, His incarnation upon earth; the third His birth in the heart of man. Compare the Roman Missal: also Kellner, "Heortology" (English translation, London, 1908), p. 156.

249. Eckhart, Pred. i., "Mystische Schriften," p. 13. Compare Tauler, Sermon on the Nativity of Our Lady ("The Inner Way," p. 167).

250. This idea of re-birth is probably of Oriental origin. It can be traced back to Egypt, being found in the Hermetic writings of the third century, B.C. See Petrie, "Personal Religion in Egypt before Christianity," p. 167.

251. F. von Hügel, "The Life of Prayer," p. 24.

252. Supra , p. 53.

253. "The Cloud upon the Sanctuary," p. 77.

254. The Enochian Walks with God," p. 3.

255. Op. cit ., p. 81.

256. "De Signatura Rerum," viii. 47.

257. "De Itinerado Mentis in Deo," cap. vii.

CHAPTER VI

In our study of theology we saw the Christian mystic adopting, as chart and pilot book of his voyages and adventures, the scheme of faith, and diagram of the spiritual world, which is accepted by ordinary Christian men. We saw that he found in it a depth and richness of content which the conventional believer in that theology, the "good churchman," seldom suspects: and that which is true of the Christian mystic is also true in its measure and as regards their respective theologies, of the Pagan, the Mahommedan and the Buddhist.

But since the spiritual adventures of the mystic are not those of ordinary men, it will follow that this map, though always true for him, is not complete. He can press forward to countries which unmystical piety must mark as unexplored, Pushing out from harbour to "the vast and stormy sea of the divine," he can take soundings, and mark dangers the existence of which such piety never needs to prove. Hence it is not strange that certain maps, artistic representations or symbolic schemes, should have come into being which describe or suggest the special experiences of the mystical consciousness, and the doctrines to which these experiences have given birth. Many of these maps have an uncouth, even an impious appearance in the eyes of those unacquainted with the facts which they attempt to translate: as the charts of the deep-sea sailor seem ugly and unintelligible things to those who have never been out of sight of land. Others--and these the most pleasing, most easily understood--have already been made familiar, perhaps tiresomely familiar, to us by the poets; who, intuitively recognizing their suggestive qualities, their links with truth, have borrowed and adapted them to their own business of translating Reality into terms of rhythm and speech. Ultimately, however, they owe their origin to the mystics, or to that mystical sense which is innate in all true poets: and in the last resort it is the mystic's kingdom, and the mystic's experience, which they affect to describe.

These special mystical diagrams, these symbolic and artistic descriptions of man's inward history--his secret adventures with God--are almost endless in their variety: since in each we have a picture of the country of the soul seen through a different temperament. To describe all would be to analyse the whole field of mystical literature, and indeed much other literature as well; to epitomize in fact all that has been dreamed and written concerning the so-called "inner life"--a dreary and a lengthy task. But the majority of them, I think, express a comparatively small number of essential doctrines or fundamental ways of seeing things; and as regards their imagery, they fall into three great classes, representative of the three principal ways in which man's spiritual consciousness reacts to the touch of Reality, the three primary if paradoxical facts of which that consciousness must be aware. Hence a consideration of mystic symbols drawn from each of these groups may give us a key with which to unlock some at least of the verbal riddles of the individual adventurer.

Thanks to the spatial imagery inseparable from human thinking and human expression, no direct description of spiritual experience is or can be possible to man. It must always be symbolic, allusive, oblique: always suggest, but never tell, the truth: and in this respect there is not much to choose between the fluid and artistic language of vision and the arid technicalities of philosophy. In another respect, however, there is a great deal to choose between them: and here the visionary, not the philosopher, receives the palm. The greater the suggestive quality of the symbol used, the more answering emotion it evokes in those to whom it is addressed, the more truth it will convey. A good symbolism, therefore, will be more than mere diagram or mere allegory: it will use to the utmost the resources of beauty and of passion, will bring with it hints of mystery and wonder, bewitch with dreamy periods the mind to which it is addressed. Its appeal will not be to the clever brain, but to the desirous heart, the intuitive sense, of man.

The three great classes of symbols which I propose to consider, appeal to three deep cravings of the self, three great expressions of man's restlessness, which only mystic truth can fully satisfy. The first is the craving which makes him a pilgrim and wanderer. It is the longing to go out from his normal world in search of a lost home, a "better country"; an Eldorado, a Sarras, a Heavenly Syon. The next is that craving of heart for heart, of the soul for its perfect mate, which makes him a lover. The third is the craving for inward purity and perfection, which makes him an ascetic, and in the last resort a saint.

These three cravings, I think, answer to three ways in which mystics of different temperaments attack the problem of the Absolute: three different formulae under which their transcendence of the sense-world can be described. In describing this transcendence, and the special adventures involved in it, they are describing a change from the state of ordinary men, in touch with the sense-world, responding to its rhythms, to the state of spiritual consciousness in which, as they say, they are "in union" with Divine Reality, with God. Whatever be the theological creed of the mystic, he never varies in declaring this close, definite, and actual intimacy to be the end of his quest. "Mark me like the tulip with Thine own streaks," says the Sufi. [258] "I would fain be to the Eternal Goodness what his own hand is to a man," says the German contemplative. [259] "My me isGod, nor do I know my self-hood save in Him," says the Italian saint. [260]

But, since this Absolute God is for him substance, ground or underlying Reality of all that is : present yet absent, near yet far: He is already as truly immanent in the human soul as in the Universe. The seeker for the Real may therefore objectify his quest in two apparently contradictory, yet really mutually explanatory ways. First he may see it as an outgoing journey from the world of illusion to the real or transcendental world: a leaving of the visible for the invisible. Secondly, it may appear to him as an inward alteration, remaking or regeneration, by which his personality or character is so changed as to be able to enter into communion with that Fontal Being which he loves and desires; is united with and dominated by the indwelling God who is the fount of his spiritual life. In the first case, the objective idea "God" is the pivot of his symbolism: the Blazing Star, or Magnet of the Universe which he has seen far off, and seeing, has worshipped and desired. In the second case, the emphasis falls on the subjective idea "Sanctity," with its accompanying consciousness of a disharmony to be abolished. The Mystic Way will then be described, not as a journey, but as an alteration of personality, the transmuting of "earthly" into "heavenly" man. Plainly these two aspects are obverse and reverse of one whole. They represent that mighty pair of opposites, Infinite and Finite, God and Self, which it is the business of mysticism to carry up into a higher synthesis. Whether the process be considered as outward search or inward change, its object and its end are the same. Man enters into that Order of Reality for which he was made, and which is indeed the inciting cause of his pilgrimage and his purification: for however great the demand on the soul's own effort may be, the initiative always lies with the living Divine World itself. Man's small desire is evoked, met, and fulfilled by the Divine Desire, his "separated will" or life becomes one with the great Life of the All.

From what has been said in the last chapter, it will be clear that the symbolism of outward search and of inward change will be adopted respectively by the two groups of selves whose experience of "union with the Divine" leans (1) to the Transcendent or external, (2) to the Immanent or internal way of apprehending Reality. A third or intermediate group of images will be necessary to express the experience of those to whom mystic feeling--the satisfaction of love--is the supreme factor in the mystic life. According, then, to whether man's instinct prompts him to describe the Absolute Reality which he knows and craves for as a Place, a Person, or a State--all three of course but partial and inadequate translations of the one Indescribable Truth--so will he tend to adopt a symbolism of one or other of these three types.

A. Those who conceive the Perfect as a beatific vision exterior to them and very far off, who find in the doctrine of Emanations something which answers to their inward experience, will feel the process of their entrance into reality to be a quest, an arduous journey from the material to the spiritual world. They move away from, rather than transmute to another form, the life of sense. The ecstasies of such mystics will answer to the root-meaning of that much perverted word, as a "standing out" from themselves; a flight to happier countries far away. For them, the soul is outward bound towards its home.

B. Those for whom mysticism is above all things an intimate and personal relation, the satisfaction of a deep desire--who can say with Gertrude More, "never was there or can there be imagined such a love, as is between an humble soul and Thee"--will fall back upon imagery drawn largely from the language of earthly passion. Since the Christian religion insists upon the personal aspect of the Godhead, and provides in Christ an object of such intimacy, devotion and desire, an enormous number of Christian mystics inevitably describe their experiences under symbolism of this kind.

C. Those who are conscious rather of the Divine as a Transcendent Life immanent in the world and the self, and of a strange spiritual seed within them by whose development man, moving to higher levels of character and consciousness, attains his end, will see the mystic life as involving inward change rather than outgoing search. Regeneration is their watchword, and they will choose symbols of growth or transmutation: saying with St. Catherine of Genoa, "my Being is God, not by simple participation, but by a true transformation of my Being." [261]

These three groups of mystics, then, stand for three kinds of temperament; and we may fairly take as their characteristic forms of symbolic expression the Mystic Quest, the Marriage of the Soul, and the "Great Work" of the Spiritual Alchemists.

The pilgrimage idea, the outgoing quest, appears in mystical literature under two different aspects. One is the search for the "Hidden Treasure which desires to be found." Such is the "quest of the Grail" when regarded in its mystic aspect as an allegory of the adventures of the soul. The other is the long, hard journey towards a known and definite goal or state. Such are Dante's "Divine Comedy" and Bunyan's "Pilgrim's Progress"; each in their manner faithful descriptions of the Mystic Way. The goal of the quest--the Empyrean of Dante, the Beatific Vision or fulfilment of love--is often called Jerusalem by the Christian mystics: naturally enough since that city was for the mediaeval mind the supreme end of pilgrimage. By Jerusalem they mean not only the celestial country Heaven, but also the spiritual life, which is "itself a heaven." [262] "Right as a true pilgrim going to Jerusalem," says Hilton, "leaveth behind him house and land, wife and child, and maketh himself poor and bare from all that he hath, that he may go lightly without letting: right so, if thou wilt be a ghostly pilgrim, thou shalt make thyself naked from all that thou hast . . . then shalt thou set in thy heart wholly and fully that thou wouldst be at Jerusalem, and at none other place but there." "Jerusalem," he says in this same chapter, "is as much as to say a sight of peace; and betokeneth contemplation in perfect love of God." [263]

Under this image of a pilgrimage--an image as concrete and practical, as remote from the romantic and picturesque, for the mediaeval writers who used it, as a symbolism of hotel and railway train would be to us--the mystics contrived to summarize and suggest much of the life history of the ascending soul; the developing spiritual consciousness. The necessary freedom and detachment of the traveller, his departure from his normal life and interests, the difficulties, enemies, and hardships encountered on the road--the length of the journey, the variety of the country, the dark night which overtakes him, the glimpses of destination far away--all these are seen more and more as we advance in knowledge to constitute a transparent allegory of the incidents of man's progress from the unreal to the real. Bunyan was but the last of a long series of minds which grasped this fact.

The Traveller, says the Sufi Aziz bin Mahommed Nafasi, in whose book, "The Remotest Aim," the pilgrimage-symbolism is developed in great detail, is the Perceptive or Intuitive Sense of Man. The goal to which he journeys is Knowledge of God. This mysterious traveller towards the only country of the soul may be known of other men by his detachment, charity, humility, and patience. These primary virtues, however--belonging to ethical rather than to spiritual life--are not enough to bring his quest to a successful termination. They make him, say the Sufis, "perfect in knowledge of his goal but deficient in the power of reaching it." Though he has fraternal love for his fellow-pilgrims, detachment from wayside allurements, untiring perseverance on the road, he is still encumbered and weakened by unnecessary luggage. The second stage of his journey, therefore, is initiated like that of Christian by a casting off of his burden: a total self-renouncement, the attainment of a Franciscan poverty of spirit whereby he becomes "Perfectly Free."

Having got rid of all impediments to the spiritual quest, he must now acquire or develop in their stead the characteristic mystical qualities, or Three Aids of the Pilgrim; which are called in this system Attraction, Devotion, and Elevation. Attraction is consciousness of the mutual desire existing between man's spirit and the Divine Spirit: of the link of love which knits up reality and draws all things to their home in God. This is the universal law on which all mysticism is based. It is St. Augustine's "Thou hast made us for Thyself and our hearts can find no rest except in Thee." This "natural magnetism," then, once he is aware of it, will draw the pilgrim irresistibly along the road from the Many to the One. His second aid, Devotion, says the "Remotest Aim" in a phrase of great depth and beauty, is "the prosecution of the journey to God and in God." [264] It embraces, in fact, the whole contemplative life. It is the next degree of spiritual consciousness after the blind yielding to the attraction of the Real, and the setting in order of man's relation to his source.

The Traveller's journey to God is complete when he attains knowledge of Him--"Illumination," in the language of European mystics. The point at which this is reached is called the Tavern or resting-place upon the road, where he is fed with the Divine Mysteries. There are also "Wine Shops" upon the way, where the weary pilgrim is cheered and refreshed by a draught of the wine of Divine Love. [265] Only when the journey to God is completed begins the "Journey in God"--that which the Christian mystics call the Unitive Way--and this, since it is the essence of Eternal Life, can have no end. Elevation, the pilgrim's third aid, is the exalted or ecstatic form of consciousness peculiar to the contemplative, and which allows the traveller a glimpse of the spiritual city towards which he goes. [266]

The Sufi poet Attar, in his mystical poem, "The Colloquy of the Birds," has described the stages of this same spiritual pilgrimage with greater psychological insight, as the journey through "Seven Valleys." The lapwing, having been asked by other birds what is the length of the road which leads to the hidden Palace of the King, replies that there are Seven Valleys through which every traveller must pass: but since none who attain the End ever come back to describe their adventures, no one knows the length of the way.

(1) The first valley, says the lapwing, is the Valley of the Quest. It is long and toilsome: and there the traveller must strip himself of all earthly things, becoming poor, bare, and desolate: and so stay till

the Supernal Light casts a ray on his desolation. It is in fact, Dante's Purgatorio, the Christian Way of Purgation: the period of self-stripping and purification which no mystic system omits.

(2) When the ray of Supernal Light has touched the pilgrim he enters the limitless Valley of Love: begins, that is to say, the mystic life. It is Dante's "Earthly Paradise," or, in the traditional system of the mystics, the onset of Illumination.

(3) Hence he passes to the Valley of Knowledge or Enlightenment--the contemplative state--where each finds in communion with Truth the place that belongs to him. No Dante student will fail to see here a striking parallel with those planetary heavens where each soul partakes of the Divine, "not supremely in the absolute sense," as St. Bonaventura has it, but "supremely in respect of himself." The mystery of Being is now revealed to the traveller. He sees Nature's secret, and God in all things. It is the height of illumination.

(4) The next stage is the Valley of Detachment, of utter absorption in Divine Love--the Stellar Heaven of the Saints--where Duty is seen to be all in all. This leads to--

(5) The Valley of the Unity, where the naked Godhead is the one object of contemplation. This is the stage of ecstasy, or the Beatific Vision: Dante's condition in the last canto of the "Paradiso." It is transient, however, and leads to--

(6) The Valley of Amazement; where the Vision, far transcending the pilgrim's receptive power, appears to be taken from him and he is plunged in darkness and bewilderment. This is the state which Dionysius the Areopagite, and after him many mediaeval mystics, called the Divine Dark, and described as the truest and closest of all our apprehensions of the Godhead. It is the Cloud of Unknowing, "dark from excessive bright." The final stage is--

(7) The Valley of Annihilation of Self: the supreme degree of union or theopathetic state, in which the self is utterly merged "like a fish in the sea" in the ocean of Divine Love. [267]

Through all these metaphors of pilgrimage to a goal--of a road followed, distance overpassed, fatigue endured--there runs the definite idea that the travelling self in undertaking the journey is fulfilling a destiny, a law of the transcendental life; obeying an imperative need. The chosen Knights are destined or called to the quest of the Grail. "All men are called to their origin," says Rulman Merswin, and the fishes which he sees in his Vision of Nine Rocks are impelled to struggle, as it were "against nature," uphill from pool to pool towards their source. [268]

All mystical thinkers agree in declaring that there is a mutual attraction between the Spark of the Soul, the free divine germ in man, and the Fount from which it came forth. "We long for the Absolute," says Royce, "only in so far as in us the Absolute also longs, and seeks, through our very temporal striving, the peace that is nowhere in Time, but only, and yet Absolutely, in Eternity." [269] So, many centuries before the birth of American philosophy, Hilton put the same truth of experience in lovelier words. "He it is that desireth in thee, and He it is that is desired. He is all and He doth all if thou might see Him." [270]

The homeward journey of man's spirit, then, may be thought of as due to the push of a divine life within, answering to the pull of a divine life without. [271] It is only possible because there is already in that spirit a certain kinship with the Divine, a capacity for Eternal Life; and the mystics, in undertaking it, are humanity's pioneers on the only road to rest. Hence that attraction which the Moslem mystic discerned as the traveller's necessary aid, is a fundamental doctrine of all mysticism: and as a consequence, the symbolism of mutual desire is here inextricably mingled with that of pilgrimage. The spiritual pilgrim goes because he is called; because he wants to go, must go, if he is to find rest and peace. "God needs man," says Eckhart. It is Love calling to love: and the journey, though in one sense a hard pilgrimage, up and out, by the terraced mount and the ten heavens to God, in another is the inevitable rush of the roving comet, caught at last, to the Central Sun. "My weight is my love," said St. Augustine. [272] Like gravitation, it inevitably compels, for good or evil, every spirit to its own place. According to another range of symbols, that love flings open a door, in order that the larger Life may rush in and it and the soul be "one thing."

Here, then, we run through the whole gamut of symbolic expression; through Transcendence, Desire, and Immanence. All are seen to point to one consummation, diversely and always allusively expressed: the need of union between man's separated spirit and the Real, his remaking in the interests of transcendent life, his establishment in that Kingdom which is both "near and far."

"In the book of Hidden Things it is written," says Eckhart, "I stand at the door and knock and wait' . . . thou needst not seek Him here or there: He is no farther off than the door of the heart. There He stands and waits and waits until He finds thee ready to open and let Him in. Thou needst not call Him from a distance; to wait until thou openest is harder for Him than for thee. He needs thee a thousand times more than thou canst need Him. Thy opening and His entering are but one moment ." [273] "God," he says in another place, "can as little do without us, as we without Him." [274] Our attainment of the Absolute is not a one-sided ambition, but the fulfilment of a mutual desire. "For our natural Will," says Lady Julian, "is to have God, and the Good will of God is to have us; and we may never cease from longing till we have Him in fullness of joy." [275]

So, in the beautiful poem or ritual called the "Hymn of Jesus," contained in the apocryphal "Acts of John" and dating from primitive Christian times, the Logos, or Eternal Christ, is thus represented as matching with His own transcendent, self-giving desire every need of the soul. [276]

The Soul says:--

"I would be saved.'"

Christ replies:--

"And I would save.' Amen."

The Dialogue continues:--

"I would be loosed.'
And I would loose.' Amen.
I would be pierced.'
And I would pierce.' Amen.
I would be born.'
And I would bear.' Amen.
I would eat.'
And I would be eaten.' Amen.
I would hear.'
And I would be heard.' Amen."
"I am a Lamp to thee who beholdest Me,
I am a Mirror to thee who perceivest Me,
I am a Door to thee, who knockest at Me,
I am a Way to thee a wayfarer.'"

The same fundamental idea of the mutual quest of the Soul and the Absolute is expressed in the terms of another symbolism by the great Mahommedan mystic:--

"No lover ever seeks union with his beloved,
But his beloved is also seeking union with him.
But the lover's love makes his body lean
While the beloved's love makes her fair and lusty.
When in this heart the lightning spark of love arises,
Be sure this love is reciprocated in that heart.
When the love of God arises in thy heart,
Without doubt God also feels love for thee." [277]

The mystic vision, then, is of a spiritual universe held within the bonds of love: [278] and of the free and restless human soul, having within it the spark of divine desire, the "tendency to the Absolute," pnly finding satisfaction and true life when united with this Life of God. Then, in Patmore's lovely image, "the babe is at its mother's breast," "the lover has returned to the beloved." [279]

Whatever their outward sense, all true mystic symbols express aspects of this "secret of the world," this primal verity. But whereas such great visionary schemes as those of Attar and of Dante show it in its cosmic form, in many symbolic descriptions--particularly those which we meet in the writings of the ecstatic saints--the personal subjective note, the consciousness of an individual relation between that one self and the Supernal Self, overpowers all general applications. Then philosophy and formal allegory must step aside: the sacramental language of exalted emotion, of profoundly felt experience, takes its place. The phases of mutual love, of wooing and combat, awe and delight--the fevers of desire, the ecstasy of surrender--are drawn upon and made to contribute something to the description of the great and secret drama of the soul.

To such symbolic transcripts of intimate experience belongs one amazing episode of the spiritual life-history which, because it has been given immortal expression by the greatest mystical poet of modern times, is familiar to thousands of readers who know little or nothing of the more normal adventures incidental to man's attainment of the Absolute. In "The Hound of Heaven" Francis Thompson described with an almost terrible power, not the self's quest of adored Reality, but Reality's quest of the unwilling self. He shows to us the remorseless, untiring seeking and following of the soul by the Divine Life to which it will not surrender: the inexorable onward sweep of "this tremendous Lover," hunting the separated spirit, "strange piteous futile thing" that flees Him "down the nights and down the days." This idea of the love-chase, of the spirit rushing in terror from the overpowering presence of God, but followed, sought, conquered in the end, is common to all the mediaeval mystics: it is the obverse of their general doctrine of the necessary fusion of human and divine life, "escape from the flame of separation."

"I chased thee, for in this was my pleasure," says the voice of Love to Mechthild of Magdeburg; "I captured thee, for this was my desire; I bound thee, and I rejoice in thy bonds; I have wounded thee, that thou mayst be united to me. If I gave thee blows, it was that I might be possessed of thee." [280]

So in the beautiful Middle English poem of "Quia amore langueo,"--

"I am true love that fals was nevere,
Mi sistyr, mannis soule, I loved hir thus;
Bicause we wolde in no wise discevere
I lefte my Kyngdom glorious.
I purveyde for hir a paleis precious;
She fleyth, I folowe, I sought hir so.
I suffride this peyne piteous
Quia amore langueo," [281]

Meister Eckhart has the same idea of the inexorable Following Love, impossible to escape, expressed under less personal images. "Earth," he says, "cannot escape the sky; let it flee up or down, the sky flows into it, and makes it fruitful whether it will or no. So God does to man. He who will escape Him only runs to His bosom; for all corners are open to Him." [282]

We find in all the mystics this strong sense of a mysterious spiritual life--a Reality--over against man, seeking him and compelling him to Its will. It is not for him, they think, to say that he will or will not aspire to the transcendental world. [283] Hence sometimes this inversion of man's long quest of God. The self resists the pull of spiritual gravitation, flees from the touch of Eternity; and the Eternal seeks it, tracks it ruthlessly down. The Following Love, the mystics say, is a fact of experience, not a poetic idea. "Those strong feet that follow, follow after," once set upon the chase, are bound to win. Man, once conscious of Reality, cannot evade it. For a time his separated spirit, his disordered loves, may wilfully frustrate the scheme of things: but he must be conquered in the end. Then the mystic process unfolds itself: Love triumphs: the "purpose of the worlds" fulfils itself in the individual life.

II

It was natural and inevitable that the imagery of human love and marriage should have seemed to the mystic the best of all images of his own "fulfilment of life"; his soul's surrender, first to the call, finally to the embrace of Perfect Love. It lay ready to his hand: it was understood of all men: and moreover, it certainly does offer, upon lower levels, a strangely exact parallel to the sequence of states in which man's spiritual consciousness unfolds itself, and which form the consummation of the mystic life.

It has been said that the constant use of such imagery by Christian mystics of the mediaeval period is traceable to the popularity of the Song of Songs, regarded as an allegory of the spiritual life. I think that the truth lies rather in the opposite statement: namely, that the mystic loved the Song of Songs because he there saw reflected, as in a mirror, the most secret experiences of his soul. The sense of a desire that was insatiable, of a personal fellowship so real, inward, and intense that it could only be compared with the closest link of human love, of an intercourse that was no mere spiritual self-indulgence, but was rooted in the primal duties and necessities of life--more, those deepest, most intimate secrets of communion, those self-giving ecstasies which all mystics know, but of which we, who are not mystics, may not speak--all these he found symbolized and suggested, their unendurable glories veiled in a merciful mist, in the poetry which man has invented to honour that august passion in which the merely human draws nearest to the divine.

The great saints who adopted and elaborated this symbolism, applying it to their pure and ardent passion for the Absolute, were destitute of the prurient imagination which their modern commentators too often possess. They were essentially pure of heart; and when they "saw God" they were so far from confusing that unearthly vision with the products of morbid sexuality, that the dangerous nature of the imagery which they employed did not occur to them. They knew by experience the unique nature of spiritual love: and no one can know anything about it in any other way.

Thus for St. Bernard, throughout his deeply mystical sermons on the Song of Songs, the Divine Word is the Bridegroom, the human soul is the Bride: but how different is the effect produced by his use of these symbols from that with which he has been charged by hostile critics! In the place of that "sensuous imagery" which is so often and so earnestly deplored by those who have hardly a nodding acquaintance with the writings of the saints, we find images which indeed have once been sensuous; but which are here anointed and ordained to a holy office, carried up, transmuted, and endowed with a radiant purity, an intense and spiritual life.

" Let Him kiss me with the kisses of His mouth.' Who is it speaks these words? It is the Bride. Who is the Bride? It is the Soul thirsting for God. . . . She who asks this is held by the bond of love to him from whom she asks it. Of all the sentiments of nature, this of love is the most excellent, especially when it is rendered back to Him who is the principle and fountain of it--that is, God. Nor are there found any expressions equally sweet to signify the mutual affection between the Word of God and the soul, as those of Bridegroom and of Bride; inasmuch as between individuals who stand in such relation to each other all things are in common, and they possess nothing separate or divided. They have one inheritance, one dwelling-place, one table, and they are in fact one flesh. If, then, mutual love is especially befitting to a bride and bridegroom, it is not unfitting that the name of Bride is given to a soul which loves." [284]

To women mystics of the Catholic Church, familiar with the antique and poetic metaphor which called every cloistered nun the Bride of Christ, that crisis in their spiritual history in which they definitely vowed themselves to the service of Transcendent Reality seemed, naturally enough, the veritable betrothal of the soul. Often, in a dynamic vision, they saw as in a picture the binding vows exchanged between their spirits and their God. [285] That further progress on the mystic way which brought with it a sharp and permanent consciousness of union with the Divine Will, the constant sustaining presence of a Divine Companion, became, by an extension of the original simile, Spiritual Marriage. The elements of duty, constancy, irrevocableness, and loving obedience involved in the mediaeval conception of the marriage tie, made it an apt image of a spiritual state in which humility, intimacy, and love were the dominant characteristics. There is really no need to seek a pathological explanation of these simple facts. [286] Moreover with few exceptions, the descriptions of spiritual marriage which the great mystics have left are singularly free from physical imagery. "So mysterious is the secret," says St. Teresa, "and so sublime the favour that God thus bestows instantaneously on the soul, that it feels a supreme delight, only to be described by saying that our Lord vouchsafes for the moment to reveal to it His own heavenly glory in a far more subtle way than by any vision or spiritual delight. As far as can be understood, the soul, I mean the spirit of this soul, is made one with God, who is Himself a spirit, and Who has been pleased to show certain persons how far His love for us extends in order that we may praise His greatness. He has thus deigned to unite Himself to His creature: He has bound Himself to her as firmly as two human beings are joined in wedlock and will never separate Himself from her." [287]

The great Richard of St. Victor, in one of his most splendid mystical treatises, [288] has given us perhaps the most daring and detailed application of the symbolism of marriage to the adventures of the spirit of man. He divides the "steep stairway of love," by which the contemplative ascends to union with the Absolute, into four stages. These he calls the betrothal, the marriage, the wedlock, and the fruitfulness of the soul. [289] In the betrothal, he says, the soul "thirsts for the Beloved"; that is to say, it longs to experience the delights of Reality. "The Spirit comes to the Soul, and seems sweeter than honey." It is conversion, the awakening to mystical truth; the kindling of the passion for the Absolute. "Then the Soul with pertinacity demands more": and because of her burning desire she attains to pure contemplation, and so passes to the second degree of love. In this she is "led in bridal" by the Beloved. Ascending "above herself" in contemplation, she "sees the Sun of Righteousness." She is now confirmed in the mystic life; the irrevocable marriage vows are made between her spirit and her God. At this point she can "see the Beloved," but "cannot yet come in to Him," says Richard. This degree, as we shall see later, answers more or less to that which other mystics call the Illuminative Way: but any attempt to press these poetic symbols into a cast-iron series, and establish exact parallels, is foredoomed to failure, and will merely succeed in robbing them of their fragrance and suggestive power. In Richard's "third stage," however, that of union, or wedlock, it is clear that the soul enters upon the "Unitive Way." She has passed the stages of ecstatic and significant events, and is initiated into the Life. She is "deified," "passes utterly into God, and is glorified in Him": is transfigured, he says, by immediate contact with the Divine Substance, into an utterly different quality of being. "Thus," says St. John of the Cross, "the soul, when it shall have driven away from itself all that is contrary to the divine will, becomes transformed in God by love. [290]

"The Soul," says Richard again, "is utterly concentrated on the One." She is "caught up to the divine light." The expression of the personal passion, the intimate relation, here rises to its height. But this is not enough. Where most mystical diagrams leave off, Richard of St. Victor's "steep stairway of Love" goes on: with the result that this is almost the only symbolic system bequeathed to us by the great contemplatives in which all the implications contained in the idea of the spiritual marriage have been worked out to their term. He saw clearly that the union of the soul with its Source could not be a barren ecstasy. That was to mistake a means for an end; and to frustrate the whole intention of life, which is, on all levels, fruitful and creative. Therefore he says that in the fourth degree, the Bride who has been so greatly honoured, caught up to such unspeakable delight, sinks her own will and "is humiliated below herself." She accepts the pains and duties in the place of the raptures of love; and becomes a source, a "parent" of fresh spiritual life. The Sponsa Dei develops into the Mater Divinae gratiae. That imperative need of life, to push on, to create, to spread, is here seen operating in the spiritual sphere. This forms that rare and final stage in the evolution of the great mystics, in which they return to the world which they forsook; and there live, as it were, as centres of transcendental energy, the creators of spiritual families, the partners and fellow-labourers with the Divine Life. [291]

III

We come now to the symbols which have been adopted by those mystics in whom temperamental consciousness of their own imperfection, and of the unutterable perfection of the Absolute Life for which they longed, has overpowered all other aspects of man's quest of reality. The "seek, and ye shall find" of the pilgrim, the "by Love shall He be gotten and holden" of the bride, can never seem an adequate description of experience to minds of this type. They are intent on the inexorable truth which must be accepted in some form by both these classes: the crucial fact that "we behold that which we are," or, in other words, that "only the Real can know Reality." Hence the state of the inward man, the "unrealness" of him when judged by any transcendental standard, is their centre of interest. His remaking or regeneration appears to them as the primal necessity, if he is ever to obtain rights of citizenship in the "country of the soul."

We have seen that this idea of the New Birth, the remaking or transmutation of the self, clothed in many different symbols, runs through the whole of mysticism and much of theology. It is the mystic's subjective reading of those necessary psychological and moral changes which he observes within himself as his spiritual consciousness grows. His hard work of renunciation, of detachment from the things which that consciousness points out as illusory or impure, his purifications and trials, all form part of it. If that which is whole or perfect is to come, then that which is in part must be done away: "for in what measure we put off the creature, in the same measure are we able to put on the Creator: neither more nor less." [292]

Of all the symbolic systems in which this truth has been enshrined none is so complete, so picturesque, and now so little understood as that of the "Hermetic Philosophers" or Spiritual Alchemists. This fact would itself be sufficient to justify us in examining some of the chief features of their symbolism. There is a further excuse for this apparently eccentric proceeding, however, in the fact that the language of alchemy was largely--though not always accurately and consistently--used by the great mystic Jacob Boehme, and after him by his English disciple, William Law. Without, then, some knowledge of the terms which they employed, but seldom explained, the writings of this important school can hardly be understood.

The alchemic symbols, especially as applied to the mystic life, are full of an often deliberate obscurity; which makes their exact interpretation a controversial matter at the best. Moreover, the authors of the various Hermetic writings do not always use them in the same sense, and whilst many of these writings are undoubtedly mystical, others clearly deal with the physical quest of gold: nor have we any sure standard by which to divide class from class. The elements from which the spiritual alchemists built up their allegories of the mystic life are, however, easily grasped: and these elements, with the significance generally attributed to them, are as much as those who are not specialists can hope to unravel from this very tangled skein. First, there are the metals; of course the obvious materials of physical alchemy. These are usually called by the names of their presiding planets: thus in Hermetic language Luna means silver, Sol gold, etc. Then there is the Vessel, or Athanor, in which the transmutation of base metal to gold took place: an object whose exact nature is veiled in much mystery. The Fire, and various solvents and waters, peculiar to the different alchemistic recipes, complete the apparatus necessary to the "Great Work."

The process of this work, sometimes described in chemical, and sometimes in astrological terms, is more often than not disguised in a strange heraldic and zoological symbolism dealing with Lions, Dragons, Eagles, Vultures, Ravens and Doves: which, delightful in its picturesqueness, is unequalled in its power of confusing the anxious and unwary inquirer. It is also the subject of innumerable and deliberate allegories, which were supposed to convey its secrets to the elect, whilst most certainly concealing them from the crowd. Hence it is that the author of "A Short Enquiry concerning the Hermetic Art" speaks for all investigators of this subject when he describes the "Hermetic science" as a "great Labyrinth, in which are abundance of enquirers rambling to this day, many of them undiscerned by one another." Like him, I too "have taken several Turns in it myself, wherein one shall meet with very few; for tis so large, and almost every one taking a different Path, that they seldom meet. But finding it a very melancholy place, I resolved to get out of it, and rather content myself to walk in the little garden before the entrance, where many things, though not all, were orderly to be seen. Choosing rather to stay there, and contemplate on the Metaphor set up, than venture again into the wilderness."[293]

Coming, then, to the "contemplation of the Metaphor set up,"--by far the most judicious course for modern students of the Hermetic art--we observe first that the prime object of alchemy was held to be the production of the Philosopher's Stone, that perfect and incorrupt substance or "noble Tincture," never found upon our imperfect earth in its natural state, which could purge all baser metals of their dross, and turn them to pure gold. The quest of the Stone, in fact, was but one aspect of man's everlasting quest of perfection, his hunger for the Absolute; and hence an appropriate symbol of the mystic life. But this quest was not conducted in some far off transcendental kingdom. It was prosecuted in the Here and Now within the physical world.

Gold, the Crowned King, or Sol, as it is called in the planetary symbolism of the alchemists, was their standard of perfection, the "Perfect Metal." Towards it, as the Christian towards sanctity, their wills were set. It had for them a value not sordid but ideal. Nature, they thought, is always trying to make gold, this incorruptible and perfect thing; and the other metals are merely the results of the frustration of her original design. Nor is this aiming at perfection and achieving of imperfection limited to the physical world. Quod superius, sicut quod inferius. Upon the spiritual plane also they held that the Divine Idea is always aiming at "Spiritual Gold"--divine humanity, the New Man, citizen of the transcendental world--and "natural man" as we ordinarily know him is a lower metal, silver at best. He is a departure from the "plan," who yet bears within himself, if we could find it, the spark or seed of absolute perfection: the "tincture" which makes gold. "The smattering I have of the Philosopher's Stone," says Sir Thomas Browne, "(which is something more than the perfect exaltation of gold) hath taught me a great deal of divinity, and instructed my belief how that immortal spirit and incorruptible substance of my soul may lie obscure, and sleep awhile within this house of flesh." [294] This "incorruptible substance" is man's goldness, his perfect principle: for "the highest mineral virtue resides in Man," says Albertus Magnus, "and God may be found everywhere." [295] Hence the prosecution of a spiritual chemistry is a proper part of the true Hermetic science.

The art of the alchemist, whether spiritual or physical, consists in completing the work of perfection, bringing forth and making dominant, as it were, the "latent goldness" which "lies obscure" in metal or man. The ideal adept of alchemy was therefore an "auxiliary of the Eternal Goodness." By his search for the "Noble Tincture" which should restore an imperfect world, he became a partner in the business of creation, assisting the Cosmic Plan. Thus the proper art of the Spiritual Alchemist, with whom alone we are here concerned, was the production of the spiritual and only valid tincture or Philosopher's Stone; the mystic seed of transcendental life which should invade, tinge, and wholly transmute the imperfect self into spiritual gold. That this was no fancy of seventeenth-century allegorists, but an idea familiar to many of the oldest writers upon alchemy--whose quest was truly a spiritual search into the deepest secrets of the soul--is proved by the words which bring to an end the first part of the antique "Golden Treatise upon the Making of the Stone," sometimes attributed to Hermes Trismegistus. "This, O Son," says that remarkable tract, "is the Concealed Stone of Many Colours, which is born and brought forth in one colour; know this and conceal it . . . it leads from darkness into light, from this desert wilderness to a secure habitation, and from poverty and straits to a free and ample fortune." [296]

Man, then, was for the alchemists "the true laboratory of the Hermetic art"; which concealed in an entanglement of vague and contradictory symbols the life-process of his ascension to that perfect state in which he was able to meet God. This state must not be confused with a merely moral purity, but is to be understood as involving utter transmutation into a "new form." It naturally followed from this that the indwelling Christ, the "Corner Stone," the Sun of Righteousness, became, for many of the Christian alchemists, identified with the Lapis Philosophorum and with Sol: and was regarded both as the image and as the earnest of this "great work." His spirit was the "noble tincture" which "can bring that which is lowest in the death to its highest ornament or glory;" [297] transmuting the natural to the supernatural, operating the "New Birth." "This," says Boehme, "is the noble precious Stone (Lapis Philosophorum), the Philosopher's Stone, which the Magi (or wise men) find which tinctureth nature, and generateth a new son in the old. He who findeth that, esteemeth more highly of it than of this (outward) world. For the Son is many thousand times greater than the Father." Again, "If you take the spirit of the tincture, then indeed you go on a way in which many have found Sol; but they have followed on the way to the heart of Sol, where the spirit of the heavenly tincture hath laid hold on them, and brought them into the liberty, into the Majesty, where they have Known the Noble Stone, Lapis Philosophorum, the Philosopher's Stone, and have stood amazed at man's blindness, and seen his labouring in vain. Would you fain find the Noble Stone? Behold, we will show it you plain enough, if you be a Magus, and worthy, else you shall remain blind still: therefore fall to work thus: for it hath no more but three numbers. First tell from one till you come to the Cross, which is ten (X) . . . and there lieth the Stone without any great painstaking, for it is pure and not defiled with any earthly nature."

"In this stone there lieth hidden, whatsoever God and the Eternity, also heaven, the stars and elements contain and are able to do. There never was from eternity anything better or more precious than this, and it is offered by God and bestowed upon man; every one may have it . . . it is in a simple form, and hath the power of the whole Deity in it." [298]

Boehme is here using alchemic symbols, according to his custom, in a loose and artistic manner; for the true Hermetic Philosopher's Stone is not something which can be found but something which must be made. The alchemists, whether their search be for a physical or a spiritual "tincture," say always that this tincture is the product of the furnace and Athanor: and further that it is composed of "three numbers" or elements, which they call Sulphur, Salt, and Mercury. These, when found, and forced into the proper combination, form the "Azoth" or "Philosopher's Egg"--the stuff or First Matter of the Great Work. Sulphur, Salt, and Mercury, however, must not be understood in too literal a sense. "You need not look for our metallic seed among the elements," says Basil the Monk, "it need not be sought so far back. If you can only rectify the Mercury, Sulphur, and Salt (understand those of the sages) until the metallic spirit and body are inseparably joined together by means of the metallic soul, you thereby firmly rivet the chain of love and prepare the palace for the Coronation." [299]

Of these three ingredients, the important one is the spiritual principle, the unseizable Mercury; which is far from being the metal which we ordinarily know by that name. The Mercury which the alchemists sought--often in strange places--is a hidden and powerful substance. They call it "Mercury of the Wise"; and he who can discover it, they say, is on the way towards success. The reader in search of mystical wisdom already begins to be bewildered; but if he persevere in this labyrinth of symbolism, he presently discovers--as Basil the Monk indeed hints--that the Sulphur and the Salt, or "metallic soul and body" of the spiritual chemistry, represent something analogous to the body and mind of man--Sulphur his earthly nature, seasoned with intellectual Salt. The Mercury is Spirit in its most mystic sense, the Synteresis or holy Dweller in the Innermost, the immanent spark or Divine Principle of his life. Only the "wise," the mystically awakened, can know this Mercury, the agent of man's transmutation: and until it has been discovered, brought out of the hiddenness, nothing can be done. "This Mercury or Snowy Splendour, is a Celestial Body drawn from the beams of the Sun and the Moon. It is the only Agent in the world for this art." [300] It is the divine-human "spark of the soul," the bridge between Gold and Silver, God and man.

The Three Principles being enclosed in the vessel, or Athanor, which is man himself, and subjected to a gentle fire--the Incendium Amoris --the process of the Great Work, the mystic transmutation of natural into spiritual man, can begin. This work, like the ingredients which compose it, has "three numbers": and the first matter, in the course of its transmutation, assumes three successive colours: the Black, the White, and the Red. These three colours are clearly analogous to the three traditional stages of the Mystic Way: Purgation, Illumination, Union.

The alchemists call the first stage, or Blackness, Putrefaction. In it the three principles which compose the "whole man" of body, soul and spirit, are "sublimated" till they appear as a black powder full of corruption, and the imperfect body is "dissolved and purified by subtle Mercury"; as man is purified by the darkness, misery, and despair which follows the emergence of his spiritual consciousness. As psychic uproar and disorder seems part of the process of mental growth, so " Solve et coagula "--break down that you may build up--is the watchword of the spiritual alchemist. The "black beast," the passional element, of the lower nature must emerge and be dealt with before anything further can be done. "There is a black beast in our forest," says the highly allegorical "Book of Lambspring," "his name is Putrefaction, his blackness is called the Head of the Raven; when it is cut off, Whiteness appears." [301] This Whiteness, the state of Luna, or Silver, the "chaste and immaculate Queen," is the equivalent of the Illuminative Way: the highest point which the mystic can attain short of union with the Absolute. This White Stone is pure, and precious; but in it the Great Work of man's spiritual evolution has not yet reached its term. That term is the attainment of the Red, the colour of Perfection or alchemic gold; a process sometimes called the "Marriage of Luna and Sol"--the fusion of the human and divine spirit. Under this image is concealed the final secret of the mystic life: that ineffable union of finite and infinite--that loving reception of the inflowing vitality of God--from which comes forth the Magnum Opus: deified or spiritual man.

"This," says the author of "A Suggestive Enquiry," "is the union supersentient, the nuptials sublime, Mentis et Universi . . . . Lo! behold I will open to thee a mystery, cries the Adept, the bridegroom crowneth the bride of the north [i.e. , she who comes out of the cold and darkness of the lower nature]. In the darkness of the north, out of the crucifixion of the cerebral life, when the sensual dominant is occultated in the Divine Fiat, and subdued, there arises a Light wonderfully about the summit, which wisely returned and multiplied according to the Divine Blessing, is made substantial in life." [302]

I have said, that side by side with the metallic and planetary language of the alchemists, runs a strange heraldic symbolism in which they take refuge when they fear--generally without reason--that they are telling their secrets too plainly to an unregenerate world. Many of these heraldic emblems are used in an utterly irresponsible manner; and whilst doubtless conveying a meaning to the individual alchemist and the disciples for whom he wrote, are, and must ever be, unintelligible to other men. But others are of a more general application; and appear so frequently in seventeenth-century literature, whether mystical or non-mystical, that some discussion of them may well be of use.

Perhaps the quaintest and most celebrated of all these allegories is that which describes the quest of the Philosopher's Stone as "the hunting of the Green Lion." [303] The Green Lion, though few would divine it, is the First Matter of the Great Work: hence, in spiritual alchemy, natural man in his wholeness--Salt, Sulphur, and Mercury in their crude state. He is called green because, seen from the transcendent standpoint, he is still unripe, his latent powers undeveloped; and a Lion, because of his strength, fierceness, and virility. Here the common opinion that a pious effeminacy, a diluted and amiable spirituality, is the proper raw material of the mystic life, is emphatically contradicted. It is not by the education of the lamb, but by the hunting and taming of the wild intractable lion, instinct with vitality, full of ardour and courage, exhibiting heroic qualities on the sensual plane, that the Great Work is achieved. The lives of the saints enforce the same law.

> "Our lyon wanting maturitie
> Is called greene for his unripeness trust me:
> And yet full quickly he can run,
> And soon can overtake the Sun." [304]

The Green Lion, then, in his strength and wholeness is the only creature potentially able to attain Perfection. It needs the adoption and purification of all the wealth and resources of man's nature, not merely the encouragement of his transcendental tastes, if he is to "overtake the Sun" and achieve the Great Work. The Kingdom of Heaven is taken by violence, not by amiable aspiration. "The Green Lion," says one alchemist, "is the priest by whom Sol and Luna are wed." In other words, the raw stuff of indomitable human nature is the means by which man is to attain union with the Absolute. The duty of the alchemist, the transmuting process, is therefore described as the hunting of the Green Lion through the forest of the sensual world. He, like the Hound of Heaven, is on a love chase down the nights and down the days.

When the lion is caught, when Destiny overtakes it, its head must be cut off as the preliminary to the necessary taming process. This is called by the alchemists "the head of the Raven," the Crow, or the Vulture, "for its blackness." It represents the fierce and corrupt life of the passions: and its removal is that "death of the lower nature" which is the object of all asceticism-- i.e. , Purgation. The lion, the whole man, Humanity in its strength, is as it were "slain to the world," and then resuscitated; but in a very different shape. By its passage through this mystic death or the "putrefaction of the Three Principles" the "colour of unripeness" is taken away. Its taming completed, it receives wings, wherewith it may fly up to Sol, the Perfect or Divine; and is transmuted, say the alchemists, into the Red Dragon. This is to us a hopelessly grotesque image: but to the Hermetic philosophers, whose sense of wonder was uncorrupt, it was the deeply mystical emblem of a new, strange, and transcendental life, powerful alike in earth and in heaven. As the angel to the man, so was the dragon to the world of beasts: a creature of splendour and terror, a super-brute, veritably existent if seldom seen. We realize something of the significance of this symbol for the alchemic writers, if we remember how sacred a meaning it has for the Chinese: to whom the dragon is the traditional emblem of free spiritual life, as the tiger represents the life of the material plane in its intensest form. Since it is from China that alchemy is supposed to have reached the European world, it may yet be found that the Red Dragon is one of the most antique and significant symbols of the Hermetic Art.

For the Spiritual Chemistry, then, the Red Dragon represents Deified Man; whose emergence must always seem like the birth of some monstrous and amazing creature when seen from the standpoint of the merely natural world. With his coming forth, the business of the alchemist, in so far as he be a mystic, is done. Man has transcended his lower nature, has received wings wherewith to live on higher levels of reality. The Tincture, the latent goldness, has been found and made dominant, the Magnum Opus achieved. That the trite and inward business of that Work, when stripped of its many emblematic veils, was indeed the reordering of spiritual rather than material elements, is an opinion which rests on a more solid foundation than personal interpretations of old allegories and alchemic-tracts. The Norwich physician--himself deeply read in the Hermetic science--has declared to us his own certainty concerning it in few but lovely words. In them is contained the true mystery of man's eternal and interior quest of the Stone: its reconciliation with that other, outgoing quest of "the Hidden Treasure that desires to be found."

"Do but extract from the corpulency of bodies, or resolve things beyond their First Matter, and you discover the habitation of Angels: which, if I call it the ubiquitary and omnipresent Essence of God, I hope I shall not offend Divinity." [305]

Footnotes:

258. Jámi, "Joseph and Zulaikha. The Poet's Prayer."
259. "Theologia Germanica," cap. x.

260. St. Catherine of Genoa, " Vita e Dottrina," cap. xiv.

261. "Vita e Dottrina," p. 36.

262. This image seems first to have been elaborated by St. Augustine, from whom it was borrowed by Hugh of St. Victor, and most of the mediaeval mystics.

263. "The Scale of Perfection," bk. ii. cap. xxi.

264. So too Ruysbroeck says that "the just man goes towards God by inward love in perpetual activity and in God in virtue of his fruitive affection in eternal rest" ("De Ornatu Spiritalium Nuptiarum," l. ii. cap. lxv).

265] I need not remind the reader of the fact that this symbolism, perverted to the purposes of his skeptical philosophy, runs through the whole of the Rubaiyat of Omar Khayyám.

266. See Palmer's "Oriental Mysticism," pt. I. caps. i., ii., iii., and v.

267. An abridged translation of Attar's allegory of the Valleys will be found in "The Conference of the Birds," by R. P. Masani (1924). See also W. S. Lilly's "Many Mansions," p. 130.

268. Jundt, "Rulman Merswin," p. 27.

269. Royce, "The World and the Individual," vol. ii. p. 386.

270. "The Scale of Perfection," bk. ii. cap. xxiv.

271. Compare Récéjac ("Fondements de la Connaissance Mystique," p. 252). "According to mysticism, morality leads the soul to the frontiers of the Absolute and even gives it an impulsion to enter, but this is not enough. This movement of pure Freedom cannot succeed unless there is an equivalent movement within the Absolute itself."

272. Aug. Conf., bk. xiii. cap. 9. "All those who love," says Ruysbroeck, "feel this attraction: more or less according to the degree of their love." ("De Calculo sive de Perfectione filiorum Dei.")

273. Meister Eckhart, Pred. iii.

274. Ibid ., Pred. xiii.

275. "Revelations of Divine Love," cap. vi.

276. The Greek and English text will be found in the "Apocrypha Anecdota" of Dr. M. R. James, series 2 (Cambridge, 1897), pp. 1-25. I follow his translation. It will be seen that I have adopted the hypotheses of Mr. G. R. S. Mead as to the dramatic nature of this poem. See his "Echoes from the Gnosis," 1896.

277. Jalalu d' Din Rumi (Wisdom of the East Series), p. 77.

278. So Dante--

" Nel suo profondo vidi che s'interna
legato con amore in un volume
cio che per l'universo si squaderna." (Par. xxxiii. 85.)

279. "The Rod, the Root, and the Flower," "Aurea Dicta," ccxxviii.

280. "Das Fliessende Licht der Gottheit," pt. i. cap. iii.

281. "Quia amore langueo," an anonymous fifteenth-century poem. Printed from the Lambeth MS. by the E.E.T.S., 1866-67.

282. Pred. lxxxviii.

283. So we are told of St. Francis of Assisi, that in his youth he "tried to flee God's hand." Thomas of Celano, Legenda Prima, cap. ii.

284. Sr. Bernard, "Cantica Canticorum," Sermon vii. For a further and excellent discussion of St. Bernard's mystical language, see Dom Cuthbert Butler, "Western Mysticism," 2nd ed., pp. 160 seq .

285. Vide infra, Pt. II. cap. v.

286. Professor Pratt, by no means an enthusiastic witness, most justly observes "There are several excellent reasons why the mystics almost inevitably make use of the language of human love in describing the joy of the love of God. The first and simplest is this: that they have no other language to use . . . the mystic must make use of expressions drawn from earthly love to describe his experience, or give up the attempt of describing it at all. It is the only way he has of even suggesting to the non-mystical what he has felt" ("The Religious Consciousness," p. 418).

287. "El Castillo Interior," Moradas Sétimas, cap ii.

288. "De Quatuor Gradibus Violentae Charitatis" (Migne, Patrologia Latina, vol. cxcvi. col. 1207).

289. "In primo gradu fit desponsatio, in secundo nuptiae, in tertio copula, in quarto puerperium. . . . De quarto dicitur, Coucepimus, et quasi parturivimus et peperimus spiritum" (Isa. xviii . 26). (Op. cit., 1216, D.)

290. "Subida del Monte Carmelo," lii. cap. v.

291. Vide infra , pt. ii. caps. i. and x.

292. "Theologia Germanica," cap. i.

293. "A Short Enquiry Concerning the Hermetic Art," p. 29.

294. "Religio Medici," pt. i.

295. "A Suggestive Enquiry into the Hermetic Mystery," p. 143. This rare and curious study of spiritual alchemy was the anonymous work of the late Mrs. Atwood. She attempted to suppress it soon

after publication under the impression--common amongst mystics of a certain type--that she had revealed matters which might not be spoken of; as Coventry Patmore for the same reason destroyed his masterpiece, "Sponsa Dei."

296. Quoted in "A Suggestive Enquiry into the Hermetic Mystery," p. 107. The whole of the "Golden Treatise" will be found set out in this work.

297. Jacob Boehme, "The Threefold Life of Man," cap. iv. § 23.

298. Boehme, "The Threefold Life of Man," cap. vi. § 98; cap. x. §§ 3, 4; and cap. xiii. § 1.

299. "The Golden Tripod of the Monk Basilius Valentinus" ("The Hermetic Museum, " vol. i. p. 319).

300. "A Short Enquiry Concerning the Hermetic Art," p. 17.

301. "The Hermetic Museum," vol. i. p. 272.

302. "A Suggestive Enquiry," p. 345.

303. See "A Short Enquiry," p. 17, and "A Suggestive Enquiry," pp. 297 et seq ., where the rhymed Alchemic tract called "Hunting the Greene Lyon" is printed in full.

304. Op. cit.

305. Sir Thomas Browne, "Religio Medici," pt. i.

CHATPER VII

It is unnecessary to examine in detail the mistakes--in ecclesiastical language, the heresies--into which men have been led by a feeble, a deformed, or an arrogant mystical sense. The number of these mistakes is countless; their wildness almost inconceivable to those who have not been forced to study them. Too often the loud voices and strange declarations of their apostles have drowned the quieter accents of the orthodox.

It seems as though the moment of puberty were far more critical in the spiritual than it is in the physical life: the ordinary dangers of adolescence being intensified when they appear upon the higher levels of consciousness. In the condition of psychic instability which is characteristic of his movement to new states, man is unusually at the mercy of the suggestions and impressions which he receives. Hence in every period of true mystical activity we find an outbreak of occultism, illuminism, or other perverted spirituality and--even more dangerous and confusing for the student--a borderland region where the mystical and psychical meet. In the youth of the Christian Church, side by side with genuine mysticism descending from the Johannine writings or brought in by the Christian Neoplatonists, we have the arrogant and disorderly transcendentalism of the Gnostics: their attempted fusion of the ideals of mysticism and magic. During the Middle Ages and the Renaissance there are the spurious mysticism of the Brethren of the Free Spirit, the occult propaganda of Paracelsus, the Rosicrucians, the Christian Kabalists; and the innumerable pantheistic, Manichean, mystery-making, and Quietist heresies which made war upon Catholic tradition. In the modern world, Theosophy in its various forms is probably the most widespread and respectable representative of the occult tradition.

The root idea from which these varied beliefs and practices develop is always the same; and, since right doctrine is often most easily defined by contrast with its opposite, its study is likely to help us to fix more precisely the true characters of mysticism. Leaving therefore the specifically mystical error of Quietism until we come to the detailed discussion of the contemplative states, we will consider here some of those other supernormal activities of the self which we have already agreed to classify as magic: and learn through them more of those hidden and half-comprehended forces which she has at her command.

The word "magic" is out of fashion, though its spirit was never more widely diffused than at the present time. Thanks to the gradual debasement of the verbal currency, it suggests to the ordinary reader the production of optical illusions and other parlour tricks. It has dragged with it in its fall the terrific verb "to conjure," which, forgetting that it once undertook to compel the spirits of men and angels, is now content to produce rabbits from top-hats. These facts would have little importance, were it not that modern occultists--annoyed, one supposes, by this abuse of their ancient title--constantly arrogate to their tenets and practices the name of "Mystical Science." Vaughan, in his rather supercilious survey of the mystics, classed all forms of white magic, alchemy, and occult philosophy as "theurgic mysticism," [306] and, on the other side of the shield, the occultists display an increasing eagerness to claim the mystics as masters in their school. [307] Even the "three-fold way" of mysticism has been adopted by them and relabelled "Probation, Enlightenment, Initiation." [308]

In our search for the characteristics of mysticism we have already marked the boundary which separates it from magic: and tried to define the true nature and intention of occult philosophy. [309] We saw that it represented the instinctive human "desire to know more" applied to suprasensible things. For good or ill this desire, and the occult sciences and magic arts which express it, have haunted humanity from the earliest times. No student of man can neglect their investigation, however distasteful to his intelligence their superficial absurdities may be. The starting-point of all magic, and of all magical religion--the best and purest of occult activities--is, as in mysticism, man's inextinguishable conviction that there are other planes of being than those which his senses report to him; and its proceedings represent the intellectual and individualistic results of this conviction--his craving for the hidden knowledge. It is, in the eyes of those who really practise it, a moyen de parvenir: not the performance of illicit tricks, but a serious attempt to solve the riddle of the world. Its result, according to a modern writer upon occult philosophy, "comprises an actual, positive, and realizable knowledge concerning the worlds which we denominate invisible, because they transcend the imperfect and rudimentary faculties of a partially developed humanity, and concerning the latent potentialities which constitute--by the fact of their latency--the interior man. In more strictly philosophical language, the Hermetic science is a method of transcending the phenomenal world and attaining to the reality which is behind phenomena."[310]

Though fragments of this enormous claim seem able to justify themselves in experience, the whole of it cannot be admitted. The last phrase in particular is identical with the promise which we have seen to be characteristic of mysticism. It presents magic as a pathway to reality; a promise which it cannot fulfil, for the mere transcending of phenomena does not entail the attainment of the Absolute. Magic even at its best extends rather than escapes the boundaries of the phenomenal world. It stands, where genuine, for that form of transcendentalism which does abnormal things, but does not lead anywhere: and we are likely to fall victims to some kind of magic the moment that the declaration "I want to know" ousts the declaration "I want to be" from the chief place in our consciousness. The true "science of ultimates" must be a science of pure Being, for reasons which the reader is now in a position to discover for himself. But magic is merely a system whereby the self tries to assuage its transcendental curiosity by extending the activities of the will beyond their usual limits; sometimes, according to its own account, obtaining by this means an experimental knowledge of planes of existence usually--but inaccurately--regarded as "supernatural."

Even this modified claim needs justification. For most persons who do not specialize in the eccentric sciences the occultist can only be said to exist in either the commercial or the academic sense. The fortune-teller represents one class; the annotator of improper grimoires the other. In neither department is the thing supposed to be taken seriously: it is merely the means of obtaining money, or of assuaging a rather morbid curiosity.

Such a view is far from accurate. In magic, whether regarded as a superstition or a science, we have at any rate the survival of a great and ancient tradition, the true meaning of whose title should hardly have been lost in a Christian country; for it claims to be the science of those Magi whose quest of the symbolic Blazing Star brought them once, at least, to the cradle of the Incarnate God. Its laws, and the ceremonial rites which express those laws, have come down from immemorial antiquity. They appear to enshrine a certain definite knowledge, and a large number of less definite theories, concerning the sensual and supersensual worlds, and concerning powers which man, according to occult thinkers, may develop if he will. Orthodox persons should be careful how they condemn the laws of magic: for they unwittingly conform to many of them whenever they go to church. All ceremonial religion contains some elements of magic. The art of medicine will never wholly cast it off: many centuries ago it gave birth to that which we now call modern science. It seems to possess inextinguishable life. This is not surprising when we perceive how firmly occultism is rooted in psychology: how perfectly it is adapted to certain perennial characteristics of the human mind--its curiosity, its arrogance, its love of mystery.

Magic, in its uncorrupted form, claims to be a practical, intellectual, highly individualistic science; working towards the declared end of enlarging the sphere on which the human will can work, and obtaining experimental knowledge of planes of being usually regarded as transcendental. It is the last descendant of a long line of teaching--the whole teaching, in fact, of the mysteries of Egypt and Greece--which offered to initiate man into a certain secret knowledge and understanding of things. "In every man," says a modern occultist, "there are latent faculties by means of which he can acquire for himself knowledge of the higher worlds . . . as long as the human race has existed there have always been schools in which those who possessed these higher faculties gave instruction to those who were in search of them. Such are called the occult schools, and the instruction which is imparted therein is called esoteric science or the occult teaching." [311]

These occult schools, as they exist in the present day, state their doctrine in terms which seem distressingly prosaic to the romantic inquirer; borrowing from physics and psychology theories of vibration, attraction, mental suggestion and subconscious activity which can be reapplied for their own purposes. According to its modern teachers, magic is simply an extension of the theory and practice of volition beyond the usual limits. The will, says the occultist, is king, not only of the House of Life, but of the universe outside the gates of sense. It is the key to "man limitless" the true "ring of Gyges," which can control the forces of nature known and unknown. This aspect of occult philosophy informs much of the cheap American transcendentalism which is so lightly miscalled mystical by its teachers and converts; Menticulture, "New" or "Higher Thought," and the scriptures of the so-called "New Consciousness." The ingenious authors of "Volo," "The Will to be Well," and "Just How to Wake the Solar Plexus," the seers who assure their eager disciples that by "Concentration" they may acquire not only health, but also that wealth which is "health of circumstance," are no mystics. They are magicians; and teach, though they know it not, little else but the cardinal doctrines of Hermetic science, omitting only their picturesque ceremonial accompaniments. [312]

These cardinal doctrines, in fact, have varied little since their first appearance early in the world's history: though, like the doctrines of theology, they have needed re-statement from time to time. In discussing them I shall quote chiefly from the works of Eliphas Lévi; the pseudonym under which Alphonse Louis Constant, the most readable occult philosopher of the nineteenth century, offered his conclusions to the world.

The tradition of magic, like most other ways of escape which man has offered to his own soul, appears to have originated in the East. It was formulated, developed, and preserved by the religion of Egypt. It made an early appearance in that of Greece. It has its legendary grand master in Hermes Trismegistus, who gave to it its official name of Hermetic Science, and whose status in occultism is much the same as that occupied by Moses in the tradition of the Jews. Fragmentary writings attributed to this personage and said to be derived from the Hermetic books, are the primitive scriptures of occultism: and the probably spurious Table of Emerald, which is said to have been discovered in his tomb, ranks as the magician's Table of Stone. [313] In Gnosticism, in the allegories of the Kabalah, in theosophy, in secret associations which still exist in England, France, and Germany--and even in certain practices embedded in the ceremonial of the Christian Church-- the main conceptions which constitute the "secret wisdom" of magical tradition have wandered down the centuries. The baser off-shoots of that tradition are but too well known, and need not be particularized. [314]

Like the world which it professes to interpret, magic has a body and a soul: an outward vesture of words and ceremonies and an inner doctrine. The outward vesture, which is all that the uninitiated are permitted to perceive, consists of a series of confusing and often ridiculous symbolic veils: of strange words and numbers, grotesque laws and ritual acts, personifications and mystifications. The outward vestures of our religious, political, and social systems--which would probably appear equally irrational to a wholly ignorant yet critical observer--offer an instructive parallel to this aspect of occult philosophy. Stripped of these archaic formulae, symbols, and mystery-mongerings, however, magic as described by its apologists, is found to rest upon three fundamental axioms which can hardly be dismissed as ridiculous by those who listen respectfully to the ever-shifting hypotheses of psychology and physics.

(1) The first axiom declares the existence of an imponderable "medium" or "universal agent," which is described as beyond the plane of our normal sensual perceptions yet interpenetrating and binding up the material world. This agent, which is not luminous and has nothing to do with the stars, is known to the occultists by the unfortunate name of "Astral Light": a term originally borrowed from the Martinists by Eliphas Lévi. To live in conscious communication with the "Astral Light" is to live upon the "Astral Plane," or in the Astral World: to have achieved, that is to say, a new level of consciousness. The education of the occultist is directed towards this end.

This doctrine of the Astral Plane, like most of our other diagrams of the transcendent, possesses a respectable ancestry, and many prosperous relations in the world of philosophic thought. Traces of it may even be detected under veils in the speculations of orthodox physics. It is really identical with the "Archetypal World" or Yesod of the Kabalah--the "Perfect Land" of old Egyptian religion--in which the true or spirit forms of all created things are held to exist. It may be connected with the "real world" described by such visionaries as Boehme and Blake, many of whose experiences are far more occult than mystical in character. [315] A persistent tradition as to the existence of such a plane of being or of consciousness is found all over the world: in Indian, Greek Egyptian, Celtic, and Jewish thought. "Above this visible nature there exists another, unseen and eternal, which, when all things created perish, does not perish," says the Bhagavad Gita. According to the Kabalists it is "the seat of life and vitality, and the nourishment of all the world." [316] Vitalism might accept it as one of those aspects of the universe which can be perceived by a more extended rhythm than that of normal consciousness. Various aspects of the Astral have been identified with the "Burning Body of the Holy Ghost" of Christian Gnosticism and with the Odic force of the old-fashioned spiritualists.

Further, the Astral Plane is regarded as constituting the "Cosmic Memory," where the images of all beings and events are preserved, as they are preserved in the memory of man.

"The high that proved too high, the heroic for earth too hard
The passion that left the ground to lose itself in the sky"--

all are living in the Astral World. There too the concepts of future creation are present in their completeness in the Eternal Now before being brought to birth in the material sphere. On this theory prophecy, and also clairvoyance--one of the great objects of occult education--consist in opening the eyes of the mind upon this timeless Astral World: and spiritualists, evoking the phantoms of the dead, merely call them up from the recesses of universal instead of individual remembrance. The reader who feels his brain to be whirling amidst this medley of solemn statement and unproven fairy tale must remember that the dogmatic part of the occult tradition can only represent the attempt of an extended or otherwise abnormal consciousness to find an explanation of its own experiences.

Further, our whole selves--not merely our sentient selves--are regarded as being bathed in the Astral Light, as in the ether of physics. Hence in occult language it is a "universal agent" connecting soul with soul, and becomes the possible vehicle of hypnotism, telepathy, clairvoyance, and all those supernormal phenomena which are the subject-matter of "psychical research." This hypothesis also accounts for the confusing fact of an initial similarity of experience in many of the proceedings of mystic and occultist. Both must pass through the plane of consciousness which the concept of the "Astral" represents, because this plane of perception is the one which lies "next beyond" our normal life. The transcendental faculties may become aware of this world; only, in the case of the mystic, to pass through it as quickly as they can. But the occultist, the medium, the psychic, rest in the "Astral" and develop their perceptions of this aspect of the world. It is the medium in which they work.

From earliest times, occult philosophy has insisted on the existence of this medium: as a scientific fact, outside the range of our normal senses, but susceptible of verification by the trained powers of the "initiate." The possessor of such trained powers, not the wizard or the fortune-teller, is regarded as the true magician: and it is the declared object of occult education, or initiation, to actualize this supersensual plane of experience, to give the student the power of entering into conscious communion with it, and teach him to impose upon its forces the directive force of his own will, as easily as he imposes that will upon the "material" things of senses. [317]

(2) This brings us to the second axiom of magic, which also has a curiously modern air: for it postulates simply the limitless power of the disciplined human will. This dogma has been "taken over" without acknowledgment from occult philosophy to become the trump card of menticulture, "Christian Science," and "New Thought." The preachers of "Joy Philosophy" and other dilute forms of mental discipline, the Liberal Catholic "priest" producing "a vast bubble of etheric astromental matter, a thought-edifice, ethereal, diaphanous, a bubble which just includes the congregation. . ." [318] these are the true hierophants of magic in the modern world. [319]

The first lesson of the would-be magus is self-mastery. "By means of persevering and gradual athletics," says Eliphas Lévi, "the powers of the body can be developed to an amazing extent. It is the same with the powers of the soul. Would you govern yourself and others? Learn how to will. How may one learn how to will? This is the first secret of magical initiation; and it was to make the foundations of this secret thoroughly understood that the antique keepers of the mysteries surrounded the approach to the sanctuary with so many terrors and illusions. They did not believe in a will until it had given its proofs; and they were right. Strength cannot prove itself except by conquest. Idleness and negligence are the enemies of the will, and this is the reason why all religions have multiplied their practices and made their cults difficult and minute. The more trouble one gives oneself for an idea, the more power one acquires in regard to that idea. . . . Hence the power of religions resides entirely in the inflexible will of those who practise them." [320]

This last sentence alone is enough to define the distinction between mysticism and magic, and clear the minds of those who tend to confuse the mystical and magical elements of religion. In accordance with it, real "magical initiation" is in essence a form of mental discipline, strengthening and focussing the will. This discipline, like that of the religious life, consists partly in physical austerities and a deliberate divorce from the world, partly in the cultivation of will-power: but largely in a yielding of the mind to the influence of suggestions which have been selected and accumulated in the course of ages because of their power over that imagination which Eliphas Lévi calls "The eye of the soul." There is nothing supernatural about it. Like the more arduous, more disinterested self-training of the mystic, it is character-building with an object, conducted upon an heroic scale. In magic the "will to know" is the centre round which the personality is rearranged. As in mysticism, unconscious factors are dragged from the hiddenness to form part of that personality. The uprushes of thought, the abrupt intuitions which reach us from the subliminal region, are developed, ordered, and controlled by rhythms and symbols which have become traditional because the experience of centuries has proved, though it cannot explain, their efficacy: and powers of apprehension which normally lie below the threshold may thus be liberated and enabled to report their discoveries.

"The fundamental principle," says A. E. Waite, speaking of occult evocations, "was in the exercise of a certain occult force resident in the magus, and strenuously exerted for the establishment of such a correspondence between two planes of nature as would effect his desired end. This exertion was termed the evocation, conjuration, or calling of the spirit, but that which in reality was raised was the energy of the inner man ; tremendously developed and exalted by combined will and aspiration, this energy germinated by sheer force a new intellectual faculty of sensible psychological perception. To assist and stimulate this energy into the most powerful possible operation, artificial means were almost invariably used. . . . The synthesis of these methods and processes was called Ceremonial Magic, which in effect was a tremendous forcing-house of the latent faculties of man's spiritual nature." [321]

This is the psychological explanation of those apparently absurd rituals of preparation, doctrines of signs and numbers, pentacles, charms, angelical names, the "power of the word" which made up ceremonial magic. The power of such artifices is known amongst the Indian mystics; who, recognizing in the Mantra, or occult and rhythmic formula, consciously held and repeated, an invaluable help to the attainment of the true ecstatic state, are not ashamed to borrow from the magicians. So, too, the modern American schools of mental healing and New Thought recommend concentration upon a carefully selected word as the starting-point of efficacious meditation. This fact of the psychical effect of certain verbal combinations, when allowed to dominate the field of consciousness, may have some bearing upon that need of a formal liturgy which is felt by nearly every great religion; for religion, on its ceremonial side, has certain affinities with magic. It, too, seeks by sensible means to stimulate suprasensible energies. The true magic "word" or spell is untranslatable; because its power resides only partially in that outward sense which is apprehended by the reason, but chiefly in the rhythm, which is addressed to the subliminal mind. Symbols, religious and other, and symbolic acts which appear meaningless when judged by the intellect alone, perform a similar office. They express the deep-seated instinct of the human mind that it must have a focus on which to concentrate its volitional powers, if those powers are to be brought to their highest state of efficiency. The nature of the focus matters little: its office matters much.

". . . All these figures, and acts analogous to them," says Lévi, "all these dispositions of numbers and of characters [i.e. sacred words, charms, pentacles, etc.] are, as we have said, but instruments for the education of the will, of which they fix and determine the habits. They serve also to concentrate in action all the powers of the human soul, and to strengthen the creative power of the imagination. . . . A practice, even though it be superstitious and foolish, may be efficacious because it is a realization of the will. . . . We laugh at the poor woman who denies herself a ha'porth of milk in the morning, that she may take a little candle to burn upon the magic triangle in some chapel. But those who laugh are ignorant, and the poor woman does not pay too dearly for the courage and resignation which she thus obtains. [322]

Magic symbols, therefore, from penny candles to Solomon's seal, fall in modern technical language into two classes. The first contains instruments of self-suggestion, exaltation, and will direction. To this belong all spells, charms, rituals, perfumes: from the magician's vervain wreath to the "Youth! Health! Strength!" which the student of New Thought repeats when she is brushing her hair in the morning. The second class contains autoscopes: i.e. , material objects which focus and express the subconscious perceptions of the operator. The dowser's divining rod, fortuneteller's cards, and crystal-gazer's ball, are characteristic examples. Both kinds are rendered necessary rather by the disabilities of the human than by the peculiarities of the superhuman plane: and the great adept may attain heights at which he dispenses with these "outward and visible signs." "Ceremonies being, as we have said, artificial methods of creating certain habits of the will, they cease to be necessary when these habits have become fixed." [323] These facts, now commonplaces of psychology, have long been known and used by students of magic. Those who judge the philosophy by the apparent absurdity of its symbols and ceremonies should remember that the embraces, gestures, grimaces, and other ritual acts by which we all concentrate, liberate, or express love, wrath, or enthusiasm, will ill endure the cold revealing light of a strictly rational inquiry.

(3) The dogmas of the "Astral Light" or universal agent and the "power of the will" are completed by a third: the doctrine of Analogy, of an implicit correspondence between appearance and reality, the microcosm of man and the macrocosm of the universe the seen and the unseen worlds. In this, occultism finds the basis of its transcendental speculations. Quod superius sicut quod inferius --the first words of that Emerald Table which was once attributed to Hermes Trismegistus himself--is an axiom which must be agreeable to all Platonists. It plays a great part in the theory of mysticism; which, whilst maintaining an awed sense of the total "otherness" and incomprehensibility of the Divine, has always assumed that the path of the individual soul towards loving union with the Absolute is somehow analogous with the path on which the universe moves to its consummation in God.

The notion of analogy ultimately determines the religious concepts of every race, and resembles the verities of faith in the breadth of its application. It embraces alike the appearances of the visible world--which thus become the mirrors of the invisible--the symbols of religion, the tiresome arguments of Butler's "Analogy," the allegories of the Kabalah and the spiritual alchemists, and that childish "doctrine of signatures" on which much of mediaeval science was built. "Analogy," says Lévi, [324] "is the last word of science and the first word of faith . . . the sole possible mediator between the visible and the invisible, between the finite and the infinite." Here Magic clearly defines her own limitations; stepping incautiously from the useful to the universal, and laying down a doctrine which no mystic could accept--which, carried to its logical conclusion, would turn the adventure of the infinite into a guessing game.

The argument by analogy is carried by the occultists to lengths which cannot be described here. Armed with this torch, they explore the darkest, most terrible mysteries of life: and do not hesitate to cast the grotesque shadows of these mysteries upon the unseen world. The principle of correspondence is no doubt sound so long as it works within reasonable limits. It was admitted into the system of the Kabalah, though that profound and astute philosophy was far from giving to it the importance which it assumes in Hermetic "science." It has been eagerly accepted by many of the mystics. Boehme and Swedenborg availed themselves of its method in presenting their intuitions to the world. It is implicitly acknowledged by thinkers of many other schools: its influence permeates the best periods of literature. Sir Thomas Browne spoke for more than himself when he said, in a well-known passage of the "Religio Medici": "The severe schools shall never laugh me out of the philosophy of Hermes [i.e. , Trismegistus] that this visible world is but a picture of the invisible, wherein, as in a portrait, things are not truly but in equivocal shapes, and as they counterfeit some real substance in that invisible framework." Such a sense of analogy, whatever the "severe schools" may say, is indeed the foundation of every perfect work of art. "Intuitive perception of the hidden analogies of things," says Hazlitt in "English Novelists," "or, as it may be called, his instinct of the imagination, is perhaps what stamps the character of genius on the productions of art more than any other circumstance."

The central doctrine of magic may now be summed up thus:--

(1) That a supersensible and real "cosmic medium" exists, which interpenetrates, influences, and supports the tangible and apparent world, and is amenable to the categories both of philosophy and of physics.

(2) That there is an established analogy and equilibrium between the real and unseen world, and the illusory manifestations which we call the world of sense.

(3) That this analogy may be discerned, and this equilibrium controlled, by the disciplined will of man, which thus becomes master of itself and of fate.

We must now examine in more detail the third of these propositions--that which ascribes abnormal powers to the educated and disciplined will--for this assumption lies at the root of all magical practices, old and new. "Magical operations," says Eliphas Lévi, "are the exercise of a power which is natural, but superior to the ordinary powers of nature. They are the result of a science, and of habits, which exalt the human will above its usual limits." [325] This power of the will is now recognized as playing an important part both in the healing of the body and the healing of the soul; for our most advanced theories on these subjects are little more than the old wine of magic in new bottles. The ancient occultists owed much of their power, and also of their evil reputation, to the fact that they were psychologists before their time. Effective methods of suggestion, recipes for the alteration and exaltation of personality and enhancement of will-power, the artificial production of hypnotic states, photisms, automatism and ecstasy, with the opening up of the subliminal field which accompanies these phenomena--concealed from the profane by a mass of confusing allegories and verbiage--form the backbone of all genuine occult rituals. Their authors were aware that ceremonial magic has no objective importance, but depends solely on its effect upon the operator's mind. That this effect might be enhanced, it was given an atmosphere of sanctity and mystery; its rules were strict, its higher rites difficult of attainment. These rules and rites constituted at once a test of the student's earnestness and a veil guarding the sanctuary from the profane. The long and difficult preparations, majestic phrases, and strange ceremonies of an evocation had power, not over the spirit of the dead, but over the consciousness of the living; who was thus caught up from the world of sense to a new plane of perception. Thus, according to its apologists, the education of the genuine occult student tends to awaken in him a new view and a new attitude. It adjusts the machinery of his cinematograph to the registering of new intervals in the stream of things, which passed it by before; and thus introduces new elements into that picture by which ordinary men are content to know and judge the--or rather their-- universe.

So much for the principles which govern occult education. Magic therapeutics, or as it is now called, "mental healing," is but the application of these principles upon another plane. It results, first, from a view of humanity which sees a difference only of degree between diseases of body and of soul, and can state seriously and in good faith that "moral maladies are more contagious than physical, and there are some triumphs of infatuation and fashion which are comparable to leprosy or cholera." [326] Secondly, it is worked by that enhancement of will power, that ability to alter and control weaker forms of life, which is claimed as the reward of the occult discipline. "All the power of the occult healer lies in his conscious will and all his art consists in producing faith in the patient." [327]

This simple truth was in the possession of occult thinkers at a time when Church and State saw no third course between the burning or beatification of its practitioners. Now, under the polite names of mental hygiene, suggestion, and psycho-therapeutics, it is steadily advancing to the front rank of medical shibboleths. Yet it is still the same "magic art" which has been employed for centuries, with varying ritual accompaniments, by the adepts of occult science. The methods of Brother Hilarian Tissot, who is described as curing lunacy and crime by "the unconscious use of the magnetism of Paracelsus," who attributed his cases "either to disorder of the will or to the perverse influence of external wills," and would "regard all crimes as acts of madness and treat the wicked as diseased," [328] anticipated in many respects those of the most modern psychologists.

The doctrine of magic which has here been described shows us the "Secret Wisdom" at its best and sanest. But even on these levels, it is dogged by the defects which so decisively separate the occultist from the mystic. The chief of these is the peculiar temper of mind, the cold intellectual arrogance, the intensely individual point of view which occult studies seem to induce by their conscious quest of exclusive power and knowledge, their implicit neglect of love. At bottom, every student of occultism is striving towards a point at which he may be able to "touch the button" and rely on the transcendental world "springing to do the rest." In this hard-earned acquirement of power over the Many, he tends to forget the One. In Levi's words, "Too deep a study of the mysteries of nature may estrange from God the careless investigator, in whom mental fatigue paralyses the ardours of the heart."[329] When he wrote this sentence Lévi stood, as the greater occultists have often done, at the frontiers of mysticism. The best of the Hermetic philosophers, indeed, are hardly ever without such mystical hankerings, such flashes of illumination; as if the transcendental powers of man, once roused from sleep, cannot wholly ignore the true end for which they were made.

In Levi's case, as is well known, the discord between the occult and mystical ideals was resolved by his return to the Catholic Church. Characteristically, he "read into" Catholicism much that the orthodox would hardly allow; so that it became for him, as it were, a romantic gloss on the occult tradition. He held that the Christian Church, nursing mother of the mystics, was also the heir of the magi; and that popular piety and popular magic veiled the same ineffable truths. He had more justification than at first appears probable for this apparently wild and certainly heretical statement. Religion, as we have seen, can never entirely divorce herself from magic: for her rituals and sacraments must have, if they are to be successful in their appeal to the mind, a certain magical character. All persons who are naturally drawn towards the ceremonial aspect of religion are acknowledging the strange power of subtle rhythms, symbolic words and movements, over the human will. An "impressive service" conforms exactly to the description which I have already quoted of a magical rite: it is "a tremendous forcing-house of the latent faculties of man's spiritual nature." Sacraments, too, however simple their beginnings, always tend, as they evolve, to assume upon the phenomenal plane a magical aspect--a fact which does not invalidate their claim to be the vehicles of supernatural grace. Those who have observed with understanding, for instance, the Roman rite of baptism, with its spells and exorcisms, its truly Hermetic employment of salt, anointing chrism and ceremonial lights, must have seen in it a ceremony far nearer to the operations of white magic than to the simple lustrations practiced by St. John the Baptist.

There are obvious objections to the full working out of this subject in a book which is addressed to readers of all shades of belief; but any student who is interested in this branch of religious psychology may easily discover for himself the occult elements in the liturgies of the Christian--or indeed of any other--Church. There are invocative arrangements of the Names of God which appear alike in grimoire and in Missal. Sacred numbers, ritual actions, perfumes, purifications, words of power, are all used, and rightly used by institutional religion in her work of opening up the human mind to the messages of the suprasensible world. In certain minor observances, and charm-like prayers, we seem to stand on the very borderland between magician and priest.

It is surely inevitable that this should be so. The business of the Church is to appeal to the whole man, as she finds him living in the world of sense. She would hardly be adequate to this task did she neglect the powerful weapons which the occultist has developed for his own ends. She, who takes the simplest and most common gifts of nature and transmutes them into heavenly food, takes also every discovery which the self has made concerning its own potentialities, and turns them to her own high purposes. Founding her external system on sacraments and symbols, on rhythmic invocations and ceremonial acts of praise, insisting on the power of the pure and self-denying will and the "magic chain" of congregational worship, she does but join hands with those Magi whose gold, frankincense, and myrrh were the first gifts that she received.

But she pays for this; sharing some of the limitations of the system which her Catholic nature has compelled her to absorb. It is true, of course, that she purges it of all its baser elements--its arrogance, its curiosity--true also that she is bound to adopt it, because it is the highest common measure which she can apply to the spirituality of that world to which she is sent. But she cannot--and her great teachers have always known that she cannot--extract finality from a method which does not really seek after ultimate things. This method may and does teach men goodness, gives them happiness and health. It can even induce in them a certain exaltation in which they become aware, at any rate for a moment, of the existence of the supernatural world--a stupendous accomplishment. But it will not of itself make them citizens of that world: give to them the freedom of Reality.

"The work of the Church in the world," says Patmore, "is not to teach the mysteries of life, so much as to persuade the soul to that arduous degree of purity at which God Himself becomes her teacher. The work of the Church ends when the knowledge of God begins." [330]

Footnotes:

306. R. A. Vaughan, "Hours with the Mystics," vol. i. bk. i. ch. v.

307. In a list published by Papus from the archives of the Martinists, we find such diverse names

as Averroes, St. Thomas Aquinas, Vincent of Beauvais, and Swedenborg, given as followers of the occult tradition!

308. See R. Steiner, "The Way of Initiation," p. 111.

309. Supra, pp. 70 seq .

310. A. E. Waite, "The Occult Sciences," p. 1.

311. Steiner, "The Way of Initiation," p. 66.

312. See E. Towne, "Joy Philosophy" (1903) and "Just How to Wake the Solar Plexus" (1904); R. D. Stocker, "New Thought Manual" (1906) and "Soul Culture" (1905); Floyd Wilson, "Man Limitless" (1905). The literature of these sects is enormous. For a critical and entertaining account, see C. W. Ferguson, The Confusion of Tongues." (1929).

313. It must here be pointed out that the genuine "Hermetica"--a body of ancient philosophic and religious pieces collected under this general title--are entirely unconnected with occultism. Cf. "Hermetica," ed. with English translation by W. Scott. 3 vols. 1924-8.

314. A. E. Waite, a life-long student of these byeways of thought, gives, as the main channels by which "an arcane knowledge is believed to have been communicated to the West," Magic, Alchemy, Astrology, the occult associations which culminated in Freemasonry, and, finally, "an obscure sheaf of hieroglyphs known as Tarot cards." He places in another class "the bewitchments and other mummeries of Ceremonial Magic." ("The Holy Kabbalah," pp. 518-19.)

315. For a discussion of the Gnostic and Theosophic elements in Blake's work see D. Surat, "Blake and Modern Thought" (1929).

316. A. E. Waite, "Doctrine and Literature of the Kabbalah," p. 48.

317. I offer no opinion as to the truth or falsity of these "occult" claims. For a more detailed discussion the reader is referred to Steiner's curious little book, "The Way of Initiation."

318. C. W. Leadbeater, "The Science of the Sacraments," p. 38.

319. Compare the following: "Imagine that all the world and the starry hosts are waiting, alert and with shining eyes, to do your bidding. Imagine that you are to touch the button now, and instantly they will spring to do the rest. The instant you say, I can and I will,' the entire powers of the universe are to be set in motion" (E. Towne, "Joy Philosophy," p. 52).

320. "Rituel de la Haute Magie," pp. 35, 36.

321. "The Occult Sciences," p. 14. But references in Mr. Waite's most recent work to "the puerilities and imbecility of ceremonial magic" suggest that he has modified his views. Cf. "The Holy Kabbalah" (1929), p. 521.

322. "Rituel de la Haute Magie," p. 71.

323. "Rituel de la Haute Magie," p. 139.

324. "Dogme de la Haute Magie," p. 361 et seq.

325. "Rituel de la Haute Magie," p. 32.

326. "Dogme de la Haute Magie," p. 129.

327. "Rituel," p. 312.

328. "Dogma," p. 134.

329. "Histoire de la Magie," p. 514.

330. "The Rod, the Root, and the Flower," "Knowledge and Science," xxii.

PART TWO: THE MYSTIC WAY

"As the Pilgrim passes while the Country permanent remains
So Men pass on; but the States remain permanent forever."
Blake, "Jerusalem."

CHAPTER I

We are now to turn from general principles and study those principles in action: to describe the psychological process, or "Mystic Way," by which that peculiar type of personality which is able to set up direct relations with the Absolute is usually developed. The difficulty of this description will lie in the fact that all mystics differ one from another; as all the individual objects of our perception, "living" and "not living," do. The creative impulse in the world, so far as we are aware of it, appears upon ultimate analysis to be free and original not bound and mechanical: to express itself, in defiance of the determinists, with a certain artistic spontaneity. Man, when he picks out some point of likeness as a basis on which to arrange its productions in groups, is not discovering its methods; but merely making for his own convenience an arbitrary choice of one or two--not necessarily characteristic--qualities, which happen to appear in a certain number of different persons or things. Hence the most scientific classification is a rough-and-ready business at the best. [331]

When we come to apply such classification to so delicate and elusive a series of psychological states as those which accompany the "contemplative life," all the usual difficulties are increased. No one mystic can be discovered in whom all the observed characteristics of the transcendental consciousness are resumed, and who can on that account be treated as typical. Mental states which are distinct and mutually exclusive in one case, exist simultaneously in another. In some, stages which have been regarded as essential are entirely omitted: in others, their order appears to be reversed. We seem at first to be confronted by a group of selves which arrive at the same end without obeying any general law.

Take, however, a number of such definitely mystical selves and make of them, so to speak, a "composite portrait": as anthropologists do when they wish to discover the character of a race. From this portrait we may expect a type to emerge, in which all the outstanding characteristics contributed by the individual examples are present together, and minor variations are suppressed. Such a portrait will of course be conventional: but it will be useful as a standard, which can be constantly compared with, and corrected by, isolated specimens.

The first thing we notice about this composite portrait is that the typical mystic seems to move towards his goal through a series of strongly marked oscillations between "states of pleasure" and "states of pain." The existence and succession of these states--sometimes broken and confused, sometimes crisply defined--can be traced, to a greater or less degree, in almost every case of which we possess anything like a detailed record. Gyrans gyrando radii spiritus . The soul, as it treads the ascending spiral of its road towards reality, experiences alternately the sunshine and the shade. These experiences are "constants" of the transcendental life. "The Spiritual States of the Soul are all Eternal," said Blake, with the true mystical genius for psychology. [332]

The complete series of these states--and it must not be forgotten that few individuals present them all in perfection, whilst in many instances several are blurred or appear to be completely suppressed--will be, I think, most conveniently arranged under five heads. This method of grouping means, of course, the abandonment of the time-honoured threefold division of the Mystic Way, and the apparent neglect of St. Teresa's equally celebrated Seven Degrees of Contemplation; but I think that we shall gain more than we lose by adopting it. The groups, however, must be looked upon throughout as diagrammatic, and only as answering loosely and generally to experiences which seldom present themselves in so rigid and unmixed a form. These experiences, largely conditioned as they are by surroundings and by temperament, exhibit all the variety and spontaneity which are characteristic of life in its highest manifestations: and, like biological specimens, they lose something of their essential reality in being prepared for scientific investigation. Taken all together, they constitute phases in a single process of growth; involving the movement of consciousness from lower to higher levels of reality, the steady remaking of character in accordance with the "independent spiritual world." But as the study of physical life is made easier for us by an artificial division into infancy, adolescence, maturity, and old age, so a discreet indulgence of the human passion for map-making will increase our chances of understanding the nature of the Mystic Way.

Here, then, is the classification under which we shall study the phases of the mystical life.

(1) The awakening of the Self to consciousness of Divine Reality. This experience, usually abrupt and well-marked, is accompanied by intense feelings of joy and exaltation.

(2) The Self, aware for the first time of Divine Beauty, realizes by contrast its own finiteness and imperfection, the manifold illusions in which it is immersed, the immense distance which separates it from the One. Its attempts to eliminate by discipline and mortification all that stands in the way of its progress towards union with God constitute Purgation: a state of pain and effort.

(3) When by Purgation the Self has become detached from the "things of sense," and acquired those virtues which are the "ornaments of the spiritual marriage," its joyful consciousness of the Transcendent Order returns in an enhanced form. Like the prisoners in Plato's "Cave of Illusion," it has awakened to knowledge of Reality, has struggled up the harsh and difficult path to the mouth of the cave. Now it looks upon the sun. This is Illumination: a state which includes in itself many of the stages of contemplation, "degrees of orison," visions and adventures of the soul described by St. Teresa and other mystical writers. These form, as it were, a way within the Way: a moyen de parvenir, a training devised by experts which will strengthen and assist the mounting soul. They stand, so to speak, for education; whilst the Way proper represents organic growth. Illumination is the "contemplative state" par excellence. It forms, with the two preceding states, the "first mystic life." Many mystics never go beyond it; and, on the other hand, many seers and artists not usually classed amongst them, have shared, to some extent, the experiences of the illuminated state. Illumination brings a certain apprehension of the Absolute, a sense of the Divine Presence: but not true union with it. It is a state of happiness.

(4) In the development of the great and strenuous seekers after God, this is followed--or sometimes intermittently accompanied--by the most terrible of all the experiences of the Mystic Way: the final and complete purification of the Self, which is called by some contemplatives the "mystic pain" or "mystic death," by others the Purification of the Spirit or Dark Night of the Soul. The consciousness which had, in Illumination, sunned itself in the sense of the Divine Presence, now suffers under an equally intense sense of the Divine Absence: learning to dissociate the personal satisfaction of mystical vision from the reality of mystical life. As in Purgation the senses were cleansed and humbled, and the energies and interests of the Self were concentrated upon transcendental things: so now the purifying process is extended to the very centre of I-hood, the will. The human instinct for personal happiness must be killed. This is the "spiritual crucifixion" so often described by the mystics: the great desolation in which the soul seems abandoned by the Divine. The Self now surrenders itself, its individuality, and its will, completely. It desires nothing, asks nothing, is utterly passive, and is thus prepared for

(5) Union: the true goal of the mystic quest. In this state the Absolute Life is not merely perceived and enjoyed by the Self, as in Illumination: but is one with it. This is the end towards which all the previous oscillations of consciousness have tended. It is a state of equilibrium, of purely spiritual life; characterized by peaceful joy, by enhanced powers, by intense certitude. To call this state, as some authorities do, by the name of Ecstasy, is inaccurate and confusing: since the term Ecstasy has long been used both by psychologists and ascetic writers to define that short and rapturous trance--a state with well-marked physical and psychical accompaniments--in which the contemplative, losing all consciousness of the phenomenal world, is caught up to a brief and immediate enjoyment of the Divine Vision. Ecstasies of this kind are often experienced by the mystic in Illumination, or even on his first conversion. They cannot therefore be regarded as exclusively characteristic of the Unitive Way. In some of the greatest mystics--St. Teresa is an example--the ecstatic trance seems to diminish rather than increase in frequency after the state of union has been attained: whilst others achieve the heights by a path which leaves on one side all abnormal phenomena.

Union must be looked upon as the true goal of mystical growth; that permanent establishment of life upon transcendent levels of reality, of which ecstasies give a foretaste to the soul. Intense forms of it, described by individual mystics, under symbols such as those of Mystical Marriage, Deification, or Divine Fecundity, all prove on examination to be aspects of this same experience "seen through a temperament."

It is right, however, to state here that Oriental Mysticism insists upon a further stage beyond that of union, which stage it regards as the real goal of the spiritual life. This is the total annihilation or reabsorption of the individual soul in the Infinite. Such an annihilation is said by the Sufis to constitute the "Eighth Stage of Progress," in which alone they truly attain to God. Thus stated, it appears to differ little from the Buddhist's Nirvana, and is the logical corollary of that pantheism to which the Oriental mystic always tends. Thus Jalalu d'Din:

"O, let me not exist! for Non-Existence
Proclaims in organ tones, To Him we shall return.'"[333]

It is at least doubtful, however, whether the interpretation which has been put by European students upon such passages as this be correct. The language in which Al Ghazzali attempts to describe the Eighth Stage is certainly more applicable to the Unitive Life as understood by Christian contemplatives, than to the Buddhistic annihilation of personality. "The end of Sufi-ism," he says, "is total absorption in God. This is at least the relative end to that part of their doctrine which I am free to reveal and describe. But in reality it is but the beginning of the Sufi life, for those intuitions and other things which precede it are, so to speak, but the porch by which they enter. . . . In this state some have imagined themselves to be amalgamated with God, others to be identical with Him, others again to be associated with Him: but all this is sin ." [334]

The doctrine of annihilation as the end of the soul's ascent, whatever the truth may be as to the Moslem attitude concerning it, is decisively rejected by all European mystics, though a belief in it is constantly imputed to them by their enemies: for their aim is not the suppression of life, but its intensification, a change in its form. This change, they say in a paradox which is generally misunderstood, consists in the perfecting of personality by the utter surrender of self. It is true that the more Orientally-minded amongst them, such as Dionysius the Areopagite, do use language of a negative kind which seems almost to involve a belief in the annihilation rather than the transformation of the self in God: but this is because they are trying to describe a condition of supersensible vitality from the point of view of the normal consciousness to which it can only seem a Nothing, a Dark, a Self-loss. Further it will be found that this language is often an attempt to describe the conditions of transitory perception, not those of permanent existence: the characteristics, that is to say, of the Ecstatic Trance, in which for a short time the whole self is lifted to transcendent levels, and the Absolute is apprehended by a total suspension of the surface consciousness. Hence the Divine Dark, the Nothing, is not a state of non-being to which the mystic aspires to attain: it is rather a paradoxical description of his experience of that Undifferentiated Godhead, that Supernal Light whence he may, in his ecstasies, bring down fire from heaven to light the world.

In the mystics of the West, the highest forms of Divine Union impel the self to some sort of active, rather than of passive life: and this is now recognized by the best authorities as the true distinction between Christian and non-Christian mysticism. "The Christian mystics," says Delacroix, "move from the Infinite to the Definite; they aspire to infinitize life and to define Infinity; they go from the conscious to the subconscious, and from the subconscious to the conscious. The obstacle in their path is not consciousness in general, but self -consciousness, the consciousness of the Ego. The Ego is the limitation, that which opposes itself to the Infinite: the states of consciousness free from self, lost in a vaster consciousness, may become modes of the Infinite, and states of the Divine Consciousness." [335] So Starbuck: "The individual learns to transfer himself from a centre of self-activity into an organ of revelation of universal being, and to live a life of affection for and one-ness with, the larger life outside." [336]

Hence, the ideal of the great contemplatives, the end of their long education, is to become "modes of the Infinite." Filled with an abounding sense of the Divine Life, of ultimate and adorable reality, sustaining and urging them on, they wish to communicate the revelation, the more abundant life, which they have received. Not spiritual marriage, but divine fecundity is to be their final state. In a sense St. Teresa in the Seventh Habitation, Suso when his great renunciation is made, have achieved the quest, yet there is nothing passive in the condition to which they have come. Not Galahad, but the Grail-bearer is now their type: and in their life, words or works they are impelled to exhibit that "Hidden Treasure which desires to be found."

"You may think, my daughters," says St. Teresa, "that the soul in this state [of union] should be so absorbed that she can occupy herself with nothing. You deceive yourselves. She turns with greater ease and ardour than before to all that which belongs to the service of God, and when these occupations leave her free again, she remains in the enjoyment of that companionship." [337]

No temperament is less slothful than the mystical one; and the "quiet" to which the mystics must school themselves in the early stages of contemplation is often the hardest of their tasks. The abandonment of bodily and intellectual activity is only undertaken in order that they may, in the words of Plotinus, "energize enthusiastically" upon another plane. Work they must but this work may take many forms--forms which are sometimes so wholly spiritual that they are not perceptible to practical minds. Much of the misunderstanding and consequent contempt of the contemplative life comes from the narrow and superficial definition of "work" which is set up by a muscular and wage-earning community.

All records of mysticism in the West, then, are also the records of supreme human activity. Not only of "wrestlers in the spirit" but also of great organizers, such as St. Teresa and St. John of the Cross; of missionaries preaching life to the spiritually dead, such as St. Francis of Assisi, St. Ignatius Loyola, Eckhart, Suso Tauler, Fox; of philanthropists, such as St. Catherine of Genoa or St. Vincent de Paul; poets and prophets, such as Mechthild of Magdeburg, Jacopone da Todi and Blake, finally, of some immensely virile souls whose participation in the Absolute Life has seemed to force on them a national destiny. Of this St. Bernard, St. Catherine of Siena, and Saint Joan of Arc are the supreme examples.

"The soul enamoured of My Truth," said God's voice to St. Catherine of Siena, "never ceases to serve the whole world in general." [338]

Utterly remade in the interests of Reality, exhibiting that dual condition of fruition and activity which Ruysbroeck described as the crowning stage of human evolution, the "Supreme summit of the Inner Life," [339] all these lived, as it were, with both hands towards the finite and towards the Infinite, towards God and man. It is true that in nearly every case such "great actives" have first left the world, as a necessary condition of establishing communion with that Absolute Life which reinforced their own: for a mind distracted by the many cannot apprehend the One. Hence something equivalent to the solitude of the wilderness is an essential part of mystical education. But, having established that communion, re-ordered their inner lives upon transcendent levels--being united with their Source not merely in temporary ecstasies, but in virtue of a permanent condition of the soul, they were impelled to abandon their solitude; and resumed, in some way, their contact with the world in order to become the medium whereby that Life flowed out to other men. To go up alone into the mountain and come back as an ambassador to the world, has ever been the method of humanity's best friends. This systole-and-diastole motion of retreat as the preliminary to a return remains the true ideal of Christian Mysticism in its highest development. Those in whom it is not found, however great in other respects they may be, must be considered as having stopped short of the final stage.

Thus St. Catherine of Siena spent three years in hermit-like seclusion in the little room which we still see in her house in the Via Benincasa, entirely cut off from the ordinary life of her family. "Within her own house," says her legend, "she found the desert; and a solitude in the midst of people." [340] There Catherine endured many mortifications, was visited by ecstasies and visions: passed, in fact, through the states of Purgation and Illumination, which existed in her case side by side. This life of solitude was brought to an abrupt end by the experience which is symbolized in the vision of the Mystic Marriage, and the Voice which then said to her, "Now will I wed thy soul, which shall ever be conjoined and united to Me!" Catherine, who had during her long retreat enjoyed illumination to a high degree, now entered upon the Unitive State, in which the whole of her public life was passed. Its effect was immediately noticeable. She abandoned her solitude, joined in the family life, went out into the city to serve the poor and sick, attracted and taught disciples, converted sinners, and began that career of varied and boundless activity which has made her name one of the greatest in the history of the fourteenth century. Nor does this mean that she ceased to live the sort of life which is characteristic of mystical consciousness: to experience direct contact with the Transcendental World, to gaze into "the Abyss of Love Divine." On the contrary, her practical genius for affairs, her immense power of ruling men, drew its strength from the long series of visions and ecstasies which accompanied and supported her labours in the world. She "descended into the valley of lilies to make herself more fruitful," says her legend.[341] The conscious vehicle of some "power not herself," she spoke and acted with an authority which might have seemed strange enough in an uneducated daughter of the people, were it not justified by the fact that all who came into contact with her submitted to its influence.

Our business, then, is to trace from its beginning a gradual and complete change in the equilibrium of the self. It is a change whereby that self turns from the unreal world of sense in which it is normally immersed, first to apprehend, then to unite itself with Absolute Reality: finally, possessed by and wholly surrendered to this Transcendent Life, becomes a medium whereby the spiritual world is seen in a unique degree operating directly in the world of sense. In other words, we are to see the human mind advance from the mere perception of phenomena, through the intuition--with occasional contact--of the Absolute under its aspect of Divine Transcendence, to the entire realization of, and union with, Absolute Life under its aspect of Divine Immanence.

The completed mystical life, then, is more than intuitional: it is theopathetic. In the old, frank language of the mystics, it is the deified life .

Footnotes:

331. Science seems more and more inclined to acquiesce in this judgment. See especially A. N. Whitehead: "Man and the Modern World" and "Religion in the Making."

332. "Jerusalem," pt. iii.

333. Quoted by R. A. Nicholson, "The Mystics of Islam," p. 168.

334. Schmölders, "Les Écoles Philosophiques chez les Arabes," p. 61.

335. "Études sur le Mysticisme," p. 235.

336. "The Psychology of Religion," p. 147.

337. "El Castillo Interior," Moradas Sétimas, cap. i.

338. Dialogo, cap. vii.

339. "De Ornatu Spiritalium Nuptiarum," I. ii. cap. lxxiii.

340. E. Gardner, "St. Catherine of Siena," p. 15.

341. S. Catherine Senensis Vitae (Acta SS. Aprilis t. iii.), ii. ii. § 4.

CHAPTER II

First in the sequence of the mystic states, we must consider that decisive event, the awakening of the transcendental consciousness.

This awakening, from the psychological point of view, appears to be an intense form of the phenomenon of "conversion"; and closely akin to those deep and permanent conversions of the adult type which some religious psychologists call "sanctification." [342] It is a disturbance of the equilibrium of the self, which results in the shifting of the field of consciousness from lower to higher levels, with a consequent removal of the centre of interest from the subject to an object now brought into view: the necessary beginning of any process of transcendence. It must not, however, be confused or identified with religious conversion as ordinarily understood: the sudden and emotional acceptance of theological beliefs which the self had previously either rejected or treated as conventions dwelling upon the margin of consciousness and having no meaning for her actual life. The mechanical process may be much the same; but the material involved, the results attained, belong to a higher order of reality.

"Conversion," says Starbuck, in words which are really far more descriptive of mystical awakening than of the revivalistic phenomena encouraged by American Protestantism, "is primarily an unselfing. The first birth of the individual is into his own little world. He is controlled by the deep-seated instincts of self-preservation and self-enlargement--instincts which are, doubtless, a direct inheritance from his brute ancestry. The universe is organized around his own personality as a centre." Conversion, then, is "the larger world-consciousness now pressing in on the individual consciousness. Often it breaks in suddenly and becomes a great new revelation. This is the first aspect of conversion: the person emerges from a smaller limited world of existence into a larger world of being. His life becomes swallowed up in a larger whole." [343]

All conversion entails the abrupt or gradual emergence of intuitions from below the threshold, the consequent remaking of the field of consciousness, an alteration in the self's attitude to the world. "It is," says Pratt, "a change of taste--the most momentous one that ever occurs in human experience." [344] But in the mystic this process is raised to the nth degree of intensity, for in him it means the first emergence of that passion for the Absolute which is to constitute his distinctive character: an emergence crucial in its effect on every department of his life. Those to whom it happens, often enough, are already "religious": sometimes deeply and earnestly so. Rulman Merswin, St. Catherine of Genoa, George Fox, Lucie-Christine--all these had been bred up in piety, and accepted in its entirety the Christian tradition. They were none the less conscious of an utter change in their world when this opening of the soul's eye took place.

Sometimes the emergence of the mystical consciousness is gradual, unmarked by any definite crisis. The self slides gently, almost imperceptibly, from the old universe to the new. The records of mysticism, however, suggest that this is exceptional: that travail is the normal accompaniment of birth. In another type, of which George Fox is a typical example, there is no conversion in the ordinary sense; but a gradual and increasing lucidity, of which the beginning has hardly been noticed by the self, intermittently accompanies the pain, misery of mind, and inward struggles characteristic of the entrance upon the Way of Purgation. Conversion and purification then go hand in hand, finally shading off into the serenity of the Illuminated State. Fox's "Journal" for the year 1647 contains a vivid account of these "showings" or growing transcendental perceptions of a mind not yet at one with itself, and struggling towards clearness of sight. "Though my exercises and troubles," he says, "were very great, yet were they not so continual but I had some intermissions, and was sometimes brought into such a heavenly joy that I thought I had been in Abraham's bosom. . . . Thus in the deepest miseries, and in the greatest sorrows and temptations that many times beset me, the Lord in His mercy did keep me. I found that there were two thirsts in me, the one after the creatures to get help and strength there; and the other after the Lord, the Creator. . . . It was so with me, that there seemed to be two pleadings in me. . . . One day when I had been walking solitarily abroad and was come home, I was wrapped up in the love of God, so that I could not but admire the greatness of his love. While I was in that condition it was opened unto me by the eternal Light and Power, and I saw clearly therein. . . . But O! then did I see my troubles, trials, and temptations more clearly than ever I had done." [345]

The great oscillations of the typical mystic between joy and pain are here replaced by a number of little ones. The "two thirsts" of the superficial and spiritual consciousness assert themselves by turns.

Each step towards the vision of the Real brings with it a reaction. The nascent transcendental powers are easily fatigued, and the pendulum of self takes a shorter swing. "I was swept up to Thee by Thy Beauty, and torn away from Thee by my own weight," says St. Augustine, crystallizing the secret of this experience in an unforgettable phrase. [346]

Commonly, however, if we may judge from those first-hand accounts which we possess, mystic conversion is a single and abrupt experience, sharply marked off from the long, dim struggles which precede and succeed it. It usually involves a sudden and acute realization of a splendour and adorable reality in the world--or sometimes of its obverse, the divine sorrow at the heart of things--never before perceived. In so far as I am acquainted with the resources of language, there are no words in which this realization can be described. It is of so actual a nature that in comparison the normal world of past perception seems but twilit at the best. Consciousness has suddenly changed its rhythm and a new aspect of the universe rushes in. The teasing mists are swept away, and reveal, if only for an instant, the sharp outline of the Everlasting Hills. "He who knows this will know what I say, and will be convinced that the soul has then another life." [347]

In most cases, the onset of this new consciousness seems to the self so sudden, so clearly imposed from without rather than developed from within, as to have a supernatural character. The typical case is, of course, that of St. Paul: the sudden light, the voice, the ecstasy, the complete alteration of life. We shall see, however, when we come to study the evidence of those mystics who have left a detailed record of their preconverted state, that the apparently abrupt conversion is really, as a rule, the sequel and the result of a long period of restlessness, uncertainty, and mental stress. The deeper mind stirs uneasily in its prison, and its emergence is but the last of many efforts to escape. The temperament of the subject, his surroundings, the vague but persistent apprehensions of a supersensual reality which he could not find yet could not forget; all these have prepared him for it. [348]

When, however, the subconscious intuitions, long ago quickened, are at last brought to birth and the eyes are opened on new light--and it is significant that an actual sense of blinding radiance is a constant accompaniment of this state of consciousness--the storm and stress, the vague cravings and oscillations of the past life are forgotten. In this abrupt recognition of reality "all things are made new": from this point the life of the mystic begins. Conversion of this sort has, says De Sanctis, three marked characteristics: a sense of liberation and victory: a conviction of the nearness of God: a sentiment of love towards God. [349] We might describe it as a sudden, intense, and joyous perception of God immanent in the universe; of the divine beauty and unutterable power and splendour of that larger life in which the individual is immersed, and of a new life to be lived by the self in correspondence with this now dominant fact of existence. "Suddenly," says the French contemplative Lucie-Christine of the beginning of her mystical life, "I saw before my inward eyes these words-- God only . . . they were at the same time a Light, an Attraction and a Power. A Light which showed me how I could belong completely to God alone in this world, and I saw that hitherto I had not well understood this; an Attraction by which my heart was subdued and delighted; a Power which inspired me with a generous resolution and somehow placed in my hands the means of carrying it out." [350]

I will here set down for comparison a few instances of such mystical conversion; quoting, where this is available, the actual description left by the subject of his own experience, or in default of it, the earliest authentic account. In these cases, when grouped together, we shall see certain constant characteristics, from which it may be possible to deduce the psychological law to which they owe their peculiar form.

First in point of time, and perhaps also in importance, amongst those I have chosen, is the case of that great poet and contemplative, that impassioned lover of the Absolute, St. Francis of Assisi. The fact that St. Francis wrote little and lived much, that his actions were of unequalled simplicity and directness, long blinded his admirers to the fact that he is a typical mystic: the only one, perhaps, who forced the most trivial and sordid circumstances of sensual life to become perfect expressions of Reality.

Now the opening of St. Francis's eyes, which took place in A.D. 1206 when he was twenty-four years old, had been preceded by a long, hard struggle between the life of the world and the persistent call of the spirit. His mind, in modern language, had not unified itself. He was a high-spirited boy, full of vitality: a natural artist, with all the fastidiousness which the artistic temperament involves. War and pleasure both attracted him, and upon them, says his legend, he "miserably squandered and wasted his time." [351] Nevertheless, he was vaguely dissatisfied. In the midst of festivities, he would have sudden fits of abstraction: abortive attempts of the growing transcendental consciousness, still imprisoned below the threshold but aware of and in touch with the Real, to force itself to the surface and seize the reins. "Even in ignorance," says Thomas of Celano again, "he was being led to perfect knowledge." He loved beauty, for he was by nature a poet and a musician, and shrank instinctively from contact with ugliness and disease. But something within ran counter to this temperamental bias, and sometimes conquered it. He would then associate with beggars, tend the leprous, perform impulsive acts of charity and self-humiliation. [352]

When this divided state, described by the legend as "the attempt to flee God's hand," had lasted for some years, it happened one day that he was walking in the country outside the gates of Assisi, and passed the little church of S. Damiano, "the which" (I again quote from Thomas of Celano's "Second Life") "was almost ruinous and forsaken of all men. And, being led by the Spirit, he went in to pray; and he fell down before the Crucifix in devout supplication, and having been smitten by unwonted visitations, found himself another man than he who had gone in."

Here, then, is the first stage of conversion. The struggle between two discrepant ideals of life has attained its term. A sudden and apparently "irrational" impulse to some decisive act reaches the surface-consciousness from the seething deeps. The impulse is followed; and the swift emergence of the transcendental sense results. This "unwonted visitation" effects an abrupt and involuntary alteration in the subject's consciousness: whereby he literally "finds himself another man." He is as one who has slept and now awakes. The crystallization of this new, at first fluid apprehension of Reality in the form of vision and audition: the pointing of the moral, the direct application of truth to the awakened self, follow. "And whilst he was thus moved, straightway--a thing unheard of for long ages!--the painted image of Christ Crucified spoke to him from out its pictured lips. And, calling him by his name, "Francis," it said, "go, repair My house, the which as thou seest is falling into decay." And Francis trembled, being utterly amazed, and almost as it were carried away by these words. And he prepared to obey, for he was wholly set on the fulfilling of this commandment. But forasmuch as he felt that the change he had undergone was ineffable, it becomes us to be silent concerning it. . . ." From this time he "gave untiring toil to the repair of that Church. For though the words which were said to him concerned that divine Church which Christ bought with His own Blood, he would not hasten to such heights, but little by little from things of the flesh would pass to those of the Spirit." [353]

In a moment of time, Francis's whole universe has suffered complete rearrangement. There are no hesitations, no uncertainties. The change, which he cannot describe, he knows to be central for life. Not for a moment does he think of disobeying the imperative voice which speaks to him from a higher plane of reality and demands the sacrifice of his career.

Compare now with the experience of St. Francis that of another great saint and mystic, who combined, as he did, the active with the contemplative life. Catherine of Genoa, who seems to have possessed from childhood a religious nature, was prepared for the remaking of her consciousness by years of loneliness and depression, the result of an unhappy marriage. She, like St. Francis--but in sorrow rather than in joy--had oscillated between the world, which did not soothe her, and religion, which helped her no more. At last, she had sunk into a state of dull wretchedness, a hatred alike of herself and of life.

Her emancipation was equally abrupt. In the year 1474, she being twenty-six years old, "The day after the feast of St. Benedict (at the instance of her sister that was a nun), Catherine went to make her confession to the confessor of that nunnery; but she was not disposed to do it. Then said her sister, At least go and recommend yourself to him, because he is a most worthy religious'; and in fact he was a very holy man. And suddenly, as she knelt before him, she received in her heart the wound of the unmeasured Love of God, with so clear a vision of her own misery and her faults, and of the goodness of God, that she almost fell upon the ground. And by these sensations of infinite love, and of the offenses that had been done against this most sweet God, she was so greatly drawn by purifying affection away from the poor things of this world that she was almost beside herself, and for this she cried inwardly with ardent love, No more world! no more sin!' And at this point if she had possessed a thousand worlds, she would have thrown all of them away. . . . And she returned home, kindled and deeply wounded with so great a love of God, the which had been shown her inwardly, with the sight of her own wretchedness, that she seemed beside herself. And she shut herself in a chamber, the most secluded she could find, with burning sighs. And in this moment she was inwardly taught the whole practice of orison: but her tongue could say naught but this--O Love, can it be that thou has called me with so great a love, and made me to know in one instant that which worlds cannot express?'" This intuition of the Absolute was followed by an interior vision of Christ bearing the Cross, which further increased her love and self-abasement. "And she cried again, O Love, no more sins! no more sins!' And her hatred of herself was more than she could endure." [354]

Of this experience Von Hügel says, "If the tests of reality in such things are their persistence and large and rich spiritual applicability and fruitfulness, then something profoundly real and important took place in the soul of that sad and weary woman of six-and-twenty, within that convent-chapel, at that Annunciation-tide." [355] It is certain that for St. Catherine, as for St. Francis, an utterly new life did, literally, begin at this point. The centre of interest was shifted and the field of consciousness remade. She "knew in an instant that which words cannot express." Some veil about her heart was torn away; so abruptly, that it left a wound behind. For the first time she saw and knew the Love in which life is bathed; and all the energy and passion of a strong nature responded to its call.

The conversion of Madame Guyon to the mystic life, as told by herself in the eighth chapter of Part I. of her Autobiography--"How a holy Religious caused her to find God within her heart, with

Admirable Results," is its characteristic title--is curiously like a dilute version of this experience of St. Catherine's. It, too, followed upon a period of mental distress; also the result of an uncongenial marriage. But since Madame Guyon's unbalanced, diffuse, and sentimental character entirely lacks the richness and dignity, the repressed ardours and exquisite delicacy of St. Catherine's mind, so, too, her account of her own interior processes is marred by a terrible and unctuous interest in the peculiar graces vouchsafed to her. [356]

Madame Guyon's value to the student of mysticism partly consists in this feeble quality of her surface-intelligence, which hence had little or no modifying or contributory effect upon her spiritual life and makes her an ideal "laboratory specimen" for the religious psychologist. True to her great principle of passivity or "quiet," it lets the uncriticized interior impulses have their way; thus we are able to observe their workings uncomplicated by the presence of a vigorous intellect or a disciplined will. The wind that bloweth where it listeth whistles through her soul: and the response which she makes is that of a weathercock rather than a windmill. She moves to every current; she often mistakes a draught for the divine breath; she feels her gyrations to be of enormous importance. But in the description of her awakening to the deeper life, even her effusive style acquires a certain dignity. [357]

Madame Guyon had from her childhood exhibited an almost tiresome taste for pious observances. At twelve years old she studied St. François de Sales and St. Jeanne Françoise de Chantal; begged her confessor to teach her the art of mental prayer; and when he omitted to do so, tried to teach herself, but without result. [358] She wished at this time to become a nun of the Visitation, as St. Catherine at the same age wanted to be an Augustinian canoness; but as the longings of little girls of twelve for the cloister are seldom taken seriously, we are not surprised to find the refusal of her parents' consent chronicled in the chapter which is headed " Diverses croix chez M. son père ." Growing up into an unusually beautiful young woman, she went into society, and for a short time enjoyed life in an almost worldly way. Her marriage with Jacques Guyon, however--a marriage of which she signed the articles without even being told the bridegroom's name--put an end to her gaiety. "The whole town was pleased by this marriage; and in all this rejoicing only I was sad . . . hardly was I married, when the remembrance of my old desire to be a nun overcame me." [359]

Her early married life was excessively unhappy. She was soon driven to look for comfort in the practices of religion. "Made to love much, and finding nothing to love around her, she gave her love to God," says Guerrier tersely. [360] But she was not satisfied: like most of her fellow-contemplatives, she was already vaguely conscious of something that she missed, some vital power unused, and identified this something with the "orison of quiet," the "practice of the presence of God" which mystically minded friends had described to her. She tried to attain to it deliberately, and naturally failed. "I could not give myself by multiplicity that which Thou Thyself givest, and which is only experienced in simplicity." [361]

When these interior struggles had lasted for nearly two years, and Madame Guyon was nineteen, the long desired, almost despaired of, apprehension came--as it did to St. Catherine--suddenly, magically almost; and under curiously parallel conditions. It was the result of a few words spoken by a Franciscan friar whom a "secret force" acting in her interest had brought into the neighbourhood, and whom she had been advised to consult. He was a recluse, who disliked hearing the confessions of women, and appears to have been far from pleased by her visit; an annoyance which he afterwards attributed to her fashionable appearance, "which filled him with apprehension." "He hardly came forward, and was a long time without speaking to me. I, however, did not fail to speak to him and to tell him in a few words my difficulties on the subject of orison. He at once replied, Madame, you are seeking without that which you have within. Accustom yourself to seek God in your own heart, and you will find him.' Having said this, he left me. The next morning he was greatly astonished when I again visited him and told him the effect which these words had had upon my soul: for, indeed, they were as an arrow, which pierced my heart through and through. I felt in this moment a profound wound, which was full of delight and of love--a wound so sweet that I desired that it might never heal. These words had put into my heart that which I sought for so many years, or, rather, they caused me to find that which was there. O, my Lord, you were within my heart, and you asked of me only that I should return within, in order that I might feel your presence. O, Infinite Goodness, you were so near, and I running here and there to seek you, found you not!" She, too, like St. Catherine, learned in this instant the long-sought practice of orison, or contemplation. "From the moment of which I have spoken, my orison was emptied of all form, species, and images; nothing of my orison passed through the mind; but it was an orison of joyous possession in the Will, where the taste for God was so great, pure, and simple that it attracted and absorbed the two other powers of the soul in a profound recollection without action or speech." [362]

Take now the case of a less eminent mystic, who has also left behind him a vivid personal description of his entrance upon the Mystic Way. Rulman Merswin was a wealthy, pious, and respected merchant of Strassburg. In the year 1347, when he was about thirty-six years old, he retired from business in order that he might wholly devote himself to religious matters. It was the time of that spiritual revival within the Catholic Church in Germany which, largely influenced by the great Rhenish mystics Suso and Tauler, is identified with the "Friends of God"; and Merswin himself was one of Tauler's disciples. [363]

One evening, in the autumn which followed his retirement, "about the time of Martinmas," he was strolling in his garden alone. Meditating as he walked, a picture of the Crucifix suddenly presented itself to his mind. In such an imaginary vision as this there is nothing, of course, that we can call abnormal. The thoughts of a devout Catholic, influenced by Tauler and his school, must often have taken such a direction during his solitary strolls. This time, however, the mental image of the Cross seems to have released subconscious forces which had long been gathering way. Merswin was abruptly filled with a violent hatred of the world and of his own free-will. "Lifting his eyes to heaven he solemnly swore that he would utterly surrender his own will, person, and goods to the service of God." [364]

This act of complete surrender, releasing as it were the earthbound self, was at once followed by the onset of pure mystical perception. "The reply from on high came quickly. A brilliant light shone about him: he heard in his ears a divine voice of adorable sweetness; he felt as if he were lifted from the ground and carried several times completely round his garden." [365] Optical disturbance, auditions, and the sense of levitation, are of course frequent physical accompaniments of these shiftings of the level of consciousness. There are few cases in which one or other is not present; and in some we find all. Coming to himself after this experience, Merswin's heart was filled by a new consciousness of the Divine; and by a transport of intense love towards God which made him undertake with great energy the acts of mortification which he believed necessary to the purification of his soul. From this time onwards, his mystical consciousness steadily developed. That it was a consciousness wholly different in kind from the sincere piety which had previously caused him to retire from business in order to devote himself to religious truth, is proved by the name of Conversion which he applies to the vision of the garden; and by the fact that he dates from this point the beginning of his real life.

The conversion of Merswin's greater contemporary, Suso, seems to have been less abrupt. Of its first stage he speaks vaguely at the beginning of his autobiography, wherein he says that "he began to be converted when in the eighteenth year of his age." [366] He was at this time, as St. Francis had been, restless, dissatisfied; vaguely conscious of something essential to his peace, as yet unfound. His temperament, at once deeply human and ardently spiritual, passionately appreciative of sensuous beauty yet unable to rest in it, had not "unified itself": nor did it do so completely until after a period of purgation which is probably unequalled for its austerity in the history of the mysticism of the West. "He was kept of God in this, that when he turned to those things that most enticed him he found neither happiness nor peace therein. He was restless, and-it seemed to him that something which was as yet unknown could alone give peace to his heart. And he suffered greatly of this restlessness. . . . God at last delivered him by a complete conversion. His brothers in religion were astonished by so quick a change: for the event took them unawares. Some said of it one thing, and some another: but none could know the reason of his conversion. It was God Who, by a hidden light, had caused this return to Himself." [367]

This secret conversion was completed by a more violent uprush of the now awakened and active transcendental powers. Suso, whom one can imagine as a great and highly nervous artist if his genius had not taken the channel of sanctity instead, was subject all his life to visions of peculiar richness and beauty. Often these visions seem to have floated up, as it were, from the subliminal region without disturbing the course of his conscious life; and to be little more than pictorial images of his ardour towards and intuition of, divine realities. The great ecstatic vision--or rather apprehension--with which the series opens, however, is of a very different kind; and represents the characteristic experience of Ecstasy in its fullest form. It is described with a detail and intensity which make it a particularly valuable document of the mystical life. It is doubtful whether Suso ever saw more than this: the course of his long education rather consisted in an adjustment of his nature to the Reality which he then perceived.

"In the first days of his conversion it happened upon the Feast of St. Agnes, when the Convent had breakfasted at midday, that the Servitor went into the choir. He was alone, and he placed himself in the last stall on the prior's side. And he was in much suffering, for a heavy trouble weighed upon his heart. And being there alone, and devoid of all consolations--no one by his side, no one near him--of a sudden his soul was rapt in his body, or out of his body. Then did he see and hear that which no tongue can express.

"That which the Servitor saw had no form neither any manner of being; yet he had of it a joy such as he might have known in the seeing of the shapes and substances of all joyful things. His heart was hungry, yet satisfied, his soul was full of contentment and joy: his prayers and hopes were all fulfilled. And the Friar could do naught but contemplate this Shining Brightness, and he altogether forgot himself and all other things. Was it day or night? He knew not. It was, as it were, a manifestation of the sweetness of Eternal Life in the sensations of silence and of rest. Then he said, If that which I see and feel be not the Kingdom of Heaven, I know not what it can be: for it is very sure that the endurance of all possible pains were but a poor price to pay for the eternal possession of so great a joy.'"

The physical accompaniments of ecstasy were also present. "This ecstasy lasted from half an hour to an hour, and whether his soul were in the body or out of the body he could not tell. But when he came to his senses it seemed to him that he returned from another world. And so greatly did his body suffer in this short rapture that it seemed to him that none, even in dying, could suffer so greatly in so short a time. The Servitor came to himself moaning, and he fell down upon the ground like a man who swoons. And he cried inwardly, heaving great sighs from the depth of his soul and saying, Oh, my God, where was I and where am I?' And again, Oh, my heart's joy, never shall my soul forget this hour!' He walked, but it was but his body that walked, as a machine might do. None knew from his demeanour that which was taking place within. But his soul and his spirit were full of marvels; heavenly lightnings passed and repassed in the deeps of his being, and it seemed to him that he walked on air. And all the powers of his soul were full of these heavenly delights. He was like a vase from which one has taken a precious ointment, but in which the perfume long remains."

Finally, the last phrases of the chapter seem to suggest the true position of this exalted pleasure-state as a first link in the long chain of mystical development. "This foretaste of the happiness of heaven," he says, "the which the Servitor enjoyed for many days, excited in him a most lively desire for God." [368]

Mystical activity, then, like all other activities of the self, opens with that sharp stimulation of the will, which can only be obtained through the emotional life.

Suso was a scholar, and an embryo ecclesiastic. During the period which elapsed between his conversion and his description of it, he was a disciple of Meister Eckhart, a student of Dionysius and St. Thomas Aquinas. His writings show familiarity with the categories of mystical theology; and naturally enough this circumstance, and also the fact that they were written for purposes of edification, may have dictated to some extent the language in which his conversion-ecstasy is described. As against this, I will give two first-hand descriptions of mystical conversion in which it is obvious that theological learning plays little or no part. Both written in France within a few years of one another, they represent the impact of Reality on two minds of very different calibre. One is the secret document in which a great genius set down, in words intended only for his own eyes, the record of a two hours' ecstasy. The other is the plain, unvarnished statement of an uneducated man of the peasant class. The first is, of course, the celebrated Memorial, or Amulet, of Pascal; the second is the Relation of Brother Lawrence.

The Memorial of Pascal is a scrap of parchment on which, round a rough drawing of the Flaming Cross, there are written a few strange phrases, abrupt and broken words; all we know about one of the strangest ecstatic revelations chronicled in the history of the mystic type. After Pascal's death a servant found a copy of this little document, now lost, sewn up in his doublet. He seems always to have worn it upon his person: a perpetual memorial of the supernal experience, the initiation into Reality, which it describes. Though Bremand has shown that the opening of Pascal's spiritual eyes had begun, on his own declaration, eleven months earlier, "d'une manière douce et obligeante," [369] the conversion thus prepared was only made actual by this abrupt illumination; ending a long period of spiritual stress, in which indifference to his ordinary interests was counterbalanced by an utter inability to feel the attractive force of that Divine Reality which his great mind discerned as the only adequate object of desire.

The Memorial opens thus:--

"L'an de grace 1654
lundi, 23 novembre, jour de Saint Clément, pape
et martyr, et autres au martyrologe,
veille de Saint Chrysogone, martyr et autres
depuis environ dix heures et demie du soir jusques
environ minuit et demie,
Feu."

"From half-past ten till half-past twelve, Fire!" That is all, so far as description is concerned; but enough, apparently, to remind the initiate of all that passed. The rest tells us only the passion of joy and conviction which this nameless revelation--this long, blazing vision of Reality--brought in its train. It is but a series of amazed exclamations, crude, breathless words, placed there helter-skelter, the artist in him utterly in abeyance; the names of the overpowering emotions which swept him, one after the other, as the Fire of Love disclosed its secrets, evoked an answering flame of humility and rapture in his soul.

"Dieu d'Abraham, Dieu d'Isaac, Dieu de Jacob,
Non des philosophes et des savants.
Certitude. Certitude. Sentiment. Joie. Paix".

"Not the God of philosophers and of scholars!" cries in amazement this great scholar and philosopher abruptly turned from knowledge to love.

"Oubli du monde et de tout hormis Dieu," he says again, seeing his universe suddenly swept clean of all but this Transcendent Fact. Then, "Le monde ne t'a point connu, mais je t'ai connu. Joie! joie joie! pleurs de joie!" Compare with the classic style, the sharp and lucid definition of the "Pensées," the irony and glitter of the "Provinciales," these little broken phrases--this child-like stammering speech--in which a supreme master of language has tried to tell his wonder and his delight. I know few things in the history of mysticism at once more convincing, more poignant than this hidden talisman; upon which the brilliant scholar and stylist, the merciless disputant, has jotted down in hard, crude words, which yet seem charged with passion--the inarticulate language of love--a memorial of the certitude, the peace, the joy, above all, the reiterated, all-surpassing joy, which accompanied his ecstatic apprehension of God.

" Mon Dieu, me quitterez vous?" he says again; the fire apparently beginning to die down, the ecstasy drawing to an end. " Que je n'en sois pas séparé éternellement!" "Are you going to leave me? Oh, let me not be separated from you for ever!--the one unendurable thought which would, said Aquinas, rob the Beatific Vision of its glory, were we not sure that it can never fade. [370] But the rhapsody is over, the vision of the Fire has gone; and the rest of the Memorial clearly contains Pascal's meditations upon his experience, rather than a transcript of the experience itself. It ends with the watchword of all mysticism, Surrender--" Renonciation, totale et douce" in Pascal's words--the only way, he thinks, in which he can avoid continued separation from Reality. [371]

Pascal's vision of Light, Life, and Love was highly ecstatic; an indescribable, incommunicable experience, which can only be suggested by his broken words of certitude and joy. By his simple contemporary, Brother Lawrence, that Transcendent Reality Who "is not the God of philosophers and scholars," was perceived in a moment of abrupt intuition, peculiarly direct, unecstatic and untheological in type, but absolutely enduring in its results. Lawrence was an uneducated young man of the peasant class; who first served as a soldier, and afterwards as a footman in a great French family, where he annoyed his masters by breaking everything. When he was between fifty and sixty years of age, he entered the Carmelite Order as a lay brother; and the letters, "spiritual maxims," and conversations belonging to this period of his life were published after his death in 1691. "He told me," says the anonymous reporter of the conversations, supposed to be M. Beaufort, who was about 1660 Grand Vicar to the Cardinal de Noailles, "that God had done him a singular favour in his conversion at the age of eighteen. That in the winter, seeing a tree stripped of its leaves, and considering that within a little time the leaves would be renewed, and after that the flowers and fruit appear, he received a high view of the Providence and Power of God, which has never since been effaced from his soul. That this view had set him perfectly loose from the world and kindled in him such a love for God that he could not tell whether it had increased in above forty years that he had lived since." [372]

Such use of visible nature as the stuff of ontological perceptions, the medium whereby the self reaches out to the Absolute, is not rare in the history of mysticism. The mysterious vitality of trees, the silent magic of the forest, the strange and steady cycle of its life, possess in a peculiar degree this power of unleashing the human soul: are curiously friendly to its cravings, minister to its inarticulate needs. Unsullied by the corroding touch of consciousness, that life can make a contact with the "great life of the All"; and through its mighty rhythms man can receive a message concerning the true and timeless World of "all that is, and was, and evermore shall be." Plant life of all kinds, indeed, from the "flower in the crannied wall" to the "Woods of Westermain" can easily become, for selves of a certain type, a "mode of the Infinite." So obvious does this appear when we study the history of the mystics, that Steiner has drawn from it the hardly warrantable inference that "plants are just those natural phenomena whose qualities in the higher world are similar to their qualities in the physical world." [373]

Though the conclusion be not convincing, the fact remains. The flowery garment of the world is for some mystics a medium of ineffable perception, a source of exalted joy, the veritable clothing of God. I need hardly add that such a state of things has always been found incredible by common sense. "The tree which moves some to tears of joy," says Blake, who possessed in an eminent degree this form of sacramental perception, "is in the Eyes of others only a green thing that stands in the Way." [374]

Such a perception of the Divine in Nature, of the true and holy meaning of that rich, unresting life in which we are immersed, is really a more usual feature of Illumination than of Conversion. All the most marked examples of it must be referred to that state; and will be discussed when we come to its consideration. Sometimes, however, as in the case of Brother Lawrence, the first awakening of the self to consciousness of Reality does take this form. The Uncreated Light manifests Itself in and through created things. This characteristically immanental discovery of the Absolute occurs chiefly in two classes: in unlettered men who have lived close to Nature, and to whom her symbols are more familiar than those of the Churches or the schools, and in temperaments of the mixed or mystical type, who are nearer to the poet than to the true contemplative, for whom as a rule the Absolute "hath no image." "It was like entering into another world, a new state of existence," says a witness quoted by Starbuck, speaking of his own conversion. "Natural objects were glorified. My spiritual vision was so clarified that I saw beauty in every material object in the universe. The woods were vocal with heavenly music." "Oh, how I was changed! Everything became new. My horses and hogs and everybody became changed!" exclaims with naive astonishment another in the same collection.[375] "When I went in the morning into the fields to work," says a third, "the glory of God appeared in all His visible creation. I well remember we reaped oats, and how every straw and head of the oats seemed, as it were, arrayed in a kind of rainbow glory, or to glow, if I may so express it, in the glory of God."[376]

Amongst modern men, Walt Whitman possessed in a supreme degree the permanent sense of this glory, the "light rare, untellable, lighting the very light."[377] But evidences of its existence, and the sporadic power of apprehending it, are scattered up and down the literature of the world. Its discovery constitutes the awakening of the mystical consciousness in respect of the World of Becoming: a sharp and sudden break with the old and obvious way of seeing things. The human cinematograph has somehow changed its rhythm, and begins to register new and more real aspects of the external world. With this, the self's first escape from the limitations of its conventional universe, it receives an immense assurance of a great and veritable life surrounding, sustaining, explaining its own. Thus Richard Jefferies says, of the same age as that at which Suso and Brother Lawrence awoke to sudden consciousness of Reality, "I was not more than eighteen when an inner and esoteric meaning began to come to me from all the visible universe." "I now became lost, and absorbed into the being or existence of the universe . . . and losing thus my separateness of being, came to seem like a part of the whole." "I feel on the margin of a life unknown, very near, almost touching it--on the verge of powers which, if I could grasp, would give men an immense breadth of existence."[378]

What was this "life unknown" but the Life known to the great mystics, which Richard Jefferies apprehended in these moments of insight, yet somehow contrived to miss?

Such participation in the deep realities of the World of Becoming, the boundless existence of a divine whole--which a modern psychologist has labelled and described as "Cosmic Consciousness"[379] --whilst it is not the final object of the mystic's journey, is a constant feature of it. It may represent one-half of his characteristic consciousness: an entrance into communion with the second of the Triune Powers of God, the Word which "is through all things everlastingly." Jefferies stood, as so many mystically minded men have done, upon the verge of such a transcendental life. The "heavenly door," as Rolle calls it, was ajar but not pushed wide. He peeped through it to the greater world beyond; but, unable to escape from the bonds of his selfhood, he did not pass through to live upon the independent spiritual plane.

Rolle, Jefferies's fellow countryman, and his predecessor by close upon six hundred years in the ecstatic love and understanding of natural things, shall be our last example of the mystical awakening. He, like his spiritual brother St. Francis, and other typical cases, had passed through a preliminary period of struggle and oscillation between worldly life and a vague but growing spirituality: between the superficial and the deeper self. "My youth was fond, my childhood vain, my young age unclean,"[380] but "when I should flourish unhappily, and youth of wakeful age was now come, the grace of my Maker was near, the which lust of temporal shape restrained, and unto ghostly supplications turned my desires, and the soul, from low things lifted, to heaven has borne."[381]

The real "life-changing," however, was sharply and characteristically marked off from this preparatory state. Rolle associates it with the state which he calls "Heat": the form in which his ardour of soul was translated to the surface consciousness. "Heat soothly I call when the mind truly is kindled in Love Everlasting, and the heart on the same manner to burn not hopingly but verily is felt. The heart truly turned into fire, gives feeling of burning love."[382] This burning heat is not merely a mental experience. In it we seem to have an unusual but not unique form of psychophysical parallelism: a bodily expression of the psychic travail and distress accompanying the "New Birth."[383] "More have I marvelled than I show, forsooth," he says in his prologue, "when I first felt my heart wax warm, and truly, not imaginingly, but as it were with a sensible fire , burned. I was forsooth marvelled, as this burning burst up in my soul, and of an unwonted solace; for in my ignorance of such healing abundance, oft have I groped my breast, seeing whether this burning were of any bodily cause outwardly. But when I knew that only it was kindled of ghostly cause inwardly, and this burning was naught of fleshly love or desire, in this I conceived it was the gift of my Maker."[384] Further on, he gives another and more detailed account. "From the beginning, forsooth, of my life-changing and of my mind, to the opening of the heavenly door which Thy Face showed, that the heart might behold heavenly things and see by what way its Love it might seek and busily desire, three years are run except three months or four. The door, forsooth, biding open, a year near-by I passed unto the time in which the heat of Love Everlasting was verily felt in heart. I sat forsooth in a chapel and whilst with sweetness of prayer and meditation greatly I was delighted, suddenly in me I felt a merry heat and unknown. But at first I wondered, doubting of whom it should be; but a long time I am assured that not of the Creature but of my Maker it was, for more hot and gladder I found it."[385]

To this we must add a passage which I cannot but think one of the most beautiful expressions of spiritual joy to be found in mystical literature. Based though it certainly is upon a passage in St. Augustine--for the nightingale is not a Yorkshire bird--its sketch of the ideal mystic life, to the cultivation of which he then set himself, reveals in a few lines the most charming aspect of Rolle's spirituality, its poetic fervour, its capacity for ardent love.

"In the beginning truly of my conversion and singular purpose, I though I would be like the little bird that for love of her lover longs, but in her longing she is gladdened when he comes that she loves. And joying she sings, and singing she longs, but in sweetness and heat. It is said the nightingale to song and melody all night is given, that she may please him to whom she is joined. How muckle more with greatest sweetness to Christ my Jesu should I sing, that is spouse of my soul by all this present life, that is night in regard of clearness to come." [386]

Glancing back at the few cases here brought together, we can see in them, I think, certain similarities and diversities which are often of great psychological interest and importance: and have their influence upon the subsequent development of the mystic life. We see in particular at this point--before purification, or the remaking of character, begins--the reaction of the natural self, its heart and its mind, upon that uprush of new truth which operates "mystical conversion." This reaction is highly significant, and gives us a clue not only to the future development of the mystic, but to the general nature of man's spiritual consciousness.

We have said [387] that this consciousness in its full development seems to be extended not in one but in two directions. These directions, these two fundamental ways of apprehending Reality may be called the eternal and temporal, transcendent and immanent, absolute and dynamic aspects of Truth. They comprise the twofold knowledge of a God Who is both Being and Becoming near and far: pairs of opposites which the developed mystical experience will carry up into a higher synthesis. But the first awakening of the mystic sense, the first breaking in of the suprasensible upon the soul, commonly involves the emergence of one only of these complementary forms of perception. One side always wakes first: the incoming message always choosing the path of least resistance. Hence mystical conversion tends to belong to one of two distinctive types: tends also, as regards its expression, to follow that temperamental inclination to objectivize Reality as a Place, a Person, or a State which we found to govern the symbolic systems of the mystics. [388]

There is first, then, the apprehension of a splendour without: an expansive, formless, ineffable vision, a snatching up of the self, as it were, from knowledge of this world to some vague yet veritable knowledge of the next. The veil parts, and the Godhead is perceived as transcendent to, yet immanent in, the created universe. Not the personal touch of love transfiguring the soul, but the impersonal glory of a transfigured world, is the dominant note of this experience: and the reaction of the self takes the form of awe and rapture rather than of intimate affection. Of such a kind was the conversion of Suso, and in a less degree of Brother Lawrence. Of this kind also were the Light which Rulman Merswin saw, and the mystical perception of the Being of the universe reported by Richard Jefferies and countless others.

This experience, if it is to be complete, if it is to involve the definite emergence of the self from "the prison of I-hood," its setting out upon the Mystic Way, requires an act of concentration on the self's part as the complement of its initial act of expansion. It must pass beyond the stage of metaphysical rapture or fluid splendour, and crystallize into a willed response to the Reality perceived; a definite and personal relation must be set up between the self and the Absolute Life. To be a spectator of Reality is not enough. The awakened subject is not merely to perceive transcendent life, but to participate therein; and for this, a drastic and costly life-changing is required. In Jefferies's case this crystallization, this heroic effort towards participation did not take place, and he never therefore laid hold of "the glory that has been revealed." In Suso's it did, "exciting in him a most lively desire for God."

In most cases this crystallization, the personal and imperative concept which the mind constructs from the general and ineffable intuition of Reality, assumes a theological character. Often it presents itself to the consciousness in the form of visions or voices: objective, as the Crucifix which spoke to St. Francis, or mental, as the visions of the Cross experienced by Rulman Merswin and St. Catherine of Genoa. Nearly always, this concept, this intimate realization of the divine, has reference to the love and sorrow at the heart of things, the discord between Perfect Love and an imperfect world; whereas the complementary vision of Transcendence strikes a note of rapturous joy. "The beatings of the Heart of God sounded like so many invitations which thus spake: Come and do penance, come and be reconciled, come and be consoled, come and be blessed; come, My love, and receive all that the Beloved can give to His beloved. . . . Come, My bride, and enjoy My Godhead." [389]

It is to this personal touch, to the individual appeal of an immediate Presence, not to the great light and the Beatific Vision, that the awakened self makes its most ardent, most heroic response. Not because he was rapt from himself, but because the figure on the Cross called him by name, saying, "Repair My Church" did St. Francis, with that simplicity, that disregard of worldly values which constituted his strength, accept the message in a literal sense and set himself instantly to the work demanded; bringing stones, and, in defiance alike of comfort and convention, building up with his own hands the crumbling walls.

In many conversions to the mystic life, the revelation of an external splendour, the shining vision of the transcendent spiritual world, is wholly absent. The self awakes to that which is within, rather than to that which is without: to the immanent not the transcendent God, to the personal not the cosmic relation. Where those who look out receive the revelation of Divine Beauty, those who look in receive rather the wound of Divine Love: another aspect of the "triple star." Emotional mystics such as Richard Rolle and Madame Guyon give us this experience in an extreme form. We find in St. Catherine of Genoa a nobler example of the same type of response. That inward revelation in its anguish and abruptness, its rending apart of the hard tissues of I-hood and vivid disclosures of the poverty of the finite self, seemed, says the legend of St. Catherine "the wound of Unmeasured Love," an image in which we seem to hear the very accents of the saint. "A wound full of delight," says the effusive Madame Guyon, "I wished that it might never heal." Rolle calls this piercing rapture a great heat: the heat which is to light the Fire of Love. "As it were if the finger were put in fire, it should be clad with feeling of burning so the soul with love (as aforesaid) set afire, truly feels most very heat." [390]

Love, passionate and all-dominant, here takes the place of that joyous awe which we noticed as the characteristic reaction upon reality in conversions of the Transcendent type. In the deep and strong temperaments of the great mystics this love passes quickly--sometimes instantly--from the emotional to the volitional stage. Their response to the voice of the Absolute is not merely an effusion of sentiment, but an act of will: an act often of so deep and comprehensive a kind as to involve the complete change of the outward no less than of the inward life. "Divine love," says Dionysius "draws those whom it seizes beyond themselves: and this so greatly that they belong no longer to themselves but wholly to the Object loved." [391]

Merswin's oath of self-surrender: St. Catherine of Genoa's passionate and decisive "No more world! no more sins!": St. Francis's naive and instant devotion to church-restoration in its most literal sense: these things are earnests of the reality of the change. They represent--symbolize as well as they can upon the sensual plane--the spontaneous response of the living organism to a fresh external stimulus: its first effort of adjustment to the new conditions which that stimulus represents. They complete the process of conversion; which is not one-sided, not merely an infusion into the surface-consciousness of new truth, but rather the beginning of a life-process, a breaking down of the old and building up of the new. A never to be ended give-and-take is set up between the individual and the Absolute. The Spirit of Life has been born: and the first word it learns to say is Abba, Father. It aspires to its origin, to Life in its most intense manifestation: hence all its instincts urge it to that activity which it feels to be inseparable from life. It knows itself a member of that mighty family in which the stars are numbered: the family of the sons of God, who, free and creative, sharing the rapture of a living, striving Cosmos, "shout for joy."

So, even in its very beginning, we see how active, how profoundly organic, how deeply and widely alive is the true contemplative life; how truly on the transcendent as on the phenomenal plane, the law of living things is action and reaction, force and energy. The awakening of the self is to a new and more active plane of being, new and more personal relations with Reality; hence to a new and more real work which it must do.

Footnotes:

342. See Starbuck, "The Psychology of Religion," cap. xxix.

343. Op. cit., cap. xii.

344. J. B. Pratt, "The Religious Consciousness," cap. xiii. The whole chapter deserve careful study.

345. Journal of George Fox, cap. i.

346. Aug. Conf., bk. vii. cap. xvii. We can surely trace the influence of such an experience in St. Paul's classic description of the "endopsychic conflict": Rom. vii. 14-25.

347. Plotinus, Ennead vi. 9.

348. "It is certain," says De Sanctis, "that when we attempt to probe deeper in our study of sudden converts, we discover that the coup de foudre , which in the main is observable in only a small minority of conversions, is in fact the least significant, though the most Esthetic, moment of the conversion." ("Religious Conversion," Eng. trans., p. 65. Compare St. Augustine's Confessions, with their description of the years of uncertainty and struggle which prepared him for the sudden and final "Tolle, lege!" that initiated him into the long-sought life of Reality.)

349. Op. cit. , p. 171.

350. "Journal Spirituel de Lucie-Christine," p. 11.

351. Thomas of Celano, Legenda Prima, cap. 1.

352. Thomas of Celano, Legenda Secunda, cap. v. Compare P. Sabatier. "Vie de S. François d'Assise," cap. ii., where the authorities are fully set out.

353. Thomas of Celano, Legenda Secunda, cap. vi.

354. "Vita e Dottrina di Santa Caterina da Genova," cap ii.

355. Von Hügel, "The Mystical Element of Religion," vol. ii p. 29.

356. It is clear from the heading of cap. x. (pt. i.) of her Autobiography that Madame Guyon's editors were conscious, if she was not, of some of the close coincidences between her experiences and those of St. Catherine of Genoa. The parallel between their early years is so exact and descends to such minute details that I am inclined to think that the knowledge of this resemblance, and the gratification with which she would naturally regard it, has governed or modified her memories of this past. Hence a curious and hitherto unnoticed case of "unconscious spiritual plagiarism."

357. For a thoroughly hostile account see Leuba: The Psychology of Religious Mysticism," cap. iv.

358. Vie, pt. i. cap. iv.

359. Op. cit., pt. i. cap. vi.

360. "Madame Guyon," p. 36.

361. Vie, pt. i. cap. viii.

362. Op. cit., loc. cit.

363. One of the best English accounts of this movement and the great personalities concerned in it is in Rufus Jones, "Studies in Mystical Religion," cap. xiii.

364. A. Jundt, "Rulman Merswin," p. 19. M. Jundt has condensed his account which I here translate, from Merswin's autobiographical story of his conversion, published in Breiträge zu den theologischen Wissenschaften , v . (Jena, 1854). Our whole knowledge of Merswin's existence depends on the group of documents which includes this confession, the "Book of Two Men," the "Vision of Nine Rocks," and his other reputed works. The authenticity of these documents has been much questioned, and they have doubtless suffered severely from the editorial energy of his followers. Some critics even regard them as pious fictions, useless as evidence of the incidents of Merswin's life. With this view, upheld by Karl Reider ("Der Gottesfreund von Oberland," 1905), I cannot agree. A possible solution of the many difficulties is that of M. Jundt, who believes that we have in Merswin and the mysterious "Friend of God of the Oberland," who pervades his spiritual career, a remarkable case of dissociated personality. Merswin's peculiar psychic make up, as described in his autobiography, supports this view: the adoption of which I shall assume in future references to his life. It is incredible that the vivid account of his conversion which I quote should be merely "tendency-literature," without basis in fact. Compare Jundt's monograph, and also Rufus Jones, op. cit. pp . 245-253, where the whole problem is discussed.

365. Jundt, op. cit., loc. cit.

366. "Leben und Schriften" (Diepenbrock), cap. i. Suso's autobiography is written in the third person. He refers to himself throughout under the title of "Servitor of the Eternal Wisdom."

367. Op. cit., loc. cit.

368. Leben, cap. iii.

369. Bremond, "Histoire Littérario du Sentiment Religieux en France." vol. iv. pp. 359 seq.

370. "Summa contra Gentiles," l. iii. cap. lxii.

371. The complete test of the Memorial isprinted, among other places, in Faugère's edition of the "Pensées, Fragments et Lettres de Blaise Pascal," 2nd ed., Paris, 1897. Tome i. p. 269; and is reproduced in facsimile by Bremond loc. cit. Bremond holds that the Memorial is the record of two distinct experiences: a "mystical experience in the proper meaning of the word," and an "affective meditation arising from it." This view does not seem incompatible with my original description, which I therefore retain. (Note to 12th ed.)

372. Brother Lawrence, "The Practice of the Presence of God," p. 9.

373. "The Way of Initiation," p. 134.

374. "Letters of William Blake," p. 62.

375. "The Psychology of Religion," p. 120.

376. James, "Varieties of Religion Experience," p. 253. This phenomenon receives brilliant literary expression in John Masefield's poem "The Everlasting Mercy" (1911).

377. Whitman, "The Prayer of Colombus."

378. "The Story of My Heart," pp. 8, 9, 45, 181.

379. Bucke, "Cosmic Consciousness, a Study in the Evolution of the Human Mind." Philadelphia. 1905.

380. "Fire of Love," bk. i. cap. xii.

381. Ibid. , bk. i. cap. xv.

382. Ibid., cap. xiv.

383. Hilton and the author of "The Cloud of Unknowing" both refer to "sensible heat" as a well-known but dubious concomitant of spiritual experience. Compare the confession of a modern convert, "I was siezed and possessed by an interior flame, for which nothing had prepared me; waves of fire succeeding one another for more than two hours." ("Madeleine Sémer, Convertie et Mystique," 1874-1921, p. 71.)

384. "Fire of Love," bk. i. Prologue.

385. Ibid ., bk. i. cap. xv.
386. Ibid ., bk. ii. cap. xii.
387. Supra , p. 35.
388. Ibid ., p. 128.
389. St. Mechthild of Hackborn, "Liber Specialis Gratiae," I. ii. cap. i
390. "The Fire of Love," bk. i. cap. i.
391. Dionysius the Areopagite, "De Divinis Nominibus," iv. 13.

CHAPTER III

Here , then, stands the newly awakened self: aware, for the first time, of reality, responding to that reality by deep movements of love and of awe. She sees herself, however, not merely to be thrust into a new world, but set at the beginning of a new road. Activity is now to be her watchword, pilgrimage the business of her life. "That a quest there is, and an end, is the single secret spoken." Under one symbol or another, the need of that long slow process of transcendence, of character building, whereby she is to attain freedom, become capable of living upon high levels of reality, is present in her consciousness. Those in whom this growth is not set going are no mystics, in the exact sense in which that word is here used; however great their temporary illumination may have been.

What must be the first step of the self upon this road to perfect union with the Absolute? Clearly, a getting rid of all those elements of normal experience which are not in harmony with reality: of illusion, evil, imperfection of every kind. By false desires and false thoughts man has built up for himself a false universe: as a mollusk by the deliberate and persistent absorption of lime and rejection of all else, can build up for itself a hard shell which shuts it from the external world, and only represents in a distorted and unrecognisable form the ocean from which it was obtained. This hard and wholly unnutritious shell, this one-sided secretion of the surface-consciousness, makes as it were a little cave of illusion for each separate soul. A literal and deliberate getting out of the cave must be for every mystic, as it was for Plato's prisoners, the first step in the individual hunt for reality.

In the plain language of old-fashioned theology "man's sin is stamped upon man's universe." We see a sham world because we live a sham life. We do not know ourselves; hence do not know the true character of our senses and instincts; hence attribute wrong values to their suggestions and declarations concerning our relation to the external world. That world, which we have distorted by identifying it with our own self-regarding arrangements of its elements, has got to reassume for us the character of Reality, of God. In the purified sight of the great mystics it did reassume this character: their shells were opened wide, they knew the tides of the Eternal Sea. This lucid apprehension of the True is what we mean when we speak of the Illumination which results from a faithful acceptance of the trials of the Purgative Way.

That which we call the "natural" self as it exists in the "natural" world--the "old Adam" of St. Paul--is wholly incapable of supersensual adventure. All its activities are grouped about a centre of consciousness whose correspondences are with the material world. In the moment of its awakening, it is abruptly made aware of this disability. It knows itself finite. It now aspires to the infinite. It is encased in the hard crust of individuality: it aspires to union with a larger self. It is fettered: it longs for freedom. Its every sense is attuned to illusion: it craves for harmony with the Absolute Truth. "God is the only Reality," says Patmore, "and we are real only as far as we are in His order and He is in us." [392] Whatever form, then, the mystical adventure may take it, must begin with a change in the attitude of the subject; a change which will introduce it into the order of Reality, and enable it to set up permanent relations with an Object which is not normally part of its universe. Therefore, though the end of mysticism is not adequately defined as goodness, it entails the acquirement of goodness. The virtues are the "ornaments of the spiritual marriage" because that marriage is union with the Good no less than with the Beautiful and the True.

Primarily, then, the self must be purged of all that stands between it and goodness: putting on the character of reality instead of the character of illusion or "sin." It longs ardently to do this from the first moment in which it sees itself in the all-revealing radiance of the Uncreated Light. "When love openeth the inner eyes of the soul for to see this truth," says Hilton, "with other circumstances that come withal then beginneth the soul for sooth to be vastly meek. For then by the sight of God it feeleth and seeth itself as it is, and then doth the soul forsake the beholding and leaning to itself." [393]

So, with Dante, the first terrace of the Mount of Purgatory is devoted to the cleansing of pride and the production of humility: the inevitable--one might almost say mechanical--result of a vision, however fleeting, of Reality, and an undistorted sight of the earthbound self. All its life that self has been measuring its candlelight by other candles. Now for the first time it is out in the open air and sees the sun. "This is the way," said the voice of God to St. Catherine of Siena in ecstasy. "If thou wilt arrive at a perfect knowledge and enjoyment of Me, the Eternal Truth, thou shouldst never go outside the knowledge of thyself; and by humbling thyself in the valley of humility thou wilt know Me and thyself, from which knowledge thou wilt draw all that is necessary. . . . In self knowledge, then, thou wilt humble thyself; seeing that, in thyself, thou dost not even exist." [394]

The first thing that the self observes, when it turns back upon itself in that awful moment of lucidity--enters, as St. Catherine says, into "the cell of self-knowledge,"--is the horrible contrast between its clouded contours and the pure sharp radiance of the Real; between its muddled faulty life, its perverse self-centred drifting, and the clear onward sweep of that Becoming in which it is immersed. It is then that the outlook of rapture and awe receives the countersign of repentance. The harbinger of that new self which must be born appears under the aspect of a desire: a passionate longing to escape from the suddenly perceived hatefulness of selfhood, and to conform to Reality, the Perfect which it has seen under its aspect of Goodness, of Beauty, or of Love--to be worthy of it, in fact to be real. "This showing," says Gerlac Petersen of that experience, "is so vehement and so strong that the whole of the interior man, not only of his heart but of his body, is marvellously moved and shaken, and faints within itself, unable to endure it. And by this means, his interior aspect is made clear without any cloud, and conformable in its own measure to Him whom he seeks." [395]

The lives of the mystics abound in instances of the "vehemence of this showing": of the deep-seated sense of necessity which urges the newly awakened self to a life of discomfort and conflict, often to intense poverty and pain, as the only way of replacing false experience by true. Here the transcendental consciousness, exalted by a clear intuition of its goal, and not merely "counting" but perceiving the world to be obviously well lost for such a prize, takes the reins. It forces on the unwilling surface mind a sharp vision of its own disabilities, its ugly and imperfect life; and the thirst for Perfection which is closely bound up with the mystic temperament makes instant response. "No more sins!" was the first cry of St. Catherine of Genoa in that crucial hour in which she saw by the light of love her own self-centred and distorted past. She entered forthwith upon the Purgative Way, in which for four years she suffered under a profound sense of imperfection, endured fasting, solitude and mortification; and imposed upon herself the most repulsive duties in her efforts towards that self-conquest which should make her "conformable in her own measure" to the dictates of that Pure Love which was the aspect of reality that she had seen. It is the inner conviction that this conformity--this transcendence of the unreal--is possible and indeed normal which upholds the mystic during the terrible years of Purgation: so that "not only without heaviness, but with a joy unmeasured he casts back all thing that may him let." [396]

To the true lover of the Absolute, Purgation no less than Illumination is a privilege, a dreadful joy. It is an earnest of increasing life. "Let me suffer or die!" said St. Teresa: a strange alternative in the ears of common sense, but a forced option in the spiritual sphere. However harsh its form, however painful the activities to which it spurs him, the mystic recognizes in this breakup of his old universe an essential part of the Great Work: and the act in which he turns to it is an act of loving desire, no less than an act of will. "Burning of love into a soul truly taken all vices purgeth: . . . for whilst the true lover with strong and fervent desire into God is borne, all things him displease that from the sight of God withdrawn." [397] His eyes once opened, he is eager for that costly ordering of his disordered loves which alone can establish his correspondences with Transcendental Life. "Teach me, my only joy," cries Suso, "the way in which I may bear upon my body the marks of Thy Love." "Come, my soul, depart from outward things and gather thyself together into a true interior silence, that thou mayst set out with all thy courage and bury and lose thyself in the desert of a deep contrition." [398]

It is in this torment of contrition, this acute consciousness of unworthiness, that we have the first swing back of the oscillating self from the initial state of mystic pleasure to the complementary state of pain. It is, so to speak, on its transcendental side, the reflex action which follows the first touch of God. Thus, we read that Rulman Merswin, "swept away by the transports of Divine Love," did not surrender himself to the passive enjoyment of this first taste of Absolute Being, but was impelled by it to diligent and instant self-criticism. He was "seized with a hatred of his body, and inflicted on himself such hard mortifications that he fell ill." [399] It is useless for lovers of healthy-mindedness to resent this and similar examples of self-examination and penance: to label them morbid or mediaeval. The fact remains that only such bitter knowledge of wrongness of relation, seen by the light of ardent love, can spur the will of man to the hard task of readjustment.

"I saw full surely," says Julian of Norwich, "that it behoveth needs to be that we should be in longing and in penance, until the time that we be led so deep into God that we verily and truly know our own soul." [400]

Dante's whole journey up the Mount of Purgation is the dramatic presentation of this one truth. So, too, the celebrated description of Purgatory attributed to St. Catherine of Genoa [401] is obviously founded upon its author's inward experience of this Purgative Way. In it, she applies to the souls of the dead her personal consciousness of the necessity of purification; its place in the organic process of spiritual growth. It is, as she acknowledges at the beginning, the projection of her own psychological adventures upon the background of the spiritual world: its substance being simply the repetition after death of that eager and heroic acceptance of suffering, those drastic acts of purification, which she has herself been compelled to undertake under the whip of the same psychic necessity--that of removing the rust of illusion, cleansing the mirror in order that it may receive the divine light. "It is," she says, "as with a covered object, the object cannot respond to the rays of the sun, not because the sun ceases to shine--for it shines without intermission--but because the covering intervenes. Let the covering be destroyed, and again the object will be exposed to the sun, and will answer to the rays which beat against it in proportion as the work of destruction advances. Thus the souls are covered by a rust--that is, by sin--which is gradually consumed away by the fire of purgatory. The more it is consumed, the more they respond to God their true Sun. Their happiness increases as the rust falls off and lays them open to the divine ray . . . the instinctive tendency to seek happiness in God develops itself, and goes on increasing through the fire of love which draws it to its end with such impetuosity and vehemence that any obstacle seems intolerable; and the more clear its vision, the more extreme its pain." [402]

"Mostratene la via di gire al monte!" cry the souls of the newly-dead in Dante's vision, [403] pushed by that "instinctive tendency" towards the purifying flames. Such a tendency, such a passionate desire, the aspiring self must have. No cool, well-balanced knowledge of the need of new adjustments will avail to set it on the Purgative Way. This is a heroic act, and demands heroic passions in the soul.

"In order to overcome our desires," says St. John of the Cross, who is the classic authority upon this portion of the mystic quest, "and to renounce all those things, our love and inclination for which are wont so to inflame the will that it delights therein, we require a more ardent fire and a nobler love--that of the Bridegroom. Finding her delight and strength in Him, the soul gains the vigour and confidence which enable her easily to abandon all other affections. It was necessary, in her struggle with the attractive force of her sensual desires, not only to have this love for the Bridegroom, but also to be filled with a burning fervour, full of anguish . . . if our spiritual nature were not on fire with other and nobler passions we should never cast off the yoke of the senses, nor be able to enter on their night, neither should we have the courage to remain in the darkness of all things, and in denial of every desire." [404]

"We must be filled with a burning fervour full of anguish." Only this deep and ardent passion for a perceived Object of Love can persuade the mystic to those unnatural acts of abnegation by which he kills his lesser love of the world of sense, frees himself from the "remora of desire," unifies all his energies about the new and higher centre of his life. His business, I have said, is transcendence: a mounting up, an attainment of a higher order of reality. Once his eyes have been opened on Eternity, his instinct for the Absolute roused from its sleep, he sees union with that Reality as his duty no less than his joy: sees too, that this union can only be consummated on a plane where illusion and selfhood have no place.

The inward voice says to him perpetually, at the least seasonable moments, "Dimitte omnia transitoria, quaere aeterna." [405] Hence the purgation of the senses, and of the character which they have helped to build is always placed first in order in the Mystic Way; though sporadic flashes of illumination and ecstasy may, and often do, precede and accompany it. Since spiritual no less than physical existence, as we know it, is an endless Becoming, it too has no end. In a sense the whole of the mystical experience in this life consists in a series of purifications, whereby the Finite slowly approaches the nature of its Infinite Source: climbing up the cleansing mountain pool by pool, like the industrious fish in Rulman Merswin's vision, until it reaches its Origin. The greatest of the contemplative saints, far from leaving purgation behind them in their progress, were increasingly aware of their own inadequateness, the nearer they approached to the unitive state: for the true lover of the Absolute, like every other lover, is alternately abased and exalted by his unworthiness and his good fortune. There are moments of high rapture when he knows only that the banner over him is Love: but there are others in which he remains bitterly conscious that in spite of his uttermost surrender there is within him an ineradicable residuum of selfhood, which "stains the white radiance of eternity."

In this sense, then, purification is a perpetual process. That which mystical writers mean, however, when they speak of the Way of Purgation, is rather the slow and painful completion of Conversion. It is the drastic turning of the self from the unreal to the real life: a setting of her house in order, an orientation of the mind to Truth. Its business is the getting rid, first of self-love; and secondly of all those foolish interests in which the surface-consciousness is steeped.

"The essence of purgation," says Richard of St. Victor, "is self-simplification." Nothing can happen until this has proceeded a certain distance: till the involved interests and tangled motives of the self are simplified, and the false complications of temporal life are recognized and cast away.

"No one," says another authority in this matter, "can be enlightened unless he be first cleansed or purified and stripped." [406] Purgation, which is the remaking of character in conformity with perceived reality, consists in these two essential acts: the cleansing of that which is to remain, the stripping of that which is to be done away. It may best be studied, therefore, in two parts: and I think that it will be in the reader's interest if we reverse the order which the "Theologia Germanica" adopts, and first consider Negative Purification, or self-stripping, and next Positive Purification, or character-adjustment. These, then, are the branches into which this subject will here be split. (1) The Negative aspect, the stripping or purging away of those superfluous, unreal, and harmful things which dissipate the precious energies of the self. This is the business of Poverty, or Detachment . (2) The Positive aspect: a raising to their highest term, their purest state, of all that remains--the permanent elements of character. This is brought about by Mortification, the gymnastic of the soul: a deliberate recourse to painful experiences and difficult tasks.

I. Detachment

Apart from the plain necessity of casting out imperfection and sin, what is the type of "good character" which will best serve the self in its journey towards union with the Absolute?

The mystics of all ages and all faiths agree in their answer. Those three virtues which the instinct of the Catholic Church fixed upon as the necessities of the cloistered life--the great Evangelical counsel of voluntary Poverty with its departments, Chastity, the poverty of the senses, and Obedience, the poverty of the will--are also, when raised to their highest term and transmuted by the Fire of Love, the essential virtues of the mystical quest.

By Poverty the mystic means an utter self-stripping, the casting off of immaterial as well as material wealth, a complete detachment from all finite things. By Chastity he means an extreme and limpid purity of soul, cleansed from personal desire and virgin to all but God: by Obedience, that abnegation of selfhood, that mortification of the will, which results in a complete self-abandonment, a "holy indifference" to the accidents of life. These three aspects of perfection are really one: linked together as irrevocably as the three aspects of the self. Their common characteristic is this: they tend to make the subject regard itself, not as an isolated and interesting individual, possessing desires and rights, but as a scrap of the Cosmos, an ordinary bit of the Universal Life, only important as a part of the All, an expression of the Will Divine. Detachment and purity go hand in hand, for purity is but detachment of the heart; and where these are present they bring with them that humble spirit of obedience which expresses detachment of will. We may therefore treat them as three manifestations of one thing: which thing is Inward Poverty. "Blessed are the poor in spirit, for theirs is the Kingdom of Heaven," is the motto of all pilgrims on this road.

"God is pure Good in Himself," says Eckhart, "therefore will He dwell nowhere but in a pure soul. There He can pour Himself out: into that He can wholly flow. What is Purity? It is that a man should have turned himself away from all creatures and have set his heart so entirely on the Pure Good that no creature is to him a comfort, that he has no desire for aught creaturely, save so far as he may apprehend therein the Pure Good, which is God. And as little as the bright eye can endure aught foreign in it, so little can the pure soul bear anything in it, any stain on it, that comes between it and God. To it all creatures are pure to enjoy; for it enjoyeth all creatures in God, and God in all creatures." [407]

"To it all creatures are pure to enjoy!" This is hardly the popular concept of the mystic; which credits him, in the teeth of such examples as St. Francis, St. Mechthild of Magdeburg, Rolle, Suso, and countless others, with a hearty dread of natural things. Too many examples of an exaggerated asceticism--such as the unfortunate story told of the holy Curé d'Ars, who refused to smell a rose for fear of sin--have supported in this respect the vulgar belief; for it is generally forgotten that though most mystics have practised asceticism as a means to an end, all ascetics are not mystics. Whatever may be the case with other deniers of the senses, it is true that the soul of the great mystic, dwelling on high levels of reality, his eyes set on the Transcendental World, is capable of combining with the perfection of detachment that intense and innocent joy in natural things, as veils and vessels of the divine, which results from seeing "all creatures in God and God in all creatures." "Whoso knows and loves the nobleness of My Freedom," said the voice of God to Mechthild of Magdeburg, "cannot bear to love Me alone, he must love also Me in the creatures." [408] That all-embracing love is characteristic of the illumination which results from a faithful endurance of the Purgative Way; for the corollary of "blessed are the pure in heart" is not merely a poetic statement. The annals of mysticism prove it to be a psychological law.

How then is this contradiction to be resolved: that the mystic who has declared the fundamental necessity of "leaving all creatures" yet finds them pure to enjoy? The answer to the riddle lies in the ancient paradox of Poverty: that we only enjoy true liberty in respect of such things as we neither possess nor desire. "That thou mayest have pleasure in everything, seek pleasure in nothing. That thou mayest know everything, seek to know nothing. That thou mayest possess all things, seek to possess nothing. . . . In detachment the spirit finds quiet and repose, for coveting nothing, nothing wearies it by elation, and nothing oppresses it by dejection, because it stands in the centre of its own humility. For as soon as it covets anything, it is immediately fatigued thereby." [409]

It is not love but lust--the possessive case, the very food of selfhood--which poisons the relation between the self and the external world and "immediately fatigues" the soul. Divide the world into "mine" and "not mine," and unreal standards are set up, claims and cravings begin to fret the mind. We are the slaves of our own property. We drag with us not a treasure, but a chain. "Behold," says the "Theologia Germanica," "on this sort must we cast all things from us and strip ourselves of them: we must refrain from claiming anything for our own. When we do this, we shall have the best, fullest, clearest, and noblest knowledge that a man can have, and also the noblest and purest love and desire." [410]

"Some there are," says Plotinus, "that for all their effort have not attained the Vision. . . . They have received the authentic Light, all their soul has gleamed as they have drawn near, but they come with a load on their shoulders which holds them back from the place of Vision. They have not ascended in the pure integrity of their being, but are burdened with that which keeps them apart. They are not yet made one within." [411] Accept Poverty, however, demolish ownership, the verb "to have" in every mood and tense, and this downward drag is at an end. At once the Cosmos belongs to you, and you to it. You escape the heresy of separateness, are "made one," and merged in "the greater life of the All." Then, a free spirit in a free world, the self moves upon its true orbit; undistracted by the largely self-imposed needs and demands of ordinary earthly existence.

This was the truth which St. Francis of Assisi grasped, and applied with the energy of a reformer and the delicate originality of a poet to every circumstance of the inner and the outer life. This noble liberty it is which is extolled by his spiritual descendant, Jacopone da Todi, in one of his most magnificent odes:--

"Povertá, alto sapere,
a nulla cosa sojacere,
en desprezo possedere
tutte le cose create. . . .
Dio non alberga en core stretto,
tant'é grande quant' hai affetto,
povertate ha si gran petto
che ci alberga deitate. . . .
Povertate è nulla avere
e nulla cosa poi volere;
ad omne cosa possedere
en spirito de libertate." [412]

"My little sisters the birds," said St. Francis, greatest adept of that high wisdom, "Brother Sun, Sister Water, Mother Earth." [413] Not my servants, but my kindred and fellow-citizens; who may safely be loved so long as they are not desired. So, in almost identical terms, the dying Hindu ascetic:--

"Oh Mother Earth, Father Sky,
Brother Wind, Friend Light, Sweetheart Water,
Here take my last salutation with folded hands!
For to-day I am melting away into the Supreme
Because my heart became pure,
And all delusion vanished,
Through the power of your good company."

It is the business of Lady Poverty to confer on her lovers this freedom of the Universe, to eradicate delusion, cut out the spreading growth of claimfulness, purify the heart, and initiate them into the "great life of the All." Well might St. Francis desire marriage with that enchantress, who gives back ten-fold all that she takes away. "Holy poverty," he said, "is a treasure so high excelling and so divine that we be not worthy to lay it up in our vile vessels; since this is that celestial virtue whereby all earthly things and fleeting are trodden underfoot, and whereby all hindrances are lifted from the soul, so that freely she may join herself to God Eternal." [414]

Poverty, then, prepares man's spirit for that union with God to which it aspires. She strips off the clothing which he so often mistakes for himself, transvaluates all his values, and shows him things as they are. "There are," says Eckhart, "four ascending degrees of such spiritual poverty. 1. The soul's contempt of all things that are not God. 2. Contempt of herself and her own works. 3. Utter self-abandonment. 4. Self-loss in the incomprehensible Being of God." [415] So, in the "Sacrum Commercium," when the friars, climbing "the steeps of the hill," found Lady Poverty at the summit "enthroned only in her nakedness," she "preventing them with the blessings of sweetness," said, "Why hasten ye so from the vale of tears to the mount of light? If, peradventure, it is me that ye seek, lo, I am but as you behold, a little poor one, stricken with storms and far from any consolation." Whereto the brothers answer, " Only admit us to thy peace; and we shall be saved ." [416]

The same truth: the saving peace of utter detachment from everything but Divine Reality--a detachment which makes those who have it the citizens of the world, and enabled the friars to say to Lady Poverty as they showed her from the hill of Assisi the whole countryside at her feet, "Hoc est claustrum nostrum, Domina," [417] --is taught by Meister Eckhart in a more homely parable.

"There was a learned man who, eight years long, desired that God would show him a man who would teach him the truth. And once when he felt a very great longing, a voice from God came to him and said, Go to the church, and there shalt thou find a man who shalt show thee the way to blessedness.' And he went thence and found a poor man whose feet were torn and covered with dust and dirt: and all his clothes were hardly worth three farthings. And he greeted him, saying:--

"God give you good day!'

"He answered: I have never had a bad day.'

"God give you good luck.'

"I have never had ill luck.'

"May you be happy! but why do you answer me thus?'

"I have never been unhappy.'

"Pray explain this to me, for I cannot understand it.'

"The poor man answered, Willingly. You wished me good day. I never had a bad day; for if I am hungry I praise God; if it freezes, hails, snows, rains, if the weather is fair or foul, still I praise God; am I wretched and despised, I praise God, and so I have never had an evil day. You wished that God would send me luck. But I never had ill luck, for I know how to live with God, and I know that what He does is best; and what God gives me or ordains for me, be it good or ill, I take it cheerfully from God as the best that can be, and so I have never had ill luck. You wished that God would make me happy. I was never unhappy; for my only desire is to live in God's will, and I have so entirely yielded my will to God's, that what God wills, I will.'

"But if God should will to cast you into hell,' said the learned man, what would you do then?'

"Cast me into hell? His goodness forbids! But if He did cast me into hell, I should have two arms to embrace Him. One arm is true humility, that I should lay beneath Him, and be thereby united to His holy humanity. And with the right arm of love, which is united with His holy divinity, I should so embrace Him that He would have to go to hell with me. And I would rather be in hell and have God, then in heaven and not have God.'

"Then the Master understood that true abandonment with utter humility is the nearest way to God.

"The Master asked further: Whence are you come?'

"From God.'

"Where did you find God?'

"When I forsook all creatures.'

"Where have you left God?'

"In pure hearts, and in men of good will.'

"The Master asked: What sort of man are you?'

"I am a king.'

"Where is your kingdom?'

"My soul is my kingdom, for I can so rule my senses inward and outward, that all the desires and power of my soul are in subjection, and this kingdom is greater than a kingdom on earth.' [418]

"What brought you to this perfection?'

"My silence, my high thoughts, and my union with God. For I could not rest in anything that was less than God. Now I have found God; and in God have eternal rest and peace.'" [419]

Poverty, then, consists in a breaking down of man's inveterate habit of trying to rest in, or take seriously, things which are "less than God": i.e. , which do not possess the character of reality. Such a habit is the most fertile of all causes of "world-weariness," disillusion and unrest: faults, or rather spiritual diseases, which the mystics never exhibit, but which few who are without all mystic feeling can hope to escape. Hence the sharpened perceptions of the contemplatives have always seen poverty as a counsel of prudence, a higher form of common sense. It was not with St. Francis, or any other great mystic, a first principle, an end in itself. It was rather a logical deduction from the first principle of their science--the paramount importance to the soul of an undistracted vision of reality.

Here East and West are in agreement: "Their science," says Al Ghazzali of the Sufis, who practised, like the early Franciscans, a complete renunciation of worldly goods, "has for its object the uprooting from the soul of all violent passions, the extirpation from it of vicious desires and evil qualities; so that the heart may become detached from all that is not God, and give itself for its only occupation meditation upon the Divine Being." [420]

All those who have felt themselves urged towards the attainment of this transcendental vision, have found that possessions interrupt the view; that claims, desires, attachments become centres of conflicting interest in the mind. They assume a false air of importance, force themselves upon the attention, and complicate life. Hence, in the interest of self-simplification, they must be cleared away: a removal which involves for the real enthusiast little more sacrifice than the weekly visit of the dustman. "Having entirely surrendered my own free-will," says Al Ghazzali of his personal experience," my heart no longer felt any distress in renouncing fame, wealth, or the society of my children." [421]

Others have reconciled self-surrender with a more moderate abandonment of outward things; for possessions take different rank for almost every human soul. The true rule of poverty consists in giving up those things which enchain the spirit, divide its interests, and deflect it on its road to God--whether these things be riches, habits, religious observances, friends, interests, distastes, or desires--not in mere outward destitution for its own sake. It is attitude, not act, that matters; self-denudation would be unnecessary were it not for our inveterate tendency to attribute false value to things the moment they become our own. "What is poverty of spirit but meekness of mind, by which a man knows his own infirmity?" says Rolle, "seeing that to perfect stableness he may not come but by the grace of God, all thing that him might let from that grace he forsakes, and only in joy of his Maker he sets his desire. And as of one root spring many branches, so of wilful poverty on this wise taken proceed virtues and marvels untrowed. Not as some, that change their clothes and not their souls; riches soothly it seems these forsake, and vices innumerable they cease not to gather. . . . If thou truly all thing for God forsake, see more what thou despised than what thou forsaketh. " [422]

The Poverty of the mystics, then, is a mental rather than a material state. Detachment of the will from all desire of possessions is the inner reality, of which Franciscan poverty is a sacrament to the world. It is the poor in spirit, not the poor in substance, who are to be spiritually blessed. "Let all things be forsaken of me," says Gerlac Petersen, "so that being poor I may be able in great inward spaciousness, and without any hurt, to suffer want of all those things which the mind of man can desire; out of or excepting God Himself." [423]

"The soul," says St. John of the Cross, "is not empty, so long as the desire for sensible things remains. But the absence of this desire for things produces emptiness and liberty of soul; even when there is an abundance of possessions." [424]

Every person in whom the mystical instinct awakes soon discovers in himself certain tastes or qualities which interrupt the development of that instinct. Often these tastes and qualities are legitimate enough upon their own plane; but they are a drain upon the energy of the self, preventing her from attaining that intenser life for which she was made and which demands her undivided zest. They distract her attention, fill the field of perception, stimulate her instinctive life: making of the surface-consciousness so active a thing that it can hardly be put to sleep. "Where can he have that pure and naked vision of unchangeable Truth whereby he see into all things," says Petersen again, "who is so busied in other things, not perhaps evil, which operate . . . upon his thoughts and imagination and confuse and enchain his mind . . . that his sight of that unique One in Whom all things are is overclouded?" [425]

The nature of these distracting factors which "confuse and enchain the mind" will vary with almost every individual. It is impossible to predict what those things will be which a self must give up, in order that the transcendental consciousness may grow. "It makes little difference whether a bird be held by a slender thread or by a rope; the bird is bound, and cannot fly until the cord that holds it is broken. It is true that a slender thread is more easily broken; still notwithstanding, if it is not broken the bird cannot fly. This is the state of a soul with particular attachments: it never can attain to the liberty of the divine union, whatever virtues it may possess. Desires and attachments affect the soul as the remora is said to affect a ship; that is but a little fish, yet when it clings to the vessel it effectually hinders its progress." [426]

Thus each adventurer must discover and extirpate all those interests which nourish selfhood, however innocent or even useful these interests may seem in the eyes of the world. The only rule is the ruthless abandonment of everything which is in the way. "When any man God perfectly desires to love, all things as well inward as outward that to God's love are contrary and from His love do let, he studies to do away." [427] This may mean the prompt and utter self-stripping of St. Francis of Assisi, who cast off his actual clothing in his relentless determination to have nothing of his own: [428] the reluctant bit-by-bit renunciations which at last set his follower Angela of Foligno free, or the drastic proceedings of Antoinette Bourignan, who found that a penny was enough to keep her from God.

"Being one night in a most profound Penitence," says the biographer of this extraordinary woman, "she said from the bottom of her Heart, O my Lord! what must I do to please Thee? For I have nobody to teach me. Speak to my soul and it will hear Thee.'" At that instant she heard, as if another had spoken within her "Forsake all earthly things. Separate thyself from the love of the creatures. Deny thyself." From this time, the more she entered into herself the more she was inclined to abandon all. But she had not the courage necessary for the complete renunciation towards which her transcendental consciousness was pressing her. She struggled to adjust herself to the inner and the outer life, but without success. For such a character as hers, compromise was impossible. "She asked always earnestly, When shall I be perfectly thine, O my God? and she thought He still answered her, When thou shalt no longer possess anything, and shalt die to thyself. And where shall I do that, Lord? He answered, In the Desert." At last the discord between her deeper and her superficial self became intolerable. Reinforced by the miseries of an unsympathetic home, still more by a threat of approaching marriage, the impulse to renunciation got its way. She disguised herself in a hermit's dress--she was only eighteen, and had no one to help or advise her--and "went out of her chamber about Four in the Morning, taking nothing but one Penny to buy Bread for that Day and it being said to her in the going out, Where is thy Faith? In a Penny? she threw it away. . . . Thus she went away wholly delivered from the heavy burthen of the

Cares and Good Things of this World." [429]

An admirable example of the mystic's attitude towards the soul-destroying division of interests, the natural but hopeless human struggle to make the best of both worlds, which sucks at its transcendental vitality, occurs in St. Teresa's purgative period. In her case this war between the real and the superficial self extended over many years; running side by side with the state of Illumination, and a fully developed contemplative life. At last it was brought to an end by a "Second Conversion" which unified her scattered interests and set her firmly and for ever on the Unitive Way. The virile strength of Teresa's character, which afterwards contributed to the greatness of her achievement, opposed the invading transcendental consciousness; disputed every inch of territory; resisted every demand made upon it by the growing spiritual self. Bit by bit it was conquered, the sphere of her deeper life enlarged; until the moment came in which she surrendered, once for all, to her true destiny. [430]

During the years of inward stress, of penance and growing knowledge of the Infinite, which she spent in the Convent of the Incarnation, and which accompanied this slow remaking of character, Teresa's only self-indulgence--as it seems, a sufficiently innocent one--was talking to the friends who came down from Avila to the convent-parlour, and spoke to her through the grille. Her confessors, unaccustomed to the education of mystical genius, saw nothing incompatible between this practice and the pursuit of a high contemplative life. But as her transcendental consciousness, her states of orison grew stronger, Teresa felt more and more the distracting influence of these glimpses of the outer world. They were a drain upon the energy which ought to be wholly given to that new, deep, more real life which she felt stirring within her, and which could only hope to achieve its mighty destiny by complete concentration upon the business in hand. No genius can afford to dissipate his energies: the mystic genius least of all. Teresa knew that so long as she retained these personal satisfactions, her life had more than one focus; she was not whole-hearted in her surrender to the Absolute. But though her inward voices, her deepest instincts, urged her to give them up, for years she felt herself incapable of such a sacrifice. It was round the question of their retention or surrender that the decisive battle of her life was fought.

"The devil," says her great Augustinian eulogist, Fray Luis de Leon, in his vivid account of these long interior struggles, "put before her those persons most sympathetic by nature; and God came, and in the midst of the conversation discovered Himself aggrieved and sorrowful. The devil delighted in the conversation and pastime, but when she turned her back on them and betook herself to prayer, God redoubled the delight and favours, as if to show her how false was the lure which charmed her at the grating, and that His sweetness was the veritable sweetness. . . . So that these two inclinations warred with each other in the breast of this blessed woman, and the authors who inspired them each did his utmost to inflame her most, and the oratory blotted out what the grating wrote, and at times the grating vanquished and diminished the good fruit produced by prayer, causing agony and grief which disquieted and perplexed her soul: for though she was resolved to belong entirely to God, she knew not how to shake herself free from the world: and at times she persuaded herself that she could enjoy both, which ended mostly, as she says, in complete enjoyment of neither. For the amusements of the locutorio were embittered and turned into wormwood by the memory of the secret and sweet intimacy with God; and in the same way when she retired to be with God, and commenced to speak with Him, the affections and thoughts which she carried with her from the grating took possession of her." [431]

Compare with these violent oscillations between the superficial and mystical consciousness--characteristic of Teresa's strong volitional nature, which only came to rest after psychic convulsions which left no corner of its being unexplored--the symbolic act of renunciation under which Antoinette Bourignan's "interior self" vanquished the surface intelligence and asserted its supremacy. Teresa must give up her passionate delight in human friendship. Antoinette, never much tempted in that direction, must give up her last penny. What society was to Teresa's generous, energetic nature, prudence was to the temperamentally shrewd and narrow Antoinette: a distraction, a check on the development of the all-demanding transcendental genius, an unconquered relic of the "lower life."

Many a mystic, however, has found the perfection of detachment to be consistent with a far less drastic renunciation of external things than that which these women felt to be essential to their peace. The test, as we have seen, does not lie in the nature of the things which are retained, but in the reaction which they stimulate in the self. "Absolute poverty is thine," says Tauler, "when thou canst not remember whether anybody has ever owed thee or been indebted to thee for anything; just as all things will be forgotten by thee in the last journey of death." [432] Poverty, in this sense, may be consistent with the habitual and automatic use of luxuries which the abstracted self never even perceives. Thus we are told that St. Bernard was reproached by his enemies with the inconsistency of preaching evangelical poverty whilst making his journeys from place to place on a magnificently caparisoned mule, which had been lent to him by the Cluniac monks. He expressed great contrition: but said that he had never noticed what it was that he rode upon. [433]

Sometimes, the very activity which one self has rejected as an impediment becomes for another the channel of spiritual perception. I have mentioned the Curé d'Ars, who, among other inhibitions, refused to allow himself to smell a rose. Yet St. Francis preached to the flowers, [434] and ordered a plot to be set aside for their cultivation when the convent garden was made, "in order that all who saw them might remember the Eternal Sweetness." [435] So, too, we are told of his spiritual daughter, St. Douceline, that "out of doors one day with her sisters, she heard a bird's note. What a lovely song!' she said: and the song drew her straight way to God. Did they bring her a flower, its beauty had a like effect ." [436] "To look on trees, water, and flowers," says St. Teresa of her own beginnings of contemplation, "helped her to recollect the Presence of God." [437] Here we are reminded of Plato. "The true order of going is to use the beauties of Earth as steps along which one mounts upwards for the sake of that other Beauty." This, too, is the true order of Holy Poverty: the selfless use, not the selfish abuse of lovely and natural things.

To say that some have fallen short of this difficult ideal and taken refuge in mere abnegation is but to say that asceticism is a human, not a superhuman art, and is subject to "the frailty of the creature." But on the whole, these excesses are mainly found amongst saintly types who have not exhibited true mystic intuition. This intuition, entailing as it does communion with intensest Life, gives to its possessors a sweet sanity, a delicate balance, which guards them, as a rule, from such conceptions of chastity as that of the youthful saint who shut himself in a cupboard for fear he should see his mother pass by: from the obedience which identifies the voice of the director with the voice of God; from detachment such as that exhibited by the Blessed Angela of Foligno, who, though a true mystic, viewed with almost murderous satisfaction the deaths of relatives who were "impediments." [438] The detachment of the mystic is just a restoration to the liberty in which the soul was made: it is a state of joyous humility in which he cries, "Nought I am, nought I have, nought I lack." To have arrived at this is to have escaped from the tyranny of selfhood: to be initiated into the purer air of that universe which knows but one rule of action--that which was laid down once for all by St. Augustine when he said, in the most memorable and misquoted of epigrams: "Love, and do what you like."

II. Mortification

By mortification, I have said, is to be understood the positive aspect of purification: the remaking in relation to reality of the permanent elements of character. These elements, so far, have subserved the interests of the old self, worked for it in the world of sense. Now they must be adjusted to the needs of the new self and to the transcendent world in which it moves. Their focal point is the old self; the "natural man" and his self-regarding instincts and desires. The object of mortification is to kill that old self, break up his egoistic attachments and cravings, in order that the higher centre, the "new man," may live and breathe. As St. Teresa discovered when she tried to reconcile the claims of worldly friendships and contemplation, one or other must go: a house divided against itself cannot stand. "Who hinders thee more," says Thomas a Kempis, "than the unmortified affections of thy own heart? . . . if we were perfectly dead unto ourselves, and not entangled within our own breasts, then should we be able to taste Divine things, and to have some experience of heavenly contemplation." [439]

In psychological language, the process of mortification is the process of setting up "new paths of neural discharge." That is to say, the mystic life has got to express itself in action: and for this new paths must be cut and new habits formed--all, in spite of the new self's enthusiasm, "against the grain"--resulting in a complete sublimation of personality. The energy which wells up incessantly in every living being must abandon the old road of least resistance and discharge itself in a new and more difficult way. In the terms of the hormic psychology, the conative drive of the psyche must be concentrated on new objectives; and the old paths, left to themselves, must fade and die. When they are dead, and the new life has triumphed, Mortification is at an end. The mystics always know when this moment comes. Often an inner voice then warns them to lay their active penances aside.

Since the greater and stronger the mystic, the stronger and more stubborn his character tends to be, this change of life and turning of energy from the old and easy channels to the new is often a stormy matter. It is a period of actual battle between the inharmonious elements of the self, its lower and higher springs of action: of toil, fatigue, bitter suffering, and many disappointments. Nevertheless, in spite of its etymological associations, the object of mortification is not death but life: the production of health and strength, the health and strength of the human consciousness viewed sub specie aeternitatis . "In the truest death of all created things, the sweetest and most natural life is hidden." [440]

"This dying," says Tauler again, "has many degrees, and so has this life. A man might die a thousand deaths in one day and find at once a joyful life corresponding to each of them. This is as it must be: God cannot deny or refuse this to death. The stronger the death the more powerful and thorough is the corresponding life; the more intimate the death, the more inward is the life. Each life brings strength, and strengthens to a harder death. When a man dies to a scornful word, bearing it in God's name, or to some inclination inward or outward, acting or not acting against his own will, be it in love or grief, in word or act, in going or staying; or if he denies his desires of taste or sight, or makes no excuses when wrongfully accused; or anything else, whatever it may be, to which he has not yet died, it is harder at first to one who is unaccustomed to it and unmortified than to him who is mortified. . . . A great life makes reply to him who dies in earnest even in the least things, a life which strengthens him immediately to die a greater death; a death so long and strong, that it seems to him hereafter more joyful, good and pleasant to die than to live, for he finds life in death and light shining in darkness."[441]

No more than detachment, then, is mortification an end in itself. It is a process, an education directed towards the production of a definite kind of efficiency, the adjustment of human nature to the demands of its new life. Severe, and to the outsider apparently unmeaning--like their physical parallels the exercises of the gymnasium--its disciplines, faithfully accepted, do release the self from the pull of the lower nature, establish it on new levels of freedom and power. "Mortification," says the Benedictine contemplative Augustine Baker, "tends to subject the body to the spirit and the spirit to God. And this it does by crossing the inclinations of sense, which are quite contrary to those of the Divine Spirit . . . by such crossing and afflicting of the body, self-love and self-will (the poison of our spirits) are abated, and in time in a sort destroyed; and instead of them there enter into the soul the Divine love and Divine will, and take possession thereof." [442] This transformation accomplished, mortification may end, and often does, with startling abruptness. After a martyrdom which lasted sixteen years, says Suso--speaking as usual in the third person--of his own experience, "On a certain Whitsun Day a heavenly messenger appeared to him, and ordered him in God's name to continue it no more. He at once ceased, and threw all the instruments of his sufferings [irons, nails, hair-shirt, etc.] into a river." [443] From this time onward, austerities of this sort had no part in Suso's life.

The Franco-Flemish mystic who wrote, and the English contemplative who translated, "The Mirror of Simple Souls," have between them described and explained in bold and accurate language the conditions under which the soul is enabled to abandon that "hard service of the virtues" which has absorbed it during the Purgative Way. The statement of the "French Book" is direct and uncompromising: well calculated to startle timid piety. "Virtues, I take leave of you for evermore!" exclaims the Soul. "Now shall mine heart be more free and more in peace than it hath been before. I wot well your service is too travaillous. . . . Some time I laid mine heart in you without any dissevering: ye wot well this: I was in all things to you obedient. O I was then your servant, but now I am delivered out of your thraldom."

To this astounding utterance the English translator has added a singularly illuminating gloss. "I am stirred here," he says, "to say more to the matter, as thus: First: when a soul giveth her to perfection, she laboureth busily day and night to get virtues, by counsel of reason, and striveth with vices at every thought, at every word and deed that she perceiveth cometh of them, and busily searcheth vices, them to destroy. Thus the virtues be mistresses, and every virtue maketh her to war with its contrary, the which be vices. Many sharp pains and bitterness of conscience feeleth the soul in this war. . . . But so long one may bite on the bitter bark of the nut, that at last he shall come to the sweet kernel. Right so, ghostly to understand, it fareth by these souls that be come to peace. They have so long striven with vices and wrought by virtues, that they be come to the nut kernel, that is, to the love of God, which is sweetness. And when the soul hath deeply tasted this love, so that this love of God worketh and hath his usages in her soul, then the soul is wondrous light and gladsome. . . . Then is she mistress and lady over the virtues, for she hath them all within herself. . . . And then this soul taketh leave of virtues, as of the thraldom and painful travail of them that she had before, and now she is lady and sovereign, and they be subjects." [444]

Jacopone da Todi speaks to the same effect:--

"La guerra è terminata
de le virtu battaglia,
de la mente travaglia
cosa nulla contende". [445]

Thus, St. Catherine of Genoa, after a penitential period of four years, during which she was haunted by a constant sense of sin, and occupied by incessant mortifications, found that "all thought of such mortifications was in an instant taken from her mind: in such a manner that, had she even wished to continue such mortifications, she would have been unable to do so . . . the sight of her sins was now taken from her mind, so that henceforth she did not catch a glimpse of them: it was as though they had all been cast into the depths of the sea." [446] In other words, the new and higher centre of consciousness, finally established, asserted itself and annihilated the old. "La guerra e teminata,"all the energy of a strong nature flows freely in the new channels; and mortification ceases, mechanically, to be possible to the now unified, sublimated, or "regenerated" self.

Mortification takes its name from the reiterated statement of all ascetic writers that the senses, or "body of desire," with the cravings which are excited by different aspects of the phenomenal world, must be mortified or killed; which is, of course, a description of psychological necessities from their special point of view. All those self-regarding instincts--so ingrained that they have become automatic--which impel the self to choose the more comfortable part, are seen by the awakened intuition of the embryo mystic as gross infringements of the law of love. "This is the travail that a man behoveth, to draw out his heart and his mind from the fleshly love and the liking of all earthly creatures, from vain thoughts and from fleshly imaginations, and out from the love and the vicious feeling of himself, that his soul should find no rest in no fleshly thought, nor earthly affection." [447] The rule of Poverty must be applied to the temper of normal consciousness as well as to the tastes and possessions of the self. Under this tonic influence, real life will thrive, unreal life will wither and die.

This mortifying process is necessary, not because the legitimate exercise of the senses is opposed to Divine Reality, but because those senses have usurped a place beyond their station; become the focus of energy, steadily drained the vitality of the self. "The dogs have taken the children's meat." The senses have grown stronger than their masters, monopolized the field of perception, dominated an organism which was made for greater activities, and built up those barriers of individuality which must be done away if true personality is to be achieved, and with it some share in the boundless life of the One. It is thanks to this wrong distribution of energy, this sedulous feeding of the cuckoo in the nest, that "in order to approach the Absolute, mystics must withdraw from everything, even themselves." [448] "The soul is plunged in utter ignorance, when she supposes that she can attain to the high estate of union with God before she casts away the desire of all things, natural and supernatural, which she may possess," says St. John of the Cross, "because the distance between them and that which takes place in the state of pure transformation in God is infinite." [449] Again, "until the desires be lulled to sleep by the mortification of sensuality, and sensuality itself be mortified in them, so that it shall war against the spirit no more, the soul cannot go forth in perfect liberty to union with the Beloved." [450]

The death of selfhood in its narrow individualistic sense is, then, the primary object of mortification. All the twisted elements of character which foster the existence of this unreal yet complex creature are to be pruned away. Then, as with the trees of the forest, so with the spirit of man, strong new branches will spring into being, grow towards air and light. "I live, yet not I" is to be the declaration of the mystic who has endured this "bodily death." The self-that-is-to-be will live upon a plane where her own prejudices and preferences are so uninteresting as to be imperceptible. She must be weaned from these nursery toys: and weaning is a disagreeable process. The mystic, however, undertakes it as a rule without reluctance: pushed by his vivid consciousness of imperfection, his intuition of a more perfect state, necessary to the fulfilment of his love. Often his entrance upon the torments of the Purgative Way, his taking up of the spiritual or material instruments of mortification, resembles in ardour and abruptness that "heroic plunge into Purgatory" of the newly dead when it perceives itself in the light of Love Divine, which is described in the "Treatise" of St. Catherine of Genoa as its nearest equivalent. "As she, plunged in the divine furnace of purifying love, was united to the Object of her love, and satisfied with all he wrought in her, so she understood it to be with the souls in Purgatory." [451]

This "divine furnace of purifying love" demands from the ardent soul a complete self-surrender, and voluntary turning from all impurity, a humility of the most far-reaching kind: and this means the deliberate embrace of active suffering, a self-discipline in dreadful tasks. As gold in the refiner's fire, so "burning of love into a soul truly taken all vices purgeth." Detachment may be a counsel of prudence, a practical result of seeing the true values of things; but the pain of mortification is seized as a splendid opportunity, a love token, timidly offered by the awakened spirit to that all-demanding Lover from Whom St. Catherine of Siena heard the terrible words "I, Fire, the Acceptor of sacrifices, ravishing away from them their darkness, give the light." [452] "Suffering is the ancient law of love," says the Eternal Wisdom to Suso, "there is no quest without pain, there is no lover who is not also a martyr. Hence it is inevitable that he who would love so high a thing as Wisdom should sometimes suffer hindrances and griefs." [453]

The mystics have a profound conviction that Creation, Becoming, Transcendence, is a painful process at the best. Those who are Christians point to the Passion of Christ as a proof that the cosmic journey to perfection, the path of the Eternal Wisdom, follows of necessity the Way of the Cross. That law of the inner life, which sounds so fantastic and yet is so bitterly true--"No progress without pain"--asserts itself. It declares that birth pangs must be endured in the spiritual as well as in the material world: that adequate training must always hurt the athlete. Hence the mystics' quest of the Absolute drives them to an eager and heroic union with the reality of suffering, as well as with the reality of joy.[454]

This divine necessity of pain, this necessary sharing in the travail of a World of Becoming, is beautifully described by Tauler in one of those "internal conversations" between the contemplative soul and its God, which abound in the works of the mystics and are familiar to all readers of "The Imitation of Christ." "A man once thought," says Tauler, "that God drew some men even by pleasant paths, while other were drawn by the path of pain. Our Lord answered him thus, What think ye can be pleasanter or nobler than to be made most like unto Me? that is by suffering. Mark, to whom was ever offered such a troubled life as to Me? And in whom can I better work in accordance with My true nobility than in those who are most like Me? They are the men who suffer. . . . Learn that My divine nature never worked so nobly in human nature as by suffering; and because suffering is so efficacious, it is sent out of great love. I understand the weakness of human nature at all times, and out of love and righteousness I lay no heavier load on man than he can bear. The crown must be firmly pressed down that is to bud and blossom in the Eternal Presence of of My Heavenly Father. He who desires to be wholly immersed in the fathomless sea of My Godhead must also be deeply immersed in the deep sea of bitter sorrow. I am exalted far above all things, and work supernatural and wonderful works in Myself: the deeper and more supernaturally a man crushes himself beneath all things the more supernaturally will he be drawn far above all things.'" [455]

Pain, therefore, the mystics always welcome and often court: sometimes in the crudely physical form which Suso describes so vividly and horribly in the sixteenth chapter of his Life, more frequently in those refinements of torture which a sensitive spirit can extract from loneliness, injustice, misunderstanding--above all, from deliberate contact with the repulsive accidents of life. It would seem from a collation of the evidence that the typical mystical temperament is by nature highly fastidious. Its passionate apprehension of spiritual beauty, its intuitive perception of divine harmony, is counterbalanced by an instinctive loathing of ugliness, a shrinking from the disharmonies of squalor and disease. Often its ideal of refinement is far beyond the contemporary standards of decency: a circumstance which is alone enough to provide ample opportunity of wretchedness. This extreme sensitiveness, which forms part of the normal psychophysical make-up of the mystic, as it often does of the equally highly-strung artistic type, is one of the first things to be seized upon by the awakened self as a disciplinary instrument. Then humility's axiom, "Naught is too low for love" is forced to bear the less lovely gloss, "Naught must be too disgusting."

Two reasons at once appear for this. One is the contempt for phenomena, nasty as well as nice--the longing to be free from all the fetters of sense--which often goes with the passion for invisible things. Those mystics to whom the attractions of earth are only illusion, are inconsistent if they attribute a greater reality to the revolting and squalid incidents of life. St. Francis did but carry his own principles to their logical conclusion, when he insisted that the vermin were as much his brothers as the birds. Real detachment means the death of preferences of all kinds: even of those which seem to other men the very proofs of virtue and fine taste.

The second reason is nobler. It is bound up with that principle of self-surrender which is the mainspring of the mystic life. To the contemplative mind, which is keenly conscious of unity in multiplicity--of Gods in the world--all disinterested service is service of the Absolute which he loves: and the harder it is, the more opposed to his self-regarding and aesthetic instincts, the more nearly it approaches his ideal. The point to which he aspires--though he does not always know it--is that in which all disharmony, all appearance of vileness, is resolved in the concrete reality which he calls the Love of God. Then, he feels dimly, everything will be seen under the aspect of a cosmic and charitable beauty; exhibiting through the woof of corruption the web of eternal life.

It is told of St. Francis of Assisi, in whom the love of lovely things was always paramount, how he forced himself to visit the lepers whose sight and smell disgusted him: how he served them and even kissed them. [456] "Then as he departed, in very truth that which had aforetime been bitter unto him, to wit, the sight and touch of lepers, now changed into sweetness. For, as he confessed, the sight of lepers had been so grievous unto him that he had been minded to avoid not only seeing them, but even going nigh their dwelling. And if at any time he chanced to pass their abodes, or to see them, albeit he were moved by compassion to do them an alms through another person, yet alway would he turn aside his face, stopping his nostrils with his hand. But through the grace of God he became so intimate a friend of the lepers that, even as he recorded in his will, he did sojourn with them and did humbly serve them."

Also, after his great renunciation of all property, he, once a prosperous young man who had been "dainty in his father's home," accustomed himself to take a bowl and beg scraps of food from door to door: and here too, as in the case of the lepers, that which at first seemed revolting became to him sweet. "And when he would have eaten that medley of various meats," says the legend, "at first he shrank back, for that he had never been used willingly even to see, much less to eat, such scraps. At length, conquering himself, he began to eat; and it seemed to him that in eating no rich syrup had he ever tasted aught so delightsome." [457]

The object, then, of this self-discipline is, like the object of all purgation, freedom: freedom from the fetters of the senses, the "remora of desire," from the results of environment and worldly education, from pride and prejudice, preferences and distaste: from selfhood in every form. Its effect is a sharp reaction to the joy of self-conquest. The very act that had once caused in the enchained self a movement of loathing becomes not merely indifferent, but an occasion of happiness. So Margery Kempe "had great mourning and sorrowing if she might not kiss a leper when she met them in the way for the love of our Lord, which was all contrary to her disposition in the years of her youth and prosperity, for then she abhorred them most." [458]

I spare the sensitive reader a detailed account of the loathsome ordeals by which St. Catherine of Genoa and Madame Guyon strove to cure themselves of squeamishness and acquire this liberty of spirit. [459] They, like St. Francis, St. Elizabeth of Hungary, and countless other seekers for the Real, sought out and served with humility and love the sick and the unclean; deliberately associated themselves with life in its meanest forms; compelled themselves to contact with the most revolting substances; and mortified the senses by the traditional ascetic expedient of deliberately opposing all--even their most natural and harmless--inclinations. "In the first four years after she received the sweet wound from her Lord," says the Life of St. Catherine of Genoa, she "made great penances: so that all her senses were mortified. And first, so soon as she perceived that her nature desired anything at once she deprived it thereof, and did so that it should receive all those things that it abhorred. She wore harsh hair, ate no meat nor any other thing that she liked; ate no fruit, neither fresh nor dried . . . and she lived greatly submitted to all persons, and always sought to do all those things which were contrary to her own will; in such a way that she was always inclined to do more promptly the will of others than her own." . . . "And while she worked such and so many mortifications of all her senses it was several times asked of her Why do you do this?' And she answered I do not know, but I feel myself drawn inwardly to do this . . . and I think it is God's will.'" [460]

St. Ignatius Loyola, in the world a highly bred Spanish gentleman of refined personal habits, found in those habits an excellent opportunity of mortification. "As he was somewhat nice about the arrangement of his hair, as was the fashion of those days and became him not ill, he allowed it to grow naturally, and neither combed it nor trimmed it nor wore any head covering by day or night. For the same reason he did not pare his finger or toe nails; for on these points he had been fastidious to an extreme." [461]

Madame Guyon, a delicate girl of the leisured class, accustomed to the ordinary comforts of her station, characteristically chose the most crude and immoderate forms of mortification in her efforts towards the acquirement of "indifference." But the peculiar psychic constitution which afterwards showed itself in the forms of automatism and clairvoyance, seems to have produced a partial anesthesia. "Although I had a very delicate body, the instruments of penitence tore my flesh without, as it seemed to me, causing pain. I wore girdles of hair and of sharp iron, I often held wormwood in my mouth." "If I walked, I put stones in my shoes. These things, my God, Thou didst first inspire me to do, in order that I might be deprived even of the most innocent satisfactions." [462]

In the earlier stages of their education, a constant agere contra, even in apparently indifferent things, seems essential to the mystics; till the point is reached at which the changes and chances of mortal life are accepted with a true indifference and do not trouble the life of the soul. This established ascendancy of the "interior man," the transcendental consciousness, over "sensitive nature"--the self in its reactions to the ups and downs and manifold illusions of daily life--is the very object of Purgation. It is, then, almost impossible that any mystic, whatever his religion, character or race, should escape its battles: for none at the beginning of their growth are in a position to dispense with its good offices. Neoplatonists and Mahommedans, no less than the Christian ascetics, are acquainted with the Purgative Way. All realize the first law of Spiritual Alchemy, that you must tame the Green Lion before you give him wings. Thus in Attar's allegory of the Valleys, the valley of self-stripping and renunciation comes first. [463] So too Al Ghazzali, the Persian contemplative, says of the period immediately following his acceptance of the principles of Sufi ism and consequent renunciation of property, "I went to Syria, where I remained more than two years; without any other object than that of living in seclusion and solitude, conquering my desires, struggling with my passions, striving to purify my soul, to perfect my character, and to prepare my heart to meditate upon God." At the end of this period of pure purgation circumstances forced him to return to the world; much to his regret, since he "had not yet attained to the perfect ecstatic state, unless it were in one or two isolated moments." [464]

Such gleams of ecstatic vision, distributed through the later stages of purification, seem to be normal features of mystical development. Increasing control of the lower centres, of the surface intelligence and its scattered desires, permits the emergence of the transcendental perceptions. We have seen that Fox in his early stages displayed just such an alternation between the light and shade of the mystic way. [465] So too did that least ascetic of visionaries, Jacob Boehme. "Finding within myself a powerful contrarium, namely the desires that belong to the flesh and blood," he says, "I began to fight a hard battle against my corrupted nature, and with the aid of God I made up my mind to overcome the inherited evil will, to break it, and to enter wholly into the Love of God. . . . This, however, was not possible for me to accomplish, but I stood firmly by my earnest resolution, and fought a hard battle with myself. Now while I was wrestling and battling, being aided by God, a wonderful light arose within my soul. It was a light entirely foreign to my unruly nature, but in it I recognized the true nature of God and man, and the relation existing between them, a thing which heretofore I had never understood, and for which I would never have sought." [466]

In these words Boehme bridges the gap between Purgation and Illumination: showing these two states or ways as coexisting and complementary one to another, the light and dark sides of a developing mystic consciousness. As a fact, they do often exist side by side in the individual experience: [467] and any treatment which exhibits them as sharply and completely separated may be convenient for purposes of study, but becomes at best diagrammatic if considered as a representation of the mystic life. The mystical consciousness, as we have seen, belongs--from the psychological point of view--to that mobile or "unstable" type in which the artistic temperament also finds a place. It sways easily between the extremes of pleasure and pain in its gropings after transcendental reality. It often attains for a moment to heights in which it is not able to rest: is often flung from some rapturous vision of the Perfect to the deeps of contrition and despair.

The mystics have a vivid metaphor by which to describe that alternation between the onset and the absence of the joyous transcendental consciousness which forms as it were the characteristic intermediate stage between the bitter struggles of pure Purgation, and the peace and radiance of the Illuminative Life. They call it Ludus Amoris , the "Game of Love" which God plays with the desirous soul. It is the "game of chess," says St. Teresa, "in which game Humility is the Queen without whom none can checkmate the Divine King." [468] "Here," says Martensen, "God plays a blest game with the soul." [469] The "Game of Love" is a reflection in consciousness of that state of struggle, oscillation and unrest which precedes the first unification of the self. It ceases when this has taken place and the new level of reality has been attained. Thus St. Catherine of Siena, that inspired psychologist, was told in ecstasy, "With the souls who have arrived at perfection, I play no more the Game of Love, which consists in leaving and returning again to the soul; though thou must understand that it is not, properly speaking, I, the immovable GOD, Who thus elude them, but rather the sentiment that My charity gives them of Me." [470] In other terms, it is the imperfectly developed spiritual perception which becomes tired and fails, throwing the self back into the darkness and aridity whence it has emerged. So we are told of Rulman Merswin [471] that after the period of harsh physical mortification which succeeded his conversion came a year of "delirious joy alternating with the most bitter physical and moral sufferings." It is, he says, "the Game of Love which the Lord plays with His poor sinful creature." Memories of all his old sins still drove him to exaggerated penances: morbid temptations "made me so ill that I feared I should lose my reason." These psychic storms reacted upon the physical organism. He had a paralytic seizure, lost the use of his lower limbs, and believed himself to be at the point of death. When he was at his worst, however, and all hope seemed at an end, an inward voice told him to rise from his bed. He obeyed, and found himself cured. Ecstasies were frequent during the whole of this period. In these moments of exaltation he felt his mind to be irradiated by a new light, so that he knew, intuitively, the direction which his life was bound to take, and recognized the inevitable and salutary nature of his trials. "God showed Himself by turns harsh and gentle: to each access of misery succeeded the rapture of supernatural grace." In this intermittent style, torn by these constant fluctuations between depression and delight, did Merswin, in whom the psychic instability of the artistic and mystic types is present in excess, pass through the purgative and illuminated states. [472] They appear to have coexisted in his consciousness, first one and then the other emerging and taking control. Hence he did not attain the peaceful condition which is characteristic of full illumination, and normally closes the "First Mystic Life"; but passed direct from these violent alternations of mystical pleasure and mystical pain to the state which he calls "the school of suffering love." This, as we shall see when we come to its consideration, is strictly analogous to that which other mystics have called the "Dark Night of the Soul," and opens the "Second Mystic Life" or Unitive Way.

Such prolonged coexistence of alternating pain and pleasure states in the developing soul, such delay in the attainment of equilibrium, is not infrequent, and must be taken into account in all analyses of the mystic type. Though it is convenient for purposes of study to practise a certain dissection, and treat as separate states which are, in the living subject, closely intertwined, we should constantly remind ourselves that such a proceeding is artificial. The struggle of the self to disentangle itself from illusion and attain the Absolute is a life-struggle. Hence, it will and must exhibit the freedom and originality of life: will, as a process, obey artistic rather than scientific laws. It will sway now to the light and now to the shade of experience: its oscillations will sometimes be great, sometimes small. Mood and environment, inspiration and information, will all play their part.

There are in this struggle three factors.

(1) The unchanging light of Eternal Reality: that Pure Being "which ever shines and nought shall ever dim."

(2) The web of illusion, here thick, there thin; which hems in, confuses, and allures the sentient self.

(3) That self, always changing, moving, struggling--always, in fact, becoming-- alive in every fibre, related at once to the unreal and to the real; and, with its growth in true being, ever more conscious of the contrast between them.

In the ever-shifting relations between these three factors, the consequent energy engendered, the work done, we may find a cause of the innumerable forms of stress and travail which are called in their objective form the Purgative Way. One only of the three is constant: the Absolute to which the soul aspires. Though all else may fluctuate, that goal is changeless. That Beauty so old and so new, "with whom is no variableness, neither shadow of turning," which is the One of Plotinus, the All of Eckhart and St. John of the Cross, the Eternal Wisdom of Suso, the Unplumbed Abyss of Ruysbroeck, the Pure

Love of St. Catherine of Genoa, awaits yesterday, to-day, and for ever the opening of Its creature's eyes.

In the moment of conversion those eyes were opened for an instant: obtained, as it were, a dazzling and unforgettable glimpse of the Uncreated Light. They must learn to stay open: to look steadfastly into the eyes of Love: so that, in the beautiful imagery of the mystics, the "faithful servant" may become the "secret friend." [473] Then it is, says Boehme, that "the divine glimpse and beam of joy ariseth in the soul, being a new eye, in which the dark, fiery soul conceiveth the Ens and Essence of the divine light." [474] So hard an art is not at once acquired in its perfection. It is in accordance with all that we know of the conditions of development that a partial achievement should come first; bewildering moments of lucidity, splendid glimpses, whose brevity is due to the weakness of the newly opened and unpractised "eye which looks upon Eternity," the yet undisciplined strength of the "eye which looks upon Time." Such is that play of light and dark, of exaltation and contrition, which often bridges the gap between the Purgative and the Illuminative states. Each by turn takes the field and ousts the other; for "these two eyes of the soul of man cannot both perform their work at once." [475]

To use another and more domestic metaphor, that Divine Child which was, in the hour of the mystic conversion, born in the spark of the soul, must learn like other children to walk. Though it is true that the spiritual self must never lose its sense of utter dependence on the Invisible; yet within that supporting atmosphere, and fed by its gifts, it must "find its feet." Each effort to stand brings first a glorious sense of growth, and then a fall: each fall means another struggle to obtain the difficult balance which comes when infancy is past. There are many eager trials, many hopes, many disappointments. At last, as it seems suddenly, the moment comes: tottering is over, the muscles have learnt their lesson, they adjust themselves automatically, and the new self suddenly finds itself--it knows not how--standing upright and secure. That is the moment which marks the boundary between the purgative and the illuminative states.

The process of this passage of the "new" or spiritual man from his awakening to the illuminated life, has been set out by Jacob Boehme in language which is at once poetic and precise. "When Christ the Corner-Stone [i.e. , the divine principle latent in man] stirreth himself in the extinguished Image of Man in his hearty Conversion and Repentance," he says, "then Virgin Sophia appeareth in the stirring of the Spirit of Christ in the extinguished Image, in her Virgin's attire before the Soul; at which the Soul is so amazed and astonished in its Uncleanness that all its Sins immediately awake in it, and it trembleth before her; for then the judgment passeth upon the Sins of the Soul, so that it even goeth back in its unworthiness, being ashamed in the Presence of its fair Love, and entereth into itself, feeling and acknowledging itself utterly unworthy to receive such a Jewel. This is understood by those who are of our tribe and have tasted of this heavenly Gift, and by none else. But the noble Sophia draweth near in the Essence of the Soul, and kisseth it in friendly Manner, and tinctureth its dark Fire with her Rays of Love, and shineth through it with her bright and powerful Influence. Penetrated with the strong Sense and Feeling of which, the Soul skippeth in its Body for great Joy, and in the strength of this Virgin Love exulteth, and praiseth the great God for his blest Gift of Grace. I will set down here a short description how it is when the Bride thus embraceth the Bridegroom, for the consideration of the Reader, who perhaps hath not yet been in this wedding chamber. It may be he will be desirous to follow us, and to enter into the Inner Choir, where the Soul joineth hands and danceth with Sophia, or the Divine Wisdom." [476]

Footnotes:

392. "The Rod, the Root, and the Flower," "Magna Moralia," xxii.

393. "The Scale of Perfection," bk. ii. cap. xxxvii.

394. Dialogo, cap. iv.

395. "Ignitum cum Deo Soliloquium." cap. xi.

396. Richard Rolle, "The Mending of Life," cap. i.

397. Ibid ., "The Fire of Love," bk. i. cap, xxiii.

398. "Buchlein von der ewigen Weisheit," cap. v.

399. Jundt, "Rulman Merswin," p. 19.

400. Revelations of Divine Love," cap. lvi.

401. I offer no opinion upon the question of authorship. Those interested may consult Von Hügel, "The Mystical Element of Religion," vol. i., Appendix. Whoever may be responsible for its present form, the Treatise is clearly founded upon first-hand mystic experience: which is all that our present purpose requires.

402. "Trattato di Purgatorio," caps. ii. and iii.

403. Purg. ii., 60.

404. "Subida del Monte Carmelo I. i. cap. xiv.

405. "De Imitatione Christi," I. iii. cap. i.

406. "Theologia Germanica," cap. xiv.

407. Meister Eckhart, quoted by Wackernagel, "Altdeutsches Lesebuch," p. 891.

408. "Das Fliessende Licht der Gottheit." pt. vi., cap. 4.

409. St. John of the Cross, "Subida del Monte Carmelo," bk. i. cap. xiii.

410. "Theologia Germanica," cap. v.

411. Ennead vi. 9.

412. "Oh Poverty, high wisdom! to be subject to nothing, and by despising all to possess all created things. . . . God will not lodge in a narrow heart; and it is as great as thy love. Poverty has so ample a bosom that Deity Itself may lodge therein. . . . Poverty is naught to have, and nothing to desire: but all things to possess in the spirit of liberty."-- Jacopone da Todi. Lauda lix.

413. "Fioretti," cap. xvi., and "Speculum," cap. cxx.

414. Ibid ., cap. xiii. (Arnold's translation).

415. Pfeiffer, Tractato x. (Eng. translation., p, 348).

416. "Sacrum Commercium Beati Francisci cum Domina Paupertate," caps. iv. and v. (Rawnsley's translation).

417. Op. cit ., cap. xxii.

418. So Ruysbroeck, "Freewill is the king of the soul . . . he should dwell in the chief city of that kingdom: that is to say, the desirous power of the soul" ("De Ornatu Spiritalium Nuptiarum," I. i. cap. xxiv.).

419. Meister Eckhart. Quoted in Martensen's monograph, p. 107.

420. Schmölders, "Essai sur les Écoles Philosophiques chez les Arabes," p. 54.

421. Schmölders, "Essai sur les Écoles Philosophiques chez les Arabes," op. cit., p. 58.

422. Richard Rolle, "The Mending of Life," cap. iii.

423. "Ignitum cum Deo Soliloquium," cap. i.

424. "Subida del Monte Carmelo," I. i. cap. iii.

425. Gerlac Petersen, op. cit., cap. xi.

426. St. John of the Cross, op. cit ., cap. xi.

427. Richard Rolle, "The Fire of Love," bk. i. cap. xix.

428. Thomas of Celano, Legenda Prima, cap. vi.

429. "An Apology for Mrs. Antoinette Bourignan," pp. 269-70.

430. St. Teresa's mystic states are particularly difficult to classify. From one point of view these struggles might be regarded as the preliminaries of conversion. She was, however, proficient in contemplation when they occurred, and I therefore think that my arrangement is the right one.

431. Quoted by G. Cunninghame Graham, "Santa Teresa," vol. i. p. 139. For St. Teresa's own account, see Vida, caps. vii-ix.

432. Sermon on St. Paul ("The Inner Way," p. 113).

433. Cotter Morison, "Life and Times of St. Bernard," p. 68.

434. Thomas of Celano, Legenda Prima, cap. xxix.

435. Ibid ., Legenda Secunda, cap. cxxiv.

436. Anne Macdonell, "St. Douceline," p. 30.

437. Vida, cap. ix., p. 6.

438. "In that time and by God's will there died my mother, who was a great hindrance unto me in following the way of God: soon after my husband died likewise, and also all my children. And because I had commenced to follow the Aforesaid Way, and had prayed God that He would rid me of them, I had great consolation of their deaths. (Ste Angèle de Foligno: "Le Livre de l'Expérience des Vrais Fidèles." Ed. M. J. Ferry p. 10.)

439. "De Imitatione Christi," I. i. caps. iii. and ix.

440. Tauler, Sermon on St. Paul ("The Inner Way," p. 114).

441. Tauler, Second Sermon for Easter Day. (This is not included in either of the English collections.)

442. Augustine Baker, "Holy Wisdom," Treatise ii. Sect. i., cap. 3.

443. Suso, Leben. cap. xvii.

444. "The Mirror of Simple Souls," edited by Clare Kirchberger, p. 12.

445. "The war is at an end: in the battle of virtues, in travail of mind, there is no more striving" (Lauda xci.).

446. "Vita e Dottrina," cap. v.

447. Walter Hilton "The Scale of Perfection," bk. i. cap. 8, xlii.

448. Récéjac, "Fondements de la Connaissance Mystique," p. 78. This, however, is to be understood of the initial training of the mystic; not of his final state.

449. "Subida del Monte Carmelo," I. i. cap. v.

450. Op. cit., bk. i. cap. xv.

451. S. Caterina di Genova, "Trattato di Purgatorio," cap. i.

452. Dialogo, cap. lxxxv.

453. Leben, cap. iv.

454. "This truth, of which she was the living example," says Huysmans of St. Lydwine, "has been and will be true for every period. Since the death of Lydwine, there is not a saint who has not confirmed it. Hear them formulate their desires. Always to suffer, and to die! cries St. Teresa; always to suffer, yet not to die, corrects St. Magdalena dei Pazzi; yet more, oh Lord, yet more! exclaims St. Francis Xavier, dying in anguish on the coast of China; I wish to be broken with suffering in order that I may prove my love to God, declares a seventeenth century Carmelite, the Ven. Mary of the Trinity. The desire for suffering is itself an agony, adds a great servant of God of our own day, Mother Mary Du Bourg; and she confided to her daughters in religion that if they sold pain in the market she would hurry to buy it there.'" (J. K. Huysmans, "Sainte Lydwine de Schiedam," 3rd edition, p. 225).Examples can be multiplied indefinitely from the lives and works of the mystics of all periods.

455. Tauler, Sermon on St. Paul ("The Inner Way," p. 114).

456. Thomas of Celano, Legenda Prima, cap. vii.; 3 Soc. cap. iv.

457. 3 Soc. cap. vii.

458. "A Short Treatise of Contemplation taken out of the boke of Margery Kempe ancresse of Lynne." London, 1521. Reprinted and ed. by F. Gardner in "The Cell of Self-Knowledge," 1910, p. 49.

459. The curious are referred to the original authorities. For St. Catherine chapter viii. of the "Vita e Dottrina": for Madame Guyon, Vie, pt. i. ch. x.

460. "Vita e Dottrina," cap. v.

461. Testament, cap. ii. (Rix's translation).

462. Vie, pt. i. cap. x.

463. Supra , p. 131.

464. Schmölders, "Essay sur les Écoles Philosophiques chez les Arabes," p. 59.

465. Supra , p. 177.

466. Hartmann, "Life and Doctrines of Jacob Boehme," p. 50.

467. Compare the case of St. Teresa already cited, supra , p. 213.

468. "Camino de Perfeccion," cap. xvii.

469. Martensen, "Meister Eckhart," p. 75.

470. Dialogo, cap. lxxviii.

471. Jundt, "Rulman Merswin," pp. 10 and 20.

472. We recognize here the chief symptoms of the "cyclic type" of mentality, with its well-marked alternations of depression and exaltation. This psychological type is found frequently, but not invariably, among the mystics: and its peculiarities must be taken into account when studying their experiences. For a technical description, see W. McDougall: "An Introduction to Abnormal Psychology," caps. xxii and xxviii.

473. See Ruysbroeck, "De Calculo," cap. vii. The metaphor is an ancient one and occurs in many patristic and mediaeval writers.

474. "The Epistles of Jacob Boehme," p. 19.

475. "Theologia Germanica," cap. vii.

476. Jacob Boehme, "The Way to Christ," pt. i. p. 23 (vol. iv. of the complete English translation of Boehme's works).

CHAPTER IV

In illumination we come to that state of consciousness which is popularly supposed to be peculiar to the mystic: a form of mental life, a kind of perception, radically different from that of "normal" men. His preceding adventures and experiences cannot be allowed this quality. His awakening to consciousness of the Absolute--though often marked by a splendour and intensity which seem to distinguish it from other psychic upheavals of that kind--does but reproduce upon higher levels those characteristic processes of conversion and falling in love which give depth and actuality to the religious and passional life. The purification to which he then sets himself--though this possesses as a rule certain features peculiar to mystical development--is again closely related to the disciplines and mortifications of ascetic, but not necessarily mystical, piety. It is the most exalted form with which we are acquainted of that catharsis-- that pruning and training of the human plant--which is the essence of all education, and a necessary stage in every kind of transcendence. Here, the mystic does but adopt in a more drastic form the principles which all who would live with an intense life, all seekers after freedom, all true lovers must accept: though he may justly claim with Ophelia that these wear their rue with a difference.[477]

But in the great swing back into sunshine which is the reward of that painful descent into the "cell of self-knowledge," he parts company with these other pilgrims. Those who still go with him a little way--certain prophets, poets, artists, dreamers do so in virtue of that mystical genius, that instinct for transcendental reality, of which all seers and creators have some trace. The initiates of beauty or of wisdom, as the great mystic is the initiate of love, they share in some degree the experiences of the way of illumination. But the mystic has now a veritable foothold in that transcendental world into which they penetrate now and again: enjoys a certain fellowship--not yet union--with the "great life of the All," and thence draws strength and peace. Really and actually, as one whose noviciate is finished, he has "entered the Inner Choir, where the Soul joineth hands and danceth with Sophia, the Divine Wisdom": and, keeping time with the great rhythms of the spiritual universe, feels that he has found his place.

This change of consciousness, however abrupt and amazing it may seem to the self which experiences it, seems to the psychologist a normal phase in that organic process of development which was initiated by the awakening of the transcendental sense. Responding to the intimations received in that awakening, ordering itself in their interest, concentrating its scattered energies on this one thing, the self emerges from long and varied acts of purification to find that it is able to apprehend another order of reality. It has achieved consciousness of a world that was always there, and wherein its substantial being--that Ground which is of God--has always stood. Such a consciousness is "Transcendental Feeling" in excelsis : a deep, intuitional knowledge of the "secret plan."

"We are like a choir who stand round the conductor," says Plotinus, "but do not always sing in tune, because their attention is diverted by looking at external things. So we always move round the One--if we did not, we should dissolve and cease to exist--but we do not always look towards the One." Hence, instead of that free and conscious co-operation in the great life of the All which alone can make personal life worth living, we move like slaves or marionettes, and, oblivious of the whole to which our little steps contribute, fail to observe the measure "whereto the worlds keep time." Our minds being distracted from the Corypheus in the midst the "energetic Word" who sets the rhythm, we do not behold Him. We are absorbed in the illusions of sense; the "eye which looks on Eternity" is idle. "But when we do behold Him," says Plotinus again, "we attain the end of our existence and our rest. Then we no longer sing out of tune, but form a truly divine chorus about Him; in the which chorus dance the soul beholds the Fountain of life the Fountain of intellect, the Principle of Being, the cause of good the root of soul." [478] Such a beholding, such a lifting of consciousness from a self-centred to a God-centred world, is of the essence of illumination.

It will be observed that in these passages the claim of the mystic is not yet to supreme communion; the "Spiritual Marriage" of the Christian mystic, or that "flight of the Alone to the Alone" which is the Plotinian image for the utmost bliss of the emancipated soul. He has now got through preliminaries; detached himself from his chief entanglements; re-orientated his instinctive life. The result is a new and solid certitude about God, and his own soul's relation to God: an "enlightenment" in which he is adjusted to new standards of conduct and thought. In the traditional language of asceticism he is "proficient" but not yet perfect. He achieves a real vision and knowledge, a conscious harmony with the divine World of Becoming: not yet self-loss in the Principle of Life, but rather a willing and harmonious revolution about Him, that "in dancing he may know what is done." This character distinguishes almost every first-hand description of illumination: and it is this which marks it off from mystic union in all its forms. All pleasurable and exalted states of mystic consciousness in which the sense of I-hood persists, in which there is a loving and joyous relation between the Absolute as object and the self as subject, fall under the head of Illumination: which is really an enormous development of the intuitional life at high levels. All veritable and first-hand apprehensions of the Divine obtained by the use of symbols, as in the religious life; all the degrees of prayer lying between meditation and the prayer of union; many phases of poetic inspiration and "glimpses of truth," are activities of the illuminated mind.

To "see God in nature," to attain a radiant consciousness of the "otherness" of natural things, is the simplest and commonest form of illumination. Most people, under the spell of emotion or of beauty, have known flashes of rudimentary vision of this kind. Where such a consciousness is recurrent, as it is in many poets, [479] there results that partial yet often overpowering apprehension of the Infinite Life immanent in all living things, which some modern writers have dignified by the name of "nature-mysticism." Where it is raised to its highest denomination, till the veil is obliterated by the light behind, and "faith has vanished into sight," as sometimes happened to Blake, we reach the point at which the mystic swallows up the poet.

"Dear Sir," says that great genius in one of his most characteristic letters, written immediately after an onset of the illuminated vision which he had lost for many years, "excuse my enthusiasm, or rather madness, for I am really drunk with intellectual vision whenever I take a pencil or graver into my hand." [480] Many a great painter, philosopher, or poet, perhaps every inspired musician, has known this indescribable inebriation of Reality in those moments of transcendence in which his masterpieces were conceived. This is the "saving madness" of which Plato speaks in the "Phaedrus"; the ecstasy of the "God-intoxicated man," the lover, the prophet, and the poet "drunk with life." When the Christian mystic, eager for his birthright, says "Sanguis Christi, inebria me!" he is asking for just such a gift of supernal vitality, a draught of that Wine of Absolute Life which runs in the arteries of the world. Those to whom that cup is given attain to an intenser degree of vitality, hence to a more acute degree of perception, a more vivid consciousness, than that which is enjoyed by other men. For though, as Ruysbroeck warns us, this "is not God," yet it is for many selves "the Light in which we see Him." [481]

Blake conceived that it was his vocation to bring this mystical illumination, this heightened vision of reality, within the range of ordinary men: to "cleanse the doors of perception" of the race. They thought him a madman for his pains.

". . . I rest not upon my great task
To open the Eternal Worlds, to open the immortal Eyes
Of Man inwards into the Worlds of Thought: into Eternity
Ever expanding in the Bosom of God, the Human Imagination.
O Saviour, pour upon me thy Spirit of meekness and love,
Annihilate the Selfhood in me: be thou all my life." [482]

The Mysteries of the antique world appear to have been attempts--often by way of a merely magical initiation--to "open the immortal eyes of man inwards": exalt his powers of perception until they could receive the messages of a higher degree of reality. In spite of much eager theorizing, it is impossible to tell how far they succeeded in this task. To those who had a natural genius for the Infinite, symbols and rituals which were doubtless charged with ecstatic suggestions, and often dramatized the actual course of the Mystic Way, may well have brought some enhancement of consciousness: [483] though hardly that complete rearrangement of character which is an essential of the mystic's entrance on the true Illuminated State. Hence Plato only claims that "he whose initiation is recent" can see Immortal Beauty under mortal veils.

"O blessèd he in all wise,
Who hath drunk the Living Fountain
Whose life no folly staineth
And whose soul is near to God:
Whose sins are lifted pall-wise
As he worships on the Mountain." [484]

Thus sang the initiates of Dionysus; that mystery-cult in which the Greeks seem to have expressed all they knew of the possible movement of consciousness through rites of purification to the ecstasy of the Illuminated Life. The mere crude rapture of illumination has seldom been more vividly expressed. With its half-Oriental fervours, its self-regarding glory in personal purification achieved, and the spiritual superiority conferred by adeptship, may be compared the deeper and lovelier experience of the Catholic poet and saint, who represents the spirit of Western mysticism at its best. His sins, too, had been "lifted pall-wise" as a cloud melts in the sunshine of Divine Love: but here the centre of interest is not the little self which has been exalted, but the greater Self which deigns thus to exalt.

"O burn that burns to heal!
O more than pleasant wound!
And O soft hand, O touch most delicate
That dost new life reveal
That dost in grace abound
And, slaying, dost from death to life translate." [485]

Here the joy is as passionate, the consciousness of an exalted life as intense: but it is dominated by the distinctive Christian concepts of humility, surrender, and intimate love.

We have seen that all real artists, as well as all pure mystics, are sharers to some degree in the Illuminated Life. They have drunk, with Blake, from that cup of intellectual vision which is the chalice of the Spirit of Life: know something of its divine inebriation whenever Beauty inspires them to create. Some have only sipped it. Some, like John of Parma, have drunk deep, accepting in that act the mystic heritage with all its obligations. But to all who have seen Beauty face to face, the Grail has been administered; and through that sacramental communion they are made participants in the mystery of the world.

In one of the most beautiful passages of the "Fioretti" it is told how Brother Jacques of la Massa, "unto whom God opened the door of His secrets," saw in a vision this Chalice of the Spirit of Life delivered by Christ into the hands of St. Francis, that he might give his brothers to drink thereof.

"Then came St. Francis to give the chalice of life to his brothers. And he gave it first to Brother John of Parma: who, taking it drank it all in haste, devoutly; and straightway he became all shining like the sun. And after him St. Francis gave it to all the other brothers in order: and there were but few among them that took it with due reverence and devotion and drank it all. Those that took it devoutly and drank it all, became straightway shining like the sun; but those that spilled it all and took it not devoutly, became black, and dark, and misshapen and horrible to see; but those that drank part and spilled part, became partly shining and partly dark, and more so or less according to the measure of their drinking or spilling thereof. But the aforesaid Brother John was resplendent above all the rest; the which had more completely drunk the chalice of life, whereby he had the more deeply gazed into the abyss of the infinite light divine ." [486]

No image, perhaps, could suggest so accurately as this divine picture the conditions of perfect illumination: the drinking deeply, devoutly, and in haste--that is, without prudent and self-regarding hesitation--of the heavenly Wine of Life; that wine of which Rolle says that it "fulfils the soul with a great gladness through a sweet contemplation." [487] John of Parma, the hero of those Spiritual Franciscans in whose interest this exquisite allegory was composed, stands for all the mystics, who, "having completely drunk," have attained the power of gazing into the abyss of the infinite light divine. In those imperfect brothers who dared not drink the cup of sacrifice to the dregs, but took part and spilled part, so that they became partly shining and partly dark, "according to the measure of their drinking or spilling thereof," we may see an image of the artist, musician, prophet, poet, dreamer, more or less illuminated according to the measure of courage and self-abandonment in which he has drunk the cup of ecstasy: but always in comparison with the radiance of the pure contemplative, "partly shining and partly dark." "Hinder me not," says the soul to the senses in Mechthild of Magdeburg's vision, "I would drink for a space of the unmingled wine." [488] In the artist, the senses have somewhat hindered the perfect inebriation of the soul.

We have seen that a vast tract of experience--all the experience which results from contact between a purged and heightened consciousness and the World of Becoming in which it is immersed; and much, too, of that which results from contact set up between such a consciousness and the Absolute Itself--is included in that stage of growth which the mystics call the Illuminative Way. This is the largest and most densely populated province of the mystic kingdom. Such different visionaries as Suso and Blake, Boehme and Angela of Foligno, Mechthild of Magdeburg, Fox, Rolle, St. Teresa, and countless others have left us the record of their sojourn therein. Amongst those who cannot be called pure mystics we can detect in the works of Plato and Heracleitus, Wordsworth, Tennyson, and Walt Whitman indications that they too were acquainted, beyond most poets and seers, with the phenomena of the illuminated life. In studying it then, we shall be confronted by a mass of apparently irreconcilable material: the results of the relation set up between every degree of lucidity, every kind of character, and the suprasensible world.

To say that God is Infinite is to say that He may be apprehended and described in an infinity of ways. That Circle whose centre is everywhere and whose circumference is nowhere, may be approached from every angle with a certainty of being found. Mystical history, particularly that which deals with the Illuminative Way, is a demonstration of this fact. Here, in the establishment of the "first mystic life," of conscious correspondence with Reality, the self which has oscillated between two forms of consciousness, has alternately opposed and embraced its growing intuitions of the Absolute, comes for a time to rest. To a large extent, the discordant elements of character have been purged away. Temporally at least the mind has "unified itself" upon high levels, and attained, as it believes, a genuine consciousness of the divine and veritable world. The depth and richness of its own nature will determine how intense that consciousness shall be.

Whatever its scope, however, this new apprehension of reality generally appears to the illuminated Self as final and complete. As the true lover is always convinced that he has found in his bride the one Rose of the World, so the mystic, in the first glow of his initiation, is sure that his quest is now fulfilled. Ignorant as yet of that consummation of love which overpasses the proceedings of the inward eye and ear, he exclaims with entire assurance "Beati oculi qui exterioribus clausi, interioribus autem sunt intenti," [489] and, absorbed in this new blissful act of vision, forgets that it belongs to those who are still in via . He has yet to pass through that "night of the senses" in which he learns to distinguish the substance of Reality from the accidents under which it is perceived; to discover that the heavenly food here given cannot satisfy his "hunger for the Absolute." [490] His true goal lies far beyond this joyful basking in the sunbeams of the Uncreated Light. Only the greatest souls learn this lesson, and tread the whole of that "King's Highway" which leads man back to his Source. "For the many that come to Bethlehem, there be few that will go on to Calvary." The rest stay here, in this Earthly Paradise, these flowery fields; where the liberated self wanders at will, describing to us as well as it can now this corner, now that of the Country of the Soul.

It is in these descriptions of the joy of illumination--in the outpourings of love and rapture belonging to this state--that we find the most lyrical passages of mystical literature. Here poet, mystic, and musician are on common ground: for it is only by the oblique methods of the artist, by the use of aesthetic suggestion and musical rhythm, that the wonder of that vision can be expressed. When essential goodness, truth, and beauty--Light, Life, and Love--are apprehended by the heart, whether the heart be that of poet, painter, lover, or saint, that apprehension can only be communicated in a living, that is to say, an artistic form. The natural mind is conscious only of succession: the special differentia of the mystic is the power of apprehending simultaneity. In the peculiarities of the illuminated consciousness we recognize the effort of the mind to bridge the gap between Simultaneity and Succession: the characters of Creator and Creation. Here the successive is called upon to carry the values of the Eternal.

Here, then, genius and sanctity kiss one another; and each, in that sublime encounter, looks for an instant through the other's eyes. Hence it is natural and inevitable that the mystic should here call into play all the resources of artistic expression: the lovely imagery of Julian and Mechthild of Magdeburg, Suso's poetic visions, St. Augustine's fire and light, the heavenly harmonies of St. Francis and Richard Rolle. Symbols, too, play a major part, not only in the description, but also in the machinery of illumination: the intuitions of many mystics presenting themselves directly to the surface-mind in a symbolic form. We must therefore be prepared for a great variety and fluidity of expression, a constant and not always conscious recourse to symbol and image, in those who try to communicate the secret of this state of consciousness. We must examine, and even classify so far as possible, a wide variety of experience--some which is recognized by friends and foes alike as purely "mystical," some in which the operation of poetic imagination is clearly discernible, some which involves "psychic phenomena" and other abnormal activities of the mind--refusing to be frightened away from investigation by the strange, and apparently irreconcilable character of our material.

There are three main types of experience which appear again and again in the history of mysticism; nearly always in connection with illumination, rather than any other phase of mystical development. I think that they may fairly be regarded as its main characteristics, though the discussion of them cannot cover all the ground. In few forms of spiritual life is the spontaneity of the individual so clearly seen as here: and in few is the ever-deadly process of classification attended with so many risks.

These three characteristics are:--

1. A joyous apprehension of the Absolute: that which many ascetic writers call "the practice of the Presence of God." This, however, is not to be confused with that unique consciousness of union with the divine which is peculiar to a later stage of mystical development. The self, though purified, still realizes itself as a separate entity over against God. It is not immersed in its Origin, but contemplates it. This is the "betrothal" rather than the "marriage" of the soul.

2. This clarity of vision may also be enjoyed in regard to the phenomenal world. The actual physical perceptions seem to be strangely heightened, so that the self perceives an added significance and reality in all natural things: is often convinced that it knows at last "the secret of the world." In Blake's words "the doors of perception are cleansed" so that "everything appears to man as it is , infinite." [491]

In these two forms of perception we see the growing consciousness of the mystic stretching in two directions, until it includes in its span both the World of Being and the World of Becoming; [492] that dual apprehension of reality as transcendent yet immanent which we found to be one of the distinguishing marks of the mystic type.

3. Along with this two-fold extension of consciousness, the energy of the intuitional or transcendental self may be enormously increased. The psychic upheavals of the Purgative Way have tended to make it central for life: to eliminate from the character all those elements which checked its activity. Now it seizes upon the ordinary channels of expression; and may show itself in such forms as (a) auditions, (b) dialogues between the surface consciousness and another intelligence which purports to be divine, (c) visions, and sometimes (d) in automatic writings. In many selves this automatic activity of those growing but still largely subconscious powers which constitute the "New Man," increases steadily during the whole of the mystic life.

Illumination, then, tends to appear mainly under one or all of these three forms. Often all are present; though, as a rule, one is dominant. The balance of characteristics will be conditioned in each case by the self's psychic make-up; its temperamental leaning towards "pure contemplation," "lucid vision," or automatic expression; emanation or immanence, the metaphysical, artistic, or intimate aspects of truth. The possible combinations between these various factors are as innumerable as the possible creations of Life itself.

In the wonderful rhapsodies of St. Augustine, in St. Bernard's converse with the Word, in Angela of Foligno's apprehensions of Deity, in Richard Rolle's "state of song," when "sweetest heavenly melody he took, with him dwelling in mind," or in Brother Lawrence's "practice of the Presence of God," we may see varied expressions of the first type of illuminated consciousness. Jacob Boehme is rightly looked upon as a classic example of the second; which is also found in one of its most attractive forms in St. Francis of Assisi. Suso and St. Teresa, perhaps, may stand for the third, since in them the visionary and auditory phenomena were peculiarly well marked. A further study of each characteristic in order, will help us to disentangle the many threads which go to the psychical make-up of these great and complex mystic types. The rest of this chapter will, then, be given to the analysis of the two chief forms of illuminated consciousness: the self's perception of Reality in the eternal and temporal worlds. The important subject of voices and visions demands a division to itself.

I. The Consciousness of the Absolute, or "Sense of the Presence of God"

This consciousness, in its various forms and degrees, is perhaps the most constant characteristic of Illumination; and makes it, for the mystic soul, a pleasure-state of the intensest kind. I do not mean by this that the subject passes months or years in a continuous ecstasy of communion with the Divine. Intermittent periods of spiritual fatigue or "aridity"--renewals of the temperamental conflicts experienced in purgation--the oncoming gloom of the Dark Night--all these may be, and often are, experienced at intervals during the Illuminated Life; as flashes of insight, indistinguishable from illumination, constantly break the monotony of the Purgative Way. But a deep certitude of the Personal Life omnipresent in the universe has been achieved; and this can never be forgotten, even though it be withdrawn. The "spirit stretching towards God" declares that it has touched Him; and its normal condition henceforth is joyous consciousness of His Presence with "many privy touchings of sweet spiritual sights and feeling, measured to us as our simpleness may bear it." [493] Where he prefers less definite or more pantheistic language, the mystic's perceptions may take the form of "harmony with the Infinite"--the same divine music transposed to a lower key.

This "sense of God" is not a metaphor. Innumerable declarations prove it to be a consciousness as sharp as that which other men have, or think they have, of colour, heat, or light. It is a well-known though usually transitory experience in the religious life: like the homing instinct of birds, a fact which can neither be denied nor explained. "How that presence is felt, it may better be known by experience than by any writing," says Hilton, "for it is the life and the love, the might and the light, the joy and the rest of a chosen soul. And therefore he that hath soothfastly once felt it he may not forbear it without pain; he may not undesire it, it is so good in itself and so comfortable. . . . He cometh privily sometimes when thou art least aware of Him, but thou shalt well know Him or He go; for wonderfully He stirreth and mightily He turneth thy heart into beholding of His goodness, and doth thine heart melt delectably as wax against the fire into softness of His love." [494]

Modern psychologists have struggled hard to discredit this "sense of the presence"; sometimes attributing it to the psychic mechanism of projection, sometimes to "wish-fulfilments" of a more unpleasant origin. [495] The mystics, however, who discriminate so much more delicately than their critics between true and false transcendental experience, never feel any doubt about its validity. Even when their experience seems inconsistent with their theology, they refuse to be disturbed.

Thus St. Teresa writes of her own experience, with her usual simplicity and directness, "In the beginning it happened to me that I was ignorant of one thing--I did not know that God was in all things: and when He seemed to me to be so near, I thought it impossible. Not to believe that He was present was not in my power; for it seemed to me, as it were, evident that I felt there His very presence. Some unlearned men used to say to me, that He was present only by His grace. I could not believe that, because, as I am saying, He seemed to me to be present Himself: so I was distressed. A most learned man, of the Order of the glorious Patriarch St. Dominic, delivered me from this doubt, for he told me that He was present, and how He communed with us: this was a great comfort to me." [496]

Again, "An interior peace, and the little strength which either pleasures or displeasures have to remove this presence (during the time it lasts) of the Three Persons, and that without power to doubt of it, continue in such a manner that I clearly seem to experience what St. John says, That He will dwell in the soul, and this not only by grace, but that He will also make her perceive this presence." [497] St. Teresa's strong "immanental" bent comes out well in this passage.

Such a sense of the divine presence may go side by side with the daily life and normal mental activities of its possessor; who is not necessarily an ecstatic or an abstracted visionary, remote from the work of the world. It is true that the transcendental consciousness has now become, once for all, his centre of interest, its perceptions and admonitions dominate and light up his daily life. The object of education, in the Platonic sense, has been achieved: his soul has "wheeled round from the perishing world" to "the contemplation of the real world and the brightest part thereof." [498] But where vocation and circumstances require it, the duties of a busy outward life continue to be fulfilled with steadiness and success: and this without detriment to the soul's contemplation of the Real.

In many temperaments of the unstable or artistic type, however, this intuitional consciousness of the Absolute becomes ungovernable: it constantly breaks through, obtaining forcible possession of the mental field and expressing itself in the "psychic" phenomena of ecstasy and rapture. In others, less mobile, it wells up into an impassioned apprehension, a "flame of love" in which the self seems to "meet God in the ground of the soul." This is "pure contemplation": that state of deep orison in which the subject seems to be "seeing, feeling and thinking all at once." By this spontaneous exercise of all his powers under the dominion of love, the mystic attains that "Vision of the Heart" which, "more interior, perhaps, than the visions of dream or ecstasy," [499] stretches to the full those very faculties which it seems to be holding in suspense; as a top "sleeps" when it is spinning fast. Ego dormio et cor meum vigilat . This act of contemplation, this glad surrender to an overwhelming consciousness of the Presence of God, leaves no sharp image on the mind: only a knowledge that we have been lifted up, to a veritable gazing upon That which eye hath not seen.

St. Bernard gives in one of his sermons a simple, ingenuous and obviously personal account of such "privy touchings," such convincing but elusive contacts of the soul with the Absolute. "Now bear with my foolishness for a little," he says, "for I wish to tell you, as I have promised, how such events have taken place in me. It is, indeed, a matter of no importance. But I put myself forward only that I may be of service to you; and if you derive any benefit I am consoled for my egotism. If not, I shall but have displayed my foolishness. I confess, then, though I say it in my foolishness, that the Word has visited me, and even very often. But, though He has frequently entered into my soul, I have never at any time been sensible of the precise moment of His coming. I have felt that He was present, I remember that He has been with me; I have sometimes been able even to have a presentiment that He would come: but never to feel His coming nor His departure. For whence He came to enter my soul, or whither He went on quitting it, by what means He has made entrance or departure, I confess that I know not even to this day; according to that which is said, Nescis unde veniat aut quo vadat . Nor is this strange, because it is to Him that the psalmist has said in another place, Vestigia tua non cognoscentur .

"It is not by the eyes that He enters, for He is without form or colour that they can discern; nor by the ears, for His coming is without sound; nor by the nostrils, for it is not with the air but with the mind that He is blended. . . . By what avenue then has He entered? Or perhaps the fact may be that He has not entered at all, nor indeed come at all from outside: for not one of these things belongs to outside. Yet it has not come from within me, for it is good, and I know that in me dwelleth no good thing. I have ascended higher than myself, and lo! I have found the Word above me still. My curiosity has led me to descend below myself also, and yet I have found Him still at a lower depth. If I have looked without myself, I have found that He is beyond that which is outside of me, and if within, He was at an inner depth still. And thus have I learned the truth of the words I have read, In ipso enim vivimus et movemur et sumus ." [500]

Such a lifting up, such a condition of consciousness as that which St. Bernard is here trying to describe, seems to snatch the spirit for a moment into a state which it is hard to distinguish from that of true "union." This is what the contemplatives call passive or infused contemplation, or sometimes the "orison of union": a brief foretaste of the Unitive State, often enjoyed for short periods in the Illuminative Way, which reinforces their conviction that they have now truly attained the Absolute. It is but a foretaste, however, of that attainment: the precocious effort of a soul still in that stage of "Enlightening" which the "Theologia Germanica" declares to be "belonging to such as are growing."[501]

This distinction between the temporary experience of union and the achievement of the Unitive Life is well brought out in a fragment of dialogue between Soul and Self in Hugh of St. Victor's mystical tract, "De Arrha Animae."

The Soul says, "Tell me, what can be this thing of delight that merely by its memory touches and moves me with such sweetness and violence that I am drawn out of myself and carried away, I know not how? I am suddenly renewed: I am changed: I am plunged into an ineffable peace. My mind is full of gladness, all my past wretchedness and pain is forgot. My soul exults: my intellect is illuminated: my heart is afire: my desires have become kindly and gentle: I know not where I am, because my Love has embraced me. Also, because my Love has embraced me I seem to have become possessed of something, and I know not what it is; but I try to keep it, that I may never lose it. My soul strives in gladness that she may not be separated from That which she desires to hold fast for ever: as if she had found in it the goal of all her desires. She exults in a sovereign and ineffable manner, seeking nought, desiring nought, but to rest in this. Is this, then, my Beloved? Tell me that I may know Him, and that if He come again I may entreat Him to leave me not, but to stay with me for ever."

Man says, "It is indeed thy Beloved who visits thee; but He comes in an invisible shape, He comes disguised, He comes incomprehensibly. He comes to touch thee, not to be seen of thee: to arouse thee, not to be comprehended of thee. He comes not to give Himself wholly, but to be tasted by thee: not to fulfil thy desire, but to lead upwards thy affection. He gives a foretaste of His delights, brings not the plenitude of a perfect satisfaction: and the earnest of thy betrothal consists chiefly in this, that He who shall afterwards give Himself to be seen and possessed by thee perpetually, now permits Himself to be sometimes tasted, that thou mayest learn how sweet He is. This shall console thee for His absence: and the savour of this gift shall keep thee from all despair." [502]

The real distinction between the Illuminative and the Unitive Life is that in Illumination the individuality of the subject--however profound his spiritual consciousness, however close his apparent communion with the Infinite--remains separate and intact. His heightened apprehension of reality lights up rather than obliterates the rest of his life: and may even increase his power of dealing adequately with the accidents of normal existence. Thus Brother Lawrence found that his acute sense of reality, his apprehension of the Presence of God, and the resulting detachment and consciousness of liberty in regard to mundane things, upheld and assisted him in the most unlikely tasks; as, for instance, when he was sent into Burgundy to buy wine for his convent, "which was a very unwelcome task to him, because he had no turn for business, and because he was lame, and could not go about the boat but by rolling himself over the casks. That, however, he gave himself no uneasiness about it, nor about the purchase of the wine. That he said to God, It was His business he was about: and that he afterwards found it very well performed. . . . So likewise in his business in the kitchen, to which he had naturally a great aversion." [503]

The mind, concentrated upon a higher object of interest, is undistracted by its own anxieties, likes, or dislikes; and hence performs the more efficiently the work that is given it to do. Where it does not do so, then the normal make-up or imperfect discipline of the subject, rather than its mystical proclivities, must be blamed. St. Catherine of Genoa found in this divine companionship the power which made her hospital a success. St. Teresa was an administrator of genius and an admirable housewife, and declared that she found her God very easily amongst the pots and pans. [504] Appearances notwithstanding, Mary would probably have been a better cook than Martha, had circumstances required of her this form of activity.

In persons of feeble or diffuse intelligence, however, and above all in victims of a self-regarding spirituality, this deep absorption in the sense of Divine Reality may easily degenerate into monoideism. Then the "shady side" of Illumination, a selfish preoccupation with transcendental joys, the "spiritual gluttony" condemned by St. John of the Cross, comes out. "I made many mistakes," says Madame Guyon pathetically, "through allowing myself to be too much taken up by my interior joys. . . . I used to sit in a corner and work, but I could hardly do anything, because the strength of this attraction made me let the work fall out of my hands. I spent hours in this way without being able to open my eyes or to know what was happening to me: so simply, so peacefully, so gently that sometimes I said to myself, Can heaven itself be more peaceful than I?'" [505]

Here we see Madame Guyon basking like a pious tabby cat in the beams of the Uncreated Light, and already leaning to the extravagances of Quietism, with its dangerous "double character of passivity and beatitude." The heroic aspect of the mystic vocation is in abeyance. Those mystical impressions which her peculiar psychic make-up permitted her to receive, have been treated as a source of personal and placid satisfactions; not as a well-spring, whence new vitality might be drawn for great and self-giving activities.

It has been claimed by the early biographers of St. Catherine of Genoa, that she passed in the crisis of her conversion directly through the Purgative to the Unitive Life; and never exhibited the characteristics of the Illuminative Way. This has been effectually disproved by Baron von Hügel, [506] though he too is inclined in her case to reject the usual sequence of the mystic states. Yet the description of Catherine's condition after her four great penitential years were ended, as given in cap. vi. of the "Vita e Dottrina," is an almost perfect picture of healthy illumination of the inward or "immanental" type; and makes an effective foil to the passage which I have quoted from Madame Guyon's life.

No doubt there were hours in which St. Catherine's experience, as it were, ran ahead; and she felt herself not merely lit up by the Indwelling Light, but temporally merged in it. These moments are responsible for such passages as the beautiful fragment in cap. v.; which does, when taken alone, seem to describe the true unitive state. "Sometimes," she said, "I do not see or feel myself to have either soul, body, heart, will or taste, or any other thing except Pure Love." [507] Her normal condition of consciousness, however, was clearly not yet that which Julian of Norwich calls being "oned with bliss"; but rather an intense and continuous communion with an objective Reality which was clearly realized as distinct from herself. "After the aforesaid four years," says the next chapter of the "Vita," "there was given unto her a purified mind, free, and filled with God: insomuch that no other thing could enter into it. Thus, when she heard sermons or Mass, so much was she absorbed in her interior feelings, that she neither heard nor saw that which was said or done without. But within, in the sweet divine light, she saw and heard other things, being wholly absorbed by that interior light: and it was not in her power to act otherwise." St. Catherine, then, is still a spectator of the Absolute, does not feel herself to be one with it. "And it is a marvellous thing that with so great an interior recollection, the Lord never permitted her to go beyond control. But when she was needed, she always came to herself: so that she was able to reply to that which was asked of her: and the Lord so guided her, that none could complain of her. And she had her mind so filled by Love Divine, that conversation became hard to her: and by this continuous taste and sense of God, several times she was so greatly transported, that she was forced to hide herself, that she might not be seen." It is clear, however, that Catherine herself was aware of the transitory and imperfect nature of this intensely joyous state. Her growing transcendental self, unsatisfied with the sunshine of the Illuminative Way, the enjoyment of the riches of God, already aspired to union with the Divine. With her, as with all truly heroic souls, it was love for love, not love for joy. "She cried to God because He gave her so many consolations, Non voglio quello che esce da te, ma sol voglio te, O dolce Amore !'" [508]

"Non voglio quello che esce da te." When the growing soul has reached this level of desire, the Illuminative Way is nearly at an end. It has seen the goal, "that Country which is no mere vision, but a home," [509] and is set upon the forward march. So Rabia, the Moslem saint: "O my God, my concern and my desire in this world, is that I should remember thee above all the things of this world, and in the next that out of all who are in that world, I should meet with thee alone." [510] So Gertrude More: "No knowledge which we can here have of thee can satisfy my soul seeking and longing without ceasing after thee. . . . Alas, my Lord God, what is all thou canst give to a loving soul which sigheth and panteth after thee alone, and esteemeth all things as dung that she may gain thee? What is all I say, whilst thou givest not thyself, who art that one thing which is only necessary and which alone can satisfy our souls? Was it any comfort to St. Mary Magdalen, when she sought thee, to find two angels which presented themselves instead of thee? verily I cannot think it was any joy unto her. For that soul that hath set her whole love and desire on thee can never find any true satisfaction but only in thee." [511]

What is the nature of this mysterious mystic illumination? Apart from the certitude it imparts, what is the form which it most usually assumes in the consciousness of the self? The illuminatives seem to assure us that its apparently symbolic name is really descriptive; that they do experience a kind of radiance, a flooding of the personality with new light. A new sun rises above the horizon, and transfigures their twilit world. Over and over again they return to light-imagery in this connection. Frequently, as in their first conversion, they report an actual and overpowering consciousness of radiant light, ineffable in its splendour, as an accompaniment of their inward adjustment.

"Sopr' onne lengua amore,
bontá senza figura,
lume fuor di mesura
resplende nel mio core," [512]

sang Jacopone da Todi. "Light rare, untellable!" said Whitman. "The flowing light of the Godhead," said Mechthild of Magdeburg, trying to describe what it was that made the difference between her universe and that of normal men. "Lux vixens dicit," said St. Hildegarde of her revelations, which she described as appearing in a special light, more brilliant than the brightness round the sun. [513] It is an "infused brightness," says St. Teresa, "a light which knows no night; but rather, as it is always light, nothing ever disturbs it." [514]

"De subito parve giorno a giorno
essere aggiunto!"
exclaims Dante, initiated into the atmosphere of heaven; "Lume è lassù"is his constant declaration:
"Cio ch' io dico è un semplice lume,"

his last word, in the effort to describe the soul's apprehension of the Being of God. [515]

It really seems as though the mystics' attainment of new levels of consciousness did bring with it the power of perceiving a splendour always there, but beyond the narrow range of our poor sight; to which it is only a "luminous darkness" at the best. "In Eternal Nature, or the kingdom of Heaven," said Law, "materiality stands in life and light." [516] The cumulative testimony on this point is such as would be held to prove, in any other department of knowledge, that there is indeed an actual light, "lighting the very light" and awaiting the recognition of men. [517]

Consider the accent of realism with which St. Augustine speaks of his own experience of Platonic contemplation; a passage in which we seem to see a born psychologist desperately struggling by means of negations to describe an intensely positive state. "I entered into the secret closet of my soul, led by Thee; and this I could do because Thou wast my helper. I entered, and beheld with the mysterious eye of my soul the Light that never changes, above the eye of my soul, above my intelligence. It was not the common light which all flesh can see, nor was it greater yet of the same kind, as if the light of day were to grow brighter and brighter and flood all space. It was not like this, but different: altogether different from all such things. Nor was it above my intelligence in the same way as oil is above water, or heaven above earth; but it was higher because it made me, and I was lower because made by it. He who knoweth the truth knoweth that Light: and who knoweth it, knoweth eternity. Love knoweth it." [518]

Here, as in the cases of St. Teresa, St. Catherine of Genoa, and Jacopone da Todi, we have a characteristically "immanental" description of the illuminated state. The self, by the process which mystics call "introversion," the deliberate turning inwards of its attention, its conative powers, discerns Reality within the heart: "the rippling tide of love which flows secretly from God into the soul, and draws it mightily back into its source." [519] But the opposite or transcendental tendency is not less frequent. The cosmic vision of Infinity, exterior to the subject--the expansive, outgoing movement towards a Divine Light,

> "Che visible face
> lo Creatore a quella creatura,
> che solo in lui vedere ha la sua pace," [520]

wholly other than anything the earth-born creature can conceive--the strange, formless absorption in the Divine Dark to which the soul is destined to ascend--all these modes of perception are equally characteristic of the Illuminative Way. As in conversion, so here Reality may be apprehended in either transcendent or immanent, positive or negative terms. It is both near and far; "closer to us than our most inward part, and higher than our highest"; [521] and for some selves that which is far is easiest to find. To a certain type of mind, the veritable practice of the Presence of God is not the intimate and adorable companionship of the personal Comrade or the Inward Light, but the awestruck contemplation of the Absolute, the "naked Godhead," source and origin of all that Is. It is an ascent to the supernal plane of perception, where "the simple, absolute and unchangeable mysteries of heavenly Truth lie hidden in the dazzling obscurity of the secret Silence, outshining all brilliance with the intensity of their darkness, and surcharging our blinded intellects with the utterly impalpable and invisible fairness of glories which exceed all beauty." [522]

With such an experience of eternity, such a vision of the triune all-including Absolute which "binds the Universe with love," Dante ends his "Divine Comedy": and the mystic joy with which its memory fills him is his guarantee that he has really seen the Inviolate Rose, the flaming heart of things.

> "O abbondante grazia, ond' io presunsi
> ficcar lo viso per la luce eterna
> tanto che la veduta vi consunsi!
> Nel suo profondo vidi che s' interna,
> legato con amore in un volume,
> ciò che per l'universo si squaderna;
> Sustanzia ed accidenti, e lor costume,
> quasi conflati insieme per tal modo
> che ciò ch' io dico è un semplice lume.
> La forma universal di questo nodo
> credo ch' io vidi, perchè più di largo,
> dicendo questo, mi sento ch' io godo.
> . . . . .
> O, quanto è corto il dire, e come fioco
> al mio concetto! e questo, a quel ch' io vidi,
> è tanto che non basta a dicer poco.
> O luce eterna, che sola in te sidi,
> sola t' intendi, e, da te intelletta

ed intendente te, ami ed arridi!" [523]

In Dante, the transcendent and impersonal aspect of illumination is seen in its most exalted form. It seems at first sight almost impossible to find room within the same system for this expansive vision of the Undifferentiated Light and such intimate and personal apprehensions of Deity as Lady Julian's conversations with her "courteous and dearworthy Lord," or St. Catherine's companionship with Love Divine. Yet all these are really reports of the same psychological state: describe the attainment by selves of different types, of the same stage in the soul's progressive apprehension of reality.

In a wonderful passage, unique in the literature of mysticism, Angela of Foligno has reported the lucid vision in which she perceived this truth: the twofold revelation of an Absolute at once humble and omnipotent, personal and transcendent--the unimaginable synthesis of "unspeakable power" and "deep humility."

"The eyes of my soul were opened, and I beheld the plenitude of God, wherein I did comprehend the whole world, both here and beyond the sea, and the abyss and ocean and all things. In all these things I beheld naught save the divine power, in a manner assuredly indescribable; so that through excess of marvelling the soul cried with a loud voice, saying This whole world is full of God!' [524] Wherefore I now comprehended how small a thing is the whole world, that is to say both here and beyond the seas, the abyss, the ocean, and all things; and that the Power of God exceeds and fills all. Then He said unto me: I have shown thee something of My Power,' and I understood, that after this I should better understand the rest. He then said Behold now My humility.' Then was I given an insight into the deep humility of God towards man. And comprehending that unspeakable power and beholding that deep humility, my soul marvelled greatly, and did esteem itself to be nothing at all." [525]

It must never be forgotten that all apparently one-sided descriptions of illumination--more, all experiences of it--are governed by temperament. "That Light whose smile kindles the Universe" is ever the same; but the self through whom it passes, and by whom we must receive its report, has already submitted to the moulding influences of environment and heredity, Church and State. The very language of which that self avails itself in its struggle for expression, links it with half a hundred philosophies and creeds. The response which it makes to Divine Love will be the same in type as the response which its nature would make to earthly love: but raised to the n th degree. We, receiving the revelation, receive with it all those elements which the subject has contributed in spite of itself. Hence the soul's apprehension of Divine Reality may take almost any form, from the metaphysical ecstasies which we find in Dionysius, and to a less degree in St. Augustine, to the simple, almost "common-sense" statements of Brother Lawrence, the emotional ardours of St. Gertrude, or the lovely intimacies of Julian or Mechthild.

Sometimes--so rich and varied does the nature of the great mystic tend to be--the exalted and impersonal language of the Dionysian theology goes, with no sense of incongruity, side by side with homely parallels drawn from the most sweet and common incidents of daily life. Suso, in whom illumination and purgation existed side by side for sixteen years, alternately obtaining possession of the mental field, and whose oscillations between the harshest mortification and the most ecstatic pleasure-states were exceptionally violent and swift, is a characteristic instance of such an attitude of mind. His illumination was largely of the intimate and immanental type; but, as we might expect in a pupil of Eckhart, it was not without touches of mystical transcendence, which break out with sudden splendour side by side with those tender and charming passages in which the Servitor of the Eternal Wisdom tries to tell his love.

Thus, he describes in one of the earlier chapters of his life how "whilst he was thinking, according to his custom, of the most lovable Wisdom, he questioned himself, and interrogated his heart, which sought persistently for love, saying, O my heart, whence comes this love and grace, whence comes this gentleness and beauty, this joy and sweetness of the heart? Does not all this flow forth from the Godhead, as from its origin? Come! let my heart, my senses and my soul immerse themselves in the deep Abyss whence come these adorable things. What shall keep me back? To-day I will embrace you, even as my burning heart desires to do.' And at this moment there was within his heart as it were an emanation of all good, all that is beautiful, all that is lovable and desirable was there spiritually present, and this in a manner which cannot be expressed. Whence came the habit that every time he heard God's praises sung or said, he recollected himself in the depths of his heart and soul, and thought on that Beloved Object, whence comes all love. It is impossible to tell how often, with eyes filled with tears and open heart, he has embraced his sweet Friend, and pressed Him to a heart overflowing with love. He was like a baby which a mother holds upright on her knees, supporting it with her hands beneath its arms. The baby, by the movements of its little head, and all its little body, tries to get closer and closer to its dear mother, and shows by its little laughing gestures the gladness in its heart. Thus did the heart of the Servitor ever seek the sweet neighbourhood of the Divine Wisdom, and thus he was as it were altogether filled with delight." [526]

II. The Illuminated Vision of the World

Closely connected with the sense of the "Presence of God," or power of perceiving the Absolute, is the complementary mark of the illuminated consciousness; the vision of "a new heaven and a new earth," or an added significance and reality in the phenomenal world. Such words as those of Julian, "God is all thing that is good as to my sight, and the goodness that all thing hath, it is He," [527] seem to supply the link between the two. Here again we must distinguish carefully between vaguely poetic language--"the light that never was," "every common bush afire with God"--and descriptions which can be referred to a concrete and definite psychological experience. This experience, at its best, balances and completes the experience of the Presence of God at its best. That is to say, its "note" is sacramental, not ascetic. It entails the expansion rather than the concentration of consciousness; the discovery of the Perfect One self-revealed in the Many, not the forsaking of the Many in order to find the One. Its characteristic expression is--

"The World is charged with the grandeur of God;
It will flame out, like shining from shook foil,"

not "turn thy thoughts into thy own soul, where He is hid." It takes, as a rule, the form of an enhanced mental lucidity--an abnormal sharpening of the senses--whereby an ineffable radiance, a beauty and a reality never before suspected, are perceived by a sort of clairvoyance shining in the meanest things.

"From the moment in which the soul has received the impression of Deity in infused orison," says Malaval, "she sees Him everywhere, by one of love's secrets which is only known of those who have experienced it. The simple vision of pure love, which is marvellously penetrating, does not stop at the outer husk of creation: it penetrates to the divinity which is hidden within." [528]

Thus Browning makes David declare--

"I but open my eyes,--and perfection, no more and no less
In the kind I imagined full-fronts me, and God is seen God
In the star, in the stone, in the flesh, in the soul and the clod." [529]

Blake's "To see a world in a grain of sand," Tennyson's "Flower in the crannied wall," Vaughan's "Each bush and oak doth know I AM," and the like, are exact though over-quoted reports of "things seen" in this state of consciousness, this "simple vision of pure love": the value of which is summed up in Eckhart's profound saying, "The meanest thing that one knows in God--for instance if one could understand a flower as it has its Being in God--this would be a higher thing than the whole world!"[530] Mystical poets of the type of Wordsworth and Walt Whitman seem to possess in a certain degree this form of illumination. It is this which Bucke, the American psychologist, analysed under the name of "Cosmic Consciousness." [531] It is seen at its full development in the mystical experiences of Boehme, Fox, and Blake.

We will take first the experience of Jacob Boehme, a mystic who owed little or nothing to the influence of tradition, and who furnishes one of the best recorded all-round examples of mystical illumination; exhibiting, along with an acute consciousness of divine companionship, all those phenomena of visual lucidity, automatism, and enhanced intellectual powers which properly belong to it, but are seldom developed simultaneously in the same individual.

In Boehme's life, as described in the Introduction to the English translation of his collected works,[532] there were three distinct onsets of illumination; all of the pantheistic and external type. In the first, which seems to have happened whilst he was very young, we are told that "he was surrounded by a divine Light for seven days, and stood in the highest contemplation and Kingdom of Joy." This we may perhaps identify with mystical awakening, of the kind experienced by Suso. About the year 1600 occurred the second illumination, initiated by a trance-like state of consciousness, the result of gazing at a polished disc. To this I have already referred. [533] This experience brought with it that peculiar and lucid vision of the inner reality of the phenomenal world in which, as he says, "he looked into the deepest foundations of things." "He believed that it was only a fancy, and in order to banish it from his mind he went out upon the green. But here he remarked that he gazed into the very heart of things, the very herbs and grass, and that actual Nature harmonized with what he had inwardly seen." [534] Of this same experience and the clairvoyance which accompanied it, another biographer says, "Going abroad in the fields to a green before Neys Gate, at Görlitz, he there sat down, and, viewing the herbs and grass of the field in his inward light, he saw into their essences, use and properties, which were discovered to him by their lineaments, figures and signatures. . . . In the unfolding of these mysteries before his understanding, he had a great measure of joy, yet returned home and took care of his family and lived in great peace and silence, scarce intimating to any these wonderful things that had befallen him." [535]

So far as we can tell from his own scattered statements, from this time onwards Boehme must have enjoyed a frequent and growing consciousness of the transcendental world: though there is evidence that he, like all other mystics, knew seasons of darkness, "many a shrewd Repulse," and times of struggle with that "powerful contrarium" the lower consciousness. In 1610--perhaps as the result of such intermittent struggles--the vivid illumination of ten years before was repeated in an enhanced form: and it was in consequence of this, and in order that there might be some record of the mysteries upon which he had gazed, that he wrote his first and most difficult book, the "Aurora," or "Morning Redness." The passage in which the "inspired shoemaker" has tried to tell us what his vision of Reality was like, to communicate something of the grave and enthusiastic travail of his being, the unspeakable knowledge of things which he attained, is one of those which arouse in all who have even the rudiments of mystical perception the sorrow and excitement of exiles who suddenly hear the accents of home. Like absolute music, it addresses itself to the whole being, not merely to the intellect. Those who will listen and be receptive will find themselves repaid by a strange sense of extended life, an exhilarating consciousness of truth. Here, if ever, is a man who is struggling to "speak as he saw": and it is plain that he saw much--as much, perhaps, as Dante, though he lacked the poetic genius which was needed to give his vision an intelligible form. The very strangeness of the phrasing, the unexpected harmonies and dissonances which worry polite and well-regulated minds, are earnests of the Spirit of Life crying out for expression from within. Boehme, like Blake, seems "drunk with intellectual vision"--"a God-intoxicated man."

"In this my earnest and Christian Seeking and Desire," he says, "(wherein I suffered many a shrewd Repulse, but at last resolved rather to put myself in Hazard, than give over and leave off) the Gate was opened to me, that in one Quarter of an Hour I saw and knew more than if I had been many years together at an University, at which I exceedingly admired, and thereupon turned my Praise to God for it. For I saw and knew the Being of all Beings, the Byss and the Abyss, and the Eternal Generation of the Holy Trinity, the Descent and Original of the World, and of all creatures through the Divine Wisdom: knew and saw in myself all the three Worlds, namely, The Divine, angelical and paradisical; and the dark World, the Original of the Nature to the Fire; and then, thirdly, the external; and visible World, being a Procreation or external Birth from both the internal and spiritual Worlds. And I saw and knew the whole working Essence in the Evil and the Good, and the Original and Existence of each of them; and likewise how the fruitful bearing Womb of Eternity brought forth. . . . Yet however I must begin to labour in these great mysteries, as a Child that goes to School. I saw it as in a great Deep in the Internal. For I had a thorough view of the Universe, as in a Chaos, wherein all things are couched and wrapped up, but it was impossible for me to explain the same. Yet it opened itself to me, from Time to Time, as in a Young Plant; though the same was with me for the space of twelve years, and as it was as it were breeding, and I found a powerful Instigation within me, before I could bring it forth into external Form of Writing: and whatever I could apprehend with the external Principle of my mind, that I wrote down." [536]

Close to this lucid vision of the reality of things--this sudden glimpse of the phenomenal in the light of the intelligible world--is George Fox's experience at the age of twenty-four, as recorded in his Journal. [537] Here, as in Boehme's case, it is clear that a previous and regrettable acquaintance with the "doctrine of signatures" has to some extent determined the language and symbols under which he describes his intuitive vision of actuality as it exists in the Divine Mind.

"Now was I come up in spirit through the flaming sword into the Paradise of God. All things were new: and all the creation gave another smell unto me than before, beyond what words can utter. . . . The creation was opened to me; and it was showed me how all things had their names given them, according to their nature and virtue. And I was at a stand in my mind whether I should practise physic for the good of mankind, seeing the nature and virtue of the creatures were so opened to me by the Lord. . . . Great things did the Lord lead me unto, and wonderful depths were opened unto me beyond what can by words be declared; but as people come into subjection to the Spirit of God, and grow up in the image and power of the Almighty, they may receive the word of wisdom that opens all things, and come to know the hidden unity in the Eternal Being."

"To know the hidden unity in the Eternal Being"--know it with an invulnerable certainty, in the all-embracing act of consciousness with which we are aware of the personality of those we truly love--is to live at its fullest the Illuminated Life, enjoying "all creatures in God and God in all creatures." Lucidity of this sort seemes to be an enormously enhanced form of the poetic consciousness of "otherness" in natural things--the sense of a unity in separateness, a mighty and actual Life beyond that which eye can see, a glorious reality shining through the phenomenal veil--frequent in those temperaments which are at one with life. The self then becomes conscious of the living reality of that World of Becoming, the vast arena of the Divine creativity, in which the little individual life is immersed. Alike in howling gale and singing cricket it hears the crying aloud of that "Word which is through all things everlastingly." It participates, actively and open-eyed, in the mighty journey of the Son towards the Father's heart: and seeing with purged sight all things and creatures as they are in that transcendent order, detects in them too that striving of Creation to return to its centre which is the secret of the Universe.

A harmony is thus set up between the mystic and Life in all its forms. Undistracted by appearance, he sees, feels, and knows it in one piercing act of loving comprehension. "And the bodily sight stinted," says Julian, "but the spiritual sight dwelled in mine understanding, and I abode with reverent dread joying in that I saw." [538] The heart outstrips the clumsy senses, and sees--perhaps for an instant, perhaps for long periods of bliss--an undistorted and more veritable world. All things are perceived in the light of charity, and hence under the aspect of beauty: for beauty is simply Reality seen with the eyes of love. As in the case of another and more beatific Vision, essere in caritate è qui necesse [539] For such a reverent and joyous sight the meanest accidents of life are radiant. The London streets are paths of loveliness; the very omnibuses look like coloured archangels, their laps filled full of little trustful souls.

Often when we blame our artists for painting ugly things, they are but striving to show us a beauty to which we are blind. They have gone on ahead of us, and attained that state of "fourfold vision to which Blake laid claim; in which the visionary sees the whole visible universe transfigured, because he has "put off the rotten rags of sense and memory," and "put on Imagination uncorrupt." [540] In this state of lucidity symbol and reality, Nature and Imagination, are seen to be One: and in it are produced all the more sublime works of art, since these owe their greatness to the impact of Reality upon the artistic mind. "I know," says Blake again, "that this world is a world of imagination and vision. I see everything I paint in this world, but everybody does not see alike. To the eye of a miser a guinea is far more beautiful than the sun and a bag worn with the use of money has more beautiful proportions than a vine filled with grapes. The tree which moves some to tears of joy is in the eyes of others only a green thing which stands in the way. Some see Nature all ridicule and deformity, and by these I shall not regulate my proportions; and some scarce see Nature at all. But to the eyes of the man of imagination Nature is Imagination itself. As a man is, so he sees. As the eye is formed, such are its powers. You certainly mistake, when you say that the visions of fancy are not to be found in this world. To me this world is all one continued vision of fancy or imagination, and I feel flattered when I am told so." [541]

If the Mystic Way be considered as an organic process of transcendence, this illuminated apprehension of things, this cleansing of the doors of perception, is surely what we might expect to occur as man moves towards higher centres of consciousness. It marks the self's growth towards free and conscious participation in the Absolute Life; its progressive appropriation of that life by means of the contact which exists in the deeps of man's being--the ground or spark of the soul--between the subject and the transcendental world. The surface intelligence, purified from the domination of the senses, is invaded more and more by the transcendent personality; the "New Man" who is by nature a denizen of the independent spiritual world, and whose destiny, in mystical language, is a "return to his Origin." Hence an inflow of new vitality, a deeper and wider apprehension of the mysterious world in which man finds himself, an exaltation of his intuitive powers.

In such moments of clear sight and enhanced perception as that which Blake and Boehme describe, the mystic and the artist do really see sub specie aeternitatis the Four-fold River of Life--that World of Becoming in which, as Erigena says, "Every visible and invisible creature is a theophany or appearance of God"-- as all perhaps might see it, if prejudice, selfhood, or other illusion did not distort our sight. From this loving vision there comes very often that beautiful sympathy with, that abnormal power over, all living natural things, which crops up again and again in the lives of the mystical saints; to amaze the sluggish minds of common men, barred by "the torrent of Use and Wont" [542] from all free and deep communion alike with their natural and supernatural origin.

Yet it is surely not very amazing that St. Francis of Assisi, feeling and knowing--not merely "believing"--that every living creature was veritably and actually a "theophany or appearance of God," should have been acutely conscious that he shared with these brothers and sisters of his the great and lovely life of the All. Nor, this being so, can we justly regard him as eccentric because he acted in accordance with his convictions, preached to his little sisters the birds, [543] availed himself of the kindly offices of the falcon, [544] enjoyed the friendship of the pheasant, [545] soothed the captured turtledoves, his "simple-minded sisters, innocent and chaste," [546] or persuaded his Brother Wolf to a better life. [547]

The true mystic, so often taunted with "a denial of the world," does but deny the narrow and artificial world of self: and finds in exchange the secrets of that mighty universe which he shares with Nature and with God. Strange contacts, unknown to those who only lead the life of sense, are set up between his being and the being of all other things. In that remaking of his consciousness which follows upon the "mystical awakening," the deep and primal life which he shares with all creation has been roused from its sleep. Hence the barrier between human and non-human life, which makes man a stranger on earth as well as in heaven, is done away. Life now whispers to his life: all things are his intimates, and respond to his fraternal sympathy.

Thus it seems quite a simple and natural thing to the Little Poor Man of Assisi, whose friend the pheasant preferred his cell to "the haunts more natural to its state," that he should be ambassador from the terrified folk of Gubbio to his formidable brother the Wolf. The result of the interview, reduced to ordinary language, could be paralleled in the experience of many persons who have possessed this strange and incommunicable power over animal life.

"O wondrous thing! whereas St. Francis had made the sign of the Cross, right so the terrible wolf shut his jaws and stayed his running: and when he was bid, came gently as a lamb and laid him down at the feet of St. Francis. . . . And St. Francis stretching forth his hand to take pledge of his troth, the wolf lifted up his right paw before him and laid it gently on the hand of St. Francis, giving thereby such sign of good faith as he was able. Then quoth St. Francis, Brother Wolf, I bid thee in the name of Jesu Christ come now with me, nothing doubting, and let us go stablish this peace in God's name.' And the wolf obedient set forth with him, in fashion as a gentle lamb; whereat the townsfolk made mighty marvel, beholding. . . . And thereafter this same wolf lived two years in Agobio; and went like a tame beast in and out the houses from door to door, without doing hurt to any, or any doing hurt to him, and was courteously nourished by the people; and as he passed thus wise through the country and the houses, never did any dog bark behind him. At length after a two years space, brother wolf died of old age: whereat the townsfolk sorely grieved, sith marking him pass so gently through the city, they minded them the better of the virtue and the sanctity of St. Francis." [548]

In another mystic, less familiar than St. Francis to English readers--Rose of Lima, the Peruvian saint--this deep sympathy with natural things assumed a particularly lovely form. To St. Rose the whole world was a holy fairyland, in which it seemed to her that every living thing turned its face towards Eternity and joined in her adoration of God. It is said in her biography that "when at sunrise, she passed through the garden to go to her retreat, she called upon nature to praise with her the Author of all things. Then the trees were seen to bow as she passed by, and clasp their leaves together, making a harmonious sound. The flowers swayed upon their stalks, and opened their blossoms that they might scent the air; thus according to their manner praising God. At the same time the birds began to sing, and came and perched upon the hands and shoulders of Rose. The insects greeted her with a joyous murmur, and all which had life and movement joined in the concert of praise she addressed to the Lord." [549]

Again--and here we catch an echo of the pure Franciscan spirit, the gaiety of the Troubadours of God--during her last Lent, "each evening at sunset a little bird with an enchanting voice came and perched upon a tree beside her window, and waited till she gave the sign to him to sing. Rose, as soon as she saw her little feathered chorister, made herself ready to sing the praises of God, and challenged the bird to this musical duel in a song which she had composed for this purpose. Begin, dear little bird,' she said, begin thy lovely song! Let thy little throat, so full of sweet melodies, pour them forth: that together we may praise the Lord. Thou dost praise thy Creator, I my sweet Saviour: thus we together bless the Deity. Open thy little beak, begin and I will follow thee: and our voices shall blend in a song of holy joy.'

"At once the little bird began to sing, running through his scale to the highest note. Then he ceased, that the saint might sing in her turn . . . thus did they celebrate the greatness of God, turn by turn, for a whole hour: and with such perfect order, that when the bird sang Rose said nothing, and when she sang in her turn the bird was silent, and listened to her with a marvellous attention. At last, towards the sixth hour, the saint dismissed him, saying, Go, my little chorister, go, fly far away. But blessed be my God who never leaves me!'" [550]

The mystic whose illumination takes such forms as these, who feels with this intensity and closeness the bond of love which "binds in one book the scattered leaves of all the universe," dwells in a world unknown to other men. He pierces the veil of imperfection, and beholds Creation with the Creator's eye. The "Pattern is shown him in the Mount." "The whole consciousness," says Récéjac, "is flooded with light to unknown depths, under the gaze of love, from which nothing escapes. In this stage, intensity of vision and sureness of judgment are equal: and the things which the seer brings back with him when he returns to common life are not merely partial impressions, or the separate knowledge of science' or poetry.' They are rather truths which embrace the world, life and conduct: in a word, the whole consciousness ." [551]

It is curious to note in those diagrams of experience which we have inherited from the more clear-sighted philosophers and seers, indications that they have enjoyed prolonged or transitory periods of this higher consciousness; described by Récéjac as the marriage of imaginative vision with moral transcendence. I think it at least a reasonable supposition that Plato's doctrine of Ideas owed something to an intuition of this kind; for a philosophy, though it may claim to be the child of pure reason, is usually found to owe its distinctive character to the philosopher's psychological experience. The Platonic statements as to the veritable existence of the Idea of a house, a table, or a bed, and other such concrete and practical applications of the doctrine of the ideal, which have annoyed many metaphysicians, become explicable on such a psychological basis. That illuminated vision in which "all things are made new" can afford to embrace the homeliest as well as the sublimest things; and, as a matter of experience, it does do this, seeing all objects, as Monet saw the hayrick, as "modes of light." Blake said that his cottage at Felpham was a shadow of the angels' houses, [552] and I have already referred to the converted Methodist who saw his horses and hogs on the ideal plane. [553]

Again, when Plotinus, who is known to have experienced ecstatic states, speaks with the assurance of an explorer of an "intelligible world," and asks us, "What other fire could be a better image of the fire which is there, than the fire which is here? Or what other earth than this, of the earth which is there?"[554]

we seem to detect behind the language of Neoplatonic philosophy a hint of the same type of first-hand experience. The minds to whom we owe the Hebrew Kabalah found room for it too in their diagram of the soul's ascent towards Reality. The first "Sephira" above Malkuth, the World of Matter, or lowest plane upon that Tree of Life which is formed by the ten emanations of the Godhead is, they say, "Yesod," the "archetypal universe." In this are contained the realities, patterns, or Ideas, whose shadows constitute the world of appearance in which we dwell. The path of the ascending soul upon the Tree of Life leads him first from Malkuth to Yesod: i.e. , human consciousness in the course of its transcendence passes from the normal illusions of men to a deeper perception of its environment--a perception which is symbolized by the "archetypal plane" or world of Platonic Ideas. "Everything in temporal nature," says William Law, "is descended out of that which is eternal, and stands as a palpable visible outbirth of it, so when we know how to separate the grossness, death, and darkness of time from it, we find what it is in its eternal state. . . . In Eternal Nature, or the Kingdom of Heaven, materiality stands in life and light; it is the light's glorious Body, or that garment wherewith light is clothed, and therefore has all the properties of light in it, and only differs from light as it is its brightness and beauty, as the holder and displayer of all its colours, powers, and virtues." [555] When Law wrote this, he may have believed that he was interpreting to English readers the unique message of his master, Jacob Boehme. As a matter of fact he was reiterating truths which a long line of practical mystics had been crying for centuries into the deaf ears of mankind. He was saying in the eighteenth century what Gregory of Nyssa had said in the fourth and Erigena in the ninth; telling the secret of that "Inviolate Rose" which can never be profaned because it can only be seen with the eyes of love.

That serene and illuminated consciousness of the relation of things inward and outward--of the Hidden Treasure and its Casket, the energizing Absolute and its expression in Time and Space--which we have been studying in this chapter, is at its best a state of fine equilibrium; a sane adjustment of the inner and outer life. By that synthesis of love and will which is the secret of the heart, the mystic achieves a level of perception in which the whole world is seen and known in God, and God is seen and known in the whole world. It is a state of exalted emotion: being produced by love, of necessity it produces love in its turn. The sharp division between its inlooking and outlooking forms which I have adopted for convenience of description, is seldom present to the minds which achieve it. They, "cleansed, fed, and sanctified," are initiated into a spiritual universe where such clumsy distinctions have little meaning. All is alike part of the "new life" of peaceful charity: and that progressive abolition of selfhood which is of the essence of mystical development, is alone enough to prevent them from drawing a line between the inward personal companionship and outward impersonal apprehension of the Real. True Illumination, like all real and vital experience, consists rather in the breathing of a certain atmosphere, the living at certain levels of consciousness, than in the acquirement of specific information. It is, as it were, a resting-place upon "the steep stairway of love"; where the self turns and sees all about it a transfigured universe, radiant with that same Light Divine which nests in its own heart and leads it on.

"When man's desires are fixed immovably on his Maker as far as for deadliness and corruption of the flesh he is let," says Rolle of the purified soul which has attained the illuminated state, "then it is no marvel that his strength manly using, first as it were heaven being opened, with his understanding he beholds high heavenly citizens; and afterwards sweetest heat, as it were burning fire, he feels. Then with marvellous sweetness he is taught, and so forth in songful noise he is joyed. This, therefore, is perfect charity, which no man knows but he that hath it took. And he that it has taken, it never leaves: sweetly he lives and sickerly he shall die." [556]

Sweetly, it is true, the illuminated mystic may live; but not, as some think, placidly. Enlightenment is a symptom of growth: and growth is a living process, which knows no rest. The spirit, indeed, is invaded by a heavenly peace; but it is the peace, not of idleness, but of ordered activity. "A rest most busy," in Hilton's words: a progressive appropriation of the Divine. The urgent push of an indwelling spirit, aspiring to its home in the heart of Reality, is felt more and more, as the invasion of the normal consciousnesss by the transcendental personality--the growth of the New Man--proceeds towards its term.

Therefore the great seekers for reality are not as a rule long delayed by the exalted joys of Illumination. Intensely aware now of the Absolute Whom they adore, they are aware too that though known He is unachieved. Even whilst they enjoy the rapture of the Divine Presence--of life in a divine, ideal world--something, they feel, makes default. Sol voglio Te, O dolce Amore. Hence for them that which they now enjoy, and which passes the understanding of other men, is not a static condition; often it coexists with that travail of the heart which Tauler has called "stormy love." The greater the mystic, the sooner he realizes that the Heavenly Manna which has been administered to him is not yet That with which the angels are full fed. Nothing less will do: and for him the progress of illumination is a progressive consciousness that he is destined not for the sunny shores of the spiritual universe, but for "the vast and stormy sea of the divine."

"Here," says Ruysbroeck of the soul which has been lit by the Uncreated Light, "there begins an eternal hunger, which shall never more be satisfied. It is the inward craving and hankering of the affective power and created spirit after an Uncreated Good. And as the spirit longs for fruition, and is invited and urged thereto by God, she must always desire to attain it. Behold! here begin an eternal craving and continual yearning in eternal insatiableness! These men are poor indeed: for they are hungry and greedy, and their hunger is insatiable! Whatsoever they eat and drink they shall never be satisfied, for this hunger is eternal. . . . Here are great dishes of food and drink, of which none know but those who taste them; but full satisfaction in fruition is the one dish that lacks them, and this is why their hunger is ever renewed. Nevertheless in this contact rivers of honey full of all delight flow forth; for the spirit tastes these riches under every mode that it can conceive or apprehend. But all this is according to the manner of the creatures, and is below God: and hence there remains an eternal hunger and impatience. If God gave to such a man all the gifts which all the saints possess, and all that He is able to give, but without giving Himself, the craving desire of the spirit would remain hungry and unsatisfied."[557]

Footnotes:

477. For the relation between catharsis and poetic and mystical knowledge, see Bremond, "Prière et Poesie," caps xvi. and xvii.

478. Plotinus, Ennead vi. 9. Compare with this image of the rhythmic dance of things about a divine Corypheus in the midst, those passages in the Apocryphal "Hymn of Jesus" where the Logos or Christ, standing within the circle of disciples, says, "I am the Word who did play and dance all things," "Now answer to My dancing," "Understand by dancing what I do." Again, "Who danceth not knoweth not what is being done." "I would pipe, dance ye all!" and presently the rubric declares, "All whose Nature is to dance, doth dance!" (See Dr. M. R. James, "Apocrypha Anecdota," series 2; and G. R. S. Mead, "Echoes from the Gnosis: the Dance of Jesus." Compare supra, p. 134.)

479. For instance, Keats Shelley, Wordsworth, Tennyson, Browning, Whitman.

480. "Letters of William Blake," p. 171.

481. Ruysbroeck, "De vera Contemplatione," cap. xi.

482. "Jerusalem," cap. i.

483. Compare E. Rhode, "Psyche," and J. E. Harrison, "Prolegomena to the Study of Greek Religion," caps, ix., x., and xi.; a work which puts the most favourable construction possible on the meaning of Orphic initiation.

484. The "Bacchae" of Euripides (translated by Gilbert Murray), p. 83.

485. St. John of the Cross, "Llama de Amor Viva" (translated by Arthur Symons).

486. "Fioretti," cap. xlviii. (Arnold's translation).

487. Horstman, "Richard Rolle of Hampole," vol. ii. p. 79.

488. "Das Fliessende Licht der Gottheit," pt. i. cap. 43.

489. "De Imitatione Christi," I. iii. cap. i.

490. For the decisive character of this "night of the senses," see St. John of the Cross, "Noche escura del Alma," I. i.

491. "The Marriage of Heaven and Hell," xxii.

492. Vide supra, pp. 42-50 .

493. Julian of Norwich, "Revelations," cap. xliii.

494. "The Scale of Perfection," bk. ii. cap. xli.

495. See Delacroix, "Études sur le Mysticisme," Appendix I. "Sentiment de Présence." For a balanced view, Maréchal, "Studies in the Psychology of the Mystics," p. 55. See also Poulain, "Les Grâces d'Oraison," cap. v.

496. Vida, cap. xviii. § 20.

497. "Letters of St. Teresa" (1581), Dalton's translation, No. VII.

498. "Republic," vii. 518.

499. Récéjac, "Fondements de la Connaissance Mystique," p. 151.

500. St. Bernard, "Cantica Canticorum," Sermon lxxiv.

501. "Theologia Germanica," cap. xiv.

502. Hugh of St. Victor, "De Arrha Animae" (Migne, Patrologia Latina, vol. clxxvi.).

503. "The Practice of the Presence of God," Second Conversation.

504. St. Teresa, "Las Fundaciones," cap, v. p. 8.

505. Vie, pt. i. cap. xvii.

506. "Mystical Element of Religion," vol. i. p. 105.

507. "Vita e Dottrina" loc. cit.

508. "I desire not that which comes forth from Thee; but only I desire Thee, O sweetest Love!" ("Vita e Dottrina," cap. vi).

509. Aug. Conf., bk. vii. cap. xx. Compare St. Teresa: "Rapture is a great help to recognize our

true home and to see that we are pilgrims here; it is a great thing to see what is going on there, and to know where we have to live, for if a person has to go and settle in another country, it is a great help to him in undergoing the fatigues of his journey that he has discovered it to be a country where he may live in the most perfect peace" (Vida, cap. xxxviii., § 8).

510. M. Smith, "Rabia the Mystic," p. 30.

511. "Spiritual Exercises," pp. 26 and 174.

512. "Love above all language, goodness unimagined, light without measure shines in my heart" (Jacopone da Todi. Lauda xci.).

513. Pitra, "Analecta S. Hildegardis opera," p. 332.

514. St. Teresa, Vida, cap. xxviii. §§ 7, 8.

515. Par. i. 61, xxx. 100, xxxiii. 90.

516. "An Appeal to All who Doubt." I give the whole passage below, p. 263.

517. It is, of course, arguable that the whole of this light-imagery is ultimately derived from the Prologue of the Fourth Gospel: as the imagery of the Spiritual Marriage is supposed to be derived from the Song of Songs. Some hardy commentators have even found in it evidence of the descent of Christian Mysticism from sun-worship. (See H. F. Dunbar, "Symbolism in Mediaeval Thought".) But it must be remembered that mystics are essentially realists, always seeking for language adequate to their vision of truth: hence their adoption of this imagery is most simply explained by the fact that it represent something which they know and are struggling to describe.

518. Aug. Conf., bk. vii. cap. x.

519. Mechthild of Magdeburg, op. cit ., pt. vii. 45.

520. Par. xxx. 100, "Which makes visible the creator to that creature who only in beholding Him finds its peace."

521. Aug. Conf., bk. iii. cap. 6.

522. Dionysius the Areopagite, "De Mystica Theologia," i. 1. (Rolt's translation.)

523. Par. xxxiii. 82, 121:-- "O grace abounding! wherein I presumed to fix my gaze on the eternal light so long that I consumed my sight thereon! In its depths I saw ingathered the scattered leaves of the universe, bound into one book by love. Substance and accident and their relations: as if fused together in such a manner that what I tell of is a simple light. And I believe that I saw the universal form of this complexity; because, as I say this, I feel that I rejoice more deeply. . . . Oh, but how scant the speech and how faint to my concept! and that to what I saw is such, that it suffices not to call it little.' O Light Eternal, Who only in Thyself abidest, only Thyself dost comprehend, and, of Thyself comprehended and Thyself comprehending, dost love and smile!"

524. The Latin is more vivid: "Est iste mundus pregnans de Deo."

525. Ste. Angèle de Foligno, "Le Livre de l'Expérience des Vrais Fidèles," p. 124 (English translation, p. 172).

526. Suso, Leben, cap. iv.

527. "Revelations," cap. viii.

528. Malaval, "De l'Oraison Ordinaire" ("La Pratique de la Vraye Theologie Mystique," vol. i. p. 342).

529. "Saul," xvii.

530. Meister Eckhart ("Mystische Schriften," p. 137).

531. Vide supra, pt. II. Cap. II., the cases of Richard Jefferies, Brother Lawrence, and others.

532. The Works of Jacob Boehme, 4 vols., 1764, vol. i. pp. xii., etc.

533. Supra , p. 58.

534. Martensen, "Jacob Boehme," p. 7.

535. "Life of Jacob Boehme," pp. xiii. and xiv. in vol. i. of his Collected Works, English translation.

536. Op. cit ., p. xv.

537. Vol. I. cap. ii.

538. "Revelations," cap. viii.

539. Par. iii. 77.

540. "Letters of William Blake," p. 111.

541. Op. cit., p. 62.

542. Aug. Conf., bk. I. cap. xvi.

543. "Fioretti," cap. xiv.

544. Ibid., "Delle Istimate," 2, and Thomas of Celano, Vita Secunda, cap. xccvii.

545. Thomas of Celano, op. cit., cap. cxxix.

546. "Fioretti," cap. xxii.

547. Ibid., cap. xxi.

548. Fioretti," cap. xxi (Arnold's translation). Perhaps I may be allowed to remind the incredulous reader that the discovery of a large wolf's scull in Gubbio close to the spot in which Brother Wolf is said

to have lived in a cave for two years after his taming by the Saint, has done something to vindicate the truth of this beautiful story.

549. De Bussierre, "Le Pérou et Ste. Rose de Lime," p. 256.
550. De Bussierre, "Le Pérou et Ste. Rose de Lime," p. 415.
551. "Fondements de la Connaissance Mystique," p. 113.
552. Letters, p. 75.
553. Vide supra, p. 192.
554. Ennead ii. 9. 4.
555. "An Appeal to All who Doubt" (Liberal and Mystical Writings of William Law, p. 52).
556. Rolle, "The Fire of love," bk. i. cap. xix.
557. "De Ornatu Spiritalium Nuptiarum," I. ii. cap, liii.

CHAPTER V

We now come to that eternal battle-ground, the detailed discussion of those abnormal psychic phenomena which appear so persistently in the history of the mystics. That is to say, visions, auditions, automatic script, and those dramatic dialogues between the Self and some other factor--the Soul, Love, Reason, of the Voice of God--which seem sometimes to arise from an exalted and uncontrolled imaginative power, sometimes to attain the proportions of auditory hallucination.

Here, moderate persons are like to be hewn in pieces between the two "great powers" who have long disputed this territory. On the one hand we have the strangely named rationalists, who feel that they have settled the matter once for all by calling attention to the obvious parallels which exist between the bodily symptoms of acute spiritual stress and the bodily symptoms of certain forms of disease. These considerations, reinforced by those comfortable words "auto-suggestion" "psychosensorial hallucination" and "association neurosis"--which do but reintroduce mystery in another and less attractive form--enable them to pity rather than blame the peculiarities of the great contemplatives. French psychology, in particular, revels in this sort of thing: and would, if it had its way, fill the wards of the Salpêtriére with patients from the Roman Calendar. The modern interpreter, says Rufus Jones, finds in the stigmata of St. Francis of Assisi a point of weakness rather than a point of strength: not "the marks of a saint," but "the marks of emotional and physical abnormality." [558] This is a very moderate statement of the "rational" position, by a writer who is in actual sympathy with certain aspects of mysticism. Yet it may well be doubted whether that flame of living love which could, for one dazzling instant, weld body and soul in one, was really a point of weakness in a saint: whether Blake was quite as mad as some of his interpreters, or the powers of St. Paul and St. Teresa are fully explained on a basis of epilepsy or hysteria: whether, finally, it is as scientific as it looks, to lump together all visions and voices--from Wandering Willy to the Apocalypse of St. John--as examples of unhealthy cerebral activity.

As against all this, the intransigeant votaries of the supernatural seem determined to play into the hands of their foes. They pin themselves, for no apparent reason, to the objective reality and absolute value of visions, voices, and other experiences which would be classed, in any other department of life, as the harmless results of a vivid imagination: and claim as examples of miraculous interference with "natural law" psychic phenomena which may well be the normal if rare methods by which a certain type of intuitive genius actualizes its perceptions of the spiritual world. [559]

Materialistic piety of this kind, which would have us believe that St. Anthony of Padua really held the Infant Christ in his arms, and that the Holy Ghost truly told the Blessed Angela of Foligno that He loved her better than any other woman in the Vale of Spoleto, and she knew Him more intimately than the Apostles themselves, [560] is the best friend the "rationalists" possess. It turns dreams into miracles and drags down the symbolic visions of genius to the level of pious hallucination. Even the profound and beautiful significance of St. Margaret Mary Alacoque's vision of the Sacred Heart--a pictured expression of one of the deepest intuitions of the human soul, caught up to the contemplation of God's love--has been impaired by the grossly material interpretation which it has been forced to bear. So, too, the beautiful reveries of Suso, the divine visitations experienced by Francis, Catherine, Teresa and countless other saints, have been degraded in the course of their supposed elevation to the sphere called "supernatural"--a process as fatal to their truth and beauty as the stuffing of birds. [561]

All this, too, is done in defiance of the great mystics themselves, who are unanimous in warning their disciples against the danger of attributing too much importance to "visions" and "voices," or accepting them at their face value as messages from God. Nevertheless, these visions and voices are such frequent accompaniments of the mystic life, that they cannot be ignored. The messengers of the invisible world knock persistently at the doors of the senses: and not only at those which we refer to hearing and to sight. In other words, supersensual intuitions--the contact between man's finite being and the Infinite Being in which it is immersed--can express themselves by means of almost any kind of sensory automatism. Strange sweet perfumes and tastes, physical sensations of touch, inward fires, are reported over and over again in connection with such spiritual adventures. [562] Those symbols under which the mystic tends to approach the Absolute easily become objectivized, and present themselves to the consciousness as parts of experience, rather than as modes of interpretation. The knowledge which is obtained in such an approach is wholly transcendental. It consists in an undifferentiated act of the whole consciousness, in which under the spur of love life draws near to Life. Thought, feeling, vision, touch--all are hopelessly inadequate to it: yet all, perhaps, may hint at that intense perception of which they are the scattered parts. "And we shall endlessly be all had in God," says Julian of this supreme experience, "Him verily seeing and fully feeling, Him spiritually hearing and Him delectably smelling and sweetly swallowing." [563]

All those so-called "hallucinations of the senses" which appear in the history of mysticism must, then, be considered soberly, frankly, and without prejudice in the course of our inquiry into the psychology of man's quest of the Real. The question for their critics must really be this: do these automatisms, which appear so persistently as a part of the contemplative life, represent merely the dreams and fancies, the old digested percepts of the visionary, objectivized and presented to his surface-mind in a concrete form; or, are they ever representations--symbolic, if you like--of some fact, force, or personality, some "triumphing spiritual power," external to himself? Is the vision only a pictured thought, an activity of the dream imagination: or, is it the violent effort of the self to translate something impressed upon its deeper being, some message received from without, [564] which projects this sharp image and places it before the consciousness?

The answer seems to be that the voice or vision may be either of these two things: and that pathology and religion have both been over-hasty in their eagerness to snatch at these phenomena for their own purposes. Many--perhaps most--voices do but give the answer which the subject has already suggested to itself; [565] many--perhaps most--visions are the picturings of dreams and desires. [566] Some are morbid hallucinations: some even symptoms of insanity. All probably borrow their shape, as apart from their content, from suggestions already present in the mind of the seer. [567]

But there are some, experienced by minds of great power and richness, which are crucial for those who have them. These bring wisdom to the simple and ignorant, sudden calm to those who were tormented by doubts. They flood the personality with new light: accompany conversion, or the passage from one spiritual state to another: arrive at moments of indecision, bringing with them authoritative commands or counsels, opposed to the inclination of the self: confer a convinced knowledge of some department of the spiritual life before unknown. Such visions, it is clear, belong to another and higher plane of experience from the radiant appearances of our Lady, the piteous exhibitions of the sufferings of Christ, which swarm in the lives of the saints, and contain no feature which is not traceable to the subject's religious enthusiasms or previous knowledge. [568] These, in the apt phrase of Godfernaux, are but "images floating on the moving deeps of feeling," [569] not symbolic messages from another plane of consciousness. Some test, then, must be applied, some basis of classification discovered, if we are to distinguish the visions and voices which seem to be symptoms of real transcendental activity from those which are only due to imagination raised to the n th power, to intense reverie, or to psychic illness. That test, I think, must be the same as that which we shall find useful for ecstatic states; namely, their life-enhancing quality.

Those visions and voices which are the media by which the "seeing self" truly approaches the Absolute; which are the formula under which ontological perceptions are expressed; are found by that self to be sources of helpful energy, charity, and, courage. They infuse something new in the way of strength, knowledge, direction; and leave it--physically, mentally, or spiritually--better than they found it. Those which do not owe their inception to the contact of the soul with external reality--in theological language, do not "come from God"--do not have this effect. At best, they are but the results of the self's turning over of her treasures: at worst, they are the dreams--sometimes the diseased dreams--of an active, rich, but imperfectly controlled subliminal consciousness.

Since it is implicit in the make-up of the mystical temperament, that the subliminal consciousness should be active and rich--and since the unstable nervous organization which goes with it renders it liable to illness and exhaustion--it is not surprising to find that the visionary experience even of the greatest mystics is mixed in type. Once automatism has established itself in a person, it may as easily become the expression of folly as of wisdom. In the moments when inspiration has ebbed, old forgotten superstitions may take its place. When Julian of Norwich in her illness saw the "horrible showing" of the Fiend, red with black freckles, which clutched at her throat with its paws: [570] when St. Teresa was visited by Satan, who left a smell of brimstone behind, or when she saw him sitting on the top of her breviary and dislodged him by the use of holy water: [571] it is surely reasonable to allow that we are in the presence of visions which tend towards the psychopathic type, and which are expressive of little else but an exhaustion and temporary loss of balance on the subject's part, which allowed her intense consciousness of the reality of evil to assume a concrete form. [572]

Because we allow this, however, it does not follow that all the visionary experience of such a subject is morbid: any more than "Oedipus Tyrannus" invalidates "Prometheus Unbound," or occasional attacks of dyspepsia invalidate the whole process of nutrition. The perceptive power and creative genius of mystics, as of other great artists, sometimes goes astray. That visions or voices should sometimes be the means by which the soul consciously assimilates the nourishment it needs, is conceivable: it is surely also conceivable that by the same means it may present to the surface-intelligence things which are productive of unhealthy rather than of healthy reactions.

If we would cease, once for all, to regard visions and voices as objective, and be content to see in them forms of symbolic expression, ways in which the subconscious activity of the spiritual self reaches the surface-mind, many of the disharmonies noticeable in visionary experience, which have teased the devout, and delighted the agnostic, would fade away. Visionary experience is--or at least may be--the outward sign of a real experience. It is a picture which the mind constructs, it is true, from raw materials already at its disposal: as the artist constructs his picture with canvas and paint. But, as the artist's paint and canvas picture is the fruit, not merely of contact between brush and canvas, but also of a more vital contact between his creative genius and visible beauty or truth; so too we may see in vision, where the subject is a mystic, the fruit of a more mysterious contact between the visionary and a transcendental beauty or truth. Such a vision, that is to say, is the "accident" which represents and enshrines a "substance" unseen: the paint and canvas picture which tries to show the surface consciousness that ineffable sight, that ecstatic perception of good or evil--for neither extreme has the monopoly--to which the deeper, more real soul has attained. The transcendental powers take for this purpose such material as they can find amongst the hoarded beliefs and memories of the self. [573] Hence Plotinus sees the Celestial Venus, Suso the Eternal Wisdom, St. Teresa the Humanity of Christ, Blake the strange personages of his prophetic books: others more obviously symbolic objects. St. Ignatius Loyola, for instance, in a moment of lucidity, "saw the most Holy Trinity as it were under the likeness of a triple plectrum or of three spinet keys" and on another occasion "the Blessed Virgin without distinction of members." [574]

Visions and voices, then, may stand in the same relation to the mystic as pictures, poems, and musical compositions stand to the great painter, poet, musician. They are the artistic expressions and creative results (a) of thought, (b) of intuition, (c) of direct perception. All would be ready to acknowledge how conventional and imperfect of necessity are those transcripts of perceived Goodness, Truth, and Beauty which we owe to artistic genius: how unequal is their relation to reality. But this is not to say that they are valueless or absurd. So too with the mystic, whose proceedings in this respect are closer to those of the artist than is generally acknowledged. In both types there is a constant and involuntary work of translation going on, by which Reality is interpreted in the terms of appearance. In both, a peculiar mental make-up conduces to this result.

In artistic subjects, the state of reverie tends easily to a visionary character: thought becomes pictorial, auditory or rhythmic as the case may be. Concrete images, balanced harmonies, elusive yet recognizable, surge up mysteriously without the intervention of the will, and place themselves before the mind. Thus the painter really sees his impainted picture, the novelist hears the conversation of his characters, the poet receives his cadences ready-made, the musician listens to a veritable music which "pipes to the spirit ditties of no tone." In the mystic, the same type of activity constantly appears. Profound meditation takes a pictorial or dramatic form. Apt symbols which suggest themselves to his imagination become objectivized. The message that he longs for is heard within his mind. Hence, those "interior voices" and "imaginary visions" which are sometimes--as in Suso--indistinguishable from the ordinary accompaniments of intense artistic activity.

Where, however, artistic "automatisms" spend themselves upon the artist's work, mystical "automatisms" in their highest forms have to do with that transformation of personality which is the essence of the mystic life. They are media by which the self receives spiritual stimulus; is reproved, consoled, encouraged and guided on its upward way. Moreover, they are frequently coordinated. The voice and the vision go together: corroborate one another, and "work out right" in relation to the life of the self. Thus St. Catherine of Siena's "mystic marriage" was preceded by a voice, which ever said in answer to her prayers, "I will espouse thee to Myself in faith"; and the vision in which that union was consummated was again initiated by a voice saying, "I will this day celebrate solemnly with thee the feast of the betrothal of thy soul, and even as I promised I will espouse thee to Myself in faith." [575] "Such automatisms as these," says Delacroix, "are by no means scattered and incoherent. They are systematic and progressive: they are governed by an interior aim; they have, above all, a teleological character. They indicate the continuous intervention of a being at once wiser and more powerful than the ordinary character and reason; they are the realization, in visual and auditory images, of a secret and permanent personality of a superior type to the conscious personality. They are its voice, the exterior projection of its life. They translate to the conscious personality the suggestions of the subconscious: and they permit the continuous penetration of the conscious personality by these deeper activities. They establish a communication between these two planes of existence, and, by their imperative nature, they tend to make the inferior subordinate to the superior." [576]

Audition

The simplest and as a rule the first way in which automatism shows itself, is in "voices" or auditions. The mystic becomes aware of Something which speaks to him either clearly or implicitly; giving him abrupt and unexpected orders and encouragements. The reality of his contact with the Divine Life is thus brought home to him by a device with which the accidents of human intercourse have made him familiar. His subliminal mind, open as it now is to transcendental impressions, "at one with the Absolute," irradiated by the Uncreated Light, but still dissociated from the surface intelligence which it is slowly educating, seems to that surface self like another being. Hence its messages are often heard, literally, as Voices: either (1) the "immediate" or inarticulate voice, which the auditive mystic knows so well, but finds it so difficult to define; (2) the distinct interior voice, perfectly articulate, but recognized as speaking only within the mind; (3) by a hallucination which we have all experienced in dream or reverie, the exterior voice, which appears to be speaking externally to the subject and to be heard by the outward ear. This, the traditional classification of auditions, also answers exactly to she three main types of vision--(1) intellectual, (2) imaginary, (3) corporeal.

Of these three kinds of voices the mystics are unanimous in their opinion that the first and least "marvellous" is by far the best: belonging indeed to an entirely different plane of consciousness from the uttered interior or exterior "word," which few of the great contemplatives are willing to accept without scrutiny as a "message from God." The articulate word is inevitably subject to some degree of illusion, even at the best; since so far as it possesses transcendental content it represents the translation of the simultaneous into successive speech.

"Let Thy good Spirit enter my heart and there be heard without utterance, and without the sound of words speak all truth," says a prayer attributed to St. Ambrose, [577] exactly describing the function of these unmediated or "intellectual words." Dynamic messages of this kind, imperative intuitions which elude the containing formula of speech, are invariably attributed by the self to the direct action of the Divine. They are indeed their own guarantee, bringing with them an infusion of new knowledge or new life. Their character is less that of messages than of actual "invasions" from beyond the threshold; transcending succession and conveying "all at once" fresh truth or certitude. "Intellectual words," in fact, are a form of inspiration. Eternal truth bursts in upon the temporally-conditioned human mind. Thus St. Hildegarde tells us that each of her great revelations was received "in an instant" and St. Bridget of Sweden that the whole substance of her 5th Book was given "in a flash." [578]

"Distinct interior words," on the other hand, lack this character of simultaneity. Nor are they invariably authoritative for those who hear them. St. Teresa, whose brilliant self-criticisms are our best source of information on mystical auditions, considers that, though they often "come from God," they are not due to direct contact with the Divine; and agrees with all the great mystics on the need of subjecting them to criticism. She hesitated long before obeying the Voice which told her to leave the Convent of the Incarnation and make the first foundation of her Reform. Genuine locutions may however be distinguished from those "words" which result merely from voluntary activity of the imagination, as much by the sense of certitude, peace and interior joy which they produce, as by the fact that they force themselves upon the attention in spite of its resistance, and bring with them knowledge which was not previously within the field of consciousness. That is to say, they are really automatic presentations of the result of mystic intuition, not mere rearrangements of the constituents of thought.[579] Hence they bring to the surface-self new conviction or material: have a positive value for life.

Those purely self-created locutions, or rearrangements of thought "which the mind self-recollected forms and fashions within itself"--often difficult to distinguish from true automatic audition--are called by Philip of the trinity, St. John of the Cross and other mystical theologians "successive words." They feel it to be of the highest importance that the contemplative should learn to distinguish such hallucinations from real transcendental perceptions presented in auditive form.

"I am really terrified," says St. John of the Cross, with his customary blunt common sense, "by what passes among us in these days. Anyone who has barely begun to meditate, if he becomes conscious of words of this kind during his self-recollection, pronounces them forthwith to be the work of God; [580] and, convinced that they are so, goes about proclaiming God has told me this,' or I have had that answer from God.' But all is illusion and fancy; such an one has only been speaking to himself. Besides, the desire for these words, and the attention they give to them, end by persuading men that all the observations which they address to themselves are the responses of God." [581] These are the words of one who was at once the sanest of saints and the most penetrating of psychologists: words which our modern unruly amateurs of the "subconscious" might well take to heart.

True auditions are usually heard when the mind is in a state of deep absorption without conscious thought: that is to say, at the most favourable of all moments for contact with the transcendental world. They translate into articulate language some aspect of that ineffable apprehension of Reality which the contemplative enjoys: crystallize those clairvoyant intuitions, those prophetic hints which surge in on him so soon as he lays himself open to the influence of the supra-sensible. Sometimes, however, mystical intuition takes the form of a sudden and ungovernable uprush of knowledge from the deeps of personality. Then, auditions may break in upon the normal activities of the self with startling abruptness. It is in such cases that their objective and uncontrollable character is most sharply felt. However they may appear, they are, says St. Teresa, "very distinctly formed; but by the bodily ear they are not heard. They are, however, much more clearly understood than if they were heard by the ear. It is impossible not to understand them, whatever resistance we may offer. . . . The words formed by the understanding effect nothing, but when our Lord speaks, it is at once word and work. . . . The human locution [i.e. , the work of imagination] is as something we cannot well make out, as if we were half asleep: but the divine locution is a voice so clear, that not a syllable of its utterance is lost. It may occur, too, when the understanding and the soul are so troubled and distracted that they cannot form one sentence correctly: and yet grand sentences, perfectly arranged such as the soul in its most recollected state never could have formed, are uttered: and at the first word, as I have said, change it utterly." [582]

St. Teresa's mystic life was governed by voices: her active career as a foundress was much guided by them. They advised her in small things as in great. Often they interfered with her plans, ran counter to her personal judgment, forbade a foundation on which she was set, or commanded one which appeared imprudent or impossible. They concerned themselves with journeys, with the purchase of houses; they warned her of coming events. [583] As her mystical life matured, Teresa seems to have learned to discriminate those locutions on which action should properly be based. She seldom resisted them, though it constantly happened that the action on which they insisted seemed the height of folly: and though they frequently involved her in hardships and difficulties, she never had cause to regret this reliance upon decrees which she regarded as coming direct from God, and which certainly did emanate from a life greater than her own. So too St. Hildegarde, when she prefaced her prophecies and denunciations by "Thus saith the Living Light" was not making use of a poetic metaphor. She lived under the direction of a Power which was precise and articulate in its communications, and at her peril disobeyed its commands.

So far from mere vague intuitions are the "distinct interior words" which the mystic hears within his mind, that Suso is able to state that the hundred meditations on the Passion thus revealed to him were spoken in German and not in Latin. [584] St. Teresa's own auditions were all of this interior kind--some "distinct" and some "substantial" or inarticulate--as her corresponding visions were nearly all of the "intellectual" or "imaginary" sort: that is to say, she was not subject to sensible hallucination. Often, however, the boundary is overpassed, and the locution seems to be heard by the mystic's outward ear; as in the case of those voices which guided the destinies of St. Joan of Arc, or the Figure upon the Cross which spoke to St. Francis of Assisi. We then have the third form--"exterior words"--which the mystics for the most part regard with suspicion and dislike.

Sometimes audition assumes a musical rather than a verbal character: a form of perception which probably corresponds to the temperamental bias of the self, the ordered sweetness of Divine Harmony striking responsive chords in the music-loving soul. The lives of St. Francis of Assisi, St. Catherine of Siena, and Richard Rolle provide obvious instances of this: [585] but Suso, in whom automatism assumed its richest and most varied forms, has also given in his autobiography some characteristic examples.

"One day . . . whilst the Servitor was still at rest, he heard within himself a gracious melody by which his heart was greatly moved. And at the moment of the rising of the morning star, a deep sweet voice sang within him these words, Stella Maria maris, hodie processit ad ortum . That is to say, Mary Star of the Sea is risen today. And this song which he heard was so spiritual and so sweet, that his soul was transported by it and he too began to sing joyously. . . . And one day--it was in carnival time--the Servitor had continued his prayers until the moment when the bugle of the watch announced the dawn. Therefore he said to himself, Rest for an instant, before you salute the shining Morning Star. And, whilst that his senses were at rest, behold! angelic spirits began to sing the fair Respond: Illuminare, illuminare, Jerusalem !'And this song was echoed with a marvellous sweetness in the deeps of his soul. And when the angels had sung for some time his soul overflowed with joy: and his feeble body being unable to support such happiness, burning tears escaped from his eyes." [586]

Closely connected on the one hand with the phenomena of automatic words, on the other with those of prophecy and inspiration, is the prevalence in mystical literature of revelations which take the form of dialogue: intimate colloquies between Divine Reality and the Soul. The Revelations of Julian of Norwich and St. Catherine of Siena, and many of those of the Blessed Angela of Foligno and of the modern mystic Lucie-Christine appear to have been received by them in this way. We seem as we read them to be present at veritable outpourings of the Divine Mind, crystallized into verbal form on their way through the human consciousness. We feel on the one hand a "one-ness with the Absolute" on the part of the mystic which has made her really, for the time being, the "voice of God": whilst on the other we recognize in her the persistence of the individual--exalted, but not yet wholly absorbed in the Divine--whose questions, here and there, break in upon the revelation which is mediated by the deeper mind.

Duologues of this sort are reported with every appearance of realism and good faith by Suso, Tauler, Mechthild of Magdeburg, Angela of Foligno, St. Teresa, and countless other mystics. The third book of the "Imitation of Christ" contains some conspicuously beautiful examples, which may or may not be due to literary artifice. The self, wholly absorbed by the intimate sense of divine companionship, receives its messages in the form of "distinct interior words"; as of an alien voice, speaking within the mind with such an accent of validity and spontaneity as to leave no room for doubt as to its character. Often, as in Julian's Revelations, the discourses of the "Divine Voice," its replies to the eager questions of the self, are illustrated by imaginary visions. Since these dialogues are, on the whole, more commonly experienced in the illuminative than the unitive way, that self--retaining a clear consciousness of its own separateness, and recognizing the Voice as personal and distinct from its own soul--naturally enters into a communion which has an almost conversational character, replies to questions or asks others in its turn: and in this dramatic style the content of its intuitions is gradually expressed. We have then an extreme form of that dissociation which we all experience in a slight degree when we "argue with ourselves." But in this case one of the speakers is become the instrument of a power other than itself, and communicates to the mind new wisdom and new life.

The peculiar rhythmical language of genuine mystic dialogue of this kind--for often enough, as in Suso's "Book of the Eternal Wisdom," it is deliberately adopted as a literary device--is an indication of its automatic character. [587] Expression, once it is divorced from the critical action of the surface intelligence, always tends to assume a dithyrambic form. Measure and colour, exaltation of language, here take a more important place than the analytic intellect will generally permit. This feature is easily observable in prophecy, and in automatic writing. It forms an interesting link with poetry; which--in so far as it is genuine and spontaneous--is largely the result of subliminal activity. Life, which eludes language, can yet--we know not why--be communicated by rhythm: and the mystic fact is above all else the communication of a greater Life. Hence we must not take it amiss if the voice of the Absolute, as translated to us by those mystics who are alone capable of hearing it, often seems to adopt the "grand manner."

We pass from the effort of man's deeper mind to speak truth to his surface-intelligence, to the effort of the same mysterious power to show truth: in psychological language, from auditory to visual automatism. "Vision," that vaguest of words, has been used by the friends and enemies of the mystics to describe or obscure a wide range of experience: from formless intuition, through crude optical hallucination, to the voluntary visualizations common to the artistic mind. In it we must include that personal and secret vision which is the lover's glimpse of Perfect Love, and the great pictures seen by clairvoyant prophets acting in their capacity as eyes of the race. Of these, the two main classes of vision, says Denis the Carthusian, the first kind are to be concealed, the second declared. The first are more truly mystic, the second prophetic: but excluding prophetic vision from our inquiry, a sufficient variety of experience remains in the purely mystical class. St. Teresa's fluid and formless apprehension of the Trinity, her concrete visions of Christ, Mechthild of Madeburg's poetic dreams, Suso's sharply pictured allegories, even Blake's soul of a flea, all come under this head.

Since no one can know what it is really like to have a vision but the visionaries themselves, it will be interesting to see what they have to say on this subject: and notice the respects in which these self-criticisms agree with the conclusions of psychology. We forget, whilst arguing on these matters, that it is as impossible for those who have never heard a voice or seen a vision to discuss these experiences with intelligence, as it is for stay-at-homes to discuss the passions of the battle-field on the material supplied by war correspondents. No second-hand account can truly report the experience of the person whose perceptions or illusions present themselves in this form. "We cannot," says Récéjac, "remind ourselves too often that the mystic act consists in relations between the Absolute and Freedom which are incommunicable. We shall never know, for instance, what was the state of consciousness of some citizen of the antique world when he gave himself without reserve to the inspiring suggestions of the Sacred Fire, or some other image which evoked the infinite." [588] Neither shall we ever know, unless it be our good fortune to attain to it, the secret of that consciousness which is able to apprehend the Transcendent in visionary terms.

The first thing we notice when we come to this inquiry is that the mystics are all but unanimous in their refusal to attribute importance to any kind of visionary experience. [589] The natural timidity and stern self-criticism with which they approach auditions is here greatly increased: and this, if taken to heart, might well give pause to their more extreme enemies and defenders. "If it be so," says Hilton of automatisms in general, "that thou see any manner of light or brightness with thy bodily eye or in imagining, other than every man may see; or if thou hear any merry sounding with thy ear, or in thy mouth any sweet sudden savour, other than of kind [nature], or any heat in thy breast as it were fire, or any manner delight in any part of thy body, or if a spirit bodily appeareth to thee as it were an angel, for to comfort thee and kiss thee, or any such feeling, which thou wost well that it cometh not of thyself, nor of no bodily creature, be then wary in that time or soon after, and wisely behold the stirrings of thy heart. If thou be stirred because of that liking that thou feelest for to draw out thine heart . . . from the inward desire of virtues and of ghostly knowing and feeling of God, for to set the sight of thy heart and thine affection, thy delight and thy rest, principally therein, weening that bodily feeling should be a part of heavenly joy and of angels' bliss . . . this feeling is suspect and of the enemy. And therefore, though it be never so liking and wonderful, refuse it, and assent not thereto." [590] Nearly every master of the contemplative life has spoken to the same effect: none, perhaps, more strongly than that stern and virile lover of the invisible, St. John of the Cross, who was relentless in hunting down even the most "spiritual" illusions, eager to purge mind as well as morals of all taint of the unreal.

"It often happens," he says "that spiritual men are affected supernaturally by sensible representations and objects. They sometimes see the forms and figures of those of another life, saints or angels, good and evil, or certain extraordinary lights and brightness. They hear strange words, sometimes seeing those who utter them and sometimes not. They have a sensible perception at times of most sweet odours, without knowing whence they proceed. . . . Still, though all these experiences may happen to the bodily senses in the way of God, we must never delight in them nor encourage them; yea, rather we must fly from them, without seeking to know whether their origin be good or evil. For, inasmuch as they are exterior and physical, the less is the likelihood of their being from God. That which properly and generally comes from God is a purely spiritual communication; wherein there is greater security and profit for the soul than through the senses, wherein there is usually much danger and delusion, because the bodily sense decides upon, and judges, spiritual things, thinking them to be what itself feels them to be, when in reality they are as different as body and soul, sensuality and reason." [591]

Again, "in the high state of the union of love, God does not communicate Himself to the soul under the disguise of imaginary visions, similitudes or figures, neither is there place for such, but mouth to mouth. . . . The soul, therefore, that will ascend to this perfect union with God, must be careful not to lean upon imaginary visions, forms, figures, and particular intelligible objects, for these things can never serve as proportionate or proximate means towards so great an end; yea, rather they are an obstacle in the way, and therefore to be guarded against and rejected." [592]

So, too, St. Teresa. "In such matters as these there is always cause to fear illusion; until we are assured that they truly proceed from the Spirit of God. Therefore at the beginning it is always best to resist them. If it is indeed God who is acting, the soul will but progress still more quickly, for the trial will favour her advancement." [593]

Vision, then, is recognized by the true contemplative as at best an imperfect, oblique, and untrustworthy method of apprehension: it is ungovernable, capricious, liable to deception, and the greater its accompanying hallucination the more suspicious it becomes. All, however, distinguish different classes of visionary experience; and differentiate sharply between the value of the vision which is "felt" rather than seen, and the true optical hallucination which is perceived, exterior to the subject, by the physical sight.

We may trace in visions, as in voices--for these, from the psychologist's point of view, are strictly parallel phenomena--a progressive externalization on the self's part of those concepts or intuitions which form the bases of all automatic states. Three main groups have been distinguished by the mystics, and illustrated again and again from their experiences. These are (1) Intellectual (2) Imaginary, and (3) Corporeal vision: answering to (1) Substantial or inarticulate, (2) Interior and distinct, (3) Exterior words. With the first two we must now concern ourselves. As to corporeal vision, it has few peculiarities of interest to the student of pure mysticism. Like the "exterior word" it is little else than a more or less uncontrolled externalization of inward memories, thoughts, or intuitions--even of some pious picture which has become imprinted on the mind--which may, in some subjects, attain the dimensions of true sensorial hallucination.

(1) Intellectual Vision.-- The "intellectual vision," like the "substantial word" as described to us by the mystics, is of so elusive, spiritual, and formless a kind that it is hard to distinguish it from that act of pure contemplation in which it often takes its rise. These moods and apprehensions of the soul are so closely linked together--the names applied to them are so often little more than the struggles of different individuals to describe by analogy an experience which is one-- that we risk a loss of accuracy the moment that classification begins. The intellectual vision, so far as we can understand it, seems to be a something not sought but put before the mind, and seen or perceived by the whole self by means of a sense which is neither sight nor feeling, but partakes of the character of both. It is intimate but indescribable: definite, yet impossible to define. There is a passage in the Revelations of Angela of Foligno which vividly describes the sequence of illuminated states leading up to and including the intuitions which constitute the substance of this "formless vision" and its complement the "formless word": and this does far more towards making us realize its nature than the most painstaking psychological analysis could ever do. "At times God comes into the soul without being called; and He instills into her fire, love, and sometimes sweetness; and the soul believes this comes from God, and delights therein. But she does not yet know, or see, that He dwells in her; she perceives His grace, in which she delights. And again God comes to the soul, and speaks to her words full of sweetness, in which she has much joy, and she feels Him. This feeling of God gives her the greatest delight; but even here a certain doubt remains; for the soul has not the certitude that God is in her. . . . And beyond this the soul receives the gift of seeing God. God says to her, Behold Me!' and the soul sees Him dwelling within her. She sees Him more clearly than one man sees another. For the eyes of the soul behold a plenitude of which I cannot speak: a plenitude which is not bodily but spiritual, of which I can say nothing. And the soul rejoices in that sight with an ineffable joy; and this is the manifest and certain sign that God indeed dwells in her. And the soul can behold nothing else, because this fulfils her in an

unspeakable manner. This beholding, whereby the soul can behold no other thing, is so profound that it grieves me that I can say nothing of it. It is not a thing which can be touched or imagined, for it is ineffable." [594]

Intellectual vision, then, seems to be closely connected with that "consciousness of the Presence of God" which we discussed in the last chapter: though the contemplatives themselves declare that it differs from it. [595] It is distinguished apparently from that more or less diffused consciousness of Divine Immanence by the fact that although unseen of the eyes, it can be exactly located in space. The mystic's general awareness of the divine is here focussed upon one point--a point to which some theological or symbolic character is at once attached. The result is a sense of presence so concrete defined, and sharply personal that, as St. Teresa says, it carries more conviction than bodily sight. This invisible presence is generally identified by Christian mystics rather with the Humanity of Christ than with the unconditioned Absolute. "In the prayer of union and of quiet," says St. Teresa, "certain inflowings of the Godhead are present; but in the vision, the Sacred Humanity also, together with them, is pleased to be our companion and to do us good." [596] "A person who is in no way expecting such a favour," she says again, "nor has ever imagined herself worthy of receiving it, is conscious that Jesus Christ stands by her side; although she sees Him neither with the eyes of the body nor of the soul. This is called an intellectual vision; I cannot tell why. This vision, unlike an imaginary one, does not pass away quickly but lasts for several days and even sometimes for more than a year. . . . Although I believe some of the former favours are more sublime, yet this brings with it a special knowledge of God; a most tender love for Him results from being constantly in His company while the desire of devoting one's whole being to His service is more fervent than any hitherto described. The conscience is greatly purified by the knowledge of His perpetual and near presence, for although we know that God sees all we do, yet nature inclines us to grow careless and forgetful of it. This is impossible here, since our Lord makes the soul conscious that He is close at hand." [597]

In such a state--to which the term "vision" is barely applicable--it will be observed that consciousness is at its highest, and hallucination at its lowest point. Nothing is seen, even with the eyes of the mind: as, in the parallel case of the "substantial word," nothing is said. It is pure apprehension: in the one case of Personality, in the other of knowledge. "The immediate vision of the naked Godhead," says Suso of this, "is without doubt the pure truth: a vision is to be esteemed the more noble the more intellectual it is, the more it is stripped of all image and approaches the state of pure contemplation."[598]

We owe to St. Teresa our finest first-hand account of this strange condition of "awareness." It came upon her abruptly, after a period of psychic distress, and seemed to her to be an answer to her unwilling prayers that she might be "led" by some other way than that of "interior words"; which were, in the opinion of her director, "so suspicious." "I could not force myself," she says, "to desire the change, nor believe that I was under the influence of Satan. Though I was doing all I could to believe the one and to desire the other, it was not in my power to do so." She resolved this divided state by making an act of total surrender to the will of God: and it seems to have been as the result of this release of stress, this willing receptivity, that the new form of automatism suddenly developed itself, reinforcing and justifying her auditions and bringing peace and assurance to the distracted surface-self.

"At the end of two years spent in prayer by myself and others for this end, namely, that our Lord would either lead me by another way, or show the truth of this--for now the locutions of our Lord were extremely frequent--this happened to me. I was in prayer one day--it was the feast of the glorious St. Peter--when I saw Christ close by me, or, to speak more correctly, felt Him; for I saw nothing with the eyes of the body, nothing with the eyes of the soul. He seemed to me to be close beside me; and I saw, too, as I believe, that it was He who was speaking to me. As I was utterly ignorant that such a vision was possible, I was extremely afraid at first, and did nothing but weep; however, when He spoke to me but one word to reassure me, I recovered myself, and was, as usual, calm and comforted, without any fear whatever. Jesus Christ seemed to be by my side continually. As the vision was not imaginary, I saw no form, but I had a most distinct feeling that He was always on my right hand, a witness of all I did; and never at any time, if I was but slightly recollected, or not too much distracted, could I be ignorant of His near presence. I went at once to my confessor in great distress, to tell him of it. He asked in what form I saw our Lord. I told him I saw no form. He then said: How did you know that it was Christ?' I replied that I did not know how I knew it; but I could not help knowing that He was close beside me . . . there are no words whereby to explain--at least, none for us women, who know so little; learned men can explain it better.

"For if I say that I see Him neither with the eyes of the body nor those of the soul--because it was not an imaginary vision--how is it that I can understand and maintain that He stand beside me, and be more certain of it than if I saw Him ? If it be supposed that it is as if a person were blind, or in the dark, and therefore unable to see another who is close to him, the comparison is not exact. There is a certain likelihood about it, however, but not much, because the other senses tell him who is blind of that presence: he hears the other speak or move, or he touches him; but in these visions there is nothing like this. The darkness is not felt; only He renders Himself present to the soul by a certain knowledge of

Himself which is more clear than the sun. I do not mean that we now see either a sun or any other brightness, only that there is a light not seen, which illumines the understanding, so that the soul may have the fruition of so great a good. This vision brings with it great blessings." [599]

(2) In Imaginary Vision, as in "interior words," there is again no sensorial hallucination. The self sees sharply and clearly, it is true: but is perfectly aware that it does so in virtue of its most precious organ--"that inward eye which is the bliss of solitude." [600] Imaginary Vision is the spontaneous and automatic activity of a power which all artists, all imaginative people, possess. So far as the machinery employed in it is concerned, there is little real difference except in degree between Wordsworth's imaginary vision of the "dancing daffodils" and Suso's of the dancing angels, who "though they leapt very high in the dance, did so without any lack of gracefulness." [601] Both are admirable examples of "passive imaginary vision": though in the first the visionary is aware that the picture seen is supplied by memory, whilst in the second it arises spontaneously like a dream from the subliminal region, and contains elements which may be attributed to love, belief, and direct intuition of truth.

Such passive imaginary vision--by which I mean spontaneous mental pictures at which the self looks, but in the action of which it does not participate--takes in the mystics two main forms: (a) symbolic, (b) personal.

(a) In the symbolic form there is no mental deception: the self is aware that it is being shown truth "under an image." Many of the visions of the great prophetic mystics--e.g., St. Hildegarde--have so elaborate a symbolic character, that much intellectual activity is involved in their interpretation. This interpretation is sometimes "given" with the vision. Rulman Merswin's "Vision of Nine Rocks" is thus described to us as being seen by him in a sharp picture, the allegorical meaning of which was simultaneously presented to his mind. In Suso's life these symbolic visions abound: he seems to have lived always on the verge of such a world of imagination, and to have imbibed truth most easily in this form. Thus: "It happened one morning that the Servitor saw in a vision that he was surrounded by a troop of heavenly spirits. He therefore asked one of the most radiant amongst these Princes of the Sky to show him how God dwelt in his soul. The angel said to him, Do but fix your eyes joyously upon yourself, and watch how God plays the game of love within your loving soul.' And he looked quickly, and saw that his body in the region of his heart was pure and transparent like crystal: and he saw the Divine Wisdom peacefully enthroned in the midst of his heart, and she was fair to look upon. And by her side was the soul of the Servitor, full of heavenly desires; resting lovingly upon the bosom of God, Who had embraced it, and pressed it to His Heart. And it remained altogether absorbed and inebriated with love in the arms of God its well-beloved." [602]

In such a vision as this, we see the mystic's passion for the Absolute, his intuition of Its presence in his soul, combining with material supplied by a poetic imagination, and expressing itself in an allegorical form. It is really a visualized poem, inspired by a direct contact with truth. Of the same kind are many of those reconstructions of Eternity in which mystics and seers of the transcendent and outgoing type actualized their profound apprehensions of reality. In such experiences, as Beatrice told Dante when he saw the great vision of the River of Light, the thing seen is the shadowy presentation of a transcendent Reality which the self is not yet strong enough to see.

"E vidi lume in forma di rivera
fulvido di fulgore, intra due rive
dipinte di mirabil primavera.
Di tal fiumana uscian faville vive,
e d' ogni parte si mettean nei fiori,
quasi rubin che oro circonscrive.
Poi, come inebriate dagli odori,
riprofondavan sè nel miro gurge,
e, s'una entrava, un' altra n' uscia fuori."
. . . .
"il sol degli occhi miei
anco soggiunse: Il fiume, e li topazii
ch' entrano ed escono, e il rider dell' erbe
son di lor vero ombriferi prefazii.
Non che da sè sien queste cose acerbe:
ma è difetto dalla parte tua,
che non hai viste ancor tanto superbe." [603]

In the last two lines of this wonderful passage, the whole philosophy of vision is expressed. It is an accommodation of the supra-sensible to our human disabilities, a symbolic reconstruction of reality on levels accessible to sense. This symbolic reconstruction is seen as a profoundly significant, vivid, and dramatic dream: and since this dream conveys transcendental truth, and initiates the visionary into the atmosphere of the Eternal, it may well claim precedence over that prosaic and perpetual vision which we call the "real world." In it--as in the less significant dreams of our common experience--vision and audition are often combined. Many of the visions of St. Mechthild of Hackborn are of this complex type. Thus--"She saw in the Heart of God, as it were a virgin exceeding fair, holding a ring in her hand on which was a diamond: with which, incessantly, she touched the Heart of God. Moreover, the soul asked why that virgin thus touched the Heart of God. And the virgin answered, I am Divine Love, and this stone signifieth the sin of Adam. . . . As soon as Adam sinned, I introduced myself and intercepted the whole of his sin, and by thus ceaselessly touching the Heart of God and moving Him to pity, I suffered Him not to rest until the moment when I took the Son of God from His Father's Heart and laid him in the Virgin Mother's womb.' . . . Another time, she saw how Love, under the likeness of a fair Virgin, went round about the consistory singing Alone I have made the circuit of heaven, and I have walked on the waves of the sea. In these words she understood how Love had subjected to herself the Omnipotent Majesty of God, had inebriated His Unsearchable Wisdom, had drawn forth all His most sweet goodness; and, by wholly conquering His divine justice and changing it into gentleness and mercy, had moved the Lord of all Majesty." [604]

Imaginary vision of this kind is probably far more common than is generally supposed: and can exist without any disturbance of that balance of faculties which is usually recognized as "sane." "If," says Pratt, "there be any truth in Freud's insistence upon the symbolic nature of normal dreams, it is the less surprising that the dream imagination of the Christian mystic should work up visions of a symbolic sort. . . . Our modern tendency to consider visions quite extraordinary and pathological is probably mistaken. [605] It is certain that the meditations of those persons who are "good visualizers" often take a pictorial form; and indeed St. Ignatius Loyola, the great teacher of meditation, advised a deliberate effort so to visualize the subject dwelt upon. The picture may appear involuntarily, at the summit of a train of thought, which it sometimes illustrates and sometimes contradicts. It may show itself faintly against a background of mist; or start into existence sharply focussed, well-lighted, and alive. It always brings with it a greater impression of reality than can be obtained by the operations of the discursive mind.

(b) The symbolic and artistic character of the visions we have been discussing is obvious. There is, however, another form of imaginary vision which must be touched on with a gentler hand. In this, the imagery seized upon by the subliminal powers, or placed before the mind by that Somewhat Other of which the mystic is always conscious over against himself, is at once so vivid, so closely related to the concrete beliefs and spiritual passions of the self, and so perfectly expresses its apprehensions of God, that it is not always recognized as symbolic in kind. A simple example of this is the vision of Christ at the moment of consecration at Mass, experienced by so many Catholic ecstatics. [606] Another is St. Margaret Mary Alacoque's vision of the Sacred Heart. St. Teresa is one of the few mystics who have detected the true character of automatisms of this sort: which bring with them--like their purer forms, the intellectual visions of God--a vivid apprehension of Personality, the conviction of a living presence, rather than the knowledge of new facts. "Now and then," she says of her own imaginary visions of Christ, "it seemed to me that what I saw was an image: but most frequently it was not so. I thought it was Christ Himself, judging by the brightness in which He was pleased to show Himself. Sometimes the vision was so indistinct, that I thought it was an image: but still, not like a picture, however well painted, and I have seen a good many pictures. It would be absurd to suppose that the one bears any resemblance whatever to the other, for they differ as a living person differs from his portrait, which, however well drawn, cannot be lifelike, for it is plain that it is a dead thing." [607]

"The vision," she says in another place, "passes as quickly as a flash of lightning, yet this most glorious picture makes an impression on the imagination that I believe can never be effaced until the soul at last sees Christ to enjoy Him for ever. Although I call it a picture,' you must not imagine that it looks like a painting: Christ appears as a living Person, Who sometimes speaks and reveals deep mysteries." [608]

It seems, then, that this swift and dazzling vision of Divine Personality may represent a true contact of the soul with the Absolute Life--a contact immediately referred to the image under which the self is accustomed to think of its God. Obviously in the case of Christian contemplatives this image will most usually be the historical Person of Christ, as He is represented in sacred literature and art. [609] The life-enhancing quality of such an abrupt apprehension, however, the profound sense of reality which it brings, permit of its being classed not amongst vivid dreams, but amongst those genuine mystic states in which "the immanent God, formless, but capable of assuming all forms, expresses Himself in vision as He had expressed Himself in words." [610] Certainty and joy are the feeling-states accompanying this experience; which is as it were a love-letter received by the ardent soul, bringing with it the very fragrance of personality, along with the sign-manual of the beloved.

This concrete vision of Christ has the true mystic quality of ineffability, appearing to the self under a form of inexpressible beauty, illuminated with that unearthly light which is so persistently reported as a feature of transcendent experience. The artist's exalted consciousness of Beauty as a form of Truth is here seen operating on the transcendental plane. Thus when St. Teresa saw only the Hands of God, she was thrown into an ecstasy of adoration by their shining loveliness. [611] "If I were to spend many years in devising how to picture to myself anything so beautiful," she says of the imaginary vision of Christ, "I should never be able, nor even know how, to do it; for it is beyond the scope of any possible imagination here below: the whiteness and brilliancy alone are inconceivable. It is not a brightness which dazzles, but a delicate whiteness, an infused brightness, giving excessive delight to the eyes, which are never wearied thereby nor by the visible brightness which enables us to see a beauty so divine. It is a light so different from any light here below, that the very brightness of the sun we see, in comparison with the brightness and light before our eyes, seems to be something so obscure that no one would ever wish to open his eyes again. . . . In short, it is such that no man, however gifted he may be, can ever in the whole course of his life arrive at any imagination of what it is. God puts it before us so instantaneously, that we could not open our eyes in time to see it, if it were necessary for us to open them at all. But whether our eyes be open or shut, it makes no difference whatever: for when our Lord wills, we must see it, whether we will or not." [612]

There is another and highly important class of visual automatisms: those which I have chosen to call Active Imaginary Visions. Whereas vision of the passive kind is the expression of thought, perception, or desire on the part of the deeper self: active vision is the expression of a change in that self, and generally accompanies some psychological crisis. In this vision, which always has a dramatic character, the self seems to itself to act, not merely to look on. Such visions may possess many of the characters of dreams; they may be purely symbolic; they may be theologically "realistic." They may entail a journey through Hell, Purgatory and Heaven, an excursion into fairyland, a wrestling with the Angel in the Way. Whatever their outward form, they are always connected with inward results. They are the automatic expressions of intense subliminal activity: not merely the media by which the self's awareness of the Absolute is strengthened and enriched, but the outward and visible signs of its movement towards new levels of consciousness. Hence we are not surprised to find that a dynamic vision of this sort often initiates the Unitive Life. Such are the imaginary visions reported by St. Francis of Assisi and St. Catherine of Siena at the moment of their stigmatization: the transverberation of St. Teresa; the heavenly visitor who announced to Suso his passage from the "lower school" to the "upper school" of the Holy Spirit. [613] But perhaps the most picturesque and convincing example of all such dramas of the soul, is that which is known in art as the "Mystic Marriage of St. Catherine of Siena."

We have seen that Catherine, who was subject from childhood to imaginary visions and interior words, had long been conscious of a voice reiterating the promise of this sacred bretrothal; and that on the last day of the Carnival, A.D. 1366, it said to her, "I will this day celebrate solemnly with thee the feast of the betrothal of thy soul, and even as I promised I will espouse thee to Myself in faith." "Then," says her legend, "whilst the Lord was yet speaking, there appeared the most glorious Virgin His Mother, the most blessed John, Evangelist, the glorious Apostle Paul, and the most holy Dominic, father of her order; and with these the prophet David, who had the psaltery set to music in his hands; and while he played with most sweet melody the Virgin Mother of God took the right hand of Catherine with her most sacred hand, and, holding out her fingers towards the Son, besought Him to deign to espouse her to Himself in faith. To which graciously consenting the Only Begotten of God drew out a ring of gold, which had in its circle four pearls enclosing a most beauteous diamond; and placing this ring upon the ring finger of Catherine's right hand He said, Lo, I espouse thee to Myself, thy Creator and Saviour in the faith, which until thou dost celebrate thy eternal nuptials with Me in Heaven thou wilt preserve ever without stain. Henceforth, my daughter, do manfully and without hesitation those things which by the ordering of My providence will be put into thy hands; for being now armed with the fortitude of the faith, thou wilt happily overcome all thy adversaries.' Then the vision disappeared, but that ring ever remained on her finger, not indeed to the sight of others, but only to the sight of the virgin herself; for she often, albeit with bashfulness, confessed to me that she always saw that ring on her finger, nor was there any time when she did not see it.'" [614]

It is not difficult to discern the materials from which this vision has been composed. As far as its outward circumstances go, it is borrowed intact from the legendary history of St. Catherine of Alexandria, with which her namesake must have been familiar from babyhood. [615] Caterina Benincasa showed a characteristic artistic suggestibility and quickness in transforming the stuff of this old story into the medium of a profound personal experience: as her contemporaries amongst the Sienese painters took subject, method, and composition from the traditional Byzantine source, yet forced them to become expressions of their overpowering individuality. The important matter for us, however, is not the way in which the second Catherine adapted a traditional story to herself, actualized it in her experience: but the fact that it was for her the sacramental form under which she became acutely and permanently conscious of union with God. Long prepared by that growing disposition of her deeper self which caused her to hear the reiterated promise of her Beloved, the vision when it came was significant, not for its outward circumstances, but for its permanent effect upon her life. In it she passed to a fresh level of consciousness; entering upon that state of spiritual wedlock, of close and loving identification with the interests of Christ, which Richard of St. Victor calls the "Third Stage of Ardent Love."

Of the same active sort is St. Teresa's great and celebrated vision, or rather experience, of the Transverberation; in which imagery and feeling go side by side in their effort towards expressing the anguish of insatiable love. "I saw," she says, "an angel close by me, on my left side, in bodily form. This I am not accustomed to see unless very rarely. Though I have visions of angels frequently, yet I see them only by an intellectual vision, such as I have spoken of before. It was our Lord's will that in this vision I should see the angel in this wise. He was not large, but small of stature, and most beautiful--his face burning, as if he were one of the highest angels, who seem to be all of fire: they must be those whom we call Cherubim. . . . I saw in his hand a long spear of gold, and at the iron's point there seemed to be a little fire. He appeared to me to be thrusting it at times into my heart, and to pierce my very entrails; when he drew it out, he seemed to draw them out also and to leave me all on fire with a great love of God. The pain was so great that it made me moan; and yet so surpassing was the sweetness of this excessive pain that I could not wish to be rid of it. The soul is satisfied now with nothing less than God. The pain is not bodily, but spiritual; though the body has its share in it, even a large one. It is a caressing of love so sweet which now takes place between the soul and God, that I pray God of His goodness to make him experience it who may think that I am lying." [616]

Finally it should be added that dynamic vision may assume a purely intellectual form; as in the case of the Blessed Angela of Foligno. "During last Lent I found myself," she says, "altogether in God, without knowing how, and in a way more exalted than was customary for me. I seemed to be in the midst of the Trinity in a more exalted way than I had ever been before for greater than usual were the blessings I received, and I enjoyed these blessings without interruption. And thus to be absorbed in God filled me with joy and with delight. And feeling myself to be in this beatitude and this great and unspeakable delight, which were above all I had experienced before, such ineffable divine operations took place in my soul, as neither saint nor angel could describe or explain. And I see and understand that these divine operations, that unfathomable abyss, no angel or other creature howsoever great or wise, could comprehend; and all I say now of it seemeth to me so ill said that it is blasphemy." [617]

Automatic Script

The rarest of the automatic activities reported to us in connection with mysticism is that of "automatic writing." This form of subliminal action has already been spoken of in an earlier chapter; [618] where two of the most marked examples--Blake and Madame Guyon--are discussed. As with voice and vision, so this power of automatic composition may and does exist in various degrees of intensity: ranging from that "inspiration," that irresistible impulse to write, of which all artists are aware, to the extreme form in which the hand of the conscious self seems to have become the agent of another personality. We are not here in the presence of phenomena which require a "supernatural" explanation. From the point of view of the psychologist, the inspirational writing of the mystics differs in degree rather than in kind from such poetic creation as that described by de Russet: "it is not work, it is listening; it is as if some unknown person were speaking in your ear." [619] Such subliminal activity is probably present to some extent in all the literary work of the great mystics, whose creative power, like that of most poets, is largely dissociated from the control of the will and the surface intelligence.

St. Catherine of Siena, we are told, dictated her great Dialogue to her secretaries whilst in the state of ecstasy: which may mean no more than the absorbed state of recollection in which the creative faculty works most freely, or may have been a condition of consciousness resembling the "trance" of mediums, in which the deeper mind governs the tongue. Had she been more accustomed to the use of the pen--she did not learn writing until after the beginning of her apostolic life--that deeper mind would almost certainly have expressed itself by means of automatic script. As it is, in the rhythm and exaltation of its periods, the Dialogue bears upon it all the marks of true automatic composition of the highest type. The very discursiveness of its style, its loose employment of metaphor, the strangely mingled intimacy and remoteness of its tone, link it with prophetic literature; and are entirely characteristic of subliminal energy of a rich type, dissociated from the criticism and control of the normal consciousness. [620]

So too the writings of Rulman Merswin, if we accept the ingenious and interesting theory of his psychic state elaborated by M. Jundt, [621] were almost wholly of this kind. So Blake insisted that he was "under the direction of Messengers from Heaven, Daily and Nightly," [622] and stated on his deathbed that the credit for all his works belonged not to himself, but to his "celestial friends," [623] i.e. , to the inspiration of a personality which had access to levels of truth and beauty unknown to his surface mind.

St. Teresa was of much the same opinion in respect of her great mystical works: which were, she said, like the speech of a parrot repeating, though he cannot understand, the things which his master has taught him. There is little doubt that her powers of composition--as we might expect in one so apt at voice and vision--were largely of the uncontrolled, inspired, or "automatic" kind. She wrote most usually after the reception of Holy Communion--that is to say, when her mystic consciousness was in its most active state--and always swiftly, without hesitations or amendments. Ideas and images welled up from her rich and active subliminal region too quickly, indeed, for her eager, hurrying pen: so that she sometimes exclaimed, "Oh, that I could write with many hands, so that none were forgotten!" [624] In Teresa's unitive state, a slight suggestion was enough to change the condition of her consciousness, place her under the complete domination of her deeper mind. Often, she said, when composing the "Interior Castle," her work reacted upon herself. She would suddenly be caught up into the very degree of contemplation which she was trying to describe, and continued to write in this absorbed or entranced condition, clearly perceiving that her pen was guided by a power not her own, and expressed ideas unknown to her surface mind, which filled her with astonishment.

In the evidence given during the process for St. Teresa's beatification, Maria de San Francisco of Medina, one of her early nuns, stated that on entering the saint's cell whilst she was writing this same "Interior Castle" she found her so absorbed in contemplation as to be unaware of the external world. "If we made a noise close to her," said another, Maria del Nacimiento, "she neither ceased to write nor complained of being disturbed." Both these nuns, and also Ana de la Encarnacion, prioress of Granada, affirmed that she wrote with immense speed, never stopping to erase or to correct: being anxious, as she said, to "write what the Lord had given her, before she forgot it." They and many others declared that when she was thus writing she seemed like another being: and that her face, excessively beautiful in expression, shone with an unearthly splendour which afterwards faded away. [625]

As for Madame Guyon, whose temperament had in it almost as much of the medium as of the mystic, and whose passion for quietism and mental passivity left her almost wholly at the mercy of subconscious impulses, she exhibits by turns the phenomena of clairvoyance, prophecy, telephathy, and automatic writing, in bewildering profusion.

"I was myself surprised," she says, "at the letters which Thou didst cause me to write, and in which I had no part save the actual movement of my hand: and it was at this time that I received that gift of writing according to the interior mind, and not according to my own mind, which I had never known before. Also my manner of writing was altogether changed, and every one was astonished because I wrote with such great facility." [626]

Again, ". . . Thou didst make me write with so great a detachment that I was obliged to leave off and begin again as Thou didst choose. Thou didst try me in every way: suddenly Thou wouldst cause me to write, then at once to cease, and then to begin again. When I wrote during the day, I would be suddenly interrupted, and often left words half written, and afterwards Thou wouldst give me whatever was pleasing to Thee. Nothing of that which I wrote was in my mind: my mind, in fact, was so wholly at liberty that it seemed a blank, I was so detached from that which I wrote that it seemed foreign to me. . . . All the faults in my writings come from this: that being unaccustomed to the operations of God, I was often unfaithful to them, thinking that I did well to continue writing when I had time, without being moved thereto, because I had been told to finish the work. So that it is easy to distinguish the parts which are fine and sustained, and those which have neither savour nor grace. I have left them as they are; so that the difference between the Spirit of God and the human or natural spirit may be seen. . . . I continued always to write, and with an inconceivable swiftness, for the hand could hardly keep up with the dictating spirit: and during this long work, I never changed my method, nor did I make use of any book. The scribe could not, however great his diligence, copy in five days that which I wrote in a single night. . . . I will add to all that I have been saying on my writings, that a considerable part of the book on Judges' was lost. Being asked to complete it, I rewrote the lost portions. Long afterwards, when I was moving house, these were found in a place where no one could have imagined that they would be; and the old and new versions were exactly alike--a circumstance which greatly astonished those persons of learning and merit who undertook its verification." [627]

A far greater and stronger mystic than Madame Guyon, Jacob Boehme, was also in his literary composition the more or less helpless tool of some power other than his normal surface-mind. It is clear from his own words that his first book, the "Aurora," produced after the great illumination which he received in the year 1610, was no deliberate composition, but an example of inspired or automatic script. This strange work, full of sayings of a deep yet dazzling darkness, was condemned by the local tribunal; and Boehme was forbidden to write more. For seven years he obeyed. Then "a new motion from on high" seized him, and under the pressure of this subliminal impulse--which, characteristically, he feels as coming from without not from within--he began to write again.

This second outburst of composition, too, was almost purely automatic in type. The transcendental consciousness was in command, and Boehme's surface-intellect could exert but little control. "Art," he says of it himself, "has not wrote here, neither was there any time to consider how to set it punctually down, according to the Understanding of the Letters, but all was ordered according to the Direction of the Spirit, which often went in haste, so that in many words Letters may be wanting, and in some Places a Capital Letter for a Word; so that the Penman's Hand, by reason he was not accustomed to it, did often shake. And though I could have wrote in a more accurate, fair and plain Manner, yet the Reason was this, that the burning Fire often forced forward with Speed and the Hand and Pen must hasten directly after it, for it comes and goes as a sudden shower." [628]

No description could give more vividly than this the spontaneous and uncontrollable character of these automatic states; the welling-up of new knowledge, the rapid formation of sentences: so quick, that the hand of the subject can hardly keep pace with that "burning Fire," the travail of his inner mind. As in vision, so here, the contents of that inner mind, its hoarded memories will influence the form of the message. Hence, in Boehme's works, the prevalence of that obscure Kabalistic and Alchemical imagery which baffles even his most eager readers, and which is the result of an earlier acquaintance with the works of Paracelsus, Weigel, and Sebastian Franck. [629] Such language, however, no more discredits the "power behind the pen," than the form under which St. Catherine of Siena apprehended the mystic marriage discredits her attainment of the unitive life. In the fruit of such automatic travail, such a "wrestling with the Angel in the way," the mystic offers to our common humanity the chalice of the Spirit of Life. We may recognize the origins of the ornament upon the chalice: but we cannot justly charge him with counterfeiting the Wine.

We have been dealing throughout this section with means rather than with ends: means snatched at by the struggling self which has not yet wholly shaken itself free from "image," in its efforts to seize somehow--actualize, enjoy, and adore--that Absolute which is the sum of its desires. No one will ever approach an understanding of this phase of the mystical consciousness, who brings to it either a contempt for the minds which could thus simply and sometimes childishly objectivize the Divine, or a superstitious reverence for the image, apart from the formless Reality at which it hints. Between these two extremes lies our hope of grasping the true place of automatisms on the Mystic Way: of seeing in them instances of the adaptation of those means by which we obtain consciousness of the phenomenal world, to an apprehension of that other world whose attainment is humanity's sublimest end.

Footnotes:

558. "Studies in Mystical Religion," p. 165. Those who wish to study the "rationalist" argument in an extreme form are directed to Prof. Janet, "L'Automatisme psychologique" and "L'État mentale des hysteriques," and Prof. Leuba, "Introduction to the Psychology of Religious Mysticism."

559. On the difference in this respect between the "normal" and the "average," see Granger, "The Soul of a Christian," p. 12.

560. See St. Angèle de Foligno, op. cit ., p. 130 (English translation, p. 245).

561. Poulain, "Les Graces d'Oraison," cap. xx. Farges, "Mystical Phenomena," and Ribet's elaborate work, "La Mystique Divine," well represent the "supernaturalist" position. As against the "rationalistic" theory of stigmatization already described, one feels that this last-named writer hardly advances his own cause when he insists on attributing equal validity (a) to the Stigmata as marks of the Divine, (b) to the imprint of a toad, bat, spider "ou de tout autre objet exprimant l'abjection" on the bodies of those who have had commerce with the devil (tome iii. p. 482).

562. Vide infra, quotations from Hilton and St. John of the Cross. Also Rolle "The Fire of Love," Prologue. E. Gardner, "St. Catherine of Siena," p. 15. Von Hügel, "The Mystical Element of Religion," vol. i. pp. 178-181.

563. "Revelations of Divine Love," cap. xliii. I have restored the bold language of the original, which is somewhat toned down in modern versions.

564. Here as elsewhere the reader will kindly recollect that all spatial language is merely symbolic when used in connection with spiritual states.

565. For instance when Margaret Ebner, the celebrated "Friend of God," heard a voice telling her that Tauler, who was the object of great veneration in the circle to which she belonged, was the man whom God loved best and that He dwelt in him like melodious music (see Rufus Jones, op. cit ., p. 257).

566. "There are persons to be met with," says St. Teresa, "and I have known them myself, who have so feeble a brain and imagination that they think they see whatever they are thinking about, and this is a very dangerous condition." ("El Castillo Interior," Moradas Cuartas, cap. iii.)

567. The dream-theory of vision is well and moderately stated by Pratt: "The Religious Consciousness," cap. xviii, pp. 402 seq. But his statement (loc. cit.) that "the visions of the mystics are determined in content by their belief, and are due to the dream imagination working upon the mass of theological material which fills the mind" is far too absolute.

568. The book of Angela of Foligno, already cited, contains a rich series of examples.

569. "Sur la psychologie du Mysticisme" (Revue Philosophique, February, 1902).

570. "Revelations of Divine Love," cap. lxvi.

571. Vida, cap. xxxi. §§ 5 and 10.

572. Thus too in the case of St. Catherine of Siena, the intense spiritual strain of that three years' retreat which I have already described (supra, Pt. II, Cap 1.) showed itself towards the end of the period by a change in the character of her visions. These, which had previously been wholly concerned with intuitions of the good and beautiful, now took on an evil aspect and greatly distressed her (Vita (Acta SS.). i. xi. 1; see E. Gardner, "St. Catherine of Siena," p. 20). We are obliged to agree with Pratt that such visions as these are "pathological phenomena quite on a level with other hallucinations."("The

Religious Consciousness," p 405.)

573. An excellent example of such appropriation of material is related without comment by Huysmans ("Sainte Lyndwine de Schiedam," p. 258): "Lydwine found again in heaven those forms of adoration, those ceremonial practices of the divine office, which she had known here below during her years of health. The Church Militant had been, in fact, initiated by the inspiration of its apostles, its popes, and its saints into the liturgic joys of Paradise." In this same vision, which occurred on Christmas Eve, when the hour of the Nativity was rung from the belfries of heaven, the Divine Child appeared on His Mother's knee: just as the crèche is exhibited in Catholic churches the moment that Christmas has dawned.

574. Testament, cap. iii.

575. E. Gardner "St. Catherine of Siena," p. 25.

576. Delacroix, "Études sur le Mysticisme," p. 114.

577. Missale Romanum. Praeparatio ad Missam; Die Dominica.

578. Given in Poulain: "Les Grâces d'Oraison," p. 318.

579. "El Castillo Interior." Moradas Sextas, cap. iii.

580. "Subida del Monte Carmelo," I. ii. cap. xxvii.

581. "Subida del Monte Carmelo," I. ii. cap. xxvii.

582. Vida. cap. xxv. §§ 2, 5, 6. See also for a detailed discussion of all forms of auditions St. John of the Cross, op. cit ., I. ii. caps. xxviii. to xxxi.

583. "El Libro de las Fundaciones" is full of instances.

584. Suso, "Buchlein von der ewigen Weisheit," Prologue.

585. "Fioretti," "Delle Istimate," 2.; E. Gardner, "St. Catherine of Siena." p. 15; Rolle, "The Fire of Love," bk. i. cap. xvi., and other places.

586. Leben, cap. vi.

587. Compare p. 80.

588. "Les Fondements de la Connaissance Mystique." p. 149.

589. Here the exception which proves the rule is Blake. But Blake's visions differed in some important respects from those of his fellow-mystics. They seem to have been "corporeal," not "imaginary" in type, and were regarded by him as actual perceptions of that "real and eternal world" in which he held that it was man's privilege to dwell.

590. "The Scale of Perfection," bk. i. cap. xi.

591. "Subida del Monte Carmelo," I. ii. cap. xi. The whole chapter should be read in this connection.

592. "Subida del Monte Carmelo," I. ii. cap. xvi.

593. El Castillo Interior," Moradas Sextas, cap. iii.

594. St. Angels de Foligno, "Livre de l'Expérience des Vrais Fidèles," pp. 170 seq. (English translation, p. 24).

595. "It is not like that presence of God which is frequently felt . . . this is a great grace . . . but it is not vision" (St. Teresa, Vida, cap, xxvii. § 6).

596. Op. cit., loc. cit.

597. St. Teresa, "El Castillo Interior," Moradas Sextas, cap. viii.

598. Leben, cap. liv.

599. St. Teresa, Vida, cap. xxvii. §§ 2-5.

600. "For oft, when on my couch I lie In vacant or in pensive mood, They flash upon that inward eye Which is the bliss of solitude: And then my heart with pleasure fills And dances with the daffodils." Wordsworth , "The Daffodils."

601. Leben, cap. vii.

602. Suso, Leben, cap. vi.

603. Par. xxx. 61-81: "And I saw light in the form of a river blazing with radiance, streaming between banks painted with a marvellous spring. Out of that river issued living sparks and settled on the flowers on every side, like rubies set in gold. Then, as it were inebriated by the perfume, they plunged again into the wondrous flood, and as one entered another issued forth. . . . Then added the Sun of my eyes: The river, the topazes that enter and come forth, the smiling flowers are shadowy foretastes of their reality. Not that these things are themselves imperfect; but on thy side is the defect, in that thy vision cannot rise so high." This passage probably owes something to Mechthild of Magdeburg's concept of Deity as a Flowing Light.

604. Mechthild of Hackborn, "Liber Specialis Gratiae," I. ii. caps. xvii. and xxxv.

605. Pratt, "The Religious Consciousness," p. 404.

606. For instance, the Blessed Angela of Foligno, who gives in her "Revelations" a complete series of such experiences, ranging from an apprehension of Divine Beauty "shining from within and surpassing the splendour of the sun" (op. cit., p. 64, English translation, p. 222)to a concrete vision of two eyes shining in the Host (loc. cit., English translation, p. 230)."I saw Him most plainly with the eyes

of the mind," she says, "first living, suffering, bleeding, crucified, and then dead upon the Cross" (p. 326, English translation p. 223)."Another time I beheld the Child Christ in the consecrated Host. He Appeared beautiful and full of majesty, He seemed as a child of twelve years of age (p. 67. English translation, p. 229).

607. Vida, cap. xxviii. § 11.

608. "El Castillo Interior," Moradas Sextas, cap. ix.

609. "On one of the feasts of St. Paul, while I was at Mass, there stood before me the most sacred Humanity as painters represent Him after the resurrection" (St. Teresa, Vida, cap. xxviii § 4). So too the form assumed by many of the visions of Angela of Foligno is obviously due to her familiarity with the frescoed churches of Assisi and the Vale of Spoleto. "When I bent my knees upon entering in at the door of the church," she says, "I immediately beheld a picture of St. Francis lying in Christ's bosom. Then said Christ unto me, Thus closely will I hold thee and so much closer, that bodily eyes can neither perceive nor comprehend it'." (op. cit., p. 53. English translation, p. 165).

610. Delacroix. "Études sur le Mysticisme." p. 116.

611. Vida, cap. xxviii. § 2.

612. St. Teresa, op. cit ., cap. xxviii. §§ 7, 8. Angela of Foligno says of a similar vision of Christ, "His beauty and adornment were so great . . . and so great was my joy at the sight, that I think I shall never lose it. And so great was my certitude that I cannot doubt it in any point" (St. Angèle de Foligno, op. cit ., p. 66. English translation, p. 229).

613. Leben, cap. xxi.

614. E. Gardner, "St. Catherine of Siena," p. 25. Vita, i. xii. 1, 2 (Acta S.S., loc. cit .). In the ring which she always saw upon her finger. we seem to have an instance of true corporeal vision; which finds a curiously exact parallel in the life of St. Teresa. "On one occasion when I was holding in my hand the cross of my rosary, He took it from me into His own hand. He returned it, but it was then four large stones incomparably more precious than diamonds. He said to me that for the future that cross would so appear to me always: and so it did. I never saw the wood of which it was made, but only the precious stones. They were seen, however, by no one else" (Vida, cap. xxix. § 8). This class of experience, says Augustine Baker, particularly gifts of roses, rings, and jewels, is "much to be suspected," except in "souls of a long-continued sanctity" ("Holy Wisdom." Treatise iii. § iv. cap. iii.).

615. Vide "Legenda Aurea," Nov. xxv.

616. Vida, cap. xxix. §§ 16, 17.

617. St. Angèle de Foligno op. cit ., p. 232 (English translation, p. 186).

618. P. 66.

619. Quoted by Prescott, "The Poetic Mind," p. 102.

620. On this point I must respectfully differ from Mr. E. Gardner. See his "St. Catherine of Siena," p. 354.

621. Supra , p. 185.

622. Quoted by M. Wilson, "Life of William Blake," p. 135.

623. Berger, "William Blake," p. 54.

624. G. Cunninghame Graham. "Santa Teresa." vol. i, pp. 202.

625. G. Cunninghame Graham. "Santa Teresa." vol. i, pp. 203-4.

626. Vie, pt. ii. cap. ii.

627. Vie, pt. ii. cap. xxi. Those who wish to compare this vivid subjective account of automatic writing with modern attested instances may consult Myers, "Human Personality," and Oliver Lodge, "The Survival of Man."

628. Works of Jacob Boehme (English translation, vol. i. p. xiv.).

629. See E. Boutroux, "Le Philosophe Allemand, Jacob Boehme."

CHAPTER VI

In our study of the First Mystic Life, its purification and illumination, we have been analysing and considering a process of organic development; an evolution of personality. We may treat this either as a movement of consciousness towards higher levels, or as a remaking of consciousness consequent on the emergence and growth of a factor which is dormant in ordinary man, but destined to be supreme in the full-grown mystic type. We have seen the awakening of this factor--this spark of the soul--with its innate capacity for apprehending the Absolute. We have seen it attack and conquer the old sense-fed and self-centred life of the normal self, and introduce it into a new universe, lit up by the Uncreated Light. These were the events which, taken together, constituted the "First Mystic Life"; a complete round upon the spiral road which leads from man to God.

What we have been looking at, then, is a life-process, the establishment of a certain harmony between the created self and that Reality whose invitation it has heard: and we have discussed this life-process rather as if it contained no elements which were not referable to natural and spontaneous growth, to the involuntary adjustments of the organism to that extended or transcendental universe of which it gradually becomes aware. But side by side with this organic growth there always goes a specific kind of activity which is characteristic of the mystic: an education which he is called to undertake, that his consciousness of the Infinite may be stabilized, enriched and defined. Already once or twice we have been in the presence of this activity, have been obliged to take its influence into account: as, were we studying other artistic types, we could not leave on one side the medium in which they work.

Contemplation is the mystic's medium. It is an extreme form of that withdrawal of attention from the external world and total dedication of the mind which also, in various degrees and ways, conditions the creative activity of musician, painter and poet: releasing the faculty by which he can apprehend the Good and Beautiful, enter into communion with the Real. As "voice" or "vision" is often the way in which the mystical consciousness presents its discoveries to the surface-mind, so contemplation is the way in which it makes those discoveries, perceives the suprasensible over against itself. The growth of the mystic's effective genius, therefore, is connected with his growth in this art: and that growth is largely conditioned by education.

The painter, however great his natural powers, can hardly dispense with some technical training; the musician is wise if he acquaint himself at least with the elements of counterpoint. So too the mystic. It is true that he sometimes seems to spring abruptly to the heights, to be caught into ecstasy without previous preparation: as a poet may startle the world by a sudden masterpiece. But unless they be backed by discipline, these sudden and isolated flashes of inspiration will not long avail for the production of great works. "Ordina quest' amore, o tu che m'ami" is the imperative demand made by Goodness, Truth, and Beauty, by every aspect of Reality, upon the human soul. Lover and philosopher, saint, artist, and scientist, must alike obey or fail.

Transcendental genius, then, obeys the laws which govern all other forms of genius, in being susceptible of culture: and, indeed, cannot develop its full powers without an educative process of some kind. This strange art of contemplation, which the mystic tends to practise during the whole of his career--which develops step by step with his vision and his love--demands of the self which undertakes it the same hard dull work, the same slow training of the will, which lies behind all supreme achievement, and is the price of all true liberty. It is the want of such training--such "supersensual drill"--which is responsible for the mass of vague, ineffectual, and sometimes harmful mysticism which has always existed: the dilute cosmic emotion and limp spirituality which hang, as it were, on the skirts of the true seekers of the Absolute, and bring discredit upon their science.

In this, as in all the other and lesser arts which have been developed by the race, education consists largely in a humble willingness to submit to the discipline, and profit by the lessons, of the past. Tradition runs side by side with experience; the past collaborates with the present. Each new and eager soul rushing out towards the only end of Love passes on its way the landmarks left by others upon the pathway to Reality. If it be wise it observes them: and finds in them rather helps towards attainment than hindrances to that freedom which is of the essence of the mystic act. This act, it is true, is in the last resort a solitary experience, "the flight of the Alone to the Alone"; even though no achievement of the soul truly takes place in vacao, or leaves the universe of souls unchanged. At the same time, here as elsewhere, man cannot safely divorce his personal history from that of the race. The best and truest experience does not come to the eccentric and individual pilgrim whose intuitions are his only law: but rather to him who is willing to profit by the culture of the spiritual society in which he finds himself, and submit personal intuition to the guidance afforded by the general history of the mystic type. Those who refuse this guidance expose themselves to all the dangers which crowd about the individualist: from heresy at one end of the scale to madness at the other. Vae Soli! Nowhere more clearly than in the history of mysticism do we observe the essential solidarity of mankind, the penalty paid by those who will not acknowledge it.

The education which tradition has ever prescribed for the mystic, consists in the gradual development of an extraordinary faculty of concentration, a power of spiritual attention. It is not enough that he should naturally be "aware of the Absolute," unless he be able to contemplate it: just as the mere possession of eyesight or hearing, however acute, needs to be supplemented by trained powers of perception and reception, if we are really to appreciate--see or hear to any purpose--the masterpieces of Music or of Art. More, Nature herself reveals little of her secret to those who only look and listen with the outward ear and eye. The condition of all valid seeing and hearing, upon every plane of consciousness, lies not in the sharpening of the senses, but in a peculiar attitude of the whole personality: in a self-forgetting attentiveness, a profound concentration, a self-merging, which operates a real communion between the seer and the seen--in a word, in Contemplation.

Contemplation, then, in the most general sense is a power which we may--and often must--apply to the perception, not only of Divine Reality, but of anything. It is a mental attitude under which all things give up to us the secret of their life. All artists are of necessity in some measure contemplative. In so far as they surrender themselves without selfish preoccupation, they see Creation from the point of view of God. [630] "Innocence of eye" is little else than this: and only by its means can they see truly those things which they desire to show the world. I invite those to whom these statements seem a compound of cheap psychology and cheaper metaphysics to clear their minds of prejudice and submit this matter to an experimental test. If they will be patient and honest--and unless they belong to that minority which is temperamentally incapable of the simplest contemplative act--they will emerge from the experiment possessed of a little new knowledge as to the nature of the relation between the human mind and the outer world.

All that is asked is that we shall look for a little time, in a special and undivided manner, at some simple, concrete, and external thing. This object of our contemplation may be almost anything we please: a picture, a statue, a tree, a distant hillside, a growing plant, running water, little living things. We need not, with Kant, go to the starry heavens. "A little thing the quantity of an hazel nut" will do for us, as it did for Lady Julian long ago. [631] Remember, it is a practical experiment on which we are set; not an opportunity of pretty and pantheistic meditation.

Look, then, at this thing which you have chosen. Wilfully yet tranquilly refuse the messages which countless other aspects of the world are sending; and so concentrate your whole attention on this one act of loving sight that all other objects are excluded from the conscious field. Do not think, but as it were pour out your personality towards it: let your soul be in your eyes. Almost at once, this new method of perception will reveal unsuspected qualities in the external world. First, you will perceive about you a strange and deepening quietness; a slowing down of our feverish mental time. Next, you will become aware of a heightened significance, an intensified existence in the thing at which you look. As you, with all your consciousness, lean out towards it, an answering current will meet yours. It seems as though the barrier between its life and your own, between subject and object, had melted away. You are merged with it, in an act of true communion: and you know the secret of its being deeply and unforgettably, yet in a way which you can never hope to express.

Seen thus, a thistle has celestial qualities: a speckled hen a touch of the sublime. Our greater comrades, the trees, the clouds, the rivers, initiate us into mighty secrets, flame out at us "like shining from shook foil." The "eye which looks upon Eternity" has been given its opportunity. We have been immersed for a moment in the "life of the All": a deep and peaceful love unites us with the substance of all things, a "Mystic Marriage" has taken place between the mind and some aspect of the external world. Cor ad cor loquitur :Life has spoken to life, but not to the surface-intelligence. That surface-intelligence knows only that the message was true and beautiful: no more.

The price of this experience has been a stilling of that surface-mind, a calling in of all our scattered interests: an entire giving of ourselves to this one activity, without self-consciousness, without reflective thought. To reflect is always to distort: our minds are not good mirrors. The contemplative, on whatever level his faculty may operate, is contented to absorb and be absorbed: and by this humble access he attains to a plane of knowledge which no intellectual process can come near.

I do not suggest that this simple experiment is in any sense to be equated with the transcendental contemplation of the mystic. Yet it exercises on a small scale, and in regard to visible Nature, the same natural faculties which are taken up and used--it is true upon other levels, and in subjection to the transcendental sense--in his apprehension of the Invisible Real. Though it is one thing to see truthfully for an instant the flower in the crannied wall, another to be lifted up to the apprehension of "eternal Truth, true Love and loved Eternity," yet both according to their measure are functions of the inward eye, operating in the "suspension of the mind."

This humble receptiveness, this still and steady gazing, in which emotion, will, and thought are lost and fused, is the secret of the great contemplative on fire with love of that which he has been allowed to see. But whilst the contemplation of Nature entails an outgoing towards somewhat indubitably external to us, and has as its material the world of sensible experience: the contemplation of Spirit, as it seems to those who practise it, requires a deliberate refusal of the messages of the senses, an ingoing or "introversion" of our faculties, a "journey towards the centre." The Kingdom of God, they say, is within you: seek it, then, in the most secret habitations of the soul. The mystic must learn so to concentrate all his faculties, his very self, upon the invisible and intangible, that all visible things are forgot: to bring it so sharply into focus that everything else is blurred. He must call in his scattered faculties by a deliberate exercise of the will, empty his mind of its swarm of images, its riot of thought. In mystical language he must "sink into his nothingness": into that blank abiding place where busy, clever Reason cannot come. The whole of this process, this gathering up and turning "inwards" of the powers of the self, this gazing into the ground of the soul, is that which is called Introversion.

Introversion is an art which can be acquired, as gradually and as certainly, by the born mystic, as the art of piano-playing can be acquired by the born musician. In both cases it is the genius of the artist which makes his use of the instrument effective: but it is also his education in the use of the instrument which enables that genius to express itself in an adequate way. Such mystical education, of course, presumes a something that can be educated: the "New Birth," the awakening of the deeper self, must have taken place before it can begin. It is a psychological process, and obeys psychological laws. There is in it no element of the unexpected or the abnormal. In technical language, we are here concerned with "ordinary" not "extraordinary" contemplation.

In its early stages the practice of introversion is voluntary, difficult, and deliberate; as are the early stages of learning to read or write. But as reading or writing finally becomes automatic, so as the mystic's training in introversion proceeds, habits are formed: and those contemplative powers which he is educating establish themselves amongst his normal faculties. Sometimes they wholly dominate these faculties, escape the control of the will, and appear spontaneously, seizing upon the conscious field. Such violent and involuntary invasions of the transcendental powers, when they utterly swamp the surface-consciousness and the subject is therefore cut off from his ordinary "external world," constitute the typical experience of rapture or ecstasy. It is under the expansive formula of such abrupt ecstatic perception, "not by gradual steps, but by sudden ecstatic flights soaring aloft to the glorious things on high," [632] that the mystical consciousness of Divine Transcendence is most clearly expressed. Those wide, exalted apprehensions of the Godhead which we owe to the mystics have usually been obtained, not by industrious meditation, but by "a transcending of all creatures, a perfect going forth from oneself: by standing in an ecstasy of mind." [633] Hence the experiences peculiar to these ecstatic states have a great value for the student of mysticism. It will be our duty to consider them in detail in a later section of this book. The normal and deliberate practice of introversion, on the contrary, is bound up with the sense of Divine Immanence. Its emphasis is on the indwelling God Who may be found "by a journey towards the centre": on the conviction indeed that "angels and archangels are with us, but He is more truly our own who is not only with us but in us ." [634]

Contemplation--taking that term in its widest sense, as embracing all the degrees and kinds of mystical prayer--establishes communion between the soul and the Absolute by way of these complementary modes of apprehending that which is One. A. The usually uncontrollable, definitely outgoing, ecstatic experience; the attainment of Pure Being, or "flight to God." B. The more controllable ingoing experience; the breaking down of the barrier between the surface-self and those deeper levels of personality where God is met and known "in our nothingness," and a mysterious fusion of divine and human life takes place. The one, says the Christian mystic, is the "going forth to the Father"; the other is the "marriage with the Son." Both are operated by the Spirit whose dwelling is in the "spark of the soul." Yet it is probable, in spite of the spatial language which the mystics always use concerning them, that these two experiences, in their most sublime forms, are but opposite aspects of one whole: the complementary terms of a higher synthesis beyond our span. In that consummation of love which Ruysbroeck has called "the peace of the summits" they meet: then distinctions between inward and outward, near and far, cease to have any meaning, in "the dim silence where lovers lose themselves." "To mount to God," says the writer of "De Adhaerando Deo," "is to enter into one's self. For he who inwardly entereth and intimately penetrateth into himself, gets above and beyond himself and truly mounts up to God." [635]

Says Tauler of this ineffable meeting-place, which is to the intellect an emptiness, and to the heart a fulfillment of all desire, "All there is so still and mysterious and so desolate: for there is nothing there but God only, and nothing strange. . . . This Wilderness is the Quiet Desert of the Godhead, into which He leads all who are to receive this inspiration of God, now or in Eternity." [636] From this "quiet desert," this still plane of being, so near to her though she is far from it, the normal self is separated by all the "unquiet desert" of sensual existence. Yet it stretches through and in her, the stuff of Reality, the very Ground of her being, since it is, in Julian's words, "the Substance of all that is": linking that being at once with the universe and with God. "God is near us, but we are far from Him, God is within, we are without, God is at home, we are in the far country," said Meister Eckhart, struggling to express the nature of this "intelligible where." [637] Clearly, if the self is ever to become aware of it, definite work must be undertaken, definite powers of perception must be trained: and the consciousness which has been evolved to meet the exigencies of the World of Becoming must be initiated into that World of Being from which it came forth.

Plato long ago defined the necessity of such a perception, and the nature of that art of contemplation by which the soul can feed upon the Real, when he said in one of his most purely mystical passages, "When the soul returns into itself and reflects, it passes into . . . the region of that which is pure and everlasting, immortal and unchangeable: and, feeling itself kindred thereto, it dwells there under its own control, and has rest from its wanderings." [638] In the "contemplation" of Plato and of the Platonic Schools generally, however, the emphasis lies at least as much on intellect as on intuition: with him the head and not the heart is the meeting-place between man and the Real. "Anciently," says Augustine Baker, "there was a certain kind of false contemplation, which we may call philosophical, practised by some learned heathens of old, and imitated by some in these days, which hath for its last and best end only the perfection of knowledge, and a delightful complacency in it. . . . To this rank of philosophical contemplations may be referred those scholastic wits which spend much time in the study and subtle examination of the mysteries of faith, and have not for their end the increasing of divine love in their hearts." [639]

We cannot long read the works of the mystics without coming across descriptions--often first-hand descriptions of great psychological interest--of the processes through which the self must pass, the discipline which it must undertake, in the course of acquiring the art of contemplation. Most of these descriptions differ in detail; in the divisions adopted, the emotions experienced, the number of "degrees" through which the subject passes, from the first painful attempt to gather up its faculties to the supreme point at which it feels itself to be "lost in God." In each there is that quality of uniqueness which is inherent in every expression of life: in each the temperamental bias and analytical powers of the writer have exerted a further modifying influence. All, however, describe a connected experience, the progressive concentration of the entire self under the spur of love upon the contemplation of transcendental reality. As the Mystic Way involves transcendence of character, the sublimation of the instinctive life and movement of the whole man to higher levels of vitality, his attainment of freedom, so the ascent of the ladder of contemplation involves such a transcendence, or movement to high levels of liberty, of his perceptive powers.

The steps of the ladder, the substance of the progressive exercises undertaken by the developing self, its education in the art of contemplation, are usually know by the Christian mystics as the "degrees of prayer" or "orison." But the common implications of the word "prayer," with its suggestions of formal devotion, detailed petition--a definite something asked for, and a definite duty done, by means of extemporary or traditional allocutions--do not really suggest the nature of those supersensual activities which the mystics mean to express in their use of this term.

Mystical prayer, or "orison"--the term which I propose for the sake of clearness to use here--has nothing in common with petition. It is not articulate; it has no forms. "It is," says "The Mirror of St. Edmund," "naught else but yearning of soul." [640] --the expression of man's metaphysical thirst. In it, says Grou, "the soul is united to God in its ground, the created intelligence to the Intelligence Increate, without the intervention of imagination or reason, or of anything but a very simple attention of the mind and an equally simple application of the will." [641] On the psychological side its development involves a steady discipline of the mystic's rich subliminal mind, slowly preparing the channels in which the deeper consciousness is to flow. This discipline reduces to some sort of order, makes effective for life, those involuntary states of passivity, rapture and intuition which are the characteristic ways in which an uncontrolled, uncultivated genius for the Absolute breaks out. To the subject himself, however, his orison seems rather a free and mutual act of love; a supernatural intercourse between the soul and the divine, or some aspect of the divine, sometimes full of light and joy, sometimes dark and bare. [642] In some of its degrees it is a placid, trustful waiting upon messages from without. In others, it is an inarticulate communion, a wordless rapture, a silent gazing upon God. The mystics have exhausted all the resources of all tongues in their efforts to tell us of the rewards which await those who will undertake this most sublime and difficult of arts.

As we come to know our friends better by having intercourse with them, so by this deliberate intercourse the self enters more and more deeply into the Heart of Reality. Climbing like Dante step by step up the ladder of contemplation, it comes at last to the Empyrean, "ivi è perfetta, matura ed intera ciascuna disianza." [643] The true end of orison, like the true end of that mystical life within which it flowers, is the supreme meeting between Lover and Beloved, between God and the soul. Its method is the method of the mystic life, transcendence: a gradual elimination of sensible image, and bit by bit approximation of the contemplative self to reality, gradually producing within it those conditions in which union can take place. This entails a concentration, a turning inwards, of all those faculties which the normal self has been accustomed to turn outwards, and fritter upon the manifold illusions of daily life. It means, during the hours of introversion, a retreat from and refusal of the Many, in order that the mind may be able to apprehend the One. "Behold," says Boehme, "if thou desirest to see God's Light in thy Soul, and be divinely illuminated and conducted, this is the short way that thou art to take; not to let the Eye of thy Spirit enter into Matter or fill itself with any Thing whatever, either in Heaven or Earth, but to let it enter by a naked faith into the Light of the Majesty." [644]

"What this opening of the ghostly eye is," says Hilton, "the greatest clerk on earth could not imagine by his wit, nor show fully by his tongue. For it may not be got by study nor through man's travail only, but principally by grace of the Holy Ghost and with travail of man. I dread mickle to speak aught of it, for me thinketh I cannot; it passeth mine assay, and my lips are unclean. Nevertheless, for I expect love asketh and love biddeth, therefore I shall say a little more of it as I hope love teacheth. This opening of the ghostly eye is that lighty murkness and rich nought that I spake of before, and it may be called: Purity of spirit and ghostly rest, inward stillness and peace of conscience, highness of thought and onlyness of soul, a lively feeling of grace and privily of heart, the waking sleep of the spouse and tasting of heavenly savour burning in love and shining in light, entry of contemplation and reforming in feeling . . . they are divers in showing of words, nevertheless they are all one in sense of soothfastness." [645]

"Human industry," says Hilton here, must be joined to "grace." If the spiritual eye is to be opened, definite work must be done. So long as the "eye which looks upon Time" fills itself with things and usurps the conscious field, that spiritual eye which "looks upon Eternity" can hardly act at all: and this eye must not only be opened, it must be trained, so that it may endure to gaze steadfastly at the Uncreated Light. This training and purging of the transcendental sight is described under many images; "diverse in showing of words, one in sense and soothfastness." Its essence is a progressive cleaning of the mirror, a progressive self-emptying of all that is not real the attainment of that unified state of consciousness which will permit a pure, imageless apprehension of the final Reality which "hath no image" to be received by the self. "Naked orison," "emptiness," "nothingness," "entire surrender," "peaceful love in life naughted," say the mystics again and again. Where apprehension of the divine comes by way of vision or audition, this is but a concession to human weakness; a sign, they think, that "sensitive nature" is not yet wholly transcended. It is a translation of the true tongue of angels into a dialect that the normal mind can understand. A steady abolition of sense imagery, a cutting off of all possible sources of illusion, all possible encouragements of selfhood and pride--the most fertile of all sources of deception--this is the condition of pure sight; and the "degrees of orison," the "steep stairs of love" which they climb so painfully, are based upon this necessity.

The terms used by individual mystics, the divisions which they adopt in describing the self's progress in contemplation, are bewildering in their variety. Here, more than elsewhere, the mania for classification has obsessed them. We find, too, when we come to compare one with another, that the language which they employ is not always so exact as it seems: nor are traditional terms always used in the same sense. Sometimes by the word "contemplation" they intend to describe the whole process of introversion: sometimes they reserve it for the "orison of union," sometimes identify it with ecstasy. It has been pointed out by Delacroix that even St. Teresa's classification of her own states is far from lucid, and varies in each of her principal works. [646] Thus in the "Life" she appears to treat Recollection and Quiet as synonymous, whilst in "The Way of Perfection" these conditions are sharply differentiated. In "The Interior Castle" she adopts an entirely different system; the prayer of quiet being there called "tasting of God." [647] Finally, Augustine Baker, in treating of the "Prayer of Interior Silence and Quiet," insists that by the term "Quiet" St. Teresa did not mean this at all, but a form of "supernatural contemplation." [648]

Thus we are gradually forced to the conclusion that the so-called "degrees of orison" so neatly tabulated by ascetic writers are largely artificial and symbolic: that the process which they profess to describe is really, like life itself, one and continuous--not a stairway but a slope--and the parts into which they break it up are diagrammatic. Nearly every mystic makes these breaks in a different place, though continuing to use the language of his predecessors. In his efforts towards self-analysis he divides and subdivides, combines and differentiates his individual moods. Hence the confusion of mind which falls upon those who try to harmonize different systems of contemplation: to identify St. Teresa's "Four Degrees" [649] with Hugh of St. Victor's other four, [650] and with Richard of St. Victor's "four steps of ardent love": [651] or to accommodate upon this diagram Hilton's simple and poetic "three steps of contemplations--Knowing, Loving, and Knowing-and-Loving--where the adventurer rather than the map-maker speaks. Such fine shades, says Augustine Baker in this connection, are "nicely distinguished" by the author "rather out of a particular experience of the effects passing in his own soul [652] which perhaps are not the same in all" than for any more general reason. [653]

Some diagram, however, some set scheme, the writer on introversion must have, if he is to describe with lucidity the normal development of the contemplative consciousness: and so long as the methodological nature of this diagram is kept in mind, there can be little objection to the use of it. I propose then to examine under three divisions that continuous and orderly growth, that gradual process of change, by which the mystical consciousness matures, and develops its apprehension of God. We will give to these three divisions names familiar to all readers of ascetic literature: Recollection, Quiet, and Contemplation. Each of these three parts of the introversive experience may be discerned in embryo in that little experiment at which the reader has been invited to assist: the act of concentration, the silence, the new perception which results. Each has a characteristic beginning which links it with its predecessor, and a characteristic end which shades off into the next state. Thus Recollection commonly begins in Meditation and develops into the "Orison of Inward Silence or Simplicity," which again melts into the true "Quiet." "Quiet" as it becomes deeper passes into Ordinary Contemplation: and this grows through Contemplation proper to that Orison of Passive Union which is the highest of the non-ecstatic introversive states. Merely to state the fact thus is to remind ourselves how smoothly continuous is this life-process of the soul.

It is the object of contemplative prayer, as it is the object of all education, to discipline and develop certain growing faculties. Here, the faculties are those of the "transcendental self," the "new man"--all those powers which we associate with the "spiritual consciousness." The "Sons of God," however, like the sons of men, begin as babies; and their first lessons must not be too hard. Therefore the educative process conforms to and takes advantage of every step of the natural process of growth: as we, in the education of our children, make the natural order in which their faculties develop the basis of our scheme of cultivation. Recollection, Quiet, and Contemplation, then, answer to the order in which the mystic's powers unfold. Roughly speaking, we shall find that the form of spiritual attention which is called "Meditative" or "Recollective" goes side by side with the Purification of the Self; that "Quiet" tends to be characteristic of Illumination; that Contemplation proper--at any rate in its higher forms--is most fully experienced by those who have attained, or nearly attained, the Unitive Way. At the same time, just as the self in its "first mystic life," before it has passed through the dark night of the spirit, often seems to run through the whole gamut of spiritual states, and attain that immediate experience of the Absolute which it seeks--though as a fact it has not reached those higher levels of consciousness on which true and permanent union takes place--so too in its orison. At any point in its growth it may experience for brief periods that imageless and overpowering sense of identity with the Absolute Life--that loving and exalted absorption in God--which is called "passive union," and anticipates the consciousness which is characteristic of the unitive life. Over and over again in its "prayerful process" it recapitulates in little the whole great process of its life. It runs up for an instant to levels where it is not yet strong enough to dwell: "seeks God in its ground" and finds that which it seeks. Therefore we must not be too strict in our identification of the grades of education with the stages of growth.

This education, rightly understood, is one coherent process: it consists in a steady and voluntary surrender of the awakened consciousness, its feeling, thought, and will, to the play of those transcendental influences, that inflowing vitality, which it conceives of as divine. In the preparative process of Recollection, the unruly mind is brought into subjection. In "Quiet" the eager will is silenced, the "wheel of imagination" is stilled. In Contemplation, the heart at last comes to its own-- Cor ad cor loquitur . In their simplest forms, these three states involve the deliberate concentration upon, the meek resting in, the joyous communing with, the ineffable Object of man's quest. They require a progressive concentration of the mystic's powers, a gradual handing over of the reins from the surface intelligence to the deeper mind; that essential self which alone is capable of God. In Recollection the surface-mind still holds, so to speak, the leading strings: but in "Quiet" it surrenders them wholly, allowing consciousness to sink into that "blissful silence in which God works and speaks." This act of surrender, this deliberate negation of thought, is an essential preliminary of the contemplative state. "Lovers put out the candles and draw the curtains when they wish to see the god and the goddess; and in the higher communion the night of thought is the light of perception." [654] .

The education of the self in the successive degrees of orison has been compared by St. Teresa, in a celebrated passage in her Life, to four ways of watering the garden of the soul so that it may bring forth its flowers and fruits. [655] The first and most primitive of these ways is meditation. This, she says, is like drawing water by hand from a deep well: the slowest and most laborious of all means of irrigation. Next to this is the orison of quiet, which is a little better and easier: for here soul seems to receive some help, i.e. , with the stilling of the senses the subliminal faculties are brought into play. The well has now been fitted with a windlass--that little Moorish water-wheel possessed by every Castilian farm. Hence we get more water for the energy we expend: more sense of reality in exchange for our abstraction from the unreal. Also "the water is higher, and accordingly the labour is much less than it was when the water had to be drawn out of the depths of the well. I mean that the water is nearer to it, for grace now reveals itself more distinctly to the soul." In the third stage, or orison of union, we leave all voluntary activities of the mind: the gardener no longer depends on his own exertions, contact between subject and object is established, there is no more stress and strain. It is as if a little river now ran through our garden and watered it. We have but to direct the stream. In the fourth and highest stage, God Himself waters our garden with rain from heaven "drop by drop." The attitude of the self is now that of perfect receptivity, "passive contemplation," loving trust. Individual activity is sunk in the "great life of the All." [656]

The measure of the mystic's real progress is and must always be his progress in love; for his apprehension is an apprehension of the heart. His education, his watering of the garden of the soul, is a cultivation of this one flower--this Rosa Mystica which has its root in God. His advance in contemplation, then, will be accompanied step by step by those exalted feeling-states which Richard of St. Victor called the Degrees of Ardent Love. Without their presence, all the drill in the world will not bring him to the time contemplative state; though it may easily produce abnormal powers of perception of the kind familiar to students of the occult.

Thus our theory of mystic education is in close accord with our theory of mystic life. In both, there is a progressive surrender of selfhood under the steady advance of conquering love; a stilling of that "I, Me, and Mine," which is linked by all the senses, and by all its own desires, to the busy world of visible things. This progressive surrender usually appears in the practice of orison as a progressive inward retreat from circumference to centre, to that ground of the soul, that substantial somewhat in man, deep buried for most of us beneath the great rubbish heap of our surface-interests, where human life and divine life meet. To clear away the rubbish-heap so that he may get down to this treasure-house is from one point of view the initial task of the contemplative. This clearing away is the first part of "introversion": that journey inwards to his own centre where, stripped of all his cleverness and merit, reduced to his "nothingness," he can "meet God without intermediary." This ground of the soul, this strange inward sanctuary to which the normal man so seldom penetrates, is, says Eckhart, "immediately receptive of the Divine Being," and "no one can move it but God alone." [657] There the finite self encounters the Infinite; and, by a close and loving communion with and feeding on the attributes of the Divine Substance, is remade in the interests of the Absolute Life. This encounter, the consummation of mystical culture, is what we mean by contemplation in its highest form. Here we are on the verge of that great self-merging act which is of the essence of pure love: which Reality has sought of us, and we have unknowingly desired of It. Here contemplation and union are one. "Thus do we grow," says Ruysbroeck, "and, carried above ourselves, above reason, into the very heart of love, there do we feed according to the spirit; and taking flight for the Godhead by naked love, we go to the encounter of the Bridegroom, to the encounter of His Spirit, which is His love; and thus we are brought forth by God, out of our selfhood, into the immersion of love, in which we possess blessedness and are one with God."[658]

Recollection

The beginning of the process of introversion, the first deliberate act in which the self turns towards the inward path, will not merely be the yielding to an instinct, the indulgence of a natural taste for reverie; it will be a voluntary and purposeful undertaking. Like conversion, it entails a break with the obvious, which must, of necessity, involve and affect the whole normal consciousness. It will be evoked by the mystic's love, and directed by his reason; but can only be accomplished by the strenuous exercise of his will. These preparatory labours of the contemplative life--these first steps upon the ladder--are, says St. Teresa, very hard, and require greater courage than all the rest. [659] All the scattered interests of the self have here to be collected; there must be a deliberate and unnatural act of attention, a deliberate expelling of all discordant images from the consciousness a hard and ungrateful task. Since the transcendental faculties are still young and weak, the senses not wholly mortified, it needs a stern determination, a "wilful choice," if we are to succeed in concentrating our attention upon the whispered messages from within, undistracted by the loud voices which besiege us from without.

"How," says the Disciple to the Master in one of Boehme's "Dialogues," "am I to seek in the Centre this Fountain of Light which may enlighten me throughout and bring my properties into perfect harmony? I am in Nature, as I said before, and which way shall I pass through Nature and the light thereof, so that I may come into the supernatural and supersensual ground whence this true Light, which is the Light of Minds, doth arise; and this without the destruction of my nature, or quenching the Light of it, which is my reason?

"Master. Cease but from thine own activity, steadfastly fixing thine Eye upon one Point. . . . For this end, gather in all thy thoughts, and by faith press into the Centre, laying hold upon the Word of God, which is infallible and which hath called thee. Be thou obedient to this call, and be silent before the Lord, sitting alone with Him in thy inmost and most hidden cell, thy mind being centrally united in itself, and attending His Will in the patience of hope. So shall thy Light break forth as the morning, and after the redness thereof is passed, the Sun himself, which thou waitest for, shall arise unto thee, and under his most healing wings thou shalt greatly rejoice: ascending and descending in his bright and health-giving beams. Behold, this is the true Supersensual Ground of Life." [660]

In this short paragraph Boehme has caught and described the psychological state in which all introversion must begin: the primary simplification of consciousness, steadfastly fixing the soul's eye upon one point, and the turning inwards of the whole conative powers for a purpose rather believed in than known, "by faith pressing into the centre."

The unfortunate word Recollection, which the hasty reader is apt to connect with remembrance, is the traditional term by which mystical writers define just such a voluntary concentration, such a first collecting or gathering in of the attention of the self to its "most hidden cell." That self is as yet unacquainted with the strange plane of silence which so soon becomes familiar to those who attempt even the lowest activities of the contemplative life, where the self is released from succession, the noises of the world are never heard, and the great adventures of the spirit take place. It stands here between the two planes of its being; the Eye of Time is still awake. It knows that it wants to enter the inner world, that "interior palace where the King of Kings is guest": [661] but it must find some device to help it over the threshold--rather, in the language of psychology, to shift that threshold and permit its subliminal intuition of the Absolute to emerge.

This device is as a rule the practice of meditation, in which the state of Recollection usually begins: that is to say, the deliberate consideration of and dwelling upon some one aspect of Reality--an aspect most usually chosen from amongst the religious beliefs of the self. Thus Hindu mystics will brood upon a sacred word, whilst Christian contemplatives set before their minds one of the names or attributes of God, a fragment of Scripture, an incident of the life of Christ; and allow--indeed encourage--this consideration and the ideas and feelings which flow from it, to occupy the whole mental field. This powerful suggestion, kept before the consciousness by an act of will, overpowers the stream of small suggestions which the outer world pours incessantly upon the mind. The self, concentrated upon this image or idea, dwelling on it more than thinking about it--as one may gaze upon a picture that one loves--falls gradually and insensibly into the condition of reverie; and, protected by this holy day-dream from the more distracting dream of life, sinks into itself, and becomes in the language of asceticism "recollected" or gathered together. Although it is deliberately ignoring the whole of its usual "external universe," its faculties are wide awake: all have had their part in the wilful production of this state of consciousness: and this it is which marks off meditation and recollection from the higher or "infused" degrees of orison.

Such meditation as this, says Richard of St. Victor, is the activity proper to one who has attained the first degree of ardent love. By it, "God enters into the mind," and "the mind also enters into itself"; and thus receives in its inmost cell the "first visit of the Beloved." It is a kind of half-way house between the perception of Appearance and the perception of Reality. To one in whom this state is established consciousness seems like a blank field, save for the "one point" in its centre, the subject of the meditation. Towards this focus the introversive self seems to press inwards from every side; still faintly conscious of the buzz of the external world outside its ramparts, but refusing to respond to its appeals. Presently the subject of meditation begins to take on a new significance; to glow with life and light. The contemplative suddenly feels that he knows it; in the complete, vital, but indescribable way in which one knows a friend. More, through it hints are coming to him of mightier, nameless things. It ceases to be a picture, and becomes a window through which the mystic peers out into the spiritual universe, and apprehends to some extent--though how, he knows not--the veritable presence of God.

In these meditative and recollective states, the self still feels very clearly the edge of its own personality: its separateness from the Somewhat Other, the divine reality set over against the soul. It is aware of that reality: the subject of its meditation becomes a symbol through which it receives a distinct message from the transcendental world. But it is still operating in a natural way--as mystical writers would say, "by means of the faculties." There is yet no conscious fusion with a greater Life; no resting in the divine atmosphere, as in the "Quiet"; no involuntary and ecstatic lifting up of the soul to direct apprehension of truth, as in contemplation. Recollection is a definite psychic condition, which has logical psychic results. Originally induced by meditation, or absorbed brooding upon certain aspects of the Real, it develops in the Self, by way of the strenuous control exercised by the will over the understanding, a power of cutting its connection with the external world, and retreating to the inner world of the spirit.

"True recollection," says St. Teresa, "has characteristics by which it can be easily recognized. It produces a certain effect which I do not know how to explain, but which is well understood by those who have experienced it. . . . It is true that recollection has several degrees, and that in the beginning these great effects are not felt, because it is not yet profound enough. But support the pain which you first feel in recollecting yourself, despise the rebellion of nature, overcome the resistance of the body, which loves a liberty which is its ruin, learn self-conquest, persevere thus for a time, and you will perceive very clearly the advantages which you gain from it. As soon as you apply yourself to orison, you will at once feel your senses gather themselves together: they seem like bees which return to the hive and there shut themselves up to work at the making of honey: and this will take place without effort or care on your part. God thus rewards the violence which your soul has been doing to itself; and gives to it such a domination over the senses that a sign is enough when it desires to recollect itself, for them to obey and so gather themselves together. At the first call of the will, they come back more and more quickly. At last, after countless exercises of this kind, God disposes them to a state of utter rest and of perfect contemplation." [662]

This description makes it clear that "recollection" is a form of spiritual gymnastics; less valuable for itself than for the training which it gives, the powers which it develops. In it, says St. Teresa again, the soul enters with its God into that Paradise which is within itself, and shuts the door behind it upon all the things of the world. "You should know, my daughters," she continues, "that this is no supernatural act, but depends upon our will, and that therefore we can do it with that ordinary assistance of God which we need for all our acts and even for our good thoughts. For here we are not concerned with the silence of the faculties, but with a simple retreat of these powers into the ground of the soul. There are various ways of arriving at it, and these ways are described in different books. There it is said that we must abstract the mind from exterior things, in order that we may inwardly approach God: that even in our work we ought to retire within ourselves, though it be only for a moment: that this remembrance of a God who companions us within, is a great help to us; finally, that we ought little by little to habituate ourselves to gentle and silent converse with Him, so that He may make us feel His presence in the soul." [663]

Quiet

More important for us, because more characteristically mystical, is the next great stage of orison: that curious and extremely definite mental state which mystics call the Prayer of Quiet or Simplicity, or sometimes the Interior Silence. This represents the result for consciousness of a further degree of that inward retreat which Recollection began.

Out of the deep, slow brooding and pondering on some mystery, some incomprehensible link between himself and the Real, or the deliberate practice of loving attention to God, the contemplative--perhaps by way of a series of moods and acts which his analytic powers may cause him "nicely to distinguish"--glides, almost insensibly, on to a plane of perception for which human speech has few equivalents. It is a plane which is apparently characterized by an immense increase in the receptivity of the self and by an almost complete suspension of the reflective powers. The strange silence which is the outstanding quality of this state--almost the only note in regard to it which the surface-intelligence can secure--is not describable. Here, as Samuel Rutherford said of another of life's secrets, "Come and see willtell you much: come nearer will say more." Here the self passes beyond the stage at which its perceptions are capable of being dealt with by thought. It can no longer "take notes": can only surrender itself to the stream of an inflowing life, and to the direction of a larger will. Discursive thought would only interfere with this process: as it interferes with the vital processes of the body if it once gets them under its control. That thought, then, already disciplined by Recollection, gathered up, and forced to work in the interests of the transcendental mind, is now to be entirely inhibited.

As Recollection becomes deeper, the self slides into a certain dim yet vivid consciousness of the Infinite. The door tight shut on the sensual world, it becomes aware that it is immersed in a more real world which it cannot define. It rests quietly in this awareness: quite silent, utterly at peace. In the place of the struggles for complete concentration which mark the beginning of Recollection, there is now "a living, somehow self-acting recollection--with God, His peace, power, and presence, right in the midst of this rose of spiritual fragrance." [664] With this surrender to something bigger, as with the surrender of conversion, comes an immense relief of strain. This is "Quiet" in its most perfect form: this sinking, as it were, of the little child of the Infinite into its Father's arms. The giving up of I-hood, the process of self-stripping, which we have seen to be the essence of the purification of the self, finds its parallel in this phase of the contemplative experience. Here, in this complete cessation of man's proud effort to do somewhat of himself, Humility, who rules the Fourth Degree of Love, begins to be known in her paradoxical beauty and power. Consciousness loses to find, and dies that it may live. No longer, in Rolle's pungent phrase, is it a "Raunsaker of the myghte of Godd and of His Majeste." [665] Thus the act by which it passes into the Quiet is a sacrament of the whole mystic quest: of the turning from doing to being, the abolition of separateness in the interests of the Absolute Life.

The state of "Quiet," we have said, entails suspension of the surface-consciousness: yet consciousness of the subject's personality remains. It follows, generally, on a period of deliberate and loving recollection, of a slow and steady withdrawal of the attention from the channels of sense. To one who is entering this state, the external world seems to get further and further away: till at last nothing but the paramount fact of his own existence remains. So startling, very often, is the deprivation of all his accustomed mental furniture, of the noise and flashing of the transmitting instruments of sense, that the negative aspect of his condition dominates consciousness; and he can but describe it as a nothingness, a pure passivity, an emptiness, a "naked" orison. He is there, as it were poised, resting, waiting, he does not know for what: only he is conscious that all, even in this utter emptiness, is well. Presently, however, he becomes aware that Something fills this emptiness; something omnipresent, intangible, like sunny air. Ceasing to attend to the messages from without, he begins to notice That which has always been within. His whole being is thrown open to its influence: it permeates his consciousness.

There are, then, two aspects of the Orison of Quiet: the aspect of deprivation, of emptiness which begins it, and the aspect of acquisition, of something found, in which it is complete. In its description, all mystics will be found to lean to one side or the other, to the affirmative or negative element which it contains. The austere mysticism of Eckhart and his followers, their temperamental sympathy with the Neoplatonic language of Dionysius the Areopagite, caused them to describe it and also very often the higher state of contemplation to which it leads--as above all things an emptiness, a divine dark, an ecstatic deprivation. They will not profane its deep satisfactions by the inadequate terms proper to earthly peace and joy: and, true to their school, fall back on the paradoxically suggestive powers of negation. To St. Teresa, and mystics of her type, on the other hand, even a little and inadequate image of its joy seems better than none. To them it is a sweet calm, a gentle silence, in which the lover apprehends the presence of the Beloved: a God-given state over which the self has little control.

In Eckhart's writings enthusiastic descriptions of the Quiet, of inward silence and passivity as the fruit of a deliberate recollection, abound. In his view, the psychical state of Quiet is preeminently that in which the soul of man begins to be united with its "ground," Pure Being. It marks the transition from "natural" to "supernatural" prayer. The emptying of the field of consciousness, its cleansing of all images--even of those symbols of Reality which are the objects of meditation--is the necessary condition under which alone this encounter can take place.

"The soul," he says, "with all its powers, has divided and scattered itself in outward things, each according to its functions: the power of sight in the eye, the power of hearing in the ear, the power of taste in the tongue, and thus they are the less able to work inwardly, for every power which is divided is imperfect. So the soul, if she would work inwardly, must call home all her powers and collect them from all divided things to one inward work. . . . If a man will work an inward work, he must pour all his powers into himself as into a corner of the soul, and must hide himself from all images and forms, and then he can work. Then he must come into a forgetting and a not-knowing. He must be in a stillness and silence, where the Word may be heard. One cannot draw near to this Word better than by stillness and silence: then it is heard and understood in utter ignorance. When one knows nothing, it is opened and revealed. Then we shall become aware of the Divine Ignorance, and our ignorance will be ennobled and adorned with supernatural knowledge. And when we simply keep ourselves receptive, we are more perfect than when at work." [666]

The psychic state of Quiet has a further value for the mystic, as being the intellectual complement and expression of the moral state of humility and receptivity: the very condition, says Eckhart, of the New Birth. "It may be asked whether this Birth is best accomplished in Man when he does the work and forms and thinks himself into God, or when he keeps himself in Silence, stillness and peace, so that God may speak and work in him; . . . the best and noblest way in which thou mayst come into this work and life is by keeping silence, and letting God work and speak. When all the powers are withdrawn from their work and images, there is this word spoken." [667]

Eckhart's view of the primary importance of "Quiet" as essentially the introverted state is shared by all those mediaeval mystics who lay stress on the psychological rather than the objective aspect of the spiritual life. They regard it as the necessary preliminary of all contemplation; and describe it as a normal phase of the inner experience, possible of attainment by all those who have sufficiently disciplined themselves in patience, recollection, and humility.

In an old English mystical tract by the author of "The Cloud of Unknowing" there is a curious and detailed instruction on the disposition of mind proper to this orison of silence. It clearly owes much to the teaching of the Areopagite, and something surely--if we may judge by its vivid and exact instructions--to personal experience. "When thou comest by thyself," says the master to the disciple for whom this "pystle" was composed, "think not before what thou shalt do after: but forsake as well good thoughts as evil thoughts, and pray not with thy mouth, but lift thee right well. . . . And look that nothing live in thy working mind but a naked intent stretching unto God, not clothed in any special thought of God in thyself, how He is in Himself or in any of His works, but only that He is as He is. Let Him be so, I pray thee, and make Him on none otherwise speech, nor search in Him by subtilty of wit: but believe by thy ground. This naked intent freely fastened and grounded by very belief, shall be nought else to thy thought and thy feeling but a naked thought and a blind feeling of thine own being. . . . That darkness be thy mirror and thy mind whole. Think no further of thyself than I bid thee do of thy God, so that thou be oned with Him in spirit as in thought, without departing and scattering, for He is thy being and in Him thou art that thou art: not only by cause and by being, but also He is in thee both thy cause and thy being. And therefore think on God as in this work as thou dost on thyself, and on thyself as thou dost on God, that He is as He is, and thou art as thou art, and that thy thought be not scattered nor departed but privied in Him that is All." [668]

"Let Him be so, I pray thee!" It is an admonition against spiritual worry, an entreaty to the individual, already at work twisting experience to meet his own conceptions, to let things be as they are, to receive and be content. Leave off doing, that you may be. Leave off analysis, that you may know. "That meek darkness be thy mirror"--humble receptivity is the watchword of this state. "In this," says

Eckhart finely, "the soul is of equal capacity with God. As God is boundless in giving, so the soul is boundless in receiving. And as God is almighty in His work, se the soul is an abyss of receptivity: and so she is formed anew with God and in God. . . . The disciples of St. Dionysius asked him why Timotheus surpassed them all in perfection. Then said Dionysius, Timotheus is receptive of God.' And thus thine ignorance is not a defect but thy highest perfection, and thine inactivity thy highest work. And so in this work thou must bring all thy works to nought and all thy powers into silence, if thou wilt in truth experience this birth within thyself." [669]

It is interesting to contrast these descriptions of the Quiet with St. Teresa's subjective account of the same psychological state. Where the English mystic's teaching is full of an implied appeal to the will, the Spanish saint is all for the involuntary, or, as she would call it, the "supernatural" actions of the soul. "This true orison of quiet," she says, "has in it an element of the supernatural. We cannot, in spite of all our efforts, procure it for ourselves. It is a sort of peace in which the soul establishes herself, or rather in which God establishes the soul, as He did the righteous Simeon. All her powers are at rest. She understands, but otherwise than by the senses, that she is already near her God, and that if she draws a little nearer, she will become by union one with Him. She does not see this with the eyes of the body, nor with the eyes of the soul. . . . It is like the repose of a traveller who, within sight of the goal stops to take breath, and then continues with new strength upon his way. One feels a great bodily comfort, a great satisfaction of soul: such is the happiness of the soul in seeing herself close to the spring, that even without drinking of the waters she finds herself refreshed. It seems to her that she wants nothing more: the faculties which are at rest would like always to remain still, for the least of their movements is able to trouble or prevent her love. Those who are in this orison wish their bodies to remain motionless, for it seems to them that at the least movement they will lose this sweet peace . . . they are in the palace close to their King, and they see that He begins to give them His kingdom. It seems to them that they are no longer in the world, and they wish neither to hear nor to see it, but only God. . . . There is this difference between the orison of quiet and that in which the whole soul is united to God; that in this last the soul has not to absorb the Divine Food. God deposits it with her, she knows not how. The orison of quiet, on the other hand, demands, it seems to me, a slight effort; but it is accompanied by so much sweetness that one hardly feels it." [670]

"A slight effort," says St. Teresa. "A naked intent stretching," says the "Pystle of Private Counsel." These words mark the frontier between the true and healthy mystic state of "Quiet" and its morbid perversion in "Quietism": the difference between the tense stillness of the athlete and the limp passivity of the sluggard, who is really lazy, though he looks resigned. True "Quiet" is a means, not an end: is actively embraced, not passively endured. It is a phase in the self's growth in contemplation; a bridge which leads from its old and uncoordinated life of activity to its new unified life of deep action--the real "mystic life" of man. This state is desired by the mystic, not in order that consciousness may remain a blank, but in order that the "Word which is Alive" may be written thereon. Too often, however, this fact has been ignored; and the Interior Silence has been put by wayward transcendentalists to other and less admirable use.

"Quiet" is the danger-zone of introversion. Of all forms of mystical activity, perhaps this has been the most abused, the least understood. Its theory, seized upon, divorced from its context, and developed to excess, produced the foolish and dangerous exaggerations of Quietism: and these, in their turn, caused a wholesale condemnation of the principle of passivity, and made many superficial persons regard "naked orison" as an essentially heretical act. [671] The accusation of Quietism has been hurled at mystics whose only fault was a looseness of language which laid them open to misapprehension. Others, however, have certainly contrived, by a perversion and isolation of the teachings of great contemplatives on this point, to justify the deliberate production of a half-hypnotic state of passivity. With this meaningless state of "absorption in nothing at all" they were content; claiming that in it they were in touch with the divine life, and therefore exempt from the usual duties and limitations of human existence. "Quietism," usually, and rather unfairly, regarded as the special folly of Madame Guyon and her disciples, already existed in a far more dangerous form in the Middle Ages: and was described and denounced by Ruysbroeck, one of the greatest masters of true introversion whom the Christian world has known.

"Such quietude," he says, "is nought else but idleness, into which a man has fallen, and in which he forgets himself and God and all things in all that has to do with activity. This repose is wholly contrary to the supernatural repose one possesses in God; for that is a loving self-mergence and simple gazing at the Incomprehensible Brightness; actively sought with inward desire, and found in fruitive inclination. . . . When a man possesses this rest in false idleness, and all loving adherence seems a hindrance to him, he clings to himself in his quietude and lives contrary to the first way in which man is united with God; and this is the beginning of all ghostly error." [672]

There can be no doubt that for selves of a certain psychical constitution, such a "false idleness" is only too easy of attainment. They can by wilful self-suggestion deliberately produce this emptiness, this inward silence, and luxuriate in its peaceful effects. To do this from self-regarding motives, or to do it to excess--to let "peaceful enjoyment" swamp "active love"--is a mystical vice: and this perversion of the spiritual faculties, like perversion of the natural faculties, brings degeneration in its train. It leads to the absurdities of "holy indifference," and ends in the complete stultification of the mental and moral life. The true mystic never tries deliberately to enter the orison of quiet: with St. Teresa, he regards it as a supernatural gift, beyond his control, though fed by his will and love. That is to say, where it exists in a healthy form, it appears spontaneously, as a phase in normal development; not as a self-induced condition, a psychic trick.

The balance to be struck in this stage of introversion can only be expressed, it seems, in paradox. The true condition of quiet according to the great mystics, is at once active and passive: it is pure surrender, but a surrender which is not limp self-abandonment, but rather the free and constantly renewed self-giving and self-emptying of a burning love. The departmental intellect is silenced, but the totality of character is flung open to the influence of the Real. Personality is not lost: only its hard edge is gone. A "rest most busy," says Hilton. Like the soaring of an eagle, says Augustine Baker, when "the flight is continued for a good space with a great swiftness, but withal with great stillness, quietness and ease, without any waving of the wings at all, or the least force used in any member, being in as much ease and stillness as if she were reposing in her nest." [673]

"According to the unanimous teaching of the most experienced and explicit of the specifically Theistic and Christian mystics," says Von Hügel, "the appearance, the soul's own impression, of a cessation of life and energy of the soul in periods of special union with God, or of great advance in spirituality, is an appearance only. Indeed this, at such times strong, impression of rest springs most certainly from an unusually large amount of actualized energy, an energy which is now penetrating, and finding expression by ever pore and fibre of the soul. The whole moral and spiritual creature expands and rests, yes; but this very rest is produced by Action, unperceived because so fleet, so near, so all-fulfilling.'" [674]

The great teachers of Quietism, having arrived at and experienced the psychological state of "quiet": having known the ineffable peace and certainty, the bliss which follows on its act of complete surrender, its utter and speechless resting in the Absolute Life, believed themselves to have discovered in this halfway house the goal of the mystic quest. Therefore, whilst much of their teaching remains true, as a real description of a real and valid state experienced by almost all contemplatives in the course of their development, the inference which they drew from it, that in this mere blank abiding in the deeps the soul had reached the end of her course, was untrue and bad for life.

Thus Molinos gives in the "Spiritual Guide" many unexceptional maxims upon Interior Silence: "By not speaking nor desiring, and not thinking," he says justly enough of the contemplative spirit, "she arrives at the true and perfect mystical silence wherein God speaks with the soul, communicates Himself to it, and in the abyss of its own depth teaches it the most perfect and exalted wisdom. He calls and guides it to this inward solitude and mystical silence, when He says that He will speak to it alone in the most secret and hidden part of the heart." Here Molinos speaks the language of all mystics, yet the total result of his teaching was to suggest to the ordinary mind that there was a peculiar virtue in doing nothing at all, and that all deliberate spiritual activities were bad. [675]

Much of the teaching of modern "mystical" cults is thus crudely quietistic. It insists on the necessity of "going into the silence," and even, with a strange temerity, gives preparatory lessons in subconscious meditation: a proceeding which might well provoke the laughter of the saints. The faithful, being gathered together, are taught by simple exercises in recollection the way to attain the "Quiet." By this mental trick the modern transcendentalist naturally attains to a state of vacant placidity, in which he rests: and "remaining in a distracted idleness and misspending the time in expectation of extraordinary visits," believes--with a faith which many of the orthodox might envy--that he is here "united with his Principle." But, though the psychological state which contemplatives call the prayer of quiet is a common condition of mystical attainment, it is not by itself mystical at all. It is a state of preparation: a way of opening the door. That which comes in when the door is opened will be that which we truly and passionately desire. The will makes plain the way: the heart--the whole man--conditions the guest. The true contemplative, coming to this plane of utter stillness, does not desire "extraordinary favours and visitations," but the privilege of breathing for a little while the atmosphere of Love. He is about that which St. Bernard called "the business of all businesses": goes, in perfect simplicity, to the encounter of Perfection, not to the development of himself.

So, even at this apparently "passive" stage of his progress, the mystic's operations are found on analysis to have a dynamic and purposive character: his very repose is the result of stress. He is a pilgrim that still seeks his country. Urged by his innate tendency to transcendence, he is on his way to higher levels, more sublime fulfilments, greater self-giving acts. Though he may have forsaken all superficial activity, deep, urgent action still remains. "The possession of God," says Ruysbroeck, "demands and supposes active love. He who thinks or feels otherwise is deceived. All our life as it is in God is immersed in blessedness: all our life as it is in ourselves is immersed in active love. And though we live wholly in ourselves and wholly in God, it is but one life, but it is twofold and opposite according to our feeling--rich and poor hungry and fulfilled, active and quiet." [676] The essential difference between this true "active" Quiet and Quietism of all kinds has been admirably expressed by Baron von Hügel. "Quietism, the doctrine of the One Act; passivity in a literal sense, as the absence or imperfection of the power or use of initiative on the soul's part, in any and every state; these doctrines were finally condemned, and most rightly and necessarily condemned, the Prayer of Quiet and the various states and degrees of an ever-increasing predominance of Action over Activity--an action which is all the more the soul's very own, because the more occasioned, directed and informed by God's action and stimulation--these and the other chief lines of the ancient experience and practice remain as true, correct, and necessary as ever." [677]

The "ever-increasing predominance of Action over Activity"--the deep and vital movement of the whole self, too utterly absorbed for self-consciousness, set over against its fussy surface-energies--here is the true ideal of orison. This must inform all the soul's aspiration towards union with the absolute Life and Love which waits at the door. It is an ideal which includes Quiet, as surely as it excludes Quietism.

As for that doctrine of the One Act here mentioned, which was preached by the more extreme quietists; it, like all else in this movement, was the perversion of a great mystical truth. It taught that the turning of the soul towards Reality, the merging of the will in God, which is the very heart of the mystic life, was One Act, never to be repeated. This done, the self had nothing more to do but to rest in the Divine Life, be its unresisting instrument. Pure passivity and indifference were its ideal. All activity was forbidden it, all choice was a negation of its surrender, all striving was unnecessary and wrong. It needed only to rest for evermore and "let God work and speak in the silence." This doctrine is so utterly at variance with all that we know of the laws of life and growth, that it hardly seems to stand in need of condemnation. Such a state of indifference--which the quietists strove in vain to identify with that state of Pure Love which "seeketh not its own" in spiritual things--cannot coexist with any of those "degrees of ardent charity" through which man's spirit must pass on its journey to the One: and this alone is enough to prove its non-mystical character.

It is only fair to Madame Guyon to say that she cannot justly be charged with preaching this exaggeration of passivity, though a loose and fluid style has allowed many unfortunate inferences to be drawn from her works. "Some persons," she says, "when they hear of the prayer of quiet, falsely imagine that the soul remains stupid, dead, and inactive. But unquestionably it acteth therein, more nobly and more extensively than it had ever done before, for God Himself is the Mover and the soul now acteth by the agency of His Spirit. . . . Instead, then, of promoting idleness we promote the highest activity, by inculcating a total dependence on the Spirit of God as our moving principle, for in Him we live and move and have our being. . . . Our activity should therefore consist in endeavouring to acquire and maintain such a state as may be most susceptible of divine impressions, most flexile to all the operations of the Eternal Word. Whilst a tablet is unsteady, the painter is unable to delineate a true copy: so every act of our own selfish and proper spirit is productive of false and erroneous lineaments, it interrupts the work and defeats the design of this Adorable Artist." [678]

The true mystics, in whom the Orison of Quiet develops to this state of receptivity, seldom use in describing it the language of "holy indifference." Their love and enthusiasm will not let them do that. It is true, of course, that they are indifferent to all else save the supreme claims of love: but then, it is of love that they speak. Ego dormio et cor meum vigilat . "This," says St. Teresa, "is a sleep of the powers of the soul, which are not wholly lost, nor yet understanding how they are at work. . . . To me it seems to be nothing else than a death, as it were, to all the things of this world, and a fruition of God. I know of no other words whereby to describe it or explain it; neither does the soul then know what to do--for it knows not whether to speak or be silent, whether it should laugh or weep. It is a glorious folly, a heavenly madness wherein true wisdom is acquired; and to the soul a kind of fruition most full of delight. . . . The faculties of the soul now retain only the power of occupying themselves wholly with God; not one of them ventures to stir, neither can we move one of them without making great efforts to distract ourselves--and, indeed, I do not think we can do it at all at this time." [679]

Here, then, we see the Orison of Silence melting into true contemplation: its stillness is ruffled by its joy. The Quiet reveals itself as an essentially transitional state, introducing the self into a new sphere of activity.

The second degree of ardent love, says Richard of St. Victor, binds , sothat the soul which is possessed by it is unable to think of anything else: it is not only "insuperable," but also "inseparable." [680] He compares it to the soul's bridal; the irrevocable act, by which permanent union is initiated. The feeling-state which is the equivalent of the Quiet is just such a passive and joyous yielding-up of the virgin soul to its Bridegroom; a silent marriage-vow. It is ready for all that may happen to it, all that may be asked of it--to give itself and lose itself, to wait upon the pleasure of its Love. From this inward surrender the self emerges to the new life, the new knowledge which is mediated to it under the innumerable forms of Contemplation.

Footnotes:

630. "The contemplative and the artist," says Maritain, "are in a position to sympathize. . . . The contemplative, having for object the causa altissima from which all else depends, knows the place and value of art, and understands the artist. The artist as such, cannot judge the contemplative, but he can divine his greatness. If he indeed loves Beauty, and if some moral vice does not chain his heart to dulness, going over to the side of the contemplative he will recognize Love and Beauty" (J. Maritain, "Art et Scholastique," p. 139).

631. "Revelations of Divine Love," cap. v.

632. St. Bernard, "De Consideratione," bk. v. cap. iii.

633. "De Imitatione Christi," I. iii. cap. xxxi.

634. St. Bernard, op. cit ., bk. v. cap. v. So Lady Julian, "We are all in Him enclosed and He is enclosed in us" ("Revelations of Divine Love," cap. lvii.).

635. Op. cit ., cap. vii.

636. Third Instruction ("The Inner Way," p. 323).

637. Eckhart, Pred. lxix.

638. Phaedo, 79c.

639. "Holy Wisdom." Treatise iii. § iv.cap. i.

640. Cap. xvii.

641. J. N. Grou, "L'Ecole de Jésus," vol. ii., p. 8.

642. "I discover all truths in the interior of my soul," says Antoinette Bourignan, "especially when I am recollected in my solitude in a forgetfulness of all Things. Then my spirit communicates with Another Spirit, and they entertain one another as two friends who converse about serious matters. And this conversation is so sweet that I have sometimes passed a whole day and a night in it without interruption or standing in need of meat or drink" (MacEwen, "Antoinette Bourignan, Quietist," p. 109).

643. Par. xxii. 64.

644. "Dialogues of the Supersensual Life," p. 66.

645. Hilton, "The Scale of Perfection," bk. ii., cap. xi.

646. "Études sur le Mysticisme," p. 18.

647. Vida, cap. xiv.; "Camino do Perfeccion," cap. xxxi.; "El Castillo Interior," Moradas Cuartas, cap. ii.

648. "Holy Wisdom," Treatise iii. § ii. cap. vii.

649. Meditation, Quiet, a nameless "intermediate" degree, and the Orison of Union (Vida, cap. xi.).

650. Meditation, Soliloquy, Consideration, Rapture (Hugh of St. Victor, "De Contemplatione").

651. "De Quatuor Gradibus Violentae Charitatis." Vide supra, p. 139.

652. "The Scale of Perfection," bk. I. caps. iv. to viii.

653. "Holy Wisdom," loc. cit ., § ii. cap. i.

654. Coventry Patmore, The Rod, the Root, and the Flower," "Aurea Dicta," xiii.

655. Vida, cap. xi. §§ 10 and 11.

656. The detailed analysis of these four degrees fills caps. xii.-xviii. of the Vida .

657. Pred. i. This doctrine of man's latent absoluteness, expressed under a multitude of different symbols, is the central dogma of mysticism, and the guarantee of the validity of the contemplative process. In its extreme form, it can hardly be defended from the charge of pantheism; but the Christian mystics are usually careful to steer clear of this danger.

658. Ruysbroeck, "De Calculo" (condensed).

659. Vida, cap. xi. § 17.

660. "Dialogues of the Supersensual Life," p. 56.

661. St. Teresa, "Camino de Perfeccion," cap. xxx.

662. "Camino de Perfeccion," cap. xxx.

663. Op. cit ., cap. xxxi.

664. F. von Hügel. "Letters to a Niece," p. 140.

665. Prose Treatises of Richard Rolle (E.E.T.S. 20), p. 42.

666. Meister Eckhart, Pred. ii.

667. Ibid. , Pred. i.

668. "An Epistle of Private Counsel" (B.M. Harl. 674). Printed, with slight textual variations, in "The Cloud of Unknowing, and other Treatises," edited by Dom Justin McCann.

669. Eckhart, Pred. ii.

670. "Camino de Perfeccion," cap. xxxiii. The whole chapter, which is a marvel of subtle analysis, should be read in this connection.

671. Note, for instance, the cautious language of "Holy Wisdom," Treatise iii. § III. cap. vii.

672. Ruysbroeck, "De Ornatu Spiritalium Nuptiarum," l. ii. caps. lxvi. (condensed).

673. "Holy Wisdom," Treatise iii. § iii. cap. vii.

674. Von Hügel, "The Mystical Element of Religion," vol. ii. p. 132.

675. He goes so far as to say in one of his "condemned" propositions , "Oportet hominem suas potentias anshilare," and "velle operari active est Deum offendere."

676. "De Calculo," cap. ix.

677. "The Mystical Element of Religion," vol. ii. p. 143.

678. "Moyen Court," cap. xxi. Madame Guyon's vague and shifting language, however, sometimes lays her open to other and more strictly "quietistic" interpretations.

679. Vida, cap. xvi. §§ 1 and 4.

680. "De Quatuor Gradibus Violentae Charitatis" (Migne, Patrologia Latina, vol. cxcvi. col. 1215 b).

CHAPTER VII

We must now consider under the general name of Contemplation those developed states of introversion in which the mystic attains somewhat: the results and rewards of the discipline of Recollection and Quiet. If this course of spiritual athletics has done its work, he has now brought to the surface, trained and made efficient for life, a form of consciousness--a medium of communication with reality--which remains undeveloped in ordinary men. Thanks to this faculty, he is now capable of the characteristic mystic experience: temporary union with "that spiritual fount closed to all reactions from the world of sense, where, without witnesses of any kind, God and our Freedom meet." [681]

The degrees of Recollection trained the self in spiritual attention: and at the same time lifted it to a new level of perception where, by means of the symbol which formed the gathering-point of its powers, it received a new inflow of life. In the degrees of Quiet it passed on to a state characterized by a tense stillness, in which it rested in that Reality at which, as yet, it dared not look. Now, in Contemplation, it is to transcend alike the stages of symbol and of silence; and "energize enthusiastically" on those high levels which are dark to the intellect but radiant to the heart. We must expect this contemplative activity to show itself in many different ways and take many different names since its character will be largely governed by individual temperament. It appears under the forms which ascetic writers call "ordinary" and "extraordinary," "infused" or "passive" Contemplation; and as that "orison of union" which we have already discussed. [682] Sometimes, too, it shows itself under those abnormal psycho-physical conditions in which the intense concentration of the self upon its transcendental perceptions results in the narrowing of the field of consciousness to a point at which all knowledge of the external world is lost, all the messages of the senses are utterly ignored. The subject then appears to be in a state of trance, characterized by physical rigidity and more or less complete anaesthesia. These are the conditions of Rapture or Ecstasy: conditions of which the physical resemblances to certain symptoms of hysteria have so greatly reassured the enemies of mysticism.

Rapture and Ecstasy differ from Contemplation proper in being wholly involuntary states. Rapture, says St. Teresa who frequently experienced it, is absolutely irresistible; we cannot hinder it. Whereas the orison of union, which is one of the forms in which pure Contemplation appears at its highest point of development, is still controlled to a large extent by the will of the subject, and "may be hindered, although that resistance be painful and violent." [683] There is thus a sharp distinction--a distinction both physical and psychical--between the contemplative and the ecstatic states: and we shall do well to avail ourselves of it in examining their character.

First, then, as to Contemplation proper: what is it? It is a supreme manifestation of that indivisible "power of knowing" which lies at the root of all our artistic and spiritual satisfactions. In it, man's "made Trinity" of thought, love, and will, becomes a Unity: and feeling and perception are fused, as they are in all our apprehensions of beauty, our best contacts with life. It is an act, not of the Reason, but of the whole personality working under the stimulus of mystic love. Hence, its results feed every aspect of that personality: minister to its instinct for the Good the Beautiful, and the True. Psychologically it is an induced state, in which the field of consciousness is greatly contracted: the whole of the self, its conative powers, being sharply focussed, concentrated upon one thing. We pour ourselves out or, as it sometimes seems to us, in towards this over-powering interest: seem to ourselves to reach it and be merged with it. Whatever the thing may be, in this act it is given to us and we know it, as we cannot know it by the ordinary devices of thought.

The turning of our attention from that crisp and definite world of multiplicity, that cinematograph-show, with which intelligence is accustomed and able to deal, has loosed new powers of perception which we never knew that we possessed. Instead of sharply perceiving the fragment, we apprehend, yet how we know not, the solemn presence of the whole. Deeper levels of personality are opened up, and go gladly to the encounter of the universe. That universe, or some Reality hid between it and ourselves, responds to "the true lovely will of our heart." Our ingoing concentration is balanced by a great outgoing sense of expansion, of new worlds made ours, as we receive the inflow of its life. So complete is the self's absorption that it is for the time unconscious of any acts of mind or will; in technical language, its "faculties are suspended." This is the "ligature" frequently mentioned by teachers of contemplative prayer, and often regarded as an essential character of mystical states.

Delacroix has described with great subtlety the psychological character of pure contemplation.

"When contemplation appears," he says: "(a) It produces a general condition of indifference, liberty, and peace, an elevation above the world, a sense of beatitude. The Subject ceases to perceive himself in the multiplicity and division of his general consciousness. He is raised above himself. A deeper and a purer soul substitutes itself for the normal self. (b) In this state, in which consciousness of I-hood and consciousness of the world disappear, the mystic is conscious of being in immediate relation with God Himself: of participating in Divinity. Contemplation installs a method of being and of knowing. Moreover, these two things tend at bottom to become one. The mystic has more and more the impression of being that which he knows, and of knowing that which he is." [684] Temporally rising, in fact, to levels of freedom, he knows himself real, and therefore knows Reality.

Now, the object of the mystic's contemplation is always some aspect of the Infinite Life: of "God, the one Reality." Hence, that enhancement of vitality which artists or other unselfconscious observers may receive from their communion with scattered manifestations of Goodness, Truth, and Beauty, is in him infinitely increased. His uniformly rapturous language is alone enough to prove this. In the contemplative act, his whole personality, directed by love and will, transcends the sense-world, casts off its fetters, and rises to freedom: becoming operative on those high levels where, says Tauler, "reason cannot come." There it apprehends the supra-sensible by immediate contact, and knows itself to be in the presence of the "Supplier of true Life." Such Contemplation--such positive attainment of the Absolute--is the whole act of which the visions of poets, the intuition of philosophers, give us hints.

It is a brief act. The greatest of the contemplatives have been unable to sustain the brilliance of this awful vision for more than a little while. "A flash," "an instant," "the space of an Ave Maria," they say. "My mind," says St. Augustine, in his account of his first purely contemplative glimpse of the One Reality, "withdrew its thoughts from experience, extracting itself from the contradictory throng of sensuous images, that it might find out what that light was wherein it was bathed. . . . And thus with the flash of one hurried glance, it attained to the vision of That Which Is. And then at last I saw Thy invisible things understood by means of the things that are made, but I could not sustain my gaze: my weakness was dashed back, and I was relegated to my ordinary experience, bearing with me only a loving memory, and as it were the fragrance of those desirable meats on the which as yet I was not able to feed." [685]

This fragrance, as St. Augustine calls it, remains for ever with those who have thus been initiated, if only for a moment, into the atmosphere of the Real: and this--the immortal and indescribable memory of their communion with That Which Is--gives to their work the perfume of the "Inviolate Rose," and is the secret of its magic power. But they can never tell us in exact and human language what it was that they attained in their ecstatic flights towards the thought of God: their momentary mergence in the Absolute Life.

"That Which Is," says St. Augustine; "The One," "the Supplier of true Life," says Plotinus; "the energetic Word," says St. Bernard; "Eternal Light," says Dante; "the Abyss," says Ruysbroeck; "Pure Love," says St. Catherine of Genoa--Poor symbols of Perfection at the best. But, through and by these oblique utterances, they give us the assurance that the Object of their discovery is one with the object of our quest.

William James considered "ineffability" and "noetic quality" to be the constant characteristics of the contemplative experience. [686] Those who have seen are quite convinced: those who have not seen, can never be told. There is no certitude to equal the mystic's certitude: no impotence more complete than that which falls on those who try to communicate it. "Of these most excellent and divine workings in the soul, when God doth manifest Himself," says Angela of Foligno, "we can in no wise speak, or even stammer." [687] Nevertheless, the greater part of mystical literature is concerned with the attempts of the mystics to share their discoveries. Under a variety of images, by a deliberate exploitation of the musical and suggestive qualities of words--often, too, by the help of desperate paradoxes, those unfailing stimulants of man's intuitive power--they try to tell others somewhat of that veritable country which "eye hath not seen." Their success--partial though it be--can only be accounted for upon the supposition that somewhere within us lurks a faculty, a spark, a "fine point of spirit" which has known this country from its birth; which dwells in it, partakes of Pure Being, and can under certain conditions be stung to consciousness. Then "transcendental feeling," waking from its sleep, acknowledges that these explorers of the Infinite have really gazed upon the secret plan.

Contemplation is not, like meditation, one simple state, governed by one set of psychic conditions. It is a general name for a large group of states, partly governed--like all other forms of mystical activity--by the temperament of the subject, and accompanied by feeling-states which vary from the extreme of quietude or "peace in life naughted" to the rapturous and active love in which "thought into song is turned." Some kinds of Contemplation are inextricably entwined with the phenomena of "intellectual vision" and "inward voices." In others we find what seems to be a development of the "Quiet": a state which the subject describes as a blank absorption, a darkness, or "contemplation in caligine." [688] Sometimes the contemplative tells us that he passes through this darkness to the light: [689] sometimes it seems to him that he stays for ever in the "beneficent dark." [690] In some cases the soul says that even in the depths of her absorption, she "knows her own bliss": in others she only becomes aware of it when contemplation is over and the surface-intelligence reassumes the reins.

In this welter of personal experiences, it becomes necessary to adopt some basis of classification, some rule by which to distinguish true Contemplation from other introversive states. Such a basis is not easy to find. I think, however, that there are two marks of the real condition: (A) The Totality and Givenness of the Object. (B) Self-Mergence of the subject. These we may safely use in our attempt to determine its character.

(A) Whatever terms he may employ to describe it, and however faint or confused his perceptions may be, the mystic's experience in Contemplation is the experience of the All, and this experience seems to him to be given rather than attained. It is indeed the Absolute which is revealed to him: not, as in meditation or vision, some partial symbol or aspect thereof.

(B) This revealed Reality is apprehended by way of participation, not by way of observation. The passive receptivity of the Quiet is here developed into an active, outgoing self-donation, which is the self's response to the Divine initiative. By a free act, independent of man's effort, God is self-disclosed to the soul; and that soul rushes out willingly to lose itself in Him. Thus a "give and take"--a divine osmosis--is set up between the finite and the Infinite life. That dreadful consciousness of a narrow and limiting I-hood which dogs our search for freedom and full life, is done away. For a moment, at least, the independent spiritual life is achieved. The contemplative is merged in it "like a bird in the air, like a fish in the sea": loses to find and dies to live.

"We must," says Dionysius the Areopagite, "be transported wholly out of ourselves and given unto God." [691] This is the "passive union" of Contemplation: a temporary condition in which the subject receives a double conviction of ineffable happiness and ultimate reality. He may try to translate this conviction into "something said" or "something seen": but in the end he will be found to confess that he can tell nothing, save by implication. The essential fact is that he was there: as the essential fact for the returning exile is neither landscape nor language, but the homely spirit of place.

"To see and to have seen that Vision," says Plotinus in one of his finest passages, "is reason no longer. It is more than reason, before reason, and after reason, as also is the vision which is seen. . . . And perhaps we should not here speak of sight: for that which is seen is not discerned by the seer--if indeed it is possible here to distinguish seer and seen as separate things. . . .Therefore this vision is hard to tell of: for how can a man describe as other than himself that which, when he discerned it, seemed not other, but one with himself indeed?" [692]

Ruysbroeck, who continued in the mediaeval world the best traditions of Neoplatonic mysticism, also describes a condition of supreme insight, a vision of Truth, which is closely related to the Plotinian ecstasy. "Contemplation," he says, "places us in a purity and a radiance which is far above our understanding . . . and none can attain to it by knowledge, by subtlety, or by any exercise whatsoever: but he whom God chooses to unite to Himself, and to illuminate by Himself, he and no other can contemplate God. . . . But few men attain to this divine contemplation, because of our incapacity and of the hiddenness of that light in which one sees. And this is why none by his own knowledge, or by subtle consideration, will ever really understand these things. For all words and all that one can learn or understand in a creaturely way, are foreign to the truth that I mean and far below it. But he who is united to God, and illumined by this truth--he can understand Truth by Truth. [693]

This final, satisfying knowledge of reality--this understanding of Truth by Truth--is, at bottom, that which all men desire. The saint's thirst for God, the philosopher's passion for the Absolute; these are nothing else than the crying need of the spirit, variously expressed by the intellect and by the heart. The guesses of science, the diagrams of metaphysics, the intuitions of artists; all are pressing towards this. "Adam sinned when he fell from Contemplation. Since then, there has been division in man." [694]

Man's soul, says Hilton, "Feeleth well that there is somewhat above itself that it knoweth not nor hath not yet, but it would have it, and burningly yearneth for it. And that is nought else but the sight of Jerusalem without-forth, the which is like to a city that the prophet Ezechiel saw in his visions.

"He saith that he saw a city set upon an hill sloping to the south, that to his sight when it was measured was no more of length and of breadth than a rood, that was six cubits and a palm of length; but as soon as he was brought into the city and looked about him, then thought him that it was wonder mickle, for he saw many halls and chambers both open and privy, he saw gates and porches, outward and inward, and mickle more building than I say now, on length and on breadth many hundred cubits. Then was this wonder to him, how this city within was so long and so large, that was so little to his sight when he was without. This city betokeneth the perfect love of God, set in the hill of contemplation; the which unto the sight of a soul that is without the feeling of it and travaileth in desire toward, seemeth somewhat, but it seemeth but a little thing, no more than a rood, that is six cubits and a palm in length. By six cubits is understood the perfection of man's work, by the palm a little touching of contemplation. He seeth well that there is such a thing, that passeth the desert of all working of man a little, as the palm passeth over the six cubits, but he seeth not within what that is. Nevertheless, if he may come within the city of contemplation, then seeth he mickle more than he saw first." [695]

As in the case of vision, so here, all that we who "without the feeling travail in desire" can really know concerning Contemplation--its value for life, the knowledge it confers--must come from those who have "come within the city": have, in the metaphor of Plotinus, "taken flight towards the Thought of God." What, in effect, can they tell us about the knowledge of reality which they attained in that brief communion with the Absolute?

They tell us chiefly, when we come to collate their evidence, two apparently contradictory things. They speak, almost in the Same breath, of an exceeding joy, a Beatific Vision, an intense communion, and a "loving sight": and of an exceeding emptiness, a barren desert, an unfathomable Abyss, a nescience, a Divine Dark. Again and again these pairs of opposites occur in all first-hand descriptions of pure contemplation: Remoteness and Intimacy, Darkness and Light. Bearing in mind that these four metaphors all describe the same process seen "through a temperament," and represent the reaction of that temperament upon Absolute Reality, we may perhaps by their comparison obtain some faint idea of the totality of that indescribable experience at which they hint.

Note first that the emotional accompaniments of his perceptions will always and necessarily be the stuff from which the mystic draws suggestive language, by which to hint at his experience of supernal things. His descriptions will always lean to the impressionistic rather than to the scientific side. The "deep yet dazzling darkness," the "unfathomable abyss," the Cloud of Unknowing, the "embrace of the Beloved," all represent, not the Transcendent but his relation with the Transcendent; not an object observed, but an overwhelming impression felt, by the totality of his being during his communion with a Reality which is One.

It is not fair, however, to regard Contemplation on this account as pre-eminently a "feeling state"; and hence attribute to it, as many modern writers do, a merely subjective validity. It is of course accompanied, as all humanity's supreme and vital acts are accompanied, by feeling of an exalted kind: and since such emotions are the least abnormal part of it, they are the part which the subject finds easiest to describe. These elusive combinations of Fear, Amazement, Desire, and Joy are more or less familiar to him. The accidents of sensual life have developed them. His language contains words which are capable of suggesting them to other men. But his total experience transcends mere feeling, just as it transcends mere intellect. It is a complete act of perception, inexpressible by these departmental words: and its agent is the whole man, the indivisible personality whose powers and nature are only partially hinted at in such words as Love, Thought, or Will.

The plane of consciousness, however--the objective somewhat--of which this personality becomes aware in contemplation, is not familiar to it; neither is it related to its systems of thought. Man, accustomed to dwell amongst spatial images adapted to the needs of daily life, has no language that will fit it. So, a person hearing for the first time some masterpiece of classical music, would have no language in which to describe it objectively; but could only tell us how it made him feel. This is one reason why feeling-states seem to preponderate in all descriptions of the mystic act. Earthly emotions provide a parallel which enables the subject to tell us by implication something of that which he felt: but he cannot describe to us--for want of standards of comparison--that Wholly Other which induced him thus to feel. His best efforts to fit words to this elusive but objective experience generally result in the evaporation alike of its fragrance and of its truth. As St. Augustine said of Time, he knows what it is until he is asked to define it.

How symbolic and temperamental is all verbal description of mystical activity, may be seen by the aspect which contemplation took in the music-loving soul of Richard Rolle; who always found his closest parallels with Reality, not in the concepts of intimate union, or of self-loss in the Divine Abyss, but in the idea of the soul's participation in a supernal harmony--that sweet minstrelsy of God in which "thought into song is turned." "To me," he says, "it seems that contemplation is joyful song of God's love taken in mind, with sweetness of angels' praise. This is jubilation, that is the end of perfect prayer and high devotion in this life. This is that mirth in mind, had ghostily by the lover everlastingly, with great voice outbreaking. . . . Contemplative sweetness not without full great labour is gotten, and with joy untold it is possessed. Forsooth, it is not man's merit but God's gift; and yet from the beginning to this day never might man be ravished in contemplation of Love Everlasting, but if he before parfitely all the world's vanity had forsaken." [696]

We must, then, be prepared to accept, sift, and use many different descriptions of evoked emotion in the course of our inquiry into the nature of the contemplative's perceptions of the Absolute. We find on analysis that these evoked emotions separate themselves easily into two groups. Further, these two groups answer to the two directions in which the mystic consciousness of Reality is extended, and to the pairs of descriptions of the Godhead which we have found to be characteristic of mystical literature: i.e. , the personal and spatial, immanental and transcendental, indwelling Life and Unconditioned Source; (a) the strange, dark, unfathomable Abyss of Pure Being always dwelt upon by mystics of the metaphysical type, and (b) the divine and loved Companion of the soul, whose presence is so sharply felt by those selves which lean to the concept of Divine Personality.

A. The Contemplation of Transcendence.-- The first group of feeling-states, allied to those which emphasize the theological idea of Divine Transcendence, is born of the mystic's sense of his own littleness, unworthiness, and incurable ignorance in comparison with the ineffable greatness of the Absolute Godhead which he has perceived, and in which he desires to lose himself; of the total and incommunicable difference in kind between the Divine and everything else. Awe and self-abasement, and the paradoxical passion for self-loss in the All, here govern his emotional state. All affirmative statements seem to him blasphemous, so far are they from an ineffable truth which is "more than reason, before reason, and after reason." To this group of feelings, which usually go with an instinctive taste for Neoplatonism, an iconoclastic distrust of personal imagery, we owe all negative descriptions of supreme Reality. For this type of self, God is the Unconditioned, the Wholly Other for whom we have no words, and whom all our poor symbols insult. To see Him is to enter the Darkness, the "Cloud of Unknowing," and "know only that we know nought." Nothing else can satisfy this extreme spiritual humility; which easily degenerates into that subtle form of pride which refuses to acquiesce in the limitations of its own creaturely state.

"There is none other God but He that none may know, which may not be known," says this contemplative soul. "No, soothly no! Without fail, No, says she. He only is my God that none can one word of say, nor all they of Paradise one only point attain nor understand, for all the knowing that they have of Him." [697]

When they try to be geographically exact, to define and describe their apprehension of, and contact with, the Unconditioned One who is the only Country of the Soul, contemplatives of this type become, like their great master the Areopagite, impersonal and remote. They seem to have been caught up to some measureless height, where the air is too rarefied for the lungs of common men. When we ask them the nature of the life on these summits, they are compelled as a rule to adopt the Dionysian concept of Divine Darkness, or the parallel idea of the fathomless Abyss, the Desert of the Godhead, the Eckhartian "still wilderness where no one is at home."

Oddly enough, it is in their language concerning this place or plane of reality, in which union with the Super-essential Godhead takes place--this "lightsome darkness and rich nought"--that they come nearer to distinct affirmation, and consequently offer more surprises to sentimental and anthropomorphic piety, than in any other department of their work. Unquestionably this language, with its constant reference to a "still desert," a "vast sea," an "unplumbed abyss" in which the "emptiness," the "nothing," the "Dark" on which the self entered in the Orison of Quiet is infinitely increased, yet positive satisfaction is at last attained, does correspond with a definite psychological experience. It is not merely the convention of a school. These descriptions, incoherent as they are, have a strange note of certainty, a stranger note of passion, an odd realism of their own: which mean, wherever we meet them, that experience not tradition is their source. Driven of necessity to a negation of all that their surface-minds have ever known--with language, strained to the uttermost, failing them at every turn--these contemplatives are still able to communicate to us a definite somewhat; news as to a given and actual Reality, an unchanging Absolute, and a beatific union with it, most veritably attained. They agree in their accounts of it, in a way which makes it obvious that all these reporters have sojourned in the same land, and experienced the same spiritual state. Moreover, our inmost minds bear witness for them. We meet them half-way. We know instinctively and irrefutably that they tell true; and they rouse in us a passionate nostalgia, a bitter sense of exile and of loss.

One and all, these explorers of the Infinite fly to language expressive of great and boundless spaces. In their withdrawal from the busy, fretful sense-world they have sunk down to the "ground" of the soul and of the apparent universe: Being, the Substance of all that Is. Multiplicity is resolved into Unity: a unity with which the perceiving self is merged. Thus the mystic, for the time of this "union with the Divine," does find himself, in Tauler's words, to be "simply in God."

"The great wastes to be found in this divine ground," says that great master, "have neither image nor form nor condition, for they are neither here nor there. They are like unto a fathomless Abyss, bottomless and floating in itself. Even as water ebbs and flows, up and down; now sinking into a hollow, so that it looks as if there were no water there, and then again in a little while rushing forth as if it would engulf everything, so does it come to pass in this Abyss. This, truly, is much more God's Dwelling-place than heaven or man. A man who verily desires to enter will surely find God here, and himself simply in God; for God never separates Himself from this ground. God will be present with him, and he will find and enjoy Eternity here. There is no past nor present here, and no created light can reach unto or shine into this divine Ground; for here only is the dwelling-place of God and His sanctuary.

"Now this Divine Abyss can be fathomed by no creatures; it can be filled by none, and it satisfies none, God only can fill it in His Infinity. For this abyss belongs only to the Divine Abyss of which it is written: Abysses abyssum invocal . He who is truly conscious of this ground, which shone into the powers of his soul, and lighted and inclined its lowest and highest powers to turn to their pure Source and true Origin, must diligently examine himself, and remain alone, listening to the voice which cries in the wilderness of this ground. This ground is so desert and bare that no thought has ever entered there.

None of all the thoughts of man which, with the help of reason, have been devoted to meditation on the Holy Trinity (and some men have occupied themselves much with these thoughts) have ever entered this ground. For it is so close and yet so far off, and so far beyond all things, that it has neither time nor place. It is a simple and unchanging condition. A man who really and truly enters, feels as though he had been here throughout eternity, and as though he were one therewith." [698]

Many other mystics have written to the same effect: have described with splendour the ineffable joys and terrors of the Abyss of Being "where man existed in God from all Eternity," the soul's adventures when, "stripped of its very life," it "sails the wild billows of the sea divine." But their words merely amaze the outsider and give him little information. The contemplative self who has attained this strange country can only tell an astonished and incredulous world that here his greatest deprivation is also his greatest joy; that here the extremes of possession and surrender are the same, that ignorance and knowledge, light and dark, are One. Love has led him into that timeless, spaceless world of Being which is the peaceful ground, not only of the individual striving spirit, but also of the striving universe; and he can but cry with Philip, " It is enough."

"Here," says Maeterlinck, "we stand suddenly at the confines of human thought, and far beyond the Polar circle of the mind. It is intensely cold here; it is intensely dark, and yet you will find nothing but flames and light. But to those who come without having trained their souls to these new perceptions, this light and these flames are as dark and as cold as if they were painted. Here we are concerned with the most exact of sciences: with the exploration of the harshest and most uninhabitable headlands of the divine Know thyself': and the midnight sun reigns over that rolling sea where the psychology of man mingles with the psychology of God." [699]

On one hand "flames and light"--the flame of living and creative love which fills the universe--on the other the "quiet desert of Godhead," transcending all succession and dark to the single sight of earth-born men. Under these two metaphors, one affirmative, one negative, resumed in his most daring paradox nearly the whole of man's contemplative experience of the Absolute can be and is expressed. We have considered his negative description of Utmost Transcendence: that confession of "divine ignorance" which is a higher form of knowledge. But this is balanced, in a few elect spirits, by a positive contemplation of truth; an ecstatic apprehension of the "secret plan."

Certain rare mystics seem able to describe to us a Beatific Vision experienced here and now: a knowledge by contact of the flaming heart of Reality, which includes in one great whole the planes of Being and Becoming, the Simultaneous and the Successive, the Eternal Father, and His manifestation in the "energetic Word." We saw something of this power, which is characteristic of mystical genius of a high order, in studying the characteristics of Illumination. Its finest literary expression is found in that passage of the "Paradiso" where Dante tells us how he pierced, for an instant, the secret of the Empyrean. Already he had enjoyed a symbolic vision of two-fold Reality as the moving River of Light and the still white Rose. [700] Now these two aspects vanished, and he saw the One.

". . . la mia vista, venendo sincera
e più e più entrava per lo raggio
dell' alta luce, che da sè è vera.
Da quinci innanzi il mio veder fu maggio
che il parlar nostro ch' a tal vista cede,
e cede la memoria a tanto oltraggio.
Qual è colui che somniando vede,
chè dopo il sogno la passione impressa
rimane, e l' altro alla mente non riede;
cotal son io, che quasi tutta cessa
mia visione, ed ancor mi distilla
nel cor lo dolce che nacque da essa.
. . . .
Io credo, per l' acume ch' io soffersi
del vivo raggio, ch' io sarei smarrito,
se gli occhi miei da lui fossero aversi.
E mi ricorda ch' io fui più ardito
per questo a sostener tanto ch' io giunsi
l' aspetto mio col valor infinito.
Cosi la mente mia, tutta sospesa,
mirava fissa, immobile ed attenta,
e sempre del mirar faceasi accesa.
A quella luce cotal si diventa,
che volgersi da lei per altro aspetto
è impossibil che mai si consenta.

Però che il Ben, ch' è del volere obbietto,
tutto s'accoglie in lei, e fuor di quella
è difettivo cio che lì è perfetto." [701]

Intermediate between the Dantesque apprehension of Eternal Reality and the contemplative communion with Divine Personality, is the type of mystic whose perceptions of the suprasensible are neither wholly personal nor wholly cosmic and transcendental in type. To him, God is pre-eminently the Perfect--Goodness, Truth, and Beauty, Light, Life, and Love--discovered in a moment of lucidity at the very door of the seeking self. Here the symbols under which He is perceived are still the abstractions of philosophy; but in the hands of the mystic these terms cease to be abstract, are stung to life. Such contemplatives preserve the imageless and ineffable character of the Absolute, but are moved by its contemplation to a joyous and personal love.

Thus, in a striking passage of her revelations, Angela of Foligno suddenly exclaims, "I saw God!" "And I, the writing brother," says her secretary, "asked her what she saw, how she saw, and if she saw any bodily thing. She replied thus: I beheld a fullness and a clearness, and felt them within me so abundantly that I cannot describe it, or give any likeness thereof. I cannot say I saw anything corporeal. It was as though it were in heaven: a beauty so great that I can say nought concerning it, save that it was supreme Beauty and sovereign Good.'" Again, "I beheld the ineffable fullness of God: but I can relate nothing of it, save that I have seen in it the Sovereign Good." [702]

B. The Contemplation of Immanence.-- The second group of contemplatives is governed by that "Love which casteth out fear": by a predominating sense of the nearness, intimacy, and sweetness, rather than the strangeness and unattainable transcendence, of that same Infinite Life at whose being the first group could only hint by amazing images which seem to be borrowed from the poetry of metaphysics. These are, says Hilton, in a lovely image, "Feelingly fed with the savour of His invisible blessed Face." [703] All the feelings which flow from joy, confidence, and affection, rather than those which are grouped about rapture and awe--though awe is always present in some measure, as it is always present in all perfect love--here contribute towards a description of the Truth.

These contemplatives tell us of their attainment of That which Is, as the closest and most joyous of all communions; a coming of the Bridegroom; a rapturous immersion in the Uncreated Light. "Nothing more profitable, nothing merrier than grace of contemplation!" cries Rolle, "that lifts us from this low and offers to God. What is grace of contemplation but beginning of joy? what is parfiteness of joy but grace confirmed? [704] In such "bright contemplation" as this, says "The Mirror of Simple Souls," "the soul is full gladsome and jolly." Utter peace and wild delight, every pleasure-state known to man's normal consciousness, are inadequate to the description of her joy. She has participated for an instant in the Divine Life; knows all, and knows nought. She has learnt the world's secret, not by knowing, but by being: the only way of really knowing anything.

Where the dominant emotion is that of intimate affection, and where the training or disposition of the mystic inclines him to emphasize the personal and Incarnational rather than the abstract and Trinitarian side of Christianity, the contemplative of this type will always tend to describe his secret to us as above all things an experience of adorable Friendship. Reality is for him a Person, not a State. In the "orison of union" it seems to him that an actual communion, a merging of his self with this other and strictly personal Self takes place. "God," he says, then "meets the soul in her Ground": i.e. , in that secret depth of personality where she participates in the Absolute Life. Clearly, the "degree of contemplation," the psychological state, is here the same as that in which the mystic of the impersonal type attained the "Abyss." But from the point of view of the subject, this joyful and personal encounter of Lover and Beloved will be a very different experience from the soul's immersion in that "desert of Deity," as described by Eckhart and his school. "In this oning," says Hilton, "is the marriage made betwixt God and the soul, that shall never be broken." [705]

St. Teresa is the classic example of this intimate and affective type of contemplation: but St. Gertrude, Suso, Julian, Mechthild of Magdeburg, and countless others, provide instances of its operation. We owe to it all the most beautiful and touching expressions of mystic love. Julian's "I saw Him and sought Him: and I had Him, I wanted Him" expresses in epigram its combination of rapturous attainment and insatiable desire: its apprehension of a Presence at once friendly and divine. So too does her description of the Tenth Revelation of Love, when "with this sweet enjoying He showed unto mine understanding in part the blessed Godhead, stirring then the poor soul to understand, as it may be said; that is, to think on the endless Love that was without beginning, and is, and shall be ever. And with this our good Lord said full blissfully, Lo, how that I loved thee, as if He had said, My darling, behold and see thy Lord, thy God that is thy Matter, and thine endless joy." [706]

"The eyes of her soul were opened," says the scribe to whom Angela of Foligno dictated her revelations. "And she saw Love advancing gently towards her; and she saw the beginning, but not the end, for it was continuous. And there was no colour to which she could compare this Love; but directly it reached her she beheld it with the eyes of the soul, more clearly than she might do with the eyes of the body, take as towards her the semblance of a sickle. Not that there was any actual and measurable likeness, but this love took on the semblance of a sickle, because it first withdrew itself, not giving itself so fully as it had allowed itself to be understood and she had understood it; the which caused her to yearn for it the more." [707]

It is to Mechthild of Magdeburg, whose contemplation was emphatically of the intimate type, that we owe the most perfect definition of this communion of the mystic with his Friend. "Orison," she says, "draws the great God down into the small heart: it drives the hungry soul out to the full God. It brings together the two lovers, God and the soul, into a joyful room where they speak much of love." [708]

We have already seen that the doctrine of the Trinity makes it possible for Christian mystics, and, still more, for Christian mysticism as a whole, to reconcile this way of apprehending Reality with the "negative" and impersonal perception of the ineffable One; the Absolute which "hath no image." Though they seem in their extreme forms to be so sharply opposed as to justify Eckhart's celebrated distinction between the unknowable totality of the Godhead and the knowable personality of God, the "image" and the "circle" yet represent diverse apprehensions of one whole. All the mystics feel--and the German school in particular have expressed--Dante's conviction that these two aspects of reality, these two planes of being, however widely they seem to differ, are One . [709] Both are ways of describing man's partial contacts with that Absolute Truth, "present yet absent, near, yet far," that Triune Fact, di tre colori e d' una continenza , which is God. Both are necessary if we are to form any idea of that complete Reality, imperfect as any such idea must be: as, when two men go together to some undiscovered country, one will bring home news of its great spaces, its beauty of landscape, another of its geological formation, or the flora and fauna that express its life, and both must be taken into account before any just estimate of the real country can be made.

Since it is of the essence of the Christian religion to combine personal and metaphysical truth, a transcendent and an incarnate God, [710] it is not surprising that we should find in Christianity a philosophic and theological basis for this paradox of the contemplative experience. Most often, though not always, the Christian mystic identifies the personal and intimate Lover of the soul, of whose elusive presence he is so sharply aware, with the person of Christ; the unknowable and transcendent Godhead with that eterna luce, the Undifferentiated One in Whom the Trinity of Persons is resumed. Temperamentally, most practical contemplatives lean to either one or other of these apprehensions of Reality: to a personal and immanental meeting in the "ground of the soul," or to the austere joys of the "naughted soul" abased before an impersonal Transcendence which no language but that of negation can define. In some, however, both types of perception seem to exist together: and they speak alternately of light and darkness, of the rapturous encounter with Love and of supreme self-loss in the naked Abyss, the desert of the Essence of God. Ruysbroeck is the perfect example of this type of contemplative; and his works contain numerous and valuable passages descriptive of that synthetic experience which resumes the personal and transcendental aspects of the mystic fact.

"When we have become seeing," he says--that is to say, when we have attained to spiritual lucidity--"we are able to contemplate in joy the eternal coming of the Bridegroom; and this is the second point on which I would speak. What, then, is this eternal coming of our Bridegroom? It is a perpetual new birth and a perpetual new illumination: for the ground whence the Light shines and which is Itself the Light, is life-giving and fruitful: and hence the manifestation of the Eternal Light is renewed without interruption in the hiddenness of the spirit. Behold! here all human works and active virtues must cease; for here God works alone at the apex of the soul. Here there is nought else but an eternal seeing and staring at that Light, by the Light and in the Light. And the coming of the Bridegroom is so swift, that He comes perpetually, and He dwells within us with His abysmal riches, and He returns to us anew in His Person without interruption; with such new radiance, that He seems never to have come to us before. For His coming consists, outside all Time, in an Eternal Now, always welcomed with new longing and new joy. Behold! the delights and the joys which this Bridegroom brings in His coming are fathomless and limitless, for they are Himself: and this is why the eyes by which the spirit contemplates the Bridegroom, are opened so widely that they can never close again. . . . Now this active meeting, and this loving embrace, are in their essence fruitive and unconditioned; for the infinite Undifferentiation of the Godhead is so dark and so naked of all image, that it conceals within itself all the divine qualities and works, all the attributes of the Persons, in the all-enfolding richness of the Essential Unity, and brings about a divine fruition in the Abyss of the Ineffable. And here there is a death in fruition, and a melting and dying into the nudity of Pure Being; where all the Names of God, and all conditions, and all the living images which are reflected in the mirror of divine truth, are absorbed into the Ineffable Simplicity, the Absence of image and of knowledge. For in this limitless Abyss of Simplicity, all things are embraced in the bliss of fruition; but the Abyss itself remains uncomprehended, except by the Essential Unity. The Persons and all that which lives in God, must give place to this. For there is nought else here but an eternal rest in the fruitive embrace of an outpouring love: and this is the wayless Being that all interior souls have chosen above all other things. This is the dim silence where all lovers lose themselves." [711]

Here Ruysbroeck, beginning with a symbol of the Divine Personality as Bridegroom of the Soul, which would have been congenial to the mind of St. Catherine of Siena, ends upon the summits of Christian metaphysics; with a description of the loving immersion of the self in that Unconditioned One who transcends the Persons of theology and beggars human speech. We seem to see him desperately clutching at words and similes which may, he hopes, give some hint of the soul's fruition of Reality: its immeasurable difference in kind from the dreams and diagrams of anthropomorphic religion. His strange statements in respect of this Divine Abyss are on a par with those which I have already quoted from the works of other contemplatives, who, refusing to be led away by the emotional aspect of their experience, have striven to tell us--as they thought--not merely what they felt but what they beheld. Ruysbroeck's mystical genius, however, the depth and wholeness of his intuition of Reality, does not allow him to be satisfied with a merely spatial or metaphysical description of the Godhead. The "active meeting" and the "loving embrace" are, he sees, an integral part of the true contemplative act. In "the dim silence where lovers lose themselves," a Person meets a person: and this it is, not the philosophic Absolute, which "all interior souls have chosen above all other thing."

We must now look more closely at the method by which the contemplative attains to his unique communion with the Absolute Life: the kind of activity which seems to him to characterize his mergence with Reality. As we might expect, that activity, like its result, is of two kinds; personal and affirmative, impersonal and negative. It is obvious that where Divine Perfection is conceived as the soul's companion, the Bridegroom, the Beloved, the method of approach will be very different from that which ends in the self's immersion in the paradoxical splendour of the Abyss, the "still wilderness where no one is at home." It is all the difference between the preparations for a wedding and for an expedition to the Arctic Seas. Hence we find, at one end of the scale, that extreme form of personal and intimate communion--the going forth of lover to beloved--which the mystics call "the orison of union": and at the other end, the "dark contemplation," by which alone selves of the transcendent and impersonal type claim that they draw near to the Unconditioned One.

Of the dim and ineffable contemplation of Unnameable Transcendence, the imageless absorption in the Absolute, Dionysius the Areopagite of course provides the classic example. It was he who gave to it the name of Divine Darkness: and all later mystics of this type borrow their language from him. His directions upon the subject are singularly explicit: his descriptions, like those of St. Augustine, glow with an exultant sense of a Reality attained, and which others may attain if they will but follow where he leads.

"As for thee, dear Timothy," he says, "I counsel that in the earnest exercise of mystical contemplation thou leave the senses and the operations of the intellect and all things that the senses or the intellect can perceive, and all things in this world of nothingness or that world of being; and that, thine understanding being laid to rest, thou ascend (so far as thou mayest) towards union with Him whom neither being nor understanding can contain. For by the unceasing and absolute renunciation of thyself and all things, thou shalt in pureness cast all things aside, and be released from all, and so shalt be led upwards to the Ray of that Divine Darkness which exceetedth all existence." [712] Again, "The Divine Dark is nought else but that inaccessible light wherein the Lord is said to dwell. Although it is invisible because of its dazzling splendours and unsearchable because of the abundance of its supernatural brightness, nevertheless, whosoever deserves to see and know God rests therein: and, by the very fact that he neither sees nor knows, is truly in that which surpasses all truth and all knowledge."[713]

It has become a commonplace with writers on mysticism to say, that all subsequent contemplatives took from Dionysius this idea of "Divine Darkness," and entrance therein as the soul's highest privilege: took it, so to speak, ready-made and on faith, and incorporated it in their tradition. To argue thus is to forget that mystics are above all things practical people. They do not write for the purpose of handing on a philosophical scheme, but in order to describe something which they have themselves experienced: something which they feel to be of transcendent importance for humanity. If, therefore, they persist--and they do persist--in using this simile of "darkness" to describe their experience in contemplation, it can only be because it fits the facts. No Hegelian needs to be told that we shall need the addition of its opposite before we can hope to approach the truth: and it is exactly the opposite of this "dim ignorance" which is offered us by mystics of the "joyous" or "intimate" type, who find their supreme satisfaction in the positive experience of "union," the "mystical marriage of the soul."

What, then, do those who use this image of the "dark" really mean by it? They mean this: that God in His absolute Reality is unknowable--is dark--to man's intellect: which is, as Bergson has reminded us, adapted to other purposes than those of divine intuition. When, under the spur of mystic love, the whole personality of man comes into contact with that Reality, it enters a plane of experience to which none of the categories of the intellect apply. Reason finds itself, in a most actual sense, "in the dark"--immersed in the Cloud of Unknowing. This dimness and lostness of the mind, then, is a necessary part of the mystic's ascent to the Absolute. That Absolute--the Mysterium tremendum et fascinans [714] --willnot be "known of the heart" until we acknowledge that It is "unknown of the intellect"; and obey the Dionysian injunction to leave "the operations of the understanding" on one side. The movement of the contemplative must be a movement of the whole man: he is to "precipitate himself, free and unfettered," into the bosom of Reality. Only when he has thus transcended sight and knowledge, can he be sure that he has also transcended the world with which these faculties are competent to deal; and is in that Wholly Other which surpasses all image and all idea.

"This is Love: to fly heavenward,
To rend, every instant, a hundred veils,
The first moment, to renounce life;
The last step, to fare without feet.
To regard this world as invisible,
Not to see what appears to oneself." [715]

This acknowledgment of our intellectual ignorance, this humble surrender, is the entrance into the "Cloud of Unknowing": the first step towards mystical knowledge of the Absolute. "For Truth and Humility are full true sisters," says Hilton, "fastened together in love and charity, and there is no distance of counsel betwixt them two." [716]

"Thou askest me and sayest," says the author of "The Cloud of Unknowing," "How shall I think on Himself and what is He? and to this I cannot answer thee but thus: I wot not.

"For thou hast brought me with thy question, into that same darkness and into that same cloud of unknowing that I would thou wert in thyself. For of all other creatures and their works, yea and of the works of God's self may a man through grace have fulhead of knowledge, and well he can think of them; but of God Himself can no man think. And therefore I will leave all that thing that I can think, and choose to my love that thing that I cannot think. For why; He may well be loved, but not thought. By love may He be gotten and holden, but by thought never. . . . Smite upon that thick cloud of unknowing with a sharp dart of longing love; and go not thence for thing that befalleth." [717]

So long, therefore, as the object of the mystic's contemplation is amenable to thought, is something which he can "know," he may be quite sure that it is not the Absolute; but only a partial image or symbol of the Absolute. To find that final Reality, he must enter into the "cloud of unknowing"--must pass beyond the plane on which the intellect can work.

"When I say darkness," says the same great mystic, "I mean thereby a lack of knowing. . . . And for this reason it is not called a cloud of the air, but a cloud of unknowing, that is between thee and thy God." [718]

The business of the contemplative, then, is to enter this cloud: the "good dark," as Hilton calls it. The deliberate inhibition of discursive thought and rejection of images, which takes place in the "orison of quiet," is one of the ways in which this entrance is effected: personal surrender, or "self-naughting," is another. He who, by dint of detachment and introversion, enters the "nothingness" or "ground of the soul," enters also into the "Dark": a statement which seems simple enough until we try to realize what it means.

"O where," says the bewildered disciple in one of Boehme's dialogues, "is this naked Ground of the Soul void of all Self? And how shall I come at the hidden centre, where God dwelleth and not man? Tell me plainly, loving Sir, where it is, and how it is to be found of me, and entered into?

"Master. There where the soul hath slain its own Will and willeth no more any Thing as from itself. . . .

"Disciple. But how shall I comprehend it?

"Master. If thou goest about to comprehend it, then it will fly away from thee, but if thou dost surrender thyself wholly up to it, then it will abide with thee, and become the Life of thy Life, and be natural to thee." [719]

The author of "The Cloud of Unknowing" is particularly explicit as to the sense of dimness and confusion which overwhelms the self when it first enters this Dark; a proceeding which is analogous to that annihilation of thought in the interests of passive receptivity which we have studied in the "Quiet."

"At the first time when thou dost it," he says of the neophyte's first vague steps in contemplation, "thou findest but a darkness, and as it were a cloud of unknowing thou knowest not what, saving that thou feelest in thy will a naked intent unto God. This darkness and this cloud is, howsoever thou dost, betwixt thee and thy God, and letteth thee, that thou mayest neither see Him clearly by light of understanding in thy reason, nor feel Him in sweetness of love in thine affection. And therefore shape thee to bide in this darkness as long as thou mayest, evermore crying after Him that thou lovest. For if ever thou shalt feel Him or see Him as it may be here, it behoveth always to be in this cloud and this darkness." [720]

From the same century, but from a very different country and temperament, comes another testimony as to the supreme value of this dark contemplation of the Divine: this absorption, beyond the span of thought or emotion, in the "substance of all that Is." It is one of the most vivid and detailed accounts of this strange form of consciousness which we possess; and deserves to be compared carefully with the statements of "The Cloud of Unknowing," and of St. John of the Cross. We owe it to that remarkable personality, the Blessed Angela of Foligno, who was converted from a life of worldliness to become not only a Franciscan, but also a Platonic mystic. In it we seem to hear the voice of Plotinus speaking from the Vale of Spoleto.

"Whilst I was questioning her," says her secretary, "Christ's faithful one was suddenly rapt in spirit and seemed not to understand my words. And then was given her a wondrous grace. After a short time . . . she began to tell me what follows. My soul has just been rapt to a state in which I tasted unspeakable joy. I knew all I longed to know, possessed all I longed to possess. I saw all Good.' She said further: In this state the soul cannot believe that this Good will ever depart from her, or that she will depart from it, or that she will again be separated from it. But she delights herself in that Sovereign Good. My soul sees nothing whatever that can be told of the lips or the heart, she sees nothing, and she sees All . . . No good that can be described or conceived is now the object of my hope; for I have put all my hope in a secret Good, most hid and secret, which I apprehend in great darkness.' And as I, the brother, could not receive or understand this dark, Christ's faithful one wishing to explain said: If I see it in the dark, it is because it surpasses all good. All, all the rest is but darkness. All which the soul or heart can reach is inferior to this Good. That which I have told hitherto, namely, all the soul grasps when she sees all creatures filled with God, when she sees the divine power, and when she sees the divine will, is inferior to this most secret Good; because this Good which I see in the darkness is the All, and all other things are but parts.' And she added, Though inexpressible, these other things bring delight; but this vision of God in darkness brings no smile to the lips, no devotion or fervour of love to the soul. . . . All the countless and unspeakable favours God has done to me, all the words He has said to me, all you have written are, I know, so far below the Good I see in that great darkness that I do not put in them my hope' . . . Christ's faithful one told me that her mind had been uplifted but three times to this most high and ineffable mode of beholding God in great darkness, and in a vision so marvellous and complete. Certainly she had seen the Sovereign Good countless times and always darkly; yet never in such a high manner and through such great dark." [721]

These words, and indeed the whole idea which lies at the bottom of "dark contemplation," will perhaps be better understood in the light of Baron von Hügel's deeply significant saying "Souls loving God in His Infinite Individuality will necessarily love Him beyond their intellectual comprehension of Him: the element of devoted trust, of free self-donation to One fully known only through and in such an act, will thus remain to man for ever." [722] Hence, the contemplative act, which is an act of loving and self-forgetting concentration upon the Divine--the outpouring of man's little and finite personality towards the Absolute Personality of God--will, in so far as it transcends thought, mean darkness for the intellect; but it may mean radiance for the heart. Psychologically, it will mean the necessary depletion of the surface-consciousness, the stilling of the mechanism of thought, in the interests of another centre of consciousness. Since this new centre makes enormous demands on the self's stock of vitality its establishment must involve, for the time that it is active, the withdrawal of energy from other centres. Thus the "night of thought" becomes the strictly logical corollary of the "light of perception."

No one has expressed this double character of the Divine Dark--its "nothingness" for the dissecting knife of reason, its supreme fruitfulness for expansive, active love--with so delicate an insight as St. John of the Cross. In his work the Christian touch of personal rapture vivifies the exact and sometimes arid descriptions of the Neoplatonic mystics. A great poet as well as a great mystic, in his poem on the "Obscure Night," he brings to bear on the actual and ineffable experience of the introverted soul all the highest powers of artistic expression, all the resources of musical rhythm, the suggestive qualities of metaphor.

"Upon an obscure night
Fevered with Love's anxiety
(O hapless, happy plight!)
I went, none seeing me,
Forth from my house, where all things quiet be.
By night, secure from sight
And by a secret stair, disguisedly,
(O hapless, happy plight!)
By night, and privily
Forth from my house, where all things quiet be.
Blest night of wandering
In secret, when by none might I be spied,
Nor I see anything:
Without a light to guide
Save that which in my heart burnt in my side.

That light did lead me on,
More surely than the shining of noontide
Where well I knew that One
Did for my coming bide;
Where He abode might none but He abide.
O night that didst lead thus
O night more lovely than the dawn of light;
O night that broughtest us,
Lover to lover's sight,
Lover to loved, in marriage of delight!
Upon my flowery breast
Wholly for Him and save Himself for none,
There did I give sweet rest
To my beloved one:
The fanning of the cedars breathed thereon." [723]

Observe in these verses the perfect fusion of personal and metaphysical imagery; each contributing by its suggestive qualities to a total effect which conveys to us, we hardly know how, the obscure yet flaming rapture of the mystic, the affirmation of his burning love and the accompanying negation of his mental darkness and quiet--that "hapless, happy plight." All is here: the secrecy of the contemplative's true life, unseen of other men his deliberate and active abandonment of the comfortable house of the senses, the dim, unknown plane of being into which his ardent spirit must plunge--a "night more lovely than the dawn of light"--the Inward Light, the fire of mystic love, which guides his footsteps "more surely than the shining of noon-tide": the self-giving ecstasy of the consummation "wholly for Him, and save Himself for none," in which lover attains communion with Beloved "in marriage of delight."

In his book, "The Dark Night of the Soul," St. John has commented upon the opening lines of this poem; and the passages in which he does this are amongst the finest and most subtle descriptions of the psychology of contemplation which we possess.

"The soul," he says, "calls the dim contemplation, by which it ascends to the union of love, a secret stair; and that because of two properties of this contemplation which I shall explain separately. First, this dark contemplation is called secret, because it is, as I have said before, the mystical theology which theologians call secret wisdom, and which according to St. Thomas is infused into the soul more especially by love. This happens in a secret hidden way, in which the natural operations of the understanding and the other powers have no share. . . . The soul can neither discern nor give it a name, neither desires so to do; and besides, it can discover no way nor apt comparison by which to make known a knowledge so high, a spiritual impression so delicate and infused. Sothat even if the soul felt the most lively desire to explain itself, and heaped up explanations, the secret would remain a secret still. Because this interior wisdom is so simply, general, and spiritual, that it enters not into the understanding under the guise of any form or image perceptible to sense. Therefore the senses and the imagination--which have not served as intermediaries, and have perceived no sensible form or colour--cannot account for it, nor form any conception of it, so as to speak about it; though the soul be distinctly aware that it feels and tastes this strange wisdom. The soul is like a man who sees an object for the first time, the like of which he has never seen before; he perceives it and likes it, yet he cannot say what it is, nor give it a name, do what he will, though it be even an object cognisable by the senses. How much less, then can that be described which does not enter in by the senses. . . . Inexpressible in its natures as we have said, it is rightly called secret. And for yet another reason it is so called; for this mystical wisdom has the property of hiding the soul within itself. For beside its ordinary operation, it sometimes happens that this wisdom absorbs the soul and plunges it in a secret abyss wherein it sees itself distinctly as far away, and separated from, all created things; it looks upon itself as one that is placed in a profound and vast solitude whither no creature can come, and which seems an immense Wilderness without limits. And this solitude is the more delicious, sweet, and lovely, the more it is deep, vast, and empty. There the soul is the more hidden, the more it is raised up above all created things.

"This abyss of wisdom now lifts up and enlarges the soul, giving it to drink at the very sources of the science of love. Thereby it perceives how lowly is the condition of all creatures in respect to the supreme knowledge and sense of the Divine. It also understands how low, defective, and, in a certain sense, improper, are all the words and phrases by which in this life we discuss divine things; that they escape the best efforts of human art and science, and that only the mystical theology can know and taste what these things are in their reality." [724]

In this important passage we have a reconciliation of the four chief images under which contemplation has been described: the darkness and the light, the wilderness and the union of love. That is to say, the self's paradoxical sense of an ignorance which is supreme knowledge, and of a solitude which is intimate companionship. On the last of these antitheses, the "wilderness that is more delicious, sweet, and lovely, the more it is wide, vast, and empty," I cannot resist quoting, as a gloss upon the dignified language of the Spanish mystic, the quaint and simple words of Richard Rolle.

"In the wilderness . . . speaks the loved to the heart of the lover, as it were a bashful lover, that his sweetheart before men entreats not, nor friendly-wise but commonly and as a stranger he kisses. A devout soul safely from worldly business in mind and body departed . . . anon comes heavenly joy, and it marvellously making merry melody, to her springs; whose token she takes, that now forward worldly sound gladly she suffers not. This is ghostly music, that is unknown to all that with worldly business lawful or unlawful are occupied. No man there is that this has known, but he that has studied to God only to take heed." [725]

Doubtless the "dark transcendence" reported and dwelt upon by all mystics of the Dionysian type, is nearest the truth of all our apprehensions of God: [726] though it can be true only in the paradoxical sense that it uses the suggestive qualities of negation--the Dark whose very existence involves that of Light--to hint at the infinite Affirmation of All that Is. But the nearer this language is to the Absolute, the further it is from ourselves. Unless care be taken in the use of it, the elimination of falsehood may easily involve for us the elimination of everything else. Man is not yet pure spirit, has not attained the Eternal. He is in via and will never arrive if impatient amateurs of Reality insist on cutting the ground from under his feet. Like Dante, he needs a ladder to the stars, a ladder which goes the whole way from the human to the divine. Therefore the philosophic exactitude of these descriptions of the dark must be balanced, as they are in St. John of the Cross, by the personal, human, and symbolic affirmations of Love, if we would avoid a distorted notion of the Reality which the contemplative attains in his supreme "flights towards God." Consciousness has got to be helped across the gap which separates it from its Home.

The "wilderness," the dread Abyss, must be made homely by the voice of "the lover that His sweetheart before men entreats not." Approximate as we know such an image of our communion with the Absolute to be, it represents a real aspect of the contemplative experience which eludes the rule and compass of metaphysical thought. Blake, with true mystic insight, summed up the situation as between the two extreme forms of contemplation when he wrote:-- [727]

"God appears, and God is Light
To those poor souls who dwell in night:
But doth a human form display
To those who dwell in realms of day."

In the "orison of union" and the "Spiritual Marriage," those contemplatives whose temperament inclines them to "dwell in realms of day" receive just such a revelation of the "human form"--a revelation which the Christian dogma of the Incarnation brings to a point. They apprehend the personal and passionate aspect of the Infinite Life; and the love, at once intimate and expansive, all-demanding and all-renouncing, which plays like lightning between it and the desirous soul. "Thou saidst to me, my only Love, that Thou didst will to make me Thyself; and that Thou wast all mine, with all that Thou hadst and with all Paradise, and that I was all Thine. That I should leave all, or rather the nothing; and that (then) thou wouldst give me the all. And that Thou hadst given me this name--at which words I heard within me dedi te in lucem gentium'--not without good reason. And it seemed then, as though I had an inclination for nothing except the purest Union, without any means, in accordance with that detailed sight which Thou hadst given me. So then I said to Thee: These other things, give them to whom Thou wilt; give me but this most pure Union with Thee, free from every means." [728]

"Our work is the love of God," cries Ruysbroeck. "Our satisfaction lies in submission to the Divine Embrace." This utter and abrupt submission to the Divine Embrace is the essence of that form of contemplation which is called the Orison of Union. "Surrender" is its secret: a personal surrender, not only of finite to Infinite, but of bride to Bridegroom, heart to Heart. This surrender, in contemplatives of an appropriate temperament, is of so complete and ecstatic a type that it involves a more or less complete suspension of normal consciousness, an entrancement; and often crosses the boundary which separates contemplation from true ecstasy, producing in its subject physical as well as psychical effects. In this state, says St. Teresa, "There is no sense of anything: only fruition, without understanding what that may be the fruition of which is granted. It is understood that the fruition is of a certain good, containing in itself all good together at once; but this good is not comprehended. The senses are all occupied in this fruition in such a way, that not one of them is at liberty so as to be able to attend to anything else, whether outward or inward. . . . But this state of complete absorption, together with the utter rest of the imagination--for I believe that the imagination is then wholly at rest--lasts only for a short time; though the faculties do not so completely recover themselves as not to be for some hours afterwards as if in disorder. . . . He who has had experience of this will understand it in some measure, for it cannot be more clearly described, because what then takes place is so obscure. All I am able to say is, that the soul is represented as being close to God; and that there abides a conviction thereof so certain and strong that it cannot possibly help believing so. All the faculties fail now, and are suspended in such a way that, as I said before, their operations cannot be traced. . . . The will must be fully occupied in loving, but it understands not how it loves; the understanding, if it understands, does not understand how it understands. It does not understand, as it seems to me, because, as I said just now, this is a matter which cannot be understood." [729] Clearly, the psychological situation here is the same as that in which mystics of the impersonal type feel themselves to be involved in the Cloud of Unknowing, or Divine Dark.

"Do not imagine," says St. Teresa in another place, "that this orison, like that which went before [i.e. , the quiet] is a sort of drowsiness: (I call it drowsiness, because the soul seems to slumber being neither thoroughly asleep, nor thoroughly awake). In the prayer of union the soul is asleep; fast asleep as regards herself and earthly things. In fact, during the short time that this state lasts she is deprived of all feeling, and though she wishes it, she can think of nothing. Thus she needs no effort in order to suspend her thoughts; if the soul can love--she knows not how or when she loves, nor what she desires . . . she is, as it were, entirely dead to the world, the better to live in God." [730]

It may be asked, in what way does such contemplation as this differ from unconsciousness. The difference, according to St. Teresa, consists in the definite somewhat which takes place during this inhibition of the surface consciousness: a "somewhat" of which that surface-consciousness becomes aware when it awakes. True contemplation, as the mystics are constantly assuring us, must always be judged by its fruits. If it be genuine, work has been done during the period of apparent passivity. The deeper self has escaped, has risen to freedom, and returns other than it was before. We must remember that Teresa is speaking from experience, and that her temperamental peculiarities will modify the form which this experience takes. "The soul," she says, "neither sees, hears, nor understands anything while this state lasts; but this is usually a very short time, and seems to the soul even shorter than it really is. God visits the soul in a way that prevents it doubting when it comes to itself that is has been in God and God in it; and so firmly is it convinced of this truth that, though years may pass before this state recurs, the soul can never forget it nor doubt its reality. . . . But you will say, how can the soul see and comprehend that she is in God and God in her, if during this union she is not able either to see or understand? I reply, that she does not see it at the time, but that afterwards she perceives it clearly: not by a vision, but by a certitude which remains in the heart which God alone can give." [731]

Footnotes:

681. Récéjac, "Fondements de la Connaissance Mystique," p. 176.

682. Supra , p. 245.

683. St. Teresa, Vida, cap. xx. § 1 and 3.

684. "Études sur le Mysticisme," p. 370.

685. Aug. Conf., bk. vii. cap. xvii.

686. "Varieties of Religious Experience," p. 380.

687. St. Angèle de Foligno, "Le Livre de l'Expérience des Vrais Fidèles," p. 238 (English translation, p. 189).

688. Compare Baker, "Holy Wisdom," Treatise iii. § iv. cap. iv.

689. See Hilton, "The Scale of Perfection," bk. ii. cap. xxv.

690. Vide infra , p. 347.

691. "De Divinis Nominibus," vii. 1.

692. Ennead vi. 9, 10.

693. Ruysbroeck, "De Ornatu Spiritalium Nuptiarum," I. iii. cap. i.

694. J. Maritain, "Art et Scholastique," p. 141.

695. "The Scale of Perfection," bk. ii. cap. xxv.

696. Richard Rolle, "The Mending of Life," cap. xii.

697. "The Mirror of Simple Souls," Div. iii. cap. xiii.

698. Tauler, Sermon on St. John the Baptist ("The Inner Way," pp. 97-99).

699. Maeterlinck, Introduction to Ruysbroeck's "L'Ornement des Noces Spirituelles," p. v. Theologians will recognize here a poetic account of the soul's contact with that aspect of Divine Reality emphasized in the work of Rudolf Otto and of Karl Barth.

700. Par. xxx. 61-128. Compare p. 286.

701. Par. xxxiii. 52-63, 76-81, 97-105. "My vision, becoming purified, entered deeper and deeper into the ray of that Supernal Light which in itself is true. Thenceforth my vision was greater than our language, which fails such a sight; and memory too fails before such excess. As he who sees in a dream, and after the dream is gone the impression or emotion remains, but the rest returns not to the mind, such am I for nearly the whole of my vision fades, and yet there still wells within my heart the sweetness born therefrom. . . . I think that by the keenness of the living ray which I endured I had been lost, had I

once turned my eyes aside. And I remember that for this I was the bolder so long to sustain my gaze, as to unite it with the Power Infinite. . . . Thus did my mind, wholly in suspense, gaze fixedly, immovable and intent, ever enkindled by its gazing. In the presence of that Light one becomes such, that never could one consent to turn from it to any other sight. Because the Good, which is the object of the will, is therein wholly gathered; and outside of this, that is defective which therein is perfect."

702. St. Angèle de Foligno, "Le Livre de l'Expérience des Vrais Fidèles," pp. 78 and 116 (English translation, here very imperfect, pp. 169, 174).

703. "The Scale of Perfection," bk. ii. cap. xli.

704. "The Mending of Life," cap. xii.

705. Scale of Perfection," bk. i. cap. viii.

706. "Fevelations of Divine Love," cap. xxiv.

707. St. Angèle, op. cit ., p. 156 (English translations p. 178).

708. "Das Fliessende Licht der Gottheit," pt. v. cap. 13.

709. Par. xxxiii. 137.

710. Compare supra , Pt. I. Cap. V.

711. Ruysbroeck, "De Ornatu Spiritalium Nuptiarum," bk. iii. caps. ii. and iv.

712. Dionysius the Areopagite, "De Mystica Theologia," i. 1.

713. Ibid., Letter to Dorothy the Deacon. This passage seems to be the source of Vaughan's celebrated verse in "The Night"-- "There is in God, some say A deep but dazzling darkness, as men here Say it is late and dusky because they See not all clear. O for that Night! where I in Him Might live invisible and dim."

714. R. Otto, "The Idea of the Holy," caps. iii. and iv. The whole of this work should be studied in its bearing on the contemplation of supra-rational Reality.

715. Jalalu d Din, "Selected Poems from the Divan," p. 137.

716. "The Scale of Perfection," bk. ii. cap. xiii.

717. "The Cloud of Unknowing," cap. vi.

718. Ibid ., cap. iv.

719. Boehme, "Three Dialogues of the Supersensual Life," p. 71.

720. "The Cloud of Unknowing," cap. iii.

721. St. Angèle, loc. cit ., pp. 210-12 (English translation, p. 181).

722. "The Mystical Element of Religion," vol. ii. p. 257.

723. "En una Noche Escura." This translation, by Mr. Arthur Symons, will be found in vol. ii. of his Collected Poems.

724. St. John of the Cross, "Noche Escura del Alma," I. ii. cap. xvii. It is perhaps advisable to warn the reader that in this work St. John applies the image of "darkness" to three absolutely different things: i.e ., to a purgation of mind which he calls the "night of sense", to dim contemplation, or the Dionysian "Divine Dark", and to the true "dark night of the soul," which he calls the "night of the spirit." The result has been a good deal of confusion, in modern writers on mysticism upon the subject of the "Dark Night."

725. "The Fire of Love," bk. ii. cap. vii.

726. Compare Baker, "Holy Wisdom," Treatise iii. § iv. cap iv.

727. "Auguries of Innocence."

728. Colloquies of Battista Vernazza: quoted by Von Hügel, "The Mystical Element of Religion," vol. i. p. 350.

729. Vida, cap. xviii. §§ 2, 17, 19.

730. "El Castillo Interior," Moradas Quintas, cap. i.

731. Op. cit., loc. cit.

CHAPTER VIII

Since the object of all contemplation is the production of that state of intimate communion in which the mystics declare that the self is "in God and God is in her," it might be supposed that the orison of union represented the end of mystical activity, in so far as it is concerned with the attainment of a transitory but exalted consciousness of "oneness with the Absolute." Nearly all the great contemplatives, however, describe as a distinct, and regard as a more advanced phase of the spiritual consciousness, the group of definitely ecstatic states in which the concentration of interest on the Transcendent is so complete, the gathering up and pouring out of life on this one point so intense, that the subject is more or less entranced, and becomes, for the time of the ecstasy, unconscious of the external world. In ordinary contemplation he refused to attend to that external world: it was there, a blurred image, at the fringe of his conscious field, but he deliberately left it on one side. In ecstasy he cannot attend to it. None of its messages reach him: not even those most insistent of all messages which are translated into the terms of bodily pain.

All mystics agree in regarding such ecstasy as an exceptionally favourable state; the one in which man's spirit is caught up to the most immediate union with the divine. The word has become a synonym for joyous exaltation, for the inebriation of the Infinite. The induced ecstasies of the Dionysian mysteries, the metaphysical raptures of the Neoplatonists, the voluntary or involuntary trance of Indian mystics and Christian saints--all these, however widely they may differ in transcendental value, agree in claiming such value, in declaring that this change in the quality of consciousness brought with it a valid and ineffable apprehension of the Real. Clearly, this apprehension will vary in quality and content with the place of the subject in the spiritual scale. The ecstasy is merely the psycho-physical condition which accompanies it. "It is hardly a paradox to say," says Myers, "that the evidence for ecstasy is stronger than the evidence for any other religious belief. Of all the subjective experiences of religion, ecstasy is that which has been most urgently, perhaps to the psychologist most convincingly asserted; and it is not confined to any one religion. . . . From the medicine man of the lowest savages up to St. John, St. Peter, and St. Paul, with Buddha and Mahomet on the way, we find records which, though morally and intellectually much differing, are in psychological essence the same." [732]

There are three distinct aspects under which the ecstatic state may be studied: (a) the physical, (b) the psychological, (c) the mystical. Many of the deplorable misunderstandings and still more deplorable mutual recriminations which surround its discussion come from the refusal of experts in one of these three branches to consider the results arrived at by the other two.

A. Physically considered, ecstasy is a trance; more or less deep, more or less prolonged. The subject may slide into it gradually from a period of absorption in, or contemplation of, some idea which has filled the field of consciousness: or, it may come on suddenly, the appearance of the idea--or even some word or symbol suggesting the idea--abruptly throwing the subject into an entranced condition. This is the state which some mystical writers call Rapture. The distinction, however, is a conventional one: and the works of the mystics describe many intermediate forms.

During the trance, breathing and circulation are depressed. The body is more or less cold and rigid, remaining in the exact position which it occupied at the oncoming of the ecstasy, however difficult and unnatural this pose may be. Sometimes entrancement is so deep that there is complete anaesthesia, as in the case which I quote from the life of St. Catherine of Siena. [733] Credible witnesses report that Bernadette, the visionary of Lourdes, held the flaming end of a candle in her hand for fifteen minutes during one of her ecstasies. She felt no pain, neither did the flesh show any marks of burning. Similar instances of ecstatic anesthesia abound in the lives of the saints, and are also characteristic of certain pathological states. [734]

The trance includes, according to the testimony of the ecstatics, two distinct phases--(a) the short period of lucidity and (b) a longer period of complete unconsciousness, which may pass into a death like catalepsy, lasting for hours; or, as once with St. Teresa, for days. "The difference between union and trance," says Teresa, "is this: that the latter lasts longer and is more visible outwardly, because the breathing gradually diminishes, so that it becomes impossible to speak or to open the eyes. And though this very thing occurs when the soul is in union, there is more violence in a trance, for the natural warmth vanishes, I know not how, when the rapture is deep, and in all these kinds of orison there is more or less of this. When it is deep, as I was saying, the hands become cold and sometimes stiff and straight as pieces of wood; as to the body if the rapture comes on when it is standing or kneeling it remains so; and the soul is so full of the joy of that which Our Lord is setting before it, that it seems to forget to animate the body and abandons it. If the rapture lasts, the nerves are made to feel it." [735]

Such ecstasy as this, so far as its physical symptoms go, is not of course the peculiar privilege of the mystics. It is an abnormal bodily state, caused by a psychic state: and this causal psychic state may be healthy or unhealthy, the result of genius or disease. It is common in the little understood type of personality called "sensitive" or mediumistic: it is a well-known symptom of certain mental and nervous illnesses. A feeble mind concentrated on one idea--like a hypnotic subject gazing at one spot--easily becomes entranced; however trivial the idea which gained possession of his consciousness. Apart from its content, then, ecstasy carries no guarantee of spiritual value. It merely indicates the presence of certain abnormal psycho-physical conditions: an alteration of the normal equilibrium, a shifting of the threshold of consciousness, which leaves the body, and the whole usual "external world" outside instead of inside the conscious field, and even affects those physical functions--such as breathing--which are almost entirely automatic. Thus ecstasy, physically considered, may occur in any person in whom (1) the threshold of consciousness is exceptionally mobile and (2) there is a tendency to dwell upon one governing idea or intuition. Its worth depends entirely on the objective value of that idea or intuition.

In the hysterical patient, thanks to an unhealthy condition of the centres of consciousness, any trivial or irrational idea, any one of the odds and ends stored up in the subliminal region, may thus become fixed, dominate the mind, and produce entrancement. Such ecstasy is an illness: the emphasis is on the pathological state which makes it possible. In the mystic, the idea which fills his life is so great a one--the idea of God--that, in proportion as it is vivid, real, and intimate, it inevitably tends to monopolize the field of consciousness. Here the emphasis is on the overpowering strength of spirit, not on the feeble and unhealthy state of body or mind. [736] This true ecstasy, says Godferneaux, is not a malady, but "the extreme form of a state which must be classed amongst the ordinary accidents of conscious life." [737]

The mystics themselves are fully aware of the importance of this distinction. Ecstasies, no less than visions and voices, must they declare, be subjected to unsparing criticism before they are recognized as divine: whilst some are undoubtedly "of God," others are no less clearly "of the devil." "The great doctors of the mystic life," says Malaval, "teach that there are two sorts of rapture, which must be carefully distinguished. The first are produced in persons but little advanced in the Way, and still full of selfhood; either by the force of a heated imagination which vividly apprehends a sensible object, or by the artifice of the Devil. These are the raptures which St. Teresa calls, in various parts of her works, Raptures of Feminine Weakness. The other sort of Rapture is, on the contrary, the effect of pure intellectual vision in those who have a great and generous love for God. To generous souls who have utterly renounced themselves, God never fails in these raptures to communicate high things." [738]

All the mystics agree with Malaval in finding the test of a true ecstasy, not in its outward sign, but in its inward grace, its after-value: and here psychology would do well to follow their example. The ecstatic states, which are supreme instances of the close connection between body and soul, have bodily as well as mental results: and those results are as different and as characteristic as those observed in healthy and in morbid organic processes. If the concentration has been upon the highest centre of consciousness, the organ of spiritual perception--if a door has really been opened by which the self has escaped for an instant to the vision of That Which Is--the ecstasy will be good for life. The entrancement of disease, on the contrary is always bad for life. Its concentration being upon the lower instead of the higher levels of mentality, it depresses rather than enhances the vitality, the fervour, or the intelligence of its subject: and leaves behind it an enfeebled will, and often moral and intellectual chaos. [739] "Ecstasies that do not produce considerable profit either to the persons themselves or others, deserve to be suspected," says Augustine Baker, "and when any marks of their approaching are perceived, the persons ought to divert their minds some other way." [740] It is the difference between a healthy appetite for nourishing food and a morbid craving for garbage. The same organs of digestion are used in satisfying both: yet he would be a hardy physiologist who undertook to discredit all nutrition by a reference to its degenerate forms.

Sometimes both kinds of ecstasy, the healthy and the psychopathic, are seen in the same person. Thus in the cases of St. Catherine of Genoa and St. Catherine of Siena it would seem that as their health became feebler and the nervous instability always found in persons of genius increased, their ecstasies became more frequent; but these were not healthy ecstasies, such as those which they experienced in the earlier stages of their careers, and which brought with them an access of vitality. They were the results of increasing weakness of body, not of the overpowering strength of the spirit: and there is evidence that Catherine of Genoa, that acute self-critic, was conscious of this. "Those who attended on her did not know how to distinguish one state from the other. And hence on coming to; she would sometimes say, Why did you let me remain in this quietude, from which I have almost died?'" [741] Her earlier ecstasies, on the contrary, had in a high degree the positive character of exaltation and life-enhancement consequent upon extreme concentration on the Absolute; as well as the merely negative character of annihilation of the surface-consciousness. She came from them with renewed health and strength, as from a resting in heavenly places and a feeding on heavenly food: and side by side with this ecstatic life, fulfilled the innumerable duties of her active vocation as hospital matron and spiritual mother of a large group of disciples. "Many times," says her legend, "she would hide herself in some secret place and there stay: and being sought she was found upon the ground, her face hidden in her hands, altogether beyond herself, in such a state of joy as is beyond thought or speech: and being called--yea, even in a loud voice--she heard not. And at other times she would go up and down. . . . as if beyond herself, drawn by the impulse of love, she did this. And certain other times she remained for the space of six hours as if dead: but hearing herself called, suddenly she got up, and answering she would at once go about all that needed to be done even the humblest things. [742] And in thus leaving the All, she went without any grief, because she fled all selfhood (la proprietà) as if it were the devil. And when she came forth from her hiding-place her face was rosy as it might be a cherub's; and it seemed as if she might have said, Who shall separate me from the love of God?'" [743] "Very often," says St. Teresa, describing the results of such rapturous communion with Pure Love as that from which St. Catherine came joyous and rosy-faced, "he who was before sickly and full of pain comes forth healthy and even with new strength: for it is something great that is given to the soul in rapture." [744]

B. Psychologically considered, all ecstasy is a form--the most perfect form--of the state which is technically called "complete mono-ideism," That withdrawal of consciousness from circumference to centre, that deliberate attention to one thing , which we discussed in Recollection, is here pushed--voluntarily or involuntarily--to its logical conclusion. It is (1) always paid for by psycho-physical disturbances; (2) rewarded in healthy cases by an enormous lucidity, a supreme intuition in regard to the one thing on which the self's interest has been set.

Such ecstasy, then, is an exalted form of contemplation, and might be expected in appropriate subjects to develop naturally from that state. "A simple difference of degree," says Maury, "separates ecstasy from the action of forcibly fixing an idea in the mind. Contemplation implies exercise of will, and the power of interrupting the extreme tension of the mind. In ecstasy, which is contemplation carried to its highest pitch, the will, although in the strictest sense able to provoke the state, is nevertheless unable to suspend it." [745]

In "complete mono-ideism" then, the attention to one thing and the inattention to all else, is so entire that the subject is entranced. Consciousness has been withdrawn from those centres which receive and respond to the messages of the external world: he neither sees, feels, nor hears. The Ego dormio et cor meum vigilat of the contemplative ceases to be a metaphor, and becomes a realistic description. It must be remembered that the whole trend of mystical education has been toward the production of this fixity of attention. Recollection and Quiet lead up to it. Contemplation cannot take place without it. All the mystics assure us that a unification of consciousness, in which all outward things are forgot, is the necessary prelude of union with the Divine; for consciousness of the Many and consciousness of the One are mutually exclusive states. Ecstasy, for the psychologist, is such a unification in its extreme form. The absorption of the self in the one idea, the one desire, is so profound--and in the case of the great mystics so impassioned--that everything else is blotted out. The tide of life is withdrawn, not only from those higher centres which are the seats of perception and of thought, but also from those lower centres which govern the physical life. The whole vitality of the subject is so concentrated on the transcendental world--or, in a morbid ecstatic, on the idea which dominates his mind--that body and brain alike are depleted of their energy in the interests of this supreme act.

Since mystics have, as a rule, the extreme susceptibility to suggestions and impressions which is characteristic of artistic and creative types, it is not surprising that their ecstasies are often evoked, abruptly, by the exhibition of, or concentration upon, some loved and special symbol of the divine. Such symbols form the rallying-points about which are gathered a whole group of ideas and intuitions. Their presence--sometimes the sudden thought of them--will be enough, in psychological language, to provoke a discharge of energy along some particular path: that is to say, to stir to life all those ideas and intuitions which belong to the self's consciousness of the Absolute, to concentrate vitality on them, and introduce the self into that world of perception of which they are, as it were, the material keys. Hence the profound significance of symbols for some mystics: their paradoxical clinging to outward forms, whilst declaring that the spiritual and intangible alone is real.

For the Christian mystics, the sacraments and mysteries of faith have always provided such a point d'appui; and these often play a large part in the production of their ecstasies. For St. Catherine of Siena, and also very often for her namesake of Genoa, the reception of Holy Communion was the prelude to ecstasy. Julian of Norwich [746] and St. Francis of Assissi [747] became entranced whilst gazing on the crucifix. We are told of Denis the Carthusian that towards the end of his life, hearing the Veni Creator or certain verses of the psalms, he was at once rapt in God and lifted up from the earth. [748]

Of St. Catherine of Siena, her biographer says that "she used to communicate with such fervour that immediately afterwards she would pass into the state of ecstasy, in which for hours she would be totally unconscious. On one occasion, finding her in this condition, they (the Dominican friars) forcibly threw her out of the church at midday, and left her in the heat of the sun watched over by some of her companions till she came to her senses." Another, "catching sight of her in the church when she was in ecstasy, came down and pricked her in many places with a needle. Catherine was not aroused in the least from her trance, but afterwards, when she came back to her senses, she felt the pain in her body and perceived that she had thus been wounded." [749]

It is interesting to compare with this objective description, the subjective account of ecstatic union which St. Catherine gives in her "Divine Dialogue." Here, the deeper self of the mystic is giving in a dramatic form its own account of its inward experiences: hence we see the inward side of that outward state of entrancement, which was all that onlookers were able to perceive. As usual in the Dialogue, the intuitive perceptions of the deeper self are attributed by St. Catherine to the Divine Voice speaking in her soul.

"Oftentimes, through the perfect union which the soul has made with Me, she is raised from the earth almost as if the heavy body became light. But this does not mean that the heaviness of the body is taken away, but that the union of the soul with Me is more perfect than the union of the body with the soul; wherefore the strength of the spirit, united with Me, raises the weight of the body from the earth, leaving it as if immoveable and all pulled to pieces in the affection of the soul. Thou rememberest to have heard it said of some creatures, that were it not for My Goodness, in seeking strength for them, they would not be able to live; and I would tell thee that, in the fact that the souls of some do not leave their bodies, is to be seen a greater miracle than in the fact that some have arisen from the dead, so great is the union which they have with Me. I, therefore, sometimes for a space withdraw from the union, making the soul return to the vessel of her body . . . from which she was separated by the affection of love. From the body she did not depart, because that cannot be except in death; the bodily powers alone departed, becoming united to Me through affection of love. The memory is full of nothing but Me, the intellect, elevated, gazes upon the object of My Truth; the affection, which follows the intellect, loves and becomes united with that which the intellect sees. These powers being united and gathered together and immersed and inflamed in Me, the body loses its feeling, so that the seeing eye sees not, and the hearing ear hears not, and the tongue does not speak; except as the abundance of the heart will sometimes permit it, for the alleviation of the heart and the praise and glory of My Name. The hand does not touch and the feet walk not, because the members are bound with the sentiment of Love." [750]

A healthy ecstasy so deep as this seems to be the exclusive prerogative of the mystics: perhaps because so great a passion, so profound a concentration, can be produced by nothing smaller than their flaming love of God. But as the technique of contemplation is employed more or less consciously by all types of creative genius--by inventors and philosophers, by poets, prophets, and musicians, by all the followers of the "Triple Star," no less than by the mystic saints--so too this apotheosis of contemplation, the ecstatic state, sometimes appears in a less violent form, acting healthily and normally, in artistic and creative personalities at a complete stage of development. It may accompany the prophetic intuitions of the seer, the lucidity of the great metaphysician, the artist's supreme perception of beauty or truth. As the saint is "caught up to God," so these are "caught up" to their vision: their partial apprehensions of the Absolute Life. Those joyous, expansive outgoing sensations, characteristic of the ecstatic consciousness, are theirs also. Their greatest creations are translations to us, not of something they have thought, but of something they have known, in a moment of ecstatic union with the "great life of the All."

We begin, then, to think that the "pure mono-ideism," which the psychologist identifies with ecstasy, though doubtless a part, is far from being the whole content of this state, True, the ecstatic is absorbed in his one idea, his one love: he is in it and with it: it fills his universe. But this unified state of consciousness does not merely pore upon something already possessed. When it only does this, it is diseased. Its true business is pure perception. It is outgoing, expansive: its goal is something beyond itself. The rearrangement of the psychic self which occurs in ecstasy is not merely concerned with the normal elements of consciousness. It is rather a temporary unification of consciousness round that centre of transcendental perception which mystics call the "apex" or the "spark of the soul." Those deeper layers of personality which normal life keeps below the threshold are active in it: and these are fused with the surface personality by the governing passion, the transcendent love which lies at the basis of all sane ecstatic states. The result is not merely a mind concentrated on one idea nor a heart fixed on one desire, nor even a mind and a heart united in the interests of a beloved thought: but a whole being welded into one, all its faculties, neglecting their normal universe, grouped about a new centre, serving a new life, and piercing like a single flame the barriers of the sensual world. Ecstasy is the psycho-physical state which may accompany this brief synthetic act.

C. Therefore, whilst on its physical side ecstasy is an entrancement, on its mental side a complete unification of consciousness, on its mystical side it is an exalted act of perception. It represents the greatest possible extension of the spiritual consciousness in the direction of Pure Being: the "blind intent stretching" here receives its reward in a profound experience of Eternal Life. In this experience the departmental activities of thought and feeling the consciousness of I-hood, of space and time--all that belongs to the World of Becoming and our own place therein--are suspended. The vitality which we are accustomed to split amongst these various things, is gathered up to form a state of "pure apprehension": a vivid intuition of--or if you like conjunction with--the Transcendent. For the time of his ecstasy the mystic is, for all practical purposes, as truly living in the supersensual world as the normal human animal is living in the sensual world. He is experiencing the highest and most joyous of those temporary and unstable states--those "passive unions"--in which his consciousness escapes the limitations of the senses, rises to freedom, and is united for an instant with the "great life of the All."

Ecstasy, then, from the contemplative's point of view, is the development and completion of the orison of union, and he is not always at pains to distinguish the two degrees, a fact which adds greatly to the difficulties of students. [751] In both states--though he may, for want of better language, describe his experience in terms of sight--the Transcendent is perceived by contact, not by vision: as, enfolded in darkness with one whom we love, we obtain a knowledge far more complete than that conferred by the sharpest sight the most perfect mental analysis. In Ecstasy, the apprehension is perhaps more definitely "beatific" than in the orison of union. Such memory of his feeling-state as the ecstatic brings back with him is more often concerned with an exultant certainty--a conviction that he has known for once the Reality which hath no image, and solved the paradox of life--than with meek self-loss in that Cloud of Unknowing where the contemplative in union is content to meet his Beloved. The true note of ecstasy, however, its only valid distinction from infused contemplation, lies in entrancement; in "being ravished out of fleshly feeling," as St. Paul caught up to the Third Heaven, [752] not in "the lifting of mind unto God." This, of course, is an outward distinction only, and a rough one at that, since entrancement has many degrees: but it will be found the only practical basis of classification.

Probably none but those who have experienced these states know the actual difference between them. Even St. Teresa's psychological insight fails her here, and she is obliged to fall back on the difference between voluntary and involuntary absorption in the divine: a difference, not in spiritual values, but merely in the psycho-physical constitution of those who have perceived these values. "I wish I could explain with the help of God," she says, "wherein union differs from rapture, or from transport, or from flight of the spirit, as they call it, or from trance, which are all one. I mean that all these are only different names for that one and the same thing, which is also called ecstasy. It is more excellent than union, the fruits of it are much greater, and its other operations more manifold, for union is uniform in the beginning, the middle, and the end, and is so also interiorly; but as raptures have ends of a much higher kind, they produce effects both within and without [i.e. , both physical and psychical]. . . . A rapture is absolutely irresistible; whilst union, inasmuch as we are then on our own ground, may be hindered, though that resistance be painful and violent." [753]

From the point of view of mystical psychology, our interest in ecstasy will centre in two points. (1) What has the mystic to tell us of the Object of his ecstatic perception? (2) What is the nature of the peculiar consciousness which he enjoys in his trance? That is to say, what news does he bring us as to the Being of God and the powers of man?

It may be said generally that on both these points he bears out, amplifies, and expresses under formulae of greater splendour, with an accent of greater conviction, the general testimony of the contemplatives. In fact, we must never forget that an ecstatic is really nothing else than a contemplative of a special kind, with a special psycho-physical make-up. Moreover, we have seen that it is not always easy to determine the exact point at which entrancement takes place, and deep contemplation assumes the ecstatic form. The classification, like all classifications of mental states, is an arbitrary one. Whilst the extreme cases present no difficulty, there are others less complete, which form a graduated series between the deeps of the "Quiet" and the heights of "Rapture." We shall never know, for instance, whether the ecstasies of Plotinus and of Pascal involved true bodily entrancement, or only a deep absorption of the "unitive" kind. So, too, the language of many Christian mystics when speaking of their "raptures" is so vague and metaphorical that it leaves us in great doubt as to whether they mean by Rapture the abrupt suspension of normal consciousness, or merely a sudden and agreeable elevation of soul.

"Ravishing," says Rolle, "as it is showed, in two ways is to be understood. One manner, forsooth, in which a man is ravished out of fleshly feeling; so that for the time of his ravishing plainly he feels nought in flesh, nor what is done of his flesh, and yet he is not dead but quick, for yet the soul to the body gives life. And on this manner saints sometime are ravished, to their profit and other men's learning; as Paul ravished to the third heaven. And on this manner sinners also in vision sometime are ravished, that they may see joys of saints and pains of damned for their correction. [754] And many other as we read of. Another manner of ravishing there is, that is lifting of mind into God by contemplation. And this manner of ravishing is in all that are perfect lovers of God, and in none of them but that love God. And as well this is called a ravishing as the other; for with a violence it is done, and as it were against nature." [755]

It is, however, very confusing to the anxious inquirer when--as too often--"lifting of mind by contemplation" is "as well called a ravishing as the other," and ecstasy is used as a synonym for gladness of heart. Here, so far as is possible, these words will be confined to their strict meaning, and not applied generally to the description of all the outgoing and expansive states of the transcendental consciousness.

What does the mystic claim that he attains in this abnormal condition--this irresistible trance? The price that he pays is heavy, involving much psycho-physical wear and tear. He declares that his rapture or ecstasy includes a moment--often a very short, and always an indescribable moment--in which he enjoys a supreme knowledge of or participation in Divine Reality. He tells us under various metaphors that he then attains Pure Being, his Source, his Origin, his Beloved: "is engulphed in the very thing for which he longs, which is God." [756] "Oh, wonder of wonders," cries Eckhart, "when I think of the union the soul has with God! He makes the enraptured soul to flee out of herself, for she is no more satisfied with anything that can be named. The spring of Divine Love flows out of the soul and draws her out of herself into the unnamed Being, into her first source, which is God alone." [757]

This momentary attainment of the Source, the Origin, is the theme of all descriptions of mystic ecstasy. In Rulman Merswin's "Book of the Nine Rocks," that brief and overwhelming rapture is the end of the pilgrim's long trials and ascents. "The vision of the Infinite lasted only for a moment: when he came to himself he felt inundated with life and joy. He asked, Where have I been?' and he was answered, In the upper school of the Holy Spirit. There you were surrounded by the dazzling pages of the Book of Divine Wisdom. [758] Your soul plunged therein with delight, and the Divine Master of the school has filled her with an exuberant love by which even your physical nature has been transfigured.'"[759] Another Friend of God, Ellina von Crevelsheim, who was of so abnormal a psychic constitution that her absorption in the Divine Love caused her to remain dumb for seven years, was "touched by the Hand of God" at the end of that period, and fell into a five-days' ecstasy, in which "pure truth" was revealed to her, and she was lifted up to an immediate experience of the Absolute. There she "saw the interior of the Father's heart," and was "bound with chains of love, enveloped in light, and filled with peace and joy." [760]

In this transcendent act of union, the mystic sometimes says that he is "conscious of nothing." But it is clear that this expression is figurative, for otherwise he would not have known that there had been an act of union: were his individuality abolished, it could not have been aware of its attainment of God. What he appears to mean is that consciousness so changes its form as to be no longer recognizable or describable in human speech. In the paradoxical language of Richard of St. Victor, "In a wondrous fashion remembering we do not remember, seeing we do not see, understanding we not understand, penetrating we do not penetrate." [761] In this indescribable but most actual state, the whole self, exalted and at white heat, is unified and poured out in one vivid act of impassioned perception, which leaves no room for reflection or self-observation. That aloof "somewhat" in us which watches all our actions, splits our consciousness, has been submerged. The mystic is attending exclusively to Eternity, not to his own perception of Eternity. That he can only consider when the ecstasy itself is at an end.

"All things I then forgot,
My cheek on Him Who for my coming came,
All ceased, and I was not,
Leaving my cares and shame
Among the lilies, and forgetting them." [762]

This is that perfect unity of consciousness, that utter concentration on an experience of love, which excludes all conceptual and analytic acts. Hence, when the mystic says that his faculties were suspended, that he "knew all and knew nought," he really means that he was so concentrated on the Absolute that he ceased to consider his separate existence: so merged in it that he could not perceive it as an object of thought, as the bird cannot see the air which supports it, nor the fish the ocean in which it swims. He really "knows all" but "thinks" nought: "perceives all," but "conceives nought."

The ecstatic consciousness is not self-conscious: it is intuitive not discursive. Under the sway of a great passion, possessed by a great Idea, it has become "a single state of enormous intensity." [763] In this state, it transcends our ordinary processes of knowledge, and plunges deep into the Heart of Reality. A fusion which is the anticipation of the unitive life takes place: and the ecstatic returns from this brief foretaste of freedom saying, "I know, as having known, the meaning of Existence; the sane centre of the universe--at once the wonder and the assurance of the soul." [764] "This utter transformation of the soul in God," says St. Teresa, describing the same experience in the official language of theology, "continues only for an instant: yet while it continues no faculty of the soul is aware of it, or knows what is passing there. Nor can it be understood while we are living on the earth; at least God will not have us understand it, because we must be incapable of understanding it. I know is by experience. " [765] Theutterances of those who know by experience are here of more worth than all the statements of psychology, which are concerned of necessity with the "outward signs" of this "inward and spiritual grace." To these we must go if we would obtain some hint of that which ecstasy may mean to the ecstatic.

"When the soul, forgetting itself, dwells in that radiant darkness," says Suso, "it loses all its faculties and all its qualities, as St. Bernard has said. And this, more or less completely, according to whether the soul--whether in the body or out of the body--is more or less united to God. This forgetfulness of self is, in a measure, a transformation in God; who then becomes, in a certain manner, all things for the soul, as Scripture saith. In this rapture the soul disappears, but not yet entirely. It acquires, it is true, certain qualities of divinity, but does not naturally become divine. . . . To speak in the common language, the soul is rapt, by the divine power of resplendent Being, above its natural faculties, into the nakedness of the Nothing." [766]

Here Suso is trying to describe his rapturous attainment of God in the negative terms of Dionysian theology. It is probable that much of the language of that theology originated, not in the abstract philosophizings, but in the actual ecstatic experience, of the Neoplatonists, who--Christian and Pagan alike--believed in, and sometimes deliberately induced, this condition as the supreme method of attaining the One. The whole Christian doctrine of ecstasy, on its metaphysical side, really descends from that great practical transcendentalist Plotinus: who is known to have been an ecstatic, and has left in his Sixth Ennead a description of the mystical trance obviously based upon his own experiences. "Then," he says, "the soul neither sees, nor distinguishes by seeing, nor imagines that there are two things; but becomes as it were another thing, ceases to be itself and belong to itself. It belongs to God and is one with Him, like two concentric circles: concurring they are One; but when they separate, they are two. . . . Since in this conjunction with Deity there were not two things, but the perceiver was one with the thing perceived, if a man could preserve the memory of what he was when he mingled with the Divine, he would have within himself an image of God. . . . For then nothing stirred within him, neither anger, nor desire, nor even reason, nor a certain intellectual perception nor, in short, was he himself moved, if we may assert this; but being in an ecstasy, tranquil and alone with God, he enjoyed an unbreakable calm." [767] Ecstasy, says Plotinus in another part of the same treatise, is "another mode of seeing, a simplification and abandonment of oneself, a desire of contact, rest, and a striving after union." All the phases of the contemplative experience seem to be summed up in this phrase.

It has been said by some critics that the ecstasy of Plotinus was different in kind from the ecstasy of the Christian saints: that it was a philosophic rhapsody, something like Plato's "saving madness," which is also regarded on somewhat insufficient evidence as being an affair of the head and entirely unconnected with the heart. At first sight the arid metaphysical language in which Plotinus tries to tell his love, offers some ground for this view. Nevertheless the ecstasy itself is a practical matter; and has its root, not in reason, but in a deep-seated passion for the Absolute which is far nearer to the mystic's love of God than to any intellectual curiosity, however sublime. The few passages in which it is mentioned tell us what his mystical genius drove him to do: and not what his philosophical mind encouraged him to think or say. At once when we come to these passages we notice a rise of temperature, an alteration of values. Plotinus the ecstatic is sure whatever Plotinus the metaphysician may think, that the union with God is a union of hearts: that "by love He may be gotten and holden, but by thought never." He, no less than the mediaeval contemplatives, is convinced--to quote his own words--that the Vision is only for the desirous; for him who has that "loving passion" which "causes the lover to rest in the object of his love." [768] The simile of marriage, of conjunction as the soul's highest bliss, which we are sometimes told that we owe in part to the unfortunate popularity of the Song of Songs, in part to the sexual aberrations of celibate saints, is found in the work of this hardheaded Pagan philosopher: who was as celebrated for his practical kindness and robust common sense as for his transcendent intuitions of the One.

The greatest of the Pagan ecstatics then, when speaking from experience, anticipates the Christian contemplatives. His words, too, when compared with theirs, show how delicate are the shades which distinguish ecstasy such as this from the highest forms of orison. "Tranquil and alone with God"--mingled for an instant of time "like two concentric circles" with the Divine Life," "perceiver and perceived made one"--this is as near as the subtle intellect of Alexandria can come to the reality of that experience in which the impassioned mono-ideism of great spiritual genius conquers the rebellious senses, and becomes, if only for a moment, operative on the highest levels accessible to the human soul. Self-mergence, then--that state of transcendence in which, the barriers of selfhood abolished, we "receive the communication of Life and of Beatitude, in which all things are consummated and all things are renewed" [769] --is the secret of ecstasy, as it was the secret of contemplation. On their spiritual side the two states cannot, save for convenience of description, be divided. Where contemplation becomes expansive, out-going, self-giving, and receives a definite fruition of the Absolute in return, its content is already ecstatic. Whether its outward form shall be so depends on the body of the mystic, not on his soul.

"Se l' atto della mente
è tutto consopito,
en Dio stando rapito,
ch' en sé non se retrova.
. . . .
En mezo de sto mare
essendo sì abissato,
giá non ce trova lato
onde ne possa uscire,
De sé non può pensare
né dir como è formato,
però che, trasformato,
altro sí ha vestire.
Tutto lo suo sentire
en ben sí va notando,
belleza contemplando
la qual non ha colore." [770]

Thus sang Jacopone da Todi of the ecstatic soul: and here the descriptive powers of one who was both a poet and a mystic bring life and light to the dry theories of psychology.

He continues--and here, in perhaps the finest of all poetic descriptions of ecstasy, he seems to echo at one point Plotinus, at another Richard of St. Victor: at once to veil and reveal the utmost secrets of the mystic life:--

"Aperte son le porte
facta ha conjunzione,
et e in possessione
de tutto quel de Dio.
Sente que non sentio,
que non cognove vede,
possede que non crede,
gusta senza sapere.
Però ch' ha sé perduto
tutto senza misura,
possede quel' altura
de summa smesuranza.
Perché non ha tenuto
en sé altra mistura,
quel ben senza figura
recere en abondanza." [771]

This ineffable "awareness," en dio stando rapito , this union with the Imageless Good, is not the only--though it is the purest--form taken by ecstatic apprehension. Many of the visions and voices described in a previous chapter were experienced in the entranced or ecstatic state; generally when the first violence of the rapture was passed. St. Francis and St. Catherine of Siena both received the stigmata in ecstasy: almost all the entrancements of Suso and many of those of St. Teresa and Angela of Foligno, entailed symbolic vision, rather than pure perception of the Absolute. More and more, then, we are forced to the opinion that ecstasy, in so far as it is not a synonym for joyous and expansive contemplation, is really the name of the outward condition rather than of any one kind of inward experience.

Rapture

In all the cases which we have been considering--and they are characteristic of a large group--the onset of ecstasy has been seen as a gradual, though always involuntary process. Generally it has been the culminating point of a period of contemplation. The self, absorbed in the orison of quiet or of union, or some analogous concentration on its transcendental interests, has passed over the limit of these states; and slid into a still ecstatic trance, with its outward characteristics of rigid limbs, cold, and depressed respiration.

The ecstasy, however, instead of developing naturally from a state of intense absorption in the Divine Vision, may seize the subject abruptly and irresistibly, when in his normal state of consciousness. This is strictly what ascetic writers mean by Rapture. We have seen that the essence of the mystic life consists in the remaking of personality: its entrance into a conscious relation with the

Absolute. This process is accompanied in the mystic by the development of an art expressive of his peculiar genius: the art of contemplation. His practice of this art, like the practice of poetry, music, or any other form of creation, may follow normal lines, at first amenable to the control of his will, and always dependent on his own deliberate attention to the supreme Object of his quest: that is to say, on his orison. His mystic states, however they may end, will owe their beginning to some voluntary act upon his part: a deliberate response to the invitation of God, a turning from the visible to the invisible world. Sometimes, however, his genius for the transcendent becomes too strong for the other elements of character, and manifests itself in psychic disturbances--abrupt and ungovernable invasions from the subliminal region--which make its exercise parallel to the "fine frenzy" of the prophet, the composer, or the poet. Such is Rapture: a violent and uncontrollable expression of genius for the Absolute, which temporarily disorganizes and may permanently injure the nervous system of the self. Often, but not necessarily, Rapture--like its poetic equivalent--yields results of great splendour and value for life. But it is an accident, not an implicit of mystical experience: an indication of disharmony between the subject's psychophysical make-up and his transcendental powers.

Rapture, then, may accompany the whole development of selves of an appropriate type. We have seen that it is a common incident in mystical conversion. The violent uprush of subliminal intuitions by which such conversion is marked disorganizes the normal consciousness, overpowers the will and the senses, and entails a more or less complete entrancement. This was certainly the case with Suso and Rulman Merswin, and perhaps with Pascal: whose "Certitude, Peace, Joy" sums up the exalted intuition of Perfection and Reality--the conviction of a final and unforgettable knowledge--which is characteristic of all ecstatic perception.

In her Spiritual Relations, St. Teresa speaks in some detail of the different phases or forms of expression of these violent ecstatic states: trance, which in her system means that which we have called ecstasy, and transport, or "flight of the spirit," which is the equivalent of rapture. "The difference between trance and transport," she says, "is this. In a trance the soul gradually dies to outward things, losing the senses and living unto God. But a transport comes on by one sole act of His Majesty, wrought in the innermost part of the soul with such swiftness that it is as if the higher part thereof were carried away, and the soul were leaving the body." [772]

Rapture, says St. Teresa in another place, "comes in general as a shock, quick and sharp, before you can collect your thoughts, or help yourself in any way; and you see and feel it as a cloud, or a strong eagle rising upwards and carrying you away on its wings. I repeat it: you feel and see yourself carried away, you know not whither." [773] This carrying-away sensation may even assume the concrete form which is known as levitation: when the upward and outward sensations so dominate the conscious field that the subject is convinced that she is raised bodily from the ground. "It seemed to me, when I tried to make some resistance, as if a great force beneath my feet lifted me up. I know of nothing with which to compare it; but it was much more violent than the other spiritual visitations, and I was therefore as one ground to pieces . . . And further, I confess that it threw me into a great fear, very great indeed at first; for when I saw my body thus lifted up from the earth, how could I help it? Though the spirit draws it upwards after itself, and that with great sweetness if unresisted, the senses are not lost; at least I was so much myself as to be able to see that I was being lifted up ." [774]

So Rulman Merswin said that in the rapture which accompanied his conversion, he was carried round the garden with his feet off the ground: [775] and St. Catherine of Siena, in a passage which I have already quoted, speaks of the strength of the spirit, which raises the body from the earth. [776]

The subjective nature of this feeling of levitation is practically acknowledged by St. Teresa when she says, "When the rapture was over, my body seemed frequently to be buoyant, as if all weight had departed from it; so much so, that now and then I scarcely knew that my feet touched the ground. But during the rapture the body is very often as it were dead, perfectly powerless. It continues in the position it was in when the rapture came upon it--if sitting, sitting." Obviously here the outward conditions of physical immobility coexisted with the subjective sensation of being "lifted Up." [777]

The self's consciousness when in the condition of rapture may vary from the complete possession of her faculties claimed by St. Teresa to a complete entrancement. However abrupt the oncoming of the transport, it does not follow that the mystic instantly loses his surface-consciousness. "There remains the power of seeing and hearing; but it is as if the things heard and seen were at a great distance far away."[778] They have retreated, that is to say, to the fringe of the conscious field, but may still remain just within it. Though the senses may not be entirely entranced, however, it seems that the power of movement is always lost. As in ecstasy, breathing and circulation are much diminished.

"By the command of the Bridegroom when He intends ravishing the soul," says St. Teresa, "the doors of the mansions and even those of the keep and of the whole castle are closed; for He takes away the power of speech, and although occasionally the other faculties are retained rather longer, no word can be uttered. Sometimes the person is at once deprived of all the senses, the hands and body becoming as cold as if the soul had fled; occasionally no breathing can be detected. This condition lasts but a short while, I mean in the same degree, for when this profound suspension diminishes the body seems to come to itself and gain strength to return again to this death which gives more vigorous life to the soul."[779]

This spiritual storm, then, in St. Teresa's opinion, enhances the vitality of those who experience it; makes them "more living than before." It initiates them into "heavenly secrets," and if it does not do this it is no "true rapture," but a "physical weakness such as women are prone to owing to their delicacy of constitution." Its sharpness and violence, however, leave considerable mental disorder behind: "This supreme state of ecstasy never lasts long, but although it ceases, it leaves the will so inebriated, and the mind so transported out of itself that for a day, or sometimes for several days, such a person is incapable of attending to anything but what excites the will to the love of God; although wide awake enough to this, she seems asleep as regards all earthly matters." [780]

But when equilibrium is re-established, the true effects of this violent and beatific intuition of the Absolute begin to invade the normal life. The self which has thus been caught up to awareness of new levels of Reality, is stimulated to fresh activity by the strength of its impressions. It now desires an eternal union with that which it has known; with which for a brief moment it seemed to be merged. The peculiar talent of the mystic--power of apprehending Reality which his contemplations have ordered and developed, and his ecstasies express--here reacts upon his life-process, his slow journey from the Many to the One. His nostalgia has been increased by a glimpse of the homeland. His intuitive apprehension of the Absolute, which assumes in ecstasy its most positive form, spurs him on towards that permanent union with the Divine which is his goal. "Such great graces," says St. Teresa, "leave the soul avid of total possession of that Divine Bridegroom who has conferred them." [781]

Hence the ecstatic states do not merely lift the self to an abnormal degree of knowledge: they enrich her life, contribute to the remaking of her consciousness, develop and uphold the "strong and stormy love which drives her home." They give her the clearest vision she can have of that transcendent standard to which she must conform: entail her sharpest consciousness of the inflow of that Life on which her little striving life depends. Little wonder, then, that--though the violence of the onset may often try his body to the full--the mystic comes forth from a "good ecstasy" as Pascal from the experience of the Fire, humbled yet exultant, marvellously strengthened; and ready, not for any passive enjoyments, but rather for the struggles and hardships of the Way, the deliberate pain and sacrifice of love.

In the third Degree of Ardent Love, says Richard of St. Victor, love paralyses action. Union (copula) is the symbol of this state: ecstasy is its expression. The desirous soul, he says finely, no longer thirsts for God but into God. The pull of its desire draws it into the Infinite Sea. The mind is borne away into the abyss of Divine Light; and, wholly forgetful of exterior things, knows not even itself, but passes utterly into its God. In this state, all earthly desire is absorbed in the heavenly glory. "Whilst the mind is separated from itself, and whilst it is borne away into the secret place of the divine mystery and is surrounded on all sides by the fire of divine love, it is inwardly penetrated and inflamed by this fire, and utterly puts off itself and puts on a divine love: and being conformed to that Beauty which it has beheld, it passes utterly into that other glory." [782]

Thus does the state of ecstasy contribute to the business of deification; of the remaking of the soul's susbtance in conformity with the Goodness, Truth, and Beauty which is God, "Being conformed to that Beauty which it has beheld, it passes utterly into that other glory"; into the flaming heart of Reality, the deep but dazzling darkness of its home.

Footnotes:

732. "Human Personality and its Survival of Bodily Death," vol. ii. p. 260.

733. Vide infra, p. 365.

734. An interesting modern case is reported in the Lancet, 18 March, 1911.

735. Relaccion, viii. 8.

736. St. Thomas proves ecstasies to be inevitable on just this psychological ground. "The higher our mind is raised to the contemplation of spiritual things," he says, "the more it is abstracted from sensible things. But the final term to which contemplation can possibly arrive is the divine substance. Therefore the mind that sees the divine substance must be totally divorced from the bodily senses, either by death or by some rapture" ("Sultana contra Gentiles," I. iii. cap. xlvii., Rickaby's translation).

737. "Sur la Psychologie du Mysticisme" (Revue Philosophique, February, 1902).

738. Malaval, "La Pratique de la Vraye Théologie Mystique," vol. i. p. 89.

739. Pierre Janet ("The Major Symptoms of Hysteria," p. 316) says that a lowering of the mental level in an invariable symptom or "stigma" of hysteria.

740. "Holy Wisdom," Treatise iii. § iv. cap. iii.

741. Von Hügel, "The Mystical Element of Religion," vol. i. p. 206 .

742. This power of detecting and hearing the call of duty, though she was deaf to everything else, is evidently related to the peculiarity noticed by Ribot: who says that an ecstatic hears no sounds, save,

in some cases, the voice of one specific person, which is always able to penetrate the trance. ("Les Maladies de la Volonté," p. 125.)

743. Vita e Dottrina, cap. v.

744. Vida, cap. xx. § 29.

745. A. Maury, "Le Sommeil et les Rèves," p. 235.

746. "Revelations of Divine Love," cap. iii.

747] Vide supra, p. 181.

748. D. A. Mougel, "Denys le Chartreux," p. 32.

749. E. Gardner, "St. Catherine of Siena," p. 50.

750. Dialogo, cap. lxxix.

751. In the case of Dante, for instance, we do not know whether his absorption in the Eternal light did or did not entail the condition of trance.

752. 2 Cor. xii. 1-6.

753. Vida, cap. xx. §§ 1 and 3.

754. Compare Dante, Letter to Can Grande, sect. 28, where he adduces this fact of "the ravishing of sinners for their correction," in support of his claim that the "Divine Comedy" is the fruit of experience, and that he had indeed "navigated the great Sea of Being" of which he writes.

755. Richard Rolle, "The Fire of Love," bk. ii. cap. vii.

756. Dante, loc. cit.

757. Eckhart, "On the Steps of the Soul" (Pfeiffer, p. 153).

758. Compare Par. xxxiii. 85 (vide supra , p. 135).

759. Jundt, "Rulman Merswin," p. 27. Note that this was a "good ecstasy," involving healthful effects for life.

760. Jundt, "Les Amis de Dieu," p. 39. Given also by Rufus Jones, "Studies in Mystical Religixn," p. 271.

761. "Benjamin Major."

762. St. John of the Cross, "En una Noche Escura."

763. Ribot, "Psychologie de l'Attention," cap. iii.

764. B. P. Blood. See William James, "A Pluralistic Mystic," in the Hibbert Journal, July, 1910 .

765. Vida, cap. xx. § 24.

766. Leben, cap. vl.

767. Ennead vi. 9

768. Op. cit., loc. cit.

769. Ruysbroeck, "De Calculo," cap. xii.

770. "The activity of the mind is lulled to rest: rapt in God, It can no longer find itself. . . . Being so deeply engulphed in that ocean, now it can find no place to issue therefrom. Of itself it cannot think, nor can it say what it is like: because transformed, it hath another vesture. All its perceptions have gone forth to gaze upon the Good, and contemplate that Beauty which has no likeness" (Lauda xci.).

771. "The doors are flung wide: conjoined to God, it possesses all that is in Him. It feels that which it felt not: sees that which it knew not, possesses that which it believed not, tastes, though it savours not. Because it is wholly lost to itself, it possesses that height of Unmeasured Perfection. Because it has not retained in itself the mixture of any other thing, it has received in abundance that Imageless Good" (op. cit .).

772. Relaccion viii. 8 and 10.

773. Vida, cap. xx. § 3.

774. St. Teresa, op. cit., loc. cit., §§ 7 and 9.

775. Supra , p. 186.

776. Dialogo, cap. lxxix.

777. Vida, cap, xx. § 23. At the same time in the present state of our knowledge and in view of numerous attested cases of levitation, it is impossible to dogmatise on this subject. The supernaturalist view is given in its extreme form by Farges, "Mystical Phenomena," pp. 536 seq.

778. Teresa, loc. cit.

779. St. Teresa, "El Castillo Interior," Moradas Sextas, cap. iv.

780. Op. cit., loc. cit .

781. St. Teresa, op. cit., cap. vi.

782. "De Quatuor Gradibus Violentae Charitatis" (paraphrase).

CHAPTER IX

We have wandered during the last few chapters from our study of the mystical life-process in man, the organic growth of his transcendental consciousness, in order to examine the byproducts of that process, its characteristic forms of self-expression: the development of its normal art of contemplation, and the visions and voices, ecstasies and raptures which are frequent--though not essential--accompaniments of its activity.

But the mystic, like other persons of genius, is man first and artist afterwards. We shall make a grave though common mistake if we forget this and allow ourselves to be deflected from our study of his growth in personality by the wonder and interest of his art. Being, not Doing, is the first aim of the mystic; and hence should be the first interest of the student of mysticism. We have considered for convenience' sake all the chief forms of mystical activity at the half-way house of the transcendental life: but these activities are not, of course, peculiar to any one stage of that life. Ecstasy, for instance, is as common a feature of mystical conversion as of the last crisis, or "mystic marriage" of the soul: [783] whilst visions and voices--in selves of a visionary or auditive type--accompany and illustrate every phase of the inward development. They lighten and explain the trials of Purgation as often as they express the joys of Illumination, and frequently mark the crisis of transition from one mystic state to the next.

One exception, however, must be made to this rule. The most intense period of that great swing-back into darkness which usually divides the "first mystic life," or Illuminative Way, from the "second mystic life," or Unitive Way, is generally a period of utter blankness and stagnation, so far as mystical activity is concerned. The "Dark Night of the Soul," once fully established, is seldom lit by visions or made homely by voices. It is of the essence of its miseries that the once-possessed power of orison or contemplation now seems wholly lost. The self is tossed back from its hard-won point of vantage. Impotence, blankness, solitude, are the epithets by which those immersed in this dark fire of purification describe their pains. It is this episode in the life-history of the mystic type to which we have now come.

We have already noticed [784] the chief psychological characteristics of all normal mystical development. We have seen that its essence consists in the effort to establish a new equilibrium, to get, as it were, a firm foothold upon transcendent levels of reality; and that in its path towards this consummation the self experiences a series of oscillations between "states of pleasure" and "states of pain." Put in another way, it is an orderly movement of the whole consciousness towards higher centres, in which each intense and progressive affirmation fatigues the immature transcendental powers, and is paid for by a negation; a swing-back of the whole consciousness, a stagnation of intellect, a reaction of the emotions, or an inhibition of the will.

Thus the exalted consciousness of Divine Perfection which the self acquired in its "mystical awakening" was balanced by a depressed and bitter consciousness of its own inherent imperfection, and the clash of these two perceptions spurred it to that laborious effort of accommodation which constitutes the "Purgative Way." The renewed and ecstatic awareness of the Absolute which resulted, and which was the governing characteristic of Illumination, brought its own proper negation: the awareness, that is to say, of the self's continued separation from and incompatibility with that Absolute which it has perceived. During the time in which the illuminated consciousness is fully established, the self, as a rule, is perfectly content: believing that in its vision of Eternity, its intense and loving consciousness of God, it has reached the goal of its quest. Sooner or later, however, psychic fatigue sets in; the state of illumination begins to break up, the complementary negative consciousness appears, and shows itself as an overwhelming sense of darkness and deprivation. This sense is so deep and strong that it inhibits all consciousness of the Transcendent; and plunges the self into the state of negation and misery which is called the Dark Night.

We may look at the Dark Night, as at most other incidents of the Mystic Way, from two points of view: (1) We may see it, with the psychologist, as a moment in the history of mental development, governed by the more or less mechanical laws which so conveniently explain to him the psychic life of man: or (2) with the mystic himself, we may see it in its spiritual aspect as contributing to the remaking of character, the growth of the "New Man"; his "transmutation in God."

(1) Psychologically considered, the Dark Night is an example of the operation of the law of reaction from stress. It is a period of fatigue and lassitude following a period of sustained mystical

activity. "It is one of the best established laws of the nervous system," says Starbuck, "that it has periods of exhaustion if exercised continuously in one direction, and can only recuperate by having a period of rest." [785] However spiritual he may be, the mystic--so long as he is in the body--cannot help using the machinery of his nervous and cerebral system in the course of his adventures. His development, on its psychic side, consists in the taking over of this machinery, the capture of its centres of consciousness, in the interests of his growing transcendental life. In so far, then, as this is so, that transcendental life will be partly conditioned by psychic necessities, and amenable to the laws of reaction and of fatigue. Each great step forward will entail lassitude and exhaustion for that mental machinery which he has pressed unto service and probably overworked. When the higher centres have been submitted to the continuous strain of a developed illuminated life, with its accompanying periods of intense fervour, lucidity, deep contemplation--perhaps of visionary and auditive phenomena--the swing-back into the negative state occurs almost of necessity.

This is the psychological explanation of those strange and painful episodes in the lives of great saints--indeed, of many spiritual persons hardly to be classed as saints--when, perhaps after a long life passed in faithful correspondence with the transcendental order, growing consciousness of the "presence of God," the whole inner experience is suddenly swept away, and only a blind reliance on past convictions saves them from unbelief. [786] The great contemplatives, those destined to attain the full stature of the mystic, emerge from this period of destitution, however long and drastic it may be, as from a new purification. It is for them the gateway to a higher state. But persons of a less heroic spirituality, if they enter the Night at all may succumb to its dangers and pains. This "great negation" is the sorting-house of the spiritual life. Here we part from the "nature mystics," the mystic poets, and all who shared in and were contented with the illuminated vision of reality. Those who go on are the great and strong spirits, who do not seek to know, but are driven to be.

We are to expect, then, as a part of the conditions under which human consciousness appears to work that for every affirmation of the mystic life there will be a negation waiting for the unstable self. Progress in contemplation, for instance, is marked by just such an alternation of light and shade: at first between "consolation" and "aridity"; then between "dark contemplation" and sharp intuitions of Reality. So too in selves of extreme nervous instability, each joyous ecstasy entails a painful or negative ecstasy. The states of darkness and illumination coexist over a long period, alternating sharply and rapidly. Many seers and artists pay in this way, by agonizing periods of impotence and depression, for each violent outburst of creative energy.

Rapid oscillations between a joyous and a painful consciousness seem to occur most often at the beginning of a new period of the Mystic Way: between Purgation and Illumination, and again between Illumination and the Dark Night: for these mental states are, as a rule, gradually not abruptly established. Mystics call such oscillations the "Game of Love" in which God plays, as it were, "hide and seek" with the questing soul. I have already quoted a characteristic instance from the life of Rulman Merswin, [787] who passed the whole intervening period between his conversion and entrance on the Dark Night, or "school of suffering love" in such a state of disequilibrium. Thus too Madame Guyon, who has described with much elaboration of detail her symptoms and sufferings during the oncoming and duration of the Night--or, as she calls its intensest period the Mystic Death--traces its beginning in short recurrent states of privation, or dullness of feeling, such as ascetic writers call "aridity": in which the self loses all interest in and affection for those divine realities which had previously filled its life. This privation followed upon, or was the reaction from, an "illuminated" period of extreme joy and security, in which, as she says, "the presence of God never left me for an instant. But how dear I paid for this time of happiness! For this possession, which seemed to me entire and perfect--and the more perfect the more it was secret, and foreign to the senses, steadfast and exempt from change--was but the preparation for a total deprivation, lasting many years, without any support or hope of its return." [788] As Madame Guyon never attempted to control her states, but made a point of conforming to her own description of the "resigned soul" as "God's weathercock," we have in her an unequalled opportunity of study.

"I endured," she says, "long periods of privation, towards the end almost continual: but still I had from time to time inflowings of Thy Divinity so deep and intimate, so vivid and so penetrating, that it was easy for me to judge that Thou wast but hidden from me and not lost. For although during the times of privation it seemed to me that I had utterly lost Thee, a certain deep support remained, though the soul knew it not: and she only became aware of that support by her subsequent total deprivation thereof. Every time that Thou didst return with more goodness and strength, Thou didst return also with greater splendour; so that in a few hours Thou didst rebuild all the ruins of my unfaithfulness and didst make good to me with profusion all my loss." [789]

Here we have, from the psychological point of view, a perfect example of the oscillations of consciousness on the threshold of a new state. The old equilibrium, the old grouping round a centre characterized by pleasure-affirmation, has been lost; the new grouping round a centre characterized by pain-negation is not yet established. Madame Guyon is standing, or rather swinging, between two worlds, the helpless prey of her own shifting and uncontrollable psychic and spiritual states. But slowly the pendulum approaches its limit: the states of privation, "become almost continual," the reactions to illumination, become less. At last they cease entirely, the new state is established, and the Dark Night has really set in.

The theory here advanced that the "Dark Night" is, on its psychic side, partly a condition of fatigue, partly a state of transition, is borne out by the mental and moral disorder which seems, in many subjects, to be its dominant character. When they are in it everything seems to "go wrong" with them. They are tormented by evil thoughts and abrupt temptations, lose grasp not only of their spiritual but also of their worldly affairs. Thus Lucie-Christine says: "Often during my great temptations to sadness I am plunged in such spiritual darkness that I think myself utterly lost in falsehood and illusion; deceiving both myself and others. This temptation is the most terrible of all." [790] The health of those passing through this phase often suffers, they become "odd" and their friends forsake them; their intellectual life is at a low ebb. In their own words "trials of every kind," "exterior and interior crosses," abound.

Now "trials," taken en bloc , mean a disharmony between the self and the world with which it has to deal. Nothing is a trial when we are able to cope with it efficiently. Things try us when we are not adequate to them: when they are abnormally hard or we abnormally weak. This aspect of the matter becomes prominent when we look further into the history of Madame Guyon's experiences. Thanks to the unctuous and detailed manner in which she has analysed her spiritual griefs, this part of her autobiography is a psychological document of unique importance for the study of the "Dark Night" as it appears in a devout but somewhat self-occupied soul.

As her consciousness of God was gradually extinguished, a mental and moral chaos seems to have invaded Madame Guyon and accompanied the more spiritual miseries of her state. "So soon as I perceived the happiness of any state, or its beauty, or the necessity of a virtue, it seemed to me that I fell incessantly into the contrary vice: as if this perception, which though very rapid was always accompanied by love, were only given to me that I might experience its opposite. I was given an intense perception of the purity of God; and so far as my feelings went, I myself became more and more impure: for in reality this state is very purifying, but I was far from understanding this. . . . My imagination was in a state of appalling confusion, and gave me no rest. I could not speak of Thee, oh my God, for I became utterly stupid; nor could I even grasp what was said when I heard Thee spoken of. . . . I found myself hard towards God, insensible to His mercies; I could not perceive any good thing that I had done in my whole life. The good appeared to me evil; and--that which is terrible--it seemed to me that this state must last for ever." [791]

This world as well as the next seemed leagued against her. Loss of health and friendship, domestic vexations, increased and kept pace with her interior griefs. Self-control and power of attention were diminished. She seemed stupefied and impotent, unable to follow or understand even the services of the Church, incapable of all prayer and all good works; perpetually attracted by those worldly things which she had renounced, yet quickly wearied by them. The neat edifice of her first mystic life was in ruins, the state of consciousness which accompanied it was disintegrated, but nothing arose to take its place.

"It is an amazing thing," says Madame Guyon naively, "for a soul that believed herself to be advanced in the way of perfection, when she sees herself thus go to pieces all at once." [792]

So, too, Suso, when he had entered the "upper school" of the spiritual life, was tormented not only by temptations and desolations, but by outward trials and disabilities of every kind: calumnies, misunderstandings, difficulties, pains. "It seemed at this time as if God had given permission both to men and demons to torment the Servitor," he says. [793] This sense of a generally inimical atmosphere, and of the dimness and helplessness of the Ego oppressed by circumstances, is like the vague distress and nervous sensibility of adolescence, and comes in part from the same cause: the intervening period of chaos between the break-up of an old state of equilibrium and the establishment of the new. The self, in its necessary movement towards higher levels of reality, loses and leaves behind certain elements of its world, long loved but now outgrown: as children must make the hard transition from nursery to school. Destruction and construction here go together: the exhaustion and ruin of the illuminated consciousness is the signal for the onward movement of the self towards other centres: the feeling of deprivation and inadequacy which comes from the loss of that consciousness is an indirect stimulus to new growth. The self is being pushed into a new world where it does not feel at home; has not yet reached the point at which it enters into conscious possession of its second or adult life.

"Thou hast been a child at the breast, a spoiled child," said the Eternal Wisdom to Suso. "Now I will withdraw all this." In the resulting darkness and confusion, when the old and known supports are thus withdrawn, the self can do little but surrender itself to the inevitable process of things: to the operation of that unresting Spirit of Life which is pressing it on towards a new and higher state, in which it shall not only see Reality but be real.

Psychologically, then, the "Dark Night of the Soul" is due to the double fact of the exhaustion of an old state, and the growth towards a new state of consciousness. It is a "growing pain" in the organic process of the self's attainment of the Absolute. The great mystics, creative geniuses in the realm of character, have known instinctively how to turn these psychic disturbances to spiritual profit. Parallel with the mental oscillations, upheavals and readjustments, through which an unstable psycho-physical type moves to new centres of consciousness, run the spiritual oscillations of a striving and ascending spiritual type. Gyrans gyrando vadit spiritus . The machinery of consciousness, over-stretched, breaks up, and seems to toss the self back to an old and lower level, where it loses its apprehensions of the transcendental world; as the child, when first it is forced to stand alone, feels weaker than it did in its mother's arms.

"For first He not only withdraws all comfortable observable infusions of light and grace, but also deprives her of a power to exercise any perceptible operations of her superior spirit, and of all comfortable reflections upon His love, plunging her into the depth of her inferior powers," says Augustine Baker, the skilled director of souls, here anticipating the modern psychologist. "Here consequently," he continues, "her former calmness of passions is quite lost, neither can she introvert herself; sinful motions and suggestions do violently assault her, and she finds as great difficulty (if not greater) to surmount them as at the beginning of a spiritual course. . . . If she would elevate her spirit, she sees nothing but clouds and darkness. She seeks God, and cannot find the least marks or footsteps of His Presence; something there is that hinders her from executing the sinful suggestions within her but what that is she knows not, for to her thinking she has no spirit at all, and, indeed, she is now in a region of all other most distant from spirit and spiritual operations--I mean, such as are perceptible." [794]

Such an interval of chaos and misery may last for months, or even for years, before the consciousness again unifies itself and a new centre is formed. Moreover, the negative side of this new centre, this new consciousness of the Absolute, often discloses itself first. The self realizes, that is to say, the inadequacy of its old state, long before it grasps the possibility of a new and higher state. This realization will take two forms; (a) Objective: the distance or absence of the Absolute which the self seeks, (b) Subjective: the self's weakness and imperfection. Both apprehensions constitute a direct incentive to action. They present, as it were, a Divine Negation which the self must probe, combat, resolve. The Dark Night, therefore, largely the product of natural causes, is the producer in its turn of mystical energy; and hence of supernatural effects.

(2) So much for psychology. We have next to consider the mystical or transcendental aspects of the Dark Night: see what it has meant for those mystics who have endured it and for those spiritual specialists who have studied it in the interests of other men.

As in other phases of the Mystic Way, so here, we must beware of any generalization which reduces the "Dark Night" to a uniform experience; a neatly defined state which appears under the same conditions, and attended by the same symptoms, in all the selves who have passed through its pains. It is a name for the painful and negative state which normally intervenes between the Illuminative and the Unitive Life--no more. Different types of contemplatives have interpreted it to themselves and to us in different ways; each type of illumination being in fact balanced by its own appropriate type of "dark."

In some temperaments it is the emotional aspect--the anguish of the lover who has suddenly lost the Beloved--which predominates: in others, the intellectual darkness and confusion overwhelms everything else. Some have felt it, with St. John of the Cross, as a "passive purification," a state of helpless misery, in which the self does nothing, but lets Life have its way with her. Others, with Suso and the virile mysticism of the German school, have experienced it rather as a period of strenuous activity and moral conflict directed to that "total self-abandonment" which is the essential preparation of the unitive life. Those elements of character which were unaffected by the first purification of the self--left as it were in a corner when the consciousness moved to the level of the illuminated life--are here roused from their sleep, purged of illusion, and forced to join the grooving stream.

The Dark Night, then, is really a deeply human process, in which the self which thought itself so spiritual, so firmly established upon the supersensual plane, is forced to turn back, to leave the Light, and pick up those qualities which it had left behind. Only thus, by the transmutation of the whole man, not by a careful and departmental cultivation of that which we like to call his "spiritual" side, can Divine Humanity be formed: and the formation of Divine Humanity--the remaking of man "according to the pattern showed him in the mount"--is the mystic's only certain ladder to the Real. "My humanity," said the Eternal Wisdom to Suso, "is the road which all must tread who would come to that which thou seekest." [795] This "hard saying" might almost be used as a test by which to distinguish the genuine mystic life from its many and specious imitations. The self in its first purgation has cleansed the mirror of perception: hence, in its illuminated life, has seen Reality. In so doing it has transcended the normal perceptive powers of "natural" man, immersed in the illusions of sense. Now, it has got to be reality: a very different thing. For this a new and more drastic purgation is needed--not of the organs of perception, but of the very shrine of self: that "heart" which is the seat of personality, the source of its love and will. In the stress and anguish of the Night, when it turns back from the vision of the Infinite to feel again the limitations of the finite the self loses the power to Do; and learns to surrender its will to the operation of a larger Life, that it may Be. "At the end of such a long and cruel transition," says Lucie Christine, "how much more supple the soul feels itself to be in the Hand of God, how much more detached from all that is not God! She sees clearly in herself the fruits of humility and patience, and feels her love ascending more purely and directly to God in proportion as she has realized the Nothingness of herself and all things." [796]

We must remember in the midst of our analysis, that the mystic life is a life of love: that the Object of the mystic's final quest and of his constant intuition is an object of adoration and supreme desire. "With Thee, a prison would be a rose garden, oh Thou ravisher of hearts: with Thee, Hell would be Paradise, oh Thou cheerer of souls," said Jalalu d Din. [797] Hence for the mystic who has once known the Beatific Vision there can be no greater grief than the withdrawal of this Object from his field of consciousness; the loss of this companionship, the extinction of this Light. Therefore, whatever form the "Dark Night" assumes, it must entail bitter suffering: far worse than that endured in the Purgative Way. Then the self was forcibly detached from the imperfect. Now the Perfect is withdrawn, leaving behind an overwhelming yet impotent conviction of something supremely wrong, some final Treasure lost. We will now look at a few of the characteristic forms under which this conviction is translated to the surface-consciousness.

A. To those temperaments in which consciousness of the Absolute took the form of a sense of divine companionship, and for whom the objective idea "God" had become the central fact of life, it seems as though that God, having shown Himself, has now deliberately withdrawn His Presence, never perhaps to manifest Himself again. "He acts," says Eckhart, "as if there were a wall erected between Him and us." [798] The "eye which looked upon Eternity" has closed, the old dear sense of intimacy and mutual love has given place to a terrible blank.

"That which this anguished soul feels most deeply," says St. John of the Cross, "is the conviction that God has abandoned it, of which it has no doubt; that He has cast it away into darkness as an abominable thing . . . the shadow of death and the pains and torments of hell are most acutely felt, and this comes from the sense of being abandoned by God, being chastised and cast out by His wrath and heavy displeasure. All this and even more the soul feels now, for a terrible apprehension has come upon it that thus it will be with it for ever. It has also the same sense of abandonment with respect to all creatures, and that it is an object of contempt to all, especially to its friends." [799]

So, too, Madame Guyon felt this loss of her intuitive apprehension of God as one of the most terrible characteristics of the "night." "After Thou hadst wounded me so deeply as I have described, Thou didst begin, oh my God, to withdraw Thyself from me: and the pain of Thy absence was the more bitter to me, because Thy presence had been so sweet to me, Thy love so strong in me. . . . Thy way, oh my God, before Thou didst make me enter into the state of death, was the way of the dying life: sometimes to hide Thyself and leave me to myself in a hundred weaknesses, sometimes to show Thyself with more sweetness and love. The nearer the soul drew to the state of death, the more her desolations were long and weary, her weaknesses increased, and also her joys became shorter, but purer and more intimate, until the time in which she fell into total privation." [800]

When this total privation or "mystic death" is fully established, it involves not only the personal "Absence of God," but the apparent withdrawal or loss of that impersonal support, that transcendent Ground or Spark of the soul, on which the self has long felt its whole real life to be based. Hence, its very means of contact with the spiritual world vanishes; and as regards all that matters, it does indeed seem to be "dead." "When we have reached this total deprivation," says De Caussade, "what shall we do? Abide in simplicity and peace, as Job on his ash heap, repeating, Blessed are the poor in spirit; those who have nothing have all, since they have God.' Quit all, strip yourself of all,' says the great Gerson, and you will have all in God.' God felt, God tasted and enjoyed,' says Fénelon, is indeed God, but God with those gifts which flatter the soul. God in darkness, in privation, in forsakenness, in insensibility, is so much God, that He is so to speak God bare and alone. . . .' Shall we fear this death, which is to produce in us the true divine life of grace?" [801]

B. In those selves for whom the subjective idea "Sanctity"--the need of conformity between the individual character and the Transcendent--has been central, the pain of the Night is less a deprivation than a new and dreadful kind of lucidity. The vision of the Good brings to the self an abrupt sense of her own hopeless and helpless imperfection: a black "conviction of sin," far more bitter than that endured in the Way of Purgation, which swamps everything else. "That which makes her pain so terrible is that she is, as it were, overwhelmed by the purity of God, and this purity makes her see the least atoms of her imperfections as if they were enormous sins, because of the infinite distance there is between the purity of God and the creature." [802]

"This," says St. John of the Cross again, "is one of the most bitter sufferings of this purgation. The soul is conscious of a profound emptiness in itself, a cruel destitution of the three kinds of goods, natural, temporal, and spiritual, which are ordained for its comfort. It sees itself in the midst of the opposite evils, miserable imperfections, dryness and emptiness of the understanding, and abandonment of the spirit in darkness." [803]

C. Often combined with the sense of sin and the "absence of God" is another negation, not the least distressing part of the sufferings of the self suddenly plunged into the Night. This is a complete emotional lassitude: the disappearance of all the old ardours, now replaced by a callousness, a boredom, which the self detests but cannot overcome. It is the dismal condition of spiritual ennui which ascetic writers know so well under the name of "aridity," and which psychologists look upon as the result of emotional fatigue. [804] It seems incredible that the eager love of a Divine Companion, so long the focus of the self's whole being should have vanished: that not only the transcendent vision should be withdrawn, but her very desire for, and interest in, that vision should grow cold. Yet the mystics are unanimous in declaring that this is a necessary stage in the growth of the spiritual consciousness.

"When the sun begins to decline in the heavens," says Ruysbroeck, "it enters the sign Virgo; which is so called because this period of the year is sterile as a virgin." This is the autumn season in the cycle of the soul, when the summer heat grows less. "It perfects and fulfils the yearly travail of the Sun. In the same manner, when Christ, that glorious sun, has risen to His zenith in the heart of man, as I have taught in the Third degree, and afterwards begins to decline, to hide the radiance of His divine sunbeams, and to forsake the man; then the heat and impatience of love grow less. Now that occultation of Christ, and the withdrawal of His light and heat, are the first work and the new coming of this degree. Now Christ says inwardly to this man, Go ye out in the manner which I now show you: and the man goes out and finds himself to be poor, miserable, and abandoned. Here all the storm, the fury, the impatience of his love, grow cool: glowing summer turns to autumn, all its riches are transformed into a great poverty. And the man begins to complain because of his wretchedness: for where now are the ardours of love, the intimacy, the gratitude, the joyful praise, and the interior consolation, the secret joy, the sensible sweetness? How have all these things failed him? And the burning violence of his love, and all the gifts which he felt before. How has all this died in him? And he feels like some ignorant man who has lost all his learning and his works . . . and of this misery there is born the fear of being lost, and as it were a sort of half-doubt: and this is the lowest point at which a man can hold his ground without falling into despair." [805]

D. This stagnation of the emotions has its counterpart in the stagnation of the will and intelligence, which has been experienced by some contemplatives as a part of their negative state. As regards the will, there is a sort of moral dereliction: the self cannot control its inclinations and thoughts. In the general psychic turmoil, all the unpurified part of man's inheritance, the lower impulses and unworthy ideas which have long been imprisoned below the threshold, force their way into the field of consciousness. "Every vice was re-awakened within me," says Angela of Foligno, "I would have chosen rather to be roasted than to endure such pains." [806] Where visual and auditory automatism is established, these irruptions from the subliminal region often take the form of evil visions, or of voices making coarse or sinful suggestions to the self. Thus St. Catherine of Siena, in the interval between her period of joyous illumination and her "spiritual marriage," was tormented by visions of fiends, who filled her cell and "with obscene words and gestures invited her to lust." She fled from her cell to the church to escape them, but they pursued her there: and she obtained no relief from this obsession until she ceased to oppose it. She cried, "I have chosen suffering for my consolation, and will gladly bear these and all other torments in the name of the Saviour, for as long as it shall please His Majesty." With this act of surrender, the evil vision fled: Catherine swung back to a state of affirmation, and was comforted by a vision of the Cross. [807]

An analogous psychological state was experienced by St. Teresa; though she fails to recognize it as an episode in her normal development, and attributes it, with other spiritual adventures for which she can find no other explanation, to the action of the Devil. "The soul," she says, "laid in fetters, loses all control over itself, and all power of thinking of anything but the absurdities he puts before it, which, being more or less unsubstantial, inconsistent, and disconnected, serve only to stifle the soul, so that it has no power over itself; and accordingly--so it seems to me--the devils make a football of it, and the soul is unable to escape out of their hands. It is impossible to describe the sufferings of the soul in this state. It goes about in quest of relief, and God suffers it to find none. The light of reason, in the freedom of its will, remains, but it is not clear; it seems to me as if its eyes were covered with a veil. . . . Temptations seem to press it down, and make it dull, so that its knowledge of God becomes to it as that of something which it hears of far away." This dullness and dimness extends to ordinary mental activity, which shares in the lassitude and disorder of the inner life. "If it seeks relief from the fire by spiritual reading, it cannot find any, just as if it could not read at all. On one occasion it occurred to me to read the life of a saint, that I might forget myself and be refreshed with the recital of what he had suffered. Four or five times, I read as many lines, and though they were written in Spanish, I understood them less at the end than I did when I began: so I gave it up. It so happened to me on more occasions than one." [808] If we are reminded of anything here, it is of the phenomenon of "dark contemplation." That dimness of mind which we there studied, is here extended to the normal activities of the surface intelligence. The Cloud of Unknowing, rolling up, seems to envelop the whole self. Contemplation, the "way within the way," has epitomized the greater process of the mystic life. In both, the path to Light lies through a meek surrender to the confusion and ignorance of the "Dark." The stress and exasperation felt in this dark, this state of vague helplessness, by selves of an active and self-reliant type, is exhibited by Teresa in one of her half-humorous self-revealing flashes. "The Devil," she says of it, "then sends so offensive a spirit of bad temper that I think I could eat people up!" [809]

All these types of "darkness," with their accompanying and overwhelming sensations of impotence and distress, are common in the lives of the mystics. Suso and Rulman Merswin experienced them: Tauler constantly refers to them: Angela of Foligno speaks of a "privation worse than hell." It is clear that even the joyous spirit of Mechthild of Magdeburg knew the sufferings of the loss and absence of God. "Lord," she says in one place, "since Thou hast taken from me all that I had of Thee, yet of Thy grace leave me the gift which every dog has by nature: that of being true to Thee in my distress; when I am deprived of all consolation. This I desire more fervently than Thy heavenly Kingdom!" [810] In such a saying as this, the whole "value for life" of the Dark Night is revealed to us: as an education in selfless constancy, a "school of suffering love."

E. There is, however, another way in which the self's sense of a continued imperfection in its relation with the Absolute--of work yet remaining to be done--expresses itself. In persons of a very highly strung and mobile type, who tend to rapid oscillations between pain and pleasure states, rather than to the long, slow movements of an ascending consciousness, attainment of the Unitive Life is sometimes preceded by the abrupt invasion of a wild and unendurable desire to "see God," apprehend the Transcendent in Its fullness: which can only, they think, be satisfied by death. As they begin to outgrow their illuminated consciousness, these selves begin also to realize how partial and symbolic that consciousness--even at its best--has been: and their movement to union with God is foreshadowed by a passionate and uncontrollable longing for ultimate Reality. This passion is so intense, that it causes acute anguish in those who feel it. It brings with it all the helpless and desolate feelings of the Dark Night; and sometimes rises to the heights of a negative rapture, an ecstasy of deprivation. St. Teresa is perhaps the best instance of this rare method of apprehending the self's essential separation from its home; which is also the subject of a celebrated chapter in the "Traité de l'Amour de Dieu" of St. François de Sales. [811] Thanks to her exceptionally mobile temperament, her tendency to rush up and down the scale of feeling, Teresa's states of joyous rapture were often paid for by such a "great desolation"--a dark ecstasy or "pain of God." "As long as this pain lasts," she says, "we cannot even remember our own existence; for in an instant all the faculties of the soul are so fettered as to lie incapable of any action save that of increasing our torture. Do not think I am exaggerating; on the contrary, that which I say is less than the truth, for lack of words in which it may be expressed. This is a trance of the senses and the faculties, save as regards all which helps to make the agony more intense. The understanding realizes acutely what cause there is for grief in separation from God: and our Lord increases this sorrow by a vivid manifestation of Himself. The pain thus grows to such a degree that in spite of herself the sufferer gives vent to loud cries, which she cannot stifle, however patient and accustomed to pain she may be, because this is not a pain which is felt in the body, but in the depths of the soul. The person I speak of learned from this how much more acutely the spirit is capable of suffering than the body. [812]

The intense and painful concentration upon the Divine Absence which takes place in this "dark rapture" often induces all the psycho-physical marks of ecstasy. "Although this state lasts but a short time, the limbs seem to be disjointed by it. The pulse is as feeble as if one were at the point of death; which is indeed the case, for whilst the natural heat of the body fails, that which is supernatural so burns the frame that with a few more degrees God would satisfy the soul's desire for death. . . . You will say perhaps, that there is imperfection in this desire to see God: and ask why this soul does not conform herself to His will, since she has so completely surrendered herself to it. Hitherto she could do this, and consecrated her life to it; but now she cannot, for her reason is reduced to such a state that she is no longer mistress of herself and can think of nothing but her affliction. Far from her Sovereign Good, why should she desire to live? She feels an extraordinary loneliness, finds no companionship in any earthly creature; nor could she I believe among those who dwell in heaven, since they are not her Beloved. Meanwhile all company is torture to her. She is like a person suspended in mid-air, who can neither touch the earth, nor mount to heaven. She burns with a consuming thirst, and cannot reach the water. And this is a thirst which cannot be borne, but one which nothing will quench: nor would she have it quenched with any other water than that of which our Lord spoke to the Samaritan woman; and this water is denied her." [813]

All these forms of the Dark Night--the "Absence of God," the sense of sin, the dark ecstasy, the loss of the self's old passion, peace, and joy, and its apparent relapse to lower spiritual and mental levels--are considered by the mystics themselves to constitute aspects or parts of one and the same process: the final purification of the will or stronghold of personality, that it may be merged without any reserve "in God where it was first." The function of this episode of the Mystic Way is to cure the soul of the innate tendency to seek and rest in spiritual joys; to confuse Reality with the joy given by the contemplation of Reality. It is the completion of that ordering of disordered loves, that trans-valuation of values, which the Way of Purgation began. The ascending self must leave these childish satisfactions; make its love absolutely disinterested, strong, and courageous, abolish all taint of spiritual gluttony. A total abandonment of the individualistic standpoint, of that trivial and egotistic quest of personal satisfaction which thwarts the great movement of the Flowing Light, is the supreme condition of man's participation in Reality. Thus is true not only of the complete participation which is possible to the great mystic, but of those unselfish labours in which the initiates of science or of art become to the Eternal Goodness "what his own hand is to a man." "Think not," says Tauler, "that God will be always caressing His children, or shine upon their head, or kindle their hearts as He does at the first. He does so only to lure us to Himself, as the falconer lures the falcon with its gay hood. . . . We must stir up and rouse ourselves and be content to leave off learning, and no more enjoy feeling and warmth, and must now serve the Lord with strenuous industry and at our own cost." [814]

This manly view of the Dark Night, as a growth in responsibility--an episode of character-building--in which, as "The Mirror of Simple Souls" has it, "the soul leaves that pride and play wherein it was full gladsome and jolly," is characteristic of the German mystics. We find it again in Suso, to whom the angel of his tribulation gave no sentimental consolations; but only the stern command, "Viriliter agite "--"Be a man!" "Then first," says Tauler again, "do we attain to the fullness of God's love as His children, when it is no longer happiness or misery, prosperity or adversity, that draws us to Him or keeps us back from Him. What we should then experience none can utter; but it would be something far better than when we were burning with the first flame of love, and had great emotion, but less true submission." [815]

In Illumination, the soul, basking in the Uncreated Light, identified the Divine Nature with the divine light and sweetness which it then enjoyed. Its consciousness of the transcendent was chiefly felt as an increase of personal vision and personal joy. Thus, in that apparently selfless state, the "I, the Me, the Mine," though spiritualized, still remained intact. The mortification of the senses was more than repaid by the rich and happy life which this mortification conferred upon the soul. But before real and permanent union with the Absolute can take place: before the whole self can learn to live on those high levels where--its being utterly surrendered to the Infinite Will--it can be wholly transmuted in God, merged in the great life of the All, this dependence on personal joys must be done away. The spark of the soul, the fast-growing germ of divine humanity, must so invade every corner of character that the self can only say with St. Catherine of Genoa, "My me is God: nor do I know my selfhood except in God." [816]

The various torments and desolations of the Dark Night constitute this last and drastic purgation of the spirit; the doing away of separateness, the annihilation of selfhood, even though all that self now claims for its own be the Love of God. Such a claim--which is really a claim to entire felicity, since the soul which possesses it needs nothing more--is felt by these great spirits to sully the radiance of their self-giving love. "All that I would here say of these inward delights and enjoyments," says William Law, "is only this; they are not holiness, they are not piety, they are not perfection; but they are God's gracious allurements and calls to seek after holiness and spiritual perfection . . . and ought rather to convince us that we are as yet but babes, than that we are ready men of God. . . . This alone is the true Kingdom of God opened in the soul when, stripped of all selfishness, it has only one love and one will in it; when it has no motion or desire but what branches from the Love of God, and resigns itself wholly to the Will of God. . . . To sum up all in a word: Nothing hath separated us from God but our own will, or rather our own will is our separation from God. All the disorder and corruption and malady of our nature lies in a certain fixedness of our own will, imagination, and desire, wherein we live to ourselves, are our own centre and circumference, act wholly from ourselves, according to our own will, imagination, and desires. There is not the smallest degree of evil in us but what arises from this selfishness because we are thus all in all to ourselves. . . . To be humble, mortified, devout, patient in a certain degree, and to be persecuted for our virtues, is no hurt to this selfishness; nay, spiritual-self must have all these virtues to subsist upon, and his life consists in seeing, knowing and feeling the bulk, strength, and reality of them. But still, in all this show and glitter of virtue, there is an unpurified bottom on which they stand, there is a selfishness which can no more enter into the Kingdom of Heaven than the grossness of flesh and blood can enter into it. What we are to feel and undergo in these last purifications, when the deepest root of all selfishness, as well spiritual as natural, is to be plucked up and torn from us, or how we shall be able to stand in that trial, are both of them equally impossible to be known by us beforehand." [817]

The self, then, has got to learn to cease to be its "own centre and circumference": to make that final surrender which is the price of final peace. In the Dark Night the starved and tortured spirit learns through an anguish which is "itself an orison" to accept lovelessness for the sake of Love, Nothingness for the sake of the All; dies without any sure promise of life, loses when it hardly hopes to find. It sees with amazement the most sure foundations of its transcendental life crumble beneath it, dwells in a darkness which seems to hold no promise of a dawn. This is what the German mystics call the "upper school of true resignation" or of "suffering love"; the last test of heroic detachment, of manliness, of spiritual courage. Though such an experience is "passive" in the sense that the self can neither enter nor leave it at will it is a direct invitation to active endurance, a condition of stress in which work is done. Thus, when St. Catherine of Siena was tormented by hideous visions of sin, she was being led by her deeper self to the heroic acceptance of this subtle form of torture, almost unendurable to her chaste and delicate mind. When these trials had brought her to the point at which she ceased to resist them, but exclaimed, "I have chosen suffering for my consolation," their business was done. They ceased. More significant still, when she asked, "Where wast Thou, Lord, when I was tormented by this foulness?" the Divine Voice answered, "I was in thy heart." [818]

"In order to raise the soul from imperfection," said the Voice of God to St. Catherine in her Dialogue, "I withdraw Myself from her sentiment, depriving her of former consolations . . . which I do in order to humiliate her, and cause her to seek Me in truth, and to prove her in the light of faith, so that she come to prudence. Then, if she love Me without thought of self, and with lively faith and with hatred of her own sensuality, she rejoices in the time of trouble, deeming herself unworthy of peace and quietness of mind. Now comes the second of the three things of which I told thee, that is to say: how the soul arrives at perfection, and what she does when she is perfect. That is what she does. Though she perceives that I have withdrawn Myself, she does not, on that account, look back; but perseveres with humility in her exercises, remaining barred in the house of self-knowledge, and, continuing to dwell therein, awaits with lively faith the coming of the Holy Spirit, that is of Me, who am the Fire of Love. . . . This is what the soul does in order to rise from imperfection and arrive at perfection, and it is to this end, namely, that she may arrive at perfection, that I withdraw from her, not by grace, but by sentiment. Once more do I leave her so that she may see and know her defects, so that feeling herself deprived of consolation and afflicted by pain, she may recognize her own weakness, and learn how incapable she is of stability or perseverance, thus cutting down to the very root of spiritual self-love: for this should be the end and purpose of all her self-knowledge, to rise above herself, mounting the throne of conscience, and not permitting the sentiment of imperfect love to turn again in its death-struggle, but with correction and reproof digging up the root of self-love with the knife of self-hatred and the love of virtue." [819]

"Digging up the root of self-love with the knife of self-hatred"--here we see the mystical reason of that bitter self-contempt and sense of helplessness which overwhelms the soul in the Dark Night.

Such a sense of helplessness is really, the mystics say, a mark of progress: of deeper initiation into that sphere of reality to which it is not yet acclimatized, and which brings with it a growing consciousness of the appalling disparity between that Reality, that Perfection, and the imperfect soul.

The self is in the dark because it is blinded by a Light greater than it can bear--that "Divine Wisdom which is not only night and darkness to the soul, but pain and torment too." "The more clear the light, the more does it blind the eyes of the owl, and the more we try to look at the sun the feebler grows our sight and the more our weak eyes are darkened. So the divine light of contemplation, when it beats on the soul not yet perfectly purified, fills it with spiritual darkness, not only because of its brilliance, but because it paralyses the natural perception of the soul. The pain suffered by the soul is like that endured by weak or diseased eyes when suddenly struck by a strong light. Such suffering is intense when the yet unpurified soul finds itself invaded by this cleansing light. For in this pure light, which attacks its impurities to expel them, the soul perceives itself to be so unclean and miserable that it seems as if God had set Himself against it. . . . Wonderful and piteous sight! so great are the weakness and imperfection of the soul that the hand of God, so soft and so gentle, is felt to be so heavy and oppressive, though merely touching it, and that, too, most mercifully; for He touches the soul, not to chastise it, but to load it with His graces." [820]

The Dark Night then, whichever way we look at it, is a state of disharmony; of imperfect adaptation to environment. The self, unaccustomed to that direct contact of the Absolute which is destined to become the Source of its vitality and its joy, feels the "soft and gentle touch" of the Following Love as unbearable in its weight. The "self-naughting" or "purification of the will," which here takes place, is the struggle to resolve that disharmony; to purge away the somewhat which still sets itself up in the soul as separate from the Divine, and makes the clear light of reality a torment instead of a joy. So deeply has the soul now entered into the great stream of spiritual life, so dominant has her transcendental faculty become, that this process is accomplished in her whether she will or no: and in this sense it is, as ascetic writers sometimes call it, a "passive purgation." So long as the subject still feels himself to be somewhat, he has not yet annihilated selfhood and come to that ground where his being can be united with the Being of God.

Only when he learns to cease thinking of himself at all, in however depreciatory a sense; when he abolishes even such selfhood as lies in a desire for the sensible presence of God, will that harmony be attained. This is the "naughting of the soul," the utter surrender to the great movement of the Absolute Life, which is insisted upon at such length by all writers upon mysticism. Here, as in purgation, the condition of access to higher levels of vitality is a death: a deprivation, a detachment, a clearing of the ground. Poverty leaps to the Cross: and finds there an utter desolation, without promise of spiritual reward. The satisfactions of the spirit must now go the same way as the satisfactions of the senses. Even the power of voluntary sacrifice and self-discipline is taken away. A dreadful ennui, a dull helplessness, takes its place. The mystic motto, I am nothing, I have nothing, I desire nothing, must now express not only the detachment of the senses, but the whole being's surrender to the All.

The moral condition towards which the interior travail is directed is that of an utter humility. "Everything depends," says Tauler, on "a fathomless sinking in a fathomless nothingness." He continues, "If a man were to say, Lord, who art Thou, that I must follow Thee through such deep, gloomy, miserable paths?' the Lord would reply, I am God and Man, and far more God.' If a man could answer then, really and consciously from the bottom of his heart. Then I am nothing and less than nothing'; all would be accomplished, for the Godhead has really no place to work in, but ground where all has been annihilated.[821] As the schoolmen say, when a new form is to come into existence, the old must of necessity be destroyed. . . . And so I say: If a man is to be thus clothed upon with this Being, all the forms must of necessity be done away that were ever received by him in all his powers--of perception, knowledge, will, work, of subjection, sensibility and self-seeking.' When St. Paul saw nothing, he saw God. So also when Elias wrapped his face in his mantle, God came. All strong rocks are broken here, all on which the spirit can rest must be done away. Then, when all forms have ceased to exist, in the twinkling of an eye the man is transformed. Therefore thou must make an entrance. Thereupon speaks the Heavenly Father to him: "Thou shalt call Me Father, and shalt never cease to enter in; entering ever further in, ever nearer, so as to sink the deeper in an unknown and unnamed abyss; and, above all ways, images and forms, and above all powers, to lose thyself, deny thyself, and even unform thyself.' In this lost condition nothing is to be seen but a ground which rests upon itself, everywhere one Being, one Life. It is thus, man may say, that he becomes unknowing, unloving, and senseless."[822]

It is clear that so drastic a process of unselfing is not likely to take place without stress. It is the negative aspect of "deification": in which the self, deprived of "perception, knowledge, will, work, self-seeking"--the I, the Me, the Mine--loses itself, denies itself, unforms itself, drawing "ever nearer" to the One, till "nothing is to be seen but a ground which rests upon itself"--the ground of the soul, in which it has union with God.

"Everywhere one Being, one Life"--this is the goal of mystical activity; the final state of equilibrium towards which the self is moving, or rather struggling, in the dimness and anguish of the Dark Night. "The soul," says Madame Guyon in a passage of unusual beauty, "after many a redoubled death, expires at last in the arms of Love; but she is unable to perceive these arms. . . . Then, reduced to Nought, there is found in her ashes a seed of immortality, which is preserved in these ashes and will germinate in its season. But she knows not this; and does not expect ever to see herself living again." Moreover, "the soul which is reduced to the Nothing, ought to dwell therein; without wishing, since she is now but dust, to issue from this state, nor, as before, desiring to live again. She must remain as something which no longer exists: and this, in order that the Torrent may drown itself and lose itself in the Sea, never to find itself in its selfhood again: that it may become one and the same thing with the Sea."[823]

So Hilton says of the "naughted soul," "the less it thinketh that it loveth or seeth God, the nearer it nigheth for to perceive the gift of the blessed love. For then is love master, and worketh in the soul, and maketh it for to forget itself, and for to see and behold only how love doth. And then is the soul more suffering than doing, and that is clean love."[824]

The "mystic death" or Dark Night is therefore an aspect or incident of the transition from multiplicity to Unity, of that mergence and union of the soul with the Absolute which is the whole object of the mystical evolution of man. It is the last painful break with the life of illusion, the tearing away of the self from that World of Becoming in which all its natural affections and desires are rooted, to which its intellect and senses correspond; and the thrusting of it into that World of Being where at first, weak and blinded, it can but find a wilderness, a "dark." No transmutation without fire, say the alchemists: No cross, no crown, says the Christian. All the great experts of the spiritual life agree--whatever their creeds, their symbols, their explanations--in describing this stress, tribulation, and loneliness, as an essential part of the way from the Many to the One; bringing the self to the threshold of that completed life which is to be lived in intimate union with Reality. It is the Entombment which precedes the Resurrection, say the Christian mystics; ever ready to describe their life-process in the language of their faith. Here as elsewhere--but nowhere else in so drastic a sense--the self must "lose to find and die to live."

The Dark Night, as we have seen, tends to establish itself gradually; the powers and intuitions of the self being withdrawn one after another, the intervals of lucidity becoming rarer, until the "mystic death" or state of total deprivation is reached. So, too, when the night begins to break down before the advance of the new or Unitive Life, the process is generally slow, though it may be marked--as for instance in Rulman Merswin's case--by visions and ecstasies.[825] One after another, the miseries and disharmonies of the Dark Night give way: affirmation takes the place of negation: the Cloud of Unknowing is pierced by rays of light.

The act of complete surrender then, which is the term of the Dark Night, has given the self its footing in Eternity: its abandonment of the old centres of consciousness has permitted movement towards the new. In each such forward movement, the Transcendental Self, that spark of the soul which is united to the Absolute Life, has invaded more and more the seat of personality; stage by stage the remaking of the self in conformity with the Eternal World has gone on. In the misery and apparent stagnation of the Dark Night--that dimness of the spiritual consciousness, that dullness of its will and love--work has been done, and the last great phase of the inward transmutation accomplished. The self which comes forth from the night is no separated self, conscious of the illumination of the Uncreated Light, but the New Man, the transmuted humanity, whose life is one with the Absolute Life of God. "As soon as the two houses of the soul [the sensual and the spiritual]," says St. John of the Cross, "are tranquil and confirmed and merged in one by this peace, and their servants the powers, appetites and passions are sunk in deep tranquillity, neither troubled by things above nor things below, the Divine Wisdom immediately unites itself to the soul in a new bond of loving possession, and that is fulfilled which is written in the Book of Wisdom: While all things were immersed in quiet silence, and the night was in the midway of her course, Thy omnipotent Word sallied out of heaven from the royal seats' (Wisdom xviii. 14). The same truth is set before us in the Canticle, where the Bride, after passing by those who took her veil away and wounded her, saith, When I had a little passed by them I found Him Whom my soul loveth' (Cant. iii. 4)." [826]

***

So far, we have considered the Dark Night of the Soul from a somewhat academic point of view. We have tried to dissect and describe it: have seen it through the medium of literature rather than life. Such a method has obvious disadvantages when dealing with any organic process: and when it is applied to the spiritual life of man, these disadvantages are increased. Moreover, our chief example, "from the life," Madame Guyon, valuable as her passion for self analysis makes her to the student of mystic states cannot be looked upon as a satisfactory witness. Her morbid sentimentalism, her absurd "spiritual self-importance" have to be taken into account and constantly remembered in estimating the value of her psychological descriptions. If we want to get a true idea of the Dark Night, as an episode in the history of a living soul, we must see it in its context, as part of that soul's total experience. We must study the reactions of a self which is passing through this stage of development upon its normal environment the content of its diurnal existence; not only on its intuition of the Divine.

As a pendant to this chapter, then, we will look at this "state of pain" as it expressed itself in the life of a mystic whose ardent, impressionable, and poetic nature reacted to every aspect of the contemplative experience, every mood and fluctuation of the soul. I choose this particular case--the case of Suso--(1) because it contains many interesting and unconventional elements; showing us the Dark Night not as a series of specific moods and events, but as a phase of growth largely conditioned by individual temperament: (2) because, being told at first hand, in the pages of his singularly ingenuous autobiography, the record is comparatively free from the reverent and corrupting emendations of the hagiographer.

From the 22nd chapter onwards, Suso's "Life" is one of the most valuable documents we possess for the study of this period of the Mystic Way. We see in it--more clearly perhaps than its author can have done--the remaking of his consciousness, his temperamental reactions to the ceaseless travail of his deeper self: so different in type from those of St. Teresa and Madame Guyon. There is a note of virile activity about these trials and purifications, an insistence upon the heroic aspect of the spiritual life, far more attractive than Madame Guyon's elaborate discourses on resignation and holy passivity, or even St. Teresa's "dark ecstasies" of insatiable desire.

The chapter in which Suso's entrance into this "Second Mystic Life" of deprivation is described is called "How the Servitor was led into the School of True Resignation." Characteristically, this inward experience expressed itself in a series of dramatic visions; visions of that "dynamic" kind which we have noticed as a frequent accompaniment of the crisis in which the mystic self moves to a new level of consciousness. [827] It followed the long period of constant mortification and intermittent illumination which lasted, as he tells us, from his eighteenth to his fortieth year: and constituted the first cycle of his spiritual life. At the end of that time, "God showed him that all this severity and these penances were but a good beginning, that by these he had triumphed over the unruly sensual man: but that now he must exert himself in another manner if he desired to advance in the Way." [828] In two of these visions--these vivid interior dramas--we seem to see Suso's developed mystical consciousness running ahead of its experience, reading the hidden book of its own future, probing its own spiritual necessities; and presenting the results to the backward and unwilling surface-mind. This growing mystic consciousness is already aware of fetters which the normal Suso does not feel. Its eyes open upon the soul's true country, it sees the path which it must tread to perfect freedom; the difference between the quality of that freedom, and the spirituality which Suso thinks that he has attained. The first of these visions is that of the Upper School; the second is that in which he is called to put upon him the armour of a knight.

"One night after matins, the Servitor being seated in his chair, and plunged in deep thought, he was rapt from his senses. And it seemed to him that he saw in a vision a magnificent young man descend from Heaven before him, and say, "thou hast been long enough in the Lower School, and hast there sufficiently applied thyself. Come, then, with me; and I will introduce thee into the highest school that exists in this world. [829] There, thou shalt apply thyself to the study of that science which will procure thee the veritable peace of God; and which will bring thy holy beginning to a happy end.' Then the Servitor rose, full of joy; and it seemed to him that the young man took him by the hand and led him into a spiritual country, wherein there was a fair house inhabited by spiritual men: for here lived those who applied themselves to the study of this science. As soon as he entered it, these received him kindly, and amiably saluted him. And at once they went to the supreme Master, and told him that a man was come, who desired to be his disciple and to learn his science. And he said, Let him come before me, that I may see whether he please me.' And when the supreme Master saw the Servitor, he smiled on him very kindly, and said, Know that this guest is able to become a good disciple of our high science, if he will bear with patience the hard probation: for it is necessary that he be tried inwardly.'

"The Servitor did not then understand these enigmatic words. He turned toward the young man who had brought him and asked, Well, my dear comrade, what then is this Upper School and this science of which you have spoken to me?' The young man replied thus: In this Upper School they teach the science of Perfect Self-abandonment; that is to say, that a man is here taught to renounce himself so utterly that, in all those circumstances in which God is manifested, either by Himself or in His creatures, the man applies himself only to remaining calm and unmoved renouncing so far as is possible all human frailty.' And shortly after this discourse, the Servitor came to himself . . . and, talking to himself, he said, Examine thyself inwardly and thou wilt see that thou hast still much self-will: thou wilt observe, that with all thy mortifications which thou hast inflicted on thyself, thou canst not yet endure external vexations. Thou art like a hare hiding in a bush, who is frightened by the whispering of the leaves. Thou also art frightened every day by the griefs that come to thee: thou dost turn pale at the sight of those who speak against thee: when thou doest fear to succumb, thou takest flight; when thou oughtest to present thyself with simplicity, thou dost hide thyself. When they praise thee, thou art happy: when they blame thee, thou art sad. Truly is it very needful for thee that thou shouldst go to an Upper School." [830]

Some weeks later, when he had been rejoicing in the new bodily comfort which resulted from his relinquishment of all outward mortifications, Suso received a still more pointed lesson on his need of moral courage. He was sitting on his bed and meditating on the words of Job "Militia est." "The life of man upon the earth is like unto that of a knight": [831] "and during this meditation, he was once more rapt from his senses, and it seemed to him that he saw coming towards him a fair youth of manly bearing, who held in his hands the spurs and the other apparel which knights are accustomed to wear. And he drew near to the Servitor, and clothed him in a coat of mail, and said to him, Oh, knight! hitherto thou hast been but a squire, but now it is God's will that thou be raised to knighthood.' And the Servitor gazed at his spurs, and said with much amazement in his heart, Alas, my God! what has befallen me? what have I become? must I indeed be a knight? I had far rather remain in peace.' Then he said to the young man, Since it is God's will that I should be a knight I had rather have won my spurs in battle; for this would have been more glorious.' The young man turned away and began to laugh: and said to him, Have no fear! thou shalt have battles enough. He who would play a valiant part in the spiritual chivalry of God must endure more numerous and more dreadful combats than any which were encountered by the proud heroes of ancient days, of whom the world tells and sings the knightly deeds. It is not that God desires to free thee from thy burdens; He would only change them and make them far heavier than they have ever been.' Then the Servitor said, Oh, Lord, show me my pains in advance, in order that I may know them.' The Lord replied, No, it is better that thou know nothing, lest thou shouldst hesitate. But amongst the innumerable pains which thou wilt have to support, I will tell thee three. The first is this. Hitherto it is thou who hast scourged thyself, with thine own hands: thou didst cease when it seemed good to thee, and thou hadst compassion on thyself. Now, I would take thee from thyself, and cast thee without defence into the hands of strangers who shall scourge thee. Thou shalt see the ruin of thy reputation. Thou shalt be an object of contempt to blinded men; and thou shalt suffer more from this than from the wounds made by the points of thy cross. [832] When thou didst give thyself up to thy penances thou wert exalted and admired. Now thou shalt be abased and annihilated. The second pain is this: Although thou didst inflict on thyself many cruel tortures, still by God's grace there remained to thee a tender and loving disposition. It shall befall thee, that there where thou hadst thought to find a special and a faithful love, thou shalt find nought but unfaithfulness, great sufferings, and great griefs. Thy trials shall be so many that those men who have any love for thee shall suffer with thee by compassion. The third pain is this: hitherto thou hast been but a child at the breast, a spoiled child. Thou hast been immersed in the divine sweetness like a fish in the sea. Now I will withdraw all this. It is my will that thou shouldst be deprived of it, and that thou suffer from this privation, that thou shouldst be abandoned of God and of man, that thou shouldst be publicly persecuted by the friends of thine enemies. I will tell it thee in a word: all thou shalt undertake, that might bring thee joy and consolation, shall come to nothing, and all that might make thee suffer and be vexatious to thee shall succeed.'" [833]

Observe here, under a highly poetic and visionary method of presentation, the characteristic pains of the Dark Night as described by St. John of the Cross, Madame Guyon, De Caussade and almost every expert who has written upon this state of consciousness. Desolation and loneliness, abandonment by God and by man, a tendency of everything to "go wrong," a profusion of unsought trials and griefs--all are here. Suso, naturally highly strung, sensitive and poetic, suffered acutely in this mental chaos and multiplication of woes. He was tormented by a deep depression so that "it seemed as though a mountain weighed on his heart" by doubts against faith: by temptations to despair. [834] These miseries lasted for about ten years. They were diversified and intensified by external trials, such as illnesses and false accusations; and relieved, as the years of purgation had been, by occasional visions and revelations.

Suso's natural tendency was to an enclosed life: to secret asceticism, reverie, outbursts of fervent devotion, long hours of rapt communion with the Eternal Wisdom whom he loved. At once artist and recluse, utterly unpractical, he had all the dreamer's dread of the world of men. His deeper self now ran counter to all these preferences. Like the angel which said to him in the hour of his utmost prostration and misery, " Viriliter agite!" [835] it pressed him inexorably towards the more manly part; pushing him to action, sending him out from his peaceful if uncomfortable cell to the rough-and-tumble of the world. Poor Suso was little fitted by nature for that rough-and-tumble: and a large part of his autobiography is concerned with the description of all that he endured therein. The Dark Night for him was emphatically an "active night"; and the more active he was forced to be, the darker and more painful it became. Chapter after chapter is filled with the troubles of the unhappy Servitor; who, once he began to meddle with practical life, soon disclosed his native simplicity and lost the reputation for wisdom and piety which he had gained during his years of seclusion.

There was not in Suso that high-hearted gaiety, that child-like courage, which made the early Franciscans delight to call themselves God's fools. The bewildered lover of the Eternal Wisdom suffered acutely from his loss of dignity; from the unfriendliness and contempt of other men. He gives a long and dismal catalogue of the enemies that he made, the slanders which he endured, in the slow acquirement of that disinterested and knightly valour which had been revealed to him as the essential virtue of the squire who would "ride with the Eternal Wisdom in the lists." [836]

Suso was a born romantic. This dream of a spiritual chivalry haunts him: again and again he uses the language of the tournament in his description of the mystic life. Yet perhaps few ideals seem less appropriate to this timid, highly-strung, unpractical Dominican friar: this ecstatic "minnesinger of the Holy Ghost," half-poet, half-metaphysician, racked by ill-health, exalted by mystical ardours, instinctively fearing the harsh contact of his fellow-men.

There is no grim endurance about Suso: he feels every hard knock, and all the instincts of his nature are in favour of telling his griefs. A more human transcendentalist has never lived. Thanks to the candour and completeness with which he takes his readers into his confidence, we know him far more intimately than we do any of the other great contemplatives. There is one chapter in his life in which he describes with the utmost ingenuousness how he met a magnificent knight whilst crossing the Lake of Constance; and was deeply impressed by his enthusiastic descriptions of the glories and dangers of the lists. The conversation between the tough man at arms and the hypersensitive mystic is full of revealing touches. Suso is exalted and amazed by the stories of hard combats, the courage of the knights, and the ring for which they contend: but most astounded by the fortitude which pays no attention to its wounds.

"And may not one weep, and show that one is hurt, when one is hit very hard?" he says.

The knight replies, "No, even though one's heart fails, as happens to many, one must never show that one is distressed. One must appear gay and happy; otherwise one is dishonoured, and loses at the same time one's reputation and the Ring."

"These words made the Servitor thoughtful; and he was greatly moved, and inwardly sighing he said, Oh Lord, if the knights of this world must suffer so much to obtain so small a prize, how just it is that we should suffer far more if we are to obtain an eternal recompense! Oh, my sweet Lord, if only I were worthy of being Thy spiritual knight!"

Arrived at his destination, however, Suso was visited by fresh trials: and soon forgetting his valiant declarations, he began as usual to complain of his griefs. The result was a visionary ecstasy, in which he heard the voice of that deeper self to which he always attributed a divine validity, inquiring with ill-concealed irony, "Well, what has become of that noble chivalry? Who is this knight of straw, this rag-made man? It is not by making rash promises and drawing back when suffering comes, that men win the Ring of Eternity which you desire."

"Alas! Lord," said Suso plaintively, "the tournaments in which one must suffer for Thee last such a very long time!"

The voice replied, "But the reward, the honour, and the Ring which I give to My knights endure for ever." [837]

As his mystic consciousness grew, the instinct pressing him towards action and endurance grew with it. The inner voice and its visionary expression urged him on remorselessly. It mocked his weakness, encouraged him to more active suffering, more complete self-renunciation: more contact with the unfriendly world. Viriliter agile! He must be a complete personality; a whole man. Instead of the quiet cell, the secret mortifications, his selfhood was to be stripped from him, and the reality of his renunciation tested, under the unsympathetic and often inimical gaze of other men. The case of Suso is one that may well give pause to those who regard the mystic life as a progress in passivity, withdrawal from the actual world: and the "Dark Night" as one of its most morbid manifestations.

It is interesting to observe how completely human and apparently "unmystical" was the culminating trial by which Suso was "perfected in the school of true resignation." "None can come to the sublime heights of the divinity," said the Eternal Wisdom to him in one of his visions, "or taste its ineffable sweetness, if first they have not experienced the bitterness and lowliness of My humanity. The higher they climb without passing by My humanity, the lower afterward shall be their fall. My humanity is the road which all must tread who would come to that which thou seekest: My sufferings are the door by which all must come in." [838] It was by the path of humanity; by some of the darkest and most bitter trials of human experience, the hardest tests of its patience and love, that Suso "came in" to that sustained peace of heart and union with the divine will which marked his last state. The whole tendency of these trials in the "path of humanity" seems, as we look at them, to be directed towards the awakening of those elements of character left dormant by the rather specialized disciplines and purifications of his cloistered life. We seem to see the "new man" invading all the resistant or inactive corners of personality: the Servitor of Wisdom being pressed against his will to a deeply and widely human life in the interests of Eternal Love. The absence of God whom he loved, the enmity of man whom he feared, were the chief forces brought to play upon him: and we watch his slow growth, under their tonic influence, in courage, humility, and fraternal love.

Few chapters in the history of the mystics are more touching than that passage in Suso's Life.[839] "Where we speak of an extraordinary Trial which the Servitor had to bear." It tells how a malicious woman accused him of being the father of her child, and succeeded for the time in entirely destroying his reputation. "And the scandal was all the greater," says the Servitor with his customary simplicity "because the rumour of that brother's sanctity had spread so far." Poor Suso was utterly crushed by this calumny, "wounded to the depths of his heart." "Lord, Lord!" he cried, "every day of my life I have worshipped Thy holy Name in many places, and have helped to cause it to be loved and honoured by many men: and now Thou wouldst drag my name through the mud!" When the scandal was at its height, a woman of the neighbourhood came to him in secret; and offered to destroy the child which was the cause of this gossip, in order that the tale might be more quickly forgotten and his reputation restored. She said further that unless the baby were somehow disposed of, he would certainly be forced by public opinion to accept it, and provide for its upbringing. Suso, writhing as he was under the contempt of the whole neighbourhood, the apparent ruin of his career--knowing, too, that this slander of one of their leaders must gravely injure the reputation of the Friends of God--was able to meet the temptation with a noble expression of trust. "I have confidence in the God of Heaven, Who is rich, and Who has given me until now all that which was needful unto me. He will help me to keep, if need be, another beside myself." And then he said to his temptress, "Go, fetch the little child that I may see it."

"And when he had the baby, he put it on his knees and looked at it: and the baby began to smile at him. And sighing deeply, he said, Could I kill a pretty baby that smiled at me? No, no, I had rather suffer every trial that could come upon me!" And turning his face to the unfortunate little creature, he said to it, Oh my poor, poor little one! Thou art but an unhappy orphan, for thy unnatural father hath denied thee, thy wicked mother would cast thee off, as one casts off a little dog that has ceased to please! The providence of God hath given thee to me, in order that I may be thy father. I wilt accept thee, then, from Him and from none else. Ah, dear child of my heart, thou liest on my knees; thou dost gaze at me, thou canst not yet speak! As for me, I contemplate thee with a broken heart; with weeping eyes, and lips that kiss, I bedew thy little face with my burning tears! . . . Thou shalt be my son, and the child of the good God; and as long as heaven gives me a mouthful, I shall share it with thee, for the greater glory of God; and will patiently support all the trials that may come to me, my darling son!'" How different is this from the early Suso; interested in little but his own safe spirituality, and with more than a touch of the religious aesthete!

The story goes on: "And when the hard-hearted woman who had wished to kill the little one saw these tears, when she heard these tender words, she was greatly moved: and her heart was filled with pity, and she too began to weep and cry aloud. The Servitor was obliged to calm her, for fear that, attracted by the noise, some one should come and see what was going on. And when she had finished weeping the Brother gave her back the baby and blessed it, and said to it, Now may God in His goodness bless thee, and may the saints protect thee against all evil that may be!' And he enjoined the woman to care for it well at his expense."

Small wonder that after this heroic act of charity Suso's reputation went from bad to worse; that even his dearest friends forsook him, and he narrowly escaped expulsion from the religious life. His torments and miseries, his fears for the future, continued to grow until they at last came to their term in a sort of mental crisis. "His feeble nature broken by the pains which he had to endure, he went forth raving like one who has lost his sense and hid himself in a place far from men, where none could see or hear him . . . and whilst he suffered thus, several times something which came from God said within his soul, Where then is your resignation? Where is that equal humour in joy and in tribulation which you have so lightly taught other men to love? In what manner is it, then, that one should rest in God and have confidence only in Him?' He replied weeping, You ask where is my resignation? But tell me first, where is the infinite pity of God for His friends? . . . Oh Fathomless Abyss! come to my help, for without Thee I am lost. Thou knowest that Thou art my only consolation, that all my trust is only in Thee. Oh hear me, for the love of God, all you whose hearts are wounded! Behold! let none be scandalized by my insane behaviour. So long as it was only a question of preaching resignation, that was easy: but now that my heart is pierced, now that I am wounded to the marrow . . . how can I be resigned?' And after thus suffering half a day, his brain was exhausted, and at last he became calmer, and sitting down he came to himself: and turning to God, and abandoning himself to His Will, he said, If it cannot be otherwise, fiat voluntas tua .'" [1840] The act of submission was at once followed by an ecstasy and vision, in which the approaching end of his troubles was announced to him. "And in the event, God came to the help of the Servitor, and little by little that terrible tempest died away."

Thus with Suso, as with St. Catherine of Siena and other mystics whom we have considered, the travail of the Dark Night is all directed towards the essential mystic act of utter self-surrender; that fiat voluntas tua which marks the death of selfhood in the interests of a new and deeper life. He has learned the lesson of "the school of true resignation": has moved to a new stage of reality: a complete self-naughting, an utter acquiescence in the large and hidden purposes of the Divine Will.

"Anzi è formale ad esto beato esse
tenersi dentro alla divina voglia
per ch' una fansi nostre voglie stesse," [840]

says Piccarda, announcing the primary law of Paradise. Suso has passed through the fire to the state in which he too can say, "La sua voluntate è nostre pace." The old grouping of his consciousness round "spiritual self" has come to its head and at last broken down. In the midst of a psychic storm parallel to the upheavals of conversion, "mercenary love" is for ever disestablished, the new state of Pure Love is abruptly established in its place. Human pain is the price: the infinite joy peculiar to "free souls" is the reward. We may study the pain, but the nature of the joy is beyond us: as, in the Absolute Type of all mystic achievement, we see the cross clearly but can hardly guess at the true nature of the resurrection life.

Hence Suso's description of his establishment in the Unitive Way seems meagre, an anti-climax, after all that went before. "And later," he says simply, "when God judged that it was time, He rewarded the poor martyr for all his suffering. And he enjoyed peace of heart, and received in tranquillity and quietness many precious graces. And he praised the Lord from the very depths of his soul, and thanked Him for those same sufferings: which, for all the world, he would not now have been spared. And God caused him to understand that by this complete abasement he had gained more, and was made the more worthy to be raised up to God, than by all the pains which he had suffered from his youth up to that time." [841]

Footnotes:

783. Vide supra , pp. 187 seq ., the cases of Suso and Pascal.

784. Pt. ii. cap. i.

785. "Psychology of Religion," p. 24.

786. An example of this occurred in the later life of Ste. Jeanne Françoise de Chantal. See "The Nuns of Port Royal," by M. E. Lowndes, p. 284. Much valuable material bearing on the trials of the Dark Night as they appear in the experience of ordinary contemplatives will be found in the letters of direction of De Caussade. See his "L'Abandon à la Providence Divine," vol. ii.

787. Vide supra , p. 228.

788. Vie, pt. I. cap. xx.

789. Op. cit., cap. xxi.

790. "Journal Spirituel," p. 233.

791. Vie, cap. xxiii.

792. "Les Torrents," pt. i. cap. vii. § 2.

793. Leben, cap. xxii.

794. "Holy Wisdom," Treatise iii. § iv. cap. v.

795. "Buchlein von der ewigen Weisheit," cap. ii.

796. "Journal Spirituel," p. 368.

797. From the "Mesnevi." Quoted in the Appendix to The Flowers or Rose Garden of Sadi."

798. Meister Eckhart, Pred. lvii. So too St. Gertrude in one of her symbolic visions saw a thick

hedge erected between herself and Christ.

799. "Noche Escura del Alma,'" I. ii. cap. vi.

800. Vie, pt. i. cap. xxiii.

801. De Caussade, "L'Abandon à la Providence Divine," vol. ii., p. 269.

802. Madame Guyon , "Les Torrents," pt. i. cap, vii.

803. "Noche Escura del Alma," loc. cit.

804. Instructive examples in De Caussade, op. cit., vol. ii., pp. 1-82.

805. Ruysbroeck, "De Ornatu Spiritalium Nuptiarum," I. ii. cap. xxviii.

806. St. Angèle de Foligno, op. cit ., p. 197 (English translation, p. 15).

807. J. E. Gardner, "St. Catherine of Siena," p. 20.

808. Vida, cap. xxx. §§ 12 and 14.

809. Op. cit., loc. cit.

810. "Das Fliessende Licht der Gottheit," pt. ii. cap. 25.

811. L. vi. cap. xiii.

812. "El Castillo Interior," Moradas Sextas, cap. xi.

813. St. Teresa, op. cit., loc. cit. Compare the Vida, cap. xx. §§ 11 to 14.

814. Sermon for the 4th Sunday in Lent (Winkworth's translation, p. 280).

815. Op. cit , loc. cit .

816. "Vita e Dottrina," cap. xiv.

817. "Christian Regeneration" (The Liberal and Mystical Writings of William Law, pp. 158-60).

818. Vide supra , p. 392.

819. Dialogo, cap. lxiii.

820. St. John of the Cross, "Noche Escura del Alma," I. ii cap. v.

821. I.e. , the pure essence of the soul, purged of selfhood and illusion.

822. Sermon on St. Matthew ("The Inner Way." pp. 204, 205).

823. "Les Torrents" pt. i. cap, viii.

824. "The Scale of Perfection," bk. ii. cap. xxxv.

825. Jundt, "Rulman Merswin" p. 22.

826. "Noche Escura del Alma," I. ii, cap. xxiv.

827. Vide supra , p. 290.

828. Leben, cap. xx.

829. These expressions, the Upper and Lower School of the Holy Spirit, as applied to the first and second mystic life, were common to the whole group of "Friends of God," and appear frequently in their works. Vide supra , p.441, Rulman Merswin's "Vision of Nine Rocks," where the man who has "gazed upon his Origin" is said to have been in the Upper School of the Holy Spirit; i.e ., to have been united to God.

830. Leben, cap. xxi.

831. Job vii. 1 (Vulgate).

832. During the years of purgation Suso had constantly worn a sharp cross, the points of which pierced his flesh.

833. Leben, cap. xxii.

834. Leben, cap. xxiii.

835. Ibid. , cap. xxv.

836. "Buchlein von der ewigen Weisheit," cap. ii.

837. Leben, cap. xlvii. So Ruysbroeck, "The gold Ring of our Covenant is greater than Heaven or Earth" ("De Contemplatione"). Compare Vaughan the Silurist ("The World"). "I saw Eternity the other night, Like a great Ring of pure and endless light, All calm as it was bright; . . . . One whispered thus: This Ring the Bridegroom did for none provide But for His Bride.'"

838. "Buchlein von der ewigen Weisheit," cap. ii.

839. Cap. xl.

840. "Nay, it is essential to this blessed being, to hold ourselves within the Will Divine; that therewith our own wills be themselves made one."

841. Loc. cit .

CHAPTER X

What is the Unitive Life? We have referred to it often enough in the course of this inquiry. At last we are face to face with the necessity of defining its nature if we can. Since the normal man knows little about his own true personality and nothing at all about that of Deity, the orthodox description of it as "the life in which man's will is united with God," does but echo the question in an ampler form, and conveys no real meaning to the student's mind.

That we should know, by instinct, its character from within--as we know, if we cannot express, the character of our own normal human lives--is of course impossible. We deal here with the final triumph of the spirit, the flower of mysticism, humanity's top note: the consummation towards which the contemplative life, with its long slow growth and costly training, has moved from the first. We look at a small but ever-growing group of heroic figures, living at transcendent levels of reality which we immersed in the poor life of illusion, cannot attain: breathing an atmosphere whose true quality we cannot even conceive. Here, then, as at so many other points in our study of the spiritual consciousness, we must rely for the greater part of our knowledge upon the direct testimony of the mystics; who alone can tell the character of that "more abundant life" which they enjoy.

Yet we are not wholly dependent on this source of information. It is the peculiarity of the Unitive Life that it is often lived, in its highest and most perfect forms, in the world; and exhibits its works before the eyes of men. As the law of our bodies is "earth to earth" so, strangely enough, is the law of our souls. The spirit of man having at last come to full consciousness of reality, completes the circle of Being; and returns to fertilize those levels of existence from which it sprang. Hence, the enemies of mysticism, who have easily drawn a congenial moral from the "morbid and solitary" lives of contemplatives in the earlier and educative stages of the Mystic Way, are here confronted very often by the disagreeable spectacle of the mystic as a pioneer of humanity, a sharply intuitive and painfully practical person: an artist, a discoverer, a religious or social reformer, a national hero, a "great active" amongst the saints. By the superhuman nature of that which these persons accomplish, we can gauge something of the super-normal vitality of which they partake. The things done, the victories gained over circumstances by St. Bernard or St. Joan of Arc, by St. Catherine of Siena, St. Ignatius Loyola, St. Teresa, George Fox, are hardly to be explained unless these great spirits had indeed a closer, more intimate, more bracing contact than their fellows with that Life "which is the light of men."

Use have, then, these two lines of investigation open to us: first, the comparison and elucidation of that which the mystics tell us concerning their transcendent experience, secondly, the testimony which is borne by their lives to the existence within them of supernal springs of action, contact set up with deep levels of vital power. In the third place, we have such critical machinery as psychology has placed at our disposal; but this, in dealing with these giants of the spirit, must be used with peculiar caution and humility.

The Unitive Life, though so often lived in the world, is never of it. It belongs to another plane of being, moves securely upon levels unrelated to our speech; and hence eludes the measuring powers of humanity. We, from the valley, can only catch a glimpse of the true life of these elect spirits, transfigured upon the mountain. They are far away, breathing another air: we cannot reach them. Yet it is impossible to over-estimate their importance for the race. They are our ambassadors to the Absolute. They vindicate humanity's claim to the possible and permanent attainment of Reality; bear witness to the practical qualities of the transcendental life. In Eucken's words, they testify to "the advent of a triumphing Spiritual Power, as distinguished from a spirituality which merely lays the foundations of life or struggles to maintain them": [842] to the actually life-enhancing power of the Love of God, once the human soul is freely opened to receive it.

Coming first to the evidence of the mystics themselves, we find that in their attempts towards describing the Unitive Life they have recourse to two main forms of symbolic expression, both very dangerous, and liable to be misunderstood, both offering ample opportunity for harsh criticism to hostile investigators of the mystic type. We find also, as we might expect from our previous encounters with the symbols used by contemplatives and ecstatics, that these two forms of expression belong respectively to mystics of the transcendent-metaphysical and of the intimate-personal type: and that their formulae if taken alone, appear to contradict one another.

(1) The metaphysical mystic, for whom the Absolute is impersonal and transcendent, describes his

final attainment of that Absolute as deification, or the utter transmutation of the self in God. (2) The mystic for whom intimate and personal communion has been the mode under which he best apprehended Reality speaks of the consummation of this communion, its perfect and permanent form, as the Spiritual Marriage of his soul with God. Obviously, both these terms are but the self's guesses concerning the intrinsic character of a state which it has felt in its wholeness rather than analysed: and bear the same relation to the ineffable realities of that state, as our clever theories concerning the nature and meaning of life bear to the vital processes of men. It is worth while to examine them but we shall not understand them till we have also examined the life which they profess to explain.

The language of "deification" and of "spiritual marriage," then, is temperamental language: and is related to subjective experience rather than to objective fact. It describes on the one hand the mystic's astonished recognition of a profound change effected in his own personality [843] --the transmutation of his salt, sulphur, and mercury into Spiritual Gold--on the other, the rapturous consummation of his love. Hence by a comparison of these symbolic reconstructions, by the discovery and isolation of the common factor latent in each, we may perhaps learn something of the fundamental fact which each is trying to portray.

Again, the mystics describe certain symptoms either as the necessary preliminaries or as the marks and fruits of the Unitive State: and these too may help us to fix its character.

The chief, in fact the one essential, preliminary is that pure surrender of selfhood, or "self-naughting," which the trials of the Dark Night tended to produce. "This," says Julian of Norwich, "is the cause why that no soul is rested till it is naughted of all things that are made. When it is willingly made naught for love to have Him that is all, then is it able to receive spiritual rest." [844] Only the thoroughly detached, "naughted soul" is "free," says "The Mirror of Simple Souls," and the Unitive State is essentially a state of free and filial participation in Eternal Life. The capital marks of the state itself are (1) a complete absorption in the interests of the Infinite, under whatever mode It is apprehended by the self; (2) a consciousness of sharing Its strength, acting by Its authority, which results in a complete sense of freedom, an invulnerable serenity, and usually urges the self to some form of heroic effort or creative activity; (3) the establishment of the self as a "power for life," a centre of energy, an actual parent of spiritual vitality in other men. By assembling these symptoms and examining them, and the lives of those who exhibit them, in the light of psychology, we can surely get some news--however fragmentary--concerning the transcendent condition of being which involves these characteristic states and acts. Beyond this even Dante himself could not go:

Transumanar significar per verba
non si poria." [845]

We will then consider the Unitive Life (1) As it appears from the standpoint of the psychologist. (2) As it is described to us by those mystics who use (a) the language of Deification, (b) that of Spiritual Marriage. (3) Finally, we will turn to those who have lived it; and try, if we can, to realize it as an organic whole.

(1) From the point of view of the pure psychologist, what do the varied phenomena of the Unitive Life, taken together, seem to represent? He would probably say that they indicate the final and successful establishment of that higher form of consciousness which has been struggling for supremacy during the whole of the Mystic Way. The deepest, richest levels of human personality have now attained to light and freedom. The self is remade, transformed, has at last unified itself; and with the cessation of stress, power has been liberated for new purposes.

"The beginning of the mystic life," says Delacroix, "introduced into the personal life of the subject a group of states which are distinguished by certain characteristics, and which form, so to speak, a special psychological system. At its term, it has, as it were, suppressed the ordinary self, and by the development of this system has established a new personality with a new method of feeling and of action. Its growth results in the transformation of personality: it abolishes the primitive consciousness of selfhood, and substitutes for it a wider consciousness, the total disappearance of selfhood in the divine, the substitution of a Divine Self for the primitive self." [846] We give a philosophic content to this conception if we say further that man, in this Unitive State, by this substitution of the divine for the "primitive" self, has at last risen to true freedom; "entered on the fruition of reality." [847] Hence he has opened up new paths for the inflow of that Triumphing Power which is the very substance of the Real; has remade his consciousness, and in virtue of this total regeneration is "transplanted into that Universal Life, which is yet not alien but our own." [848] From contact set up with this Universal Life, this "Energetic Word of God, which nothing can contain"--from those deep levels of Being to which his shifting, growing personality is fully adapted at last--he draws that amazing strength, that immovable peace, that power of dealing with circumstance, which is one of the most marked characteristics of the Unitive Life. "That secret and permanent personality of a superior type" [849] which gave to the surface-self constant and ever more insistent intimations of its existence at every stage of the mystic's growth--his real, eternal self--has now consciously realized its destiny: and begins at last fully to be. In the travail of the Dark Night it has conquered and invaded the last recalcitrant elements of character. It is no more limited to acts of profound perception, overpowering intuitions of the Absolute: no more dependent for its emergence on the psychic states of contemplation and ecstasy. Anima and Animus are united. The mystic has at last resolved the Stevensonian paradox; and is not truly two, but truly one.

(2) The mystic, I think, would acquiesce in these descriptions, so far as they go: but he would probably translate them into his own words and gloss them with an explanation which is beyond the power and province of psychology. He would say that his long-sought correspondence with Transcendental Reality, his union with God, has now been finally established: that his self, though intact, is wholly penetrated--as a sponge by the sea--by the Ocean of Life and Love to which he has attained. "I live, yet not I but God in me." He is conscious that he is now at length cleansed of the last stains of separation, and has become, in a mysterious manner, "that which he beholds."

In the words of the Sufi poet, the mystic's journey is now prosecuted not only to God but in God. He has entered the Eternal Order, attained here and now the state to which the Magnet of the Universe draws every living thing. Moving through periods of alternate joy and anguish, as his spiritual self woke, stretched, and was tested in the complementary fires of love and pain, he was inwardly conscious that he moved towards a definite objective. In so far as he was a great mystic, he was also conscious that this objective was no mere act of knowing, however intense, exultant, and sublime, but a condition of being, fulfilment of that love which impelled him, steadily and inexorably, to his own place. In the image of the alchemists, the Fire of Love has done its work: the mystic Mercury of the Wise--that little hidden treasure, that scrap of Reality within him--has utterly transmuted the salt and sulphur of his mind and his sense. Even the white stone of illumination, once so dearly cherished, he has resigned to the crucible. Now, the great work is accomplished, the last imperfection is gone, and he finds within himself the "Noble Tincture"--the gold of spiritual humanity.

(A) We have said that the mystic of the impersonal type--the seeker of a Transcendent Absolute--tends to describe the consummation of his quest in the language of deification. The Unitive Life necessarily means for him, as for all who attain it, something which infinitely transcends the sum total of its symptoms: something which normal men cannot hope to understand. In it he declares that he "partakes directly of the Divine Nature," enjoys the fruition of reality. Since we "only behold that which we are," the doctrine of deification results naturally and logically from this claim.

"Some may ask," says the author of the "Theologia Germanica" "what is it to be a partaker of the Divine Nature, or a Godlike [vergottet , literally deified] man? Answer: he who is imbued with or illuminated by the Eternal or Divine Light and inflamed or consumed with Eternal or Divine Love, he is a deified man and a partaker of the Divine Nature." [850]

Such a word as "deification" is not, of course, a scientific term. It is a metaphor, an artistic expression which tries to hint at a transcendent fact utterly beyond the powers of human understanding, and therefore without equivalent in human speech: that fact of which Dante perceived the "shadowy preface" when he saw the saints as petals of the Sempiternal Rose. [851] Since we know not the Being of God, the mere statement that a soul is transformed in Him may convey to us an ecstatic suggestion, but will never give exact information: except of course to those rare selves who have experienced these supernal states. Such selves, however--or a large proportion of them--accept this statement as approximately true. Whilst the more clear-sighted are careful to qualify it in a sense which excludes pantheistic interpretations, and rebuts the accusation that extreme mystics preach the annihilation of the self and regard themselves as co-equal with the Deity, they leave us in no doubt that it answers to a definite and normal experience of many souls who attain high levels of spiritual vitality. Its terms are chiefly used by those mystics by whom Reality is apprehended as a state or place rather than a Person:[852] and who have adopted, in describing the earlier stages of their journey to God, such symbols as those of rebirth or transmutation.

The blunt and positive language of these contemplatives concerning deification has aroused more enmity amongst the unmystical than any other of their doctrines or practices. It is of course easy, by confining oneself to its surface sense, to call such language blasphemous: and the temptation to do so has seldom been resisted. Yet, rightly understood, this doctrine lies at the heart, not only of all mysticism, but also of much philosophy and most religion. It pushes their first principles to a logical end. Christian mysticism, says Delacroix with justice, springs from "that spontaneous and half-savage longing for deification which all religion contains." [853] Eastern Christianity has always accepted it and expressed it in her rites. "The Body of God deifies me and feeds me," says Simeon Metaphrastes, "it deifies my spirit and it feeds my soul in an incomprehensible manner." [854]

The Christian mystics justify this dogma of the deifying of man, by exhibiting it as the necessary corollary of the Incarnation--the humanizing of God. They can quote the authority of the Fathers in support of this argument. "He became man that we might be made God," says St. Athanasius. [855] "I heard," says St. Augustine, speaking of his pre-converted period, "Thy voice from on high crying unto me, I am the Food of the fullgrown: grow, and then thou shalt feed on Me. Nor shalt thou change Me into thy substance as thou changest the food of thy flesh, but thou shalt be changed into Mine."' [856] Eckhart therefore did no more than expand the patristic view when he wrote, "Our Lord says to every living soul, I became man for you. If you do not become God for me, you do me wrong.'" [857]

If we are to allow that the mystics have ever attained the object of their quest, I think we must also allow that such attainment involves the transmutation of the self to that state which they call, for want of exact language, "deified." The necessity of such transmutation is an implicit of their first position: the law that "we behold that which we are, and are that which we behold." Eckhart, in whom the language of deification assumes its most extreme form, justifies it upon this necessity. "If," he says, "I am to know God directly, I must become completely He and He I: so that this He and this I become and are one I." [858]

God, said St. Augustine, is the Country of the soul: its Home, says Ruysbroeck. The mystic in the unitive state is living in and of his native land; no exploring alien, but a returned exile, now wholly identified with it, part of it, yet retaining his personality intact. As none know the spirit of England but the English; and they know it by intuitive participation, by mergence, not by thought; so none but the "deified" know the secret life of God. This, too, is a knowledge conferred only by participation: by living a life, breathing an atmosphere, "union with that same Light by which they see, and which they see." [859] It is one of those rights of citizenship which cannot be artificially conferred. Thus it becomes important to ask the mystics what they have to tell us of their life lived upon the bosom of Reality: and to receive their reports without prejudice, however hard the sayings they contain.

The first thing which emerges from these reports, and from the choice of symbols which we find in them, is that the great mystics are anxious above all things to establish and force on us the truth that by deification they intend no arrogant claim to identification with God, but as it were a transfusion of their selves by His Self: an entrance upon a new order of life, so high and so harmonious with Reality that it can only be called divine. Over and over again they assure us that personality is not lost, but made more real. "When," says St. Augustine, "I shall cleave to Thee with all my being, then shall I in nothing have pain and labour; and my life shall be a real life, being wholly full of Thee." [860] "My life shall be a real life" because it is "full of Thee." The achievement of reality, and deification, are then one and the same thing: necessarily so, since we know that only the divine is the real. [861]

Mechthild of Magdeburg, and after her Dante, saw Deity as a flame or river of fire that filled the Universe, and the "deified" souls of the saints as ardent sparks therein, ablaze with that fire, one thing with it, yet distinct. [862] Ruysbroeck, too, saw "Every soul like a live coal, burned up by God on the heart of His Infinite Love." [863] Such fire imagery has seemed to many of the mystics a peculiarly exact and suggestive symbol of the transcendent state which they are struggling to describe. No longer confused by the dim Cloud of Unknowing, they have pierced to its heart, and there found their goal: that uncreated and energizing Fire which guided the children of Israel through the night. By a deliberate appeal to the parallel of such great impersonal forces--to Fire and Heat, Light, Water, Air--mystic writers seem able to bring out a perceived aspect of the Godhead, and of the transfigured soul's participation therein, which no merely personal language, taken alone, can touch. Thus Boehme, trying to describe the union between the Word and the soul, says, "I give you an earthly similitude of this. Behold a bright flaming piece of iron, which of itself is dark and black, and the fire so penetrateth and shineth through the iron, that it giveth light. Now, the iron doth not cease to be, it is iron still: and the source (or property) of the fire retaineth its own propriety: it doth not take the iron into it, but it penetrateth (and shineth) through the iron; and it is iron then as well as before, free in itself: and so also is the source or property of the fire. In such a manner is the soul set in the Deity; the Deity penetrateth through the soul, and dwelleth in the soul, yet the soul doth not comprehend the Deity, but the Deity comprehendeth the soul, but doth not alter it (from being a soul) but only giveth it the divine source (or property) of the Majesty." [864]

Almost exactly the same image of deification was used, five hundred years before Boehme's day, by Richard of St. Victor; a mystic whom he is hardly likely to have read. "When the soul is plunged in the fire of divine love," he says, "like iron, it first loses its blackness, and then growing to white heat, it becomes like unto the fire itself. And lastly, it grows liquid, and losing its nature is transmuted into an utterly different quality of being." "As the difference between iron that is cold and iron that is hot," he says again, "so is the difference between soul and soul: between the tepid soul and the soul made incandescent by divine love." [865] Other contemplatives say that the deified soul is transfigured by the inundations of the Uncreated Light: that it is like a brand blazing in the furnace, transformed to the likeness of the fire. "These souls," says the Divine voice to St. Catherine of Siena, "thrown into the furnace of My charity, no part of their will remaining outside but the whole of them being inflamed in Me, are like a brand, wholly consumed in the furnace, so that no one can take hold of it to extinguish it, because it has become fire. In the same way no one can seize these souls, or draw them outside of Me, because they are made one thing with Me through grace, and I never withdraw Myself from them by sentiment, as in the case of those whom I am leading on to perfection." [866]

For the most subtle and delicate descriptions of the Unitive or Deified State, understood as self-loss in the "Ocean Pacific" of God, we must go to the great genius of Ruysbroeck. He alone, whilst avoiding all its pitfalls, has conveyed the suggestion of its ineffable joys in a measure which seems, as we read, to be beyond all that we had supposed possible to human utterance. Awe and rapture, theological profundity, keen psychological insight, are here tempered by a touching simplicity. We listen to the report of one who has indeed heard "the invitation of love" which "draws interior souls towards the One" and says "Come home." A humble receptivity, a meek self-naughting is with Ruysbroeck, as with all great mystics, the gate of the City of God. "Because they have abandoned themselves to God in doing, in leaving undone, and in suffering," he says of the deified souls, "they have steadfast peace and inward joy, consolation and savour, of which the world cannot partake; neither any dissembler, nor the man who seeks and means himself more than the glory of God. Moreover, those same inward and enlightened men have before them in their inward seeing, whenever they will, the Love of God as something drawing or urging them into the Unity; for they see and feel that the Father with the Son through the Holy Ghost, embrace Each Other and all the chosen, and draw themselves back with eternal love into the unity of Their Nature. Thus the Unity is ever drawing to itself and inviting to itself everything that has been born of It, either by nature or by grace. And therefore, too, such enlightened men are, with a free spirit, lifted up above reason into a bare and imageless vision, wherein lives the eternal indrawing summons of the Divine Unity; and, with an imageless and bare understanding, they pass through all works, and all exercises, and all things, until they reach the summit of their spirits. There, their bare understanding is drenched through by the Eternal Brightness, even as the air is drenched through by the sunshine. And the bare, uplifted will is transformed and drenched through by abysmal love, even as iron is by fire. And the bare, uplifted memory feels itself enwrapped and established in an abysmal Absence of Image. And thereby the created image is united above reason in a threefold way with its Eternal Image, which is the origin of its being and its life. . . . Yet the creature does not become God, for the union takes place in God through grace and our homeward-turning love: and therefore the creature in its inward contemplation feels a distinction and an otherness between itself and God. And though the union is without means, yet the manifold works which God works in heaven and on earth are nevertheless hidden from the spirit. For though God gives Himself as He is, with clear discernment, He gives Himself in the essence of the soul, where the powers of the soul are simplified above reason, and where, in simplicity, they suffer the transformation of God. There all is full and overflowing, for the spirit feels itself to be one truth and one richness and one unity with God. Yet even here there is an essential tending forward, and therein is an essential distinction between the being of the soul and the Being of God; and this is the highest and finest distinction which we are able to feel." [867]

"When love has carried us above and beyond all things," he says in another place, "above the light, into the Divine Dark, there we are wrought and transformed by the Eternal Word Who is the image of the Father; and as the air is penetrated by the sun, thus we receive in idleness of spirit the Incomprehensible Light, enfolding us and penetrating us. And this flight is nothing else but an infinite gazing and seeing. We behold that which we are, and we are that which be behold; because our thought, life and being are uplifted in simplicity and made one with the Truth which is God." [868]

Here the personal aspect of the Absolute seems to be reduced to a minimum: yet all that we value in personality--love, action, will--remains unimpaired. We seem caught up to a plane of vision beyond the categories of the human mind: to the contemplation of a Something Other--our home, our hope, and our passion, the completion of our personality, and the Substance of all that Is. Such an endless contemplation, such a dwelling within the substance of Goodness, Truth and, Beauty, is the essence of that Beatific Vision, that participation of Eternity, "of all things most delightful and desired, of all things most loved by them who have it," [869] which theology presents to us as the objective of the soul.

Those mystics of the metaphysical type who tend to use these impersonal symbols of Place and Thing often see in the Unitive Life a foretaste of the Beatific Vision: an entrance here and now into that absolute life within the Divine Being, which shall be lived by all perfect spirits when they have cast off the limitations of the flesh and re-entered the eternal order for which they were made. For them, in fact, the "deified man," in virtue of his genius for transcendental reality, has run ahead of human history: and attained a form of consciousness which other men will only know when earthly life is past.

In the "Book of Truth" Suso has a beautiful and poetic comparison between the life of the blessed spirits dwelling within the Ocean of Divine Love, and that approximate life which is lived on earth by the mystic who has renounced all selfhood and merged his will in that of the Eternal Truth. Here we find one of the best of many answers to the ancient but apparently immortal accusation that the mystics teach the total annihilation of personality as the end and object of their quest. "Lord, tell me," says the Servitor, "what remains to a blessed soul which has wholly renounced itself." Truth says, "When the good and faithful servant enters into the joy of his Lord, he is inebriated by the riches of the house of God; for he feels, in an ineffable degree, that which is felt by an inebriated man. He forgets himself, he is no longer conscious of his selfhood; he disappears and loses himself in God, and becomes one spirit with Him, as a drop of water which is drowned in a great quantity of wine. For even as such a drop disappears, taking the colour and the taste of wine, so it is with those who are in full possession of blessedness. All human desires are taken from them in an indescribable manner, they are rapt from themselves, and are immersed in the Divine Will. If it were otherwise, if there remained in the man some human thing that was not absorbed, those words of Scripture which say that God must be all in all would be false. His being remains, but in another form, in another glory, and in another power. And all this is the result of entire and complete renunciation. . . . Herein thou shalt find an answer to thy question; for the true renunciation and veritable abandonment of a man to the Divine Will in the temporal world is an imitation and reduction of that self-abandonment of the blessed, of which Scripture speaks: and this imitation approaches its model more or less, according as men are more or less united with God and become more or less one with God. Remark well that which is said of the blessed: they are stripped of their personal initiative, and changed into another form, another glory, another power. What then is this other form, if it be not the Divine Nature and the Divine Being whereinto they pour themselves, and which pours Itself into them, and becomes one thing with them? And what is that other glory, if it be not to be illuminated and made shining in the Inaccessible Light? What is that other power, if it be not that by means of his union with the Divine Personality, there is given to man a divine strength and a divine power, that he may accomplish all which pertains to his blessedness and omit all which is contrary thereto? And thus it is that, as has been said, a man comes forth from his selfhood."[870]

All the mystics agree that the stripping off of the I, the Me, the Mine, utter renouncement, or "self-naughting"--self-abandonment to the direction of a larger Will--is an imperative condition of the attainment of the unitive life. The temporary denudation of the mind, whereby the contemplative made space for the vision of God, must now be applied to the whole life. Here, they say, there is a final swallowing up of that wilful I-hood, that surface individuality which we ordinarily recognize as ourselves. It goes for ever, and something new is established in its room. The self is made part of the mystical Body of God; and, humbly taking its place in the corporate life of Reality, would "fain be to the Eternal Goodness what his own hand is to a man." [871] That strange "hunger and thirst of God for the soul," "at once avid and generous," of which they speak in their profoundest passages, here makes its final demand and receives its satisfaction. "All that He has, all that He is He gives: all that we have, all that we are, He takes." [872] The self, they declare, is devoured, immersed in the Abyss; "sinks into God, Who is the deep of deeps." In their efforts towards describing to us this, the supreme mystic act, and the new life to which it gives birth, they are often driven to the use of images which must seem to us grotesque, were it not for the flame which burns behind: as when Ruysbroeck cries, "To eat and be eaten! this is Union! . . . Since His desire is without measure, to be devour of of Him does not greatly amaze me." [873]

(B) At this point we begin to see that the language of deification, taken alone, will not suffice to describe the soul's final experience of Reality. The personal and emotional aspect of man's relation with his Source is also needed if that which he means by "union with God" is to be even partially expressed. Hence, even the most "transcendental" mystic is constantly compelled to fall back on the language of love in the endeavour to express the content of his metaphysical raptures: and forced in the end to acknowledge that the perfect union of Lover and Beloved cannot be suggested in the precise and arid terms of religious philosophy. Such arid language eludes the most dangerous aspects of "divine union," the pantheistic on one hand, the "amoristic" on the other; but it also fails to express the most splendid side of that amazing experience. It needs some other, more personal and intimate vision to complete it: and this we shall find in the reports of those mystics of the "intimate" type to whom the Unitive Life has meant not self-loss in an Essence, but self-fulfilment in the union of heart and will.

The extreme form of this kind of apprehension of course finds expression in the well-known and heartily abused symbolism of the Spiritual Marriage between God and the Soul: a symbolism which goes back to the Orphic Mysteries, and thence descended via the Neoplatonists into the stream of Christian tradition. But there are other and less concrete embodiments of it, wholly free from the dangers which are supposed to lurk in "erotic" imagery of this kind. Thus Jalalu d Din, by the use of metaphors which are hardly human yet charged with passionate feeling, tells, no less successfully than the writer of the Song of Songs, the secret of "his union in which "heart speaks to heart."

With Thy Sweet Soul, this soul of mine
Hath mixed as Water doth with Wine.
Who can the Wine and Water part,
Or me and Thee when we combine?
Thou art become my greater self;
Small bounds no more can me confine.
Thou hast my being taken on,
And shall not I now take on Thine?
Me Thou for ever hast affirmed
That I may ever know Thee mine
Thy Love has pierced me through and through,
Its thrill with Bone and Nerve entwine.

I rest a Flute laid on Thy lips;
A lute, I on Thy breast recline.
Breathe deep in me that I may sigh:
Yet strike my strings, and tears shall shine." [874]

What the mystic here desires to tell us is, that his new life is not only a free and conscious participation in the life of Eternity--a fully-established existence on real and transcendental levels--but also the conscious sharing of an inflowing personal life greater than his own; a tightening of the bonds of that companionship which has been growing in intimacy and splendour during the course of the Mystic Way. This companionship, at once the most actual and most elusive fact of human experience, is utterly beyond the resources of speech. So too are those mysteries of the communion of love, whereby the soul's humble, active and ever-renewed self-donation becomes the occasion of her glory: and "by her love she is made the equal of Love"--the beggar maid sharing Cophetua's throne.

Thus the anonymous author of the "Mirror" writes, in one of his most daring passages, "I am God,' says Love, for Love is God, and God is Love. And this soul is God by condition of love: but I am God by Nature Divine. And this [state] is hers by righteousness of love, so that this precious beloved of me is learned, and led of Me without her [working]. . . . This [soul] is the eagle that flies high, so right high and yet more high than doth any other bird; for she is feathered with fine love.'" [875]

The simplest expression of the Unitive Life, the simplest interpretation which we can put on its declarations, is that it is the complete and conscious fulfilment here and now of this Perfect Love. In it certain elect spirits, still in the flesh, "fly high and yet more high," till "taught and led out of themselves," they become, in the exaggerated language of the "Mirror," "God by condition of love." Home-grown English mysticism tried as a rule to express the inexpressible in homelier, more temperate terms than this. "I would that thou knew," says the unknown author of the "Epistle of Prayer," "what manner of working it is that knitteth man's soul to God, and that maketh it one with Him in love and accordance of will after the word of St. Paul, saying thus: Qui adhaeret Deo, unus spiritus est cum illo ' ; that is to say: Whoso draweth near to God as it is by such a reverent affection touched before, he is one spirit with God.' That is, though all that God and he be two and sere in kind, nevertheless yet in grace they are so knit together that they are but one in spirit; and all this is one for onehead of love and accordance of will; and in this onehead is the marriage made between God and the soul the which shall never be broken, though all that the heat and the fervour of this work cease for a time, but by a deadly sin. In the ghostly feeling of this onehead may a loving soul both say and sing (if it list) this holy word that is written in the Book of Songs in the Bible, Dilectus meus mihi et ego illi, ' that is, My loved unto me, and I unto Him; understanding that God shall be knitted with the ghostly glue of grace on His party, and the lovely consent in gladness of spirit on thy party." [876]

I think no one can deny that the comparison of the bond between the soul and the Absolute to "ghostly glue," though crude, is wholly innocent. Its appearance in this passage as an alternative to the symbol of wedlock may well check the uncritical enthusiasm of those who hurry to condemn at sight all "sexual" imagery. That it has seemed to the mystics appropriate and exact is proved by its reappearance in the next century in the work of a greater contemplative. "Thou givest me," says Petersen, "Thy whole Self to be mine whole and undivided, if at least I shall be Thine whole and undivided. And when I shall be thus all Thine, even as from everlasting Thou hast loved Thyself, so from everlasting Thou hast loved me: for this means nothing more than that Thou enjoyest Thyself in me, and that I by Thy grace enjoy Thee in myself and myself in Thee. And when in Thee I shall love myself, nothing else but Thee do I love, because Thou art in me and I in Thee, glued together as one and the selfsame thing, which henceforth and forever cannot be divided." [877]

From this kind of language to that of the Spiritual Marriage, as understood by the pure minds of the mystics, is but a step. [878] They mean by it no rapturous satisfactions, no dubious spiritualizing of earthly ecstasies, but a life-long bond "that shall never be lost or broken," a close personal union of will and of heart between the free self and that "Fairest in Beauty" Whom it has known in the act of contemplation.

The Mystic Way has been a progress, a growth in love: a deliberate fostering of the inward tendency of the soul towards its source, an eradication of its disorderly tendencies to "temporal goods." But the only proper end of love is union: "a perfect uniting and coupling together of the lover and the loved into one." [879] It is "a unifying principle," the philosophers say: [880] life's mightiest agent upon every plane. Moreover, just as earthly marriage is understood by the moral sense less as a satisfaction of personal desire, than as a part of the great process of life--the fusion of two selves for new purposes--so such spiritual marriage brings with it duties and obligations. With the attainment of a new order, the new infusion of vitality, comes a new responsibility, the call to effort and endurance on a new and mighty scale. It is not an act but a state. Fresh life is imparted, by which our lives are made complete: new creative powers are conferred. The self, lifted to the divine order, is to be an agent of the divine fecundity: an energizing centre, a parent of transcendental life. "The last perfection," says Aquinas, "to supervene upon a thing, is its becoming the cause of other things. While then a creature tends by many ways to the likeness of God, the last way left open to it is to seek the divine likeness by being the cause of other things, according to what the Apostle says, Dei enim sumus adjutores ." [881]

We find as a matter of fact, when we come to study the history of the mystics, that the permanent Unitive State, or spiritual marriage, does mean for those who attain to it, above all else such an access of creative vitality. It means man's small derivative life invaded and enhanced by the Absolute Life: the appearance in human history of personalities and careers which seem superhuman when judged by the surface mind. Such activity, such a bringing forth of "the fruits of the Spirit," may take many forms: but where it is absent, where we meet with personal satisfactions, personal visions or raptures--however sublime and spiritualized--presented as marks of the Unitive Way, ends or objects of the quest of Reality, we may be sure that we have wandered from the "strait and narrow road" which leads, not to eternal rest, but to Eternal Life. "The fourth degree of love is spiritually fruitful," [882] said Richard of St. Victor. Wherever we find a sterile love, a "holy passivity," we are in the presence of quietistic heresy; not of the Unitive Life. "I hold it for a certain truth," says St. Teresa, "that in giving these graces our Lord intends, as I have often told you, to strengthen our weakness so that we may imitate Him by suffering much. . . . Whence did St. Paul draw strength to support his immense labours? We see clearly in him the effects of visions and contemplations which come indeed from our Lord, and not from our own imagination or the devil's fraud. Do you suppose St. Paul hid himself in order to enjoy in peace these spiritual consolations, and did nothing else? You know that on the contrary he never took a day's rest so far as we can learn, and worked at night in order to earn his bread. . . . Oh my sisters! how forgetful of her own ease, how careless of honours, should she be whose soul God thus chooses for His special dwelling place! For if her mind is fixed on Him, as it ought to be, she must needs forget herself; all her thoughts are bent on how to please Him better, and when and how she may show Him her love. This is the end and aim of prayer, my daughters; this is the object of that spiritual marriage whose children are always good works. Works are the best proof that the favours which we receive have come from God." [883] "To give our Lord a perfect hospitality" she says in the same chapter, "Mary and Martha must combine."

When we look at the lives of the great theopathetic mystics, the true initiates of Eternity--inarticulate as these mystics often are--we find ourselves in the presence of an amazing, a superabundant vitality: of a "triumphing force" over which circumstance has no power. The incessant production of good works seems indeed to be the object of that Spirit, by Whose presence their interior castle is now filled.

We see St. Paul, abruptly enslaved by the First and Only Fair, not hiding himself to enjoy the vision of Reality, but going out single-handed to organize the Catholic Church. We ask how it was possible for an obscure Roman citizen, without money, influence, or good health, to lay these colossal foundations: and he answers "Not I, but Christ in me."

We see St. Joan of Arc, a child of the peasant class, leaving the sheepfold to lead the armies of France. We ask how this incredible thing can be: and are told "Her Voices bade her." A message, an overpowering impulse, came from the supra-sensible: vitality flowed in on her, she knew not how or why. She was united with the Infinite Life, and became Its agent, the medium of Its strength, "what his own hand is to a man."

We see St. Francis, "God's troubadour," marked with His wounds, inflamed with His joy--obverse and reverse of the earnest-money of eternity--or St. Ignatius Loyola, our Lady's knight, a figure at once militant and romantic, go out to change the spiritual history of Europe. Where did they find--born and bred to the most ordinary of careers, in the least spiritual of atmospheres--that superabundant energy, that genius for success which triumphed best in the most hopeless situations? Francis found it before the crucifix in St. Damiano, and renewed it in the ineffable experience of La Verna; when "by mental possession and rapture he was transfigured of God." Ignatius found it in the long contemplations and hard discipline of the cave of Manresa, after the act of surrender in which he dedicated his knighthood to the service of the Mother of God.

We see St. Teresa, another born romantic, pass to the Unitive State after long and bitter struggles between her lower and higher personality. A chronic invalid over fifty years of age, weakened by long ill-health and the mortifications of the Purgative Way she deliberately breaks with her old career in obedience to the inward Voice, leaves her convent, and starts a new life: coursing through Spain, and reforming a great religious order in the teeth of the ecclesiastical world. Yet more amazing, St. Catherine of Siena, an illiterate daughter of the people, after a three years' retreat consummates the mystic marriage, and emerges from the cell of self-knowledge to dominate the politics of Italy. How came it that these apparently unsuitable men and women, checked on every side by inimical environment, ill-health, custom, or poverty achieved these stupendous destinies? The explanation can only lie in the fact that all these persons were great mystics, living upon high levels the theopathetic life. In each a character of the heroic type, of great vitality, deep enthusiasms, unconquerable will, was raised to the spiritual plane, remade on higher levels of consciousness. Each by surrender of selfhood, by acquiescence in the large destinies of life, had so furthered that self's natural genius for the Infinite that their human limitations were overpassed. Hence they rose to freedom and attained to the one ambition of the "naughted soul," "I would fain be to the Eternal Goodness what his own hand is to a man."

Even Madame Guyon's natural tendency to passive states breaks down with her entrance on the Unitive Way. Though she cannot be classed amongst the greatest of its initiates, she too felt its fertilizing power, was stung from her "holy indifference" to become, as it were, involuntarily true to type.

"The soul," she says of the self entering upon Union--and we cannot doubt that as usual she is describing her own carefully docketed "states"--"feels a secret vigour taking more and more strongly possession of all her being: and little by little she receives a new life, never again to be lost, at least so far as one can be assured of anything in this life. . . . This new life is not like that which she had before. It is a life in God. It is a perfect life. She no longer lives or works of herself: but God lives, acts and works in her, and this grows little by little till she becomes perfect with God's perfection, is rich with His riches, and loves with His love." . . . [884]

This new, intense, and veritable life has other and even more vital characteristics than those which lead to "the performance of acts" or "the incessant production of good works." It is, in an actual sense, as Richard of St. Victor reminded us, fertile, creative, as well as merely active. In the fourth degree of love, the soul brings forth its children. It is the agent of a fresh outbirth of spiritual vitality into the world; the helpmate of the Transcendent Order, the mother of a spiritual progeny. The great unitive mystics are each of them the founders of spiritual families, centres wherefrom radiates new transcendental life. The "flowing light of the Godhead" is focussed in them, as in a lens, only that it may pass through them to spread out on every side. So, too, the great creative seers and artists are the parents, not merely of their own immediate works, but also of whole schools of art, whole groups of persons who acquire or inherit their vision of beauty or truth. Thus within the area of influence of a Paul, a Francis, an Ignatius, a Teresa, an atmosphere of reality is created; and new and vital spiritual personalities gradually appear, meet for the work which these great founders set in hand. The real witness to St. Paul's ecstatic life in God, is the train of Christian churches by which his journeyings are marked. Wherever Francis passed, he left Franciscans, "fragrant with a wondrous aspect," where none had been before. [885] The Friends of God spring up, individual mystics, here and there through the Rhineland and Bavaria. Each becomes the centre of an ever widening circle of transcendent life, the parent of a spiritual family. They are come like their Master, that men may have life more abundantly: from them new mystic energy is actually born into the world. Again, Ignatius leaves Manresa a solitary: maimed, ignorant, and poor. He comes to Rome with his company already formed, and ablaze with his spirit; veritably his children, begotten of him, part and parcel of his life.

Teresa finds the order of Mount Carmel hopelessly corrupt: its friars and nuns blind to reality, indifferent to the obligations of the cloistered life. She is moved by the Spirit to leave her convent and begin, in abject poverty, the foundation of new houses, where the most austere and exalted life of contemplation shall be led. She enters upon this task to the accompaniment of an almost universal mockery. Mysteriously, as she proceeds, novices of the spiritual life appear and cluster around her. They come into existence, one knows not how, in the least favourable of atmospheres: but one and all are salted with the Teresian salt. They receive the infection of her abundant vitality: embrace eagerly and joyously the heroic life of the Reform. In the end, every city in Spain has within it Teresa's spiritual children: a whole order of contemplatives, as truly born of her as if they were indeed her sons and daughters in the flesh. Well might the Spiritual Alchemists say that the true "Lapis Philosophorum" is a tinging stone: which imparts its goldness to the base metals brought within its sphere of influence.

This reproductive power is one of the greatest marks of the theopathetic life: the true "mystic marriage" of the individual soul with its Source. Those rare personalities in whom it is found are the media through which that Triumphing Spiritual Life which is the essence of reality forces an entrance into the temporal order and begets children; heirs of the superabundant vitality of the transcendental universe.

But the Unitive Life is more than the sum total of its symptoms: more than the heroic and apostolic life of the "great active": more than the divine motherhood of new "sons and daughters of the Absolute." These are only its outward signs, its expression in time and space. I have first laid stress upon that expression, because it is the side which all critics and some friends of the mystics persistently ignore. The contemplative's power of living this intense and creative life within the temporal order, however, is tightly bound up with that other life in which he attains to complete communion with the Absolute Order, and submits to the inflow of its supernal vitality. In discussing the relation of the mystical experience to philosophy, [886] we saw that the complete mystic consciousness, and therefore, of course, the complete mystic world, had a twofold character which could hardly be reconciled with the requirements of monism. It embraced a Reality which seems from the human standpoint at once static and dynamic, transcendent and immanent, eternal and temporal: accepted both the absolute World of

Pure Being and the unresting World of Becoming as integral parts of its vision of Truth, demanding on its side a dual response. All through the Mystic Way we caught glimpses of the growth and exercise of this dual intuition of the Real. Now, the mature mystic, having come to his full stature, passed through the purifications of sense and of spirit and entered on his heritage, must and does take up as a part of that heritage not merely (a) a fruition of the Divine Goodness, Truth, and Beauty, his place within the Sempiternal Rose, nor (b) the creative activity of an agent of the Eternal Wisdom, still immersed in the River of Life: but both together--the twofold destiny of the spiritual man, called to "incarnate the Eternal in time." To use the old scholastic language, he is at once patient and agent: patient as regards God, agent as regards the world.

In a deep sense it may be said of him that he now participates according to his measure in that divine-human life which mediates between man and the Eternal, and constitutes the "salvation of the world." Therefore, though his outward heroic life of action, his divine fecundity, may seem to us the best evidence of his state, it is the inner knowledge of his mystical sonship whereby "we feel eternal life in us above all other thing," [887] which is for him the guarantee of absolute life. He has many ways of describing this central fact; this peculiar consciousness of his own transcendence, which coexists with, and depends on, a complete humility. Sometimes he says that whereas in the best moments of his natural life he was but the "faithful servant" of the eternal order, and in the illuminated way became its "secret friend," he is now advanced to the final, most mysterious state of "hidden child." "How great," says Ruysbroeck, "is the difference between the secret friend and the hidden child! For the friend makes only loving, living, but measured ascents towards God. But the child presses on to lose his own life upon the summits, in that simplicity which knoweth not itself. . . . When we transcend ourselves and become in our ascent towards God so simple that the bare supreme Love can lay hold of us, then we cease, and we and all our selfhood die in God. And in this death we become the hidden children of God, and find a new life within us." [888]

Though the outer career of the great mystic, then, be one of superhuman industry, a long fight with evil and adversity, his real and inner life dwells securely upon the heights; in the perfect fruition which he can only suggest to us by the paradoxical symbols of ignorance and emptiness. He dominates existence because he thus transcends it: is a son of God, a member of the eternal order, shares its substantial life. "Tranquillity according to His essence, activity according to His Nature: absolute repose, absolute fecundity": this, says Ruysbroeck again, is the twofold property of Godhead: and the secret child of the Absolute participates in this dual character of Reality--"for this dignity has man been made." [889]

Those two aspects of truth which he has so clumsily classified as static and dynamic, as Being and Becoming, now find their final reconciliation within his own nature: for that nature has become conscious in all its parts, has unified itself about its highest elements. That strange, tormenting vision of a perfect peace, a joyous self-loss, annihilation in some mighty Life that overpassed his own, which haunts man throughout the whole course of his history, and finds a more or less distorted expression in all his creeds, a justification in all his ecstasies, is now traced to its source: and found to be the inevitable expression of an instinct by which he recognized, though he could not attain, the noblest part of his inheritance. This recognition of his has of necessity been imperfect and oblique. It has taken in many temperaments an exaggerated form, and has been further disguised by the symbolic language used to describe it. The tendency of Indian mysticism to regard the Unitive Life wholly in its passive aspect, as a total self-annihilation, a disappearance into the substance of the Godhead, results, I believe, from such a distortion of truth. The Oriental mystic "presses on to lose his life upon the heights"; but he does not come back and bring to his fellow-men the life-giving news that he has transcended mortality in the interests of the race. The temperamental bias of Western mystics towards activity has saved them as a rule from such one-sided achievement as this; and hence it is in them that the Unitive Life, with its "dual character of activity and rest," has assumed its richest and noblest forms.

Of these Western mystics none has expressed more lucidly or splendidly than Ruysbroeck the double nature of man's reaction to Reality. It is the heart of his vision of truth. In all his books he returns to it again and again: speaking, as none familiar with his writings can doubt, the ardent, joyous, vital language of firsthand experience, not the platitudes of philosophy. He might say with Dante, his forerunner into the Empyrean:--

"La forma universal di questo nodo
credo ch' io vidi, perchè più di largo
dicendo questo, mi sento ch' io godo." [890]

It is then from Ruysbroeck that I shall make my quotations: and if they be found somewhat long and difficult of comprehension, their unique importance for the study of man's spiritual abilities must be my excuse.

First, his vision of God:--

"The Divine Persons," he says, "Who form one sole God, are in the fecundity of their nature ever active: and in the simplicity of their essence they form the Godhead and eternal blessedness. Thus God according to the Persons is Eternal Work: but according to the essence and Its perpetual stillness, He is Eternal Rest. Now love and fruition live between this activity and this rest. Love would ever be active: for its nature is eternal working with God. Fruition is ever at rest, for it consists above all will and all desire, in the embrace of the well-beloved by the well-beloved in a simple and imageless love; wherein the Father, together with the Son, enfolds His beloved ones in the fruitive unity of His Spirit, above the fecundity of nature. And that same Father says to each soul in His infinite loving kindness, Thou art Mine and I am thine: I am thine and thou art Mine, for I have chosen thee from all eternity.'" [891]

Next the vision of the self's destiny: "Our activity consists in loving God and our fruition in enduring God and being penetrated by His love. There is a distinction between love and fruition, as there is between God and His Grace. When we unite ourselves to God by love, then we are spirit: but when we are caught up and transformed by His Spirit, then we are led into fruition. And the spirit of God Himself breathes us out from Himself that we may love, and may do good works; and again He draws us into Himself, that we may rest in fruition. And this is Eternal Life; even as our mortal life subsists in the indrawing and outgoing of our breath." [892]

"Understand," he says again, "God comes to us incessantly, both with means and without means; and He demands of us both action and fruition, in such away that the action never hinders the fruition, nor the fruition the action, but they strengthen one another. And this is why the interior man [i.e., the contemplative] lives his life according to these two ways; that is to say, in rest and in work. And in each of them he is wholly and undividedly; for he dwells wholly in God in virtue of his restful fruition and wholly in himself in virtue of his active love. And God, in His communications, perpetually calls and urges him to renew both this rest and this work. And because the soul is just, it desires to pay at every instant that which God demands of it; and this is why each time it is irradiated of Him, the soul turns inward in a manner that is both active and fruitive, and thus it is renewed in all virtues and ever more profoundly immersed in fruitive rest. . . . It is active in all loving work, for it sees its rest. It is a pilgrim, for it sees its country. For love's sake it strives for victory, for it sees its crown. Consolation, peace, joy, beauty and riches, all that can give delight, all this is shown to the mind illuminated in God, in spiritual similitudes and without measure. And through this vision and touch of God, love continues active. For such a just man has built up in his own soul, in rest and in work, a veritable life which shall endure for ever, but which shall be transformed after this present life to a state still more sublime. Thus this man is just, and he goes towards God by inward love, in eternal work, and he goes in God by his fruitive inclination in eternal rest. And he dwells in God; and yet he goes out towards all creatures, in a spirit of love towards all things, in virtue and in works of righteousness. And this is she supreme summit of the inner life ." [893]

Compare this description with the careers of the theopathetic mystics, in whom, indeed, "action has not injured fruition, nor fruition action," who have by some secret adjustment contrived to "possess their lives in rest and in work" without detriment to inward joy or outward industry. Bear in mind as you read these words--Ruysbroeck's supreme effort to tell the true relation between man's created spirit and his God--the great public ministry of St. Catherine of Siena, which ranged from the tending of the plague-stricken to the reforming of the Papacy; and was accompanied by the inward fruitive consciousness of the companionship of Christ. Remember the humbler but not less beautiful and significant achievement of her Genoese namesake: the strenuous lives of St. Francis of Assisi, St. Ignatius, St. Teresa, outwardly cumbered with much serving, observant of an infinitude of tiresome details, composing rules, setting up foundations, neglecting no aspect of their business which could conduce to its practical success, yet "altogether dwelling in God in restful fruition." Are not all these supreme examples of the state in which the self, at last fully conscious, knowing Reality because she is wholly real, pays her debt? Unable to rest entirely either in work or in fruition, she seizes on this twofold expression of the superabundant life by which she is possessed: and, on the double wings of eagerness and effort, takes flight towards her Home.

In dwelling, as we have done, on the ways in which the great mystic makes actual to himself the circumstances of the Unitive State, we must not forget that this state is, in essence, a fulfilment of love; the attainment of a "heart's desire." By this attainment, this lifting of the self to free union with the Real--as by the earthly marriage which dimly prefigures it--a new life is entered upon, new powers, new responsibilities are conferred. But this is not all. The three prime activities of the normal self, feeling, intellect, and will, though they seem to be fused, are really carried up to a higher term. They are unified, it is true, but still present in their integrity; and each demands and receives full satisfaction in the attainment of this fillal "honour for which man has been made." The intellect is immersed in that mighty vision of truth, known now not as a vision but as a home; where St. Paul saw things which might not be uttered, St. Teresa found the "perpetual companionship of the Blessed Trinity," and Dante, caught to its heart for one brief moment, his mind smitten by the blinding flash of the Uncreated light, knew that he had resolved Reality's last paradox: the unity of "cerchio" and "imago" -- the infinite and personal aspects of God. [894] The enhanced will, made over to the interests of the Transcendent, receives new worlds to conquer, new strength to match its exalted destiny. But the heart too here enters on a new order, begins to live upon high levels of joy. "This soul, says Love, swims in the sea of joy: that is, in the sea of delight, the stream of divine influences." [895]

"Amans volat, currit et laetatur: liber est et non tenetur ," [896] said à Kempis: classic words, which put before us once and for ever the inward joyousness and liberty of the saints. They "fly, run, and rejoice"--those great, laborious souls, often spent with amazing mortifications, vowed to hard and never-ending tasks. They are "free, and nothing can hold them," though they seem to the world fenced in by absurd renunciations and restrictions, deprived of that cheap licence which it knows as liberty.

That fruition of joy of which Ruysbroeck speaks in majestic phrases, as constituting the interior life of mystic souls immersed in the Absolute--the translation of the Beatific Vision into the terms of a supernal feeling-state--is often realized in the secret experience of those same mystics, as the perennial possession of a childlike gaiety, an inextinguishable gladness of heart. The transfigured souls move to the measures of a "love dance" which persists in mirth without comparison, through every outward hardship and tribulation. They enjoy the high spirits peculiar to high spirituality: and shock the world by a delicate playfulness, instead of exhibiting the morose resignation which it feels to be proper to the "spiritual life." Thus St. Catherine of Siena, though constantly suffering, "was always jocund and of a happy spirit." When prostrate with illness she overflowed with gaiety and gladness, and "was full of laughter in the Lord, exultant and rejoicing. " [897]

Moreover, the most clear-sighted amongst the mystics declare such joy to be an implicit of Reality. Thus Dante, initiated into Paradise, sees the whole Universe laugh with delight as it glorifies God: [898] and the awful countenance of Perfect Love adorned with smiles. [899] Thus the souls of the great theologians dance to music and laughter in the Heaven of the Sun; [900] the loving seraphs, in their ecstatic joy, whirl about the Being of God. [901] "O luce sterna che . . . ami ed arridi, " exclaims the pilgrim, as the Divine Essence is at last revealed to him, [902] and he perceives love and joy as the final attributes of the Triune God. Thus Beatrice with "suoi occhi ridenti"-- so different from the world's idea of a suitable demeanour for the soul's supreme instructress--laughs as she mounts with him the ladder to the stars. So, if the deified soul has indeed run ahead of humanity and "according to his fruition dwells in heaven," he too, like Francis, will run, rejoice and make merry: join the eager dance of the Universe about the One. "If," says Patmore, "we may credit certain hints contained in the lives of the saints, love raises the spirit above the sphere of reverence and worship into one of laughter and dalliance: a sphere in which the soul says:--

"Shall I, a gnat which dances in Thy ray,
Dare to be reverent?'" [903]

Richard Rolle has expressed this exultant "spirit of dalliance" with peculiar insight and delicacy. "Among the delights which he tastes in so sweet love burning," he says of the true lover who "in the bond of the lovers' will stably is confirmed," "a heavenly privity inshed he feels, that no man can know but he that has received it, and in himself bears the electuary that anoints and makes happy all joyful lovers in Jesu; so that they cease not to hie in heavenly seats to sit, endlessly their Maker to enjoy. Hereto truly they yearn in heavenly sights abiding; and inwardly set afire, all their inward parts are glad with pleasant shining in light. And themselves they feel gladdened with merriest love, and in joyful song wonderfully melted. . . . But this grace generally and to all is not given, but to the holy soul imbued with the holiest is taught; in whom the excellence of love shines, and songs of lovely loving, Christ inspiring, commonly burst up, and being made as it were a pipe of love, in sight of God more goodly than can be said, joying sounds. The which (soul) the mystery of love knowing, with great cry to its Love ascends, in wit sharpest, and in knowledge and in feeling subtle; not spread in things of this world but into God all gathered and set, that in cleanness of conscience and shining of soul to Him it may serve Whom it has purposed to love, and itself to Him to give. Surely the clearer the love of the lover is, the nearer to him and the more present God is. And thereby more clearly in God he joys, and of the sweet Goodness the more he feels, that to lovers is wont Itself to inshed, and to mirth without comparison the hearts of the meek to turn." [904]

The state of burning love, said Rolle, than which he could conceive no closer reaction to Reality, was the state of Sweetness and Song: the welling up of glad music in the simple soul, man's natural expression of a joy which overpasses the descriptive powers of our untuneful speech. In the gay rhythms of that primordial art he may say something of the secret which the more decorous periods of religion and philosophy will never let him tell: something, too, which in its very childishness, its freedom from the taint of solemnity and self-importance, expresses the quality of that inward life, that perpetual youth, which the "secret child" of the Transcendent Order enjoys. "As it were a pipe of love" in the sight of God he "joying sounds." The music of the spheres is all about him: he is a part of the great melody of the Divine. "Sweetest forsooth," says Rolle again, "is the rest which the spirit takes whilst sweet goodly sound comes down, in which it is delighted: and in most sweet song and playful the mind is ravished to sing likings of love everlasting." [905]

When we come to look at the lives of the mystics, we find it literally true that such "songs of lovely loving commonly burst up" whenever we can catch them unawares; see behind the formidable and heroic activities of reformer, teacher, or leader of men the vie intime which is lived at the hearth of Love. "What are the servants of the Lord but His minstrels?" said St. Francis, [906] who saw nothing inconsistent between the Celestial Melodies and the Stigmata of Christ. Moreover the songs of such troubadours, as the hermit of Hampole learned in his wilderness, are not only sweet but playful. Dwelling always in a light of which we hardly dare to think, save in the extreme terms of reverence and awe, they are not afraid with any amazement: they are at home.

The whole life of St. Francis of Assisi, that spirit transfigured in God, who "loved above all other birds a certain little bird which is called the lark," [907] was one long march to music through the world. To sing seemed to him a primary spiritual function: he taught his friars in their preaching to urge all men to this. [908] It appeared to him appropriate and just to use the romantic language of the troubadours in praise of the perfect Love which had marked him as Its own. "Drunken with the love and compassion of Christ, blessed Francis on a time did things such as these. For the most sweet melody of spirit boiling up within him, frequently broke out in French speech, and the veins of murmuring which he heard secretly with his ears broke forth into French-like rejoicing. And sometimes he picked up a branch from the earth, and laying it on his left arm, he drew in his right hand another stick like a bow over it, as if on a viol or other instrument, and, making fitting gestures, sang with it in French unto the Lord Jesus Christ." [909]

Many a time has the romantic quality of the Unitive Life--its gaiety, freedom, assurance, and joy--broken out in "French-like rejoicings"; which have a terribly frivolous sound for worldly ears, and seem the more preposterous as coming from people whose outward circumstances are of the most uncomfortable kind. St. John of the Cross wrote love songs to his Love. St. Rose of Lima sang duets with the birds. St. Teresa, in the austere and poverty-stricken seclusion of her first foundation, did not disdain to make rustic hymns and carols for her daughters' use in the dialect of Old Castile. Like St. Francis, she had a horror of solemnity. It was only fit for hypocrites, thought these rejuvenators of the Church. The hard life of prayer and penance on Mount Carmel was undertaken in a joyous spirit to the sound of many songs. Its great Reformer was quick to snub the too-spiritual sister who "thought it better to contemplate than to sing": and was herself heard, as she swept the convent corridor, to sing a little ditty about the most exalted of her own mystical experiences: that ineffable transverberation, in which the fiery arrow of the seraph pierced her heart. [910]

But the most lovely and real, most human and near to us, of all these descriptions of the celestial exhilaration which mystic surrender brings in its train, is the artless, unintentional self-revelation of St. Catherine of Genoa, whose inner and outer lives in their balanced wholeness provide us with one of our best standards by which to judge the right proportions of the Mystic Way. Here the whole essence of the Unitive Life is summed up and presented to us by one who lived it upon heroic levels: and who was, in fruition and activity, in rest and in work, not only a great active and a great ecstatic, but one of the deepest gazers into the secrets of Eternal Love that the history of Christian mysticism contains. Yet perhaps there is no passage in the works of these same mystics which comes to so unexpected, so startling a conclusion as this; in which St. Catherine, with a fearless simplicity, shows to her fellow-men the nature of the path that she has trodden and the place that she has reached.

"When," she says, in one of her reported dialogues--and though the tone be impersonal it is clearly personal experience which speaks--"the loving kindness of God calls a soul from the world, He finds it full of vices and sins; and first He gives it an instinct for virtue, and then urges it to perfection, and then by infused grace leads it to true self-naughting, and at last to true transformation. And this noteworthy order serves God to lead the soul along the Way: but when the soul is naughted and transformed, then of herself she neither works nor speaks nor wills, nor feels nor hears nor understands, neither has she of herself the feeling of outward or inward, where she may move. And in all things it is God Who rules and guides her, without the mediation of any creature. And the state of this soul is then a feeling of such utter peace and tranquillity that it seems to her that her heart, and her bodily being, and all both within and without is immersed in an ocean of utmost peace; from when she shall never come forth for anything that can befall her in this life. And she stays immovable, imperturbable, impassible. So much so, that it seems to her in her human and her spiritual nature, both within and without, she can feel no other thing than sweetest peace. And she is so full of peace that though she press her flesh, her nerves, her bones, no other thing comes forth from them than peace. Then says she all day for joy such rhymes as these, making them according to her manner:--

"Vuoi tu che tu mostr'io
Presto che cosa è Dio?
Pace non trova chi da lui si partiò.'" [911]

"Then says she all day for joy such rhymes as these"--nursery rhymes, one might almost call them:

so infantile, so naive is their rhythm. Who would have suspected this to be the secret manner of communion between the exalted soul of Catherine and her Love? How many of those who actually saw that great and able woman labouring in the administration of her hospital--who heard that profound and instinctive Christian Platonist instructing her disciples, and declaring the law of universal and heroic love--how many of these divined that "questa santa benedetta" who seemed to them already something more than earthly, a matter of solemn congratulation and reverential approach, went about her work with a heart engaged in no lofty speculations on Eternity; no outpourings of mystic passion for the Absolute; but "saying all day for joy," in a spirit of childlike happiness, gay and foolish little songs about her Love?

Standing at the highest point of the mystic ladder which can be reached by human spirits in this world of time and space, looking back upon the course of that slow interior alchemy, that "noteworthy order" of organic transformation, by which her selfhood had been purged of imperfection, raised to higher levels, compelled at last to surrender itself to the all-embracing, all-demanding life of the Real; this is St. Catherine's deliberate judgment on the relative and absolute aspects of the mystic life. The "noteworthy order" which we have patiently followed, the psychic growth and rearrangement of character, the visions and ecstasies, the joyous illumination and bitter pain--these but "served to lead the soul along the way." In the mighty transvaluation of values which takes place when that way has at last been trod, these "abnormal events" sink to insignificance. For us, looking out wistfully along the pathway to reality, they stand out, it is true, as supreme landmarks, by which we may trace the homeward course of pilgrim man. Their importance cannot be overrated for those who would study the way to that world from this. But the mystic, safe in that silence where lovers lose themselves, "his cheek on Him Who for his coming came," remembers them no more. In the midst of his active work, his incessant spiritual creation, joy and peace enfold him. He needs no stretched and sharpened intuition now: for he dwells in that "most perfect form of contemplation" which "consists in simple and perceived contact of the substance of the soul with that of the divine." [912]

The wheel of life has made its circle. Here, at the last point of its revolution, the extremes of sublimity and simplicity are seen to meet. It has swept the soul of the mystic through periods of alternate stress and glory; tending ever to greater transcendence, greater freedom, closer contact with "the Supplier of true life." He emerges from that long and wondrous journey to find himself in rest and in work, a little child upon the bosom of the Father. In that most dear relation all feeling, will, and thought attain their end. Here all the teasing complications of our separated selfhood are transcended. Hence the eager striving, the sharp vision, are not wanted any more. In that mysterious death of selfhood on the summits which is the medium of Eternal Life, heights meet the deeps: supreme achievement and complete humility are one.

In a last brief vision, a glimpse as overpowering to our common minds as Dante's final intuition of reality to his exalted and courageous soul, we see the triumphing spirit, sent out before us the best that earth can offer, stoop and strip herself of the insignia of wisdom and power. Achieving the highest, she takes the lowest place. Initiated into the atmosphere of Eternity, united with the Absolute, possessed at last of the fullness of Its life, the soul, self-naughted becomes as a little child: for of such is the kingdom of heaven.

Footnotes:

842. Der Sinn und Wert des Lebens," p. 140.

843. Compare Dante's sense of a transmuted personality when he first breathed the air of Paradise:-- "S' io era sol di me quel che creasti novellamente, Amor che il ciel governi tu il sai, che cot tuo lume mi levasti" (Par. i. 73). "If I were only that of me which thou didst new create, oh Love who rulest heaven, thou knowest who with thy light didst lift me up."

844. "Revelations of Divine Love," cap. v.

845. Par. I. 70.

846. Delacroix. "Études sur le Mysticism," p. 197.

847. Eucken, "Der Sinn und Wert des Lebens," p. 12.

848. Ibid. , p. 96.

849. Delacroix, op. cit ., p. 114 (vide supra , p . 273).

850. "Theologia Germanica," cap. xli.

851. Par. xxx. 115-130 and xxxi. 1-12.

852. Compare, p. 128.

853. Op. cit ., ix. But it is difficult to see why we need stigmatize as "half-savage" man's primordial instinct for his destiny.

854. Divine Liturgy of the Orthodox Eastern Church. Prayers before Communion.

855. Athanasius, De Incarn. Verbi, i. 108.

856. Aug. Conf., bk. vii. cap. x.

857. Pred. lvii.

858. Pred. xcix. ("Mystische Schriften," p. 122).

859. Ruysbroeck. "De Ornatu Spiritalium Nuptiarum," I. iii. cap. iii.

860. Aug. Conf., bk. x. cap. xxviii.

861. Cf. Coventry Patmore, "The Rod, the Root, and the Flower," "Magna Moralia," xxii.

862. Par. xxx. 64.

863. "De Septem Gradibus Amoris," cap. xiv.

864. "The Threefold Life of Man," cap. vi. 88.

865. "De Quatuor Gradibus Violentae Charitatis" (Migne, Patrologia Latina cxcvi.)

866. Dialogo, cap. lxxviii.

867. Ruysbroeck. "Samuel," cap. xi. (English translation: "The Book of Truth.")

868. Ibid ., "De Calculo," cap. ix.

869. St. Thomas Aquinas, "Summa Contra Gentiles," bk. iii. cap. lxii.

870. Suso, "Buchlein von der Wahrheit," cap. iv.

871. "Theologia Germanica," cap. x.

872. Ruysbroeck, "Speculum Aeternae e Salutis," cap. vii.

873. "Regnum Deum Amantium," cap xxii.

874. Jalalu d Din, "The Festival of Spring" (Hastie's translation p. 10).

875. "The Mirror of Simple Souls," Div. iv. cap. i.

876. "The Epistle of Prayer." Printed from Pepwell's edition in "The Cell of Self-knowledge," edited by Edmund Gardner, p. 88.

877. Gerlac Petersen, "Ignitum cum Deo Soliloqium," cap. xv.

878. Compare Pt. i. Cap. vi. It seems needless to repeat here the examples there given.

879. Hilton, "The Treatise written to a Devout Man," cap. viii.

880. Cf. Ormond, "Foundations of Knowledge," p. 442. "When we love any being, we desire either the unification of its life with our own or our own unification with its life. Love in its innermost motive is a unifying principle."

881. "Summa Contra Gentiles," bk. ii. cap. xxi.

882. "De Quatuor Gradibus Violentae Charitatis" (Migne, Patrologia Latina cxcvi. col. 1216 D).

883. "El Castillo Interior," Moradas Sétimas, cap. iv.

884. "Les Torrents," pt. i. cap. ix.

885. Thomas of Celano, Legenda Secunda, cap. xii.

886. Supra , Pt. I. Cap. II.

887. Ruysbroeck, "De Calculo," cap. ix.

888. Op. cit ., cap viii. and ix. (condensed).

889. Vide supra p. 35.

890. Par. xxxiii. 91. "I believe that I beheld the universal form of this knot: because in saying this I feel my joy increased."

891. "De Septem Gradibus Amoris," Cap. xiv .

892. Ibid., loc. cit.

893. Ruysbroeck "Do Ornatu Spiritalium Nuptiarum,"" I. ii cap. lxv.

894. Par. xxxiii. 137.

895. "The Mirror of Simple Souls." p. 161.

896. "De Imitatione Christi," I. iii. cap. v.

897. Contestatio Fr. Thomae Caffarina, Processus, col. 1258 (E. Gardner, "St. Catherine of Siena," p. 48).

898. Par. xxvii. 4.

899. Ibid ., xx. 13.

900. Ibid ., x. 76, 118.

901. Ibid., xxviii. 100.

902. Ibid., xxxiii. 124-26.

903. Coventry Patmore, "The Rod, the Root, and the Flower," "Aurea Dicta."

904. Richard Rolle, "The Fire of Love," bk. ii. cap. vii.

905. Op. cit ., bk. i. cap. xi.

906. "Speculum Perfectionis," cap, c. (Steele's translation).

907. "Speculum," cap. cxiii.

908. Ibid. , cap. c.

909. Ibid. , cap. xciii., also Thomas of Celano, Vita Secunda, cap. xc.

910. Cf . G. Cunninghame Graham, "Santa Teresa," vol. i. pp. 180, 300, 304.

911. "Dost thou wish that I should show All God's Being thou mayst know? Peace is not found of those who do not with Him go." (Vita e Dottrina, cap. xviii.) Here, in spite of the many revisions to which the Vita has been subjected, I cannot but see an authentic report of St. Catherine's inner mind:

highly characteristic of the personality which "came joyous and rosy-faced" from its ecstatic encounters with Love. The very unexpectedness of its conclusion, so unlike the expressions supposed to be proper to the saints, is a guarantee of its authenticity. On the text of the "Vita" see Von Hügel, "The Mystical Element of Religion," vol. i., Appendix.

912. Coventry Patmore, "The Rod, the Root, and the Flower," "Magna Moralia," xv.

CHAPTER XI

Far from being academic or unreal, that history, I think, is vital for the deeper understanding of the history of humanity. It shows us, upon high levels, the psychological process to which every self which desires to rise to the perception of Reality must submit: the formula under which man's spiritual consciousness, be it strong or weak, must necessarily unfold. In the great mystics we see the highest and widest development of that consciousness to which the human race has yet attained. We see its growth exhibited to us on a grand scale, perceptible of all men: the stages of its slow transcendence of the sense-world marked by episodes of splendour and of terror which are hard for common men to accept or understand as a part of the organic process of life. But the germ of that same transcendent life, the spring of the amazing energy which enables the great mystic to rise to freedom and dominate his world, is latent in all of us, an integral part of our humanity. Where the mystic has a genius for the Absolute, we have each a little buried talent, some greater, some less; and the growth of this talent, this spark of the soul, once we permit its emergence, will conform in little, and according to its measure, to those laws of organic growth those inexorable conditions of transcendence which we found to govern the Mystic Way.

Every person, then, who awakens to consciousness of a Reality which transcends the normal world of sense--however small, weak imperfect that consciousness may be--is put upon a road which follows at low levels the path which the mystic treads at high levels. The success with which he follows this way to freedom and full life will depend on the intensity of his love and will, his capacity for self-discipline, his steadfastness and courage. It will depend on the generosity and completeness of his outgoing passion for absolute beauty, absolute goodness, or absolute truth. But if he move at all, he will move through a series of states which are, in their own small way, analogous to those experienced by the greatest contemplative on his journey towards that union with God which is the term of the spirit's ascent towards its home.

As the embryo of physical man, be he saint or savage, passes through the same stages of initial growth, so too with spiritual man. When the "new birth" takes place in him, the new life-process of his deeper self begins, the normal individual, no less than the mystic, will know that spiral ascent towards higher levels, those oscillations of consciousness between light and darkness, those odd mental disturbances, abrupt invasions from the subliminal region, and disconcerting glimpses of truth, which accompany the growth of the transcendental powers; though he may well interpret them in other than the mystic sense. He too will be impelled to drastic self-discipline, to a deliberate purging of his eyes that he may see: and receiving a new vision of the world, will be spurred by it to a total self-dedication, an active surrender of his whole being, to that aspect of the Infinite which he has perceived. He too will endure in little the psychic upheavals of the spiritual adolescence: will be forced to those sacrifices which every form of genius demands. He will know according to his measure the dreadful moments of lucid self-knowledge, the counter-balancing ecstasy of an intuition of the Real. More and more, as we study and collate all the available evidence, this fact--this law--is borne in on us: that the general movement of human consciousness, when it obeys its innate tendency to transcendence, is always the same. There is only one road from Appearance to Reality. "Men pass on, but the States are permanent for ever."

I do not care whether the consciousness be that of artist or musician, striving to catch and fix some aspect of the heavenly light or music, and denying all other aspects of the world in order to devote themselves to this: or of the humble servant of Science, purging his intellect that he may look upon her secrets with innocence of eye: whether the higher reality be perceived in the terms of religion, beauty, suffering; of human love, of goodness, or of truth. However widely these forms of transcendence may seem to differ, the mystic experience is the key to them all. All in their different ways are exhibitions here and now of the Eternal; extensions of man's consciousness which involve calls to heroic endeavour, incentives to the remaking of character about new and higher centres of life. Through each, man may rise to freedom and take his place in the great movement of the universe: may "understand by dancing that which is done." Each brings the self who receives its revelation in good faith, does not check it by self-regarding limitations, to a humble acceptance of the universal law of knowledge: the law that "we behold that which we are," and hence that "only the Real can know Reality." Awakening, Discipline, Enlightenment, Self-surrender, and Union, are the essential phases of life's response to this fundamental fact: the conditions of our attainment of Being, the necessary formula under which alone our consciousness of any of these fringes of Eternity--any of these aspects of the Transcendent--can unfold, develop, attain to freedom and full life.

We are, then, one and all the kindred of the mystics; and it is by dwelling upon this kinship, by interpreting--so far as we may--their great declarations in the light of our little experience, that we shall learn to understand them best. Strange and far away though they seem, they are not cut off from us by some impassable abyss. They belong to us. They are our brethren; the giants, the heroes of our race. As the achievement of genius belongs not to itself only, but also to the society that brought it forth; as theology declares that the merits of the saints avail for all; so, because of the solidarity of the human family, the supernal accomplishment of the mystics is ours also. Their attainment is the earnest-money of our eternal life.

To be a mystic is simply to participate here and now in that real and eternal life; in the fullest, deepest sense which is possible to man. It is to share, as a free and conscious agent--not a servant, but a son--in the joyous travail of the Universe: its mighty onward sweep through pain and glory towards its home in God. This gift of "sonship," this power of free co-operation in the world-process, is man's greatest honour. The ordered sequence of states, the organic development, whereby his consciousness is detached from illusion and rises to the mystic freedom which conditions instead of being conditioned by, its normal world, is the way he must tread if that sonship is to be realized. Only by this deliberate fostering of his deeper self, this transmutation of the elements of his character, can he reach those levels of consciousness upon which he hears, and responds to, the measure "whereto the worlds keep time" on their great pilgrimage towards the Father's heart. The mystic act of union, that joyous loss of the transfigured self in God, which is the crown of man's conscious ascent towards the Absolute, is the contribution of the individual to this, the destiny of the Cosmos.

The mystic knows that destiny. It is laid bare to his lucid vision, as our puzzling world of form and colour is to normal sight. He is the "hidden child" of the eternal order, an initiate of the secret plan. Hence, whilst "all creation groaneth and travaileth," slowly moving under the spur of blind desire towards that consummation in which alone it can have rest, he runs eagerly along the pathway to reality. He is the pioneer of Life on its age-long voyage to the One: and shows us, in his attainment, the meaning and value of that life.

This meaning, this secret plan of Creation, flames out, had we eyes to see, from every department of existence. Its exultant declarations come to us in all great music; its magic is the life of all romance. Its law--the law of love--is the substance of the beautiful, the energizing cause of the heroic. It lights the altar of every creed. All man's dreams and diagrams concerning a transcendent Perfection near him yet intangible, a transcendent vitality to which he can attain--whether he call these objects of desire God, grace, being, spirit, beauty, "pure idea"--are but translations of his deeper self's intuition of its destiny; clumsy fragmentary hints at the all-inclusive, living Absolute which that deeper self knows to be real. This supernal Thing, the adorable Substance of all that Is--the synthesis of Wisdom, Power, and Love--and man's apprehension of it, his slow remaking in its interests, his union with it at last; this is the theme of mysticism. That twofold extension of consciousness which allows him communion with its transcendent and immanent aspects is, in all its gradual processes, the Mystic Way. It is also the crown of human evolution; the fulfilment of life, the liberation of personality from the world of appearance, its entrance into the free creative life of the Real.

Further, Christians may well remark that the psychology of Christ, as presented to us in the Gospels, is of a piece with that of the mystics. In its pain and splendour, its dual character of action and fruition, it reflects their experience upon the supernal plane of more abundant life. Thanks to this fact, for them the Ladder of Contemplation--that ladder which mediaeval thought counted as an instrument of the Passion, discerning it as essential to the true salvation of man--stretches without a break from earth to the Empyrean. It leans against the Cross; it leads to the Secret Rose. By it the ministers of Goodness, Truth, and Beauty go up and down between the transcendent and the apparent world. Seen, then, from whatever standpoint we may choose to adopt--whether of psychology, philosophy, or religion--the adventure of the great mystics intimately concerns us. It is a master-key to man's puzzle: by its help he may explain much in his mental makeup, in his religious constructions, in his experience of life. In all these departments he perceives himself to be climbing slowly and clumsily upward toward some attainment yet unseen. The mystics, expert mountaineers, go before him: and show him, if he cares to learn, the way to freedom, to reality, to peace. He cannot rise in this, his earthly existence, to the awful and solitary peak, veiled in the Cloud of Unknowing, where they meet that "death of the summit," which is declared by them to be the gate of Perfect Life: but if he choose to profit by their explorations, he may find his level, his place within the Eternal Order. He may achieve freedom, live the "independent spiritual life."

Consider once more the Mystic Way as we have traced it from its beginning. To what does it tend if not to this?

It began by the awakening within the self of a new and embryonic consciousness: a consciousness of divine reality, as opposed to the illusory sense-world in which she was immersed. Humbled, awed by the august possibilities then revealed to her, that self retreated into the "cell of self-knowledge" and there laboured to adjust herself to the Eternal Order which she had perceived, stripped herself of all that opposed it, disciplined her energies, purified the organs of sense. Remade in accordance with her intuitions of reality, the "eternal hearing and seeing were revealed in her." She opened her eyes upon a world still natural, but no longer illusory; since it was perceived to be illuminated by the Uncreated Light. She knew then the beauty, the majesty, the divinity of the living World of Becoming which holds in its meshes every living thing. She had transcended the narrow rhythm by which common men perceive but one of its many aspects, escaped the machine-made universe presented by the cinematograph of sense, and participated in the "great life of the All." Reality came forth to her, since her eyes were cleansed to see It, not from some strange far-off and spiritual country, but gently, from the very heart of things. Thus lifted to a new level, she began again her ceaseless work of growth: and because by the cleansing of the senses she had learned to see the reality which is shadowed by the sense-world, she now, by the cleansing of her will, sought to draw nearer to that Eternal Will, that Being, which life, the World of Becoming, manifests and serves. Thus, by the surrender of her selfhood in its wholeness, the perfecting of her love, she slid from Becoming to Being, and found her true life hidden in God.

Yet the course of this transcendence, this amazing inward journey, was closely linked, first and last, with the processes of human life. It sprang from that life, as man springs from the sod. We were even able to describe it under those symbolic formulae which we are accustomed to call the "laws" of the natural world. By an extension of these formulae, their logical application, we discovered a path which led us without a break from the sensible to the supra-sensible; from apparent to absolute life. There is nothing unnatural about the Absolute of the mystics: He sets the rhythm of His own universe, and conforms to the harmonies which He has made. We, deliberately seeking for that which we suppose to be spiritual, too often overlook that which alone is Real. The true mysteries of life accomplish themselves so softly, with so easy and assured a grace, so frank an acceptance of our breeding, striving, dying, and unresting world, that the unimaginative natural man--all agog for the marvellous--is hardly startled by their daily and radiant revelation of infinite wisdom and love. Yet this revelation presses incessantly upon us. Only the hard crust of surface-consciousness conceals it from our normal sight. In some least expected moment, the common activities of life in progress, that Reality in Whom the mystics dwell slips through our closed doors, and suddenly we see It at our side.

It was said of the disciples at Emmaus, "Mensam igitur ponunt panes cibosque offerunt, et Deum, quem in Scripturae sacrae expositione non cognoverant, in panis fractione cognoscunt." So too for us the Transcendent Life for which we crave is revealed and our living within it, not on some remote and arid plane of being, in the cunning explanations of philosophy; but in the normal acts of our diurnal experience, suddenly made significant for us. Not in the backwaters of existence, not amongst subtle arguments and occult doctrines, but in all those places where the direct and simple life of earth goes on. It is found in the soul of man so long as that soul is alive and growing: it is not found in any sterile place.

This fact of experience is our link with the mystics, our guarantee of the truthfulness of their statements, the supreme importance of their adventure, their closer contact with Reality. The mystics on their part are our guarantee of the end towards which the Immanent Love, the hidden steersman which dwells in our midst, is moving: our "lovely forerunners" on the path towards the Real. They come back to us from an encounter with life's most august secret, as Mary came running from the tomb; filled with amazing tidings which they can hardly tell. We, longing for some assurance, and seeing their radiant faces, urge them to pass on their revelation if they can. It is the old demand of the dim-sighted and incredulous:--

"Dic nobis Maria
Quid vidisti in via?"

But they cannot say: can only report fragments of the symbolic vision:--

"Angelicos testes, sudarium, et vestes"--

not the inner content, the final divine certainty. We must ourselves follow in their footsteps if we would have that.

Like the story of the Cross, so too the story of man's spirit ends in a garden: in a place of birth and fruitfulness, of beautiful and natural things. Divine Fecundity is its secret: existence, not for its own sake, but for the sake of a more abundant life. It ends with the coming forth of divine humanity, never again to leave us: living in us, and with us, a pilgrim, a worker, a guest at our table, a sharer at all hazards in life. The mystics witness to this story: waking very early they have run on before us, urged by the greatness of their love. We, incapable as yet of this sublime encounter, looking in their magic mirror, listening to their stammered tidings, may see far off the consummation of the race.

According to the measure of their strength and of their passion, these, the true lovers of the Absolute, have conformed here and now to the utmost tests of divine sonship, the final demands of life. They have not shrunk from the sufferings of the cross. They have faced the darkness of the tomb. Beauty and agony alike have called them: alike have awakened a heroic response. For them the winter is over: the time of the singing of birds is come. From the deeps of the dewy garden, Life--new, unquenchable, and ever lovely--comes to meet them with the dawn.

Et hoc intellegere, quis bominum dabit bomini?
Quis angelus angelo?
Quis angelus bomini?
El te petatur,
In te quaeratur,
Eld te pulsetur,
Sic, sic accipietur invenietur, sic aperietur.

CHAPTER XII

If we try to represent the course of Mysticism in Europe during the Christian period by the common device of a chronological curve, showing by its rises and falls as it passes across the centuries the absence or preponderance in any given epoch of mystics and mystical thought, we shall find that the great periods of mystical activity tend to correspond with the great periods of artistic, material, and intellectual civilization. As a rule, they come immediately after, and seem to complete such periods: those outbursts of vitality in which man makes fresh conquests over his universe apparently producing, as their last stage, a type of heroic character which extends these victories to the spiritual sphere. When science, politics, literature, and the arts--the domination of nature and the ordering of life--have risen to their height and produced their greatest works, the mystic comes to the front; snatches the torch, and carries it on. It is almost as if he were humanity's finest flower; the product at which each great creative period of the race had aimed.

Thus the thirteenth century expressed to perfection the medieval ideal in religion, art, philosophy, and public life. It built the Gothic cathedrals, put the finishing touch to the system of chivalry, and nourished the scholastic philosophers. It has many saints, but not very many mystics; though they increase in number as the century draws on. The fourteenth century is filled by great contemplatives; who lifted this wave of activity to spiritual levels, and brought the intellectual vigour, the romance and passion of the mediaeval temperament, to bear upon the deepest mysteries of the transcendental life. Again, the sixteenth century, that period of abounding vitality which left no corner of existence unexplored, which produced the Renaissance and the Humanists and remade the mediaeval world, had hardly reached its full development before the great procession of the post-Renaissance mystics, with St. Teresa at their head, began. If life, then--the great and restless life of the race--be described under the trite metaphor of a billowy sea, each great wave as it rises from the deep bears the mystic type upon its crest.

Our curve will therefore follow close behind that other curve which represents the intellectual life of humanity. Its course will be studded and defined for us by the names of the great mystics; the possessors of spiritual genius, the pathfinders to the country of the soul. These starry names are significant not only in themselves but also as links in the chain of manes growing spiritual history. They are not isolated phenomena, but are related to one another. Each receives something from his predecessors: each by his personal adventures enriches it, and hands it on to the future. As we go on, we notice more and more this cumulative power of the past. Each mystic, original though he be, yet owes much to the inherited acquirement of his spiritual ancestors. These ancestors form his tradition, are the classic examples on which his education is based; and from them he takes the language which they have sought out and constructed as a means of telling their adventures to the world. It is by their help too, very often, that he elucidates for himself the meaning of the dim perceptions of his amazed soul. From his own experiences he adds to this store; and hands on an enriched tradition of the transcendental life to the next spiritual genius evolved by the race. Hence the names of the great mystics are connected by a thread; and it becomes possible to treat them as subjects of history rather than of biography.

I have said that this thread forms a curve, following the fluctuations of the intellectual life of the race. At its highest points, the names of the mystics are clustered most thickly, at its descents they become fewer and fewer, at the lowest points they die away. Between the first century A.D. and the nineteenth, this curve exhibits three great waves of mystical activity besides many minor fluctuations. They correspond with the close of the Classical, the Mediaeval, and the Renaissance periods in history: reaching their highest points in the third, fourteenth, and seventeenth centuries. In one respect, however, the mystic curve diverges from the historical one. It rises to its highest point in the fourteenth century, and does not again approach the level it there attains; for the mediaeval period was more favourable to the development of mysticism than any subsequent epoch has been. The fourteenth century is as much the classic moment for the spiritual history of our race as the thirteenth is for the history of Gothic, or the fifteenth for that of Italian art.

The names upon our curve, especially during the first ten centuries of the Christian era, are often separated by long periods of time. This, of course, does not necessarily mean that these centuries produced few mystics: merely that few documents relating to them have survived. We have now no means of knowing, for instance, the amount of true mysticism which may have existed amongst the initiates of the Greek or Egyptian Mysteries; how many advanced but inarticulate contemplatives there were amongst the Alexandrian Neo-platonists, amongst the pre-Christian communities of contemplatives described by Philo , the deeply mystical Alexandrian Jew (20 B.C.-A.D. 40), or the innumerable Gnostic sects which replaced in the early Christian world the Orphic and Dionysiac mystery-cults of Greece and Italy. Much real mystical inspiration there must have been, for we know that from these centres of life came many of the doctrines best loved by later mystics: that the Neoplatonists gave them the concepts of Pure Being and the One, that the New Birth and the Spiritual Marriage were foreshadowed in the Mysteries, that Philo anticipated the theology of the Fourth Gospel.

As we stand at the beginning of the Christian period we see three great sources whence its mystical tradition might have been derived. These sources are Greek, Oriental, and Christian-- i.e. , primitive Apostolic--doctrine or thought. As a matter of fact all contributed their share: but where Christianity gave the new vital impulse to transcendence, Greek and Oriental thought provided the principal forms in which it was expressed. The Christian religion, by its very nature, had a profoundly mystical side. Putting the personality of its Founder outside the limits of the present discussion, St. Paul and the author of the Fourth Gospel are obvious instances of mystics of the first rank amongst its earliest missionaries. Much of the inner history of primitive Christianity still remains unknown to us, but in what has been already made out we find numerous, if scattered, indications that the mystic life was indigenous in the Church and the natural mystic had little need to look for inspiration outside the limits of his creed. Not only the epistles of St. Paul and the Johannine writings, but also the earliest liturgic fragments which we possess, and such primitive religious poetry as the "Odes of Solomon" and the "Hymn of Jesus," show how congenial was mystical expression to the mind of the Church how easily that Church could absorb and transmute the mystic elements of Essene, Orphic, and Neoplatonic thought.

Towards the end of the second century this tendency received brilliant literary expression at the hands of Clement of Alexandria (c. 160-220)--who first adapted the language of the pagan Mysteries to the Christian theory of the spiritual life--and his great pupil Origen (c. 183-253). Nevertheless, the first person after St. Paul of whom it can now be decisively stated that he was a practical mystic of the first rank, and in whose writings the central mystic doctrine of union with God is found, is a pagan. That person is Plotinus , the great Neoplatonic philosopher of Alexandria (A.D. 205-c. 270). His mysticism owes nothing to the Christian religion, which is never mentioned in his works. Intellectually it is based on the Platonic philosophy, and also shows the influence of the Mysteries, and perhaps certain of the Oriental cults and philosophies which ran riot in Alexandria in the third century. Ostensibly a metaphysician, however, Plotinus possessed transcendental genius of a high order, and was consumed by a burning passion for the Absolute: and the importance of his work lies in the degree in which his intellectual constructions are made the vehicle of mystical experience. His disciple Porphyry has left it on record that on four occasions he saw his master rapt to ecstatic union with "the One."

The Neoplatonism of which Plotinus was the greatest exponent became the medium in which much of the mysticism--both Christian and pagan--of the first six centuries was expressed. But since mysticism is a way of life--an experience of Reality, not a philosophic account of Reality--Neoplatonism, and the mysticism which used its language, must not be identified with one another. Porphyry (233-304) the favourite pupil of Plotinus seems to have inherited something of his master's mysticism, but Neoplatonism as a whole was a confused, semi-religious philosophy, containing many inconsistent elements. Appearing when the wreck of paganism was complete, but before Christianity had conquered the educated world, it made a strong appeal to the spiritually minded; and also to those who hankered after the mysterious and the occult. It taught the illusory nature of all temporal things, and in the violence of its idealism outdid its master Plato. It also taught the existence of an Absolute God, the "Unconditioned One," who might be known in ecstasy and contemplation; and here it made a direct appeal to the mystical instincts of men. Those natural mystics who lived in the time of its greatest popularity found in it therefore a ready means of expressing their own intuitions of reality. Hence the early mysticism of Europe, both Christian and pagan, has come down to us in a Neoplatonic dress; and speaks the tongue of Alexandria rather than that of Jerusalem, Athens, or Rome.

The influence of Plotinus upon later Christian mysticism was enormous though indirect. During the patristic period all that was best in the spirit of Neoplatonism flowed into the veins of the Church. St. Augustine (A.D. 354-430) and Dionysius the Areopagite (writing between 475 and 525) are amongst his spiritual children; and it is mainly through them that his doctrine reached the mediaeval world. Proclus (412-c. 490), the last of the pagan philosophers, also derives from his teaching. Through these three there is hardly one in the long tale of the European contemplatives whom his powerful spirit has failed to reach.

The mysticism of St. Augustine is partly obscured for us by the wealth of his intellectual and practical life: yet no one can read the "Confessions" without being struck by the intensity and actuality of his spiritual experience, and the characteristically mystical formula under which he apprehended Reality. It is clear that when he composed this work he was already an advanced contemplative. The immense intellectual activities by which he is best remembered were fed by the solitary adventures of his soul. No merely literary genius could have produced the wonderful chapters in the seventh and eighth books, or the innumerable detached passages in which his passion for the Absolute breaks out. Later mystics, recognizing this fact, constantly appeal to his authority, and his influence ranks next to that of the Bible in the formation of the mediaeval school.

Second only to that of St. Augustine was the influence exercised by the strange and nameless writer who chose to ascribe his works to Dionysius the Areopagite, the friend of St. Paul, and to address his letters upon mysticism to Paul's fellow-worker, Timothy. The pseudo-Dionysius was probably a Syrian monk. The patristic quotations detected in his work prove that he cannot have written before A.D.475; it is most likely that he flourished in the early part of the sixth century. His chief works are the treatises on the Angelic Hierarchies and on the Names of God, and a short but priceless tract on mystical theology. From the ninth century to the seventeenth these writings nourished the most spiritual intuitions of men, and possessed an authority which it is now hard to realize. Medieval mysticism is soaked in Dionysian conceptions. Particularly in the fourteenth century, the golden age of mystical literature, the phrase "Dionysius saith" is of continual recurrence: and has for those who use it much the same weight as quotations from the Bible or the great fathers of the Church.

The importance of Dionysius lies in the fact that he was the first and for a long time the only, Christian writer who attempted to describe frankly and accurately the workings of the mystical consciousness, and the nature of its ecstatic attainment of God. So well did he do h s work that later contemplatives, reading him, found their most sublime experiences reflected and partly explained. Hence in describing those experiences, they adopted his language and metaphors; which afterwards became the classic terms of contemplative science. To him Christian literature owes the paradoxical concept of the Absolute Godhead as the "Divine Dark," the Unconditioned, "the negation of all that is "--i.e ., of all that the surface consciousness perceives--and of the soul's attainment of the Absolute as a "divine ignorance," a way of negation. This idea is common to Greek and Indian philosophy. With Dionysius it enters the Catholic fold.

Side by side with the Neoplatonic mysticism of St. Augustine and Dionysius runs another line of spiritual culture, hardly less important for the development of the contemplative life. This takes its rise among the Fathers of the Egyptian desert, whose heroic spirituality was a contributory factor in St. Augustine's conversion. It finds beautiful expression in the writings of St. Marcarius of Egypt (c. 295-386), the disciple of St. Anthony and friend of St. Basil, and reaches the West through the "Dialogues" of John Cassian (c. 350-), one of the most important documents for the history of Christian mysticism. The fruit of a seven-year pilgrimage among the Egyptian monasteries, and many conversations on spiritual themes with the monks, we find in these dialogues for the first time a classified and realistic description of the successive degrees of contemplative prayer, and their relation to the development of the spiritual life. Adopted by St. Benedict as part of the regular spiritual food of his monks, they have had a decisive influence on the cloistered mysticism of the Middle Ages. Their sober and orderly doctrine, destined to be characteristic of the Roman Church, received fresh emphasis in the works of St. Gregory the Great (540-604), which also helped to form the souls of succeeding generations of contemplatives.

We have therefore, at the opening of the Middle Ages, two great streams of spiritual culture; the Benedictine, moderate and practical, formed chiefly on Cassian and St. Gregory, and the Neoplatonic, represented by Dionysius the Areopagite, and in a less exclusive form by St. Augustine. The works of Dionysius were translated from Greek into Latin about A.D. 850 by the Irish philosopher and theologian, John Scotus Erigena , one of the scholars assembled at the court of Charlemagne: and this event marks the beginning of a full tradition of mysticism in Western Europe. John the Scot, many of whose own writings exhibit a strong mystical bias, is the only name in this period which the history of mysticism can claim. We are on the descending line of the "Dark Ages": and here the curve of mysticism runs parallel with the curves of intellectual and artistic activity.

The great current of medieval mysticism first shows itself in the eleventh century, and chiefly in connection with the Benedictine Order for the work of such monastic reformers as St. Romuald (c. 950-1027) St. Peter Damian (1007-1072), and St. Bruno (1032-1101), the founder of the Grande Chartreuse, was really the effort of contemplative souls to establish an environment in which the mystical life could be lived. Thus too we must regard at least a large proportion of the hermits and solitaries who became so marked a feature in the religion of the West. At this period mysticism was not sharply distinguished from the rest of the religious complex, but was rather the realistic experience of the truths on which religion rests. It spread mainly through personal instruction and discipleship. Its literary monuments were few among the most important and widely influential being the "Meditations" of St. Anselm (1033-1109), which, disentangled by recent scholarship from the spurious material passing under his name, are now seen to have been a chief channel of transmission for the Augustinian mysticism which dominated the early Middle Ages. The general religious revival of the twelfth century had its marked mystical aspect, and produced four personalities of great historical importance: the Benedictines St.

Bernard of Clairvaux (1091-1153), St. Hildegarde of Bingen (1098-1179), and Joachim of Flora (1132-1202); and the Scotch or Irish Augustinian Richard of St. Victor (ob. c. 1173), whom Dante held to be "in contemplation more than man." Richard's master and contemporary, the scholastic philosopher Hugh (1097-1141) of the same Abbey of St. Victor at Paris, is also generally reckoned amongst the mystics of thus period, but with less reason; since contemplation occupies a small place in his theological writings. In spite of the deep respect shown towards him by Aquinas and other theologians, Hugh's influence on later mystical literature was slight. The spirit of Richard and of St. Bernard, on the contrary, was destined to dominate it for the next two hundred years. With them the literature of mediaeval mysticism properly so called begins.

This literature Falls into two classes: the personal and the didactic. Sometimes, as in a celebrated sermon of St. Bernard, the two are combined; the teacher appealing to his own experience in illustration of his theme. In the works of the Victorines the attitude is didactic: one might almost say scientific. In them mysticism--that is to say, the degrees of contemplation, the training and exercise of the spiritual sense--takes its place as a recognized department of theology. It is in Richard's favourite symbolism, "Benjamin," the beloved child of Rachel, emblem of the Contemplative Life: and in his two chief works, "Benjamin Major" and "Benjamin Minor," it is classified and described in all its branches. Though mysticism was for Richard the "science of the heart" and he had little respect for secular learning, yet his solid intellectuality did much to save the medieval school from the perils of religious emotionalism. In his hands the antique mystical tradition which flowed through Plotinus and the Areopagite, was codified and transmitted to the mediaeval world. Like his master, Hugh, he had the mediaeval passion for elaborate allegory, neat arrangement, rigid classification, and significant numbers in things. As Dante parcelled out Heaven, Purgatory, and Hell with mathematical precision, and proved that Beatrice was herself a Nine, so these writers divide and subdivide the stages of contemplation, the states of the soul, the degrees of Divine Love: and perform terrible tours de force in the course of compelling the ever-variable expressions of man's spiritual vitality to fall into orderly and parallel series, conformable to the mystic numbers of Seven, Four, and Three.

The influence of Richard of St. Victor, great as it was, is exceeded by that of St. Bernard; the dominant spiritual personality of the twelfth century. Bernard's career of ceaseless and varied activity sufficiently disproves the "idleness" of the contemplative type. He continued and informed with his own spirit the Benedictine tradition, and his writings quickly took their place, with those of Richard of St. Victor, among the living forces which conditioned the development of later mysticism. Both these mystics exerted a capital influence on the formation of our national school of mysticism in the fourteenth century. Translations and paraphrases of the "Benjamin Major," "Benjamin Minor," and other works of Richard of St. Victor, and of various tracts and epistles of St. Bernard, are constantly met with in the MS. collections of mystical and theological literature written in England in the thirteenth and fourteenth centuries. An early paraphrase of the "Benjamin Minor," sometimes attributed to Richard Rolle, was probably made by the anonymous author of "The Cloud of Unknowing," who was also responsible for the first appearance of the Areopagite in English dress.

If mediaeval mysticism in the West develops mainly under the sane and enduring influence of the Victorines and St. Bernard, in Germany and Italy it appeared in a more startling form; seeking, in the prophetic activities of St. Hildegarde of Bingen and the Abbot Joachim of Flora, to influence the course of secular history. In St. Hildegarde and her fellow-Benedictine St. Elizabeth of Shönau (1138-1165) we have the first of that long line of women mystics--visionaries, prophetesses, and political reformers--combining spiritual transcendence with great practical ability, of whom St. Catherine of Siena is probably the greatest example. Exalted by the strength of their spiritual intuitions, they emerged from an obscure life to impose their wills, and their reading of events, upon the world. From the point of view of Eternity, in whose light they lived, they attacked the sins of their generation. St. Hildegarde, a woman of powerful character, apparently possessed of abnormal psychic gifts, was driven by that Living Light which was her inspiration to denounce the corruptions of Church and State. In the inspired letters which she sent like firebrands over Europe, we see German idealism and German practicality struggling together; the unflinching description of abuses, the vast poetic vision by which they are condemned. These qualities are seen again in the South German mystics of the next century: the four Benedictine women of genius, who had their home in the convent of Helfde. These are the Nun Gertrude (Abbess 1251-1291) and her sister St. Mechthild of Hackborn (ob. 1310), with her sublime symbolic visions: then, the poet of the group, the exquisite Mechthild of Magdeburg (1212-1299), who, first a béguine at Magdeburg, where she wrote the greater part of "The Flowing Light of the Godhead," came to Helfde in 1268; last the celebrated St. Gertrude the Great (1256-1311). In these contemplatives the political spirit is less marked than in St. Hildegarde: but religious and ethical activity takes its place. St. Gertrude the Great is a characteristic Catholic visionary of the feminine type: absorbed in her subjective experiences, her often beautiful and significant dreams, her loving conversations with Christ and the Blessed Virgin. Close to her in temperament is St. Mechthild of Hackborn; but her attitude as a whole is more impersonal, more truly mystic. The great symbolic visions in which her most spiritual perceptions are expressed are artistic creations rather than psycho-sensorial hallucinations, and dwell little upon the humanity of Christ, with which St. Gertrude is constantly occupied. The terms in which Mechthild of Magdeburg--an educated and well-born woman, half poet, half seer--describes her union with God are intensely individual, and apparently owe more to the romantic poets of her time than to earlier religious writers. The works of this Mechthild, early translated into Latin, were read by Dante. Their influence is traceable in the "Paradiso"; and by some scholars she is believed to be the Matilda of his Earthly Paradise, though others give this position to her sister-mystic, St. Mechthild of Hackborn.

Modern scholarship tends more and more to see in the strange personality of the Abbot Joachim of Flora, whom Dante placed among the great contemplatives in the Heaven of the Sun, the chief influence in the development of Italian mysticism. The true import of his prophecies, which proclaimed in effect the substitution of mystical for institutional Christianity, was only appreciated after his death. But their prestige grew during the course of the thirteenth century; especially after the appearance of the mendicant friars, who seemed to fulfil his prediction that the new era of the Holy Spirit would be brought in about the year 1260 by two new Orders who would live in poverty the spiritual life. From this time, Joachism found its chief vehicle of expression through Franciscan mysticism of the more revolutionary sort. Though there is no evidence that St. Francis of Assisi (1182-1226) knew the prophecies of the "Eternal Gospel," he can hardly have grown up without some knowledge of them, and also of the Cathari and other semi-mystical heresies--many of them stressing the idea of evangelical poverty--which were spreading through Italy from the north. But the mystical genius which may have received food from these sources was itself strikingly original; the spontaneous expression of a rare personality, a great spiritual realist who admitted no rival to the absolute claims of the mystical life of poverty and joy. St. Francis was untouched by monastic discipline, or the writings of Dionysius or St. Bernard. His only literary influence was the New Testament. With him, mysticism comes into the open air, seeks to transform the stuff of daily life, speaks the vernacular, turns the songs of the troubadours to the purposes of Divine love; yet remains completely loyal to the Catholic Church. None who came after him succeeded in recapturing his secret which was the secret of spiritual genius of the rarest type: but he left his mark upon the history, art and literature of Western Europe, and the influence of his spirit still lives.

In a general sense it is true to say that Italian mysticism descends from St. Francis, and in its first period seems almost to be the prerogative of his disciples; especially those of the "Spiritual" party who strove to maintain his ideals in their purity. It is here that we find Franciscan ardour and singlemindedness in alliance with apocalyptic notions deriving from Joachist ideas. In Provence, a widespread mystical movement coloured by Joachism was led by Hugues de Digne and his sister St. Douceline (n . 1214); in whom we find a spirit which, like that of Francis, could find the Divine through flowers and birds and simple natural things. In Italy, nourished by the influence of such deeply mystical friars as John of Parma (ob. 1288) and John of La Verna , this Franciscan spirituality entered into conflict with the ecclesiastical politics of the day; taking up that duty of denouncing the corruptions of the Church, which has so often attracted the mystics. Here the typical figure is that of Jacopone da Todi (1228-1306), the converted lawyer turned mystical poet. On one hand deeply influenced by St. Augustine and Dionysius the Areopagite, on the other the devoted exponent of the Founder's ideals, his "spiritual songs" lift Franciscan mysticism to the heights of ecstatic rapture and literary expression; whilst his savage castigations of the Papacy give him a place among the great mediaeval satirists. Jacopone's poems have been shown by Von Hügel to have had a formative influence on St. Catherine of Genoa; and have probably affected many other mystics, not only in Italy but elsewhere, for they quickly attained considerable circulation.

In his contemporary the Blessed Angela of Foligno (1248-1309) who was converted from a sinful life to become a tertiary hermit of the Franciscan Order we have a mystic of the first rank whose visions and revelations place her in the same class as St. Catherine of Genoa and St. Teresa. Known to her followers as the Mistress of Theologians, and numbering among her disciples the brilliant and tempestuous "spiritual" friar Ubertino da Casale, the lofty metaphysical element in Angela's mysticism suggests the high level of spiritual culture achieved in Franciscan circles of her time. By the sixteenth century her works, translated into the vernacular, had taken their place amongst the classics of mysticism. In the seventeenth they were largely used by St. François de Sales, Madame Guyon, and other Catholic contemplatives. Seventeen years older than Dante, whose great genius properly closes this line of spiritual descent, she is a link between the thirteenth and fourteenth centuries in Italian mysticism.

We now approach the Golden Age of Mysticism: and at the opening of that epoch, dominating it by their peculiar combination of intellectual and spiritual power stand the figures of the "Seraphic and Angelic Doctors," St. Bonaventura , the Franciscan (1221-1274), and St. Thomas Aquinas , the Dominican (1226-1274). As with St. Augustine, the intellectual greatness of St. Thomas has obscured his mystical side, whilst St. Bonaventura, the apostle of a wise moderation, may easily appear to the hurried reader the least mystical of the Franciscan mystics. Yet both were contemplatives, and because of this were able to interpret to the medieval world the great spiritual tradition of the past. Hence their immense influence on the mystical schools of the fourteenth century. It is sometimes stated that these schools derive mainly from St. Bonaventura, and represent an opposition to scholastic theology; but as a matter of fact their greatest personalities--in particular Dante and the German Dominicans--are soaked in the spirit of Aquinas, and quote his authority at every turn.

In Europe the mystic curve is now approaching its highest point. In the East that point has already been passed. Sufi, or Mahommedan mysticism, appearing in the eighth century in the beautiful figure of Rabi'a , the "Moslem St. Teresa" (717-801), and continued by the martyr Al Hallaj (ob. 922), attains literary expression in the eleventh in the "Confessions" of Al Ghazzali (1058-1111), and has its classic period in the thirteenth in the works of the mystic poets Attar (c. 1140-1234), Sadi (1184-1263), and the saintly Jalalu d Din (1207-1273). Its tradition is continued in the fourteenth century by the rather erotic mysticism of Hafiz (c. 1300-1388) and his successors, and in the fifteenth by the poet Jámí (1414-1492).

Whilst Hafiz already strikes a note of decadence for the mysticism of Islam, the year 1300 is for Western Europe a vital year in the history of the spiritual life. Mystics of the first rank are appearing, or about to appear. The Majorcan scholar-mystic Ramon Lull (ob. 1315) is drawing to the end of his long life. In Italy Dante (1265-1321) is forcing human language to express one of the most sublime visions of the Absolute which has ever been crystallized into speech. He inherits and fuses into one that loving and artistic reading of reality which was the heart of Franciscan mysticism, and that other ordered vision of the transcendental world which the Dominicans through Aquinas poured into the stream of European thought. For the one the spiritual world was all love: for the other all law. For Dante it was both. In the "Paradiso" his stupendous genius apprehends and shows to us a Beatific Vision in which the symbolic systems of all great mystics and many whom the world does not call mystics--of Dionysius, Richard, St. Bernard, Mechthild, Aquinas, and countless others--are included and explained.

The moment in which the "Commedia" was being written coincides with the awakening of mystical activity in Germany and Flanders. Between the years 1280 and 1309 was produced, probably in the Liege district and under Franciscan influence, the curious anonymous work which isnow only known to us in Latin and English translations-- "The Mirror of Simple Souls." This long treatise, clearly influenced by Dionysius, the Victorines, and the twelfth-century tract known as the "Letter to the Brethren of Mons Dei," is a piece of mystical literature of an advanced kind, often fringing the borders of orthodoxy and looking forward to the speculative Flemish mysticism of the fourteenth century. Its writer was probably contemporary with the founder of this school; the great Dominican scholar Meister Eckhart (1260-1327), who resembled Dante in his combination of mystical insight with intense intellectual power, and laid the foundations at once of German philosophy and German mysticism. These two giants stand side by side at the opening of the century; perfect representatives of the Teutonic and Latin instinct for transcendental reality.

Eckhart, though only a few years younger than St. Gertrude the Great, seems to belong to a different world. His commanding personality, his genius for the supra-sensible nourished by the works of Dionysius and Erigena, moulded and inspired all whom it came near. The German and Flemish mystics of the fourteenth and fifteenth centuries, differing much in temperament from their master and from each other, have yet something in common: something which is shared by no other school. This something is derived from Eckhart; for all have passed under his hand, being either his immediate disciples, or the friends or pupils of his disciples. Eckhart's doctrine is chiefly known to us by reports of his vernacular sermons delivered at Strassburg; then the religious centre of Germany. In these we see him as a teaching mystic full of pastoral zeal, but demanding a high level both of intellect and spirituality in those he addressed. Towards the end of his life he fell into disgrace. A number of propositions extracted from his writings, and representing his more extreme views, were condemned by the Church as savouring of pantheism and other heresies: and certainly the violence and daring of his language laid him open to misconstruction. In his efforts to speak of the unspeakable he was constantly betrayed into expressions which were bound to seem paradoxical and exaggerated to other men. Eckhart's influence, however, was little hurt by ecclesiastical condemnation. His pupils, though they remained loyal Catholics, contrived also to be loyal disciples. To the end of their lives their teaching was coloured--often inspired--by the doctrines of the great, if heretical, scholar whose memory they venerated as that of a saint.

The contrast in type between Eckhart and his two most famous disciples is an interesting one. All three were Dominican friars; all were devout followers of St. Augustine, the Areopagite, St. Bernard, and Aquinas; all had been trained in the schools of Cologne, where Albert the Great and St. Thomas had taught, and where their powerful influence still lived. The mysticism of Eckhart, so far as he allows us to see it in his sermons and fragmentary writings, is objective--one might almost say dogmatic. He describes with an air of almost terrible certainty and intimacy, not that which he has felt, but the place or plane of being he has known--"the desert of the Godhead were no one is at home." He is a great scholar, a natural metaphysician passionately condensed with the quest of Absolute Truth.

Of his two pupils, John Tauler (c. 1300-1361), friar-preacher of Strassburg, was a born missionary: a man who combined with great theological learning and mystical genius of a high order an overwhelming zeal for souls. He laboured incessantly to awaken men to a sense of their transcendental heritage. Without the hard intellectualism occasionally noticeable in Eckhart, or the tendency to introspection and the excessive artistic sensibility of Suso, Tauler is the most virile of the German mystics. The breadth of his humanity is only equalled by the depth of his spirituality. His sermons--his only authentic works--are trumpet-calls to heroic action upon spiritual levels. They influenced many later mystics, especially St. Teresa and St. John of the Cross. Tauler is not a subjective writer: only by implication can we assure ourselves that he speaks from personal experience. He has sometimes, though unfairly, been described as a precursor of the Reformation. Such a claim could only be made by those who look upon all pure Christianity as a form of Protestant heresy. He attacked, like St. Hildegarde, St. Catherine of Siena, and many others, the ecclesiastical corruption of his period: but his writings, if read in unexpurgated editions, prove him to have been a fervent and orthodox Catholic.

Tauler was one of the leading spirits in the great informal society of the Friends of God , which sprang into being in Strassburg, spread through the Rhenish province and beyond to Switzerland and Bavaria, and worked in this moment of religious decadence for the spiritual regeneration of the people. In a spirit of fierce enthusiasm and wholehearted devotion, the Friends of God set themselves to the mystic life as the only life worthy of the name. A great outburst of transcendental activity took place: many visions and ecstasies were reported: amazing conversions occurred. The movement had many features in common with that of the Quakers; except that it took place within, instead of without, the official Church, and was partly directed against the doctrines of the Brethren of the Free Spirit and other heretical sects. With it was connected the third of the trio of great German Dominican mystics, the Blessed Henry Suso (c. 1295-1365), a natural recluse and ascetic, and a visionary of the most exuberant Catholic type. To Suso, subjective, romantic, deeply interested in his own soul and his personal relation with God, mysticism was not so much a doctrine to be imparted to other men as an intimate personal adventure. Though a trained philosopher and theologian, and a devoted follower of Eckhart, his autobiography--a human document far more detailed and ingenuous than St. Teresa's more celebrated "Life"--is mainly the record of his griefs and joys, his pains, visions, ecstasies, and miseries. Even his mystical treatises are in dialogue form, as if he could hardly get away from the personal and dramatic aspect of the spiritual life.

Around these three--Eckhart, Tauler, Suso--are gathered other and more shadowy personalities: members of this mystical society of the Friends of God, bound to the heroic attempt to bring life--the terribly corrupt and disordered religious life of the fourteenth century--back into relation with spiritual reality, to initiate their neighbours into the atmosphere of God. From one of these nameless members comes the literary jewel of the movement: the beautiful little treatise called the "Theologia Germanica," or "Book of the Perfect Life," probably written in Frankfort about the year 1350 by a priest of the Teutonic Order. One of the most successful of many attempts to make mystic principles available for common men, this book was greatly loved by Luther, who published an incomplete edition in 1518. Other Friends of God are now only known to us as the authors of letters, descriptions of conversions, visions, and spiritual adventures--literature which the movement produced in enormous quantities. No part of the history of mysticism has been more changed by recent research than that of the Rhenish school: and the work is still but partly done. At present we can only record the principal names which we find connected with the mystical propaganda of the Friends of God. These are first the nuns Margaret Ebner (1291-1351) and her sister Christina , important personages in the movement upon whose historicity no doubts have been cast. Margaret appears to have been a psychic as well as a mystic: and to have possessed, like Madame Guyon, telepathic and clairvoyant powers. Next the rather shadowy pair of laymen, Henry of Nordlingen and Nicolas of Basle . Lastly the puzzling figure of Rulman Merswin (c. 1310-1382), author of the series of apocalyptic visions called The Book of the Nine Rocks"; whose story of his conversion and mystic life, whether it be regarded as fact or "tendency literature," is a psychological document of the first rank.

In immediate dependence on the German school, and like it drawing its intellectual vigour from the genius of Eckhart, is the mysticism of Flanders: best known to us in the work of its most sublime representative, the Blessed John Ruysbroeck (1293-1381), one of the greatest mystics whom the world has yet known. In Ruysbroeck's works the metaphysical and personal aspects of mystical truth are fused and attain their highest expression. Intellectually indebted to St. Augustine, Richard of St. Victor, and Eckhart, his value lies in the fact that the Eckhartian philosophy was merely the medium by which he expressed the results of profound experience. In his early years a priest in Brussels, in old age a recluse in the forest of Soignes, Ruysbroeck's influence on his own generation was great. Through his disciple Gerard Groot (1340-1384), founder of the Brotherhood of the Common Life, it formed the inspiration of the religious movement of the New Devotion; which carried over into the next century the spirit of the great mediaeval mystics. The mystical writings of Henry de Mande (c. 1360-1415), the "Ruysbroeck of the North," the beautiful and deeply Platonic "Fiery Soliloquy with God" of Gerlac Petersen (1378-

1411), and above all the "Imitation of Christ" of his friend Thomas à Kempis (1380-1471), in which some of Gerard Groot's meditations may be enshrined, are the chief channels through which this mystical current passed. In the next century the Franciscan Henry de Herp or Harphius (ob. 1477) and two greater personalities--the learned and holy Platonist, Cardinal Nicolas of Cusa (1401-1464), and his friend the theologian and contemplative Denis the Carthusian (1402-1471), one of the great religious figures of the fifteenth century--drew their inspiration from Ruysbroeck. Denis translated the whole of his works into Latin; and calls him "another Dionysius" but "clear where the Areopagite is obscure." It was mainly through the voluminous writings of Denis, widely read during succeeding centuries, that the doctrine of the mediaeval mystics was carried over to the Renaissance world. Ruysbroeck's works, with those of Suso, appear in English MSS. early in the fifteenth century, taking their place by the side of St. Bernard, St. Bonaventura, and the great English mystic Richard Rolle. The influence of his genius has also been detected in the mystical literature of Spain.

English mysticism seems to have its roots in the religious revival which arose during Stephen's reign. It was then, and throughout its course, closely linked with the solitary life. Its earnest literary monument, the "Ancren Riwle," was written early in the twelfth century for the use of three anchoresses. So too the "Meditations" of St. Aldred (Abbot of Rievaulx 1146-1166), and the Rule he wrote for his anchoress sister, presuppose the desire for the mystical life. But the first English mystic we can name with certainty is Margery Kempe (probably writing c. 1290), the anchoress of Lynn. Even so, we know nothing of this woman's life; and only a fragment of her "Contemplations" has survived. It is with the next name, Richard Rolle of Hampole (c. 1300-1349), that the short but brilliant procession of English mystics begins. Rolle, educated at Oxford and perhaps at Paris, and widely read in theology, became a hermit in order to live in perfection that mystic life of "Heat, Sweetness, and Song," to which he felt himself to be called. Richard of St. Victor, St. Bernard, and St. Bonaventura are the authors who have influenced him most; but he remains, in spite of this, one of the most individual of all writers on mysticism. A voluminous author, his chief works are still in MS., and he seems to have combined the careers of writer and wandering preacher with that of recluse. He laid claim to direct inspiration, was outspoken in his criticisms of religious and secular life, and in the next generation the Lollards were found to appeal to his authority. Rolle already shows the practical temper characteristic of the English school. His interest was not philosophy, but spiritual life; and especially his own experience of it. There is a touch of Franciscan poetry in his descriptions of his communion with Divine Love, and the "heavenly song" in which it was expressed, of Franciscan ardour in his zeal for souls. His works greatly influenced succeeding English mystics.

He was followed in the second half of the fourteenth century by the unknown author of "The Cloud of Unknowing" and its companion treatises, and by the gracious spirit of Walter Hilton (ob. 1396). With "The Cloud of Unknowing," the spirit of Dionysius first appears in English literature. It is the work of an advanced contemplative, deeply influenced by the Areopagite and the Victorines, who was also an acute psychologist. From the hand that wrote it came the first English translation of the "Theologia Mystica," "Dionise Hid Divinite": a work which says an old writer, "ran across England at deere rates," so ready was the religious consciousness of the time for the reception of mystical truth.

Hilton, though also influenced by Dionysius and Richard of St. Victor, addresses a wider audience. He is pre-eminently a spiritual director, the practical teacher of interior ways, not a metaphysician; and his great work "The Scale of Perfection" quickly took rank among the classics of the spiritual life. The moment of his death coincides with the completion of the most beautiful of all English mystical works, the "Revelations of Love" of the anchoress Julian of Norwich (1343-died after 1413), "theodidacta, profunda, ecstatica," whose unique personality closes and crowns the history of English mediaeval mysticism. In her the best gifts of Rolle and Hilton are transmuted by a "genius for the infinite" of a peculiarly beautiful and individual type. She was a seer, a lover, and a poet. Though considerable theological knowledge underlies her teaching, it is in essence the result of a direct and personal vision of singular intensity.

Already before the completion of Julian's revelations two other women of genius, the royal prophetess and founder St. Bridget of Sweden (1303-1373) and St. Catherine of Siena (1347-1380), had lived and died. St. Bridget, or Birgitta, a mystic and visionary of the Hildegardian type, believed herself called to end the exile of the Papacy and bring peace to the Church. Four months after her death, St. Catherine--then aged 26--took up her unfinished work. The true successor of Dante as a revealer of Reality, and next to St. Francis the greatest of Italian mystics, Catherine exhibits the Unitive Life in its richest, most perfect form. She was a great active and a great ecstatic: at once politician, teacher, and contemplative, holding a steady balance between the inner and the outer life. Well named "the mother of thousands of souls," with little education she yet contrived, in a short career dogged by persistent ill-health, to change the course of history, rejuvenate religion, and compose, in her "Divine Dialogue," one of the jewels of Italian religious literature.

With the first half of the fifteenth century it is plain that the mystic curve droops downwards. At its opening we find the influential figure of the Chancellor Gerson (1363-1429) at once a mystic in his own right and a keen and impartial critic of extravagant mystical teachings and phenomena. But the great period is over: the new life of the Renaissance, already striving in other spheres of activity, has hardly touched the spiritual plane. A transient revival of Franciscan spirituality is associated with the work of three reforming mystics; the energetic French visionary St. Colette of Corbie (1381-1447), her Italian disciple St. Bernardino of Siena (1380-1444), and the ecstatic Clarisse, St. Catherine of Bologna (1413-1463). Contemporary with this group are the careers of two strongly contrasted woman-mystics: St. Joan of Arc (1412-1431), and the suffering Flemish visionary St. Lydwine of Schiedam (1380-1432).

With the second half of the century the scene shifts to Italy, where a spiritual genius of the first rank appeared in St. Catherine of Genoa (1447-1510). She, like her namesake of Siena, was at once an eager lover and an indomitable doer. More, she was a constructive mystic, a profound thinker as well as an ecstatic: an original teacher, a busy and practical philanthropist. Her influence lived on, and is seen in the next generation in the fine, well-balanced nature of another contemplative: the Venerable Battista Vernazza (1497-1587), her goddaughter and the child of one of her most loyal friends. Catherine of Genoa stands alone in her day as an example of the sane and vigorous mystic life. Her contemporaries were for the most part visionaries of the more ordinary female type, such as Osanna Andreasi of Mantua (1449-1505), Columba Rieti (c. 1430-1501) and her disciple Lucia of Narni . They seem to represent the slow extinction of the spirit which burned so bright in St. Catherine of Siena.

That spirit reappears in the sixteenth century in Flanders in the works of the Benedictine Abbot Blosius (1506-1565); and, far more conspicuously, in Spain, a country hardly touched by the outburst of mystical life which elsewhere closed the medieval period. Spanish mysticism first appears in close connection with the religious orders: in the Franciscans Francisco de Osuna (ob. c. 1540), whose manual of contemplative prayer influenced the development of St. Teresa, and St. Peter of Alcantara (1499-1562), her friend and adviser; in the Dominican Luis de Granada (1504-1588) and the Augustinian Luis de Leon (1528-1591). It attains definite and characteristic expression in the life and personality of St. Ignatius Loyola (1491-1556), the great founder of the Society of Jesus. The concrete nature of St. Ignatius' work, and especially its later developments, has blinded historians to the fact that he was a true mystic, own brother to such great actives as St. Teresa and George Fox, actuated by the same vision of reality, passing through the same stages of psychological growth. His spiritual sons greatly influenced the inner life of the great Carmelite, St. Teresa (1515-1582).

Like St. Catherine of Siena, these mystics--and to them we must add St. Teresa's greatest disciple, the poet and contemplative St. John of the Cross (1542-1591)--seem to have arisen in direct response to the need created by the corrupt or disordered religious life of their time. They were the "saints of the counter-Reformation"; and, in a period of ecclesiastical chaos, flung the weight of their genius and their sanctity into the orthodox Catholic scale. Whilst St. Ignatius organized a body of spiritual soldiery, who should attack heresy and defend the Church, St. Teresa, working against heavy odds, infused new vitality into a great religious order and restored it to its duty of direct communion with the transcendental world. In this she was helped by St. John of the Cross; who, a psychologist and philosopher as well as a great mystic, performed the necessary function of bringing the personal experience of the Spanish school back again into touch with the main stream of mystic tradition. All three, practical organizers and profound contemplatives, exhibit in its splendour the dual character of the mystic life. They left behind them in their literary works an abiding influence which has guided the footsteps and explained the discoveries of succeeding generations of adventurers in the transcendental world. The true spiritual children of these mystics are to be found, not in their own country, where the religious life which they had lifted to transcendent levels degenerated when their overmastering influence was withdrawn, but amongst the innumerable contemplative souls of succeeding generations who have fallen under the spell of the "Spiritual Exercises," the "Interior Castle," or the "Dark Night of the Soul."

The Divine fire lit by the great Carmelites of Spain is next seen in Italy, in the lives of the Dominican nun St. Catherine dei Ricci (1522-1590) and the Florentine Carmelite St. Maria Maddelena dei Pazzi (1566-1607), the author of voluminous literary works. It appears in the New World in the beautiful figure of St. Rose of Lima (1586-1617), the Peruvian nun; and at the same moment, under a very different aspect, in Protestant Germany, in the person of one of the giants of mysticism, the "inspired shoemaker" Jacob Boehme (1575-1624).

Boehme, one of the most astonishing cases in history of a natural genius for the transcendent, has left his mark upon German philosophy as well as upon the history of mysticism. William Law, Blake, and Saint-Martin are amongst those who have sat at his feet. The great sweep of Boehme's vision includes both Man and the Universe: the nature of God and of the Soul. In him we find again that old doctrine of Rebirth which the earlier German mystics had loved. Were it not for the difficult symbolism in which his vision is expressed, his influence would be far greater than it is. He remains one of those cloud-wrapped immortals who must be rediscovered and reinterpreted by the adventurers of every age.

The seventeenth century rivals the fourteenth in the richness and variety of its mystical life. Two main currents are to be detected in it: dividing between them the two main aspects of man's communion with the Absolute. One, symbolic, constructive, activistic, bound up with the ideas of regeneration, and often using the language of the alchemists sets out from the Teutonic genius of Boehme. It achieves its successes outside the Catholic Church, and chiefly in Germany and England, where by 1650 his works were widely known. In its decadent forms it runs to the occult: to alchemy, Rosicrucianism, apocalyptic prophecy, and other aberrations of the spiritual sense. The other current arises within the Catholic Church, and in close touch with the great tradition of Christian mysticism. It achieves fullest expansion in France, and tends to emphasize the personal and intimate side of contemplation: encouraging passive receptivity and producing in its exaggerated forms the aberrations of the Quietists.

In the seventeenth century England was peculiarly rich, if not in great mystics, at any rate in mystically minded men, seekers after Reality. Mysticism, it seems, was in the air; broke out under many disguises and affected many forms of life. It produced in George Fox (1624-1690), the founder of the Quakers, a "great active" of the first rank, entirely unaffected by tradition, and in the Quaker movement itself an outbreak of genuine mysticism which is only comparable to the fourteenth-century movement of the Friends of God.

We meet in Fox that overwhelming sense of direct relationship with God, that consciousness of the transcendent characteristic of the mystic; and Quaker spirituality, in spite of its marked aversion to institutional religion, has much in common not only with those Continental Quietists who are its most obvious spiritual affinities, but also with the doctrine of the Catholic contemplatives. Mysticism crops up frequently in the writings of the school; and finds expression in the first generation in the works of Isaac Penington (1616-1679) and in the second in the Journal of the heroic American Friend John Woolman (1720-1772).

At the opposite end of the theological scale, the seventeenth century gives us a group ofEnglish mystics ofthe Catholic type, closely related to the contemporary French school. Of these, one of the most individual is the young Benedictine nun Gertrude More (1606-1633), who carries on that tradition of the communion oflove which flows from St. Augustine through St. Bernard and Thomas à Kempis, and is the very heart of Catholic mysticism. In the writings of her director, and the preserver of her works, the Venerable Augustine Baker (1575-1641)--one of the most lucid and orderly of guides to the contemplative life--we see what were still the formative influences in the environment where her mystical powers were trained. Richard of St. Victor, Hilton, and "The Cloud of Unknowing"; Angela of Foligno; Tauler, Suso, Ruysbroeck; St. Teresa and St. John of the Cross; these are the authorities to whom Augustine Baker most constantly appeals, and through these, as we know, the family tree of the mystics goes back to the Neoplatonists and the first founders of the Church.

Outside that Church, the twins Thomas Vaughan the spiritual alchemist and Henry Vaughan , Silurist, the mystical poet (1622-1695) show the reaction of two very different temperaments upon the transcendental life. Again, the group of "Cambridge Platonists," Henry More (1614-1687), John Smith (1618-1652), Benjamin Whichcote (1609-1683), Peter Sterry (c. 1614-1672), and John Norris (1657-1711) developed and preached a philosophy deeply tinged with mysticism; and Thomas Traherne (c. 1637-1674) gave poetic expression to the Platonic vision of life. In Bishop Hall (1574-1656) the same spirit takes a devotional form. Finally, the Rosicrucians, symbolists, and other spiritually minded occultists--above all the extraordinary sect of Philadelphians, ruled by Dr. Pordage (1608-1698) and the prophetess Jane Lead (1623-1704)--exhibit mysticism in its least balanced aspect mingled with mediumistic phenomena, wild symbolic visions, and apocalyptic prophecies. The influence of these Philadelphians, who were themselves strongly affected by Boehme's works, lingered for a century, appearing again in Saint-Martin the "Unknown Philosopher."

The Catholic mysticism of this period is best seen in France, where the intellectual and social expansion of the Grande Siècle had also its spiritual side. Over against the brilliant worldly life of seventeenth-century Paris and the slackness and even corruption of much organized religion there sprang up something like a cult of the inner life. This mystical renaissance seems to have originated in the work of an English Capuchin friar, William Fitch, in religion Benedict Canfield (1520-1611), who settled in Paris in old age and there became a centre of spiritual influence. Among his pupils were Madame Acarie (1566-1618) and Pierre de Bérulle (1575-1629), and through them his teaching on contemplation affected all the great religious personalities of the period. The house of Madame Acarie--a woman equally remarkable for spiritual genius and practical ability--became the gathering-point of a growing mystical enthusiasm, which also expressed itself in a vigorous movement of reform within the Church. Bérulle was one of the founders of the Oratory. Madame Acarie, known as the "conscience of Paris," visited the relaxed convents and persuaded them to a more strict and holy life. Largely by her instrumentality, the first houses of reformed Carmelites were established in France in 1604, nuns being brought to direct them from St. Teresa's Spanish convents, and French mysticism owes much to this direct contact with the Teresian school. Madame Acarie and her three daughters all became Carmelite nuns; and it was from the Dijon Carmelites that St. Jeanne Françoise de Chantal (1572-1641) received her training in contemplation. Her spiritual father, and co-founder of the Order of the Visitation, St.

François de Sales (1567-1622), had also been in youth a member of Madame Acarie's circle. He shows at its best the peculiar talent of the French school for the detailed and individual direction of souls. Outside this cultured and aristocratic group two great and pure mystics arise from humbler social levels. First the intrepid Ursuline nun Marie de l'Incarnation (1599-1672), the pioneer of education in the New World, in whom we find again St. Teresa's twin gifts for high contemplation and practical initiative. Secondly the Carmelite friar Brother Lawrence (1611-1691), who shows the passive tendency of French mysticism in its most sane, well-balanced form. He was a humble empiricist, laying claim to no special gifts: a striking contrast to his contemporary, the brilliant and unhappy genius Pascal (1623-1662), who fought his way through many psychic storms to the vision of the Absolute.

The genuine French and Flemish mysticism of this period, greatly preoccupied with the doctrines of self-naughting and passivity, constantly approached the frontiers of Quietism. The three great Capuchin teachers of contemplation, the Flemings Constantine Barbançon (1581-1632) and John Evangelist of Barluke (1588-1635), and the English Benedict Canfield, were not entirely beyond suspicion in this regard; as their careful language, and the scrutiny to which they were subjected by contemporary authority, clearly shows. The line between the true and false doctrine was a fine one, as we see in the historic controversy between Bossuet and Fenelon; and the perilous absurdities of the Quietist writers often tempted the orthodox to draw it in the wrong place.

The earliest in date and most exaggerated in type of these true Quietists is the Franco-Flemish Antoinette Bourignan (1616-1680): a strong-willed and wrong-headed woman who, having renounced the world with Franciscan thoroughness, founded a sect, endured considerable persecutions, and made a great stir in the religious life of her time. An even greater uproar resulted from the doctrinal excesses of the devout Spanish priest Miguel de Molinos (1640-1697); whose extreme teachings were condemned by the Church, and for a time brought the whole principle of passive contemplation into disrepute. Quietism, at bottom, was the unbalanced expression of that need which produced the contemporary Quaker movement in England: a need for personal contact with spiritual realities, evoked by the formal and unsatisfying quality of the official religion of the time. Unfortunately the great Quietists were not great mystics. Hence their propaganda, in which the principle of passivity--divorced from, and opposed to, all spiritual action--was pressed to its logical conclusion, resulted in a doctrine fatal not only to all organized religion but to the healthy development of the inner life.

Madame Guyon (1648-1717), the contemporary of Molinos, is usually quoted as a typical Quietist. She is an example of the unfortunate results of an alliance of mystical tendencies with a feeble surface intelligence. Had she possessed the robust common sense so often found in the great contemplatives, her temperamental inclination to passivity would have been checked, and she would hardly have made use of the exaggerated expressions which brought about the official condemnation of her works. In spite of the brilliant championship of Fenelon, and the fact that much of her writing merely reproduces orthodox teaching on contemplative prayer in an inferior form, she was involved in the general condemnation of "passive orison" which the aberrations of the extreme Quietists had called forth.

The end of the seventeenth century saw a great outburst of popular Quietism, some within and some without the official Church. Well within the frontiers of orthodoxy, and exhibiting the doctrine of passivity in its noblest form, was the Jesuit J. P. de Caussade (still living 1739). Among those who over-stepped the boundary--though all the Quietists appealed to the general tradition of mysticism in support of their one-sided doctrine--were Malaval , whose "Théologie Mystique" contains some beautiful French translations from St. Teresa, and Peter Poiret (1646-1719), once a Protestant pastor, then the devoted disciple of Antoinette Bourignan. Later generations owe much to the enthusiasm and industry of Poiret, whose belief in spiritual quiescence was combined with great literary activity. He rescued and edited all Madame Guyon's writings; and has left us, in his "Bibliotheca Mysticorum," the memorial of many lost works on mysticism. From this unique bibliography we can see how "orthodox" was the food which nourished even the most extreme of the Quietists: how thoroughly they believed themselves to represent not a new doctrine, but the true tradition of Christian mysticism.

With the close of the seventeenth century, the Quietist movement faded away. The beginning of the eighteenth sees the triumph of that other stream of spiritual vitality which arose outside the Catholic Church and flowed from the great personality of Jacob Boehme. If the idea of surrender be the mainspring of Quietism, the complementary idea of rebirth is the mainspring of this school. In Germany, Boehme's works had been collected and published by an obscure mystic, John Gichtel (1638-1710); whose life and letters constantly betray his influence. In England, where that influence had been a living force from the middle of the seventeenth century, when Boehme's writings first became known, the Anglo-German Dionysius Andreas Freher was writing between 1699 and 1720. In the early years of the eighteenth century, Freher was followed by William Law (1686-1761), the Nonjuror: a brilliant stylist, and one of the most profound of English religious writers. Law, who was converted by the reading of Boehme's works from the narrow Christianity to which he gave classic expression in the "Serious Call" to a wide and philosophic mysticism, gave, in a series of writings which burn with mystic passion, a new interpretation and an abiding place in English literature to the "inspired shoemaker's" mighty vision of Man and the Universe.

The latter part of a century which clearly represents the steep downward trend of the mystic curve gives us three strange personalities; all of whom have passed through Boehme's school, and have placed themselves in opposition to the ecclesiasticism of their day. In Germany, Eckartshausen (1752-1803), in "The Cloud upon the Sanctuary" and other works, continued upon individual lines that tradition of esoteric and mystical Christianity, and of rebirth as the price of man's entrance into Reality, which found its best and sanest interpreter in William Law. In France the troubled spirit of the transcendentalist Saint-Martin (1743-1803), the "Unknown Philosopher," was deeply affected in his passage from a merely occult to a mystical philosophy by the reading of Boehme and Eckartshausen, and also by the works of the English "Philadelphians," Dr. Pordage and Jane Lead, who had long sunk to oblivion in their native land. In England, William Blake , poet, painter, visionary, and prophet (1757-1827), shines like a solitary star in the uncongenial atmosphere of the Georgian age.

The career of Blake provides us with a rare instance of mystical genius, forcing not only rhythm and words, but also colour and form to express its vision of truth. So individual in his case was this vision, so strange the elements from which his symbolic reconstructions were built up, that he failed in the attempt to convey it to other men. Neither in his prophetic books nor in his beautiful mystical paintings does he contrive to transmit more than great and stimulating suggestions of "things seen" in some higher and more valid state of consciousness. Whilst his visionary symbolism derives to a large extent from Swedenborg, whose works were the great influence of his youth, Blake has learned much from Boehme, and probably from his English interpreters. Almost alone amongst English Protestant mystics, he has also received and assimilated the Catholic tradition of the personal and inward communion of love. In his great vision of "Jerusalem," St. Teresa and Madame Guyon are amongst the "gentle souls" whom he sees guarding that Four-fold Gate which opens towards Beulah--the gate of the contemplative life--and guiding the great "Wine-press of Love" whence mankind, at the hands of its mystics, has received, in every age, the Wine of Life.

ABOUT THE AUTHOR

EVELYN UNDERHILL (1875 -1941), English poet, novelist, and writer on mysticism, was born in England and educated at King's College for Women, London. In 1921 Miss Underhill was Upton Lecturer on the Philosophy of Religion at Manchester College, Oxford. Between 1900 and 1920 she wrote novels and light verse, but her lasting fame rests on the many books she produced on various aspects of mysticism. The most famous of these is Mysticism , which was first published in 1911. Among her other fine works are: The Mystic Way (1913), Practical Mysticism (1915), The Essentials of Mysticism (1920), The Life of the Spirit and the Life of Today (1922), Concerning the Inner Life (1926), Man and the Supernatural (1927), and The House of the Soul (1929).

First published in 1911, Mysticism remains the classic in its field and was lauded by The Princeton Theological Review as "brilliantly written [and] illuminated with numerous well-chosen extracts . . . used with exquisite skill."

Mysticism makes an in-depth and comprehensive exploration of its subject. Part One examines "The Mystic Fact," explaining the relation of mysticism to vitalism, to psychology, to theology, to symbolism, and to magic. Part Two, "The Mystic Way," explores the awakening, purification, and illumination of the self; discusses voices and visions; and delves into manifestations from ecstasy and rapture to the dark night of the soul. Rounding out the book are a useful Appendix, an exhaustive Bibliography, and an Index. Mysticism is thoroughly documented with material drawn from such great mystics as St. Teresa of Avila, Meister Eckhart, and St. John of the Cross.

--From the cover of the Image Book edition

Made in the USA
San Bernardino, CA
27 February 2017